Drawing and Detailing with SolidWorks 2012

David C. Planchard & Marie P. Planchard CSWP

ISBN: 978-1-58503-712-4

SDC
PUBLICATIONS

Schroff Development Corporation

www.SDCpublications.com

SDC Publications
P.O. Box 1334
Mission KS 66222
(913) 262-2664
www.SDCpublications.com

Publisher: Stephen Schroff

Trademarks and Disclaimer

SolidWorks® Corp. is a Dassault Systèmes S.A. (Nasdaq: DASTY) company that develops and markets software for design, analysis, and product data management applications. Microsoft® Windows, Microsoft Office® and its family of products are registered trademarks of the Microsoft Corporation. Other software applications and parts described in this book are trademarks or registered trademarks of their respective owners.

Dimensions of parts are modified for illustration purposes. Every effort is made to provide an accurate text. The authors and the manufacturers shall not be held liable for any parts or drawings developed or designed with this book or any responsibility for inaccuracies that appear in the book. Web and company information was valid at the time of the printing.

Copyright© 2012 by D & M Education LLC

Examination Copies

Teacher evaluation copies for 2012, 2010, 2009, 2008, 2007, and 2006 SolidWorks books are available with classroom support materials and initial and final SolidWorks models. Books received as examination copies are for review purposes only. Examination copies are not intended for student use. Resale of examination copies is prohibited.

Learn by doing, not just by reading! Drawing and Detailing with SolidWorks 2012 is targeted toward a beginner or intermediate user who is looking for a step-by-step project based approach. This is NOT a drawing and detailing Engineering reference book.

Electronic Files

INTRODUCTION

Drawing and Detailing with SolidWorks 2012 is written to educate and assist students, designers, engineers, and professionals in the drawing and detailing tools of SolidWorks. Explore the learning process through a series of design situations, industry scenarios, projects, and objectives target towards the beginning to intermediate SolidWorks user.

Work through numerous activities to create multiple-view, multiple-sheet, detailed drawings, and assembly drawings. Develop Drawing templates, Sheet formats, and Custom Properties. Construct drawings that incorporate part configurations, assembly configurations, and design tables with equations. Manipulate annotations in parts, drawings, assemblies, Revision tables, Bills of Materials and more.

Apply your drawing and detailing knowledge to over thirty exercises. The exercises test your usage competency as well as explore additional topics with industry examples. Advanced exercises require the ability to create parts and assemblies.

Drawing and Detailing with SolidWorks 2012 *is not a reference book* for all drafting and drawing techniques and tools. The book provides information and examples in the following areas:

- History of engineering graphics, manual sketching techniques, orthographic projection, isometric projection, multi-view drawings, dimensioning practices, fasteners in general, tolerance and fit and the history of CAD leading to the development of SolidWorks.

- Start a SolidWorks 2012 session and to understand the following interfaces: Menu bar toolbar, Menu bar menu, Drop-down menus, Context toolbars, Consolidated drop-down toolbars, System feedback icons, Confirmation Corner, Heads-up View toolbar, Document Properties and more.

- Apply Document Properties to reflect the ASME Y14 Engineering Drawing and related Drawing Practices.

- Import an AutoCAD file as a Sheet format. Insert SolidWorks System Properties and Custom Properties.

- Create new SolidWorks Document tabs.

- Create multi-sheet drawings from various part configurations and develop the following drawing views: Standard, Isometric, Auxiliary, Section, Broken Section, Detail, Half Section (Cut-away), Crop, Projected Back, with a Bill of Materials and a Revision Table and Revisions.

- Insert and edit: Dimensions, Feature Control Frames, Datums, Geometric Tolerancing, Surface Finishes, and Weld Symbols using DimXpert and manual techniques.

- Create, apply, and save Blocks and Parametric Notes in a drawing.

Chapter 10 provides a bonus section on the *Certified SolidWorks Associate CSWA program* with sample exam questions and initial and final SolidWorks models.

The book is designed to compliment the SolidWorks Users Guide, SolidWorks Reference Guide, Standards, Engineering Drawing/Design and Graphics Communications reference books.

The authors recognize that companies utilize additional drawing standards. The authors developed the industry scenarios by combining industry experience with their knowledge of engineers, sales, vendors and manufacturers. These professionals are directly involved with SolidWorks everyday. Their work goes far beyond a simple drawing with a few dimensions. They create detailed drawings, assembly drawings, marketing drawings and customer drawings. SolidWorks users work between drawings, parts, assemblies and many other documents to complete a project on time.

Note to Instructors

Please contact the publisher **www.schroff.com** for additional classroom support materials: PowerPoint presentations, Adobe files along with avi files, term projects, quizzes with initial and final SolidWorks models and tips that support the usage of this text in a classroom environment.

Trademarks, Disclaimer, and Copyrighted Material

SolidWorks® Corp. is a Dassault Systèmes S.A. (Nasdaq: DASTY) company that develops and markets software for design, analysis, and product data management applications Microsoft Windows®, Microsoft Office® and its family of products are registered trademarks of the Microsoft Corporation. Other software applications and parts described in this book are trademarks or registered trademarks of their respective owners.

Dimensions of parts and model views are modified for illustration purposes. Every effort is made to provide an accurate text. The authors and the manufacturers shall not be held liable for any parts or drawings developed or designed with this book or any responsibility for inaccuracies that appear in the book. Web and company information was valid at the time of this printing.

The Y14 ASME Engineering Drawing and Related Documentation Publications utilized in this text are as follows: ASME Y14.1 1995, ASME Y14.2M-1992 (R1998), ASME Y14.3M-1994 (R1999), ASME Y14.41-2003, ASME Y14.5-1982, ASME Y14.5M-1994, ASME B4.2

Note: By permission of The American Society of Mechanical Engineers, Codes and Standards, New York, NY, USA. All rights reserved.

Additional information references the American Welding Society, AWS 2.4:1997 Standard Symbols for Welding, Braising and Non-Destructive Examinations, Miami, Florida, USA.

About the Authors

David Planchard is the founder of D&M Education LLC. Before starting D&M Education, he spent over 27 years in industry and academia holding various engineering, marketing, and teaching positions and degrees. He holds five U.S. patents and one international patent. He has published and authored numerous papers on Machine Design, Product Design, Mechanics of Materials, and Solid Modeling. He is an active member of the SolidWorks Users Group and the American Society of Engineering Education (ASEE). David holds a BSME, MSM with the following Professional Certifications: CCAI, CCNA, CCNP, CSWA, CSWP, and CSDA. David is a SolidWorks Solution Partner, an Adjunct Faculty member and the SAE advisor at Worcester Polytechnic Institute in the Mechanical Engineering department.

Marie Planchard is the Director of World Education Markets at DS SolidWorks Corp. Before she joined SolidWorks, Marie spent over 10 years as an engineering professor at Mass Bay College in Wellesley Hills, MA. She has 14 plus years of industry software experience and held a variety of management and engineering positions. Marie holds a BSME, MSME and a Certified SolidWorks Professional (CSWP) Certification. She is an active member of the American Society of Mechanical Engineers (ASME) and the American Society for Engineering Education (ASEE).

David and Marie Planchard are co-authors of the following books:

- **A Commands Guide for SolidWorks® 2012**, 2011, 2010, 2009 and 2008

- **A Commands Guide Reference Tutorial for SolidWorks® 2007**

- **Assembly Modeling with SolidWorks® 2010**, 2009, 2008, 2006, 2005-2004, 2003 and 2001Plus

- **Drawing and Detailing with SolidWorks® 2012**, 2010, 2009, 2008, 2007, 2006, 2005, 2004, 2003, 2002 and 2001/2001Plus

- **Engineering Design with SolidWorks® with Video Instruction 2012**, 2011, 2010, 2009, 2008, 2007, 2006, 2005, 2004, 2003, 2001Plus, 2001 and 1999

- **Engineering Graphics with SolidWorks with Video Instruction 2012**, 2011, and 2010

- **SolidWorks® The Basics with Multimedia CD 2009**, 2008, 2007, 2006, 2005, 2004 and 2003

- **SolidWorks® Tutorial with Video Instruction, 2012**, 2011, 2010, 2009, 2008, 2007, 2006, 2005, 2004, 2003 and 2001/2001Plus

- **The Fundamentals of SolidWorks®: Featuring the VEXplorer robot, 2008** and 2007

- **Official Certified SolidWorks® Associate Examination Guide, Version 3; 2011, 2010, 2009,** Version 2; 2010, 2009, 2008, Version 1; 2007

- **Official Certified SolidWorks® Professional (CSWP) Certification Guide with Video Instruction DVD, 2011, 2010**

- **Applications in Sheet Metal Using Pro/SHEETMETAL & Pro/ENGINEER**

Acknowledgments

Writing this book was a substantial effort that would not have been possible without the help and support of my loving family and of my professional colleagues. I would like to thank Professor John Sullivan and Robert Norton and the community of scholars at Worcester Polytechnic Institute who have enhanced my life, my knowledge, and helped to shape the approach and content to this book.

The author is greatly indebted to my colleagues from Dassault Systèmes SolidWorks Corporation for their help and continuous support: Jeremy Luchini, Avelino Rochino, and Mike Puckett.

Thanks also to Professor Richard L. Roberts of Wentworth Institute of Technology, Professor Dennis Hance of Wright State University, and Professor Jason Durfess of Eastern Washington University who provided insight and invaluable suggestions.

Finally to my wife, who is infinitely patient for her support and encouragement and to our loving daughter Stephanie who supported me during this intense and lengthy project.

Contact the Authors

This is the sixth edition of this book. We realize that keeping software application books current is imperative to our customers. We value the hundreds of professors, students, designers, and engineers that have provided us input to enhance our book. We value your suggestions and comments. Please visit our website at **www.dmeducation.net** or contact us directly with any comments, questions or suggestions on this book or any of our other SolidWorks books at dplanchard@msn.com or planchard@wpi.edu.

References

- SolidWorks Users Guide, SolidWorks Corporation, 2012.

- SolidWorks Reference Guide, SolidWorks Corporation, 2012.

- ASME Y14 Engineering Drawing and Related Documentation Practices, ASME, NY[1].

- ASME B4.2 Dimensions Preferred Metric Limits and Fits, ASME, NY[1].

- AWS 2.4: 1997 Standard Symbols for Welding, Braising and Non-Destructive Examinations, American Weld Society, Miami, Florida[4].

- Betoline, Wiebe, Miller, Fundamentals of Graphics Communication, Irwin, 1995.

- Earle, James, Engineering Design Graphics, Addison Wesley, 1999.

- Giesecke et al. Modern Graphics Communication, Prentice Hall, 1998.

- Hoelscher, Springer, Dobrovolny, Graphics for Engineers, John Wiley, 1968.

- Jensel & Helsel, Engineering Drawing and Design, Glencoe, 1990.

- Jensen, Cecil, Interpreting Engineering Drawings, Delmar-Thomson Learning, 2002.

- Lockhart & Johnson, Engineering Design Communications, Addison Wesley, 1999.

- Madsen, David et al. Engineering Drawing and Design, Delmar Thomson Learning, 2002.

- SMC Corporation, Compact Guide Cylinder Product Manual, SMC Corporation.[2]

- Emerson-EPT Corporation, Shaft Mount Reducer Product Manual, Emerson-EPT Corporation, a division of Emerson[3].

- Walker, James, Machining Fundamentals, Goodheart Wilcox, 1999.

[1] An on-line catalog of ASME Codes and Standards is available on their web site www.asme.org.

[2] An on-line catalog of SMC parts and documents is available on their web site www.smcusa.com. Instructions to down load additional SMC components are available in the Appendix.

[3] An on-line catalog of Emerson-EPT parts and documents is available on their web site www.emerson-ept.com.

[4] An on-line catalog of AWS Standards is available on their web site www.aws.org.

Every license of SolidWorks 2012 contains a copy of SolidWorks SustainabilityXpress. SustainabilityXpress calculates environmental impact on a model in four key areas: *Carbon Footprint, Energy Consumption, Air Acidification and Water Eutrophication.* Material and Manufacturing process region and Transportation Usage region are used as input variables.

New in SolidWorks 2012 is the What's New Examples section.

All *templates, logos* and needed *models* for this book are included on the enclosed DVD. Copy the information from the DVD to your local hard drive. Work from your local hard drive.

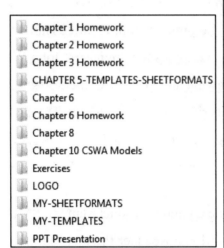

TABLE OF CONTENTS

What is SolidWorks?

SolidWorks® is a mechanical design automation software package used to build parts, assemblies and drawings that takes advantage of the familiar Microsoft® Windows graphical user interface.

SolidWorks is an easy to learn design and analysis tool, (SolidWorks SimulationXpress, SolidWorks Motion, SolidWorks Flow Simulation, etc.) which makes it possible for designers to quickly sketch 2D and 3D concepts, create 3D parts and assemblies and detail 2D drawings.

In SolidWorks, you create 2D and 3D sketches, 3D parts, 3D assemblies and 2D drawings. The part, assembly and drawing documents are related. Additional information on SolidWorks and its family of products can be obtained at their URL, www.SolidWorks.com.

Drawing refers to the SolidWorks module used to insert, add, and modify views in an engineering drawing. Detailing refers to the dimensions, notes, symbols, and Bill of Materials used to document the drawing.

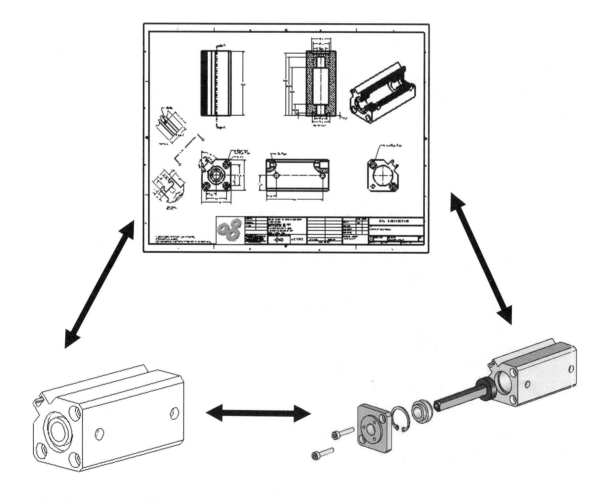

Features are the building blocks of parts. Use feature tools such as: Extruded Boss/Base, Extruded Cut, Fillet, etc. from the Features tab in the CommandManager to create 3D parts.

Extruded features begin with a 2D sketch created on a Sketch plane.

The 2D sketch is a profile or cross section. Use sketch tools such as: Line, Center Rectangle, Slot, Circle, etc. from the Sketch tab in the CommandManager to create a 2D sketch. Sketch the general shape of the profile. Add geometric relationships and dimensions to control the exact size of the geometry and your Design Intent. Design for change!

Create features by selecting edges or faces of existing features, such as a Fillet. The Fillet feature rounds sharp corners.

Dimensions drive features. Change a dimension, and you change the size of the part.

Use Geometric relationships: Vertical, Horizontal, Parallel, etc. and various End Conditions to maintain the Design Intent.

Create a hole that penetrates through a part (Through All). SolidWorks maintains relationships through the change.

The step-by-step approach used in this text allows you to create, edit and modify parts, assemblies and drawings. Change is an integral part of design!

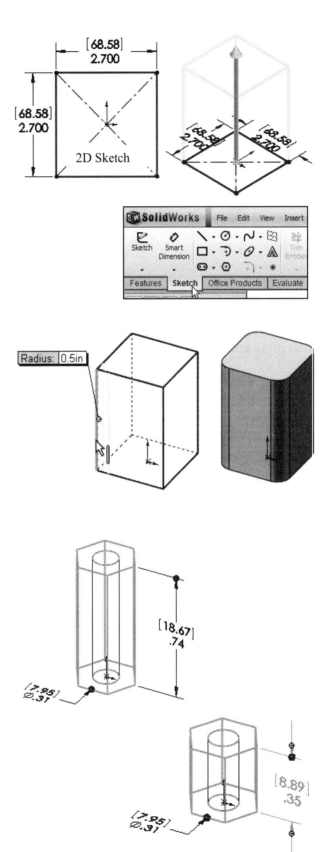

The drawing reflects the changes of the part.

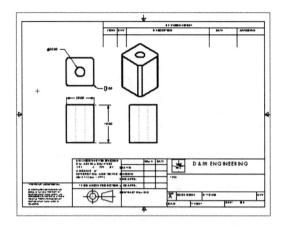 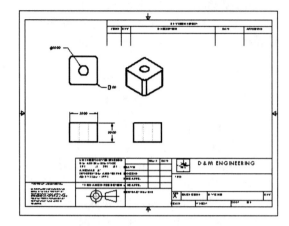

A Drawing template is the foundation for drawing information. Specified drawing standards and size, company information, manufacturing and or assembly requirements and more are included in a drawing template.

Drawing templates contain Document Properties settings such as millimeter or inch units and ANSI or ISO drawing standards.

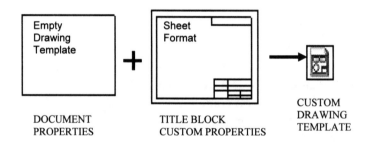

DOCUMENT PROPERTIES   TITLE BLOCK CUSTOM PROPERTIES   CUSTOM DRAWING TEMPLATE

Drawing templates also contain information included in the sheet format such as a Title block, company name, company logo, and custom properties.

A drawing is a 2D representation of a 3D part or assembly. SolidWorks utilizes various Orthographic views (Third Angle Projection or First Angle Projection) to display the 3D model on the 2D drawing. Note: All drawings in this book are displayed in Third Angle Projection.

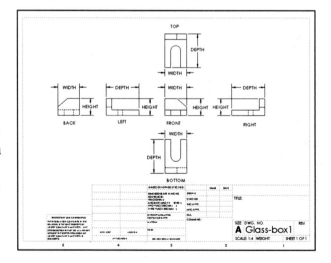

Additional views represent a 3D model or assembly. Insert views from the Drawing tools in SolidWorks such as a Section view, Auxiliary view, or Detail view. Create additional views by combining Drawing tools with different part configurations. The Half Section Isometric view utilizes second configuration that controls the state of an Extruded Cut feature.

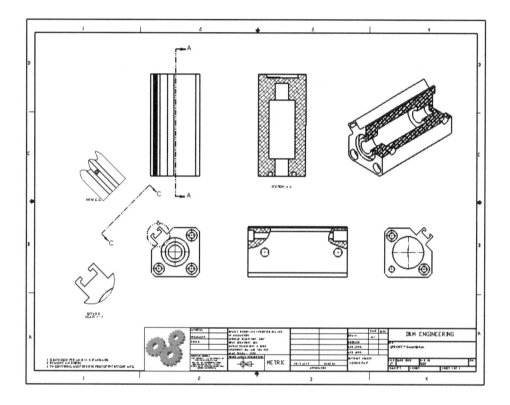

Annotations represent a text note or symbol that documents a part, assembly, or drawing.

Insert feature dimensions and annotations from the part or assembly into the drawing. Create additional reference dimensions and annotations in the drawing.

Address extension line gaps, dimension placement and line precedence.

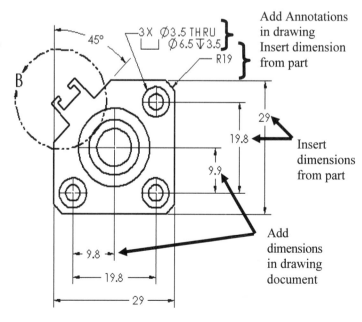

Apply different configurations in a drawing. Assign properties such as material, mass, and cost to individual parts in part and assembly Design Tables. Incorporate multiple properties into the drawing Bill of Materials.

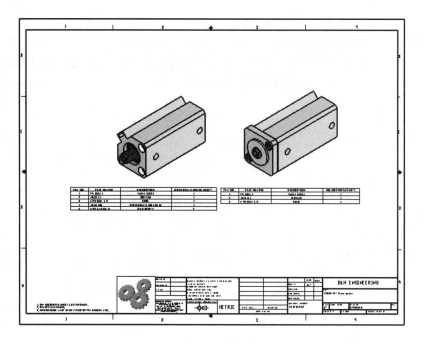

The step-by-step approach used in this text works with multiple parts and assemblies to create and to modify engineering drawings. Understanding design intent assists you in implementing changes.

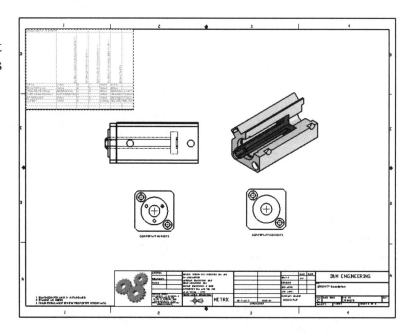

Design Intent

The SolidWorks definition of design intent is the process in which the model is developed to accept future changes.

Models behave differently when design changes occur. Design for change. Utilize geometry for symmetry, reuse common features and reuse common parts.

Build change into the following areas:

1. Sketch

2. Feature

3. Part

4. Assembly

5. Drawing

1. Design Intent in the Sketch

Build design intent in a sketch as the profile is created. A profile is determined from the selected Sketch Entity. Example: Corner Rectangle, Circle, Arc, Point, etc.

Apply symmetry into a profile through a sketch centerline, mirror entity and position about the reference planes and Origin.

Build design intent as you sketch with automatic Geometric relations. Document the decisions made during the up-front design process. This is very valuable when you modify the design later.

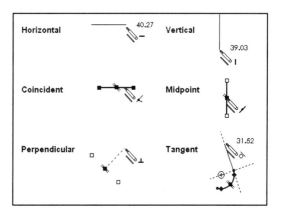

A rectangle contains Horizontal, Vertical, and Perpendicular automatic Geometric relations. Apply design intent using added Geometric relations. Example: Horizontal, Vertical, Collinear, Perpendicular, Parallel etc.

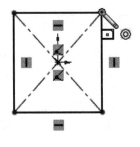

Example A: Apply design intent to create a square profile. Sketch a rectangle. Apply the Center Rectangle tool. Note: No construction reference centerline or Midpoint relation is required with the Center Rectangle tool. Insert dimensions to define the square.

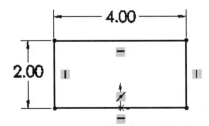

Example B: Develop a rectangular profile. Apply the Corner Rectangle tool. The bottom horizontal midpoint of the rectangular profile is located at the Origin. Add a Midpoint relation between the horizontal edge of the rectangle and the Origin. Insert two dimensions to define the width and height of the rectangle as illustrated.

2. Design Intent in the Feature

Build design intent into a feature by addressing symmetry, feature selection, and the order of feature creation.

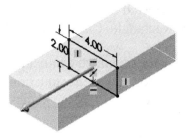

Example A: The Boss-Extrude1 feature (Base feature) remains symmetric about the Front Plane. Utilize the Mid Plane End Condition option in Direction 1. Modify the depth, and the feature remains symmetric about the Front Plane.

Example B: Do you create each tooth separate using the Extruded Cut feature? No. Create a single tooth and then apply the Circular Pattern feature. Create 34 teeth for a Circular Pattern feature. Modify the number of teeth from 32 to 24.

3. Design Intent in the Part

Utilize symmetry, feature order and reusing common features to build design intent into the part.

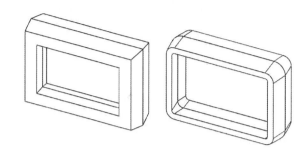

Example A: Feature order. Is the entire part symmetric? Feature order affects the part. Apply the Shell feature before the Fillet feature and the inside corners remain perpendicular.

4. Design Intent in the Assembly

Utilizing symmetry, reusing common parts and using the Mate relation between parts builds the design intent into an assembly.

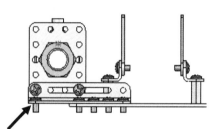

Example A: Reuse geometry in an assembly. The assembly contains a linear pattern of holes. Insert one screw into the first hole. Utilize the Component Pattern feature to copy the machine screw to the other holes.

5. Design Intent in the Drawing

Utilize dimensions, tolerance and notes in parts and assemblies to build the design intent into the Drawing.

Example A: Tolerance and material in the drawing.

Insert an outside diameter tolerance +.000/-.002 into the TUBE part. The tolerance propagates to the drawing.

Define the Custom Property MATERIAL in the part. The MATERIAL Custom Property propagates to the drawing.

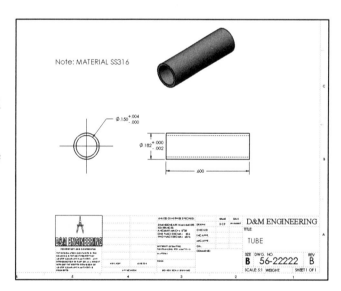

Overview of Chapters

Chapter 1: History of Engineering Graphics

Chapter 1 provides a broad discussion of the history of Engineering Graphics and the evolution from manual drawing/drafting along with an understanding of general sketching techniques, alphabet of lines, precedence of line types and Orthographic projection.

It also addresses the Glass Box method and the six principle orthographic views along with the difference between First Angle Projection and Third Angle Projection.

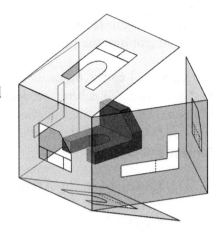

Chapter 2: Isometric Projection and Multi View Drawings

Chapter 2 provides a general introduction into Isometric Projection and sketching along with Additional Projections and arrangement of views.

It also covers advanced drawing views and an introduction to the evolution of from manual drafting to early CAD systems and finally to SolidWorks.

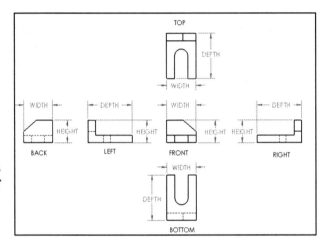

Chapter 3: Dimensioning Practices, Tolerancing and Fasteners

Chapter 3 provides a general introduction into dimensioning practices and systems, and the ASME ANSI Y14.5 standards along with fits, fasteners and general tolerancing.

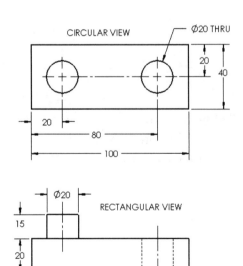

Chapter 4: SolidWorks 2012 User Interface

SolidWorks is a design software application used to model and create 2D and 3D sketches, 3D parts and assemblies, and 2D drawings. Chapter 4 introduces you to the SolidWorks 2012 User Interface and CommandManager: Menu bar toolbar, Menu bar menu, Drop-down menus, Context toolbars, Consolidated drop-down toolbars, System feedback icons, Confirmation Corner, Heads-up View toolbar, Document Properties and more.

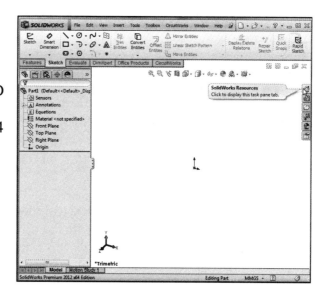

Chapter 5: Drawing Templates and Sheet Formats

Explore the SolidWorks drawing template. Apply Document Properties to reflect the ASME Y14 Engineering Drawing Standards.

Investigate the differences between a Sheet format and a Drawing template. Create two Drawing templates. Create a C-size Drawing template and an A-size Drawing template. Create a C-size Sheet format.

Import an AutoCAD drawing to create a new Sheet format. Apply SolidWorks Properties and Custom Properties in the Sheet format. Combine the Sheet format with an empty drawing template to create a custom Drawing template.

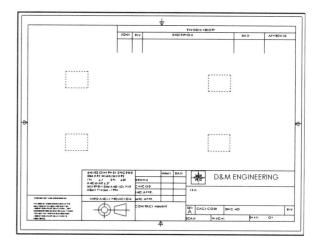

Chapter 6: Drawings and Various Drawing Views

Create three drawings: TUBE, ROD, and COVERPLATE. Insert the following drawing views: *Front Top, Right, Isometric, Auxiliary, Detail, Section, Crop, Broken Section, Half Section, Revolved Section, Offset Section, Removed, Projected, Aligned Section, and more.*

Insert, modify, suppress, unsuppressed, and delete drawing views and dimensions. Create multi-sheet drawings from various part configurations.

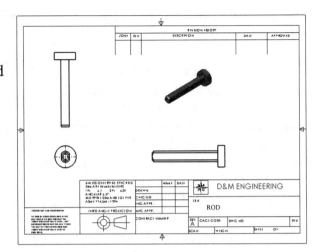

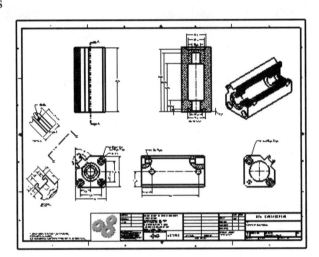

Chapter 7: Fundamentals of Detailing

Insert dimensions and annotations required to detail the TUBE and COVERPLATE drawings.

Insert, add, and modify dimensions for part features. Insert and add notes to the drawing.

Incorporate drawing standards to document specific features.

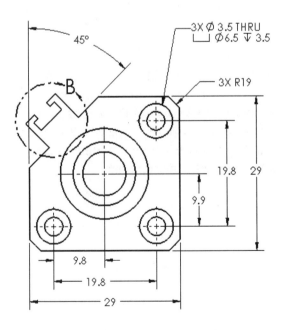

Chapter 8: Assembly Drawings

Develop the CYLINDER assembly. Combine configurations of the TUBE, ROD and COVERPLATE components.

Obtain an understanding of Custom Properties and SolidWorks Properties.

Combine Properties in a Bill of Materials.

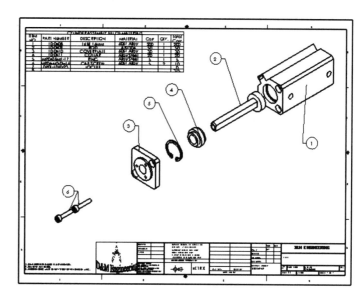

Create a design table in the assembly. Incorporate the Bill of Materials and different configurations into a multi-sheet drawing.

Chapter 9: Datums, Feature Control Frames, Geometric Tolerancing and other Drawing Symbols

Create five drawings: VALVEPLATE1, VALVEPLATE1-GDT, VALVEPLATE1-GDT eDrawing, PLATE-TUBE, PLATE-CATALOG, and modify the ASME14-41 drawing.

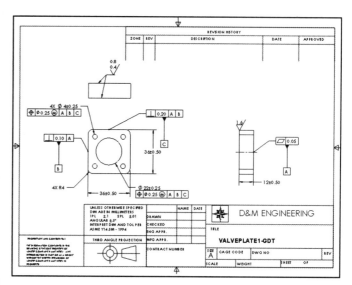

Apply DimXpert and the DimXpert Manager. Insert Feature Control Frames, Datum Feature Symbols, Geometric Tolerance, Weld Symbols, Surface Finish Symbols, and more using DimXpert and manual techniques. Format a Design Table in EXCEL.

Chapter 10: Introduction to the Certified SolidWorks Associate Exam

Chapter 10 provides a basic introduction into the curriculum and exam categories for the Certified SolidWorks Associated CSWA Certification program. Review the exam procedure, process and required model knowledge needed to take and pass the exam.

- Review the five exam categories: *Drafting Competencies, Basic Part Creation and Modification, Intermediate Part Creation and Modification, Advanced Part Creation and Modification, and Assembly Creation and Modification*

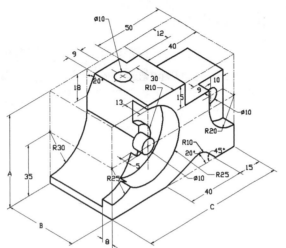

Given:
A = 63, B = 50, C = 100
Material: Copper
Units: MMGS
Density: .0089 g/mm^3
All HOLES THROUGH ALL

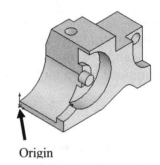

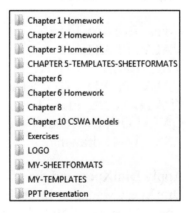

Origin

All model files for Chapter 10 are located in the Chapter 10 CSWA Models folder on the DVD.

☀ View the Certified SolidWorks Associate CSWA exam pdf file on the enclosed DVD for a sample exam.

Chapter 1 Homework
Chapter 2 Homework
Chapter 3 Homework
CHAPTER 5-TEMPLATES-SHEETFORMATS
Chapter 6
Chapter 6 Homework
Chapter 8
Chapter 10 CSWA Models
Exercises
LOGO
MY-SHEETFORMATS
MY-TEMPLATES
PPT Presentation

About the Book

The following conventions are used throughout this book:

- The term document is used to refer a SolidWorks part, drawing, or assembly file.

- The list of items across the top of the SolidWorks interface is the Menu bar menu or the Menu bar toolbar. Each item in the Menu bar has a pull-down menu. When you need to select a series of commands from these menus, the following format is used: Click **View**, check **Origins** from the Menu bar. The Origins are displayed in the Graphics window.

- The ANSI overall drafting standard and Third Angle projection is used as the default setting in this text. IPS (inch, pound, second) and MMGS (millimeter, gram, second) unit systems are used.

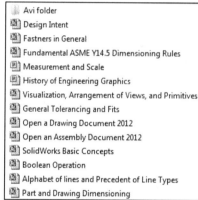

- The book is organized into various chapters. Each chapter is focused on a specific subject or feature. Additional pdf and ppt information and folders/models are provided on the enclosed DVD.

- All *templates*, *logos* and needed *model documents* for this book are included on the enclosed DVD. Copy the information from the DVD to your local hard drive. Work from your local hard drive.

- Screen shots in the book were made using SolidWorks 2012 SP0 running Windows® 7.

The following command syntax is used throughout the text. Commands that require you to perform an action are displayed in **Bold** text.

Format:	Convention:	Example:
Bold	• All commands actions. • Selected icon button. • Selected icon button. • Selected geometry: line, circle. • Value entries.	• Click **Options** from the Menu bar toolbar. • Click **Corner Rectangle** ☐ from the Sketch toolbar. • Click **Sketch** ⌇ from the Context toolbar. • Select the **centerpoint**. • Enter **3.0** for Radius.
Capitalized	• Filenames. • First letter in a feature name.	• Save the **FLATBAR** assembly. • Click the **Fillet** feature.

Windows Terminology in SolidWorks

The mouse buttons provide an integral role in executing SolidWorks commands. The mouse buttons execute commands, select geometry, display Shortcut menus and provide information feedback.

A summary of mouse button terminology is displayed below:

Item:	Description:
Click	Press and release the left mouse button.
Double-click	Double press and release the left mouse button.
Click inside	Press the left mouse button. Wait a second, and then press the left mouse button inside the text box. Use this technique to modify Feature names in the FeatureManager design tree.
Drag	Point to an object, press and hold the left mouse button down. Move the mouse pointer to a new location. Release the left mouse button.
Right-click	Press and release the right mouse button. A Shortcut menu is displayed. Use the left mouse button to select a menu command.
ToolTip	Position the mouse pointer over an Icon (button). The tool name is displayed below the mouse pointer.
Large ToolTip	Position the mouse pointer over an Icon (button). The tool name and a description of its functionality are displayed below the mouse pointer.
Mouse pointer feedback	Position the mouse pointer over various areas of the sketch, part, assembly or drawing. The cursor provides feedback depending on the geometry.

A mouse with a center wheel provides additional functionality in SolidWorks. Roll the center wheel downward to enlarge the model in the Graphics window. Hold the center wheel down. Drag the mouse in the Graphics window to rotate the model.

Visit SolidWorks website: http://www.solidworks.com/sw/support/hardware.html to view their supported operating systems and hardware requirements.

SolidWorks					
Operating Systems	SolidWorks 2009	SolidWorks 2010	SolidWorks 2011	SolidWorks 2012	(SolidWorks 2013)
Windows 7	✗	✓	✓	✓	✓
Windows Vista	✓	✓	✓	✓	✓
Windows XP	✓	✓	✓	✓	✗
Minimum Hardware	Configuring a SolidWorks Workstation				
RAM	2 GB or more				
Disk Space	5 GB or more				
Video Card	Certified cards and drivers				
Processor	Intel or AMD with SSE2 support. 64-bit operating system recommended				
Install Media	DVD Drive or Broadband Internet Connection				

The Instructors DVD contains PowerPoint presentations, Adobe files along with avi files, Term projects, quizzes with the initial and final SolidWorks models.

The book is design to expose the new user to numerous tools and procedures. It may not always use the simplest and most direct process.

The book does not cover starting a SolidWorks session in detail for the first time. A default SolidWorks installation presents you with several options. For additional information for an Education Edition, visit the following sites: http://www.solidworks.com/goedu and http://www.solidworks.com/sw/education/6443_ENU_HTML.htm.

goEDU

Installation Instructions

Education User License Agreement (EULA)

System Requirements

Product Description

Instructions to Access Instructors' Curriculum

Workgroup PDM Installation Instructions

Workgroup PDM Video Tutorials

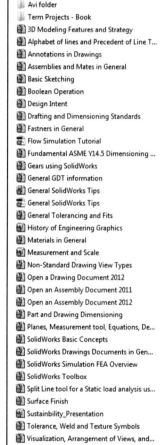

Avi folder
Term Projects - Book
3D Modeling Features and Strategy
Alphabet of lines and Precedent of Line T...
Annotations in Drawings
Assemblies and Mates in General
Basic Sketching
Boolean Operation
Design Intent
Drafting and Dimensioning Standards
Fastners in General
Flow Simulation Tutorial
Fundamental ASME Y14.5 Dimensioning ...
Gears using SolidWorks
General GDT information
General SolidWorks Tips
General SolidWorks Tips
General Tolerancing and Fits
History of Engineering Graphics
Materials in General
Measurement and Scale
Non-Standard Drawing View Types
Open a Drawing Document 2012
Open an Assembly Document 2011
Open an Assembly Document 2012
Part and Drawing Dimensioning
Planes, Measurement tool, Equations, De...
SolidWorks Basic Concepts
SolidWorks Drawings Documents in Gen...
SolidWorks Simulation FEA Overview
SolidWorks Toolbox
Split Line tool for a Static load analysis us...
Surface Finish
Sustainibility_Presentation
Tolerance, Weld and Texture Symbols
Visualization, Arrangement of Views, and...
Weldments

Notes:

Notes:

Chapter 1

History of Engineering Graphics

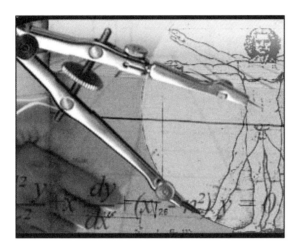 

Below are the desired outcomes and usage competencies based on the completion of Chapter 1.

Desired Outcomes:	Usage Competencies:
• Appreciate the history of Engineering Graphics.	• Identify categories and disciplines related to Engineering Graphics.
• Grasp of the Cartesian Coordinate system.	• Apply 2D and 3D Cartesian Coordinate system: Absolute, Relative, Polar, Cylindrical and Spherical.
• Understand Geometric entities. • Comprehend Free Hand Sketches.	• Points, Circles, Arcs, Planes, etc. • Solid Primitives. • Generate basic 2D shapes and objects. • Create 2D and 3D freehand sketches.
• Recognize the Alphabet of Lines and Precedence of Line types.	• Create and understand correct line precedence.
• Be familiar with Orthographic Projection using the Glass Box method.	• Explain the difference between First and Third Angle Projection type. • Identify the six principal views using the Glass Box method.

Notes:

Notes:

Chapter 1 - History of Engineering Graphics

Chapter Overview

Chapter 1 provides a broad discussion of the history of Engineering Graphics and the evolution from manual drawing/drafting along with an understanding of the Cartesian Coordinate system, Geometric entities, general sketching techniques, alphabet of lines, precedence of line types and Orthographic projection.

On the completion of this chapter, you will be able to:

- Appreciate the history of Engineering Graphics
- Understand 2D and 3D Cartesian Coordinate system:
    - Right-handed vs. Left handed
    - Absolute, Relative, Polar, Cylindrical and Spherical
- Understand Geometric entities:

    - Point, Circle, Arc, Plane, etc.

- Recognize the Alphabet of lines
- Distinguish between the Precedence of line types
- Grasp Orthographic Projection using the Glass Box method
- Identify the six Principal views
- Explain the difference between First and Third Angle Projection type

History of Engineering Graphics

Engineering Graphics is the academic discipline of creating standardized technical drawings by architects, interior designers, drafters, design engineers, and related professionals.

Standards and conventions for layout, sheet size, line thickness, text size, symbols, view projections, descriptive geometry, dimensioning, tolerencing, abbreviations, and notation are used to create drawings that are ideally interpreted in only one way.

A technical drawing differs from a common drawing by how it is interpreted. A common drawing can hold many purposes and meanings, while a technical drawing is intended to concisely and clearly communicate all needed specifications to transform an idea into physical form for manufacturing, inspection or purchasing.

We are all aware of the amazing drawings and inventions of Leonardo da Vinci (1453-1528). It is assumed that he was the father of mechanical drafting. Leonardo was probably the greatest engineer the world has ever seen. Below are a few freehand sketches from his notebooks.

Example 1:

The first freehand sketch is of a crossbow. Note the detail and notes with the freehand sketch.

Example 2:

The second freehand sketch is of an early example of an exploded assembly view.

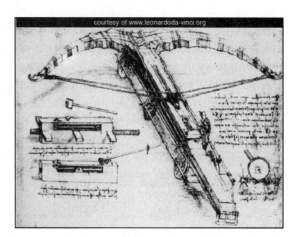

The only source for the detailed history of Leonardo's work is his own careful representations. His drawings were of an artist who was an inventor and a modern day engineer. His drawings were three-dimensional (3D) and they generally were without dimensional notations.

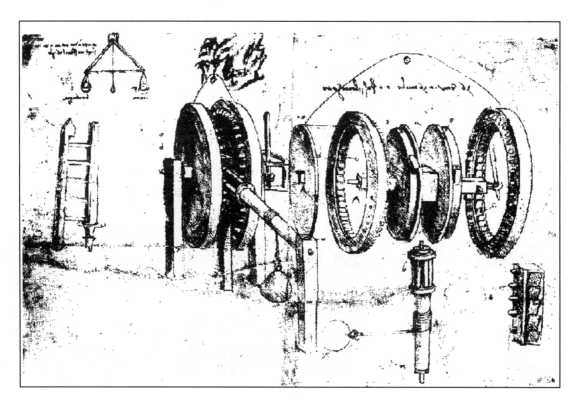

Craftsman created objects from his drawings, and each machine or device was one-of-a-kind creations. Assembly line manufacturing and interchangeable parts were not a concern.

Engineering graphics is a visual means to develop ideas and convey designs in a technical format for construction and manufacturing. Drafting is the systematic representation and dimensional specification and annotation of a design.

The basic mechanics of drafting is to place a piece of paper (or other material) on a smooth surface with right-angle corners and straight sides - typically a drafting table. A sliding straightedge known as a T-square; is then placed on one of the sides, allowing it to be slid across the side of the table, and over the surface of the paper.

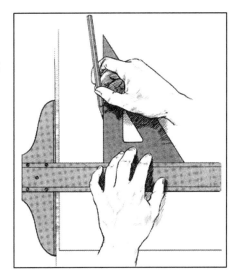

"Parallel lines" can be drawn simply by moving the T-square and running a pencil or technical pen along the T-square's edge, but more typically; the T-square is used as a tool to hold other devices such as set squares or triangles. In this case, the drafter places one or more triangles of known angles on the T-square - which is itself at right angles to the edge of the table - and can then draw lines at any chosen angle to others on the page.

Modern drafting tables (which have by now largely been replaced by CAD workstations) come equipped with a parallel rule that is supported on both sides of the table to slide over a large piece of paper. Because it is secured on both sides, lines drawn along the edge are guaranteed to be parallel.

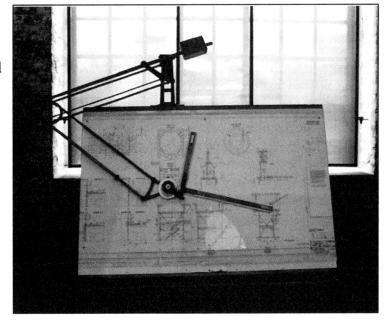

In addition, the drafter uses several tools to draw curves and circles. Primary among these are the compasses, used for drawing simple arcs and circles, the French curve, typically made out of plastic, metal or wood composed of many different curves and a spline; rubber coated articulated metal that can be manually bent to most curves.

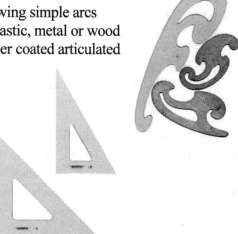

A drafting triangle always has one right angle 90°. This makes it possible to put a triangle against a T-square to draw vertical lines. A 30 60 90 triangle is used with a t-square or parallel straightedge to draw lines that are 30 60 or 90 degrees. A 45 90 triangle is used to draw lines with a T-square or parallel straightedge that are 45 or 90 degrees.

2 Dimensional Cartesian Coordinate system

A Cartesian coordinate system in two dimensions is commonly defined by two axes, at right angles to each other, forming a plane (an x,-y plane). The horizontal axis is normally labeled x, and the vertical axis is normally labeled y.

The axes are commonly defined as mutually orthogonal to each other (each at a right angle to the other). Early systems allowed "oblique" axes, that is, axes that did not meet at right angles, and such systems are occasionally used today, although mostly as theoretical exercises. All the points in a Cartesian coordinate system taken together form a so-called Cartesian plane. Equations that use the Cartesian coordinate system are called Cartesian equations.

The point of intersection, where the axes meet, is called the origin. The x and y axes define a plane that is referred to as the xy plane. Given each axis, choose a unit length, and mark off each unit along the axis, forming a grid. To specify a particular point on a two dimensional coordinate system, indicate the x unit first (abscissa), followed by the y unit (ordinate) in the form (x,-y), an ordered pair.

Example 1:

Example 1 displays an illustration of a Cartesian coordinate plane. Four points are marked and labeled with their coordinates: (2,3), (-3,1), (-1.5,-2.5), and the origin (0,0).

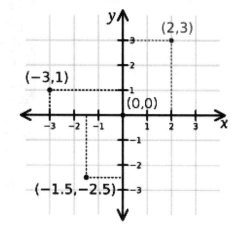

The intersection of the two axes creates four regions, called quadrants, indicated by the Roman numerals I, II, III and IV. Conventionally, the quadrants are labeled counter-clockwise starting from the upper right ("northeast") quadrant.

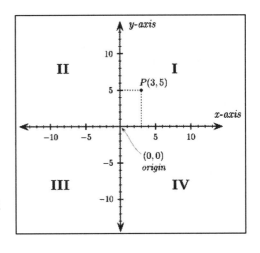

Example 2:

Example 2 displays an illustration of a Cartesian coordinate plane. Two points are marked and labeled with their coordinates: (3,5) and the origin (0,0) with four quadrants.

In the first quadrant, both coordinates are positive, in the second quadrant x-coordinates are negative and y-coordinates positive, in the third quadrant both coordinates are negative and in the fourth quadrant, x-coordinates are positive and y-coordinates negative.

3 Dimensional Cartesian Coordinate system

The three dimensional coordinate system provides the three physical dimensions of space: *height*, *width*, and *length*. The coordinates in a three dimensional system are of the form (x,y,z).

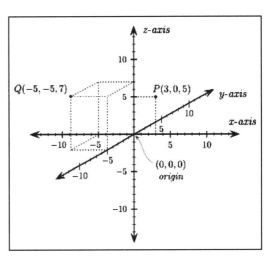

Once the x- and y-axes are specified, they determine the line along which the z-axis should lie, but there are two possible directions on this line. The two possible coordinate systems which result are called "Right-hand" and "Left-hand."

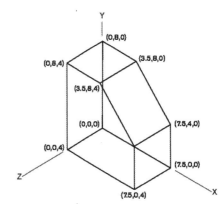

☀ Cartesian coordinates are the foundation of analytic geometry, and provide enlightening geometric interpretations for many other branches of mathematics, such as linear algebra, complex analysis, differential geometry, multivariate calculus, group theory, and more.

Most CAD systems use the Right-hand rule for a coordinate system. To use the Right-hand rule - point your thumb of your right hand in the positive direction for the x axis and your index finger in the positive direction for the y axis, your remaining fingers curl in the positive direction for the z axis as illustrated.

X- Always the thumb

  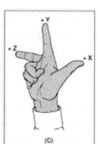

When the x,-y plane is aligned with the screen in a CAD system, the z axis is oriented horizontally (pointing towards you). In machining and many other applications, the z-axis is considered to be the vertical axis. In all cases, the coordinate axes are mutually perpendicular and oriented according to the Right-hand or Left-hand rule.

The Right-hand rule is also used to determine the direction of rotation. For rotation using the right-hand rule, point your thumb in the positive direction along the axis of rotation. Your fingers will curl in the positive direction for the rotation.

☀ Some CAD systems use a Left-hand rule. In this case, the curl of the fingers on your left hand provides the positive direction for the z axis. In this case, when the face of your computer monitor is the x,-y plane, and positive direction for the z axis would extend into the computer monitor, not towards you.

Models and drawings created in SolidWorks or a CAD system are defined and stored using sets of points in what is sometimes called World Space.

Each reference line is called a coordinate axis or just axis of the system, and the point where they meet is its origin. The coordinates can also be defined as the positions of the perpendicular projections of the point onto the two axes, expressed as a signed distance from the origin.

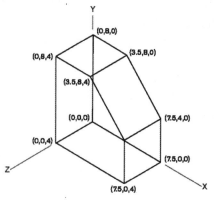

☼ The origin ⊥ in SolidWorks is displayed in blue in the center of the Graphics window. The origin represents the intersection of the three default reference planes: *Front Plane*, *Top Plane* and *Right Plane* illustrated in the FeatureManager. The positive x-axis is horizontal and points to the right of the origin in the Front view. The positive y-axis is vertical and point upward in the Front view. The FeatureManager contains a list of features, reference geometry, and settings utilized in the part.

Absolute Coordinates

Absolute coordinates are the coordinates used to store the location of points in your CAD system. These coordinates identify the location in terms of distance from the origin (0,0,0) in each of the three axis (x, y, z) directions of the Cartesian coordinate system.

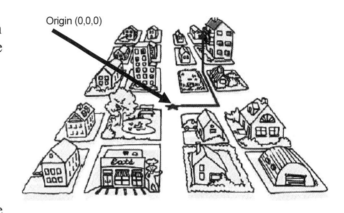

Origin (0,0,0)

As an example - someone provides directions to your house (or to a house in an area where the streets are laid out in nice rectangular blocks). A way to describe how to get to your house would be to inform the person how many blocks over and how many blocks up it is from two main streets (and how many floors up in the building, for 3D). The two main streets are like the x and y axes of the Cartesian coordinate system, with the intersection as the origin (0,0,0).

Relative Coordinates

Instead of having to specify each location from the origin (0,0,0), using relative coordinates allows you to specify a 3D location by providing the number of units from a previous location. In other words; the location is defined relative to your previous location. To understand relative coordinates, think about giving someone directions from his or her current position, not from two main streets. Using the same map as before but this time with the location of the house relative to the location of the person receiving directions.

Polar Coordinates

Polar coordinates are used to locate an object by providing an angle (from the x axis) and a distance. Polar coordinates can either be absolute, providing the angle and distance from the origin (0,0,0), or they can be relative, providing the angle and distance from the current location.

Picture the same situation of having to provide directions. You could inform the person to walk at a specified angle from the crossing of the two main streets, and how far to walk. In the illustration, it shows the angle and direction for the shortcut across the empty lot using absolute polar coordinates. Polar coordinates can also be used to provide an angle and distance relative to a starting point.

Cylindrical and Spherical Coordinates

Cylindrical and spherical coordinates are similar to polar coordinates except that you specify a 3D location instead of one on a single flat plane (such as a map). Cylindrical coordinates specify a 3D location based on a radius, angle, and distance (usually in the z axis direction). It may be helpful to think about this as giving a location as though it were on the edge of a cylinder. The radius tells how far the point is from the center (or origin); the angle is the angle from the x axis along which the point is located; and the distance gives you the height where the point is located on the cylinder. Cylindrical coordinates are similar to polar coordinates, but they add distance in the z direction.

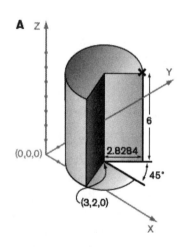

Spherical coordinates specify a 3D location by the radius, an angle from the X axis, and the angle from the x,y plane. It is helpful to think of locating a point on a sphere, where the origin of the coordinate system is at the center of the sphere. The radius gives the size of the sphere, the first angle gives a location on the equator. The second angle gives the location from the plane of the equator to the point on the sphere in line with the location specified on the equator.

Free Hand Sketching

Free hand sketching is a method of visualizing and conceptualizing your idea that allows you to communicate that idea with others. Sketches are NOT intended to be final engineering documents or drawings, but are a step in the process from an idea or thought to final design or to production.

Two types of drawings are generally associated with the four key stages of the engineering process: (1) Freehand sketches and (2) Detailed Engineering Drawings.

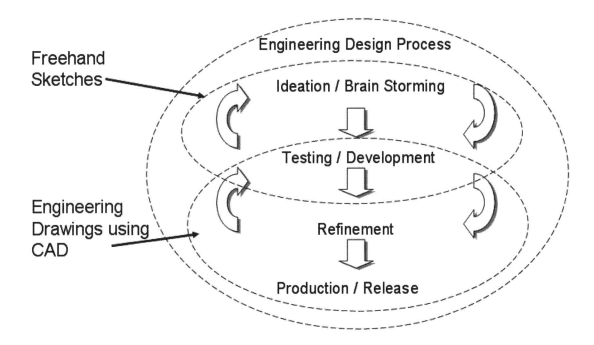

Freehand sketching is an important method to quickly document and to communicate your design ideas. Freehand sketching is a process of creating a rough, preliminary drawing to represent the main features of a design, whether it is a manufactured product, a chemical process, or a structure.

Sketches take many forms, and vary in level of detail. The designer or engineer determines the level of detail based on clarity and purpose of the sketch, as well as the intended audience. Sketches are important to record the fleeting thoughts associated with idea generation and brain storming in a group.

Freehand sketching is considered one of the most powerful methods to help develop visualization skills. The ability to sketch is helpful, not only to communicate with others, but also to work out details in ideas and to identify any potential problems.

Freehand sketching requires simple tools, a pencil, piece of paper, straight edge and can be accomplished almost anywhere. Creating freehand sketches does not require artistic ability, as some may assume.

General Sketching Techniques

Understand that it takes practice to perfect your skills in any endeavor, including freehand sketching. When sketching, you need to coordinate your eyes, hands (wrist and arm), and your brain. Chances are; you have had little opportunity in recent years to use these together, so your first experience with freehand sketching will be taxing. Some tips to ease the process include:

- Orient the paper in a comfortable position.

- Determine the most comfortable drawing direction, such as left to right, or drawing either toward or away from your body.

- Relax your hand, arm and body.

- Use the edge of the paper as a guide for straight lines.

- When using pencil, work from the top left to the lower right corner (if you are right-handed). This helps avoid smudging your work (your hand is resting on blank paper, rather than on your work).

- Remember that sketches are generally drawn without dimensions, since you are trying to represent the main features of your design concept.

- Use a wooden pencil with soft HB lead or a mechanical pencil in 5 mm or 7 mm.

Today, you may not have a T-square available, but you can still sketch in your notebook and use good sketching techniques. You should also be prepared to sketch anywhere; even on the back of a napkin.

Geometric Entities

Points

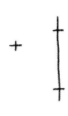

Points are geometrical constructs. Points are considered to have no width, height, or depth. Points are used to indicate locations in space. When you represent a point in a free hand sketch, the convention is to make a small cross or a bar if it is along a line, to indicate the location of the point.

In CAD drawings, a point is located by its coordinates and usually shown with some sort of marker like a cross, circle, or other representation. Many CAD systems allow you to choose the style and size of the mark that is used to represent points. Most CAD systems offer three ways to specify a point:

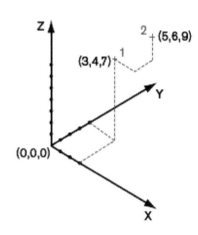

- End the coordinates for the point

- Select a point in the Graphics window

- Enter a point's location by its relationship to existing geometry (Example: a centerpoint, an endpoint of a line, or an intersection of two lines)

Picking a point from the screen is a quick way to enter points when the exact location is not important, but the accuracy of the CAD database makes it impossible to enter a location accurately in this way.

Lines

A straight line is defined as the shortest distance between two points. Geometrically, a line has length, but no other dimension such as width or thickness. Lines are used in drawings to represent the edge view of a surface, the limiting element of a contoured surface, or the edge formed where two surfaces on an object join. In CAD, 2D lines are typically stored by the coordinates (x,y) of their endpoints.

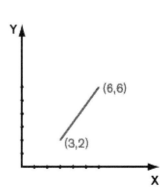

Planes

Planes are defined by:

- Two parallel lines

- Three points not lying in a straight line

- A point and a line

- Two intersecting lines

The last three ways to define a plane are all special cases of the more general case - three points not in a straight line. Knowing what can determine a plane can help you understand the geometry of solid objects - and use the geometry to work in CAD.

For example, a face on an object can is a plane that extends between the vertices and edges of the surface. Most CAD programs allow you to align new entities with an existing plane. You can use any face on the object - whether it is normal, inclined, or oblique - to define a plane for aligning a new entity. The plane can be specified using existing geometry.

Defining planes on the object or in 3D space is an important tool for working in 3D CAD. You will learn more about specifying planes to orient a user coordinate system to make it easy to create CAD geometry later in this text.

Circles

A circle is a set of points that are equidistant from a center point. The distance from the center to one of the points is the radius. The distance across the center to any two points on opposite sides is the diameter. The circumference of a circle contains 360° of arc. In a CAD file, a circle is often stored as a center point and radius. Most CAD systems allow you to define circles by specifying:

- Center and a radius

- Center and a diameter

- Two points on the diameter

- Three points on the circle

- Radius and two entities to which
  the circle is tangent

- Three entities to which the circle is tangent

As with any points, the points defining a circle can be entered with absolute, relative, polar, cylindrical, or spherical coordinates; by picking points from the screen; or by specifying existing geometry.

Arcs

An arc is a portion of a circle. An arc can be defined by specifying:

- Center, radius, and angle measure (sometimes called the included angle or delta angle)

- Center, radius, and arc length

- Center, radius, and chord length

- Endpoints and arc length

- Endpoints and a radius

- Endpoints and one other point on the arc (3 points)

- Endpoints and a chord length

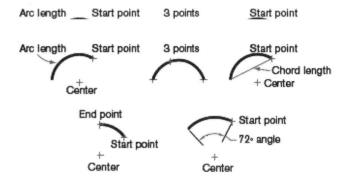

Solid Primitives

Many 3D objects can be visualized, sketched, and modeled in a CAD system by combining simple 3D shapes or primitives. Solid primitives are the building blocks for many solid objects. You should become familiar with these common primitive shapes and their geometry. The same primitives that helped you understand how to sketch objects can also help you create 3D models of them using your computer.

A common set of primitive solids that you can use to build more complex objects is illustrated: (a) box, (b) sphere, (c) cylinder, (d) cone, (e) torus, (f) wedge, and (g) pyramid.

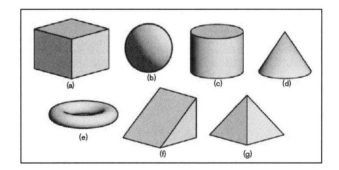

☀ Look around the room and identify some solid primitives that make up the shapes you see. The ability to identify the primitive shapes can help you model features of the objects.

Alphabet of Lines

The lines used in drafting are referred to as the alphabet of lines.

Line types and conventions for mechanical drawings are covered in ANSI Standard Y14.2M. There are four distinct thicknesses of lines: Very Thick, Thick, Medium and Thin.

Every line on your drawing has a meaning. In other words, lines are symbols that mean a specific thing. The line type determines if the line is part of the object or conveys information about the object.

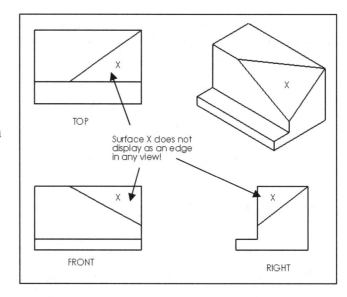

Below is a list of the most common line types and widths used in orthographic projection.

Visible lines: Visible lines (object or feature lines) are continuous lines used to represent the visible edges and contours (features) of an object. Since visible lines are the most important lines, they must stand out from all other secondary lines on the drawing. The line type is continuous and the line weight is thick (0.5 - 0.6 mm).

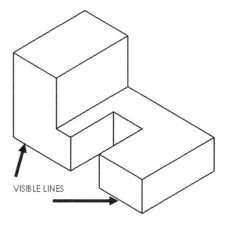

Hidden lines: Hidden lines are short-narrow dashed lines. They represent the hidden features of an object. Hidden lines should always begin and end with a dash, except when a dash would form a continuation of a visible line.

Dashes always meet at corners, and a hidden arc should start with dashes at the tangent points. When the arc is small, the length of the dash may be modified to maintain a uniform and neat appearance.

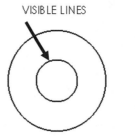

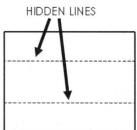

Excessive hidden lines are difficult to follow. Therefore, only lines or features that add to the clearness and the conciseness of the drawing should be displayed. Line weight is medium thick (0.35 - 0.45 mm).

Confusing and conflicting hidden lines should be eliminated. If hidden lines do not adequately define a part's configuration, a section should be taken that imaginarily cuts the part. Whenever possible, hidden lines are eliminated from the sectioned portion of a drawing. In SolidWorks, to hide a line, right click the line in a drawing view, click Hide.

Dimension lines: Dimension lines are thin lines used to show the extent and the direction of dimensions. Space for a single line of numerals is provided by a break in the dimension line.

If possible, dimension lines are aligned and grouped for uniform appearance and ease of reading. For example, parallel dimension lines should be spaced not less than (6 mm) apart, and no dimension line should be closer than (10 mm) to the outline of an object feature [(12 mm) is the preferred distance].

All dimension lines terminate with an arrowhead on mechanical engineering drawings, a slash or a dot in architecture drawings. The preferred ending is the arrowhead to an edge or a dot to a face. Line weight is thin (0.3 mm).

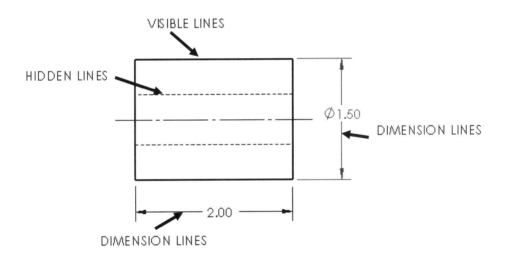

Extension lines: Extension lines are used to indicate the termination of a dimension. An extension line must not touch the feature from which it extends, but should start approximately (2 - 3mm) from the feature being dimensioned and extended the same amount beyond the arrow side of the last dimension line.

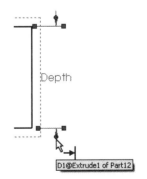

In SolidWorks, use the control points to create the needed extension line gap of ~1.5 - 2.5mms.

In SolidWorks, inserted dimensions in the drawing are displayed in gray. Imported dimensions from the part are displayed in black.

When extension lines cross other extension lines, dimension lines, leader lines, or object lines, they are usually not broken. When extension lines cross dimension lines close to an arrowhead, breaking the extension line is recommended for clarity. Line weight is thin (0.3 mm).

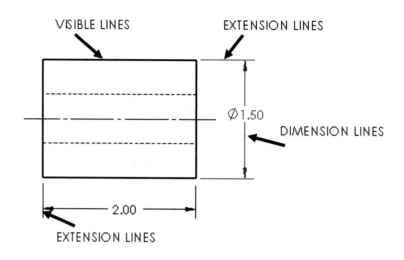

Leader lines: A leader line is a continuous straight line that extends at an angle from a note, a dimension, or other reference to a feature. An arrowhead touches the feature at that end of the leader. At the note end, a horizontal bar (6 mm) long terminates the leader approximately (3 mm) away from mid-height of the note's lettering, either at the beginning or end of the first line.

Leaders should not be bent to underline the note or dimension. Unless unavoidable, leaders should not be bent in any way except to form the horizontal terminating bar at the note end of the leader.

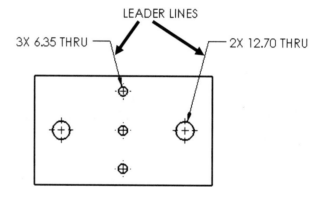

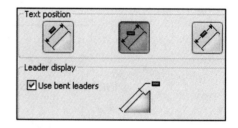

In SolidWorks, use the dimension option to control Leader display.

Leaders usually do not cross. Leaders or extension lines may cross an outline of a part or extension lines if necessary, but they usually remain continuous and unbroken at the point of intersection. When a leader is directed to a circle or a circular arc, its direction should be radial. Line weight is thin (0.3 mm).

Break lines: Break lines are applied to represent an imaginary cut in an object, so the interior of the object can be viewed or fitted to the sheet. Line weight is thick (0.5 – 0.6 mm).

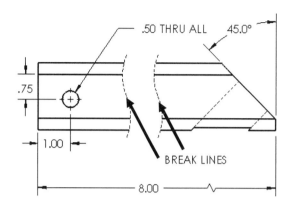

In SolidWorks, Break lines are displayed as short dashes or continuous solid lines, straight, curved or zig zag.

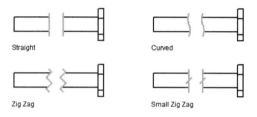

Centerlines: Centerlines are thin, long and short dashes, alternately and evenly spaced, with long dashes placed at each end of the line. The long dash is dependent on the size of the drawing and normally varies in length from (20 to 50 mm). Short dashes, depending on the length of the required centerline should be approximately (1.5 to 3.0 mm). Very short centerlines may be unbroken with dashes at both ends.

Centerlines are used to represent the axes of symmetrical parts of features, bolt circles, paths of motion, and pitch circles. They should extend about (3 mm) beyond the outline of symmetry, unless they are used as extension lines for dimensioning. Every circle, and some arcs, should have two centerlines that intersect at their center of the short dashes. Line weight is thin (0.3mm).

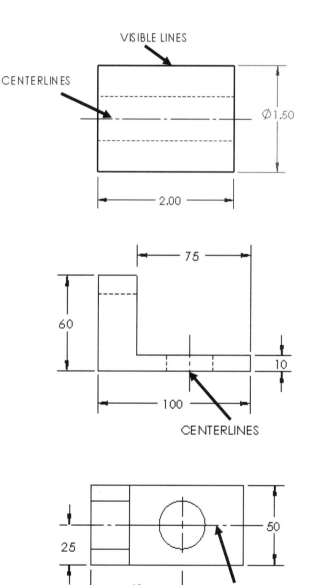

Phantom lines: Phantom lines consist of medium - thin, long and short dashes. They are used to represent alternate positions of moving parts, adjacent positions of related parts, and repeated details. They are also used to show the cast, or the rough shape, of a part before machining. The line starts and ends with the long dash of (15 mm) with about (1.5 mm) space between the long and short dashes. Line weight is usually (0.45 mm).

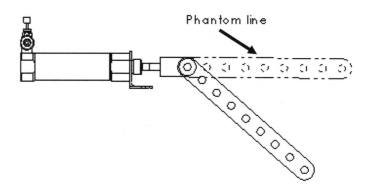

Section lines: Section lines are thin, uniformly spaced lines that indicate the exposed cut surfaces of an object in a sectional view.

Spacing should be approximately (3 mm) and at an angle of 45°. The section pattern is determined by the material being "cut" or sectioned. Section lines are commonly referred to as "cross-hatching." Line weight is thin (0.3 mm). Multiple parts in an assembly use different section angles for clarity.

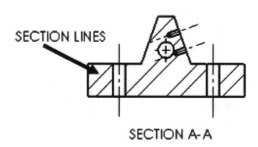

In this text, you will concentrate on creating 3D models using SolidWorks 2012. 3D modeling is an integral part of the design, manufacturing, and construction industry and contributes to increase productivity in all aspects of a project.

Section lines can serve the purpose of identifying the kind of material the part is made from.

Below are few common section line types for various materials:

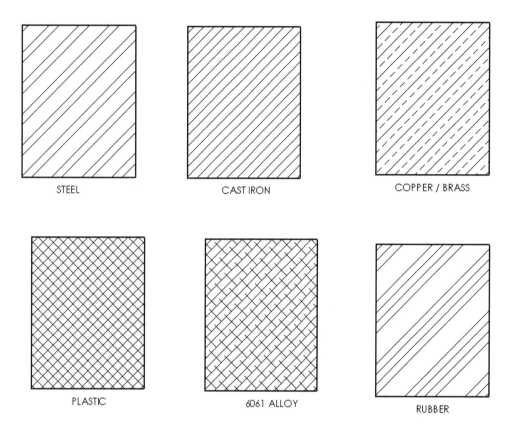

STEEL

CAST IRON

COPPER / BRASS

PLASTIC

6061 ALLOY

RUBBER

A Section lined area is always completely bounded by a visible outline.

Cutting Plane lines: Cutting Plane lines show where an imaginary cut has been made through an object in order to view and understand the interior features. Line type is phantom. Line weight is very thick (0.6 - 0.8 mm).

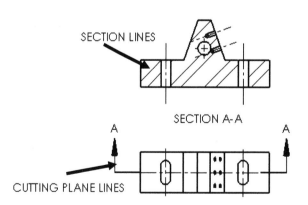

Arrows are located at the ends of the cutting plane line and the direction indicates the line of sight into the object.

Line weight (also called hierarchy) refers to thickness.

☀ In hand drafting, the contrast in lines should be in the line weight and not in the density. All lines are of equal density except for Construction lines - Light Thin so they can be erased.

Precedence of Line Types

When creating Orthographic views, it is common for one line type to overlap another line type. When this occurs, drawing conventions have established an order of precedence. For example - perhaps a visible line type belongs in the same location as a hidden line type, since the visible features of a part (object lines) are represented by thick solid lines, they take precedence over all other lines.

If a centerline and cutting plane coincides, the more important one should take precedence. Normally the cutting plane line, drawn with a thicker weight, will take precedence.

The following list gives the preferred precedence of lines on your drawing:

1. Visible (Object / Feature) Lines

2. Hidden Lines

3. Cutting Plane Lines

4. Centerlines

5. Break Lines

6. Dimension Lines

7. Extension Lines / Lead Lines

8. Section Lines / Crosshatch Lines

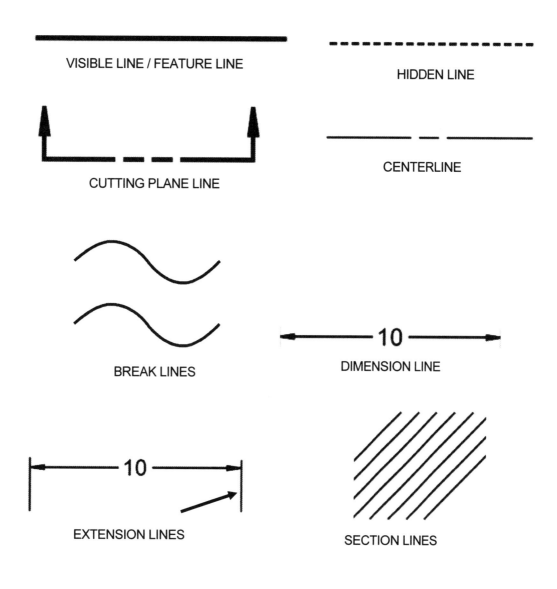

VISIBLE LINE / FEATURE LINE

HIDDEN LINE

CUTTING PLANE LINE

CENTERLINE

BREAK LINES

DIMENSION LINE

EXTENSION LINES

SECTION LINES

LEADER LINE - BENT

Alphabet of Lines Exercises:

Identify the correct line types:

Exercise 1:

Identify the number of line types and the type of lines in the below view.

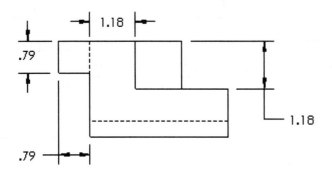

Number of Line Types:_____

Types of Lines: _____

_____

Exercise 2:

Identify the number of line types and the type of lines in the below view.

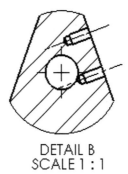

DETAIL B
SCALE 1 : 1

Number of Line Types:_____

Types of Lines: _____

_____

Exercise 3:

Identify the number of line types and the type of lines in the below view.

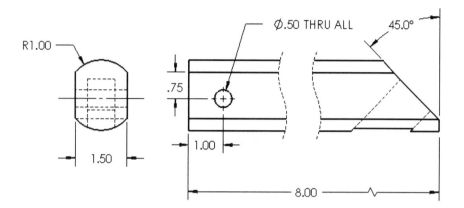

Number of Line Types:_____

Types of Lines: _____

_____

Orthographic Projection

Before an object is drawn or created, it is examined to determine which views will best furnish the information required to manufacture the object. The surface, which is to be displayed as the observer looks at the object, is called the Front view.

To obtain the front view of an object, turn the object (either physically or mentally) so that the front of the object is all you see. The top and right-side views can be obtained in a similar fashion.

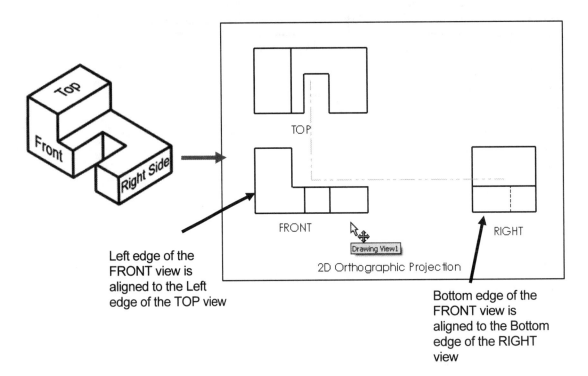

Left edge of the FRONT view is aligned to the Left edge of the TOP view

2D Orthographic Projection

Bottom edge of the FRONT view is aligned to the Bottom edge of the RIGHT view

Orthographic projection is a common method of representing three-dimensional objects, usually by three two-dimensional drawings, in each of the object is viewed along parallel lines that are perpendicular to the plane of the drawing as illustrated. These lines remain parallel to the projection plane and are not convergent.

Orthographic projection provides the ability to represent the shape of an object using two or more views. These views together with dimensions and annotations are sufficient to manufacture the part.

The six principle views of an orthographic projection are illustrated. Each view is created by looking directly at the object in the indicated direction.

Glass Box and Six Principal Orthographic Views

The Glass box method is a traditional method of placing an object in an *imaginary glass box* to view the six principle views.

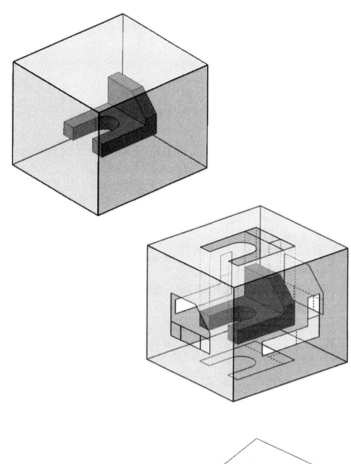

Imagine that the object you are going to draw is placed inside a glass box, so that the large flat surfaces of the object are parallel to the walls of the box.

From each point on the object, imagine a ray, or projector perpendicular to the wall of the box forming the view of the object on that wall or projection plane.

Then unfold the sides of the imaginary glass box to create the orthographic projection of the object.

There are two different types of Angle Projection: First and Third Angle Projection.

- First Angle Projection is used in Europe and Asia.

- Third Angle Projection is used in the United States.

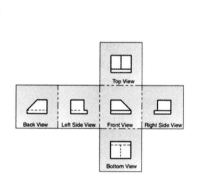

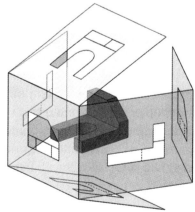

Third Angle Projection is used in the book. Imagine that the walls of the box are hinged and unfold the views outward around the front view. This will provide you with the standard arrangement of views.

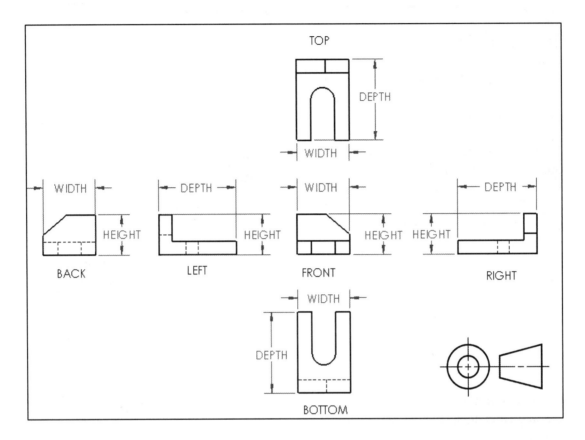

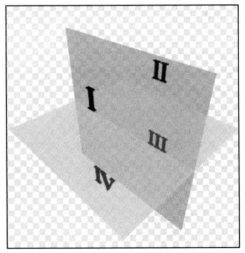

SolidWorks uses BACK view vs. REAR view.

Modern orthographic projection is derived from Gaspard Monge's descriptive geometry. Monge defined a reference system of two viewing planes, horizontal H ("ground") and vertical V ("backdrop"). These two planes intersect to partition 3D space into four quadrants. In **Third-Angle projection**, the object is conceptually located in quadrant III.

Both First Angle and Third Angle projections result in the same six views; the difference between them is the arrangement of these views around the box.

Below is an illustration of First Angle Projection.

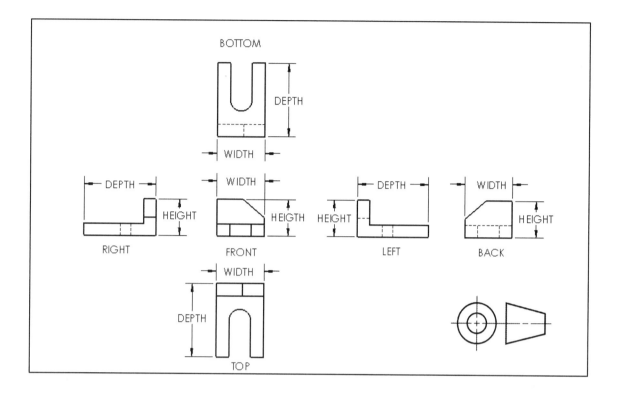

In First Angle projection, the object is conceptually located in quadrant I, i.e. it floats above and before the viewing planes, the planes are opaque, and each view is pushed through the object onto the plane furthest from it.

Both First Angle and Third Angle projections result in the same six views; the difference between them is the arrangement of these views around the box.

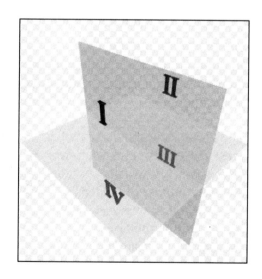

☀ SolidWorks uses BACK view vs. REAR view.

☀ In SolidWorks, when you create a new part or assembly, the three default Planes (Front, Right and Top) are align with specific views. The Plane you select for the Base sketch determines the orientation of the part or assembly.

Height, Width, and Depth Dimensions

The term height, width, and depth refer to specific dimensions or part sizes. ANSI designations for these dimensions are illustrated above. Height is the vertical distance between two or more lines or surfaces (features) which are in horizontal planes. Width refers to the horizontal distance between surfaces in profile planes. In the machine shop, the terms length and width are used interchangeably. Depth is the horizontal (front to back) distance between two features in frontal planes. Depth is often identified in the shop as the thickness of a part or feature.

No orthographic view can show height, width and depth in the same view. Each view only depicts two dimensions. Therefore, a minimum of two projections or views are required to display all three dimensions of an object. Typically, most orthographic drawings use three standard views to accurately depict the object unless additional views are needed for clarity.

The Top and Front views are aligned vertically and share the same width dimension. The Front and Right side views are aligned horizontally and share the same height dimension.

When drawing orthographic projections, spacing is usually equal between each of the views. The Front, Top, and Right views are most frequently used to depict or orthographic projection.

The Front view should show the **most features** or characteristics of the object. It usually contains the least number of hidden lines. All other views are based (projected) on the orientation chosen for the front view.

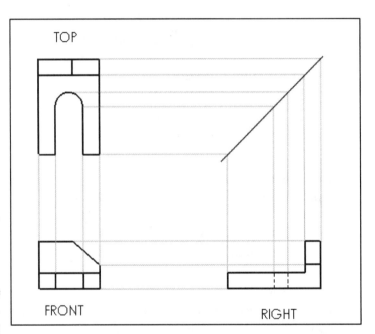

Transferring Dimensions

In SolidWorks, you can view the projection lines from the Front view placement.

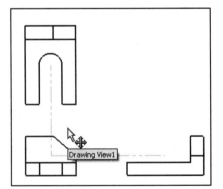

When transferring measurements between views, the width dimension can be projected from the Front view upward to the Top view or vice versa and that the height dimension can be projected directly across from the Front view to the Right view.

Depth dimensions are transferred from the Top view to the Right view or vice versa.

Height dimensions can be easily projected between two views using the grid on grid paper. Note: the grid is not displayed in the illustration to provide improved line and picture quality.

The miter line drawn at a 45° is used to transfer depth dimensions between the Top and Right view.

When constructing an Orthographic projection, you need to include enough views to completely describe the true shape of the part. You will address this later in the book.

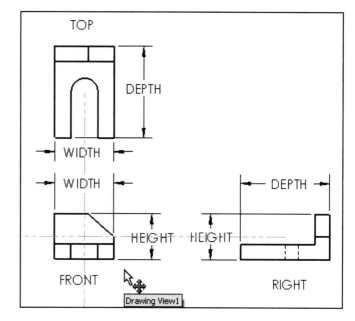

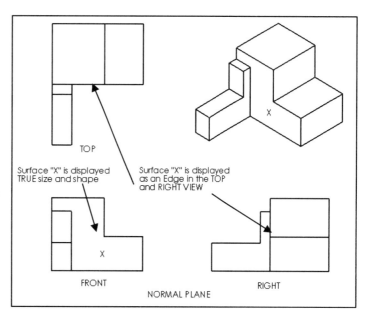

Orthographic Projection Exercises:
Exercise 1:

Label the four remaining Principle views with the appropriate view name. Identify the Angle of Projection type.

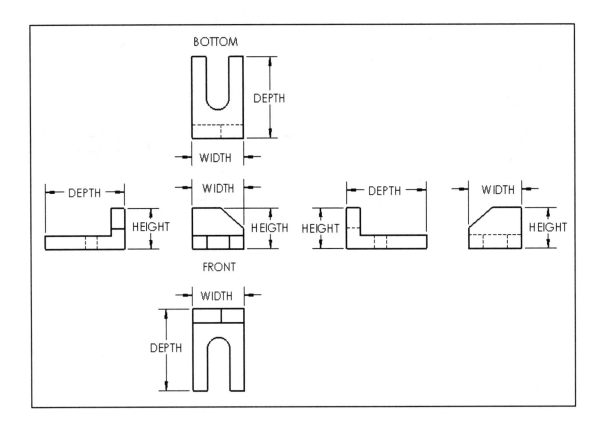

Angle of Projection type:_____

Describe the difference between the BOTTOM view and the TOP view_____

Describe the difference between the RIGHT view and the LEFT view._____

Which views have the least amount of Hidden Lines?_____

Exercise 2:

Identify the number of views required to completely describe the illustrated box.

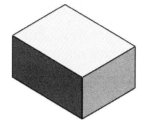

1.) One view

2.) Two views

3.) Three views

4.) Four views

5.) More than four views

Explain
Why?_____

_____

_____

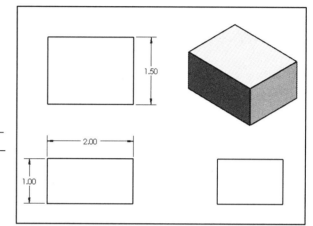

Exercise 3:

Identify the number of views required to completely describe the illustrated sphere.

1.) One view

2.) Two views

3.) Three views

4.) Four views

5.) More than four views

Explain
Why?_____

_____

_____

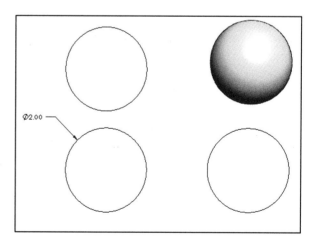

Exercise 4:

In Third Angle Projection, identify the view that displays
the most information about the illustrated model.

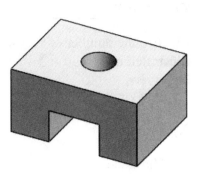

1.) FRONT view.

2.) TOP view

3.) BOTTOM view

4.) RIGHT view

Explain
Why?_____
_____

Exercise 5:

Third Angle Projection is displayed. Draw the Visible
Feature Lines of the TOP view for the model. Fill in the
missing lines in the FRONT view, RIGHT view and TOP view.

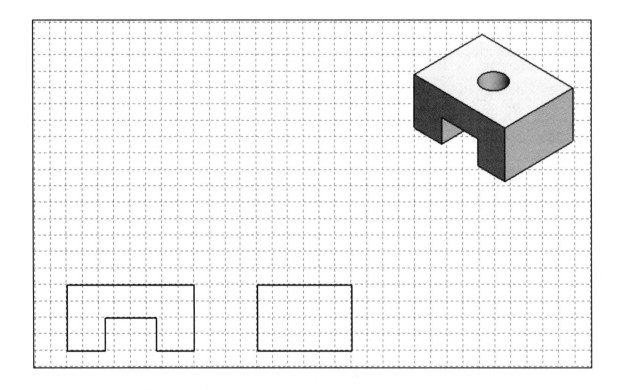

Exercise 6:

Third Angle Projection is displayed. Fill in the missing lines in the FRONT view, RIGHT view and TOP view.

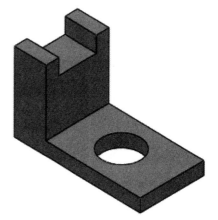

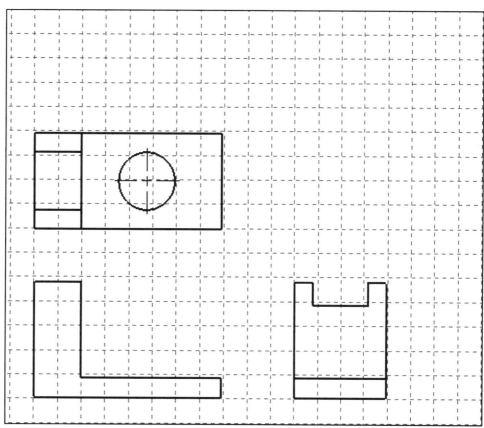

Exercise 7:

Third Angle Projection is displayed. Fill in the missing
lines in the FRONT view, RIGHT view and TOP view.

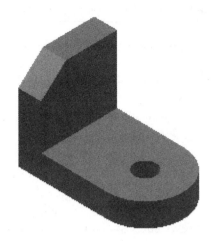

☀ Tangent Edges are displayed for educational
purposes.

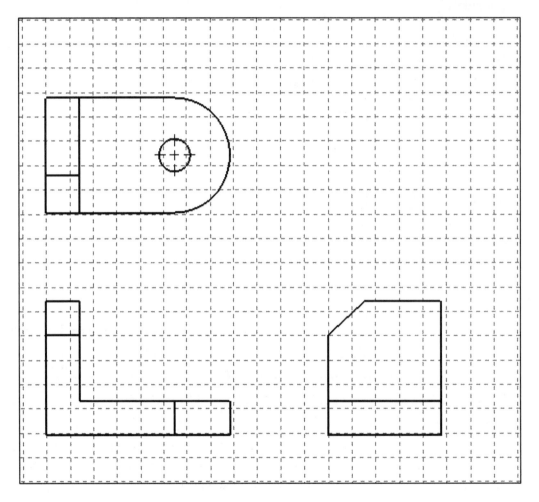

Planes (Normal, Inclined and Oblique)

Each type of plane (Normal, Inclined and Oblique) has unique characteristics when viewed in orthographic projection. To understand the three basic planes, each is illustrated.

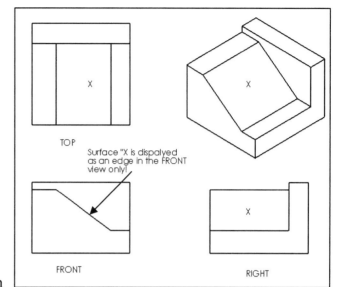

Normal planes appear as an edge in two views and a true sized in the remaining view when using three views such as the Front, Top, and Right side views.

When viewing the six possible views in an orthographic projection, a normal plane appears as an edge in four views and a true sized plane in the other two views.

Inclined Planes appear as an edge view in one of the three views as illustrated. The inclined plane is displayed as a rectangular surface in the other two views. Note: The two rectangular surfaces appear "normal" they are foreshortened and no not display the true size or shape of the object.

Oblique Planes do not display as an edge view in any of the six principle orthographic views. They are not parallel or perpendicular to the projection planes. Oblique planes are displayed as a plane and have the same number of corners in each of the six views.

☀ In SolidWorks, you can insert a sketch on any plane or face.

☀ In SolidWorks, when you create a new part or assembly, the three default Planes (Front, Right and Top) are align with specific views. The Plane you select for the Base sketch determines the orientation of the part or assembly.

Plane Exercises:
Exercise 1:

Identify the surfaces with the appropriate letter that will appear in the FRONT view, TOP view and RIGHT view.

FRONT view surfaces:_____

TOP view surfaces:_____

RIGHT view surfaces:_____

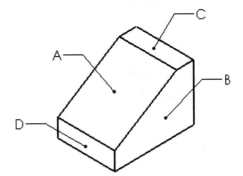

Exercise 2:

Estimate the size; draw the FRONT view, TOP view and RIGHT view of the illustrated part.

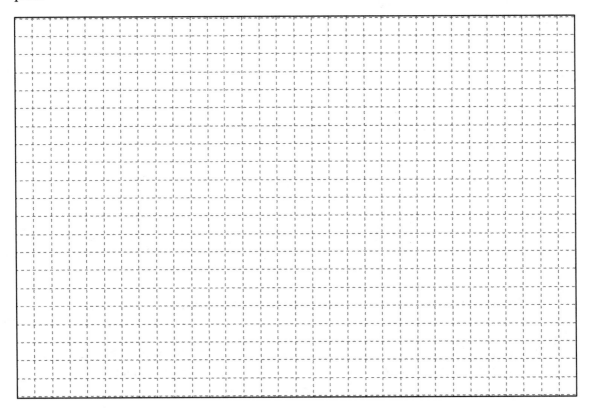

Exercise 3:

Identify the surfaces with the appropriate letter that will appear in the FRONT view, TOP view and RIGHT view.

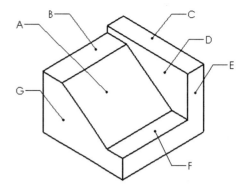

FRONT view surfaces:_____

TOP view surfaces:_____

RIGHT view surfaces:_____

Exercise 4:

Estimate the size; draw the FRONT view, TOP view and RIGHT view of the illustrated part.

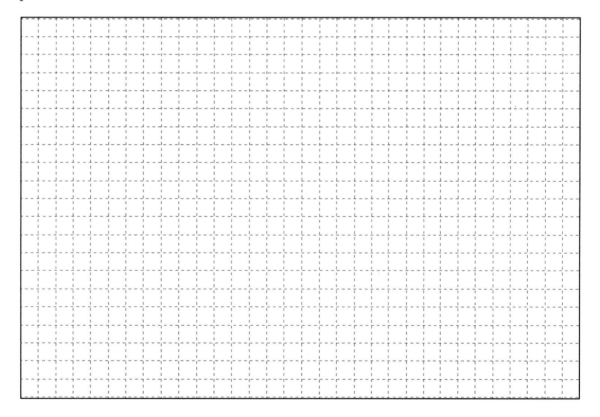

Exercise 5:

Identify the surfaces with the appropriate letter that will appear in the FRONT view, TOP view and RIGHT view.

FRONT view surfaces:_____

TOP view surfaces:_____

RIGHT view surfaces:_____

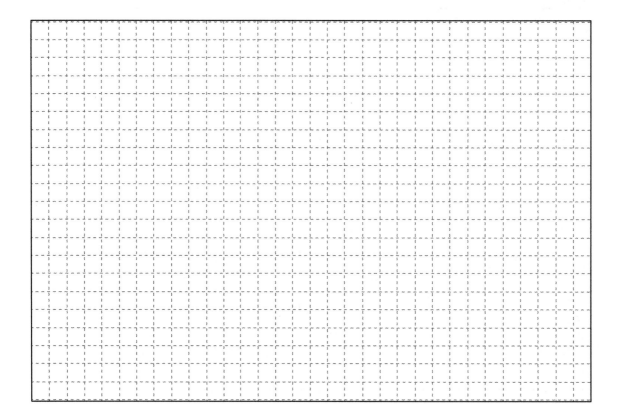

Exercise 6:

Estimate the size; draw the FRONT view, TOP view and RIGHT view of the illustrated part.

Exercise 7:

Identify the surfaces with the appropriate letter that will appear in the FRONT view, TOP view and RIGHT view.

FRONT view surfaces:_____

TOP view surfaces:_____

RIGHT view surfaces:_____

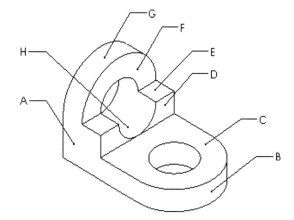

Exercise 8:

Identify the surfaces with the appropriate letter that will appear in the FRONT view, TOP view and RIGHT view.

FRONT view surfaces:_____

TOP view surfaces:_____

RIGHT view surfaces:_____

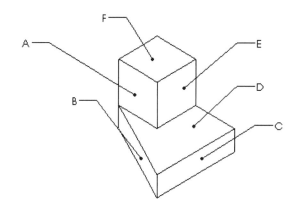

Exercise 9:

Identify the surfaces with the appropriate letter that will appear in the FRONT view, TOP view and RIGHT view.

FRONT view surfaces:_____

TOP view surfaces:_____

RIGHT view surfaces:_____

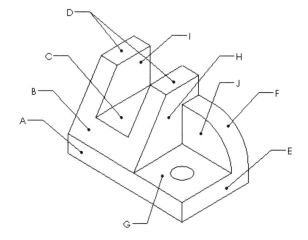

Exercise 10:

Fill in the following table for the below object.

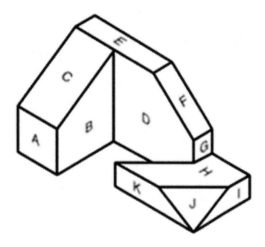

SURFACE	TOP	FRONT	RIGHT
A			
B			
C			
D			
E			
F			
G			
H			
I			
J			
K			

Exercise 11:

Fill in the following table for the below object.

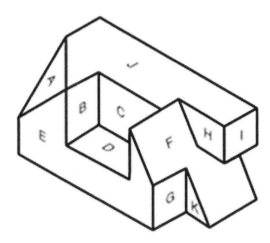

SURFACE	TOP	FRONT	RIGHT
A			
B			
C			
D			
E			
F			
G			
H			
I			
J			
K			

Chapter Summary

Chapter 1 provided a short discussion on the history of Engineering Graphics and the evolution of manual drawing/drafting. You were introduced to general sketching techniques and the 2D and 3D Cartesian Coordinate system. In engineering graphics there is a specific alphabet of lines that represent different types of geometry. In Orthographic projection, the Glass Box method was used to distinguish the six principle views. In the United State, you use Third Angle Projection. However, it is important to know First Angle Projection and other international standards.

```
Avi folder
Alphabet of lines and Precedent of Line Types
Boolean Operation
Design Intent
Fastners in General
Fundamental ASME Y14.5 Dimensioning Rules
General Tolerancing and Fits
History of Engineering Graphics
Measurement and Scale
Open a Drawing Document 2012
Open an Assembly Document 2012
Part and Drawing Dimensioning
SolidWorks Basic Concepts
Visualization, Arrangement of Views, and Primitives
```

View the files on the enclosed DVD in the book for additional information.

Chapter Terminology

Alphabet of Lines: Each line on a technical drawing has a definite meaning and is draw in a certain way. The line conventions recommended by the American National Standards Institute (ANSI) are presented in this text.

Axonometric Projection: A type of parallel projection, more specifically a type of orthographic projection, used to create a pictorial drawing of an object, where the object is rotated along one or more of its axes relative to the plane of projection.

Cartesian Coordinate system: Specifies each point uniquely in a plane by a pair of numerical coordinates, which are the signed distances from the point to two fixed perpendicular directed lines, measured in the same unit of length. Each reference line is called a coordinate axis or just axis of the system, and the point where they meet is its origin.

Depth: The horizontal (front to back) distance between two features in frontal planes. Depth is often identified in the shop as the thickness of a part or feature.

Engineering Graphics: Translates ideas from design layouts, specifications, rough sketches, and calculations of engineers & architects into working drawings, maps, plans, and illustrations which are used in making products.

First Angle Projection: In First Angle Projection the Top view is looking at the bottom of the part. First Angle Projection is used in Europe and most of the world. However America and Australia use a method known as Third Angle Projection.

French curve: A template made out of plastic, metal or wood composed of many different curves. It is used in manual drafting to draw smooth curves of varying radii.

Glass Box method: A traditional method of placing an object in an *imaginary glass box* to view the six principle views.

Grid: A system of fixed horizontal and vertical divisions.

Height: The vertical distance between two or more lines or surfaces (features) which are in horizontal planes.

Isometric Projection: A form of graphical projection, more specifically, a form of axonometric projection. It is a method of visually representing three-dimensional objects in two dimensions, in which the three coordinate axes appear equally foreshortened and the angles between any two of them are 120 °.

Precedence of Line types: When obtaining orthographic views, it is common for one type of line to overlap another type. When this occurs, drawing conventions have established an order of precedence.

Origin: The point of intersection, where the X,Y,Z axes meet, is called the origin.

Orthographic Projection: A means of representing a three-dimensional object in two dimensions. It is a form of parallel projection, where the view direction is orthogonal to the projection plane, resulting in every plane of the scene appearing in affine transformation on the viewing surface.

Right-Hand Rule: Is a common mnemonic for understanding notation conventions for vectors in 3 dimensions.

Scale: A relative term meaning "size" in relationship to some system of measurement.

T-Square: A technical drawing instrument, primarily a guide for drawing horizontal lines on a drafting table. It is used to guide the triangle that draws vertical lines. Its name comes from the general shape of the instrument where the horizontal member of the T slides on the side of the drafting table. Common lengths are 18", 24", 30", 36" and 42".

Third Angle Projection: In Third angle projection the Top View is looking at the Top of the part. First Angle Projection is used in Europe and most of the world. America and Australia use the Third Angle Projection method.

Units: Used in the measurement of physical quantities. Decimal inch dimensioning and Millimeter dimensioning are the two types of common units specified for engineering parts and drawings.

Width: The horizontal distance between surfaces in profile planes. In the machine shop, the terms length and width are used interchangeably.

Questions

1. Describe the Cartesian coordinate system.

2. Name the point of intersection, where the axes meet _____.

3. Explain the Right-hand rule in drafting.

4. Why is Freehand sketching important to understand?

5. Describe the different between First and Third Angle Projection type.

6. True or False. First Angle Projection type is used in the United States.

7. Explain the Precedent of Line types. Provide a few examples.

8. True or False. A Hidden Line has precedent over a Visible / Feature line.

9. True or False. The intersection of the two axes creates four regions, called quadrants, indicated by the Roman numerals I, II, III, and IV.

10. Explain the Glass Box method for Orthographic Projection.

11. True or False. Both First Angle and Third Angle Projection type result in the same six views; the difference between them is the arrangement of these views.

12. True or False. Section lines can serve the purpose of identifying the kind of material the part is made from.

13. True or False. All dimension lines terminate with an arrowhead on mechanical engineering drawings.

14. True or False. Break lines are applied to represent an imaginary cut in an object, so the interior of the object can be viewed or fitted to the sheet. Provide an example.

15. True or False. The Front view should show the most features or characteristics of the object. It usually contains the least number of hidden lines. All other views are based (projected) on the orientation chosen for the front view. Explain your answer.

Exercises

Exercise 1.1: Third Angle Projection type is displayed. Name the illustrated views in the below model.

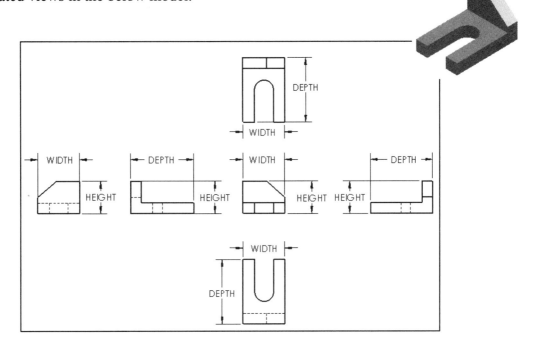

Exercise 1.2: First Angle Projection type is displayed. Name the illustrated views in the below model.

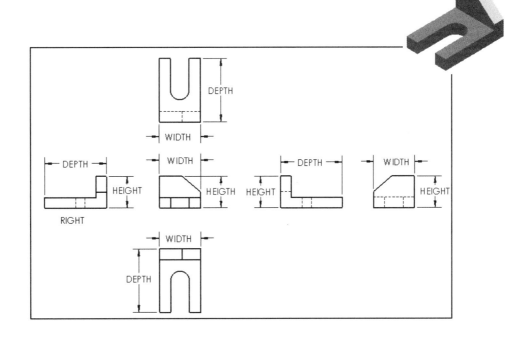

Exercise 1.3: Identify the various Line types in the below model.

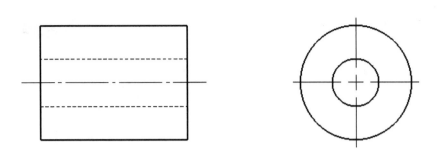

Exercise 1.4: Third Angle Projection type is displayed. Estimating the distance, draw the Visible Feature Lines of the TOP view for the model. Draw any Hidden lines or Centerlines if needed. Identify the view that displays the most information about the illustrated model.

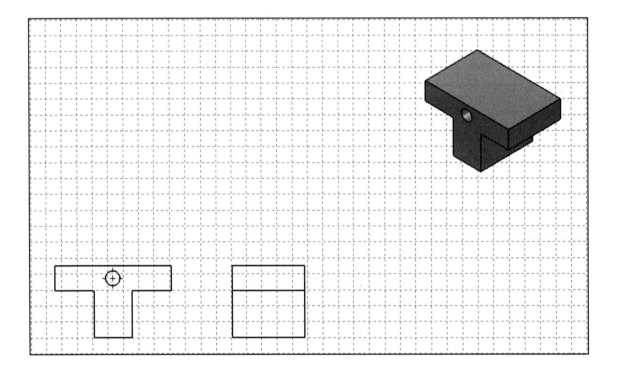

Exercise 1.5: Third Angle Projection type is displayed. Estimating the distance, draw the Visible Feature Lines of the Right view for the model. Draw any Hidden lines if needed. Identify the view that displays the most information about the illustrated model.

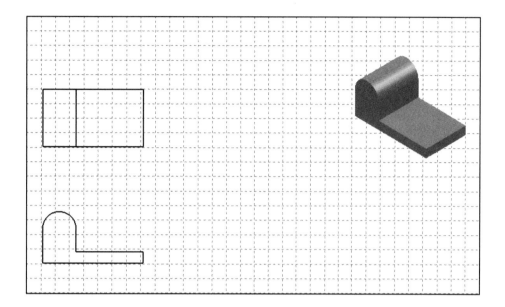

Exercise 1.6: Estimating the distance, draw the Front view, Top view and Right view. Draw the Visible Feature Lines for the model. Draw any Hidden lines if needed. Which view displays the most information about the illustrated model? Note: Third Angle Projection.

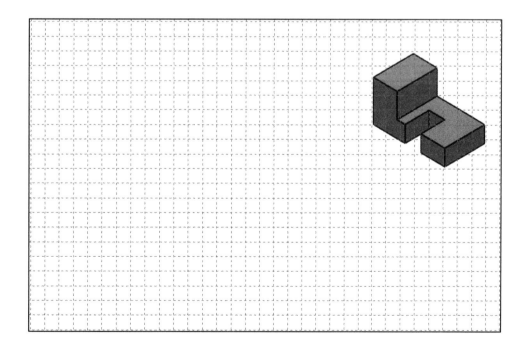

Exercise 1.7: Estimating the distance, draw the Front view, Top view and Right view. Draw the Visible Feature Lines for the model. Draw any Hidden lines or Centerlines if needed. Which view displays the most information about the illustrated model? Note: Third Angle Projection type.

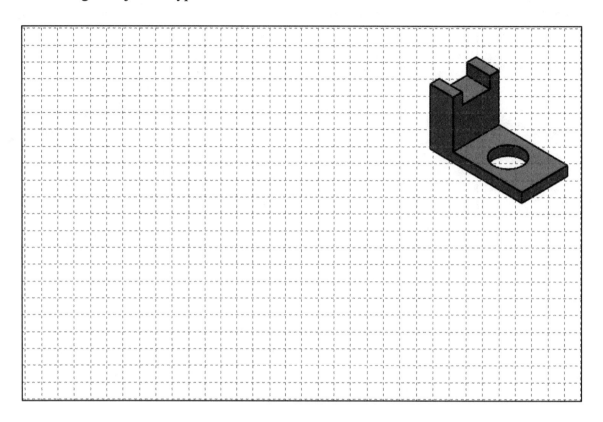

Exercise 1.8: Draw the Isometric view. Note: Third Angle Projection.

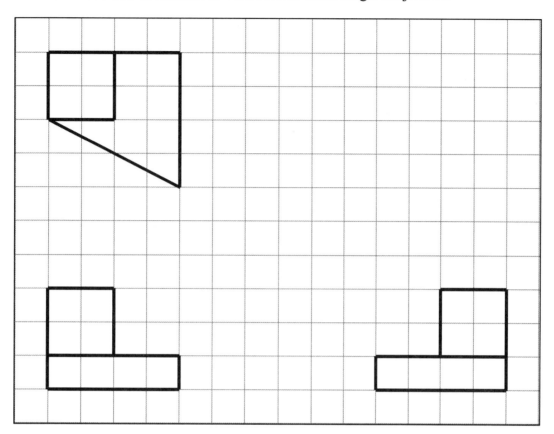

Exercise 1.9: Draw the Isometric view. Note: Third Angle Projection.

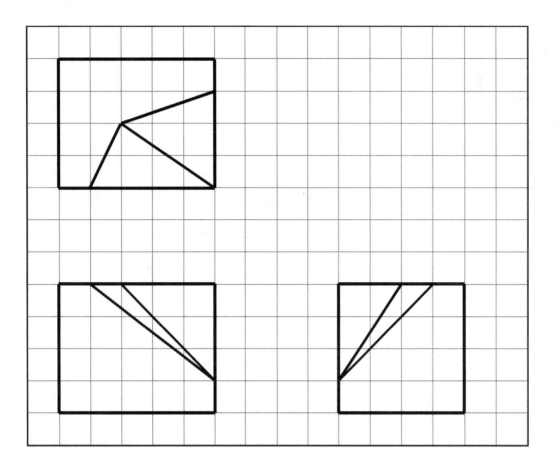

Exercise 1.10: Draw the Isometric view. Note: Third Angle Projection

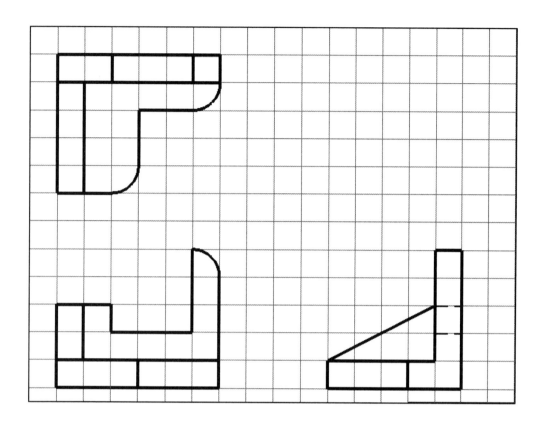

Exercise 1.11:

Identify the surfaces with the appropriate letter that will appear in the FRONT view, TOP view and RIGHT view.

FRONT view
surfaces:_____

TOP view surfaces:_____

RIGHT view
surfaces:_____

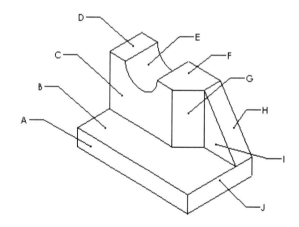

Notes:

Chapter 2

Isometric Projection and Multi View Drawings

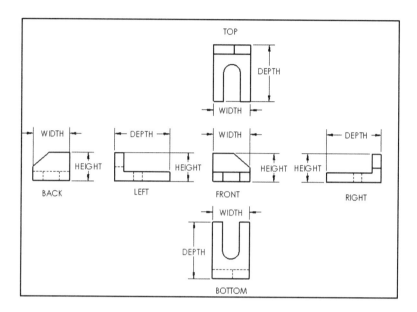

Below are the desired outcomes and usage competencies based on the completion of Chapter 2.

Desired Outcomes:	Usage Competencies:
• Understand Isometric Projection and 2D sketching.	• Identify the three main projection divisions in freehand engineering sketches and drawings: o Axonometric, Oblique, and Perspective
• Knowledge of additional Projection views and arrangement of drawing views.	• Create one and two view drawings.
• Comprehend the history and evolution of CAD and the development of SolidWorks. • Recognize Boolean operations and feature based modeling.	• Identify the development of in historic CAD systems and SolidWorks features, parameters and design intent of a sketch, part, assembly and drawing. • Apply the Boolean operation: Union, Difference and Intersection.

Notes:

Chapter 2 - Isometric Projection and Multi View Drawings

Chapter Overview

Chapter 2 provides a general introduction into Isometric Projection and Sketching along with Additional Projections and arrangement of views. It also covers advanced drawing views and an introduction from manual drafting to CAD.

On the completion of this chapter, you will be able to:

- Understand and explain Isometric Projection.

- Create an Isometric sketch.

- Identify the three main projection divisions in freehand engineering sketches and drawings:

  o Axonometric

  o Oblique

  o Perspective

- Comprehend the history and evolution of CAD.

- Recognize the following Boolean operations: Union, Difference, and Intersection.

- Understand the development of SolidWorks features, parameters and design intent of a sketch, part, assembly and drawing.

Isometric Projections

There are three main projection divisions commonly used in freehand engineering sketches and detailed engineering drawings; they are: 1.) Axonometric, with its divisions in Isometric, Dimetric and Trimetric, 2.) Oblique, and 3.) Perspective. Let's review the three main divisions.

Axonometric is a type of parallel projection, more specifically a type of Orthographic projection, used to create a pictorial drawing of an object, where the object is rotated along one or more of its axes relative to the plane of projection.

There are three main types of Axonometric projection: Isometric, Dimetric, and Trimetric projection depending on the exact angle at which the view deviates from the Orthogonal.

To display Isometric, Dimetric, or Trimetric of a 3D SolidWorks model, select the drop-down arrow from the View Orientation icon in the Heads-up view toolbar.

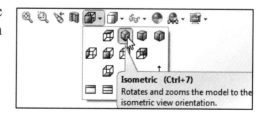

Axonometric drawings often appear distorted because they ignore the foreshortening effects of perspective (foreshortening means the way things appear to get smaller in both height and depth as they recede into the distance). Typically; Axonometric drawings use vertical lines for those lines representing height and sloping parallel edges for all other sides.

- *Isometric Projection.* Isometric projection is a method of visually representing three-dimensional objects in two dimensions, in which the three coordinate axes appear equally foreshortened and the angles between them are 120 °.

The term "Isometric" comes from the Greek for "equal measure", reflecting that the scale along each axis of the projection is the same (this is not true of some other forms of graphical projection).

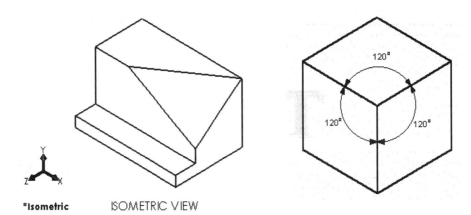

*Isometric   ISOMETRIC VIEW

- *Dimetric Projection.* A Dimetric projection is created using 3 axes but only two of the three axes have equal angles. The smaller these angles are, the less we see of the top surface. The angle is usually around 105°.

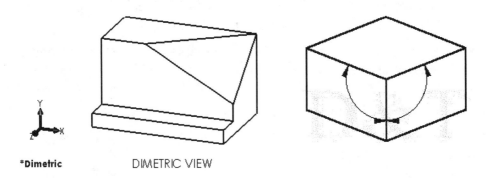

*Dimetric   DIMETRIC VIEW

- *Trimetric Projection.* A Trimetric projection is created using 3 axes where each of the angles between them is different (there are no equal angles). The scale along each of the three axes and the angles among them are determined separately as dictated by the angle of viewing. Approximations in trimetric drawings are common.

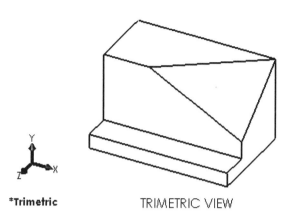

*Trimetric   TRIMETRIC VIEW

Isometric Sketching

Isometric sketches provide a 3D dimensional pictorial representation of an object. Isometric sketches helps in the visualization of an object.

The surface features or the axes of the object are drawn around three axes from a horizontal line; vertical axis, and 30° axis to the right, and a 30° axis to the left. All three axes intersect at a single point on the horizontal line.

All horizontal lines in an Isometric sketch are always drawn at 30° and parallel to each other, and are either to the left or to the right of the vertical.

For this reason, all shapes in an Isometric sketch are not true shapes, they are distorted shapes.

All vertical lines in an Isometric sketch are always drawn vertically, and they are always parallel to each other as illustrated in the following example.

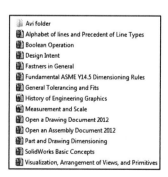

View the additional presentations on the enclosed DVD for supplementary information.

Example 1:

Exercise: Draw an Isometric sketch of a cube.

1. Draw a light horizontal axis (construction line) as illustrated on graph paper. Draw a light vertical axis. Draw a light 30° axis to the right. Draw a light 30° axis to the left.

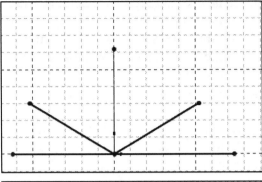

2. Measure the length along the left 30° axis, make a mark and draw a light vertical line.

3. Measure the height along the vertical axis, make a mark and draw a light 30° line to the left to intersect the vertical line drawn in step 2.

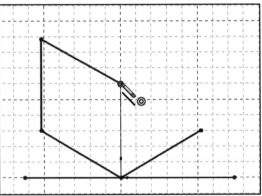

4. Measure the length along the right 30° axis, make a mark and draw a light vertical line.

5. From the height along the vertical axis, make a mark and draw a light 30° line to the right to intersect the vertical line drawn in step 4.

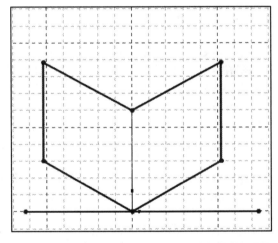

6. Draw a light 30° line to the right and a light 30° line to the left to complete the cube. Once the sketch is complete, darken the shape.

☼ In an Isometric drawing, the object is viewed at an angle, which makes circles appear as ellipses.

☼ Isometric Rule #1: Measurement can only be made on or parallel to the isometric axis.

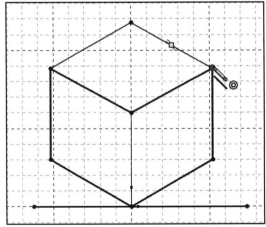

Circles drawn in Axonometric view

A circle drawn on a sloping surface in Axonometric projection will be drawn as an ellipse. An ellipse is a circle turned through an angle. All the examples shown above were box shapes without any curved surfaces. In order to draw curved surfaces we need to know how to draw an ellipse.

If you draw a circle and rotate it slowly, it will become an ellipse. As it is turned through 90° - it will eventually become a straight line. Rotate it 90° again, and it will eventually be back to a circle.

Example 1:

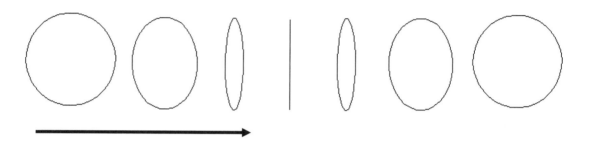

An ellipse has a major axis and a minor axis. The major axis is the axis about which the ellipse is being turned. The minor axis becomes smaller as the angle through which the ellipse is turned approaches 90°.

You can draw a cylinder using the technique shown below. The ellipses can either be sketched freehand or drawn using an ellipse template.

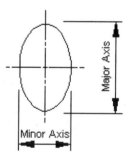

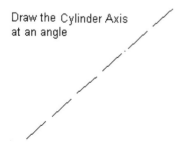

Draw the Cylinder Axis at an angle

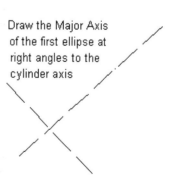

Draw the Major Axis of the first ellipse at right angles to the cylinder axis

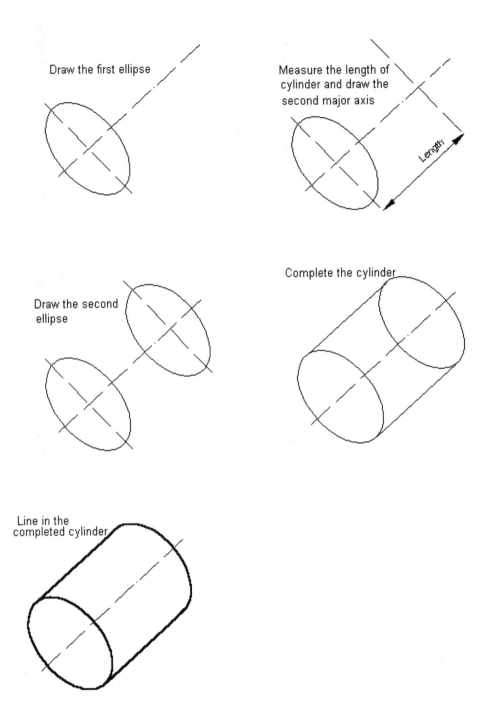

Draw the first ellipse

Measure the length of cylinder and draw the second major axis

Draw the second ellipse

Complete the cylinder

Line in the completed cylinder

💡 Isometric Rule #2: When drawing ellipses on normal isometric planes, the minor axis of the ellipse is perpendicular to the plane containing the ellipse. The minor axis is perpendicular to the corresponding normal isometric plane.

Additional Projections

Oblique Projection: In Oblique projections; the front view is drawn true size, and the receding surfaces are drawn on an angle to give it a pictorial appearance. This form of projection has the advantage of showing one face (the front face) of the object without distortion. Generally, the face with the greatest detail; faces the front.

There are two types of Oblique projection used in engineering design.

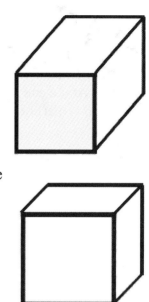

- *Cavalier*: In Cavalier Oblique drawings, all lines (including receding lines) are created to their true length or scale (1:1).

- *Cabinet*: In Cabinet Oblique drawings, the receding lines are shortened by one-half their true length or scale to compensate for distortion and to approximate more closely what the human eye would see. It is for this reason that Cabinet Oblique drawings are the most used form of Oblique drawings.

In Oblique drawings, the three axes of projection are vertical, horizontal, and receding. The front view (vertical & horizontal axis) is parallel to the frontal plane and the other two faces are oblique (receding). The direction of projection can be top-left, top-right, bottom-left, or bottom-right. The receding axis is typically drawn at 60°, 45° or 30°.

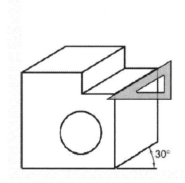
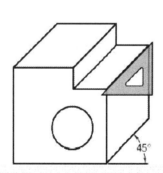
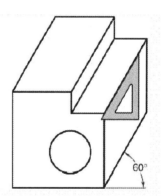

In the oblique pictorials coordinate system, only one axes is at an angle. The most commonly used angle is 45°.

Isometric Rule #1: A measurement can only be made on or parallel to the isometric axis. Therefore you cannot measure an isometric inclined or oblique line in an isometric drawing because they are not parallel to an isometric axis.

Example: Drawing cylinders in Oblique projection is quite simple if the stages outlined below are followed. In comparison with other ways of drawing cylinders (for example, perspective and isometric) using Oblique projection is relatively easy.

Step One: Draw vertical and horizontal centerlines to indicate the center of a circle, and then use a compass to draw the circle itself.

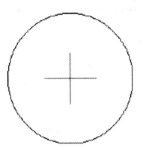

Step Two: Draw a 45° line to match the length on the cylinder. At the end of this line, draw vertical and horizontal centerlines.

Remember the general rule for Oblique is to half all distances projected backwards. If the cylinder is 100mm in length the distance back must be drawn to 50mm.

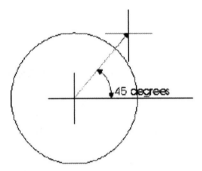

Step Three: Draw the second circle with a compass as illustrated.

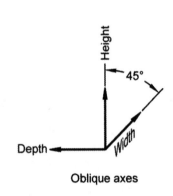

Oblique axes

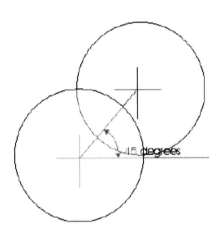

Step Four: Draw two 45° lines - to join the front and back circles.

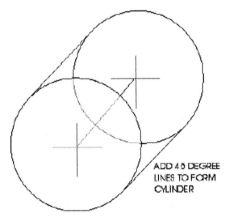

ADD 45 DEGREE
LINES TO FORM
CYLINDER

Step Five: Go over the outline of the cylinder with a fine
pen or sharp pencil. Add shading - if required.

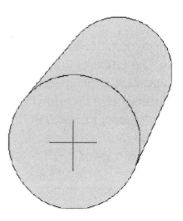

Perspective Projection: If you look along a straight road, the parallel sides of the road appear
to meet at a point in the distance. This point is called the vanishing point and has been used to
add realism. Suppose you want to draw a road that vanishes into the distance.
The rays from the points a given distance from the eye along the lines of the road, are
projected to the eye. The angle formed by the rays decreases with increasing distance from the
eye.

In SolidWorks, to display a Perspective view of the 3D model,
click View, Display, Perspective from the Main toolbar.

A perspective drawing typically aims to reproduce how humans see the world: objects that are farther away seem smaller, etc. Depending on the type of perspective (1-pt, 2-pt, 3-pt), vanishing points are established in the drawing towards which lines recede, mimicking the effect of objects diminishing in size with distance from the viewer.

One vanishing point is typically used for roads, railroad tracks, or buildings viewed so that the front is directly facing the viewer as illustrated above.

Any objects that are made up of lines either directly parallel with the viewer's line of sight or directly perpendicular (the railroad slats) can be represented with one-point perspective.

The selection of the locations of the vanishing points, which is the first step in creating a perspective sketch, will affect the looks of the resulting images.

Two-point perspective can be used to draw the same objects as one-point perspective, rotated: looking at the corner of a house, or looking at two forked roads shrink into the distance, for example. One point represents one set of parallel lines, the other point represents the other. Looking at a house from the corner, one wall would recede towards one vanishing point, the other wall would recede towards the opposite vanishing point as illustrated.

Two Point
Perspective

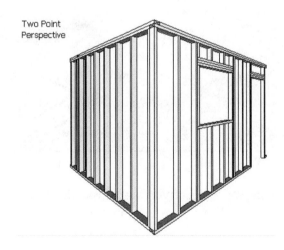

Three-point perspective is usually used for buildings seen from above (or below). In addition to the two vanishing points from before, one for each wall, there is now one for how those walls recede into the ground. This third vanishing point will be below the ground. Looking up at a tall building is another common example of the third vanishing point. This time the third vanishing point is high in space.

One-point, two-point, and three-point perspectives appear to embody different forms of calculated perspective. Despite conventional perspective drawing wisdom, perspective basically just means "position" or "viewpoint." of the viewer relative to the object.

Arrangement of Views

The main purpose of an engineering drawing is to provide the manufacturer with sufficient information needed to build, inspect or assemble the part or assembly according to the specifications of the designer. Since the selection and arrangement of views depends on the complexity of a part, only those views that are needed should be drawn.

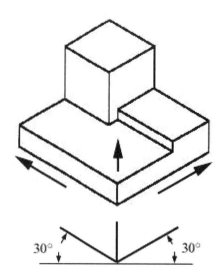

The average part drawing which includes the Front view, Top view and Right view - are known as a three-view drawing. However, the designation of the views is not as important as the fact that the combination of views must give all the details of construction in clear, correct, and concise way.

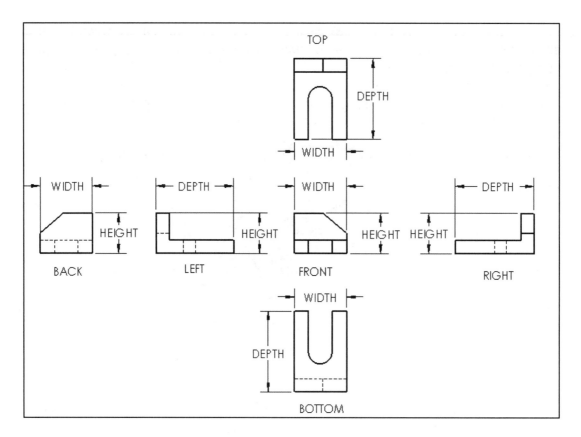

The designer usually selects as a Front view of the object that view which best describes the general shape of the part. This Front view may have no relationship to the actual front position of the part as it fits into an assembly.

The names and positions of the different views that may be used to describe an object are illustrated.

Third "3rd"Angle Projection type is displayed and used in this book.

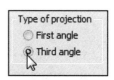

In SolidWorks, when you create a new part or assembly, the three default Planes (Front, Right and Top) are align with specific views. The Plane you select for the Base sketch determines the orientation of the part or assembly.

Two view drawing

Simple symmetrical flat objects and cylindrical parts, such as sleeves, shafts, rods, and studs require only two views to provide the full details of construction.

In the Front view, the centerline runs through the axis of the parts as a horizontal centerline. If the plug is in a vertical position, the centerline runs through the axis as vertical centerline.

The second view of the two-view drawing contains a horizontal and vertical centerline intersection at the center of the circles which make up the part in this view.

The selection of views for a two-view drawing rests largely with the designer/engineer.

Example 1:

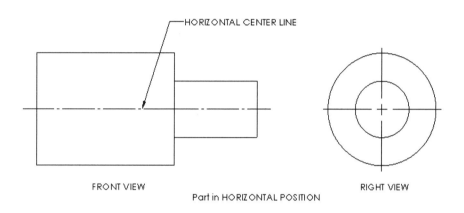

Part in HORIZONTAL POSITION

Example 2:

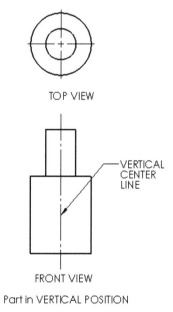

Part in VERTICAL POSITION

One view drawing

Parts that are uniform in shape often require only one view to describe them adequately. This is particularly true of cylindrical objects where a one-view drawing saves time and simplifies the drawing.

When a one-view drawing of a cylindrical part is used, the dimension for the diameter (according to ANSI standards) must be preceded by the symbol Ø, as illustrated.

Example 1:

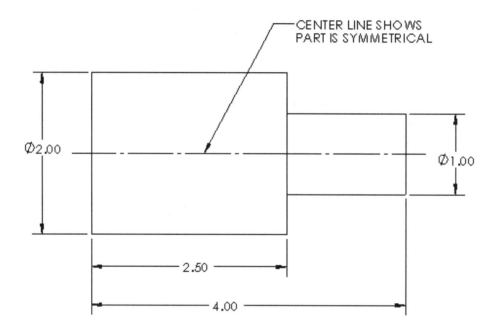

The one-view drawing is also used extensively for flat (Sheet metal) parts. With the addition of notes to supplement the dimensions on the view, the one view furnishes all the necessary information for accurately describing the part. In the first illustration, you have two view: Front view and Top view. In the section illustration, you replace the Top view with a Note: MATERIAL THICKNESS .125 INCH.

 Third Angle Projection type symbol is illustrated.

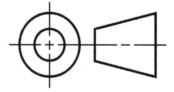

Example 1: No Note Annotation

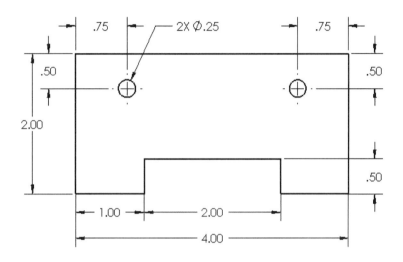

Example 2: Note Annotation to replace the TOP view

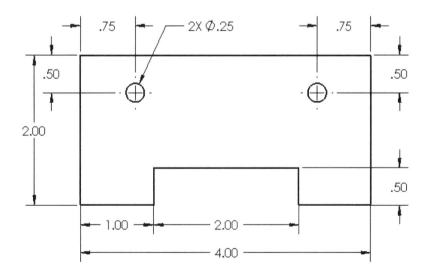

Example 3: Note Fastener Annotation

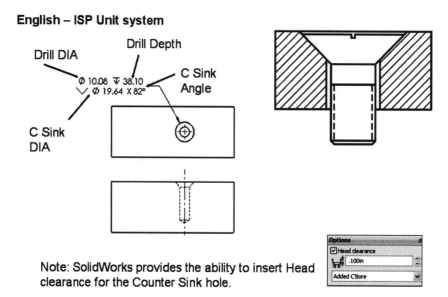

English – ISP Unit system

Drill DIA

Drill Depth

C Sink
Angle

Ø 10.08 ⊽ 38.10
Ø 19.64 X 82°

C Sink
DIA

Note: SolidWorks provides the ability to insert Head
clearance for the Counter Sink hole.

Exercises:

Exercise 1:

Draw an Isometric view. Approximate the size of the model.

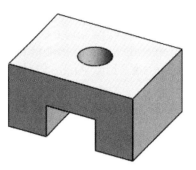

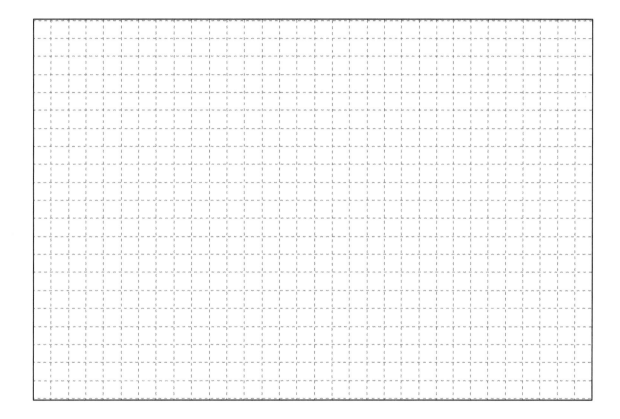

Exercise 2:

Name each view and insert the Width, Height, and Depth name. No dimensions are required in this exercise. Note: Centerlines are not displayed. Third Angle Projection is used.

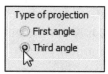

Type of projection
○ First angle
◉ Third angle

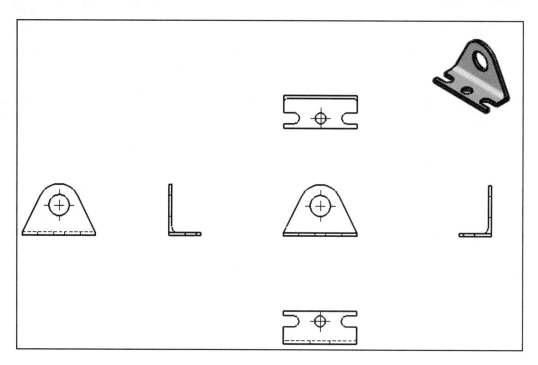

Drawing Views - Advanced

The standard views used in an orthographic projection are: Front view, Top view, Right view and Isometric view. Non-standard orthographic drawing views are used when the six principal views do not fully describe the part for manufacturing or inspection. Below are a few non-standard orthographic drawing views.

Section view

Section views are used to clarify the interior of a part that can't clearly be seen by hidden lines in a view.

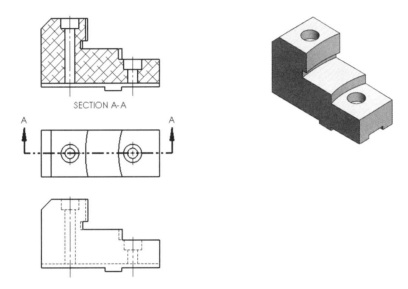

SECTION A-A

Think of an **imaginary** cutting (Plane) through the object and removing a portion. (*Imaginary)* is the key word!

A Section view is a child of the parent view. The Cutting Plane arrows used to create a Section view indicates the direction of sight. Section lines in the Section view are bounded by visible lines.

Section lines in the Section view can serve the purpose of identifying the kind of material the part is made from. Below are a few examples:

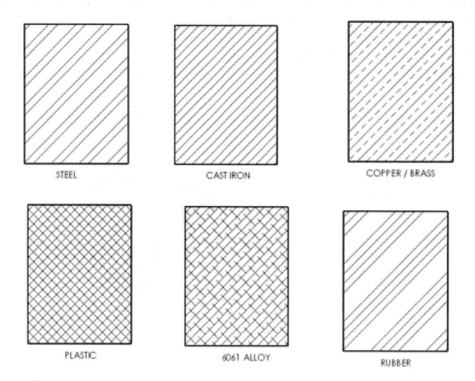

STEEL   CAST IRON   COPPER / BRASS

PLASTIC   6061 ALLOY   RUBBER

💡 To avoid a false impression of thickness, ribs are normally not sectioned.

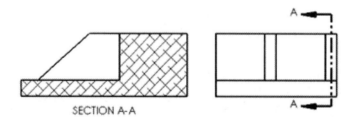

SECTION A-A

Detail View

The Detail view provides the ability to add a portion of a view, usually at an enlarged scale. A Detail view is a child of the parent view. Create a detail view in a drawing to display or highlight a portion of a view.

A Detail view may be of an Orthographic view, a non-planar (isometric) view, a Section view, a Crop view, an Exploded assembly view or another detail view.

Example 1:

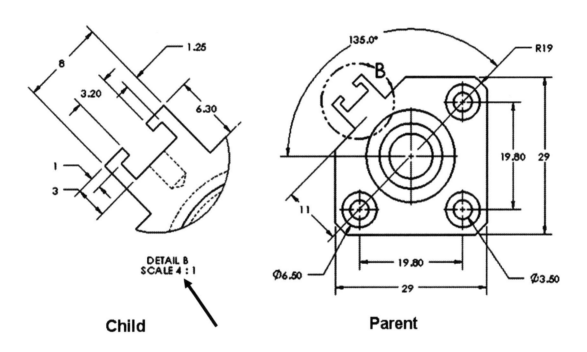

If the Detail view has a different scale than the sheet, the scale needs to be supplied as an annotation as illustrated.

☀ View the additional Power point presentations on the enclosed DVD for supplementary information.

> Avi folder
> Alphabet of lines and Precedent of Line Types
> Boolean Operation
> Design Intent
> Fastners in General
> Fundamental ASME Y14.5 Dimensioning Rules
> General Tolerancing and Fits
> History of Engineering Graphics
> Measurement and Scale
> Open a Drawing Document 2012
> Open an Assembly Document 2012
> Part and Drawing Dimensioning
> SolidWorks Basic Concepts
> Visualization, Arrangement of Views, and Primitives

Example 2:

Below is a Detail view of a Section view. The Detail view is a child view of the parent view (Detail view). The Section view cannot exist without the Detail view.

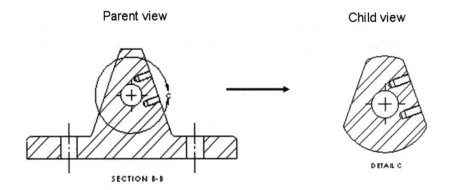

Broken out View

A Broken-out section is part of an existing drawing view, not a separate view. Material is removed to a specified depth to expose inner details. Hidden lines are displayed in the non-sectioned area of a broken section. View two examples of a Broken out View below.

Example 1:

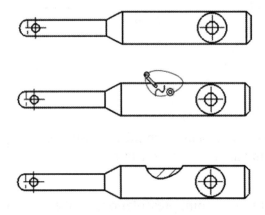

Example 2:

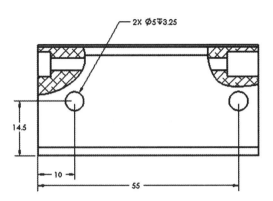

Break or Broken View

A Break view is part of an existing drawing view, not a separate view A Break view provides the ability to add a break line to a selected view. Create a Broken view to display the drawing view in a larger scale on a smaller drawing sheet size. Reference dimensions and model dimensions associated with the broken area reflect the actual model values.

Example 1:

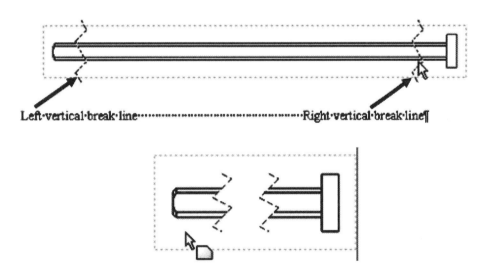

Example 2:

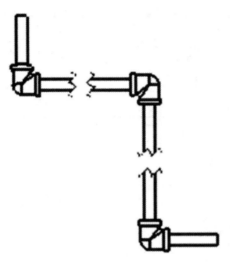

Crop View

A Crop view is a Child of the Parent view. A Crop view provides the ability to crop an existing drawing view. You can not create a Crop view on a Detail View, a view from which a Detail View has been created, or an Exploded view.

Create a Crop view to save time. Example: instead of creating a Section View and then a Detail View, then hiding the unnecessary Section View, create a Crop view to crop the Section View directly.

Example 1:

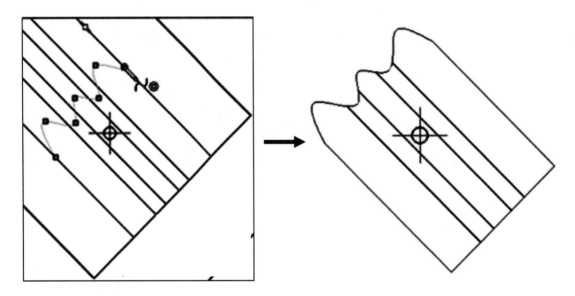

Auxiliary View

An Auxiliary view is a Child of the Parent view. An Auxiliary view provides the ability to display a plane parallel to an angled plane with true dimensions. A primary Auxiliary view is hinged to one of the six principle orthographic views.

Example 1:

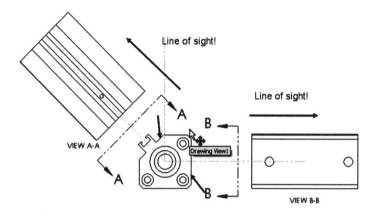

Exercises:

Exercise 1:

Label all of the name views below.

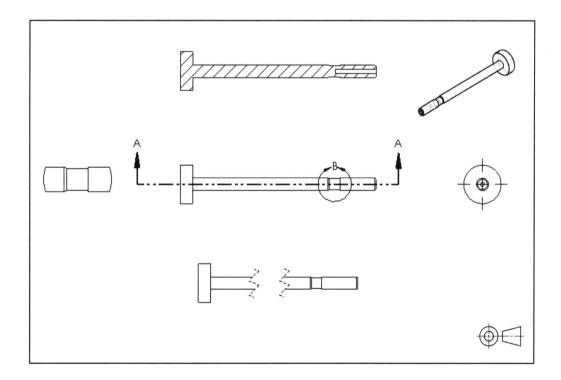

History of Computer Aided Design (CAD)

In 1963, Ivan Sutherland of MIT developed "Sketchpad", a graphical communication system, where with a light pen, Sutherland was able to select and modify geometry on a Cathode Ray System (CRT) and input values through a key pad. Geometric relationships were made between lines are arc and geometry could be moved and copied.

With aerospace and automotive technologies becoming more complex and IBM mainframe computers commercially available in the late 1960's and early 1970's, companies such as MacDonald-Douglas, Lockheed, General Motors, and Ford were utilizing their own internal CAD systems to design, manipulate and store models and drawings. Digital Equipment Corporation (DEC) and Prime Computer introduced computer hardware platforms that made CAD data storage and development more affordable. Ford's Product Design Graphics System (PDGS) developed into one of the largest integrated CAD systems in the 1980's.

By 1980, Cambridge Interact Systems (UK) introduced CIS Medusa, that was bought and distributed by Prime Computer and ran on a proprietary workstation and used Prime mini computers for data storage. Mid size companies, such as AMP and Carrier, were now using CAD in their engineering departments. Other CAD software companies also introduced new technology. Computervision utilized both proprietary hardware and SUN workstations and become a leader in 2D drafting technology.

But in the early 80's, 3D CAD used Boolean algorithms for solid geometry that were a challenge for engineers to manipulate. Other major CAD players were Integraph, GE Calma, SDRC, and IBM (Dassault Systèmes). Dassault Systèmes, with its roots in the aerospace industry, expanded development in CAD surface modeling software technology with Boeing and Ford.

In the late 80's, Parametric Technology Corporation (PTC) introduced CAD software to the market with the ability to manipulate a 3D solid model, running on a UNIX workstation platform. By changing dimensions directly on the 3D model, driven by dimensions and parameters, the model updated and was termed, parametric.

By the early 90's, the Personal Computer (PC) was becoming incorporated in the engineer's daily activities for writing reports and generating spreadsheets. In 1993, SolidWorks founder, Jon Hirschtick recruited a team of engineers to build a company and develop an affordable, 3D CAD software application that was easy to use and ran on an intuitive Windows platform, without expensive hardware and software to operate.

In 1995, SolidWorks was introduced to the market as the first 3D feature based, parametric solid modeler running on a PC. The company's rapidly growing customer base and continuous product innovation quickly established it as a strong competitor in the CAD market. The market noticed, and global product lifecycle technology giant Dassault Systèmes S.A. acquired SolidWorks for $310 million in stock in June of 1997.

SolidWorks went on to run as an independent company, incorporating finite element analysis (FEA) which has advanced dynamics, nonlinear, fatigue, thermal, steady state and turbulent fluid flow (CFD) and electromagnetic analysis capabilities, as well as design optimization. SolidWorks open software architecture as resulted in over 700 partner applications such as Computer Aided Manufacturing (CAM), robot simulation software, and process management. Today, SolidWorks software has the most worldwide users in production - more than 1,000,000 users at over 120,000 locations in more than 100 countries.

Note: There are many university researches and commercial companies that have contributed to the history of computer aided design. We developed this section on the history of CAD based on the institutions and companies that we worked for and worked with over our careers and as it relates to the founders of SolidWorks.

Boolean operations

To understand the difference between parametric solid modeling and Boolean based solid modeling you will first review Boolean operations. In the 1980s, one of the key advancements in CAD was the development of the Constructive Solid Geometry (CSG) method. Constructive Solid Geometry describes the solid model as combinations of basic three-dimensional shapes or better known as primitives. Primitives are typically simple shape: cuboids, cylinders, prisms, pyramids, spheres, and cones.

Two primitive solid objects can be combined into one using a procedure known as the Boolean operations. There are three basic Boolean operations:

- Boolean Union

- Boolean Difference

- Boolean Intersection

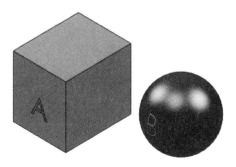
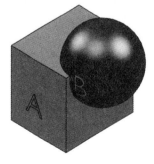

Boolean Operation	Result
Boolean Union - The merger of two separate objects into one. A + B	
Boolean Difference - The subtraction of one object from another. A - B	
Boolean Intersection - The portion common to both objects. A ∩ B	

Even today, Boolean operations assist the SolidWorks designer in creating a model with more complex geometry by combining two bodies together with a Boolean intersection.

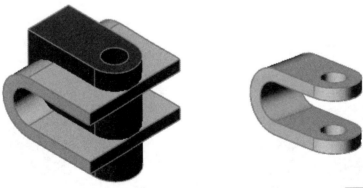

In the Help menu, the SolidWorks Tutorial, Multibody Parts provides Boolean model examples.

Mold Design
Molded Product Design - Advanced
Mouse Gestures
Multibody Parts
Pattern Features
Revolves and Sweeps

Chapter Summary

Chapter 2 provided a general introduction into isometric projection and sketching along with additional projections and the arrangement of standard views and advanced views. You explored the three main projection divisions in freehand engineering sketches and drawings: Axonometric, Oblique, and Perspective.

This chapter also introduced you to the history of CAD and the development of DS SolidWorks Corp. From early Boolean CAD software, you explored Union, Difference, and Intersection operations which are modeling techniques still used today. You were also introduced to the fundamentals of SolidWorks, its feature based modeling, driven by parameters that incorporates your design intent into a sketch, part, assembly and drawing.

Isometric Rule #1: A measurement can only be made on or parallel to the isometric axis. Therefore you cannot measure an isometric inclined or oblique line in an isometric drawing because they are not parallel to an isometric axis.

Isometric Rule #2: When drawing ellipses on normal isometric planes, the minor axis of the ellipse is perpendicular to the plane containing the ellipse. The minor axis is perpendicular to the corresponding normal isometric plane.

Avi folder
Alphabet of lines and Precedent of Line Types
Boolean Operation
Design Intent
Fastners in General
Fundamental ASME Y14.5 Dimensioning Rules
General Tolerancing and Fits
History of Engineering Graphics
Measurement and Scale
Open a Drawing Document 2012
Open an Assembly Document 2012
Part and Drawing Dimensioning
SolidWorks Basic Concepts
Visualization, Arrangement of Views, and Primitives

View the Power Point files on the enclosed DVD in the book for additional information.

Chapter Terminology

Axonometric Projection: A type of parallel projection, more specifically a type of orthographic projection, used to create a pictorial drawing of an object, where the object is rotated along one or more of its axes relative to the plane of projection.

CAD: The use of computer technology for the design of objects, real or virtual. CAD often involves more than just shapes.

Cartesian Coordinate system: Specifies each point uniquely in a plane by a pair of numerical coordinates, which are the signed distances from the point to two fixed perpendicular directed lines, measured in the same unit of length. Each reference line is called a coordinate axis or just axis of the system, and the point where they meet is its origin.

Depth: The horizontal (front to back) distance between two features in frontal planes. Depth is often identified in the shop as the thickness of a part or feature.

Engineering Graphics: Translates ideas from design layouts, specifications, rough sketches, and calculations of engineers & architects into working drawings, maps, plans, and illustrations which are used in making products.

First Angle Projection: In First Angle Projection the Top view is looking at the bottom of the part. First Angle Projection is used in Europe and most of the world. However America and Australia use a method known as Third Angle Projection.

Foreshortening: The way things appear to get smaller in both height and depth as they recede into the distance.

Grid: A system of fixed horizontal and vertical divisions.

Height: The vertical distance between two or more lines or surfaces (features) which are in horizontal planes.

Isometric Projection: A form of graphical projection, more specifically, a form of axonometric projection. It is a method of visually representing three-dimensional objects in two dimensions, in which the three coordinate axes appear equally foreshortened and the angles between any two of them are 120 °.

Oblique projection: A simple type of graphical projection used for producing pictorial, two-dimensional images of three-dimensional objects.

Origin: The point of intersection, where the X,Y,Z axes meet, is called the origin.

Orthographic Projection: A means of representing a three-dimensional object in two dimensions. It is a form of parallel projection, where the view direction is orthogonal to the projection plane, resulting in every plane of the scene appearing in affine transformation on the viewing surface.

Perspective Projection: The two most characteristic features of perspective are that objects are drawn: smaller as their distance from the observer increases and Foreshortened: the size of an object's dimensions along the line of sight are relatively shorter than dimensions across the line of sight.

Right-Hand Rule: Is a common mnemonic for understanding notation conventions for vectors in 3 dimensions.

Scale: A relative term meaning "size" in relationship to some system of measurement.

Third Angle Projection: In Third angle projection the Top View is looking at the Top of the part. First Angle Projection is used in Europe and most of the world. However America and Australia use a method known as Third Angle Projection.

Units: Used in the measurement of physical quantities. Decimal inch dimensioning and Millimeter dimensioning are the two types of common units specified for engineering parts and drawings.

Width: The horizontal distance between surfaces in profile planes. In the machine shop, the terms length and width are used interchangeably.

Questions

1. Name the three main projection divisions commonly used in freehand engineering sketches and detailed engineering drawings: _____ , _____ and _____

2. Name the projection divisions within Axonometric projection: _____, _____, and _____.

3. True or False: In oblique projections; the front view is drawn true size, and the receding surfaces are drawn on an angle to give it a pictorial appearance.

4. Name the two types of Oblique projection used in engineering design: _____, _____.

5. Describe Perspective Projection. Provide an example.

6. True or False: Parts that are uniform in shape often require only one view to describe them adequately.

7. True or False: The designer usually selects as a Front view of the object that view which best describes the general shape of the part. This Front view may have no relationship to the actual front position of the part as it fits into an assembly.

8. True or False: When a one-view drawing of a cylindrical part is used, the dimension for the diameter (according to ANSI standards) must be preceded by the symbol Ø.

9. Draw a Third Angle Projection Symbol.

10. Draw a First Angle Projection Symbol.

11. Describe the different between First and Third Angle Projection.

12. True or False. First Angle Projection is used in the United States.

13. True or False. Section lines can serve the purpose of identifying the kind of material the part is made from.

14. True or False. All dimension lines terminate with an arrowhead on mechanical engineering drawings.

15. True or False. Break lines are applied to represent an imaginary cut in an object, so the interior of the object can be viewed or fitted to the sheet. Provide an example.

Exercises

Exercise 2.1: Hand draw the Isometric view for the illustrated model below.

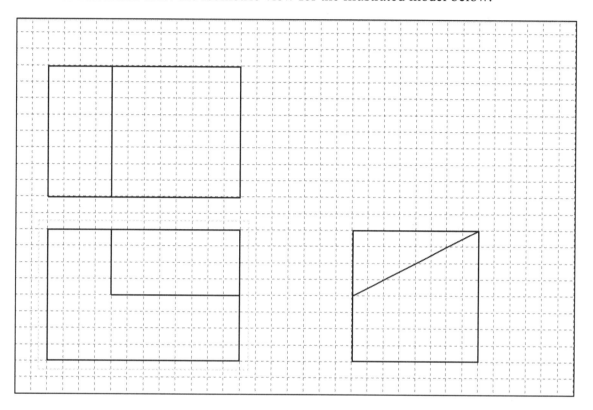

Exercise 2.2: Hand draw the Isometric view for the following models. Approximate the size of the model.

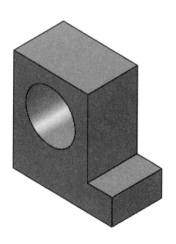

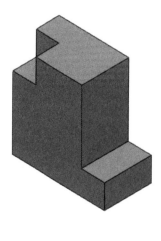

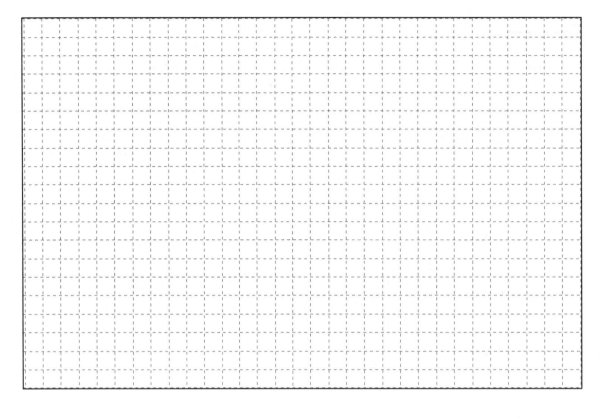

Exercise 2.3: Hand draw the Isometric view for the following models. Approximate the size of the model.

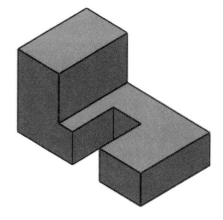

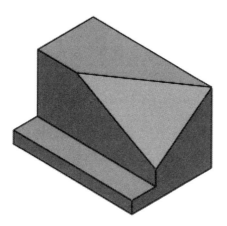

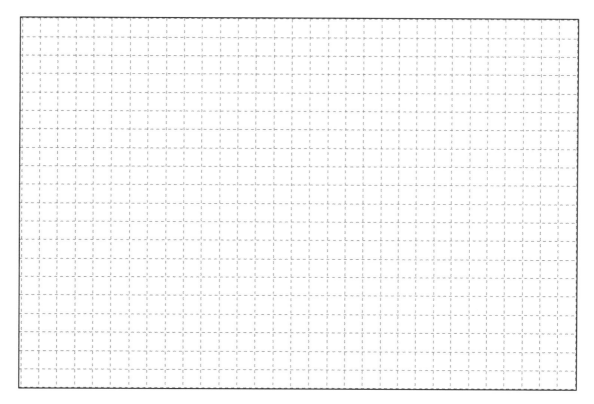

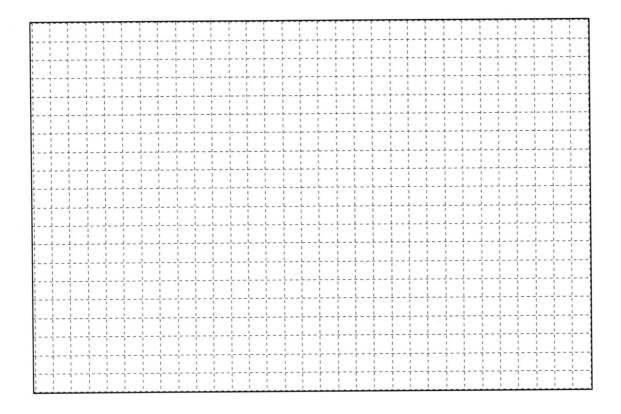

Chapter 3

Dimensioning Practices, Tolerancing, and Fasteners

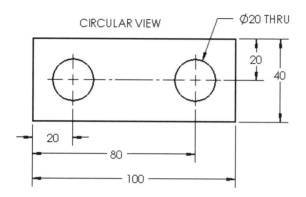

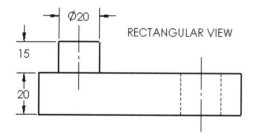

Below are the desired outcomes and usage competencies based on the completion of Chapter 3.

Desired Outcomes:	Usage Competencies:
• Knowledge of dimensioning systems and the ASME Y14.5 - 1994 standard.	• Dimension the following simple shapes: hole, cylinder, angle, point or center, arc, and chamfer.
• Awareness of the IPS Unit System, the MMGS Unit System and the Dual dimensioning system.	• Apply dual dimensioning. o IPS Unit System o MMGS Units System
• Understand Tolerancing for a drawing. • Comprehend Fasteners and hole dimensioning. • Recognize Fit types.	• Apply dimension and drawing Tolerances. • Read and understand general Fastener and hole annotations. • Apply Fit types.

Notes:

Chapter 3 - Dimensioning Practices, Tolerancing and Fasteners

Chapter Overview

Chapter 3 provides a general introduction into dimensioning systems and the ANSI Y14.5 2009 standards along with fasteners and general tolerancing.

On the completion of this chapter, you will be able to:

- Understand and apply various dimensioning systems.

- Correctly dimension the following simple shapes: hole, cylinder, angle, point or center, arc, and chamfer.

- Knowledge of dimensioning systems and the ANSI Y14.5 standards.

- Apply dual dimensioning.

- Understand and apply part and drawing Tolerance.

- Read and understand Fastener notation.

- Recognize single, double or tripe threads.

- Distinguish between Right and Left handed threads.

- Recognize annotations for a simple hole, Counterbore and Countersink in a drawing.

- Identify Fit types.

Size and Location Dimensions

To ensure some measure of uniformity in industrial drawings, the American National Standards Institute (ANSI) has established drafting standards; these standards are called the language of drafting and are in general use throughout the United States.

ANSI was originally formed in 1918, when five engineering societies and three government agencies founded the American Engineering Standards Committee (AESC). In 1928, the AESC became the American Standards Association (ASA). In 1966, the ASA was reorganized and became the United States of America Standards Institute (USASI). The present name was adopted in 1969 and the standards are published by the American Society of Mechanical Engineers (ASME).

While these drafting standards or practices may vary in some respects between industries, the principles are basically the same. The practices recommended by ANSI for dimensioning and for marking notes are followed in this book.

Dimensioning Systems

A dimension is a numerical value that is being assigned to the size, shape or location of the feature being described. There are basically three types of dimensioning systems used in creating parts and drawings:

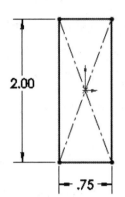

U.S. - ANSI standard for U.S. dimensioning use the decimal inch value. When the decimal inch system is used, a zero is not used to the left of the decimal point for values less than one inch, and trailing zeros are used.

The U.S. unit system is also known as the Inch, Pound, Second (IPS) unit system.

Metric - ANSI standards for the use of metric dimensioning required all the dimensions to be expressed in millimeters (mm). The (mm) is not needed on each dimension, but it is used when a dimension is used in a notation. No trailing zeros are used.

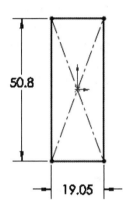

The Metric or International System of Units (S.I.) unit system in drafting is also known as the Millimeter, Gram Second (MMGS) unit system.

Dual Dimensioning - Working drawings are usually drawn with all U.S. or all metric dimensions. Sometimes the object manufactured requires using both the U.S. and metric measuring system. In this illustration, the secondary units (mm) are displayed in parenthesis. The Primary units are inches.

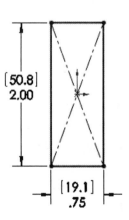

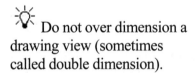 Do not over dimension a drawing view (sometimes called double dimension).

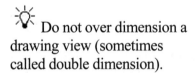 View the additional Power point presentations on the enclosed DVD for supplementary information.

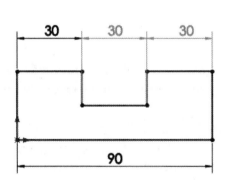

Standards for Dimensioning

All drawings should be dimensioned
completely so that a minimum of
computation is necessary, and the part
can be built without scaling the
drawing. However, there should not be a
duplication of dimensions unless such
dimensions make the drawing clearer
and easier to read. These dimensions are
called reference dimensions and are enclosed in parentheses.

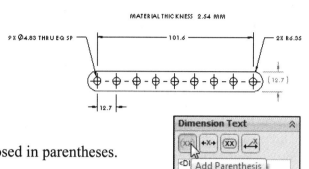

Part Dimensions / Construction Dimensions

Dimensions used in creating a part are sometimes called construction dimensions or part
dimensions. These dimensions serve two purposes: (1) indicate size, and (2) provide
exact locations. For example, to drill a through all hole in a part, the designer must know
the diameter of the hole, and the exact location of the center of the hole relative to the
origin. Note: Gaps are required between the dimension extension line and the feature line.
Do not cross Leader lines and limit the leader line length.

Example 1:

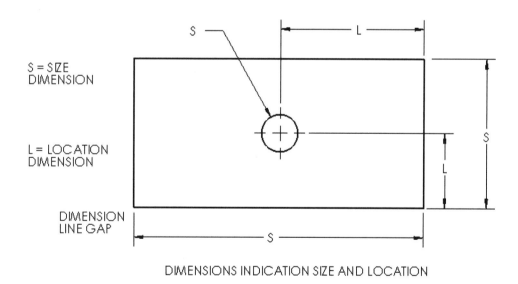

DIMENSIONS INDICATION SIZE AND LOCATION

Dimensions should not be duplicated or the same information is given in two different
ways. If a reference dimension is used, the size value is placed within parentheses (X).

Always position the diameter dimension up and off the model.

Two Place Decimal Dimensions

Dimensions may appear on drawings as two-place decimals (IPS) unit system. This is widely used when the range of dimensional accuracy of a part is between 0.01" larger or smaller than a specified dimension (nominal size). Where possible, two-place decimal dimensions are given in even hundredths of an inch.

Type	Unit	Decimals
Basic Units		
Length	inches	.12
Dual Dimension Length	millimeters	.12
Angle	degrees	.123
		.1234
Mass/Section Properties		.12345
Length	inches	.123456
		.1234567

Three and four place decimal dimensions continue to be used for more precise dimensions requiring machining accuracies in thousandths or ten-thousandths of an inch.

Size Dimensions

Every solid or part has three size dimensions: width or length, height, and depth. In the case of the Glass box method, two of the dimensions are usually placed on the Principal view and the third dimension is located on one of the other views.

Example 1:

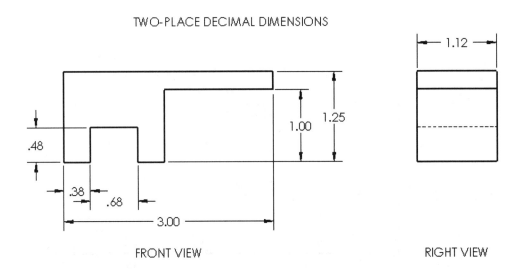

TWO-PLACE DECIMAL DIMENSIONS

FRONT VIEW   RIGHT VIEW

☼ Do not dimension inside an object and do not over dimension in a drawing.

☼ Always locate the dimensions off of the view if possible. Only place dimensions on the inside of the view if they add clarity, simplicity, and ease of reading.

☼ There should be a visible gap ~1.5mm between the object (feature) line and the beginning of each extension line.

Continuous Dimensions

Set of dimension lines and dimensions should be located on drawings close enough so they may be read easily without any possibility of confusing one dimension with another. If a series of dimensions is required, the dimensions should be placed in a line as continuous dimensions (chain dimensioning or point-to-point dimensioning) as illustrated below. This method is preferred over the staggering of dimensions, because of ease in reading, appearance, and simplified dimensioning. Note: Tolerance stack-up can be an issue with this method!

Example 1:

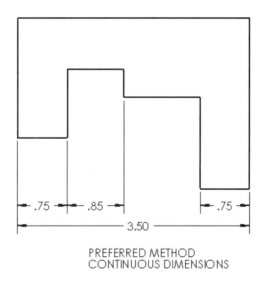

PREFERRED METHOD
CONTINUOUS DIMENSIONS

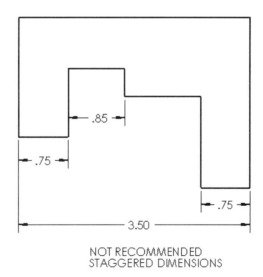

NOT RECOMMENDED
STAGGERED DIMENSIONS

 Spacing between dimension lines should be uniform throughout the drawing.

Other Dimension Placements

Dimensions should be placed in such a way as to enhance the communication of your drawing. There are a few key rules that you should know. They are:

- Place dimensions between views.

- Group dimensions whenever possible.

- Locate dimensions in the view where the shape is best shown.

- Dimension a hole in a circular view.

- Dimension a cylinder in a rectangular view.

- Dimension a hole by its diameter.

- Dimension a slot in a view where the contour of the slot is visible.

- Dimension an arc by its radius.

- Place a smaller dimension inside a larger dimension on a drawing view to avoid dimension line crossing.

- Place a smaller dimension inside a larger dimension on a drawing view to avoid dimension line crossing.

- ANSI standard states, "Dimensioning to hidden lines should be avoided wherever possible". However, sometimes it is necessary if additional views are needed to fully define the model as illustrated below.

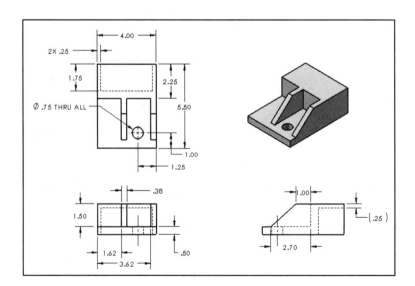

Example 1:

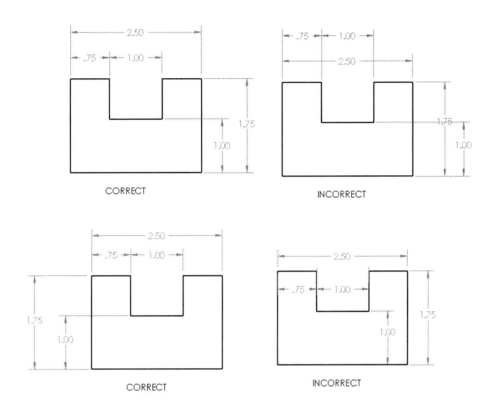

Arrowheads are drawn between extension lines if space is available. If space is limited, see the preferred arrowhead and dimension location order below.

Example 1:

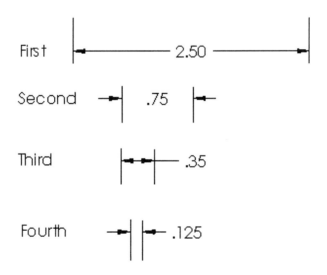

Dimension Exercises:
Exercise 1:

Identify the dimension errors in the below illustration. Circle and list the errors.

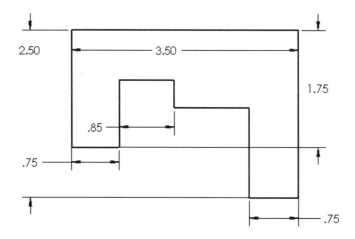

Errors:_____

_____

Exercise 2:

Identify the dimension errors in the below illustration. Circle and list the errors.

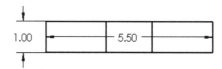

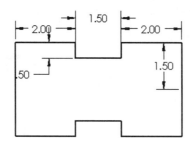

Errors:_____

_____

Exercise 3:

Identify the duplicate dimensions and cross out the ones that you feel should be omitted. Explain why. Are there any dimensioning mistakes in this drawing? Explain.

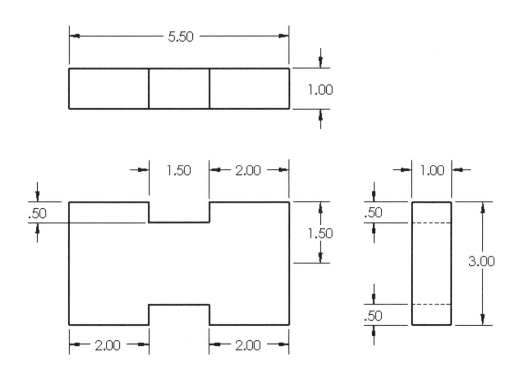

Explain:

_____

_____

_____

Dimensioning Cylinders

The length and diameter of cylinders are usually placed in the view which shows the cylinder as a rectangle as illustrated below.

Example 1:

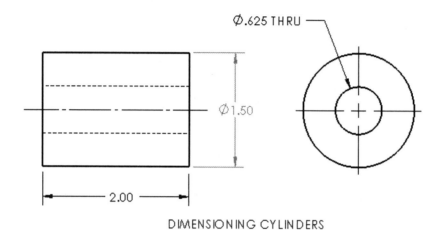

DIMENSIONING CYLINDERS

Note: Many round parts with cylindrical surface symmetrical about the axis, can be represented with a one-view drawing. A diameter is identified according to ANSI standards by using the symbol Ø preceding the dimension. Note: The below model is displayed in millimeters.

Example 2:

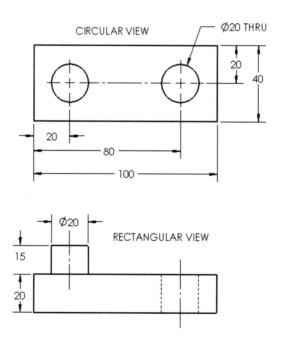

A cylinder is dimensioned by giving its diameter and length in the rectangular view, and is located in the circular view.

Holes are dimensioned by giving their diameter and location in the circular view.

Example 3:

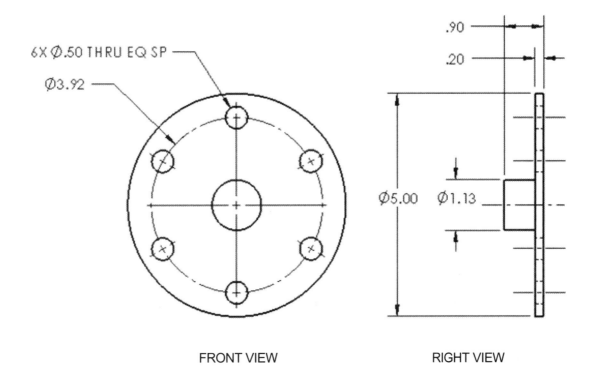

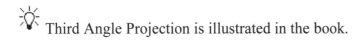

FRONT VIEW   RIGHT VIEW

🔅 Third Angle Projection is illustrated in the book.

🔅 Your choice of dimensions will directly influence the method used to manufacture the part.

🔅 Always position the diameter dimension up and off the model.

🔅 Insert the needed dimension to a single view (best view). Do not over dimension.

🔅 Dimension lines should not cross, if avoidable.

Dimensioning a Simple Hole

The diameters of holes which are to be formed by drilling, reaming, or punching should have the diameter, preferably on a leader, followed by a note indicating the operation to be performed and the number of holes to be produced, as illustrated. Note: The diameter of a hole is *placed in the view which shows the hole as a circle* as illustrated below.

Example 1:

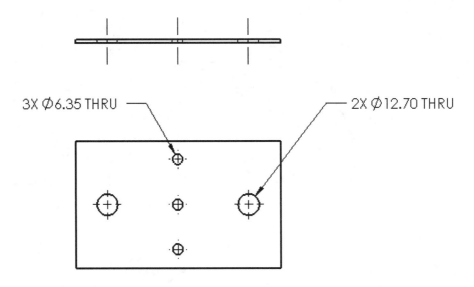

DIMENSIONING A SIMPLE HOLE

Repetitive features or dimensions can be specified by using the symbol "X" along with the number of times the feature is repeated as illustrated above. There is no space between the number of times the feature is repeated and the "X" symbol; however, there is a space between the symbol "X" and the dimension.

💡 If a hole goes completely through the feature, and it is not clearly shown on the drawing, the abbreviation "THRU" in all upper case follows the dimension. All notes should be in UPPER CASE LETTERS.

💡 The Front View should be the most descriptive view in the drawing document.

Dimensioning Angles

The design of a part may require some lines to be drawn at an angle. The amount of the divergence (the amount the lines move away from each other) is indicated by an angle measured in degrees or fractional parts of a degree. The degree is indicated by a symbol °placed after the numerical value of the angle.

Example 1:

The dimension line for an angle should be an arc whose ends terminate in arrowheads.

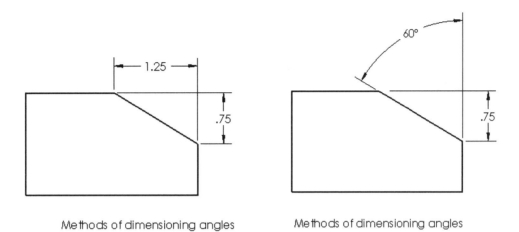

Methods of dimensioning angles   Methods of dimensioning angles

The numeral indication of the number of degrees in the angle is read in a horizontal position, except where the angle is large enough to permit the numerals to be placed along the arc.

Example 2:

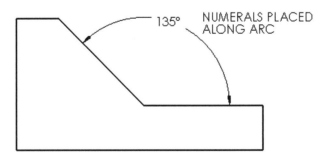

Dimensioning a Point or a Center

A point or a center of an arc or circle is generally measured from two finished surfaces. The method of location the center is preferred to making an angular measurement. As illustrated, the center of the circle and arc may be found easily be scribing the vertical and horizontal center lines from the machined surfaces.

Example 1:

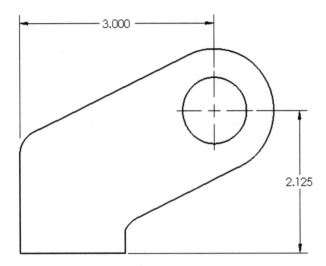

Dimensioning the center of a circle

Dimensioning equally spaced holes on a Circle

If a number of holes are to be equally spaced on a circle, then the exact location of the first hole is given by location dimension. To locate the remaining holes, the location dimension is followed by 1.) diameter of the holes, 2.) number of holes, and 3.) notation EQUALLY SPACED or "EQ SP" as illustrated.

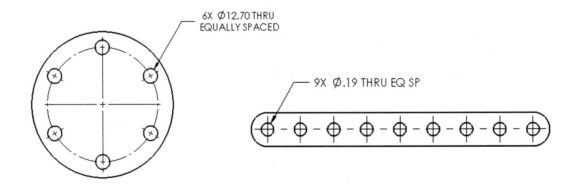

Dimensioning Holes not on a circle

Holes are often dimensioned in relation to one another and to a finished surface. Dimensions are usually given, in such cases, in the view which the shape of the holes, that is, square, round, or elongated. The preferred method of placing these dimensions is illustrated below.

Example 1:

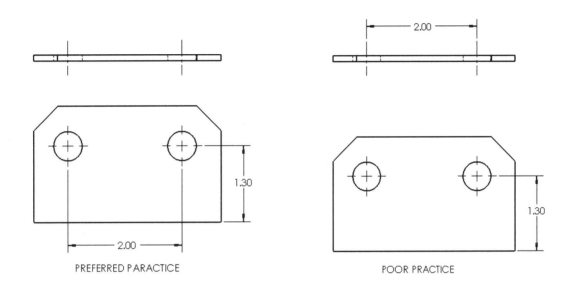

PREFERRED PARACTICE

POOR PRACTICE

Dimensioning Arcs

An arc is always dimensioned by its radius. ANSI standards require a radius dimension to be preceded by the letter (symbol) R as illustrated.

Example 1:

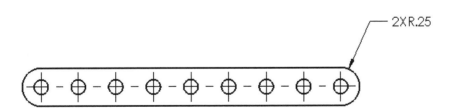

2X R.25

The radial dimension line should have only one arrowhead, and it should touch the arc.

Dimensioning Chamfers

There are two ways to dimension a chamfer feature as illustrated below.

Example 1:

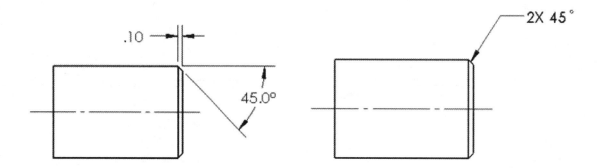

Dual Dimensioning

Working drawings are usually drawn with all U.S. or all metric dimensions. Sometimes the object is manufactured using both U.S. and metric measuring system. Dual dimensioning may be necessary. As illustrated, the primary unit system is IPS (Inch, Pounds, Second) and the secondary unit system is in MMGS (Millimeters, Grams, Second).

Example 1:

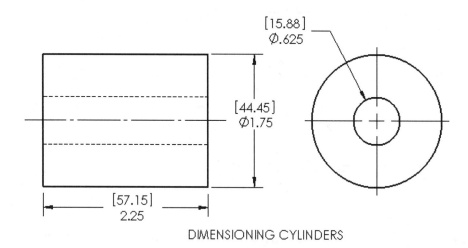

DIMENSIONING CYLINDERS

Dimension Exercises:
Exercise 1:

Identify the dimension errors in the below illustration. Circle and list the errors.

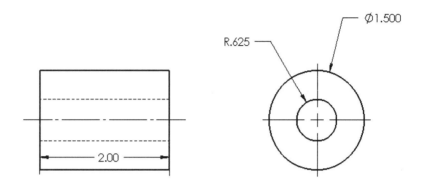

Errors:_____

_____

Exercise 2:

Identify the dimension errors in the below illustration. Circle and list the errors.

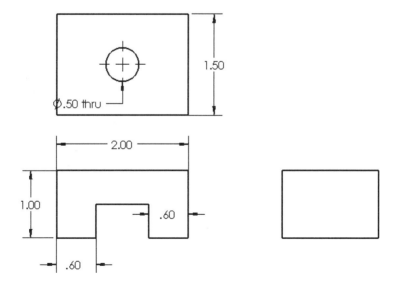

Errors:_____

_____

Exercise 3:

Identify the dimension errors in the below illustration. Circle and list the errors.

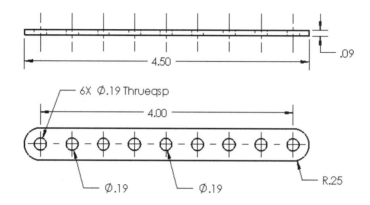

Explain:

_____

_____

Exercise 4:

Identify the dimension errors in the below illustration. Circle and list the errors.

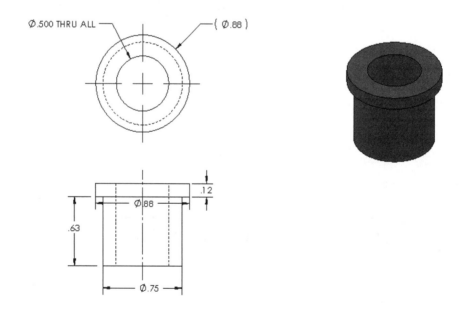

Explain:

_____

_____

Precision and Tolerance

In a manufacturing environment, quality and cost are two of the main considerations for an engineer or designer. Engineering drawings with local and general notes and dimensions often serve as purchasing documents, construction, inspection, and legal contracts to ensure the proper function and design of the product. When dimensioning a drawing, it is essential to reflect on the precision required for the model.

Precision is the degree of accuracy required during manufacturing. However, it is unfeasible to produce any dimension to an absolute, accurate measurement. Some discrepancy must be provided or allowed in the manufacturing process.

Specifying higher precision on a drawing may ensure better quality of a product, but doing so can increase the cost of the part and make it cost prohibited in being competitive with similar products.

For example, consider a design that contains cast components. A cast part usually has two types of surfaces: 1.) mating surfaces, and 2.) non-mating surfaces.

Mating surfaces work together with other surfaces, typically machined to a specified finish. Mating surfaces typical require higher precision on all corresponding dimensions.

Non-mating surfaces are usually left in the original rough-cast form. They have no significant connection with other surfaces. The dimensions on a drawing must clearly indicate which surfaces are to be finished and provide the degree of precision needed for the finishing.

The method of specifying the degree of precision is called Tolerancing. Tolerance in simple terms is the amount of *size variation* permitted and provides a useful means to achieve the precision necessary in a design. Tolerancing makes certain interchangeability in manufacturing. Parts can be manufactured by different companies in various locations while maintaining the proper functionality of the intended design.

In tolerancing; each dimension is permitted to vary within a specified amount. By assigning as large a tolerance as possible, without interfering with the functionality or intended design of a part, the production costs can be reduced and the product can be competitive in the real world. The smaller the tolerance range specified, the more expensive it is to manufacture. There is always a trade off in design.

View the additional Power point presentations on the enclosed DVD for supplementary information.

Avi folder
Alphabet of lines and Precedent of Line Types
Boolean Operation
Design Intent
Fastners in General
Fundamental ASME Y14.5 Dimensioning Rules
General Tolerancing and Fits
History of Engineering Graphics
Measurement and Scale
Open a Drawing Document 2012
Open an Assembly Document 2012
Part and Drawing Dimensioning
SolidWorks Basic Concepts
Visualization, Arrangement of Views, and Primitives

Tolerance for a drawing

The two most common Tolerance Standard agencies are: American National Standards Institute (ANSI) / (ASME) and the International Standards Organization (ISO). This book covers the ANSI (US) standards.

In this section - we will discuss Dimensional Tolerances vs. Geometric Tolerances.

General Tolerance - Title Block:

General tolerances are typically provided in the Title Block. General tolerances are applied to the dimensions in which tolerances are not given in the drawing.

As a part is designed, the engineer should consider: 1.) function either as a separate unit or as a component relation to other components in an assembly, 2.) manufacturing operations, 3.) material, 4.) quantity (run size), 5.) sustainability, and 6.) cost.

The dimensions displayed on a drawing (obtained from the part) indicate the accuracy limits for manufacturing. The limits are called tolerances and are normally displayed in decimal notation. Tolerances can be specified in various unit systems. ANSI, specifications are normally specified either in English (IPS) or Metric (MMGS).

Tolerances on decimal dimensions, which are expressed in terms of one, two, three, or more decimal places. This information can be documented on a drawing in several ways. One of the common methods of specifying a tolerance that applies to all dimensions is to use a general note in the Title block as illustrated.

Example 1 & 2:

UNLESS OTHERWISE SPECIFIED:
DIMENSIONS ARE IN INCHES TOLERANCES: ANGULAR: ± 1° ONE PLANE DECIMAL   ± .1 TWO PLACE DECIMAL   ± .01 THREE PLACE DECIMAL ± .005

UNLESS OTHERWISE SPECIFIED:
DIMENSIONS ARE IN MILLIMETERS TOLERANCES: ANGULAR: MACH± 0°30' ONE PLACE DECIMAL   ±0.5 TWO PLACE DECIMAL   ±0.15

Local Tolerance - Dimension:

A Local Tolerance note indicates a special situation which is not covered by the General Title box. A Local Tolerance is located on the drawing (NOT in the Title box) with the dimension.

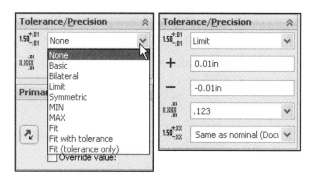

The three most common Tolerance types are: *Limit, Bilateral, and Unilateral.*

Limit Tolerance is when a dimension has a high (upper) and low (lower) limits stated. In a limit tolerance, the higher value is placed on top, and the lower value is placed on the bottom as illustrated.

$$\varnothing\,^{1.001}_{.999} \quad \text{or} \quad \varnothing.999 - 1.001$$

Limits are the maximum and minimum size that a part can obtain and still pass inspection and function in the intended assembly. When both limits are placed on a single line, the lower limit precedes the higher limit. The tolerance for the dimension illustrated above is the total amount of variation permitted or .002.

In the angle example - the dimension may vary between 60 °and 59°45'.

Note: Each degree is one three hundred and sixtieth of a circle (1/360). The degree (°) may be divided into smaller units called minutes ('). There are 60 minutes in each degree. Each minute may be divided into smaller units called seconds ("). There are 60 seconds in each minute. To simplify the dimensioning of angles, symbols are used to indicate degrees, minutes and seconds as illustrated below.

<u>Name</u>	<u>Symbol</u>
Degrees	°
Minutes	'
Seconds	"

Unilateral Tolerance is the variation of size in a single direction - either (+) or (-). The examples of Unilateral tolerances shown below indicate that the first part meets standards of accuracy when the nominal or target dimension varies in one direction only and is between 3.000" and 3.025".

Bilateral Tolerance is the variation of size in both directions. The dimensions may vary from a larger size (+) to a smaller size (-) than the basic dimension (nominal size). The basic 2.44" dimension as illustrated with a bilateral tolerance of +-.01" is acceptable within a range of 2.45" and 2.43".

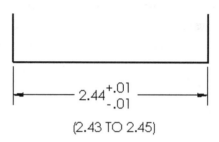

(2.43 TO 2.45)

🔅 Specify a tolerance with the degree of accuracy that is required for the design to work properly and is cost effective.

🔅 You can also create a note on the drawing referring to a specific dimension or specify general tolerances in the Title block.

Formatting Inch Tolerances

The basic dimension and the plus and minus values should have the same number of decimal places. Below are examples or *Unilateral* and *Bilateral* tolerances.

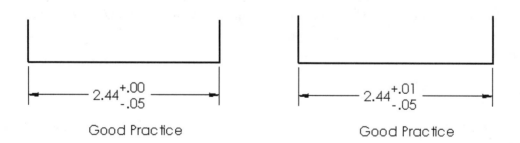

Good Practice   Good Practice

Metric Dimension Specifications

For Metric dimension specification, the book uses the Metric International System of Units (SI). The millimeter is the common unit of measurement used on engineering drawings made to the metric system.

In industry, a general note would be displayed in the Title block section of the drawing to invoke the metric system. A general note is: "UNLESS OTHERWISE SPECIFIED: DIMENSIONS ARE IN MILLIMETERS."

```
UNLESS OTHERWISE SPECIFIED:

DIMENSIONS ARE IN MILLIMETERS
TOLERANCES:
ANGULAR: MACH±  0°30'
ONE PLACE DECIMAL    ±0.5
TWO PLACE DECIMAL   ±0.15
```

Three conventions are used when specifying dimensions in metric units. They are:

1.) When a metric dimension is a whole number, the decimal point and zero are omitted.

2.) When a metric dimension is less than 1 millimeter, a zero precedes the decimal point. Example - 0.2 has a zero to the left of the decimal point.

3.) When a metric dimension is not a whole number, a decimal point with the portion of a millimeter (10ths or 100ths) is specified.

General Nomenclature

The followings are general important definitions in tolerancing as defined in the ANSI/ASME Y 14.5M standard.

- **Actual size** - The measured dimension. A shaft of nominal diameter 10 mm may be measured to be an actual size of 9.975 mm.
- **Allowance** - The minimum clearance space or maximum interference intended between two mating parts under the Maximum Material Condition (MMC).
- **Basic dimension / Basic size** - The theoretical size from which limits of size are derived. It is the size from which limits are determined for the size or location of a feature in a design.
- **Fit** - The general term used to signify the range of tightness in the design of mating parts.
- **Least Material Condition (LMC)** - The size of the part when it consists of the least material.
- **Maximum Material Condition (MMC)** - The size of the part when it consists of the most material.
- **Nominal size** - Size used for general identification – not exact size.
- **Tolerance** - The total permissible variation of a size. The tolerance is the difference between the limits.

Fit - Hole Tolerance

In the figure below, what is the minimum clearance (Allowance)? Minimum clearance is the minimum amount of space which exists between the hole and the shaft.

Minimum Clearance (Allowance) = $(0.49d_{hole})$ - $(0.51D_{shaft})$ = -0.02in

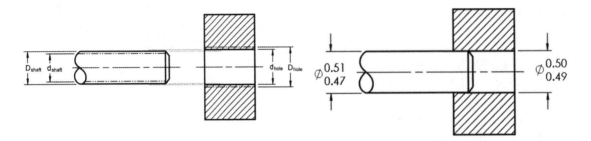

In the figure above, what is the maximum clearance (Allowance)? Maximum clearance is the difference between the largest hole diameter D_{hole} and the smallest shaft diameter d_{shaft}.

Maximum Clearance (Allowance) = $(0.50D_{hole})$ - $(0.47d_{shaft})$ = 0.03

Fit between Mating Parts

Fit is the general term used to signify the range of tightness in the design of mating parts. In ANSI/ASME Y 14.5M, four general types of fits are designated for mating parts:

1. **Clearance Fit**

2. **Interference Fit**

3. **Transition Fit**

4. **Line Fit**

Clearance Fit: The difference between the hole and shaft sizes before assembly is positive. Clearance fits have limits of size prearranged such that a clearance always results when the mating parts are assembled. Clearance fits are intended for accurate assembly of parts and bearings. The parts can be assembled by hand because the hole is always larger than the shaft. Min. Clearance > 0. Two examples: Lock and Key, Door and Door frame.

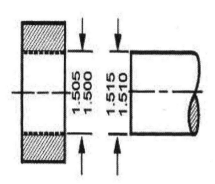

INTERFERENCE FIT

Interference Fit: The arithmetic difference between the hole and shaft sizes before assembly is negative. Interference fits have limits of size prearranged that an interference always results when mating parts are assembled. The hole is always smaller than the shaft. Interference fits are for permanent assemblies of parts which require rigidity and alignment, such as dowel pins and bearings in casting. Max. Clearance ≤ 0. Two examples: Hinge pin and pin in a bicycle chain.

Transition Fit: May provide either clearance or interference, depending on the actual value of the tolerance of individual parts. Transition fits are a compromise between the clearance and Interference fits. They are used for applications where accurate location is important, but either a small amount of clearance or interference is permissible. Max. Clearance > 0, Min. Clearance < 0.

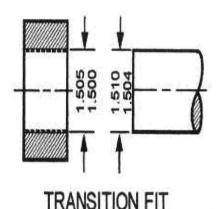

TRANSITION FIT

Line Fit: The condition in which the limits of size so that a clearance or surface contact may result between the mating parts. A space or a contact (hole diameter = shaft diameter). Max. Clearance > 0.
Min. Clearance = 0.

Why is this information important? By specifying the correct allowances and tolerances, mating components in an assembly can be completely interchangeable.

Sometimes the desired fit may require very small allowances and tolerances, and the production cost may become too high and cost prohibited. In these cases, either manual or computer-controlled selective assembly is often used. The manufactured parts are then graded as small, medium and large based on the actual sizes. In this way, very satisfactory fits are achieved at a much lower cost than to manufacturing all parts to very accurate dimensions.

Fasteners in General

Fasteners include: Bolts and Nuts (threaded), Set screws (threaded), Washers, Keys, Pins to name a few. Fasteners are not a permanent means of assembly such as welding or adhesives.

Fasteners and threaded features should be specified on your engineering drawing.

- Threaded features: Threads are specified in a thread note. In SolidWorks, apply the Hole Wizard feature.

- General Fasteners: Purchasing information must be given to allow the fastener to be ordered correctly.

Representing External (Male) Threads

Screw threads are used widely (1) to fasten two or more parts together in position, (2) to transmit power such as a feed screw on a machine, and (3) to move a scale on an instrument used for precision measurements.

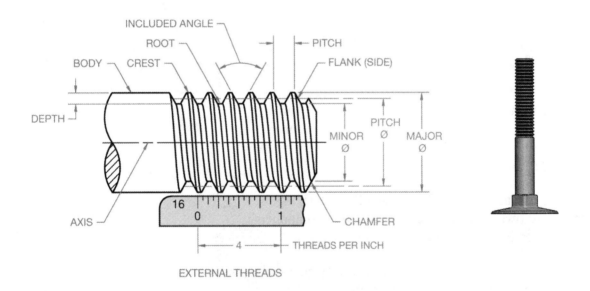

*Profile of UNIFIED and the American National Threads.

An edge of a uniform section in the form of a helix on the **external** surface of a cylinder or cone. **"A"** suffix.

Cutting External (Male) Threads

Start with a shaft the same size as the major diameter. An external thread is cut using a die or a lathe as illustrated below.

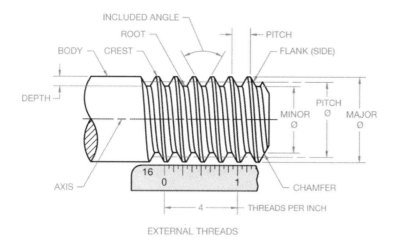

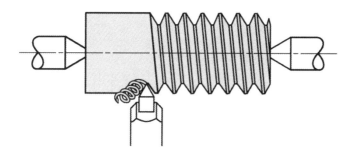

A chamfer on the end of the screw thread makes it easier to engage the nut.

Representing Internal (Female) Threads

An internal thread is a ridge of a uniform section in the form of a helix on the **internal** surface of a cylinder or cone. **"B"** suffix.

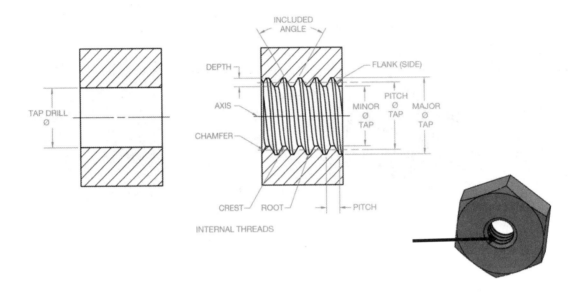

Cutting Internal (Female) Threads

In general, a tap drill hole is cut with a twist drill. The tap drill hole is a little larger than the minor diameter. Start with a shaft the same size as the major diameter as illustrated below.

Minor Diameter: The smallest diameter (fractional diameter or number) of a screw thread.

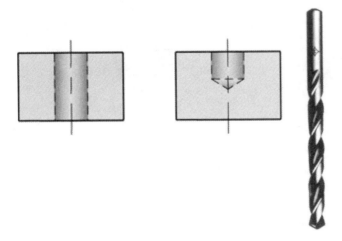

Then the threads are cut using a tap. Major tap types:

- **Taper** tap

- **Plug** tap

- **Bottoming** tap

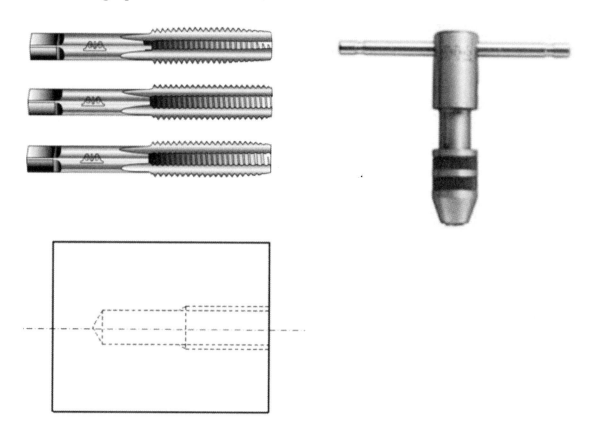

The process of cutting threads using a tap is called tapping, whereas the process using a die is called threading. Both tools can be used to clean up a thread, which is called chasing.

View the additional Power point presentations on the enclosed DVD for supplementary information.

Avi folder
Alphabet of lines and Precedent of Line Types
Boolean Operation
Design Intent
Fastners in General
Fundamental ASME Y14.5 Dimensioning Rules
General Tolerancing and Fits
History of Engineering Graphics
Measurement and Scale
Open a Drawing Document 2012
Open an Assembly Document 2012
Part and Drawing Dimensioning
SolidWorks Basic Concepts
Visualization, Arrangement of Views, and Primitives

American National Standard and Unified Screw threads

The basic profile is the theoretical profile of the thread. An essential principle is that the actual profiles of both the nut and bolt threads must never cross or transgress the theoretical profile. So bolt threads will always be equal to, or smaller than, the dimensions of the basic profile. Nut threads will always be equal to, or greater than, the basic profile. To ensure this in practice, tolerances and allowances are applied to the basic profile.

The most common screw thread form is the symmetrical V-Profile with an included angle of 60 degrees. This form is prevalent in the Unified National Screw Thread Series (UN, UNC, UNF, UNRC, UNRF) form as well as the ISO/Metric.

A thread may be either right-hand or left-hand. A right-hand thread on an external member advances into an internal thread when turned clockwise.

A left-hand thread advances when turned counterclockwise. (Bike pedal, older propane tanks, etc).

RIGHT HANDED   LEFT HANDED

Single vs. Double or Triple Threads

If a single helical groove is cut or formed on a cylinder, it is called a single-thread screw. Should the helix angle be increased sufficiently for a second thread to be cut between the grooves of the first thread, a double thread will be formed on the screw. Double, triple, and even quadruple threads are used whenever a rapid advance is desired, as on valves.

SINGLE   DOUBLE

☀ To designate a multiple thread the word "DOUBLE" (or "TRIPLE", and so on) is placed after the class of fit, like this: 3/8-16 UNC 2B DOUBLE.

Pitch and Major Diameter

Pitch and major diameter designate a thread. Lead is the distance advanced parallel to the axis when the screw is turned one revolution.

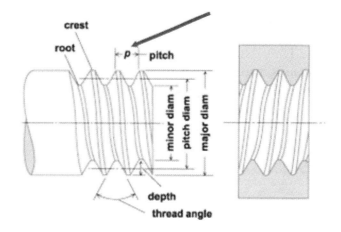

For a single thread, *lead is equal to the pitch*; for a double thread, lead is twice the pitch. For a straight thread, the pitch diameter is the diameter of an imaginary coaxial cylinder that would cut the thread forms at a height where the width of the thread and groove would be equal.

Thread Class of Fit

Classes of fit are tolerance standards; they set a plus or minus figure that is applied to the pitch diameter of bolts or nuts. The classes of fit used with almost all bolts sized in inches are specified by the ANSI/ASME Unified Screw Thread standards (which differ from the previous American National standards). There are three major Thread classes of fits, they are:

Class 1: The loosest fit. Used on parts which require assembly with a minimum of binding. Only found on bolts ¼ inch in diameter and larger.

Class 2: By far the most common class of fit. General purpose threads for bolts, nuts, and screws used in mass production.

Class 3: The closest fit. Used in precision assemblies where a close fit is desired to withstand stress and vibration.

🔅 Thread class identifies a range of thread tightness or looseness.

🔅 Classes for **External (male)** threads have an **"A"** suffix, for example, "2A" and classes for **Internal threads** have a **"B"** suffix.

General Thread Notes

The Thread note is usually applied to a drawing with a leader in the view where the thread is displayed as a circle for internal threads as illustrated below. External threads can be dimensioned with a leader with the thread length given as a dimension or at the end of the note.

English – ISP Unit system

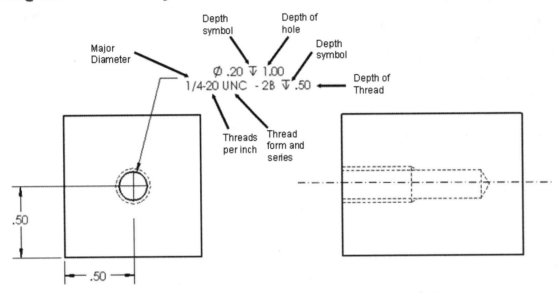

Pitch = 1/20: UNC = Unified National Series – Course: Thread Class 2: - B: = Internal. If not stated, the thread is always **Right-handed, Single**.

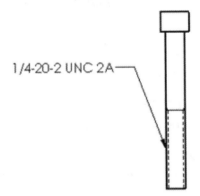

Dimensioning a Counterbore Hole

A Counterbore hole is a cylindrical flat bottom hole that has been machined to a larger diameter for a specified depth, so that a bolt or pin will fit into the recessed hole. The Counterbore provides a flat surface for the bolt or pin to seat against. In SolidWorks, use the Hole Wizard to insert the hole callout for a Counterbore.

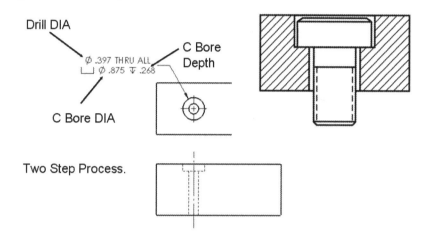

Counterbore holes are dimensioned by giving 1.) the diameter of the drill, 2.) the depth of the drill, 3.) the diameter of the counterbore , 4.) the depth of the counterbore, and 4.) the number of holes. Counterbore holes are displaced with the abbreviation C'BORE, C BORE or the symbol ⌴.

⚙ The difference between a C'BORE and a SPOTFACE is that the machining operation occurs on a curved surface.

Dimensioning a Countersunk Hole

The Countersunk hole, as illustrated below, is a cone-shaped recess machined in a part to receive a cone-shaped flat head screw or bolt.

A Countersunk hole is dimensioned by giving 1.) the diameter of the hole, 2.) the depth of the hole 3.) the diameter of the Countersunk, 4.) the angle at which the hole is to be Countersunk, 5.) the Counterbore diameter, 6.) the depth of the Counterbore, and 7.) the number of holes to be Countersunk.

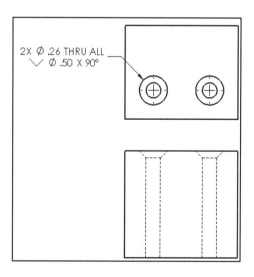

Adding a Counterbore for head clearance to a Countersink is optional. In SolidWorks, the Head Clearance option is located in the Hole Wizard Property Manager. The symbol for a Countersunk hole on a drawing annotation is CSK or ∨.

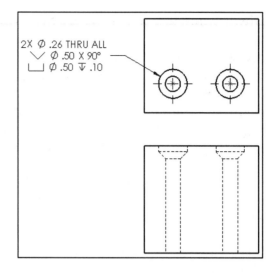

Chapter Summary

In Chapter 3 you reviewed basic dimensioning practices and were introduced to general tolerancing terminology according the ASME ANSI Y14.5 standard. You reviewed various dimensioning systems, fits and were presented with right and wrong ways to dimension simple shapes, lines, angles, circles and arcs.

Dimensioning a drawing is a means to communicate the requirements to manufacture a part. It requires special annotations for fasteners, threads, countersunk holes, counterbored holes and other types of holes.

Tolerances determine the maximum and minimum variation that a dimension on a part is manufactured to. Understanding the required tolerance can save both time and money to create a part from your drawing.

Although SolidWorks automatically generates most annotations for a part, it is up to the designer to determine if all the required information is available to manufacture the part. The annotations must be presented according to a dimensioning standard. There is no partial credit in the machine shop.

 View the pdf files on the enclosed DVD in the book for additional information.

Chapter Terminology

Depth: The horizontal (front to back) distance between two features in frontal planes. Depth is often identified in the shop as the thickness of a part or feature.

Dimensioning Standard - Metric - ASME standards for the use of metric dimensioning required all the dimensions to be expressed in millimeters (mm). The (mm) is not needed on each dimension, but it is used when a dimension is used in a notation. No trailing zeros are used. The Metric or International System of Units (S.I.) unit system in drafting is also known as the Millimeter, Gram Second (MMGS) unit system.

Dimensioning Standard - U.S. - ASME standards for U.S. dimensioning use the decimal inch value. When the decimal inch system is used, a zero is not used to the left of the decimal point for values less than one inch, and trailing zeros are used. The U.S. unit system is also known as the Inch, Pound, Second (IPS) unit system.

Engineering Graphics: Translates ideas from design layouts, specifications, rough sketches, and calculations of engineers and architects into working drawings, maps, plans, and illustrations which are used in making products.

Fasteners: Includes: Bolts and nuts (threaded), Set screws (threaded), Washers, Keys, Pins to name a few. Fasteners are not a permanent means of assembly such as welding or adhesives.

First Angle Projection: In First Angle Projection the Top view is looking at the bottom of the part. First Angle Projection is used in Europe and most of the world. However America and Australia use a method known as Third Angle Projection.

Height: The vertical distance between two or more lines or surfaces (features) which are in horizontal planes.

Origin: The point of intersection, where the X,Y,Z axes meet, is called the origin.

Part dimensions: Used in creating a part are sometimes called construction dimensions.

Thread Class or Fit: Classes of fit are tolerance standards; they set a plus or minus figure that is applied to the pitch diameter of bolts or nuts. The classes of fit used with almost all bolts sized in inches are specified by the ANSI/ASME Unified Screw Thread standards (which differ from the previous American National standards).

Thread Lead: The distance advanced parallel to the axis when the screw is turned one revolution. For a single thread, lead is equal to the pitch; for a double thread, lead is twice the pitch.

Third Angle Projection: In Third angle projection the Top View is looking at the Top of the part. First Angle Projection is used in Europe and most of the world. However America and Australia use a method known as Third Angle Projection.

Tolerance: The permissible range of variation in a dimension of an object. Tolerance may be specified as a factor or percentage of the nominal value, a maximum deviation from a nominal value, an explicit range of allowed values, be specified by a note or published standard with this information, or be implied by the numeric accuracy of the nominal value.

Questions

1. True or False: Dimensions should not be duplicated or the same information given in two different ways. If a reference dimension is used, the size value is placed within parentheses (X).

2. The U.S. unit system is also known as the (IPS) unit system. What does IPS stand for?

3. The diameter of a hole is placed in the view which shows the hole as a _____.

4. The length and diameter of cylinder are usually placed in the view which shows the cylinder as a _____.

5. Dimension a hole by its _____.

6. True or False: Dimensioning to hidden lines should be avoided wherever possible.

7. If a hole goes completely through the feature and it is not clearly shown on the drawing, the abbreviation _____ follows the dimension.

8. True or False: A dimension is said to have a *Unilateral* (single) tolerance when the total tolerance is in one direction only, either (+) or (-).

9. The degree (°) may be divided into smaller units called _____. There are 60 _____ in each degree. Each minute may be divided into smaller units called _____.

10. Classes for an **External (male thread)** have a _____ suffix.

11. Classes for an **Internal (female thread)** have a _____ suffix.

12. There are three major Thread classes of fits, they are: _____, _____, _____. Explain the differences.

13. Identify the pitch of the following Thread note: 3/8-16 UNC 2B DOUBLE_____.

14. Identify the symbol of a Counterbore and Countersunk:_____, _____.

Exercises

Exercise 3.1: Estimate the dimensions in a whole number. Dimension the below illustration. Note: There is more than one way to dimension an angle.

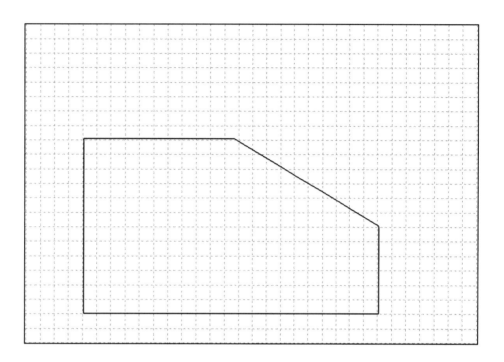

Exercise 3.2: Estimate the dimensions in a whole number. Dimension the illustration. Note: There is more than one way to dimension an angle.

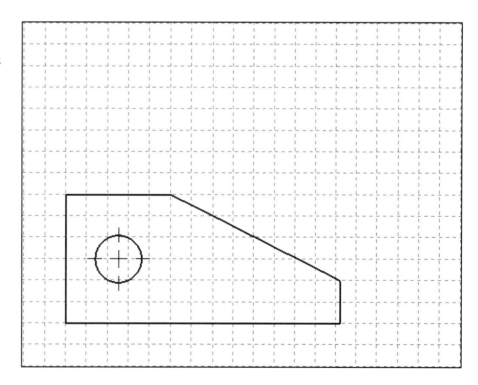

Exercise 3.3: Identify the dimension errors in the below illustration. Circle and list the errors.

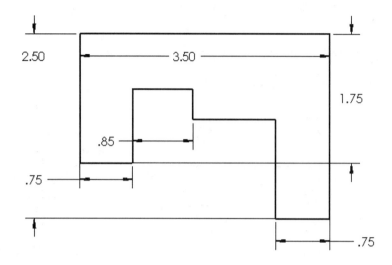

Errors:_____

_____

Exercise 3.4: Arrowheads are drawn between extension lines if space is available. If space is limited, the preferred Arrowhead and dimension location order is? List the preferred order.

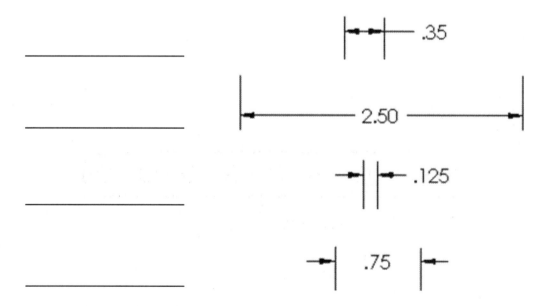

Exercise 3.5: Identify the dimension errors in the below illustration. Circle and list the errors.

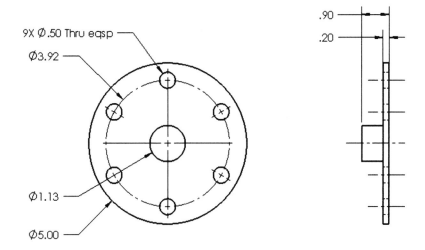

Errors:_____

_____

Exercise 3.6: Identify the dimension errors in the below illustration. Circle and list the errors.

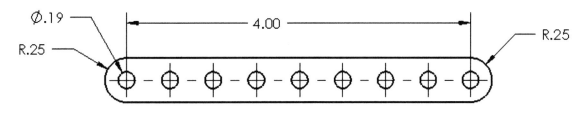

material thickness .10

Errors:_____

_____

Exercise 3.7: Place a *limit* tolerance of 002 on the below model.

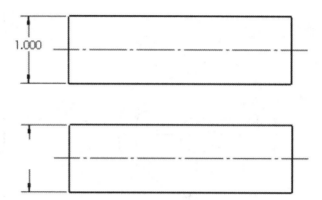

Exercise 3.8: Name three of the most common Tolerance Types.

1._____

2._____

3. _____ _

Exercise 3.9: Identify the following symbols.

_____   ⋁

_____   ⎵

_____   ⌀

_____   ⤓

Exercise 3.10: Describe the following hole callouts (symbols and meanings) in detail.

$\emptyset$ .2500 THRU ALL
$\sqcup$ $\emptyset$ .5000 $\overline{\underline{\vee}}$ .1250

$\emptyset$ .3970 THRU ALL
$\vee$ $\emptyset$ .7731 X 82°
$\sqcup$ $\emptyset$ .7731 $\overline{\underline{\vee}}$ .0402

Exercise 3.11: True / False - The loosest fit is a Class 1 fit. A Class 1 fit is used on parts which require assembly with a minimum of binding.

Exercise 3.12: The two most common Tolerance Standard agencies are: American National Standards Institute (ANSI) / (ASME) and the International Standards Organization (ISO). In the ANSI (US) standard: This is a two part question.

True or False:
T   F   The higher limit is placed below the lower limit.
T   F   When both limits are placed on one line, the lower limit precedes the higher limit.

Exercise 3.13: There are basically two types of dimensioning systems used in creating parts and drawings - **U.S.** and **Metric**.

True or False: The U.S. system uses the decimal inch value. When the decimal inch system is used, a zero is not used to the left of the decimal point for values less than one inch and trailing zeros are not used.

True or False: The Metric system normally is expressed in millimeters. When the millimeter system is used, the number is rounded to the nearest whole number. Trailing zeros are used.

Exercise 3.14: Identify the illustrated Thread Note.
Remember units!

1.) Pitch of the Thread:_____

2.) Major Thread Diameter:_____

3.) Internal or External Threads:_____

.250-20 UNC-2A-LH

Chapter 4

SolidWorks 2012 User Interface

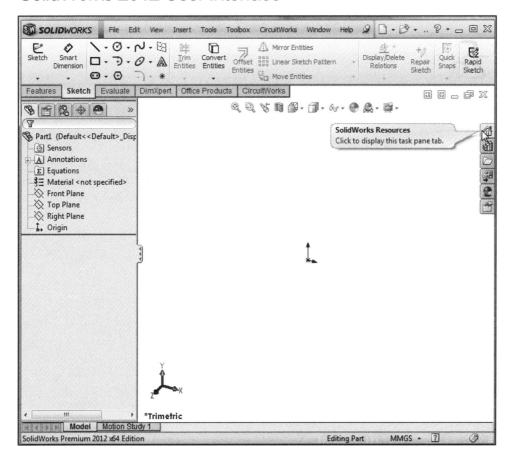

Below are the desired outcomes and usage competencies based on the completion of Chapter 4.

Desired Outcomes:	Usage Competencies:
• A comprehensive understanding of the SolidWorks 2012 User Interface and CommandManager.	• Ability to establish a SolidWorks session. • Aptitude to apply and use the following: *Menu bar toolbar, Menu bar menu, Drop-down menus, Context toolbars, Consolidated drop-down toolbars, System feedback icons, Confirmation Corner, Heads-up View toolbar, Document Properties and more.*

Notes:

Chapter 4 - SolidWorks 2012 User Interface

Chapter Objective

Provide a comprehensive understanding of the SolidWorks default User Interface and CommandManager: *Menu bar toolbar, Menu bar menu, Drop-down menu, Right-click Pop-up menus, Context toolbars / menus, Fly-out tool button, System feedback icons, Confirmation Corner, Heads-up View toolbar and an understanding of System Options, Document Properties, Part templates, File management and more.*

On the completion of this chapter, you will be able to:

- Establish a SolidWorks 2012 session.

- Comprehend the SolidWorks 2012 User Interface.

- Recognize the default Reference Planes in the FeatureManager.

- Utilize SolidWorks Help and SolidWorks Tutorials.

- Understand and apply the Task Pane tools.

- Recognize the default CommandManager tools for a Part, Assembly, and Drawing document.

- Apply the Motion Study tool.

Start a SolidWorks 2012 Session

The SolidWorks application is located in the Programs folder. SolidWorks displays the Tip of the Day box. Read the Tip of the Day every day to obtain additional information on SolidWorks.

Create a new part. Click **File, New** from the Menu bar menu or click **New** ⬜ from the Menu bar toolbar. There are two options for a new document: *Novice* and *Advanced.* Select the Advanced option. Select the Part document.

| Activity: Start a SolidWorks 2012 Session |

Start a SolidWorks 2012 session.
1) Click **Start** on the Windows Taskbar.

2) Click **All Programs**.

3) Click the **SolidWorks 2012** folder.

4) Click **SolidWorks 2012** application. The SolidWorks program window opens. Note: Do not open a document at this time.

If available, double-click the SolidWorks 2012 icon on the Windows Desktop to start a SolidWorks session.

Read the Tip of the Day dialog box.

5) If you do not see this screen, click the SolidWorks **Resources** 🏠 icon on the right side of the Graphics window located in the Task Pane.

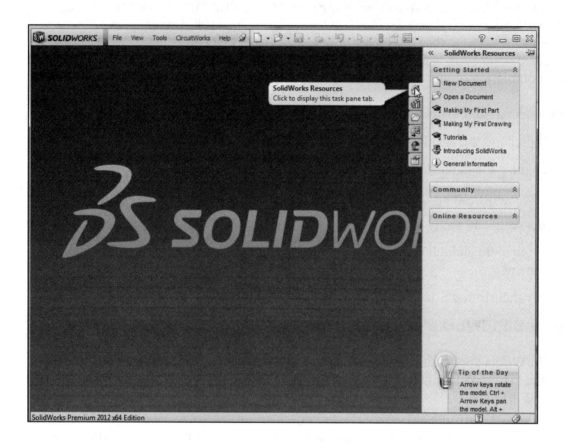

Activity: Understanding the SolidWorks UI and CommandManager

Menu bar toolbar

SolidWorks 2012 (UI) is design to make maximum use of the Graphics window area. The default Menu bar toolbar contains a set of the most frequently used tool buttons from the Standard toolbar. The available tools are: **New** □ - Creates a new document, **Open** ▷ - Opens an existing document, **Save** ⊞ - Saves an active document, **Print** ⌁ - Prints an active document, **Undo** ↺ - Reverses the last action, **Select** ⬚ - Selects Sketch entities, components and more, **Rebuild** ● - Rebuilds the active part, assembly or drawing, **File Properties** ⬚ - Shows the summary information on the active document, **Options** ⬚ - Changes system options and Add-Ins for SolidWorks.

Menu bar menu / Menu bar toolbar

Click SolidWorks in the Menu bar toolbar to display the Menu bar menu. SolidWorks provides a Context-sensitive menu structure. The menu titles remain the same for all three types of documents, but the menu items change depending on which type of document is active.

Example: The Insert menu includes features in part documents, mates in assembly documents, and drawing views in drawing documents. The display of the menu is also dependent on the workflow customization that you have selected. The default menu items for an active document are: *File, Edit, View, Insert, Tools, Window, Help* and *Pin.*

⌖ The Pin ⬚ option displays the Menu bar toolbar and the Menu bar menu as illustrated. Throughout the book, the Menu bar menu and the Menu bar toolbar are referred as the Menu bar.

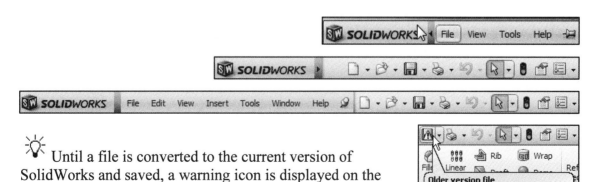

⌖ Until a file is converted to the current version of SolidWorks and saved, a warning icon is displayed on the Save tool as illustrated.

Drop-down menu

SolidWorks takes advantage of the familiar Microsoft® Windows® user interface. Communicate with SolidWorks either through the; *Drop-down menu, Pop-up menu, Shortcut toolbar, Fly-out toolbar* or the *CommandManager*.

A command is an instruction that informs SolidWorks to perform a task. To close a SolidWorks drop-down menu, press the Esc key. You can also click any other part of the SolidWorks Graphics window, or click another drop-down menu

Right-click

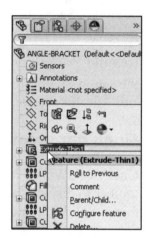

Right-click in the: *Graphics window, FeatureManager,* or *Sketch* to display a Context-sensitive toolbar. If you are in the middle of a command, this toolbar displays a list of options specifically related to that command.

Press the **s** key to view/access previous command tools in the Graphics window.

Consolidated toolbar

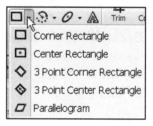

Similar commands are grouped in the CommandManager. Example: Variations of the Rectangle sketch tool are grouped in a single fly-out button as illustrated.

If you select the Consolidated toolbar button without expanding:

• For some commands such as Sketch, the most commonly used command is performed. This command is the first listed and the command shown on the button.

• For commands such as rectangle, where you may want to repeatedly create the same variant of the rectangle, the last used command is performed. This is the highlighted command when the Consolidated toolbar is expanded.

System Feedback

SolidWorks provides system feedback by attaching a symbol to the mouse pointer cursor. The system feedback symbol indicates what you are selecting or what the system is expecting you to select.

As you move the mouse pointer across your model, system feedback is provided to you in the form of symbols, riding next to the cursor arrow as illustrated.

Confirmation Corner

When numerous SolidWorks commands are active, a symbol or a set of symbols are displayed in the upper right hand corner of the Graphics window. This area is called the Confirmation Corner.

When a sketch is active, the confirmation corner box displays two symbols. The first symbol is the sketch tool icon. The second symbol is a large red X. These two symbols supply a visual reminder that you are in an active sketch. Click the sketch symbol icon to exit the sketch and to saves any changes that you made.

When other commands are active, the confirmation corner box provides a green check mark and a large red X. Use the green check mark to execute the current command. Use the large red X to cancel the command.

🔆 A goal of this book is to expose the new SolidWorks user to various design tools and features.

🔆 During the initial SolidWorks installation, you were requested to select either the ISO or ANSI drafting standard. ISO is typically; a European drafting standard and uses First Angle Projection. The book is written using the ANSI (US) overall drafting standard and Third Angle Projection for drawings.

🔆 When you create a new part or assembly, the three default Planes (Front, Right and Top) are aligned with specific views. The Plane you select for the Base sketch determines the orientation of the part or assembly.

Heads-up View toolbar

SolidWorks provides the user with numerous view options from the Standard Views, View and Heads-up View toolbar. The Heads-up View toolbar is a transparent toolbar that is displayed in the Graphics window when a document is active.

You can hide, move or modify the Heads-up View toolbar. To modify the toolbar: right-click on a tool and select or deselect the tools that you want to display. The following views are available: Note: Views are document dependent.

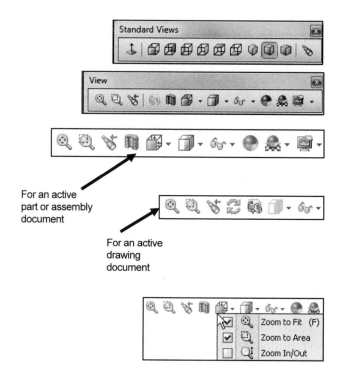

For an active part or assembly document

For an active drawing document

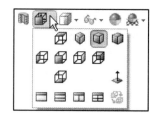

- *Zoom to Fit* : Zooms the model to fit the Graphics window.

- *Zoom to Area* : Zooms to the areas you select with a bounding box.

- *Previous View* : Displays the previous view.

- *Section View* : Displays a cutaway of a part or assembly, using one or more cross section planes.

- *View Orientation* : Provides the ability to select a view orientation or the number of viewports. The available options are: *Top, Isometric, Trimetric, Dimetric, Left, Front, Right, Back, Bottom, Single view, Two view - Horizontal, Two view - Vertical, Four view.*

- *Display Style* : Provides the ability to display the style for the active view. The available options are: *Wireframe, Hidden Lines Visible, Hidden Lines Removed, Shaded, Shaded With Edges.*

- *Hide/Show Items* : Provides the ability to select items to hide or show in the Graphics window. Note: The available items are document dependent.

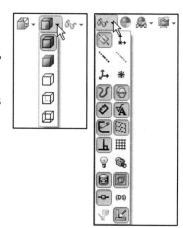

- *Edit Appearance* ● : Provides the ability to apply appearances from the Appearances PropertyManager.

- *Apply Scene* ● ▾: Provides the ability to apply a scene to an active part or assembly document. View the available options.

- *View Setting* ▾: Provides the ability to select the following: *RealView Graphics*, *Shadows in Shaded Mode* and *Perspective.*

- *Rotate* : Provides the ability to rotate a drawing view.

- *3D Drawing View* : Provides the ability to dynamically manipulate the drawing view to make a selection.

☼ To deactivate the reference planes for an active document, click **View**, uncheck **Planes** from the Menu bar. To deactivate the grid, click **Options** , **Document Properties** tab. Click **Grid/Snaps**, uncheck the **Display grid** box.

☼ Modify the Heads-up View toolbar. Press the **space** key. The Orientation dialog box is displayed. Click the **New View** tool. The Name View dialog box is displayed. Enter a new **named** view. Click **OK**. The new view is displayed in the Heads-up View toolbar.

☼ Press the **g** key to activate the Magnifying glass tool. Use the Magnifying glass tool to inspect a model and make selections without changing the overall view.

☼ This book does not cover starting a SolidWorks session in detail for the first time. A default SolidWorks installation presents you with several options. For additional information for an Education Edition, visit the following sites: http://www.solidworks.com/goedu and http://www.solidworks.com/sw/docs/EDU_2012_Inst allation_Instructions.pdf.

CommandManager

The SolidWorks CommandManager is a *Context-sensitive toolbar* that automatically updates based on the toolbar you want to access. By default, it has toolbars embedded in it based on your active document type. When you click a tab below the CommandManager, it updates to display that toolbar. For example, if you click the Sketch tab, the Sketch toolbar is displayed. The default Part tabs are: *Features, Sketch, Evaluate, DimXpert* and *Office Products*.

Below is an illustrated CommandManager for a default Part document.

 If you have SolidWorks, SolidWorks Professional, or SolidWorks Premium, the Office Products tab appears on the CommandManager as illustrated.

 Select the Add-In directly from the Office Products tab.

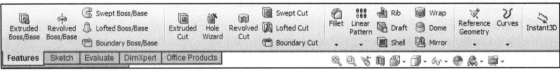

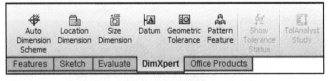

To customize the CommandManager, right-click on a tab and select Customize CommandManager.

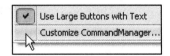

Below is an illustrated CommandManager for the default Drawing document. The default Drawing tabs are: *View Layout*, *Annotation*, *Sketch*, *Evaluate* and *Office Products*.

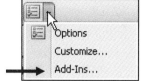

Double-clicking the CommandManager when it is docked will make it float. Double-clicking the CommandManager when it is floating will return it to its last position in the Graphics window.

Select the Add-In directly from the Office Products tab.

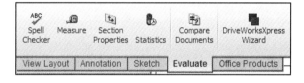

To add a custom tab to your CommandManager, right-click on a tab and click Customize CommandManager from the drop-down menu. The Customize dialog box is displayed.

You can also select to add a blank tab as illustrated and populate it with custom tools from the Customize dialog box.

Below is an illustrated CommandManager for the default Assembly document. The default Assembly tabs are: *Assembly*, *Layout*, *Sketch*, *Evaluate* and *Office Products*.

If you have SolidWorks, SolidWorks Professional, or SolidWorks Premium, the Office Products tab appears on the CommandManager

 Select the Add-In directly from the Office Products tab.

 Instant3D and the Rapid Sketch tool are active by default.

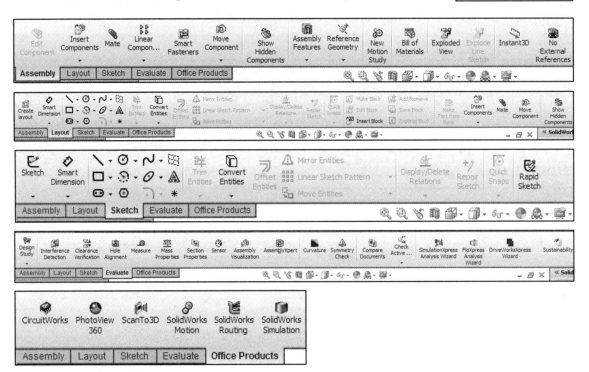

By default, the illustrated options are selected in the Customize box for the CommandManager.

Right-click on an existing tabs, and click Customize CommandManager to view your options.

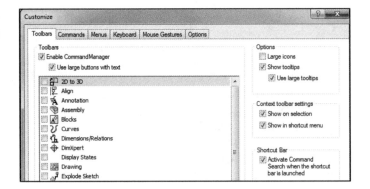

Drag or double-click the CommandManager and it becomes a separate floating window. Once it is floating, you can drag the CommandManager anywhere on or outside the SolidWorks window.

To dock the CommandManager when it is floating, perform one of the following actions:

- While dragging the CommandManager in the SolidWorks window, move the pointer over a docking icon - ⬆ Dock above , ◀ Dock left , ▶ Dock right and click the needed command.

- Double-click the floating CommandManager to revert the CommandManager to the last docking position.

Screen shots in the book were made using SolidWorks 2012 SP0 running Windows® 7 Ultimate.

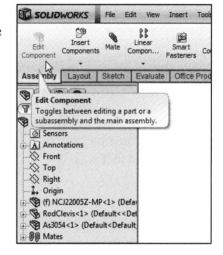

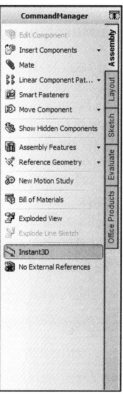

To save space in the CommandManager, right-click in the CommandManager and un-check the Use Large Buttons with Text box. This eliminates the text associated with the tool.

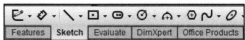

If you want to add a custom tab to your CommandManager, right-click on a tab and select the toolbar you want to insert. You can also select to add a blank tab as illustrated and populate it with custom tools from the Customize dialog box.

FeatureManager Design Tree

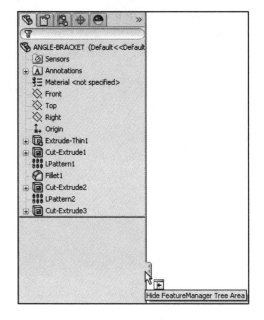

The FeatureManager design tree is located on the left side of the SolidWorks Graphics window. The FeatureManager provides a summarized view of the active part, assembly, or drawing document. The tree displays the details on how the part, assembly or drawing document was created.

Understand the FeatureManager design tree to troubleshoot your model. The FeatureManager is used extensively throughout this book.

The FeatureManager consists of five default tabs:

- *FeatureManager design tree*

- *PropertyManager*

- *ConfigurationManager*

- *DimXpertManager*

- *DisplayManager*

Select the Hide FeatureManager Tree Area

arrows as illustrated to enlarge the Graphics window for modeling.

When you create a new part or assembly, the three default Planes (Front, Right and Top) are aligned with specific views. The Plane you select for the Base sketch determines the orientation of the part or assembly.

Various commands provide the
ability to control what is displayed in
the FeatureManager design tree.
They are:

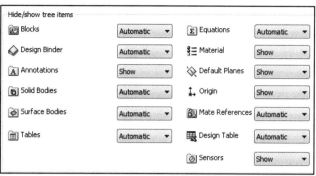

1. Show or Hide FeatureManager
items.

💡 Click **Options** 🔳 from the
Menu bar. Click **FeatureManager**
from the System Options tab.
Customize your FeatureManager
from the Hide/Show Tree Items dialog box.

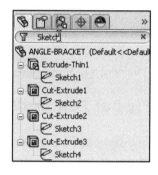

2. Filter the FeatureManager design tree. Enter information in the
filter field. You can filter by: *Type of features, Feature names,
Sketches, Folders, Mates, User-defined tags* and *Custom
properties*.

💡 Tags are keywords you can add to a
SolidWorks document to make them easier to filter
and to search. The Tags 🏷 icon is located in the
bottom right corner of the Graphics window.

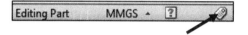

💡 To collapse all items in the FeatureManager,
right-click and select **Collapse items**, or press the **Shift +C**
keys.

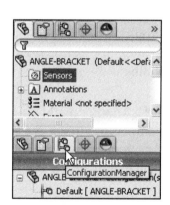

The FeatureManager design tree and the Graphics window are
dynamically linked. Select sketches, features, drawing views,
and construction geometry in either pane.

Split the FeatureManager design tree and either display two
FeatureManager instances, or combine the FeatureManager
design tree with the ConfigurationManager or
PropertyManager.

Move between the FeatureManager design tree,
PropertyManager, ConfigurationManager, and
DimXpertManager by selecting the tabs at the top of the menu.

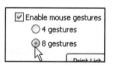

💡 Right-click and drag in the Graphics area to display the
Mouse Gesture wheel. You can customize the default commands
for a sketch, part, assembly or drawing.

The ConfigurationManager is located to the right of the FeatureManager. Use the ConfigurationManager to create, select and view multiple configurations of parts and assemblies.

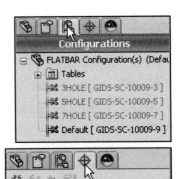

The icons in the ConfigurationManager denote whether the configuration was created manually or with a design table.

The DimXpertManager tab provides the ability to insert dimensions and tolerances manually or automatically. The DimXpertManager provides the following selections: *Auto Dimension Scheme* , *Show Tolerance Status* , *Copy Scheme* and *TolAnalyst Study* .

TolAnalyst is available in SolidWorks Premium.

Fly-out FeatureManager

The fly-out FeatureManager design tree provides the ability to view and select items in the PropertyManager and the FeatureManager design tree at the same time.

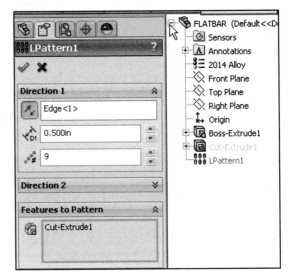

Throughout the book, you will select commands and command options from the drop-down menu, fly-out FeatureManager, Context toolbar or from a SolidWorks toolbar.

Another method for accessing a command is to use the accelerator key. Accelerator keys are special key strokes which activate the drop-down menu options. Some commands in the menu bar and items in the drop-down menus have an underlined character.

Pressing the Alt key followed by the corresponding key to the underlined character activates that command or option.

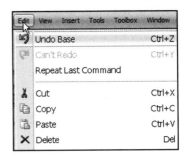

Illustrations may vary slightly depending on your SolidWorks version.

Task Pane

The Task Pane is displayed when a SolidWorks session starts. The Task Pane can be displayed in the following states: *visible or hidden*, *expanded or collapsed*, *pinned or unpinned*, *docked or floating*. The Task Pane contains the following default tabs: *SolidWorks Resources* 🏠, *Design Library* 📚, *File Explorer* 🗁, *View Palette* ⬚, *Appearances, Scenes, and Decals* ● and *Custom Properties* 🗒.

SolidWorks Resources

The basic SolidWorks Resources 🏠 menu displays the following default selections: *Getting Started*, *Community*, *Online Resources* and *Tip of the Day*.

Other user interfaces are available during the initial software installation selection: *Machine Design*, *Mold Design* or *Consumer Products Design*.

Design Library

The Design Library 📚 contains reusable parts, assemblies, and other elements, including library features. The Design Library tab contains four default selections. Each default selection contains additional sub categories. The default selections are: *Design Library*, *Toolbox*, *3D ContentCentral* and *SolidWorks Content*.

☼ To active the SolidWorks Toolbox, click **Tools**, **Add-Ins**… from the Main menu. Check the **SolidWorks Toolbox** and the **SolidWorks Toolbox Browser** box from the Add-Ins dialog box. Click **OK**.

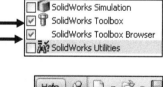

To access the Design Library folders in a non-network environment, click **Add File Location** 📚 and browse to the needed path. Paths will vary depending on your SolidWorks version and window setup. In a network environment, contact your IT department for system details.

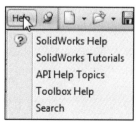

File Explorer

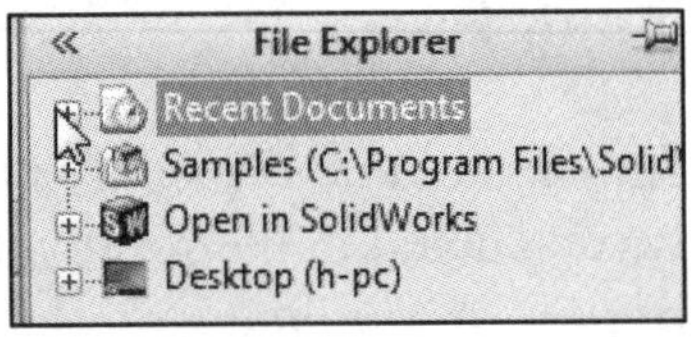

File Explorer in the Task Pane duplicates Windows Explorer from your local computer and displays the following directories: *Recent Documents, Samples, Open in SolidWorks* and *Desktop*.

Search

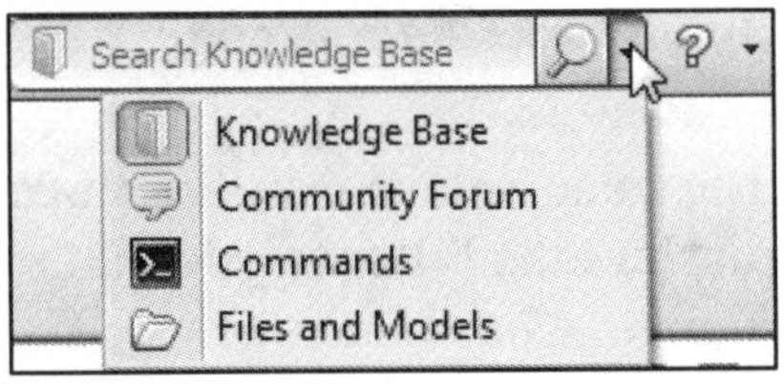

SolidWorks Search box is displayed in the upper right corner of the SolidWorks Graphics window. Enter the text or key words to search.

New search modes have been added to SolidWorks Search. In addition to searching for files and models, you can search *SolidWorks Help*, *Knowledge Base*, or *Community Forums*. Internet access is required for the Community Forums and Knowledge Base.

View Palette

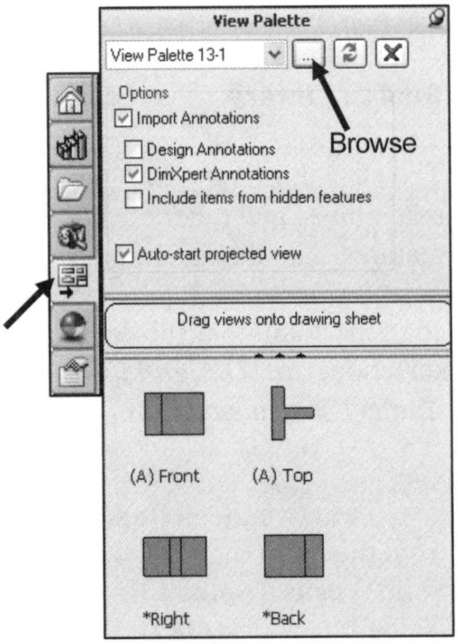

The View Palette tab located in the Task Pane provides the ability to insert drawing views of an active document, or click the Browse button to locate the desired document.

Drag and drop the view from the View Palette into an active drawing sheet to create a drawing view.

The selected model is View Palette 13-1 in the illustration. The **(A) Front** and **(A) Top** drawing views are displayed with DimXpert Annotations which was applied at the part level.

Appearances, Scenes, and Decals

Appearances, Scenes, and Decals  provide a simplified way to display models in a photo-realistic setting using a library of Appearances, Scenes, and Decals.

An appearance defines the visual properties of a model, including color and texture. Appearances do not affect physical properties, which are defined by materials.

Scenes provide a visual backdrop behind a model. In SolidWorks, they provide reflections on the model. PhotoView 360 is an Add-In. Drag and drop a selected appearance, scene, or decal on a feature, part, or assembly.

Custom Properties

The Custom Properties 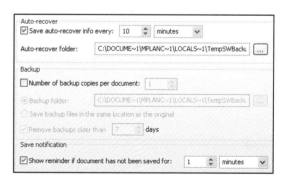 tool provides the ability to enter custom and configuration specific properties directly into SolidWorks files. In assemblies, you can assign properties to multiple parts at the same time. If you select a lightweight component in an assembly, you can view the component's custom properties in the Task Pane without resolving the component. If you edit a value, you are prompted to resolve the component so the change can be saved.

Document Recovery

If auto recovery is initiated in the System Options section and the system terminates unexpectedly with an active document, the saved information files are available on the Task Pane Document Recovery tab the next time you start a SolidWorks session.

 Run DFMXpress from the Evaluate tab or from Tools, DFMXpress in the Menu bar menu. The DFMXpress icon is displayed in the Task Pane.

Motion Study tab

Motion Studies are graphical simulations of motion for an assembly. Access MotionManager from the Motion Study tab. The Motion Study tab is located in the bottom left corner of the Graphics window.

Incorporate visual properties such as lighting and camera perspective. Click the Motion Study tab to view the MotionManager. Click the Model tab to return to the FeatureManager design tree.

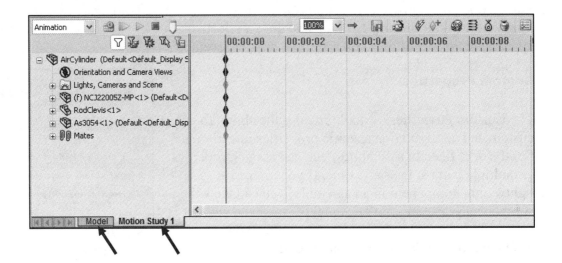

The MotionManager displays a timeline-based interface, and provides the following selections from the drop-down menu as illustrated:

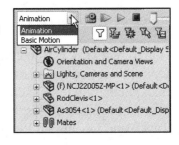

- *Animation:* Apply Animation to animate the motion of an assembly. Add a motor and insert positions of assembly components at various times using set key points. Use the Animation option to create animations for motion that do **not** require accounting for mass or gravity.

- *Basic Motion:* Apply Basic Motion for approximating the effects of motors, springs, collisions and gravity on assemblies. Basic Motion takes mass into account in calculating motion. Basic Motion computation is relatively fast, so you can use this for creating presentation animations using physics-based simulations. Use the Basic Motion option to create simulations of motion that account for mass, collisions or gravity.

If the Motion Study tab is not displayed in the Graphics window, click **View, MotionManager** from the Menu bar.

For older assemblies created before 2008, the Animation1 tab maybe displayed. View the Assembly Chapter for additional information.

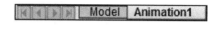

To create a new Motion Study, click **Insert, New Motion Study** from the Menu bar.

View SolidWorks Help for additional information on Motion Study.

Activity: Create a new 3D Part

A part is a 3D model which consists of features. What are features?

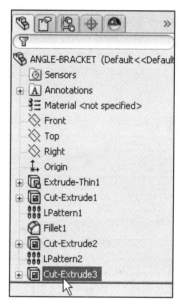

- Features are geometry building blocks.

- Features add or remove material.

- Features are created from 2D or 3D sketched profiles or from edges and faces of existing geometry.

- Features are an individual shape that combined with other features, makes up a part or assembly. Some features, such as bosses and cuts, originate as sketches. Other features, such as shells and fillets, modify a feature's geometry.

- Features are displayed in the FeatureManager as illustrated (Extrude-Thin1, Cut-Extrude1, LPattern1, Fillet1, Cut-Extrude2, Lpatern2, and Cut-Extrude3).

You can suppress a feature. A suppress feature is displayed in light gray.

The first sketch of a part is called the Base Sketch. The Base sketch is the foundation for the 3D model. The book focuses on 2D sketches and 3D features.

During the initial SolidWorks installation, you were requested to select either the ISO or ANSI drafting standard. ISO is typically; a European drafting standard and uses First Angle Projection. The book is written using the ANSI (US) overall drafting standard and Third Angle Projection for drawings.

The first sketch of a part is the Base sketch. The Base sketch is the foundation for the 3D model.

Create a new part.

6)   Click **New** ⬜ from the Menu bar. The New SolidWorks Document dialog box is displayed.

Select Advanced Mode.

7)   Click the **Advanced** button to display the New SolidWorks Document dialog box in Advance mode.

8)   The Templates tab is the default tab. Part is the default template from the New SolidWorks Document dialog box. Click **OK**.

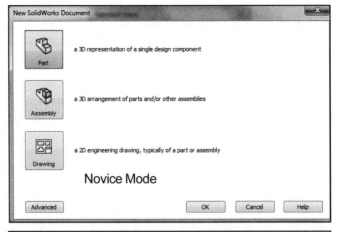

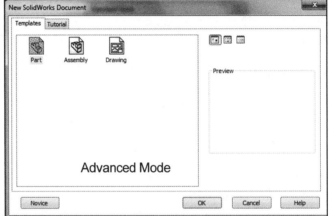

The *Advanced* mode remains selected for all new documents in the current SolidWorks session. When you exit SolidWorks, the *Advanced* mode setting is saved.

The default SolidWorks installation contains two tabs in the New SolidWorks Document dialog box: *Templates* and *Tutorial*. The *Templates* tab corresponds to the default SolidWorks templates. The *Tutorial* tab corresponds to the templates utilized in the SolidWorks Tutorials.

During the initial SolidWorks installation, you are requested to select either the ISO or ANSI drafting standard. ISO is typically a European drafting standard and uses First Angle Projection. The book is written using the ANSI (US) overall drafting standard and Third Angle Projection for all drawing documents.

Part1 is displayed in the FeatureManager and is the name of the document. Part1 is the default part window name. The Menu bar, CommandManager, FeatureManager, Heads-up View toolbar, SolidWorks Resources, SolidWorks Search, Task Pane, and the Origin are displayed in the Graphics window.

The Origin is displayed in blue in the center of the Graphics window. The Origin represents the intersection of the three default reference planes: *Front Plane*, *Top Plane* and *Right Plane*. The positive X-axis is horizontal and points to the right of the Origin in the Front view. The positive Y-axis is vertical and points upward in the Front view. The FeatureManager contains a list of features, reference geometry, and settings utilized in the part.

Edit the document units directly from the Graphics window. This is a new feature in SolidWorks 2012.

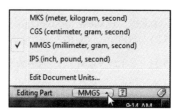

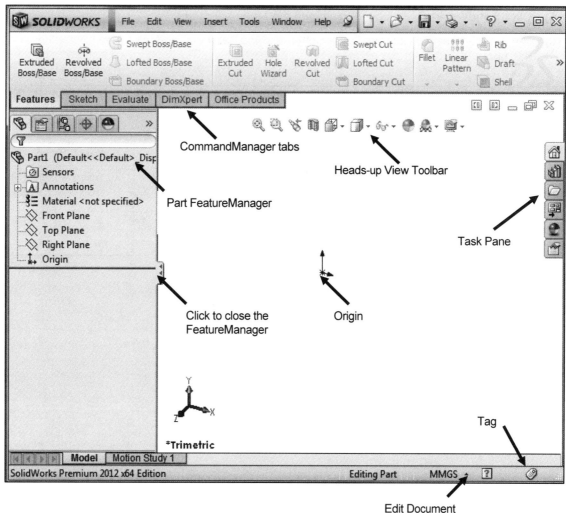

In this book, Reference planes and Grid/Snaps are deactivated in the Graphics window for improved model clarity.

Activity: Menu Bar toolbar, Menu Bar menu, Heads-up View toolbar

---

Display tools and tool tips.

9) Position the **mouse pointer** over the Heads-up View toolbar and view the tool tips.

10) **Read** the large tool tip.

11) Select the **drop-down arrow** ▼ to view the available view tools.

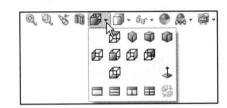

Display the View toolbar and the Menu bar.

12) Right-click in the **gray area** of the Menu bar.

13) Click **View**. The View toolbar is displayed.

14) Click and drag the **View toolbar** off the Graphics window.

15) Click **SolidWorks** as illustrated to expand the Menu bar menu.

16) **Pin** the Menu bar as illustrated. Use both the Menu bar menu and the Menu bar toolbar in this book.

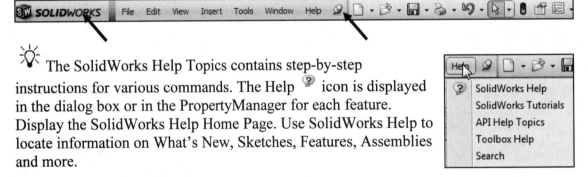

The SolidWorks Help Topics contains step-by-step instructions for various commands. The Help icon is displayed in the dialog box or in the PropertyManager for each feature. Display the SolidWorks Help Home Page. Use SolidWorks Help to locate information on What's New, Sketches, Features, Assemblies and more.

17) Click **Help** from the Menu bar.

18) Click **SolidWorks Help**. The SolidWorks Help Home Web Page is displayed by default. (Use SolidWorks Web Help is selected by default). View your options and features.

19) Click the **Home Page** icon to return to the Home Page.

20) **Close** the SolidWorks Home Page dialog box.

Display and explore the SolidWorks tutorials.

21) Click **Help** from the Menu bar.

22) Click **SolidWorks Tutorials**. The SolidWorks Tutorials are displayed. The SolidWorks Tutorials are presented by category.

23) Click the **Getting Started** category. The Getting Started category provides three 30 minute lessons on parts, assemblies, and drawings. This section also provides information for users who are switching from AutoCAD to SolidWorks. The tutorials also provide links to the CSWP and CSWA Certification programs and a new What's New Tutorials for 2012.

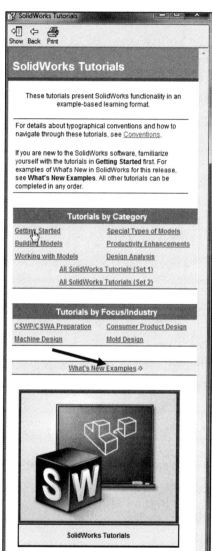

SolidWorks Corporation offers various levels of certification representing increasing levels of expertise in 3D CAD design as it applies to engineering.

The *Certified SolidWorks Associate* CSWA certification indicates a foundation in and apprentice knowledge of 3D CAD design and engineering practices and principles.

The main requirement for obtaining the CSWA certification is to take and pass the three hour, seven question on-line proctored exam at a Certified SolidWorks CSWA Provider, "university, college, technical, vocational or secondary educational institution" and to sign the SolidWorks Confidentiality Agreement.

Passing this exam provides students the chance to prove their working knowledge and expertise and to be part of a worldwide industry certification standard.

24) **Close** the ☒ Online Tutorial dialog box. Return to the SolidWorks Graphics window.

Additional information on System Options, Document Properties, File Locations, and Templates is located in SolidWorks Help Topics. Keywords: Options (detailing, units), Templates, Files (locations), menus and toolbars (features, sketch).

 Review of the SolidWorks 2012 User Interface and Part Templates

The SolidWorks 2012 User Interface and CommandManager consist of the following options: Menu bar toolbar, Menu bar menu, Drop-down menus, Context toolbars, Consolidated fly-out menus, System feedback icons, Confirmation Corner and Heads-up View toolbar.

The default CommandManager Part tabs control the display of the *Features*, *Sketch*, *Evaluate*, *DimXpert* and *Office Products* toolbars.

The FeatureManager consists of five default tabs:

- *FeatureManager design tree*

- *PropertyManager*

- *ConfigurationManager*

- *DimXpertManager*

- *DisplayManager*

The Task Pane is displayed when a SolidWorks session starts. The Task Pane can be displayed in the following states: *visible or hidden, expanded or collapsed, pinned or unpinned, docked or floating*. The Task Pane contains the following default tabs: *SolidWorks Resources*, *Design Library*, *File Explorer*, *View Palette*, *Appearances, Scenes, and Decals* and *Custom Properties*.

You created two Part Templates: **PART-MM-ISO** and **PART-IN-ANSI**. The document properties Overall drafting standard, units and decimal places were stored in the Part Templates. The File Locations System Option, Document Templates option controls the reference to the MY-TEMPLATES folder.

In some network locations and school environments, the File Locations option must be set to MY-TEMPLATES for each session of SolidWorks. You can exit SolidWorks at any time during this chapter. Save your document. Select File, Exit from the Menu bar.

When you create a new part or assembly, the three default Planes (Front, Right and Top) are aligned with specific views. The Plane you select for the Base sketch determines the orientation of the part or assembly.

Chapter Terminology

Assembly: An assembly is a document in which parts, features, and other assemblies (sub-assemblies) are put together. A part in an assembly is called a component. Adding a component to an assembly creates a link between the assembly and the component. When SolidWorks opens the assembly, it finds the component file to show it in the assembly. Changes in the component are automatically reflected in the assembly. The filename extension for a SolidWorks assembly file name is *.sldasm.

CommandManager: The CommandManager is a Context-sensitive toolbar that dynamically updates based on the toolbar you want to access. By default, it has toolbars embedded in it based on the document type. When you click a tab below the Command Manager, it updates to display that toolbar. For example, if you click the **Sketches** tab, the Sketch toolbar is displayed.

ConfigurationManager: The ConfigurationManager is located on the left side of the SolidWorks window and provides the means to create, select, and view multiple configurations of parts and assemblies in an active document. You can split the ConfigurationManager and either display two ConfigurationManager instances, or combine the ConfigurationManager with the FeatureManager design tree, PropertyManager, or third party applications that use the panel.

Coordinate System: SolidWorks uses a coordinate system with origins. A part document contains an original Origin. Whenever you select a plane or face and open a sketch, an Origin is created in alignment with the plane or face. An Origin can be used as an anchor for the sketch entities, and it helps orient perspective of the axes. A three-dimensional reference triad orients you to the X, Y, and Z directions in part and assembly documents.

Cursor Feedback: The system feedback symbol indicates what you are selecting or what the system is expecting you to select. As you move the mouse pointer across your model, system feedback is provided.

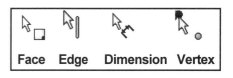

Dimension: A value indicating the size of the 2D
sketch entity or 3D feature. Dimensions in a SolidWorks drawing are associated with the model, and changes in the model are reflected in the drawing, if you DO NOT USE DimXpert.

DimXpertManager: The DimXpertManager lists the tolerance features defined by DimXpert for a part. It also displays DimXpert tools that you use to insert dimensions and tolerances into a part. You can import these dimensions and tolerances into drawings. DimXpert is not associative.

Document: In SolidWorks, each part, assembly, and drawing is referred to as a document, and each document is displayed in a separate window.

Drawing: A 2D representation of a 3D part or assembly. The extension for a SolidWorks drawing file name is .SLDDRW. Drawing refers to the SolidWorks module used to insert, add, and modify views in an engineering drawing.

Feature: Features are geometry building blocks. Features add or remove material. Features are created from 2D or 3D sketched profiles or from edges and faces of existing geometry.

FeatureManager: The FeatureManager design tree located on the left side of the SolidWorks window provides an outline view of the active part, assembly, or drawing. This makes it easy to see how the model or assembly was constructed or to examine the various sheets and views in a drawing. The FeatureManager and the Graphics window are dynamically linked. You can select features, sketches, drawing views, and construction geometry in either pane.

Graphics window: The area in the SolidWorks window where the part, assembly, or drawing is displayed.

Heads-up View toolbar: A transparent toolbar located at the top of the Graphics window.

Model: 3D solid geometry in a part or assembly document. If a part or assembly document contains multiple configurations, each configuration is a separate model.

Motion Studies: Graphical simulations of motion and visual properties with assembly models. Analogous to a configuration, they do not actually change the original assembly model or its properties. They display the model as it changes based on simulation elements you add.

Origin: The model origin is displayed in blue and represents the (0,0,0) coordinate of the model. When a sketch is active, a sketch origin is displayed in red and represents the (0,0,0) coordinate of the sketch. Dimensions and relations can be added to the model origin, but not to a sketch origin.

Part: A 3D object that consists of one or more features. A part inserted into an assembly is called a component. Insert part views, feature dimensions and annotations into 2D drawing. The extension for a SolidWorks part filename is .SLDPRT.

Plane: Planes are flat and infinite. Planes are represented on the screen with visible edges.

PropertyManager: Most sketch, feature, and drawing tools in SolidWorks open a PropertyManager located on the left side of the SolidWorks window. The PropertyManager displays the properties of the entity or feature so you specify the properties without a dialog box covering the Graphics window.

RealView: Provides a simplified way to display models in a photo-realistic setting using a library of appearances and scenes. RealView requires graphics card support and is memory intensive.

Rebuild: A tool that updates (or regenerates) the document with any changes made since the last time the model was rebuilt. Rebuild is typically used after changing a model dimension.

Relation: A relation is a geometric constraint between sketch entities or between a sketch entity and a plane, axis, edge or vertex.

Rollback: Suppresses all items below the rollback bar.

Sketch: The name to describe a 2D profile is called a sketch. 2D sketches are created on flat faces and planes within the model. Typical geometry types are lines, arcs, corner rectangles, circles, polygons, and ellipses.

Task Pane: The Task Pane is displayed when you open the SolidWorks software. It contains the following tabs: SolidWorks Resources, Design Library, File Explorer, Search, View Palette, Document Recovery and RealView/PhotoWorks.

Toolbars: The toolbars provide shortcuts enabling you to access the most frequently used commands. When you enable add-in applications in SolidWorks, you can also display their associated toolbars.

Units: Used in the measurement of physical quantities. Decimal inch dimensioning and Millimeter dimensioning are the two types of common units specified for engineering parts and drawings.

Notes:

Chapter 5

Drawing Templates and Sheet Formats

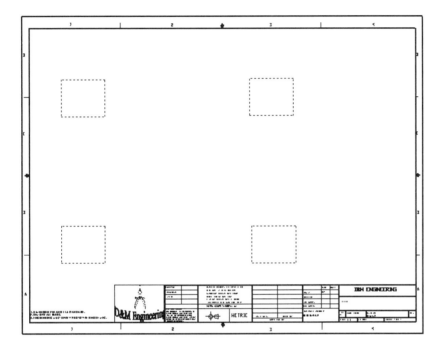

Below are the desired outcomes and usage competencies based on the completion of Chapter 5.

Desired Outcomes:	Usage Competencies:

• Two Drawing Templates:
   ○ C (ANSI) size Drawing template
   ○ A (ANSI) size Drawing template
	• Ability to apply Document Properties to reflect the ASME Y14 Engineering Drawing and Related Drawing Practices.
	
	• Understand System Options and Document Properties, which influence the drawing and Drawing template.

• One C size Sheet format.	• Import an AutoCAD file as a Sheet format. Insert SolidWorks System Properties and Custom Properties.
• New file location for Drawing templates and Sheet format.	• Ability to create new SolidWorks Document tabs.

Notes:

Chapter 5 - Drawing Templates and Sheet Formats

Chapter Objective

Create two Drawing templates. Create a C (ANSI) Landscape size Drawing template and an A (ANSI) Landscape size Drawing template. Create a C (ANSI) size Landscape Sheet format.

On the completion of this chapter, you will be able to:

- Establish a SolidWorks drawing document session.

- Distinguish between System Options and Document Properties as they relate to drawings and templates.

- Create a new SolidWorks File Location for a Drawing template.

- Set Reference Document Properties in a Drawing template.

- Create an empty C (ANSI) Landscape size Drawing template. Propagate the settings to the drawing sizes.

- Import an AutoCAD drawing as a SolidWorks C-size Sheet format.

- Combine an empty Drawing template and Sheet format to create a C-ANSI-MM Drawing template.

- Develop Linked Notes to SolidWorks Properties and Custom Properties in the Sheet format.

- Insert a company logo with a relation in the Title block.

- Create an A-ANSI-MM Drawing template by combining information from the C-size Drawing template and A-size Sheet format.

Templates are part, drawing, and assembly documents that include user-defined parameters and are the basis for new documents. You can maintain many different document templates. For example, you can create:

- A Document template using millimeters and another document template using inches.

- A Document template using ANSI and another document template using ISO dimensioning standard.

- A Document template for a Detached drawing.

A *Detached drawing* is design so you can open and work in drawing files without the model files being loaded into memory or even being present.

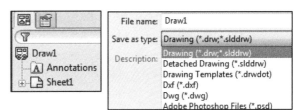

When opening a Detached drawing, SolidWorks
checks all sheets in the drawing to be sure that they
are synchronized with the model. If not, you are
warned. To save a standard drawing to a Detached
Drawing, click File, Save As, select the Save as type:
Detached Drawing (*SLDDRW).

Type of file:	SolidWorks Drawing Document (.SLDDRW)
Opens with:	🔳 SldWorks Change...

File name:	Draw1
Save as type:	Drawing (*.drw;*.slddrw)
Description:	Drawing (*.drw;*.slddrw)
	Detached Drawing (*.slddrw)
	Drawing Templates (*.drwdot)
	Dxf (*.dxf)
	Dwg (*.dwg)
	Adobe Photoshop Files (*.psd)

Chapter Overview

Your responsibilities as the designer include developing drawings that adhere to the
ASME Y14 American National Standard for Engineering Drawing and Related
Documentation Practices. The foundation for a SolidWorks drawing is the Drawing
template. Drawing size, drawing standards, units and other properties are defined in the
Drawing template.

Sheet formats contain the following: *Border, Title block, Revision block, Company name,
logo, SolidWorks Properties* and *Custom Properties*. You are under time constraints to
complete the project. Conserve drawing time. Create a custom Drawing template and
Sheet format.

Perform the following tasks in this Chapter:

- Modify Document Properties and create an empty C (ANSI) size Drawing template.

- Import an AutoCAD drawing and save the drawing as a C-size Sheet format.

- Add System Properties and Custom Properties to the Sheet format.

- Create an A-ANSI-MM Drawing template.

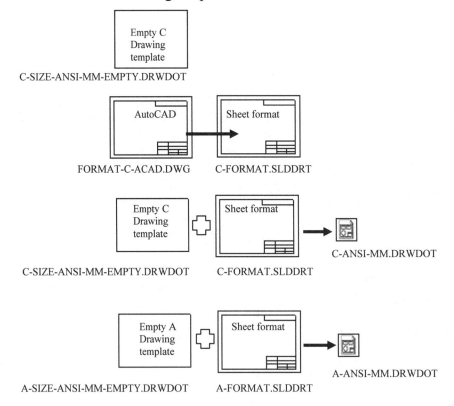

- Combine the empty drawing template and import the Sheet format to create the C-ANSI-MM Drawing template.

- Generate an empty A (ANSI) size Drawing template.

- Modify an existing SolidWorks A-size Sheet format.

Engineering Drawing and Related Documentation Practices

Drawing templates in this section are based on the American Society of Mechanical Engineers ASME Y14 American National Standard for Engineering Drawing and Related Documentation Practices.

These standards represent the drawing practices used by U.S. industry. The ASME Y14 practices supersede the American National Standards Institute ANSI standards.

The ASME Y14 Engineering Drawing and Related Documentation Practices are published by The American Society of Mechanical Engineers, New York, NY. References to the current ASME Y14 standards are used with permission.

ASME Y14 Standard Name:	American National Standard Engineering Drawing and Related Documentation:	Revision of the Standard:
ASME Y14.100M-1998	Engineering Drawing Practices	DOD-STD-100
ASME Y14.1-1995	Decimal Inch Drawing Sheet Size and Format	ANSI Y14.1
ASME Y14.1M-1995	Metric Drawing Sheet Size and Format	ANSI Y14.1M
ASME Y14.24M	Types and Applications of Engineering Drawings	ANSI Y14.24M
ASME Y14.2M(Reaffirmed 1998)	Line Conventions and Lettering	ANSI Y14.2M
ASME Y14.3M-1994	Multi-view and Sectional View Drawings	ANSI Y14.3
ASME Y14.41-2003	Digital Product Definition Data Practices	N/A
ASME Y14.5M –1994 (Reaffirmed 1999)	Dimensioning and Tolerancing	ANSI Y14.5-1982 (R1988)

This book presents a portion of the ASME Y14 American National Standard for Engineering Drawing and Related Documentation Practices. Information presented in Chapters 5 - 9 represents sample illustrations of drawings, various drawing views, and or dimension types.

The ASME Y14 Standards committee develops and maintains additional Drawing Standards. Members of these committees are from Industry, Department of Defense, and Academia.

Companies create their own drawing standards based on one or more of the following:

- ASME Y14

- ISO or other International drawing standards

- Older ANSI standards

- Military standards

☼ There is also the "We've always done it this way" drawing standard or "Go ask the Drafting supervisor" drawing standard.

File Management

File management organizes parts, assemblies and drawings. Why do you need file management? A large assembly drawing contains hundreds or even thousands of reference components.

Parts and assemblies are distributed between team members to save time. Design changes occur frequently in the development process. How do you manage and control changes? Answer: Through file management. File management is a very important tool in the development process.

Utilize file folders to organize projects, vendor parts and assemblies, templates and various libraries.

Folders exist on the local hard drive, example C:\. Folders also exist on a network drive, example Z:\. The letters C:\ and Z:\ are used as examples for a local drive and a network drive respectively. The following example utilizes the folder, "Documents" to contain the folders for your projects

---
Activity: File Management

Create a new folder in Windows to download files from the DVD and to create new ones for this book.
1)   Click **Start** from the Windows Taskbar.

2)   Click **Documents** in Windows.

3)   Click **New Folder** from the Main menu.

Enter the new folder name.
4)   Enter **DRAWING-W-SOLIDWORKS-2012**.

☼ Select the Microsoft Windows commands either from the Main menu, toolbar icons or with the right mouse button. Windows 7 is used in this section.

Return to the DRAWING-W-SOLIDWORKS-2012 folder.
5)   Click the **DRAWING-W-SOLIDWORKS-2012** folder.

Copy the files and folders from the enclosed DVD in the book to the new folder location.
6)   Right-click **Explore** on the DVD in your drive. View the available files and folders.

7)   **Copy** the files and folders to the DRAWING-W-SOLIDWORKS-2012 folder. The DRAWING-W-SOLIDWORKS-2012 folder is the working folder for this book.

Store chapter Drawing templates in the MY-TEMPLATES file folder. Store Chapter Sheet formats in the MY-SHEETFORMATS folder.

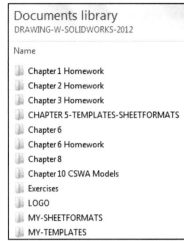

Documents library
DRAWING-W-SOLIDWORKS-2012

Name

Chapter 1 Homework
Chapter 2 Homework
Chapter 3 Homework
CHAPTER 5-TEMPLATES-SHEETFORMATS
Chapter 6
Chapter 6 Homework
Chapter 8
Chapter 10 CSWA Models
Exercises
LOGO
MY-SHEETFORMATS
MY-TEMPLATES

MY-TEMPLATES

MY-SHEETFORMATS

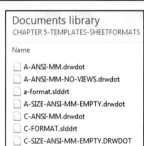

Documents library
CHAPTER 5-TEMPLATES-SHEETFORMATS

Name

A-ANSI-MM.drwdot
A-ANSI-MM-NO-VIEWS.drwdot
a-format.slddrt
A-SIZE-ANSI-MM-EMPTY.drwdot
C-ANSI-MM.drwdot
C-FORMAT.slddrt
C-SIZE-ANSI-MM-EMPTY.DRWDOT

Drawing templates and Sheet formats that are created in this chapter are located in the CHAPTER 5-TEMPLATES-SHEETFORMATS folder on the DVD. Check for proper path location on your system for created Sheet formats and Drawing templates.

Default Drawing Template, Sheet Format and Sheet Size

The foundation of a SolidWorks drawing is the Drawing template. Drawing sheet size, drawing standards, company information, manufacturing and/or assembly requirements: units, layers, line styles and other properties are defined in the Drawing template.

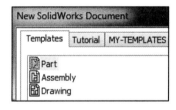

New SolidWorks Document

Templates | Tutorial | MY-TEMPLATES

Part
Assembly
Drawing

A Sheet format is incorporated into the Drawing template. The Sheet format contains a few of the following items: Sheet border, Title block, Revision block information, Company name and/or logo information, Custom Properties, SolidWorks Properties, and more.

SolidWorks starts with a default Drawing template, (*.drwdot).

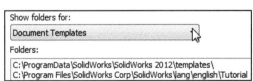

Show folders for:

Document Templates

Folders:

C:\ProgramData\SolidWorks\SolidWorks 2012\templates\
C:\Program Files\SolidWorks Corp\SolidWorks\lang\english\Tutorial

The default Drawing template is located in the C:\ProgramData\SolidWorks\SolidWork 2012\templates folder on a non-network system. SolidWorks is the name of the installation folder.

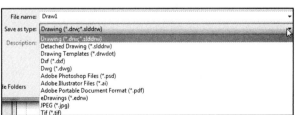

File name: Draw1

Save as type: Drawing (*.drw;*.slddrw)

Description:

Drawing (*.drw;*.slddrw)
Detached Drawing (*.slddrw)
Drawing Templates (*.drwdot)
Dxf (*.dxf)
Dwg (*.dwg)
Adobe Photoshop Files (*.psd)
Adobe Illustrator Files (*.ai)
Adobe Portable Document Format (*.pdf)
eDrawings (*.edrw)
JPEG (*.jpg)
Tif (*.tif)

New SolidWorks Document

The Templates folder corresponds to the Templates tab displayed in the New SolidWorks Document dialog box.

The Large Icons option displays the full name and a large document icon.

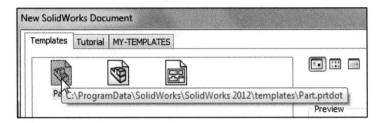

The List option displays the document icons in a list format.

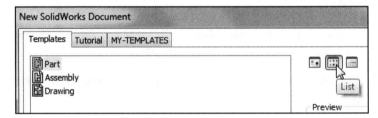

The List Details option displays the document name, size and last modified date.

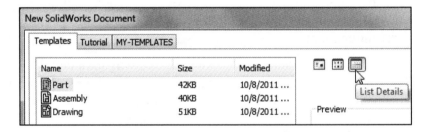

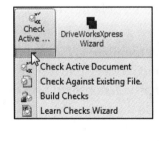 SolidWorks Design Checker verifies design elements such as dimensioning standards, fonts, materials and sketches to ensure that SolidWorks documents meet predefined designed criteria.

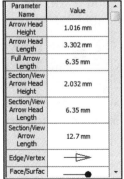

Sheet Format/Size

The Sheet Format/Size dialog box defines the Sheet format and the paper size. The U.S. default Standard Sheet Format is A (ANSI) Landscape. The Display sheet format box toggles the Sheet format display on/off.

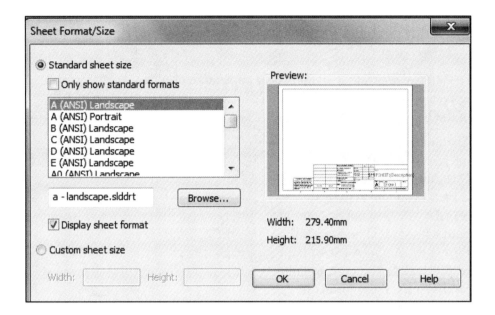

The Standard Sheet formats are located in the C:\ProgramData\SolidWorks\SolidWorks 2012\lang\english\sheetformat in a non-network system. Note: This is a hidden file.

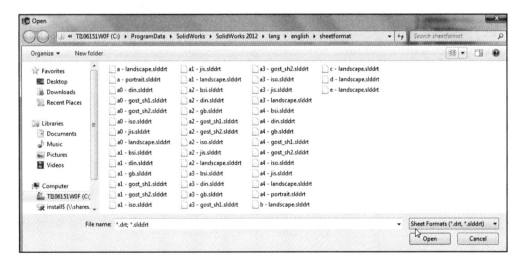

ASME Y14.1 Drawing Sheet Size and Format

There are two ASME standards that define sheet size and format. They are:

1. ASME Y14.1-1995 Decimal Inch Drawing Sheet Size and Format

2. ASME Y14.1M-1995 Metric Drawing Sheet size

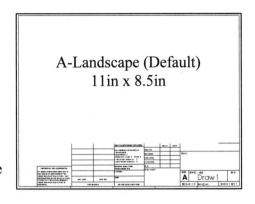

A-Landscape (Default)
11in x 8.5in

Drawing size refers to the physical paper size used to create the drawing. The most common paper size in the U.S. is the A-size: (8.5in. x 11in.).

The most common paper size internationally is the A4 size: (210mm x 297mm). The ASME Y14.1-1995 and ASME Y14.1M-1995 standards contain both a horizontal and vertical format for A and A4 size respectively. The corresponding SolidWorks Sheet format is Landscape for horizontal and Portrait for vertical.

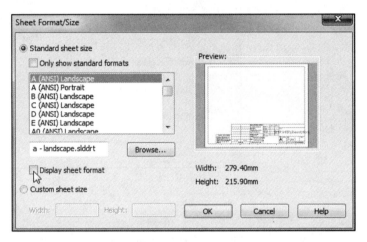

SolidWorks predefines U.S. drawing sizes A through E. Drawing sizes: F, G, H, J, & K utilize the Custom sheet size option. Enter values for width and height. SolidWorks predefines metric drawing sizes A4 through A0. Metric roll paper sizes utilize the Custom sheet size option.

The ASME Y14.1-1995 Decimal Inch Drawing and ASME Y14.1M-1995 Metric Sheet size standards are as follows:

Drawing Size: "Physical Paper"	Size in inches: Vertical	Horizontal
A horizontal (landscape)	8.5	11.0
A vertical (portrait)	11.0	8.5
B	11.0	17.0
C	17.0	22.0
D	22.0	34.0
E	34.0	44.0
F	28.0	40.0
G, H, J and K apply to roll sizes, User Defined		

Drawing Size: "Physical Paper" Metric	Size in Millimeters: Vertical	Horizontal
A0	841	1189
A1	594	841
A2	420	594
A3	297	420
A4 horizontal (landscape)	210	297
A4 vertical (portrait)	297	210

🔅 Use caution when sending electronic drawings between U.S. and International colleagues. Drawing paper sizes will vary. Example: An A-size (11in. x 8.5in.) drawing (280mm x 216mm) does not fit a A4 metric drawing (297mm x 210mm). Use a larger paper size or scale the drawing using the printer setup options.

Start a new session of SolidWorks. Create a new drawing with the default Drawing template. Utilize C (ANSI) Landscape size paper with no Sheet format displayed.

The sheet border defines the C-size drawing: 22in. x 17in, (558.80mm x 431.80mm). A new Graphics window displays the C ANSI Landscape Drawing, named Draw1.

Landscape indicates that the larger dimension is along the horizontal. A-Portrait and A4-Portrait indicate that the larger dimension is along the vertical.

Activity: Default Drawing Template

Start a SolidWorks session.

8)   Click **Start**, **All Programs** from the Windows Main menu.

9)   Click the **SolidWorks 2012** folder.

10)   Click the **SolidWorks 2012** application. The SolidWorks Graphics window is displayed.

🔅 Pin the Menu bar toolbar and the Menu bar menu to view the additional options.

Select the default Drawing template.

11)   Click **New** 🗋 from the Menu bar toolbar.

12)   Double-click **Drawing** from the Templates tab.

Create a C (ANSI) Landscape sheet.

13)   Select **C (ANSI) Landscape** from the Standard sheet size drop-down menu.

14)   **Uncheck** the Display sheet format box.

15)   Click **OK** from the Sheet Format/Size dialog box.

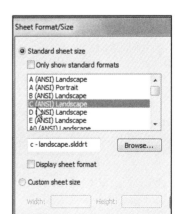

Exit the Model View PropertyManager.

16)   Click **Cancel** ✖ from the Model View PropertyManager. The FeatureManager is displayed with Draw1 as the default drawing name.

🔅 A goal of this book is to expose various SolidWorks design tools and features. The most direct way may not always be shown.

The Model View PropertyManager is displayed in the Start command when creating new drawing box is checked.

Save Draw1.

17) Click **Save As** from the Consolidated Menu bar toolbar.

18) Select the **DRAWING-W-SOLIDWORKS-2012** folder. This was the folder that you downloaded for the DVD in the book.

19) Click **Save**. The Draw1 FeatureManager is displayed.

If you do not see the above illustration, right-click inside the Sheet boundary, click Edit Sheet Format. Click Edit Sheet. SolidWorks is presently working on this reported bug.

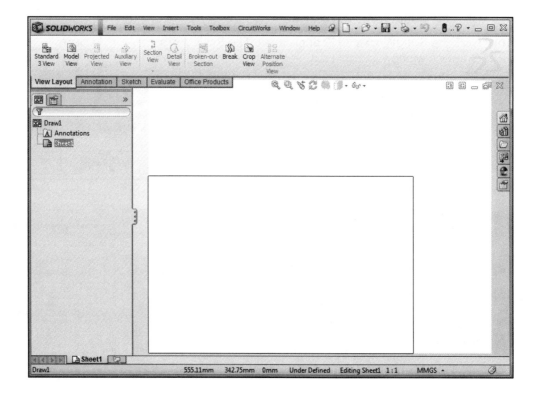

Activity: Display the Line Format Toolbar

Review the CommandManager options and display the Line Format toolbar.

20) Right-click on a **CommandManager tab** as illustrated.

21) Click **Customize**. The Customize dialog box is displayed. The Toolbars tab is displayed by default.

22) Check the **Line Format** box. The Line Format toolbar is displayed. Explore the tabs and your options to customize your options.

23) Click and drag the **Line Format toolbar** off the Graphics window.

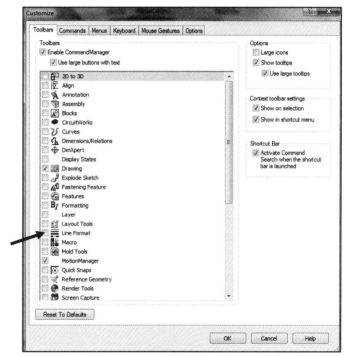

Close the Customize dialog box.

24) Click **OK**.

By default, the Show tooltips option is selected. Apply the Customize dialog box to set short cut keys from the keyboard.

Line Format Toolbar

The Line Format toolbar controls the following options: *Layer Properties* , *Line Color* , *Line Thickness* , *Line Style* , *Hide Show edges* and *Color Display Mode*  .

Utilize the Line Format toolbar when creating a Drawing template. Select the tools and menu options that are displayed in bold icons and black text.

The tools and menu options that are displayed in gray are called grayed-out. The gray icon or text cannot be selected. Additional information is required for these options.

You can also display the Line Format toolbar by clicking **View**, **Toolbars**, **Line Format** from the Menu bar menu.

Activity: Create a Keyboard Shortcut

Customize the Keyboard.

25) Click **Tools,**
Customize from the
Menu bar menu. The
Customize dialog box
is displayed.

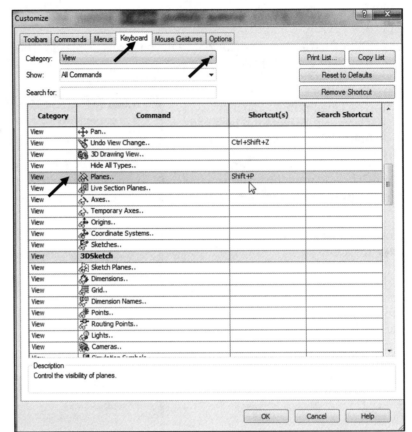

Note: There are
numerous ways to access
commands and menus in
SolidWorks.

26) Click the **Keyboard**
tab.

27) Select **View** for
Categories.

28) Select **Planes** for
Commands.

29) Click a **position**
inside the Shortcut(s)
box.

30) Enter **P** for new
shortcut key. Note:
Shift+P is displayed
in the Shortcut(s)
box.

31) Click **OK** from the Customize dialog box.

32) **Save** the drawing. Draw1 is the default name.

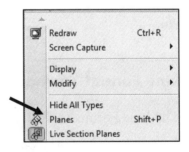

The short cut key P is displayed next to the Planes
option in the View menu. Create additional short cut keys as
an exercise.

Cursor Feedback

SolidWorks provides system feedback by attaching a symbol to the mouse pointer cursor.

The system feedback symbol indicates what you are selecting or what the system is expecting you to select.

As you move the mouse pointer across your model, system feedback is displayed in the form of a symbol, riding next to the cursor as illustrated. This is a valuable feature in SolidWorks.

The mouse pointer provides feedback in both the Drawing Sheet

and Drawing View modes. The mouse pointer displays the

Drawing Sheet icon when the Sheet properties and commands are executed.

The mouse pointer displays the Drawing View icon when the View properties and commands are executed.

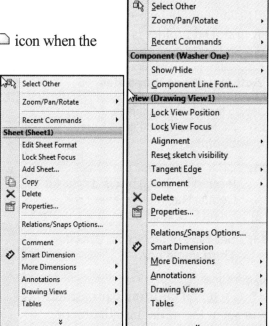

View the mouse pointer for feedback to select Sheet, View, Component and Edge properties in the Drawing.

Sheet Properties display properties of the selected sheet. Right-click in the sheet boundary.

View Properties display properties of the selected view. Right-click on the view boundary.

Use the Lock View Position command to prevent a view from being moved by dragging.

Use the Lock View Focus command when you need a view to remain active as you work within it. This allows you to add sketch entities to a view, even when the mouse pointer is close to another view. You can be sure that the items you are adding belong to the view you want.

Sheet Properties

Sheet Properties display properties of the selected sheet. Sheet Properties define the following: *Name of the Sheet, Sheet Scale, Type of Projection (First angle or Third angle), Sheet Format, Sheet Size, View label* and *Datum label.*

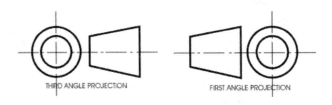

The Sheet format and Sheet size are set in the default Drawing template. Review the Sheet Properties. The Standard sheet size option is grayed out.

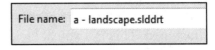

The Sheet format file extension is *.slddrt. The Sheet format option is grayed out. The C-size paper, width, and height dimensions are listed under the Custom sheet size option.

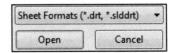

By default, sheet formats are saved in the ProgramData\SolidWorks\SolidWorks 2012\lang\english\sheetformat folder. However formats can be saved in any location. The ProgramData folder is overwritten when a new version of SolidWorks is loaded. The files will be lost if they are stored in this location.

Activity: Sheet Properties

Display the Sheet Properties.

33) Right-click inside the **Sheet boundary**.

34) Click **Properties**. The Sheet Properties dialog box is displayed. Default Name of the sheet is Sheet1. Default Scale is 1:1.

35) Set Type of projection. Click the **Third angle** box.

First or Third Angle projection was set at the initial installation of the SolidWorks software.

Exit the Sheet Properties dialog box.

36) Click **OK** from the Sheet Properties dialog box.

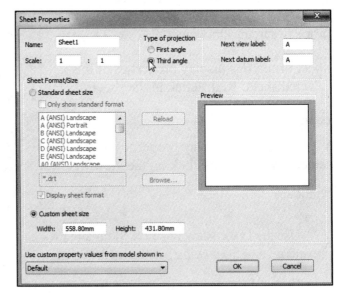

The Sheet name is Sheet1. The FeatureManager and Sheet tab display the Sheet name. The Sheet Scale is 1:1. The Preview box contains no Sheet format. Custom sheet size is 22in x 17in (558.80mm x 431.80mm).

Display Styles / Modes

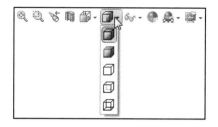

Display modes for a Drawing view are similar to a part except with the addition of the 3D Drawing view tool. This tool provides the ability to rotate the model in an existing view.

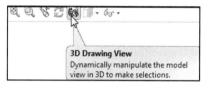

Wireframe and Shaded Display modes provide the best Graphic performance. Mechanical details require Hidden Lines Visible display and Hidden Lines Removed display. Select Shaded/Hidden Lines Removed to display Auxiliary Views to avoid confusion.

Tangent Edges Visible provides clarity for the start of a Fillet edge. Tangent Edges Removed provides the best graphic performance.

 ANSI standards prefers no Tangent Edges display, however individual company standards may display Tangents Edges for clarity.

Tangent Edges are displayed for educational purposes.

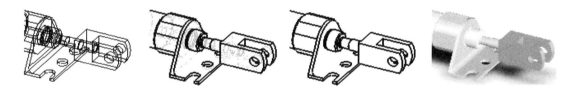

Wireframe　　　Hidden Lines Visible　　Hidden Lines Removed　　Shaded

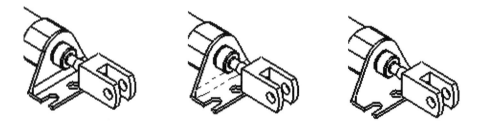

Tangent Edges Visible　Tangent Edges With Font　Tangent Edges Removed

System Options

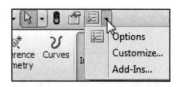

System Options are stored in the registry of the computer. System Options are not part of the document. Changes to the System Options affect all current and future documents. There are hundreds of Systems Options. Review a few of the options in this section.

Click the Options ▤ icon from the Menu bar toolbar to activate the System Options dialog box.

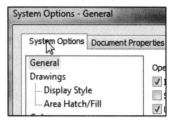

Activity: System Options - Display Style

Set the default display style.

37) Click **Options** ▤ from the Menu bar toolbar. The System Options - General dialog box is displayed.

38) Click the **Display Style** folder from the System Options tab.

39) Check the **Hidden lines removed** box for the Display style for new views.

40) Check the **Visible** box for the default Tangent edges in the new views. Note: High quality is the default option for display quality for new drawing views.

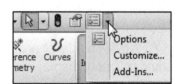

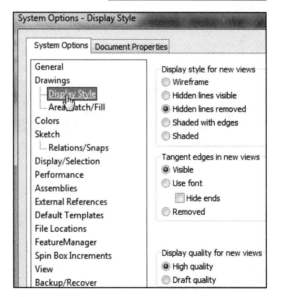

File Locations

System Options, File Locations, Document Templates option determines the path to locate a Custom Drawing template. Add the MY-TEMPLATES folder to the File Locations. The folder listed in the Document Templates option determines the tabs displayed in the New SolidWorks Document dialog box.

Activity: System Options-File Locations

Set file locations for Drawing Templates.

41) Click the **File Locations** folder from the System Options tab.

42) Select **Document Templates** from the Show folders for drop-down menu.

43) Click the **Add** button.

44) Click **Browse**.

45) Select the **DRAWING-W-SOLIDWORKS-2012\MY-TEMPLATES** folder.

46) Click **OK** from the Browse For Folder box.

47) Click **Yes**.

48) Click **OK** from the System Options dialog box.

49) Click **Yes**.

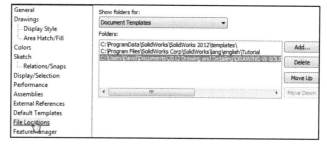

Save Draw1.

50) **Save** Draw1.

The MY-TEMPLATES tab is displayed in the New SolidWorks Drawing dialog box. The MY-TEMPLATES tab is *not displayed if the folder is empty.* The System Option, File Locations list determines the order of the tabs. Save the Drawing Templates to the MY-TEMPLATES folder.

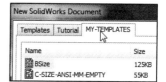

Document Properties

Document Properties apply to the current document. Set the following: *Drafting Standard, Grid/Snap, Units, Line Fonts,* and *Image Quality* in Document Properties.

When the current document is saved as a template, the current parameters are stored with the template. New documents that utilize the same template contain the stored parameters.

Conserve drawing time. Set the Document Properties in the Drawing template. Document Properties options contain hundreds of parameters. Examples are addressed in this section. Explore other parameters through SolidWorks Help Topics.

There are numerous text styles and sizes available in SolidWorks. Companies develop drawing format standards and use specific text height for Metric and English drawings.

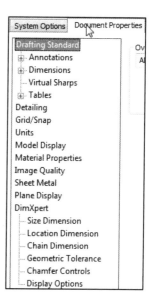

The ASME Y14.2M-1992(R1998) standard lists the following: *lettering, arrowhead, line conventions* and *lettering conventions* for engineering drawings and related documentation practices.

Font

Century Gothic is the default SolidWorks font.

Create an assessment page to test that your Printer/Plotter drivers support the default SolidWorks font.

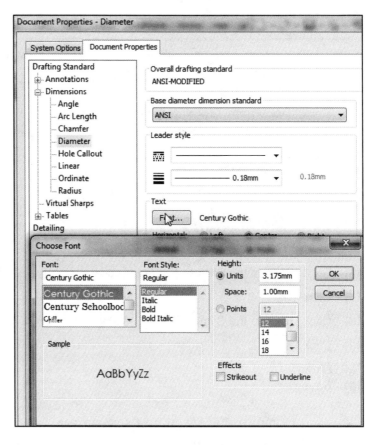

Minimum Drawing Letter Height based on ASME Y14.2.				
Annotation	Inch drawing sizes: A, B, C Metric drawing sizes: A2, A3, A4		Inch drawing sizes: D, E Metric drawing sizes: A0, A1	
	Inch	Millimeter	Inch	Millimeter
Drawing Title, Drawing Size, Cage Code, Drawing Number and Revision letter positioned inside the Title block.	.12in	3mm	.24in	6mm
Section views, Zone letter and numerals.	.24in	6mm	.24in	6mm
Drawing block headings in Title block.	.10in	2.5mm	.10mm	2.5mm
All other characters inside the Sheet boundary. Corresponds to the SW Dimension and Note font.	.12in.	3mm	.12in	3mm

Arrowheads

Control arrowheads through the Drafting Standard, Dimensions option in an active drawing document.

Utilize a solid filled arrowhead with a 3:1 ratio. The arrowhead width is proportionate to the line thickness. The Dimension line thickness is 0.3mm.

The Dimension arrow is based on the Dimension line. SolidWorks defines arrow size with three options:

- *Height*

- *Width*

- *Length*

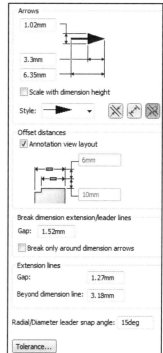

Height corresponds to the arrow width. Width corresponds to the arrow tail length. Length corresponds to the distance from the tip of the arrow to the end of the tail.

The Section line thickness, (Drafting Standard, View Labels, Section) is 0.6mm. The Section arrow is based on the Section line. The Section arrow length is 6mm. The Section arrow width is 2mm.

The illustration displays the default mm values.

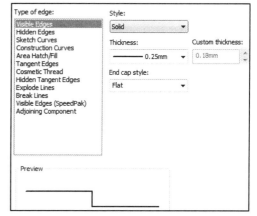

The illustrations in this book are based on SolidWorks SP1.0. The illustrations may vary slightly per your SolidWorks release.

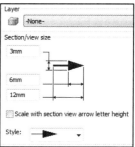

Line Widths

The ASME Y14.2M-1992 (R1998) standard recommends two line widths with a 2:1 ratio. The minimum width of a thin line is 0.3mm. The minimum width of a thick, "normal" line is 0.6mm.

A single width line is acceptable on CAD drawings. Two line widths are used in this Chapter: Thin: 0.3mm and Normal: 0.6mm.

Apply Line Styles in the Line Font Document Properties. Line Font determines the appearance of a line in the Graphics window. SolidWorks styles utilized in this chapter are as follows:

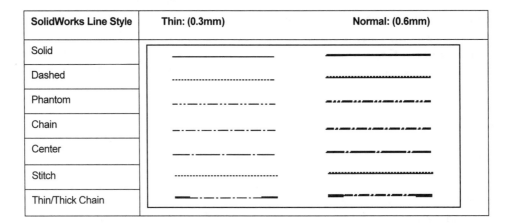

SolidWorks Line Style	Thin: (0.3mm)	Normal: (0.6mm)
Solid		
Dashed		
Phantom		
Chain		
Center		
Stitch		
Thin/Thick Chain		

Various printers/plotters provide variable Line Weight settings. Example: Thin (0.3mm), Normal (0.6mm), and Thick (0.6mm).

Refer to the printer/plotter owner's manual for Line weight setting. Utilize the Document Property, Line Style option to create, save, load, and delete line styles.

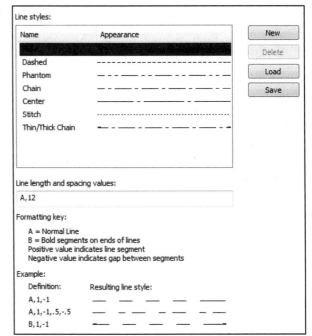

Scale large drawing sheets with the Resolution and Scale option located in the File, Page Setup Menu bar menu. Use the Scale to fit option to resize the drawing sheet to the physical paper size.

Use Scale to resize the drawing sheet by a percentage to the physical paper size.

Line Font

The ASME Y14.2M-1992(R1998) standard addresses the type and style of lines used in engineering drawings. Combine different Line Styles and use drawing layers to achieve the following types of ASME lines:

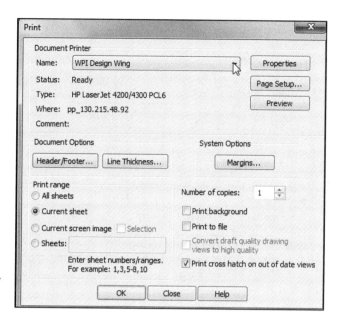

ASME Y14.2-1992(R1998) TYPE of LINE & example:	SolidWorks Line Font Type of Edge:	Style:	Thickness:
Visible line displays the visible edges or contours of a part.	Visible Edge	Solid	Thick "Normal"
Hidden line displays the hidden edges or contours of a part.	Hidden Edge	Dashed	Thin
Section lining displays the cut surface of a part assembly in a section view.	Crosshatch	Solid	Thin Different Hatch patterns relate to different materials
Center line displays the axes of center planes of symmetrical parts/features.	Construction Curves	Center	Thin
Symmetry line displays an axis of symmetry for a partial view.			Sketch Thin Center Line and Thick Visible lines on drawing layer.
Dimension lines/Extension lines/Leader lines combine to dimension drawings.	DIMENSION LINE 100 Extension Line Leader Line Dimensions	Solid	Thin
Cutting plane line or Viewing plane line display the location of a cutting plane for sectional views and the viewing position for removed views.	Section Line View Arrows D D	Phantom Solid	Thick Thick, "Normal"

Break line displays an incomplete view. Short Breaks Long Breaks		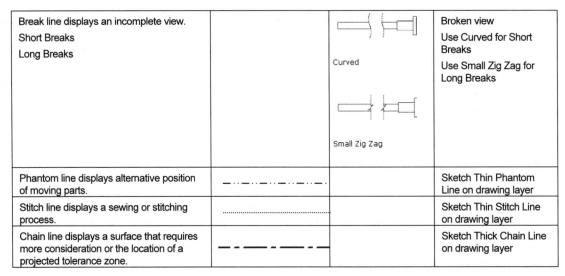 Curved Small Zig Zag	Broken view Use Curved for Short Breaks Use Small Zig Zag for Long Breaks
Phantom line displays alternative position of moving parts.	— ·· — ·· — ·· — ·		Sketch Thin Phantom Line on drawing layer
Stitch line displays a sewing or stitching process.	··············		Sketch Thin Stitch Line on drawing layer
Chain line displays a surface that requires more consideration or the location of a projected tolerance zone.	— — — · — · —		Sketch Thick Chain Line on drawing layer

The following default lines are defined in SolidWorks: Solid, Dashed, Phantom, Chain, Center, Stitch, and Thin/Thick Chain.

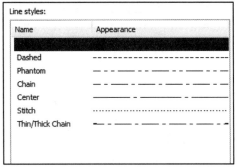

☼ Define these line types on a separate drawing layer.

Document Properties-Dimensions

Control the Dimensions options through Document Properties. The Drafting Standard, Dimensions determines the display on the drawing. Millimeter dimensioning and decimal inch dimensioning are the two key types of units specified on engineering drawings.

There are other dimension types specified for commercial commodities such as pipe sizes and lumber sizes. Develop separate Drawing templates for decimal inch units.

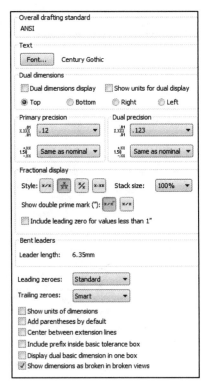

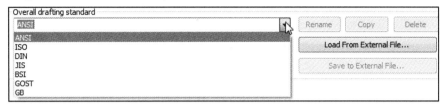 ASME Y14.2-1992(R1998) and the ASME Y14.2M Line Conventions and Lettering standard define text height, arrows and line styles for inch and metric values. Review the Detailing Document Properties options function before entering their values.

Drafting (Dimensioning) Standard

The Drafting standard options are:

- **ANSI**: American National Standards Institute

- **ISO**: International Standards Organization

- **DIN**: Deutsche Institute für Normumg (German)

- **JIS**: Japanese Industry Standard

- **BSI**: British Standards Institution

- **GOST**: Gosndarstuennye State Standard (Russian)

- **GB**: Guo Biao (Chinese)

Dual dimensions Display Option

The Dual dimensions display check box shows dimensions in two types of units on the drawing.

Select Dual dimensions display. Select the On top option. Select Dual Dimension Length units. The primary units display is 100mm. The secondary units display is [3.94]in.

Fixed Size Weld Symbols Option

The Fixed size weld symbols checkbox displays the size of the weld symbol. Scale the symbols according to the dimension font size.

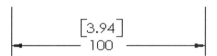

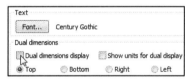

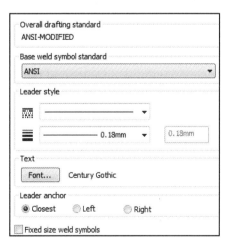

Display Datums per 1982 Option

The Display datums per 1982 checkbox displays the ANSI Y14.5M-1982 datums. Use the ASME Y14.5M-1994(R1999) datums in this text.

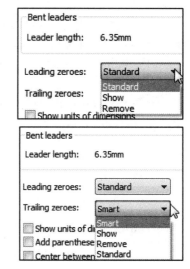

Leading Zeroes and Trailing Zeroes Option

The Leading zeroes list box contains three options:

- **Standard**: Active by default. Zeros are displayed based on the dimensioning standard.

- **Show**: Zeros before decimal points are displayed.

- **Remove**: Zeros are not displayed.

The Trailing zeroes list box contains four options:

- **Smart**: Active by default. Trailing zeros are trimmed for whole metric values. (Conforms to ANSI and ISO standards.)

- **Show**: Dimensions have trailing zeros up to the number of decimal places specified in Tools, Options, Document Properties, Units section.

- **Remove**: All trailing zeros are removed.

- **Standard**: Trims trailing zeroes to the ASME Y14.5M-1994 standard.

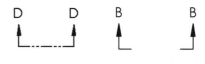

Alternative Section Display Option

The ASME Y14.2M-1992(R1998) standard supports two display styles. The default section line displays a continuous Phantom line type (D-D).

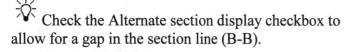

Check the Alternate section display checkbox to allow for a gap in the section line (B-B).

Centerline Extension and Center Marks Option

The Centerline extension value controls the extension length beyond the section geometry.

Centerlines are created as font lines and arcs in the drawing views.

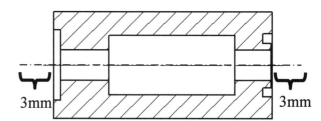

Centerlines should be added to the drawing prior to the addition of dimensions and annotations. You can resize them or modify their appearance. Resize their appearance by dragging the control points on each side of the centerline.

Center marks specify the default center mark size used with arcs and circles. Center marks are displayed with or without Center mark lines.

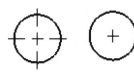

The Center mark lines extend past the circumference of the selected circle. Select the Center mark size based on the drawing size and scale.

The Center mark command creates a center mark, or a center point on selected circular edges. Selecting a circle creates a center mark. Selecting an arc creates a center point.

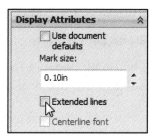

Center Marks should be added to the drawing prior to the addition of dimensions and annotations. You can resize them or modify their appearance.

☼ Center Marks and Centerlines are annotations used to mark circle centers and describe the geometry size on the drawing.

Auto Insert on View Creation Option

Auto insert on view creation locates Center marks on the appropriate entities when a new view is inserted into a drawing. By default Center marks-holes, Center marks-fillets, Center marks-slots, Centerlines, Balloons, and Dimensions marked for drawing options are not checked.

☼ Save detailing time. Uncheck the Center marks option when parts contain multiple size holes and holes positioned at angles. Insert all dimensions and then insert the Center marks tool from the Annotation toolbar.

Extension Lines Option

The ASME Y14.2M-1992(R1998) and ASME Y14.5M-1994(R1999) standard defines extension line length and gap. A visible gap exists between the extension line and the visible line. The extension line extends 3mm - 4mm past the dimension line.

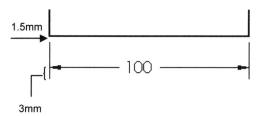

☼ The values 1.5mm and 3mm are a guide. Base the gap and extension line on the drawing size and scale.

Datum Feature Option

The Next label specifies the subsequent upper case letter used for the Datum feature symbol. The default value is A. Successive labels are in alphabetical order. The Datum Display type Per Standard option displays a filled triangular symbol on the Datum feature.

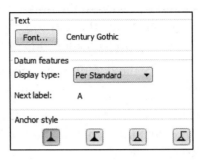
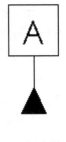

Surface Finish Symbols

For the ISO standard, Surface finish symbols display per the 2002 standard.

Break Line Option

The Break line gap specifies the size of the gap between the Broken view break lines.

Automatic Update on BOM Option

The Automatic Update on BOM option updates the Bill of Material in a drawing if related model custom properties change.

ITEM NO.	QTY.	PART NO.	MATERIAL
1	1	10-0408	ALUMINUM
2	1	10-0409	STEEL

Set the values in SolidWorks to meet the ASME standard.

💡 Set units before entering values for Detailing options. Units for the Default Templates are determined from initial SolidWorks installation options.

Visible   Hidden

Cosmetic Thread Display Option

The High quality option displays Cosmetic threads visible or hidden in a selected drawing view. A blind hole Cosmetic thread is visible in the Front view and hidden in the Back view.

The Cosmetic thread feature is used to describe the attributes of a specific hole without having to add real threads to the model. It represents the minor diameter of a tread on a boss or the major diameter of a thread on a hole and can include a hole callout.

The Cosmetic thread can be applied at the part or drawing level. Either way, a cosmetic thread differs from other annotations in that it is an absorbed feature of the item to which it is attached. For example, the cosmetic thread on a hole is in the FeatureManager design tree as Thread1 under the Hole feature, along with the sketches used to create the hole as illustrated.

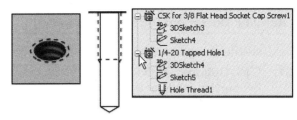

To display a Cosmetic thread, right-click the Annotations folder from the FeatureManager and click Details. The Annotation Properties dialog box is displayed. Check the Cosmetic threads box and the Shaded cosmetic threads box. Click OK. View the cosmetic thread.

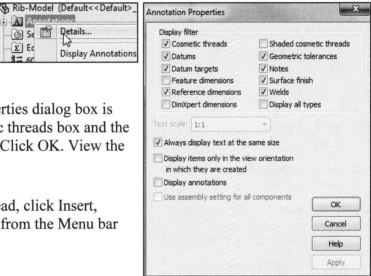

To insert a Cosmetic thread, click Insert, Annotations, Cosmetic thread from the Menu bar menu.

Review the Document Properties before inserting views, dimensions and annotations into your drawing. Modify the Document Properties that correspond to the part. For example, check/uncheck Dual dimension display if required for manufacturing. Uncheck the Auto insert on view creation, Center mark option when a part contains multiple size hole, rotated at different angles.

Modify the document units directly from the Graphics window as illustrated. This is new in SolidWorks 2012.

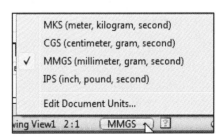

Activity: Document Properties-Detailing

Set Detailing options.

51) Click **Options** 📧 , **Document Properties** tab from the Menu bar toolbar.

52) Select **ANSI** from the Overall drafting standard drop-down menu. Various options are available depending on the selected standard.

53) Click the **Dimensions** folder.

54) Check the **Dual dimension display** box.

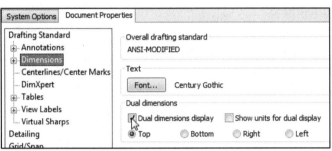

Modify the Dimension Extension line value.

55) Enter **1.5mm** for Extension lines Gap.

56) Enter **3mm** for Extension lines Beyond dimension line.

Modify the Centerline / Center Marks.

57) Click the **Centerlines/Center Marks** folder under Dimensions.

58) Enter **3mm** for the Centerline extension.

59) Enter **0.5mm** for the Center marks Size.

Modify the Break line gap.

60) Click the **Detailing** folder under Drafting Standard.

61) Enter **10mm** for the View break lines Gap.

62) Enter **3mm** for the View break lines Extension.

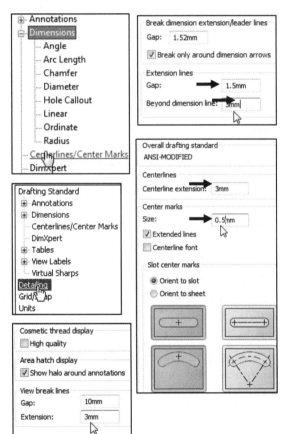

💡 There is no set value for the Break line gap. Increase the value to accommodate a revolved section.

Set units.

63) Click the **Units** folder under Drafting Standard.

64) Click the **MMGS** (millimeter, gram, second) box for Unit system.

65) Select **.12** from the drop-down menu for decimal places for Length units millimeters.

66) Select **inches** from the drop-down menu for Dual Dimension Length.

67) Select **.123** from the drop-down menu for inch Decimal places.

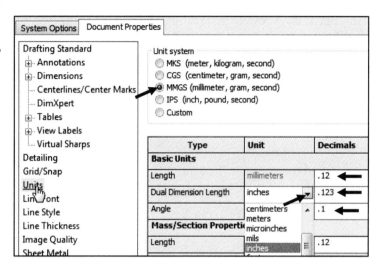

68) Select **.1** from the drop-down menu for Decimal places for Angular units.

69) Click **OK** from the Document Properties - Units dialog box.

70) Click **Save** 💾.

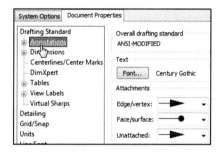

Document Properties, Annotations Font

The Annotations font controls the text height in the Drawing template for the following Annotation types: *Balloons, Datums, Geometric Tolerances, Notes, Surface Finishes* and *Weld Symbols*.

Notes Font

The Notes font option under the Annotations Font specifies the font type and size for notes and view labels.

Dimensions Font

The Dimensions font option specifies the font type and size for the dimension text.

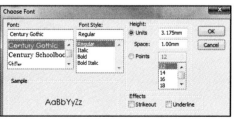

Auxiliary View / Auxiliary View Label Font

The Auxiliary View and the Auxiliary View Label fonts specify the font type and size used for the letter labels on the auxiliary arrow and the auxiliary view label text.

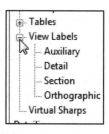

An Auxiliary View in general is similar to a Projected view, but it is unfolded normal to a reference edge in an existing view. The reference edge can be an edge of a part, a silhouette edge, an axis, or a sketched line. If you sketch a line, activate the drawing view first.

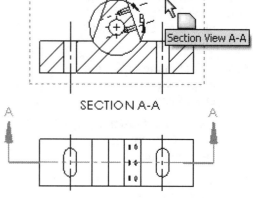

SECTION A-A

Detail View / Detail View Label Font

The Detail View and the Detail View Label fonts specify the font type and size used for the letter labels on the detail circle and the text below the detail view.

A Detail View in general is used to create a new drawing view, which is an enlarged portion of an existing view. The enlarged portion is enclosed using sketch geometry, usually a circle or other closed contour like a spline.

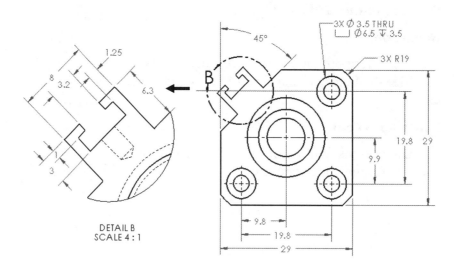

DETAIL B
SCALE 4 : 1

Section View / Section View Label Font

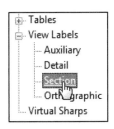

The Section View and the Section View Label fonts specify the font type and size used for the letter labels on the section lines and the text below the Section view.

A Section view is generally used to create a new drawing view that is defined by cutting an existing view with a section line (Sketch).

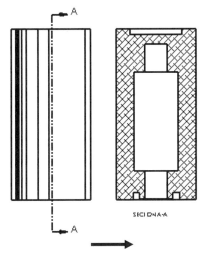

Some drawing views require or allow sketching within the view, rather than just over the view. These views, most notably sections and details require that the view be active before sketching so that the sketch geometry will be associated with the view.

Annotations Arrow Font

The Annotations font specifies the font type and size used for general annotations: *Balloons, Datums, Geometric Tolerances, Notes, Surface Finished and Weld symbols Font.*

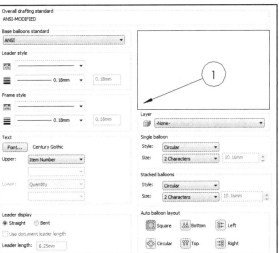

The Balloon, Datum, Geometric Tolerance, Note, Surface Finish and Weld symbol folders specifies the font type and size.

ANSI standard states that a Leader line of a balloon is displayed as an arrow that points to an edge or a dot which points to a face.

Tables Font

The Tables font varies from company to company. Tables font controls the *Bend, Bill of Materials, General, Hole, Punch, Revision* and *Weld.*

Alpha/numerical control

Select letters or numbers for bend table tag sequencing.

A, B, C	Defines the bend tag sequence as a letter.		Tag	Direction	Angle
			A	DOWN	180°
			B	DOWN	90°
1, 2, 3	Defines the bend tag sequence as a number.		Tag	Direction	Angle
			1	DOWN	180°
			2	DOWN	90°

Activity: Document Properties-Annotations Font

Set the Font.

71) Click **Options** ⬚, **Document Properties** tab from the Menu bar toolbar.

72) Expand the **Annotations** folder.

73) Click the **Notes** folder.

74) Click the **Font** button. The Choose Font dialog box is displayed.

75) Enter **3mm** for text height.

76) Click **OK** from the Choose Font dialog box.

77) Repeat the above procedure to set Font text height for **Dimensions, (View Labels - Detail circle text), Surface Finishes, Weld Symbols, Tables,** and **Balloons** font.

Set the Section and View Arrow font.

78) Click the **Detail** folder under the View Labels folder.

79) Click the **Font** button for View label text.

80) Enter **6mm** for text height.

81) Click **OK** from the Choose Font dialog box.

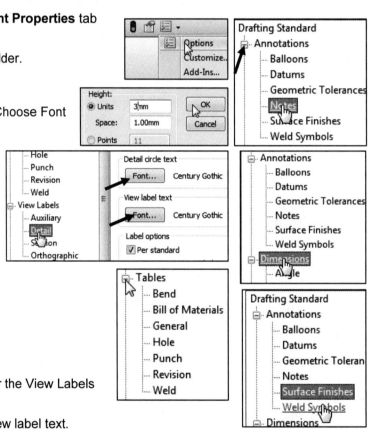

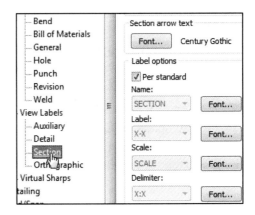

82) Repeat for the above procedure for the **Section/Section View label text**, and the **Section/Section arrow text**.

83) Click **OK** from the Document Properties dialog box.

84) Click **Save** 💾.

🔆 Companies vary the size of their default font. ASME Y14.2 lists the annotation values as minimum letter heights.

Document Properties, Dimensions Options

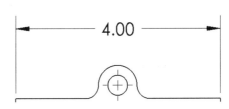

The Document Properties, Drafting Standard, Dimensions options determine the display of dimensions. The Dimensions option determines the display and position of the text and extension lines.

Reference dimensions require parentheses. Symmetric feature dimensions in the part require a redefined dimensioning scheme in the drawing.

🔆 Uncheck the Add parentheses by default to conserve design time.

🔆 Add Parenthesis to a dimension either from the Dimension PropertyManager, the Pop-up dialog box or right-click on the dimension text, click Display Options and check the Show Parentheses box.

Offset Distances Option

The ASME Y14.5M-1994(R1999) standard sets guidelines for dimension spacing. The space between the first dimension line and the part profile is 10mm or greater.

The space between subsequent parallel dimension lines is 6mm or greater. Spacing differs depending on drawing size and scale. Set the From last dimension option to 6mm. Set the From model option to 10mm.

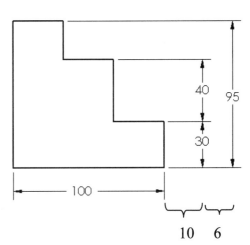

Arrows Option

The Arrows option controls the display of the Arrowheads. The ASME Y14.2M-1992(R1998) standard recommends a solid filled arrow head.

⌖ Arrowheads are drawn between extension lines if space is available. If space is limited, see the preferred arrowhead and dimension location order as illustrated.

⌖ Double-click the dimension to access the control points for the arrowheads in SolidWorks.

Break Dimension/Extension Option

The ASME Y14.5M-1994(R1999) standard states do not cross dimension lines. Break the extension line when the dimension line crosses close to an arrowhead.

Drag the extension line above the arrowhead. Sketch a new line collinear with the extension line below the arrowhead.

Uncheck the Break around dimension arrows only option. Control individual breaks in the drawing for this chapter.

Bent Leader Length Option

Create ASME leader lines with a small horizontal segment. This is called the Bent Leader length.

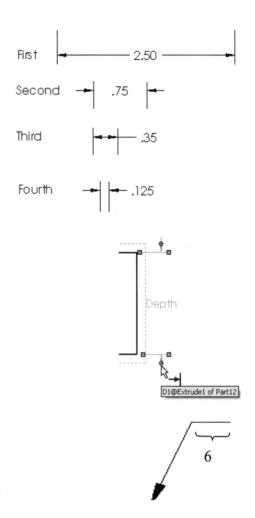

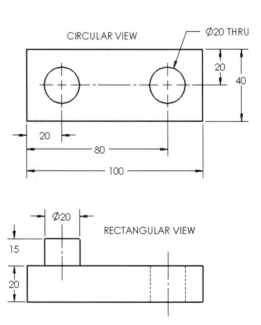

Activity: Document Properties-Dimensions

Set the Dimensions options.

85) Click **Options** ⊟ , **Document Properties** tab from the Menu bar toolbar.

86) Click the **Dimensions** folder.

87) Uncheck the **Add parentheses by default** box.

88) Uncheck the **Annotation view layout** box.

89) Set the Offset distances to **6mm** and **10mm** as illustrated.

90) Set the Arrow Style to **Solid**.

91) Select **Smart** for Trailing zeroes.

92) Enter **1.5mm** for the Gap in the Break dimension extension lines box.

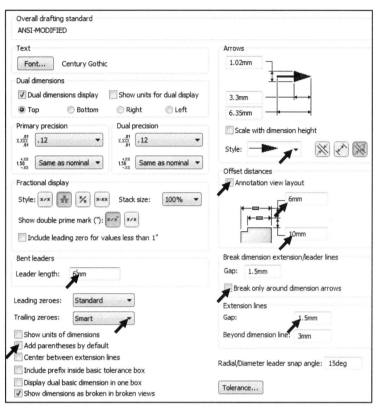

93) Uncheck the **Break around dimension arrows only** box.

94) Enter **6mm** for the Bent leader length (ASME only).

Set the Dimension Precision.

95) The primary units are millimeters. Select **.12** for two place decimal precision for Primary dimension.

96) Select **.123** for three place decimal precision for Dual precision.

97) Click **OK** from the Document Properties dialog box.

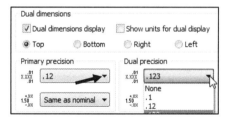

Save the drawing.

98) Click **Save** 💾 .

The Dimension Precision Value and Tolerance entries depend on drawing units and manufacturing requirements. The Tolerance button displays the Dimension Tolerance options. The Tolerance type is None by default. Control Tolerance type on individual dimensions.

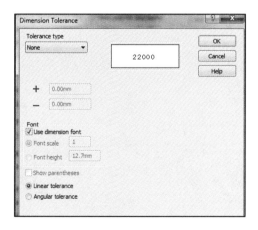

Document Properties-Notes and Balloons Option

Note text positioned on the drawing. Outside the Title block, use the same font type and height size as the Dimension font. The exceptions to the rule are:

- ASME Y14.100M-1998 Engineering Drawing Practices extended symbols.

- Use Upper case letters for all Notes unless lower case is required. Example: HCl - Hardness Critical Item requires a lower case "l".

Modify Notes Border Style to create boxes, circles, triangles and other shapes around the text. The Default Border style is set to None. Modify the border height. Use the Size option.

Balloon callouts label components in an assembly and relate them to the item numbers in the Bill of Materials. The default Balloon style is Circular.

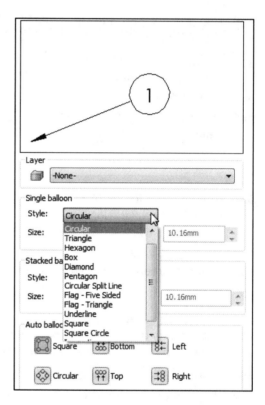

Activity: Document Properties - Notes and Balloons

Set the Notes options.

99) Click **Options**, **Document Properties** tab from the Menu bar toolbar.

100) Expand the **Annotations** folder.

101) Click the **Notes** folder.

102) Check **Bent** for Leader display.

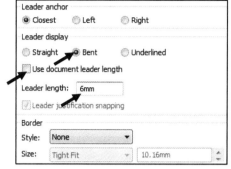

103) Un-check the **Use document leader length** box.

104) Enter **6mm** for the Leader length.

Set the drawing Balloon Properties.
105) Click the **Balloons** folder.

106) Click the **Bent** box.

107) Uncheck the **Use document leader length box**.

108) Enter **6mm** for Leader length.

109) Click **OK** from the Document Properties dialog box.

110) **Save** the drawing.

Document Properties - Arrows

Set Arrows Properties according to the ASME Y14.2M-1992(R1998) standard with a 3:1 ratio: Width to Height.

The Length value is the overall length of the arrow from the tip of the arrowhead to the end of the arrow tail. The Length is displayed when the dimension text is flipped to the inside. A Solid filled arrowhead is the preferred arrow type for dimension lines.

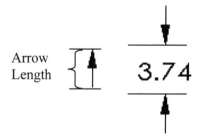

Activity: Document Properties - Arrows

Set the Dimension Arrow Properties.

111) Click **Options** 📧 , **Document Properties** tab from the Menu bar toolbar.

112) Click the **Dimensions** folder.

113) Enter **1** for the arrow Height in the Size text box.

114) Enter **3** for the arrow Width.

115) Enter **6** for the arrow Length.

Set the Section View Arrow Properties.
116) Expand the **View Labels** folder.

117) Click the **Section** folder.

Set the arrow style.
118) Under the Section/View size, enter **2** for Height.

119) Enter **6** for Width.

120) Enter **12** for Length.

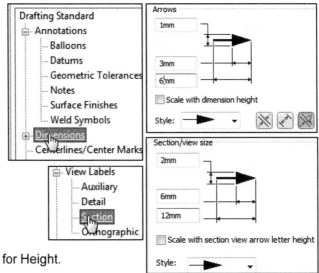

Document Properties - Line Font

The Line Font determines the style and thickness for a particular type of edge in a drawing. Modify the type of edge, style and thickness to reflect the ASME Y14.2M-1992(R1998) standard. The ASME Y14.2M-1992(R1998) standard defines two line weights: 0.3mm and 0.6mm.

Thin Thickness is 0.3mm. Thick (Normal) Thickness is 0.6mm. Review line weights as defined in the File, Page Setup or in File, Print, System Options for your particular printer/plotter. Control the line weight display in the Graphics window.

Activity: Document Properties - Line Font

Set the Line Font Properties.
121) Click the **Line Font** folder.

122) Click **Break Lines** for the Type of edge.

123) Select **Solid** for Style.

Create a Custom Line Thickness.
124) Select **Custom Size** for Thickness.

125) Enter **0.33**mm for Custom thickness.

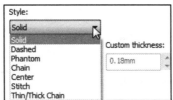

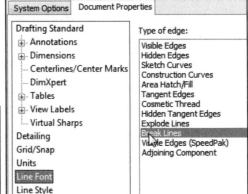

126) Click **OK** from the Document Properties - Line Font dialog box.

Save the drawing.
127) Click **Save**.

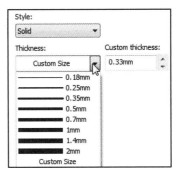

Draw1 is the current drawing. Utilize Draw1 to create a Drawing template. The empty Drawing template contains no geometry. The empty Drawing template contains the Document Properties and the Sheet Properties.

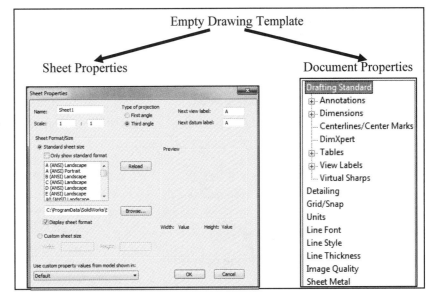

Predefined and Projected Views

In Orthographic Projection - the six principle views are *Top, Front, Right, Back, Bottom* and *Left*. Drawings commonly display the Top, Front, Right, and an Isometric view. You can define a view in a drawing sheet and then populate the view. You can save a drawing document with Predefined views as a document template.

Insert the Top, Front, Right, and Isometric views into the drawing template. Utilize the Predefined command to create the Front and Isometric view. Utilize the Projected view command to create the Right and Top view.

The Drawing template contains a Sheet format. Leave space when positioning views.

🔆 Save Predefined views with the drawing template. Save the drawing template in the next section, before you insert a part into the Predefined views.

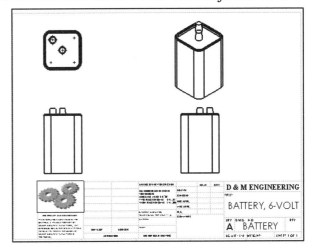

Activity: Insert Predefined and Projected Views

Insert a Front Predefined view.

128) Click **Insert**, **Drawing View**, **Predefined**  from the Menu bar menu.

129) Click the **lower left corner** of the drawing. The Drawing View1 PropertyManager is displayed.

☀ *Front view is the default view in the Orientation dialog box.

130) Click **Hidden Lines Removed** from the Display Style box.

131) Click **OK** ✔ from the Drawing View1 PropertyManager.

Insert a Top Projected view.
132) Click the **View Layout** tab from the CommandManager.

133) Click **Projected view** from the View Layout toolbar. The Projected View PropertyManager is displayed.

134) Check the **Use parent style** box to display Hidden Lines Removed.

135) Click a **position** directly above the Front view.

Insert the Right Projected view.

136) Click **Projected View** from the View Layout toolbar.

137) Click inside the **Front** view.

138) Click a **position** directly to the right of the Front view.

Insert an Isometric Predefined view.
139) Click inside the **Front** view.

140) Click **Insert**, **Drawing View**, **Predefined** from the Menu bar menu. The Drawing View PropertyManager is displayed.

141) Click a **position** in the upper right corner of the sheet as illustrated.

142) Click ***Isometric** from the Orientation box.

143) Click **OK** ✔ from the Drawing View4 PropertyManager.

144) Click **Save** 💾. View the drawing FeatureManager. Note the view icons for the Predefined and Projected views.

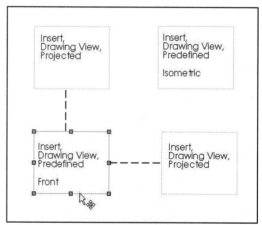

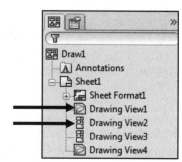

Save As

The Save As option provides the ability to save documents with various file types. The current document is a drawing named Draw1.slddrw. Save the document as a Drawing template (*.drwdot).

☼ Select the Drawing Templates (*.drwdot) option for Save as type before you browse to the MY-TEMPLATES folder. SolidWorks selects the SolidWorks\data\templates folder by default when you select Drawing Templates (*.drwdot).

Test the Drawing template located in the MY-TEMPLATES folder. Create a new drawing document.

Activity: Save As and Test Drawing Template

Save the empty Drawing Template.

145) Click **Save As** from the Menu bar menu.

146) Select **Drawing Templates (*.drwdot)** from the Save as type.

147) **Browse** and select the **DRAWING-W-SOLIDWORKS-2012\ MY-TEMPLATES** for the Save in file folder.

148) Enter **C-SIZE-ANSI-MM-EMPTY** for the File name. The file extension for the template is .drwdot.

149) Click **Save** from the Save As dialog box.

150) Click **Windows**, **Close All** from the Menu bar toolbar.

Create a new drawing.

151) Click **New** 🗋 from the Menu bar toolbar

152) Select **MY-TEMPLATES** tab from the New SolidWorks Document dialog box.

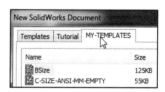

153) Double-click **C-SIZE-ANSI-MM-EMPTY**.

☼ For improved drawing visibility, the default Drawing Sheet background color is modified to white.

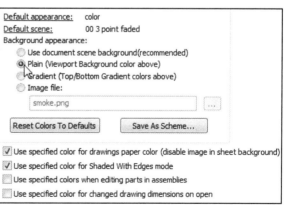

The Sheet Format/Size box displays C (ANSI) Landscape.

154) If required, click **C (ANSI) Landscape**. Click **OK**.

155) Click **Cancel** ✖ from the Model View PropertyManager. Draw2 is the current drawing document. Note the drawing view icons in the FeatureManager.

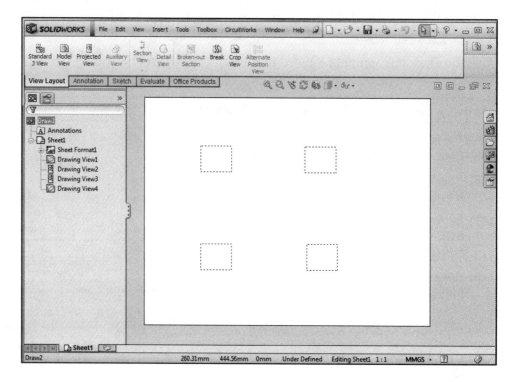

Close all documents.

156) Click **Windows**, **Close All** from the Menu bar menu.

You created a C (ANSI) size drawing with no Sheet format when you selected the C-SIZE-ANSI-MM-EMPTY template from the New SolidWorks Document box. The Drawing template controls sheet size and Document Properties. The Sheet format controls the Title block, company logo, and Custom Properties.

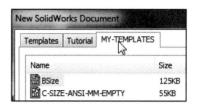

 Conserve design time. Utilize the C-SIZE-ANSI-MM-EMPTY template to create empty templates for A and B size drawings. Modify the Sheet Properties size option and utilize the Save As options for the drawing template.

Additional Information

Additional details on Sheet Properties, System Options, and Document Properties are available in SolidWorks Help Topics. Keywords: sheet properties, paper (size), drawings (display modes, edge and display), options (annotations, balloon, detailing, dimensions, file locations, font, note, and units).

Review

The Sheet Properties option displayed: Sheet name, scale, size, Type of projection, and more. You selected C (ANSI) Landscape size paper with no Sheet format.

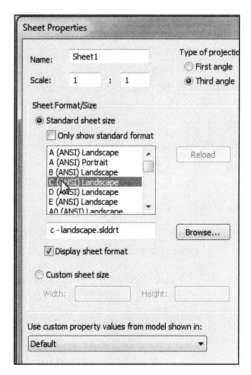

You reviewed the System Options Drawings and File Locations. The Drawings Display Style option controlled the display mode and tangent edges of the view.

The File Locations option created the MY-TEMPLATES folder tab in the New SolidWorks Document dialog box.

Document Properties are stored in the current document. You utilized the Detailing (Dimensions, Notes, Balloons, Arrows, and Annotations Font), Line Font, and Units options in the Drawing template. There are hundreds of System Options and Document Properties.

Sheet Format

Customize drawing Sheet formats to create and match your company drawing standards.

A customer requests a new product. The engineer designs the product in one location, the company produces the product in a second location and the field engineer supports the customer in a third location.

The ASME Y14.24M standard describes various types of drawings. Example: The Engineering department produces detail and assembly drawings. The drawings for machined, plastic and sheet metal parts contain specific tolerances and notes used in fabrication.

Manufacturing adds vendor item drawings with tables and notes. Field Service requires installation drawings that are provided to the customer.

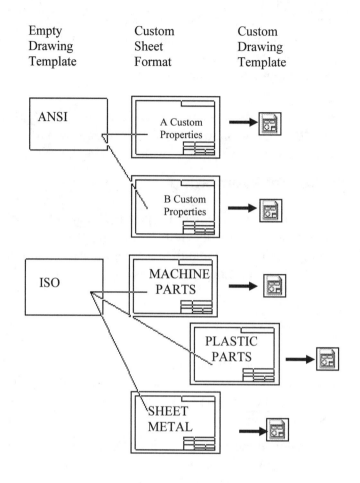

Create Sheet formats to support various standards and drawing types. There are numerous ways to create a custom Sheet format:

- Open a ".dwg" file created with another CAD application. Save the ".dwg" file as a Sheet format.

- Right-click in the Graphics window. Select Edit Sheet Format. Create drawing borders, Title block, notes, and zone locations for each drawing size. Save each drawing format.

- Right-click Properties in the Graphics window. Select Properties. Check the Display Sheet Format option from the Sheet format drop-down menu. Browse to select an existing Sheet format.

- Add an OLE supported Sheet format such as a bitmap file of the Title block and notes. Use the Insert, Object command or Insert, Picture command.

- Utilize an existing AutoCAD drawing to create a SolidWorks Sheet format.

- Open the AutoCAD drawing as the Sheet format. Save the C-FORMAT.slddrt

- Sheet format. Add the Sheet format C-FORMAT.slddrt to the empty C (ANSI) size Drawing template. Create a new Drawing template named C-ANSI-MM.drwdot.

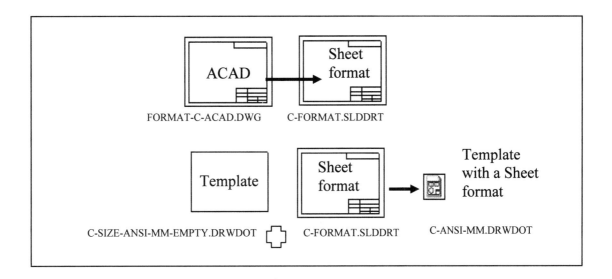

- Add an A (ANSI) size Sheet format, A-FORMAT.slddrt to an empty A (ANSI) size Drawing template. Create an A-ANSI-MM.drwdot Drawing template.

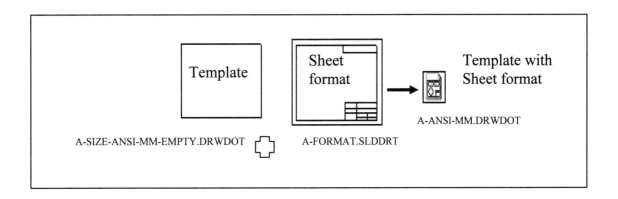

- Insert views from the part or assembly into the SolidWorks drawing.

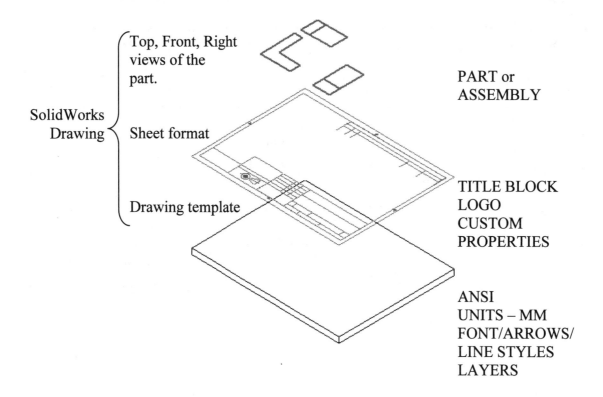

SolidWorks
Drawing
- Top, Front, Right views of the part.
- Sheet format
- Drawing template

PART or
ASSEMBLY

TITLE BLOCK
LOGO
CUSTOM
PROPERTIES

ANSI
UNITS – MM
FONT/ARROWS/
LINE STYLES
LAYERS

Data imported from other CAD systems for a Sheet format may require editing in SolidWorks. Delete extraneous lines in the imported Sheet format. The drawing sheet contains two modes:

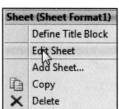

- *Edit Sheet Format*

- *Edit Sheet*

Utilize the *Edit Sheet Format* command to add or modify notes and Title block information. Edit in the *Edit Sheet Format* mode for lines and text created in the AutoCAD Title block.

Utilize the *Edit Sheet* command to insert views and dimensions. The sheet boundary and major title block headings are displayed with a THICK line style. Modify the drawing layer THICKNESS.

☼ You can create title block tables in parts and assemblies and link the table information to the configuration-specific properties of the document. Title block tables behave in a similar way to tables in drawings. As with other SolidWorks tables, you can customize title block table templates and save them for future use. See SolidWorks Help for additional information.

Activity: Sheet Format, Import From AutoCAD

Open an AutoCAD drawing: FORMAT-C-ACAD.dwg.

157) Click **Open** 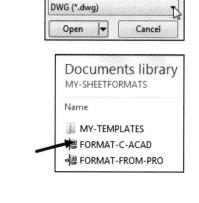 from the Menu bar toolbar.

158) Select **DWG (*.dwg)** for file type.

159) Double-click **FORMAT-C-ACAD** from the DRAWING-W-SOLIDWORKS-2012\MY-SHEETFORMATS folder. A DXF / DWG Import dialog box is displayed.

160) Accept the default settings. Click **Next>**.

161) Click **Layers selected for sheet format**.

162) Check **0**, **THICKNESS**, **THIN** and **FORMAT_TEXT** layers.

163) Check the **White background** box.

164) Click **Next>**.

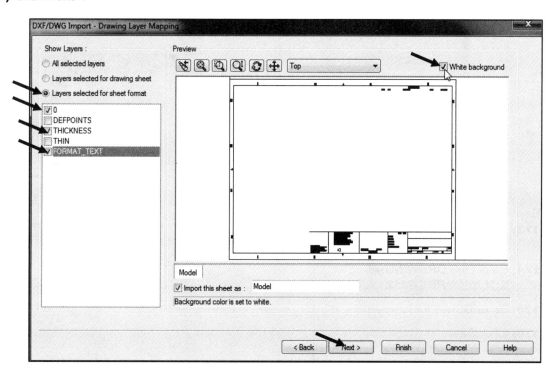

165) Select **Millimeters** for Data units.

166) Select **C-Landscape** for Paper size.

167) Click the **Browse** button.

168) Select the **MY-TEMPLATES** folder.

169) Double-click **C-SIZE-ANSI-MM-EMPTY** for Drawing Template.

170) Enter **0** for the X position.

171) Enter **0** for the Y position.

172) Click **Finish**.

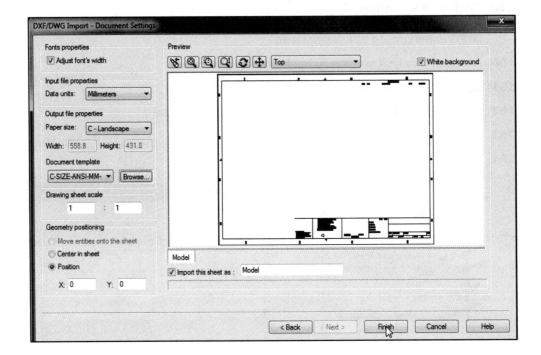

Save the Drawing.

173) Click **Save As** from the Menu bar toolbar.

174) Select the **DRAWING-W-SOLIDWORKS-2012** folder.

175) Enter **Draw3** for File name.

176) Click **Save**.

Draw# is the temporary drawing document utilized to create the Sheet format.

Edit the Title block.

177) At this time, you should be in the **Edit Sheet mode**.

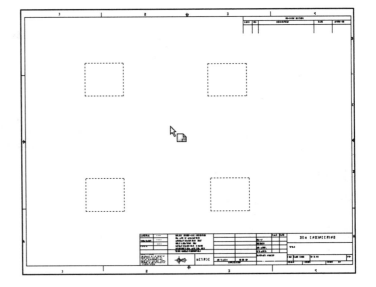

Delete the Title block lines.

178) Zoom in on the Title block.

179) Click the first **horizontal line** below the CONTRACT NUMBER.

180) Right-click **Delete**.

181) Click the second **horizontal line** below the CONTRACT NUMBER.

182) Right-click **Delete**.

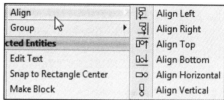

Align the NAME and DATE text.

183) Right-click **Edit Sheet Format** from the Graphics area.

184) Click and drag the **NAME** text.

185) Click and drag the **DATE** text.

You can use the Ctrl key, right-click Align and select the Align option.

Display the Layer toolbar.

186) Right-click a **position** in the gray area, to the right of the Help menu.

187) Check **Layer**. The Layer toolbar is displayed.

Modify Thick Layer properties.

188) Click the **Layer Properties** icon from the Layer toolbar.

Rename the AutoCAD layer

189) Rename Name from **THICKNESS** to **THICK**.

190) Rename Description from **THICKNESS** to **THICK BORDER**.

191) Click the **line Thickness** in the THICK layer.

192) Select the **second line**.

193) Click **OK** from the Layers dialog box.

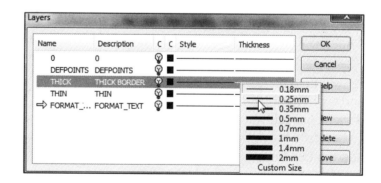

The border and Title block display the Thick line. The left line in the Title block is on the Thin layer. Modify the line layer from the Thin layer to the Thick layer.

Modify a Line layer.

194) Click on the **left line** as illustrated.

195) Click **THICK** layer from the Options box.

196) Click **OK** ✅ from the Line Properties PropertyManager.

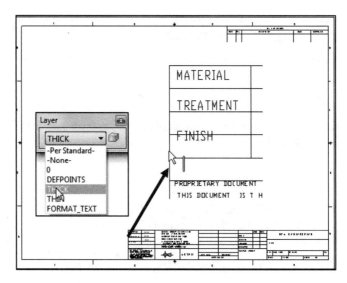

🔆 Align the MATERIAL, TREATMENT and FINISH text as an exercise. You will need to retype the MATERIAL, TREATMENT and FINISH text before you align them.

Save the Sheet.
197) Click **Save**.

The C-FORMAT requires additional information and editing in the Title block. The Title block created from AutoCAD only contains text headings such as: Drawing Number, Revision, and Drawn by. Each heading is located in a different box in the Title block.

Insert additional Notes into the Title block in the Edit Sheet Format Mode. The Notes in the Sheet Format are linked to Properties. Properties are variables shared between parts, assemblies, and drawing documents.

🔆 View Line segments clearly. The System Options, Drawings, Display sketch entity points option displays the endpoints of the line segments. Check this option before editing the lines in the Title block.

🔆 Utilize the Sketch tools to create and edit Title block lines. Utilize dimensions and geometric relations to create Title block lines for A, B, C, D, and E sheet formats according to the ASME Y14.1 Decimal Inch Drawing Sheet Size and Format and ASME Y14.1M Metric Drawing Size and Format.

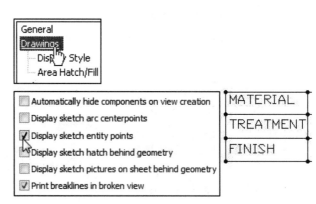

Detailing
Grid/Snap
Units
Line Font
Line Style

Utilize the Document Property, Grid/Snap for quick sketching. The ASME Y14.1 Title block is based on 0.125 increments. Set the Document Properties, Grid/Snap to 0.125 (English). The following dimensions below are recommended for A, B, C, and G sizes.

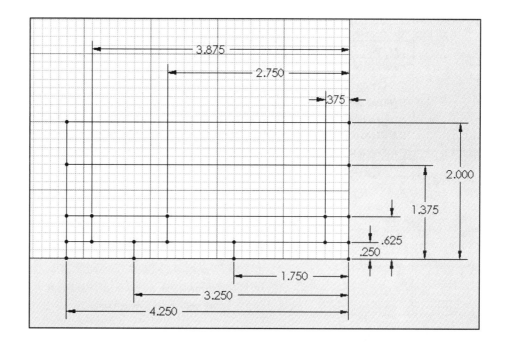

Title Block Notes and Properties

The Title block contains vital part and assembly information. Each company creates a unique version of a Title block. The imported AutoCAD sheet format contains heading names in each area of the Title block such as: TITLE, DWG NO., and SCALE.

Utilize SolidWorks System Properties and User defined Custom Properties to link Notes in the Sheet format to the drawing, part, and assembly.

System Properties

System Properties extract values from the current drawing. System Properties are determined from the SolidWorks documents. Insert System Properties as linked Notes in the Sheet Format.

System Properties begin with the prefix SW. There are two categories of Properties: System Properties and Drawing Specific System Properties.

Set System Properties in the File, Properties, Summary Information dialog box as follows:

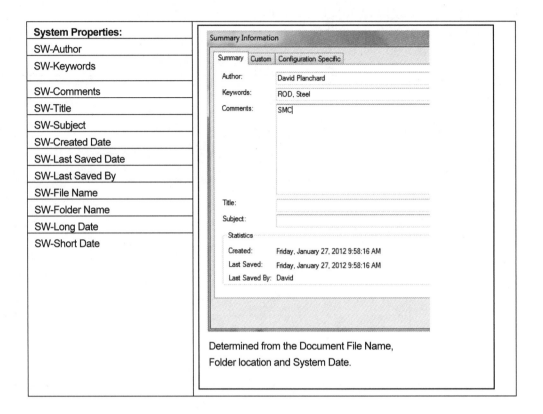

System Properties:
SW-Author
SW-Keywords
SW-Comments
SW-Title
SW-Subject
SW-Created Date
SW-Last Saved Date
SW-Last Saved By
SW-File Name
SW-Folder Name
SW-Long Date
SW-Short Date

Set Drawing Specific System Properties: SW-Sheet Name, SW-Sheet Scale, SW-Sheet Format Size and SW-Template Size in the Sheet Properties dialog box.

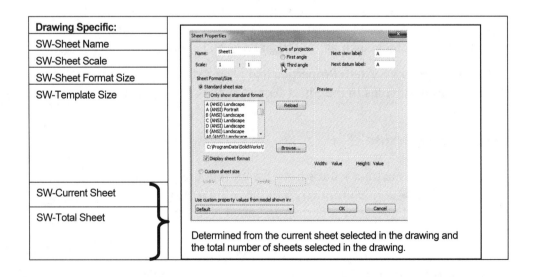

Drawing Specific:
SW-Sheet Name
SW-Sheet Scale
SW-Sheet Format Size
SW-Template Size
SW-Current Sheet
SW-Total Sheet

User Defined Properties

There are two types of User defined Properties: Custom Properties and Configuration Specific Properties. Custom Properties link all of the configurations of a part or an assembly. Configuration Specific Properties link only a single configuration of a part or an assembly.

Assign User defined Property values to named variables in the document. The default variables are listed in the text file C:\ProgramData\SolidWorks\SolidWorks 2012\lang\english, properties.txt. Create your own User defined Property named variables. The properties.txt file is a hidden file. Insert the file path into your search bar to locate a hidden file.

Conserve design time. Utilize System Properties and define Custom Properties and Configuration Specific Properties in your sheet formats.

Linked Notes

Insert Notes into the Title block. Link the Notes to SolidWorks Properties and Custom Properties.

Review your company's Engineering documentation practices to determine the Notes displayed in the Title block.

In the next activity, DWG NO. is linked to the SW-File Name System Property. Revision is linked to the Revision Custom Property in the part or assembly.

Linked Notes begin with the four different prefixes listed below:

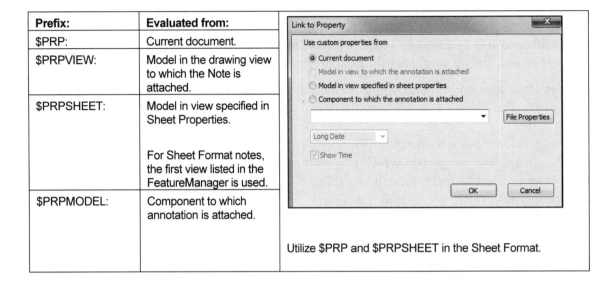

Prefix:	Evaluated from:
$PRP:	Current document.
$PRPVIEW:	Model in the drawing view to which the Note is attached.
$PRPSHEET:	Model in view specified in Sheet Properties. For Sheet Format notes, the first view listed in the FeatureManager is used.
$PRPMODEL:	Component to which annotation is attached.

Utilize $PRP and $PRPSHEET in the Sheet Format.

Linked Notes that reference Custom Properties in the drawing utilize the prefix: $PRP: Enter double quotes to define the property name: Example: $PRP:"CompanyName".

Linked Sheet Format Notes that reference Custom Properties in the part utilize the prefix: $PRPSHEET. Linked Sheet Format Notes are displayed blank in the Edit Sheet mode. Linked Sheet Format Notes are displayed with their property Name in the Edit Sheet Format mode. Example: $PRPSHEET:{Material}.

Insert the following Linked Notes:

System Properties Linked to fields in the default Sheet Format. Prefix: $PRP	Custom Properties of drawings linked to fields in the default Sheet Formats. Prefix: $PRP	Custom Properties copied from the default SW Sheet Format to a Custom Sheet Format. Prefix: $PRP		Custom Properties of parts and assemblies linked to the fields in default Sheet Formats. Prefix:$PRPSHEET
SW-File Name (in DWG. NO. field)	CompanyName	DrawnBy	DrawnDate	Description (in TITLE field):
SW-Sheet Scale	CONTRACT NUMBER	CheckedBy	CheckedDate	Weight
SW-Current Sheet		EngineeringApproval	EngAppDate	Material, Finish and TREATMENT
SW-Total Sheets		ManufacturingApproval	MfgAppDate	Revision

User-defined Custom Property Names CONTRACT NUMBER and TREATMENT are displayed in capital letters for clarity. Utilize Large and small letters for Custom Property Names. Create a new layer for the Title block notes. The large yellow arrow in the Name column indicates the current layer.

Activity: Title Block and SW-File Name

Insert the Title block TEXT layer.

198) Click the **Layer Properties** 🗐 icon.

199) Click the **New** button.

200) Enter **TB TEXT** for Name.

201) Enter **TITLE BLOCK TEXT** for Description.

202) Click **OK** from the Layers box.

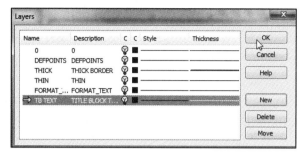

Create a Linked Note for the DWG NO System Property.

203) Click **Note** A from the Annotation toolbar.

204) Click a **point** below the DWG NO. text.

205) Click **Link to Property** 🖾 from the Text Format box.

206) Select **SW-File Name** from the drop-down menu.

207) Click **OK** from the Link to Property dialog box.

208) Click **OK** ✔ from the Note PropertyManager.

209) Position the mouse pointer on the **Draw3** text. The variable name $PRP:"SW-File Name" is displayed.

Save the Drawing.

210) **Rebuild** the drawing.

211) Click **Save**.

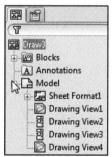

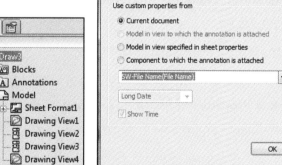

Draw3 is the current file name. The default Draw number varies depending on the number of drawings opened in a SolidWorks session.

The $PRP:"SW-File Name(File Name)" property updates to contain the part or assembly filename. Example: Insert the part 10-0408 into a Drawing template. The filename 10-0408 is linked to the SW-FileName property and is displayed in the DWG NO. box.

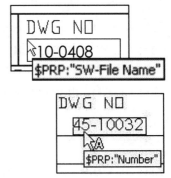

What action do you take to control the DWG NO. by a separate property not linked to the part filename? Answer: Create a Note linked to the Custom Property $PRP: "Number" in the Sheet format. Enter the value 45-10032 for the Number Custom Property in the drawing document.

Size, Sheet and Scale Properties

Additional Linked Notes are required in the Title block. Create the SIZE, SHEET and SCALE text with Linked Properties. Position the text below the headings.

The Sheet Scale value changes to reflect the sheet scale properties in the drawing. The Sheet box combines two System Properties: SW-Current Sheet and SW-Total Sheets. The Current Sheet value and Total Sheets value change as additional sheets are added to the drawing.

Activity: Size, Sheet and Scale Properties

Create a Linked Property to the SIZE text.

212) Click **Note** **A** from the Annotation toolbar.

213) Click a **point** below the SIZE text.

214) Click **Link to Property** from the Text Format box.

215) Select **SW-Sheet Format Size** from the drop-down menu.

216) Click **OK** from the Link to Property dialog box.

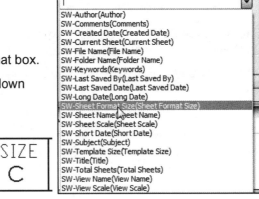

Modify the font size and style of the SIZE text.

217) Double-click **C** in the SIZE box. Enter **3** for font height.

218) Click **Bold** for style.

219) Click **OK** ✓ from the Note PropertyManager.

Create a Linked Property to SCALE.

220) Click **Note** **A** from the Annotation toolbar.

221) Click a **point** to the right of the SCALE text.

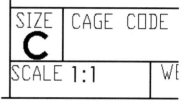

222) Click **Link to Property** 📷 from the Text Format box.

223) Select **SW-Sheet Scale** from the drop-down menu.

224) Click **OK**. 1:1 is displayed.

225) Click **OK** ✓ from the Note PropertyManager.

Delete text in the Title box. Note: You need to be in the Edit Sheet Format mode.

226) Click the **OF** text in the lower right corner of the title box.

227) Press the **Delete** key.

Combine Link Properties for the SHEET text.
228) Double-click the **SHEET** text.

229) Position the **cursor** at the end of the text.

230) Press the **space bar**.

231) Click **Link to Property** 📷 from the Text Format box.

232) Select **SW-Current Sheet** from the drop-down menu.

233) Click **OK**. Press the **space bar**.

234) Enter the text **OF**.

235) Press the **space bar**.

236) Click **Link to Property** 📷 from the Text Format box.

237) Select **SW-Total Sheets** from the drop-down menu.

238) Click **OK**.

239) Click **OK** ✓ from the Note PropertyManager.

Save the Drawing.
240) Click **Save**.

Custom Property and Logo Picture

Utilize D&M ENGINEERING or your own logo for
CompanyName in the next step. The CompanyName
Property is controlled through a Custom Property in the
Sheet format.

Activity: Custom Property and Logo Picture

Delete the current Company Name Note text.

241) Right-click on the **D&M ENGINEERING** text in the
drawing.

242) Click **Edit Text in Window**.

243) Delete **D&M ENGINEERING**.

Insert the CompanyName Property.

244) Enter **$PRP:"CompanyName"** in the Note
text box. Click **OK**.

245) Click **Link to Property**  from the Text
Format dialog box.

246) Click the **File Properties** button from the
Link to Property box.

247) Click the **Custom** tab from the Summary
Information box.

248) Click inside the **Property Name** box.

249) Select **CompanyName**.

250) Click inside the **Value / Text Expression** box.

251) Enter **D&M ENGINEERING** for CompanyName.

252) Click inside the **Evaluated Value** box.

253) Click **OK** from the Summary Information box.

254) Click **OK** from the dialog box.

255) Click **OK** ✓ from the Note PropertyManager. View the results.

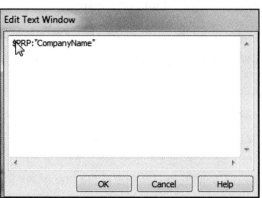

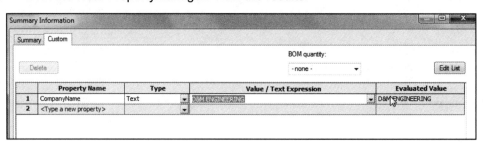

The Title block displays the CompanyName Linked Note. The current document stores the CompanyName Property. Select Custom Properties through the Link to Property drop-down menu.

Modify the font of D&M ENGINEERING.
256) Double-click the **D&M ENGINEERING** text.

257) Click **Bold**.

258) Click **OK** ✓ from the Note Property Manager.

Position the mouse pointer over the Linked Note to display the Custom Property value. Utilize Ctrl-A to select all the text in the Note text box.

A company logo is normally located in the Title block. Create a company logo by inserting a picture file or a file as an OLE object into the Title block. Example: The file COMPASS.doc is located in the MY-SHEETFORMATS folder. Utilize any picture file, scanned image, or bitmap.

Insert a picture file for the Sheet Logo. Note: You should be in the Edit Sheet Format mode.
259) Click **Insert**, **Object** from the Menu bar menu. Note: You can insert a picture as a logo. Click **Create from File**.

260) Click **Browse**.

261) Double-click **MY-SHEETFORMATS\Compass.doc**.

262) Right-click **OK.** The picture file is displayed on the Sheet.

263) Size the **picture** by dragging the picture handles in Sheet1 as illustrated.

Save the Drawing.
264) Click **Save** 🖫.

If needed, you can add relations in the sheet format so that any modifications can be easily applied. For instance if you wanted to modify the format for different sheet sizes, or needed to extend a text area

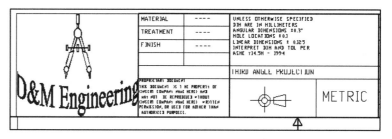

to accommodate a large amount of information in the Title block, then it would be easier to achieve if there were defined sketch entities.

User Defined Custom Property

Your company has a policy that a contract number must be contained in the Title block for all associated drawings in the chapter. The contract number is not a predefined SolidWorks Custom Property. Create a user defined Custom Property named CONTRACT NUMBER. Add it to the drawing Title block. The Custom Property is contained in the sheet format.

Activity: User Defined Custom Property

Create a User defined Custom Property.

265) Click **Note** A from the Annotation toolbar.

266) Click a **point** in the upper left hand corner below the CONTRACT NUMBER text.

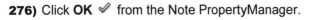

267) Click **Link to Property** from the Text Format box.

268) Click the **File Properties** button.

269) Click the **Custom** tab.

270) Click inside the **Property Name** spin box.

271) Enter **CONTRACT NUMBER** for Name.

272) Click inside the **Value / Text Expression** box.

273) Enter **101045-PAP** for Value. Click inside the **Evaluated Value** box.

274) Click **OK** from the Summary Information box.

	Property Name	Type	Value / Text Expression	Evaluated Value
1	CompanyName	Text	D&M ENGINEERING	D&M ENGINEERING
2	CONTRACT NUMBER	Text	101045-PAP	101045-PAP

275) Select **CONTRACT NUMBER** in the Property Name text box. Click **OK** from the Link to Property box. View the results.

276) Click **OK** ✔ from the Note PropertyManager.

Fit the drawing to the Graphics window.
277) Press the **f** key.

278) Click **Save**.

Copy/Paste Custom Properties

Conserve design time. Share information from Templates and Sheet Formats. Copy DrawnBy, DrawnDate, CheckedBy, CheckedDate, EngineeringApproval, EngAppDate, ManufacturingApproval and MfgAppDate from a default SolidWorks C-Sheet format to the Custom C-Format.

Activity: Copy/Paste Custom Properties

Open the default SolidWorks C-size Drawing template.

279) Click **New** ⬜ from the Menu bar toolbar.

280) Select the **Templates** tab.

281) Double-click **Drawing**.

282) Select **C (ANSI) Landscape** for the Sheet format.

283) Check **Display sheet format**. Click **OK**.

284) If needed, click **Cancel** ✖ from the Model View PropertyManager.

285) Zoom in on the NAME and DATE area in the Title block.

Display the Linked text.

286) Click **View**, **Annotation Link Errors** from the Menu bar menu. An Error indicates the value for the Custom Property is empty.

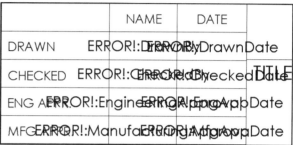

Edit the Sheet format.

287) Right-click in the **sheet boundary**.

288) Click **Edit Sheet Format**.

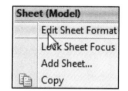

Copy the drawing Custom Properties.

289) Hold the **Ctrl** key down.

290) Select the **text** in the columns under Name and Date. Do not select the QA text row.

291) Release the **Ctrl** key.

292) Press **Ctrl + C**.

293) Return to the active custom C-Sheet format drawing.

294) Click a **position** between the NAME and DATE column and the CHECKED and ENG APPR. row.

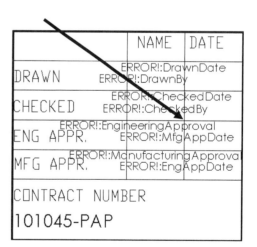

Paste the information.

295) Press **Ctrl + V**.

296) Drag the **text** to center in the NAME column and DATE column.

297) Position the **mouse pointer** on the DrawnBy text. The Custom Property $PRP:"DrawnBy" is displayed.

Hide the Linked text.

298) Click **View**, uncheck **Annotation Link Errors** from the Menu bar menu.

Insert Custom Property DrawnBy.

299) Click **File**, **Properties** from the Menu bar menu.

300) Click the **Custom** tab.

301) Select **DrawnBy** for Property Name.

302) Enter your name, example **DCP,** in the Value / Text Expression box.

303) Click inside the **Evaluated Value** box.

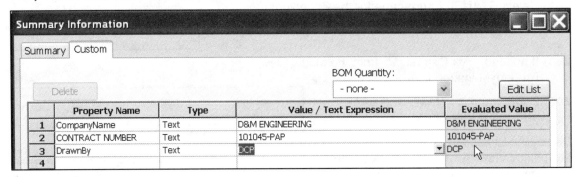

Summary Information

	Property Name	Type	Value / Text Expression	Evaluated Value
1	CompanyName	Text	D&M ENGINEERING	D&M ENGINEERING
2	CONTRACT NUMBER	Text	101045-PAP	101045-PAP
3	DrawnBy	Text	DCP	DCP
4				

304) Click **OK**.

305) Click **Save** 🖫 .

☼ In this example, you saved the DrawnBy Custom Property with the Sheet format. The DrawnBy Custom Property may also be left blank in the Sheet format and entered by the designer in the drawing.

	NAME	DATE
DRAWN	DCP	
CHECKED		

Custom Properties in Parts and Assemblies

Define Custom Properties in parts and assemblies through the ConfigurationManager, Properties option. Insert Custom Properties from a part or assembly into the drawing. Create Description, Weight, Material, and Revision Custom Properties as Linked Notes in the sheet format. Enter values for these Custom Properties in the part or assembly.

Activity: Custom Properties in Parts and Assemblies

Insert the Description Property.

306) Click **Note** **A** from the Annotation toolbar.

307) Click a **position** to the right of the TITLE.

308) Enter **$PRPSHEET:"Description"**.

309) Click **OK** ✔ from the Note PropertyManager.

TITLE $PRPSHEET:{Description}

$PRPSHEET:"Description"

The Note displays $PRPSHEET:{Description}. Enter the Description value in the part or assembly Custom Properties. The value is linked to the TITLE box Note.

Insert the Revision Property.

310) Click **Note A** from the Annotation toolbar.

311) Click a **position** below the REV text.

312) Enter **$PRPSHEET:"Revision"**.

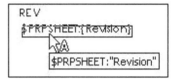

313) Click **OK** ✅ from the Note PropertyManager. The Note displays $PRPSHEET:{Revision}.

Enter the Revision value in the part or assembly Custom Properties. Edit the WEIGHT text and append the text $PRPSHEET:"WEIGHT".

Insert the Weight Property.

314) Right-click the **WEIGHT** text on Sheet1.

315) Click **Edit Text in Window**.

316) Delete the **WEIGHT** text.

317) Enter **$PRPSHEET:"Weight"**.

318) Click **OK** from the Edit Text Window dialog box.

319) Click **OK** ✅ from the Note PropertyManager.

Insert the Material Property.

320) Delete the ------ to the right of the MATERIAL box.

321) Click **Note A** from the Annotation toolbar.

322) Enter **$PRPSHEET:"Material"** to the right of the MATERIAL box.

323) Click **OK** ✅ from the Note PropertyManager.

324) **Repeat** for TREATMENT.

325) Enter **$PRPSHEET:"Treatment"** to the right of the TREATMENT box.

326) **Repeat** for FINISH.

327) Enter **$PRPSHEET:"Finish"** to the right of the FINISH box.

328) Click **Save** 💾.

MATERIAL	$PRPSHEET:{Material}
TREATMENT	$PRPSHEET:{Treatment}
FINISH	$PRPSHEET:{Finish}

Description, Revision, Weight, Material, and Finish are predefined Custom Properties. Assign values in the part and assembly. The TREATMENT Custom Property is not defined. Create the TREATMENT Custom Property Name and value in the part through the ConfigurationManager, Custom Properties, or a Design Table.

General Notes

General notes are annotations that describe additional information on a drawing. Conserve drawing time. Place common general notes in the Sheet format. The Engineering department stores general notes in a Notepad file, GENERALNOTES.TXT. General notes are usually located in a corner of a drawing.

Activity: General Notes

329) Minimize the **SolidWorks window**. Do not close.

Create general notes from a text file.
330) Double-click on the Notepad file, **MY-SHEETFORMATS\GENERALNOTES.TXT**.

331) Click **Ctrl + A** to select the text in the Notepad file.

332) Click **Ctrl + C** to copy the text into the windows clipboard.

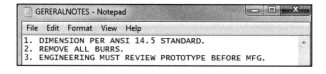

333) Return to the open document in SolidWorks. Click the **Alt + tab**.

334) Click **Note** A from the Annotation toolbar.

335) Click a **point** in the lower left hand corner of the Sheet.

336) Click **inside** the Note text box.

Paste the three lines of text.
337) Click **Ctrl + V**.

1. DIMENSION PER ANSI 14.5 STANDARD.
2. REMOVE ALL BURRS.
3. ENGINEERING MUST REVIEW PROTOTYPE BEFORE MFG.

338) Click **OK** ✅ from the Note PropertyManager.

339) Click **Save** 💾.

Tables

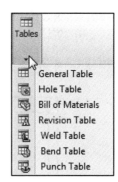

Various general SolidWorks tables are available: *General Table, Hole Table, Bill of Materials, Revision Table, Weld Table, Bend Table and Punch Table*. Each table contains an Anchor point. An Anchor point locates the Table position in the Sheet format. Access to the Anchor point is through the Table entry in the FeatureManager.

The Revision Table documents the history of a drawing. Locate the Revision Table Anchor point in the upper right corner of the sheet format. Address other tables in future projects.

Activity: Revision Table-Anchor Point

Delete the current Revision Table created in the AutoCad format.
340) Zoom in on the upper right corner of the Sheet Format.

341) Window-select the **Revision Table**.

342) Right-click **Delete** to remove all imported table lines and text.

Return to the drawing sheet.
343) Right-click in the **Graphics window**.

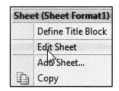

344) Right-click **Edit Sheet**.

Fit the drawing to the Graphics window.
345) Press the **f** key.

Set the default layer.
346) Click **None** from the Layer text box.

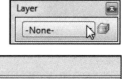

Set the Revision Table anchor point.
347) Expand Sheet Format1 in the Drawing FeatureManager.

348) Right-click **Revision Table Anchor1**.

349) Click **Set Anchor**.

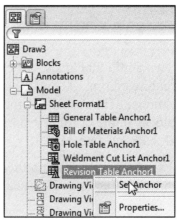

350) Click a **position** in the upper right corner of the Title block. You are in the Edit Sheet Format mode.

351) Click **Save** .

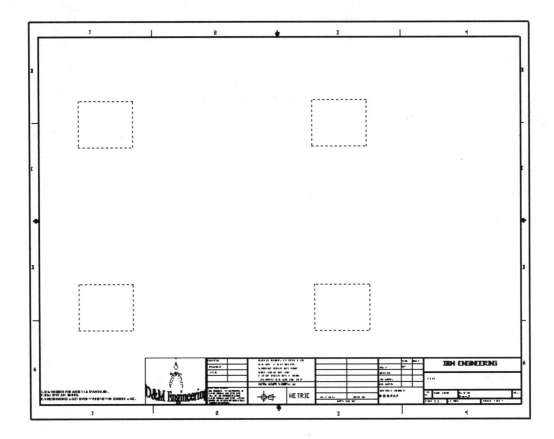

Two additional areas of the Title block require editing. Address this action as an exercise. The AutoCAD format utilized blocks in the original Proprietary Document statement.

The paragraph was imported. Letters are missing. Each line is a separate block.

PROPRIETARY DOCUMENT

THIS DOCUMENT IS T HE PROPERTY OF
<INSERT COMPANY NAME HERE> AND
MAY NOT BE REPRODCUED WTHOUT
<INSERT COMPANY NAME HERE> WRITTEN
PERMISSION, OR USED FOR AOTHER THAN
AUTHORIZED PURPOSES.

Imported from Autocad, in block format.

Delete the old note. Retype the note in SolidWorks. Modify the text font to Century Gothic.

PROPRIETARY DOCUMENT

THIS DOCUMENT IS THE PROPERTY OF D&M ENGINEERING AND MAY NOT BE REPRODUCED WITHOUT D&M ENGINEERING WRITTEN PERMISSION, OR USED FOR ANY OTHER UN-AUTHORIZED PURPOSES.

Recreated in SolidWorks in paragraph format.

The Tolerance block is located in the Title block. The Tolerance block provides information to the manufacturer on the minimum and maximum variation for each dimension on the drawing. If a specific tolerance or note is provided on the drawing, the specific tolerance or note will override the information in the Tolerance block.

UNLESS OTHERWISE SPECIFIED
DIM ARE IN MILLIMETERS
ANGULAR DIMENSIONS ±0.3°
HOLE LOCATIONS ±0.1
LINEAR DIMENSIONS ± 0.2|
INTERPRET DIM AND TOL PER
ASME Y14.5M — 1994

The design requirements and the manufacturing process determine the general tolerance values. The original Tolerance block lists values for inch parts. The Sheet format is developed for a metric part. Modify the LINEAR DIMENSIONS tolerance to +/- 0.2mm.

New in SolidWorks 2012 is the ability to modify the document units directly from the Graphics window as illustrated.

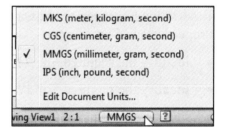

Review

The Sheet format contains System Properties, Custom Properties and General Notes. SW-File Name, SW-Sheet Scale, SW-Current Sheet and SW-Total Sheets were Notes in the Sheet format linked to System Properties.

CompanyName, CONTRACT NUMBER, DrawnBy, and DrawnDate were Notes in the sheet format linked to the Drawing Custom Properties. DrawnBy and DrawingDate were copied from an existing default Sheet format.

Description, Revision, Material, Weight, Finish and TREATMENT were Notes in the sheet format linked to Custom Properties in the part and assembly.

You inserted a file for a company logo and General Notes from a text file. You utilized a table anchor point to position future Revision Tables in the Title block.

Create Sheet formats for different parts types. Example: sheet metal parts, plastic parts and high precision machined parts. Create Sheet formats for each category of the parts that are manufactured with unique sets of Notes and Custom Properties.

The illustrations are based on SolidWorks SP1.0. The illustrations may vary slightly per your SolidWorks release.

Review the Engineering Drawing Practices in your company as they relate to Custom Properties and Sheet formats. Create a table. List the following:

- Identify the required Sheet formats.

- Identify the required SolidWorks Properties to control the design process.

- Identify the required Custom Properties to control the design process.

- Determine the required values for each Property.

- Determine the correct location to define the Property: part, assembly, or drawing.

You can create title block tables in parts and assemblies and link the table information to the configuration-specific properties of the document. Title block tables behave in a similar way to tables in drawings. As with other SolidWorks tables, you can customize title block table templates and save them for future use. See SolidWorks Help for additional information.

Save Sheet Format and Drawing Template

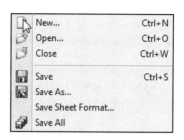

The Sheet format (*.slddrt) and Drawing template (*.drwdot) utilize two different commands to save the current drawing document (.drw). Utilize the File, Save Sheet Format option to create the Sheet format. Store Sheet formats in your MY-SHEETFORMATS folder.

Utilize the Save As command and select the Drawing template option to create the Drawing template. Combine the C-FORMAT Sheet format with the empty Drawing template. The C-FORMAT Sheet format is contained in every sheet of the drawing in the C-ANSI-MM Drawing template.

Save the Sheet format and Drawing templates in the Edit Sheet mode. Insert Views into the drawing in Edit Sheet mode. Views can't be displayed in the Edit Sheet Format mode. Set the layer option to None. The current layer is saved in the Drawing template.

Create a new drawing to test the Sheet format and the Drawing template. The Add Sheet option inserts a second sheet into the current drawing.

Activity: Save Sheet Format and Save Drawing Template

Set the Layer.
352) If needed, click **None** from the Layers toolbar.

Save the Sheet format.
353) Click **File**, **Save Sheet Format** from the Menu bar menu.

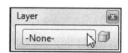

354) Enter **C-FORMAT** in the MY-SHEETFORMATS folder.

355) Click **Save**.

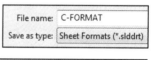

Close all documents.
356) Click **Windows**, **Close All** from the Menu bar menu.

Combine the C-SIZE-ANSI-MM-EMPTY template with the C-FORMAT Sheet format.

357) Click **New** ⬜ from the Menu bar menu.

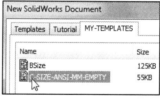

358) Double-click **C-SIZE-ANSI-MM-EMPTY** from the MY-TEMPLETES folder.

359) Right-click in the **Graphics window**.

360) Click **Properties**.

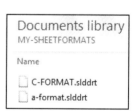

361) Click the **Standard Sheet size** box.

362) Click **Browse**.

363) Double-click **C-FORMAT** from the MY-SHEETFORMATS folder.

364) Check **Display sheet format**.

365) Click **OK** from the Sheet Properties dialog box.

Save the Drawing Template.
366) Click **Save As** from the Menu bar toolbar.

367) Select **Drawing Template (*drwdot)** for Save as type.

368) Select **MY-TEMPLATES** for Save in folder.

369) Enter **C-ANSI-MM** for File name.

370) Click **Save**.

Close all documents.
371) Click **Windows, Close All** from the Menu bar menu.

Verify the template.
372) Click **New** ☐ from the Menu bar toolbar.

373) Click the **MY-TEMPLATES** tab.

374) Double-click the **C-ANSI-MM** template. The C-ANSI-MM
Drawing template is displayed with the Sheet format.

Add Sheet2
375) Right-click in **Sheet1**.

376) Click **Add Sheet**.

377) Click **No**. Sheet2 is displayed.

Save the drawing.
378) Click **Save As** from the Menu bar toolbar.

379) Select the **DRAWING-W-SOLIDWORKS-2012** folder.

380) Enter **Draw6** for Filename.

Close all files.
381) Click **Windows, Close All** from the Menu bar menu.

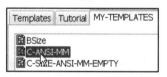

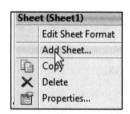

☀️ Drawing sheets are ordered as they are created. The names
are displayed in the FeatureManager design tree and as Excel-style
tabs at the bottom of the Graphics window. Activate a sheet by
right-clicking in FeatureManager design tree and clicking Activate
or click the tab name.

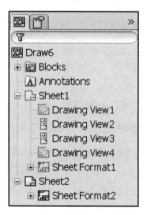

☀️ *When adding a sheet, if the system can't locate the Sheet
format, add the Sheet format in File Location under System
Options or Browse to the correct Sheet format location.*

Reorder sheets by using the standard drag and drop technique with the tabs.

 Rename a sheet by right-clicking the drawing tab, click Rename.

A (ANSI) Size Drawing Template

Create an A (ANSI) size Drawing template and an A (ANSI) size Sheet format. Text size for an A (ANSI) size drawing is the same as a C (ANSI) size drawing. Utilize the empty C (ANSI) size Drawing template to copy the Document Properties.

Create an A-ANSI-MM Drawing template. Add an A (ANSI) size Sheet format. SolidWorks copies the Document Properties in the C (ANSI) size Drawing template to the A-size Drawing template. The MY-SHEETFORMATS folder contains a predefined Sheet format named, A-FORMAT. The A-FORMAT contains geometry, text, and dimensions. The current layer is set to None. The Drawing template controls the units.

Activity: A (ANSI) Drawing Template

Create a new A (ANSI) Drawing template.

382) Click **New** ⬜ from the Menu bar toolbar.

383) Double-click **C-SIZE-ANSI-MM-EMPTY**.

384) Select **A (ANSI) Landscape** for Standard sheet size.

385) Uncheck **Display Sheet Format**.

386) Click **OK**.

387) Click and drag the **pre-determined views** into the Sheet boundary.

Fit the template to the Graphics window.
388) Press the **f** key.

Save the A-size Drawing Template.
389) Click **Save As** from the Menu bar toolbar.

390) Select **Drawing Templates** for Save as type.

391) **Browse** to the MY-TEMPLATES file folder.

392) Enter **A-SIZE-ANSI-MM-EMPTY** for File name.

393) Click **Save**.

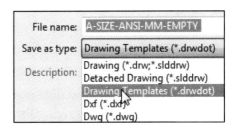

Load the Custom A-size Sheet format.
394) Right-click in the **Graphics window**.

395) Click **Properties**.

396) Click **Standard sheet size** for the Sheet format.

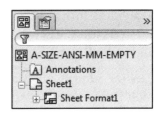

397) Click **Browse**.

398) Double-click **a-format** in the MY-SHEETFORMATS folder.

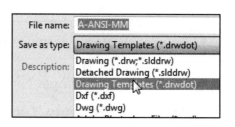

399) Check **Display sheet format**.

400) Click **OK**. Note: The current layer is set to None.

Save the new Drawing Template.
401) Click **Save As** from the Menu bar toolbar.

402) Select **Drawing Templates(*.drwdot)** for Save as type.

403) Select the **MY-TEMPLATES** file folder.

404) Enter **A-ANSI-MM**.

405) Click **Save**.

Close all documents.
406) Click **Windows**, **Close All** from the Menu bar toolbar.

Verify the template.
407) Click **New** ⬜ from the Menu bar toolbar.

408) Click the **MY-TEMPLATES** tab.

409) Double-click the **A-ANSI-MM** template. The new drawing is displayed in the Graphics window.

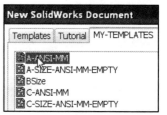

Close all documents.
410) Click **Windows**, **Close All** from the Menu bar menu.

Chapter Summary

In this chapter, you created a Custom C-size and A-size Drawing template and Sheet format. The Drawing template and Sheet format contained global drawing and detailing standards.

You obtained and applied drawing properties that reflect the ASME Y14 Engineering Drawing and Related Drawing Practices. You performed the task of importing an AutoCAD drawing to create and modify a Custom Sheet format.

The Sheet format utilized System Properties and User defined Custom Properties through Linked Notes. The A-ANSI-MM and C-ANSI-MM Drawing templates and A-FORMAT and C-FORMAT Sheet formats are used in the next Chapter.

Review additional topics in the chapter exercise. Example: Create drawing templates for inch Document Properties. Import a Pro\ENGINEER Sheet format into SolidWorks.

Chapter Terminology

ANSI: American National Standards Institute.

ASME: American Society of Mechanical Engineers. ASME is the publisher of the Y14 Engineering Drawing and Related Documentation Practices. ASME Y14.5M-1994 is a revision of ANSI Y14.5-1982.

CommandManager: The CommandManager is a Context-sensitive toolbar that dynamically updates based on the toolbar you want to access. By default, it has toolbars embedded in it based on the document type. When you click a tab below the Command Manager, it updates to display that toolbar. For example, if you click the **Sketches** tab, the Sketch toolbar is displayed.

Coordinate System: SolidWorks uses a coordinate system with origins. A part document contains an original Origin. Whenever you select a plane or face and open a sketch, an Origin is created in alignment with the plane or face. An Origin can be used as an anchor for the sketch entities, and it helps orient perspective of the axes. A three-dimensional reference triad orients you to the X, Y, and Z directions in part and assembly documents.

Cursor Feedback: The system feedback symbol indicates what you are selecting or what the system is expecting you to select. As you move the mouse pointer across your model, system feedback is provided.

DimXpertManager: The DimXpertManager lists the tolerance features defined by DimXpert for a part. It also displays DimXpert tools that you use to insert dimensions and tolerances into a part. You can import these dimensions and tolerances into drawings. DimXpert is not associative.

Drawing: A 2D representation of a 3D part or assembly. The extension for a SolidWorks drawing file name is .SLDDRW. Drawing refers to the SolidWorks module used to insert, add, and modify views in an engineering drawing.

Drawing Template: A document that is the foundation of a new drawing. The drawing template contains document properties and user-defined parameters such as sheet format. The extension for the drawing template filename is .DRWDOT.

Drawing Sheet: A page in a drawing document.

FeatureManager: The FeatureManager design tree located on the left side of the SolidWorks window provides an outline view of the active part, assembly, or drawing. This makes it easy to see how the model or assembly was constructed or to examine the various sheets and views in a drawing. The FeatureManager and the Graphics window are dynamically linked. You can select features, sketches, drawing views, and construction geometry in either pane.

Heads-up View toolbar: A transparent toolbar located at the top of the Graphic window.

Hidden Lines Removed (HLR): A view mode. All edges of the model that are not visible from the current view angle are removed from the display.

Hidden Lines Visible (HLV): A view mode. All edges of the model that are not visible from the current view angle are shown gray or dashed.

Import: The ability to open files from other software applications into a SolidWorks document. The A-size sheet format was created as an AutoCAD file and imported into SolidWorks.

Layers: Simplifies a drawing by combining dimensions, annotations, geometry and components. Properties such as: display, line style, and thickness are assigned to a named layer.

Menus: Menus provide access to the commands that the SolidWorks software offers. Menus are Context-sensitive and can be customized through a dialog box.

Model: 3D solid geometry in a part or assembly document. If a part or assembly document contains multiple configurations, each configuration is a separate model.

Mouse Buttons: The left, middle, and right mouse buttons have distinct meanings in SolidWorks. Use the middle mouse button to rotate and Zoom in/out on the part or assembly document.

OLE (Object Linking and Embedding): A Windows file format. A company logo or EXCEL spreadsheet placed inside a SolidWorks document are examples of OLE files.

Origin: The model origin is displayed in blue and represents the (0,0,0) coordinate of the model. When a sketch is active, a sketch origin is displayed in red and represents the (0,0,0) coordinate of the sketch. Dimensions and relations can be added to the model origin, but not to a sketch origin.

Part: A 3D object that consists of one or more features. A part inserted into an assembly is called a component. Insert part views, feature dimensions and annotations into 2D drawings. The extension for a SolidWorks part filename is .SLDPRT.

Plane: To create a sketch, choose a plane. Planes are flat and infinite. Planes are represented on the screen with visible edges.

Properties: Variables shared between documents through linked notes.

Sheet: A page in a drawing document.

Sheet Format: A document that contains the following: page size and orientation, standard text, borders, logos, and Title block information. Customize the Sheet format to save time. The extension for the Sheet format filename is .SLDDRT.

Sheet Properties: Sheet Properties display properties of the selected sheet. Sheet Properties define the following: Name of the Sheet, Sheet Scale, Type of Projection (First angle or Third angle), Sheet Format, Sheet Size, View label, and Datum label.

System Feedback: Feedback is provided by a symbol attached to the cursor arrow indicating your selection. As the cursor floats across the model, feedback is provided in the form of symbols riding next to the cursor.

System Options: System Options are stored in the registry of the computer. System Options are not part of the document. Changes to the System Options affect all current and future documents. There are hundreds of Systems Options.

Templates: Templates are part, drawing, and assembly documents that include user-defined parameters and are the basis for new documents.

Toolbars: The toolbar menus provide shortcuts enabling you to access the most frequently used commands. Toolbars are Context-sensitive and can be customized through a dialog box.

Questions

1. Name the drawing options defined in the Drawing template.

2. Name five drawing items that are contained in the Sheet format.

3. Identify the paper dimensions required for an A (ANSI) Landscape size horizontal drawing.

4. Identify the paper dimensions required for an A4 horizontal drawing.

5. Name the Size option you select in order to define a custom paper width and height.

6. Identify the primary type of projection utilized in a drawing in the United States.

7. Describe the steps to display and modify the Properties in a drawing sheet.

8. Identify the location of the stored System Options.

9. Name five Display Modes for drawing views.

10. True or False. SolidWorks Line Font Types define all ASME Y14.2 type and style of lines.

11. Identify all Dimensioning Standards Options supported by SolidWorks.

12. Identify 10 drawing items that are contained in a Title block.

13. SolidWorks Properties are saved with the _____ format.

14. The Drawing template ends with the SolidWorks file extension _____.

15. A Sheet format ends with the SolidWorks file extension _____.

16. An AutoCAD drawing ends with the file extension _____.

17. Describe the procedure to insert a picture into the Sheet format.

18. True or False. Custom Properties are defined only in the Drawing template.

Exercises

Notes for Exercise 5.1 through Exercise 5.3:

Create Drawing templates for both inch and metric units. ASME Y14.5M has different rules for English and Metric unit decimal display.

English decimal display: If a dimension value is less than 1in, no leading zero is displayed before the decimal point. See Table 1 for details.

Metric decimal display: If a dimension value is less than 1mm, a leading zero is displayed before the decimal point. See Table 1 for details.

Specify General Tolerances in the Title block. Specific tolerances are applied to an individual dimension.

Select ANSI for the SolidWorks Dimensioning Standard. Select inch or metric for Drawing units.

Table 1		
Tolerance Display for INCH and METRIC DIMENSIONS (ASME Y14.5M)		
Display	Inch	Metric
Dimensions less than 1	.5	0.5
Unilateral Tolerance	$1.417^{+.005}_{-.000}$	$36^{0}_{-0.5}$
Bilateral Tolerance	$1.417^{+.010}_{-.020}$	$36^{+0.25}_{-0.50}$
Limit Tolerance	.571 .463	14.50 11.50

Exercise 5.1:

Create an A-size ANSI Drawing template using inch units. Use an A-FORMAT Sheet format. Create a C-size ANSI Drawing template using inch units. Use a C-FORMAT Sheet format.

The minimum ASME Y14.2M letter height for the Title block is displayed in Table 2. Create three new Layers named:

- DETAILS

- HIDE DIMS

- CNST DIMS (Construction Dimensions)

Create new Layers to display the CHAIN, PHANTOM, and STITCH lines.

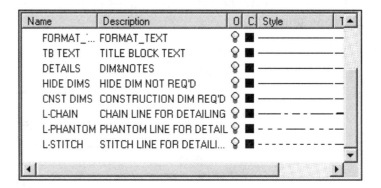

TABLE 2	
Minimum Letter Height for TITLE BLOCK	
(ASME Y14.2M)	
Title Block Text	Letter Height (inches) for A, B, C Drawing Size
Drawing Title, Drawing Size, Cage Code, Drawing Number, Revision Letter	.12
Section and view letters	.24
Drawing block letters	.10
All other characters	.10

Exercise 5.2:

Create an A4(horizontal) ISO Drawing template. Use Document Properties to set the ISO dimension standard and millimeter units.

Exercise 5.3:

Modify the SolidWorks drawing template A4-ISO. Edit Sheet Format to include a new Sheet Metal & Weldment Tolerances box on the left hand side of the Sheet format, Figure EX5.3.

Display sketched end points to create new lines for the Tolerance box. Click Options, System Options, Sketch from the Menu bar toolbar. Check Display entity points. The endpoints are displayed for the Sketched lines.

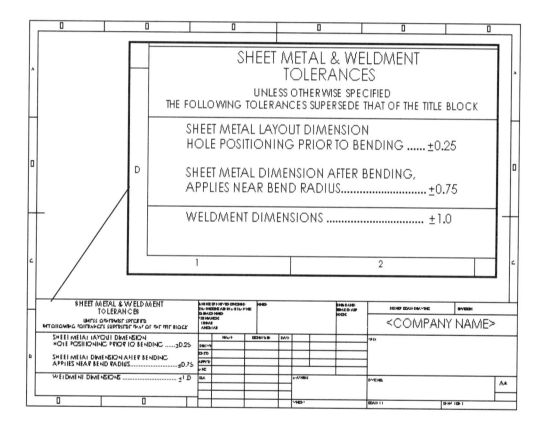

Figure EX 5.3

SHEET METAL & WELDMENT TOLERANCES box

Courtesy of Ismeca, USA Inc. Vista, CA.

Exercise 5.4:

You are not required to have Pro/E to perform the following exercise. Your company uses SolidWorks and Pro/ENGINEER to manufacture sheet metal parts, Figure EX 5.4. Import the empty A-size drawing format, FORMAT-A-PRO-E.DWG located in the DRAWING-W-SOLIDWORKS-2012 file folder. The document was exported from Pro/E as a DWG file. Save the Pro/E drawing format as a SolidWorks Sheet format.

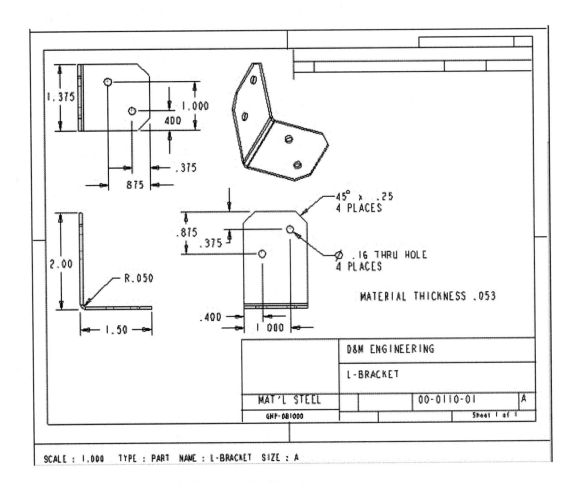

Figure EX 5.4
Sheet Metal Strong Tie Reinforcing Bracket,
Courtesy of Simpson Strong Tie Corporation, CA, USA.

Exercise 5.5:

You are required to have AutoCAD to perform the following exercise. Your company uses SolidWorks and AutoCAD. Open an A-size Drawing template from AutoCAD. Review the Dimension Variables (DIMVARS) in AutoCAD. Record the DIMSTATUS for the following variables:

AutoCAD:	Function:
DIMTXSTY	Dimensioning Text Style
DIMASZ	Arrow size
DIMCEN	Center Mark size
DIMDEC	Decimal Places
DIMTDEC	Tolerance Decimal Places
DIMTXT	Text Height
DIMDLI	Space between dimension lines for Baseline dimensioning

Identify the corresponding values in SolidWorks Document Properties to contain the AutoCAD dimension variables. Utilize Help, Moving from AutoCAD to SolidWorks. Use CommandMap, Draw Toolbar, and Dimension Toolbar in this exercise.

Define Favorite dimension style settings for a particular dimension. Apply Favorite dimension styles to other dimensions on the drawing, part and assembly documents.

Early AutoCAD drawing formats contain fonts not supported in a Windows environment. These fonts imported into SolidWorks will be misaligned in the Sheet Format. Modify older AutoCAD formats to a True Type Font in SolidWorks.

For additional information on the transition between 2D AutoCAD and 3D SolidWorks, Use the Draw Toolbar option in SolidWorks help.

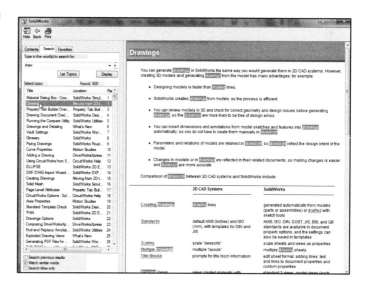

Notes:

Chapter 6

Drawings and Various Drawing Views

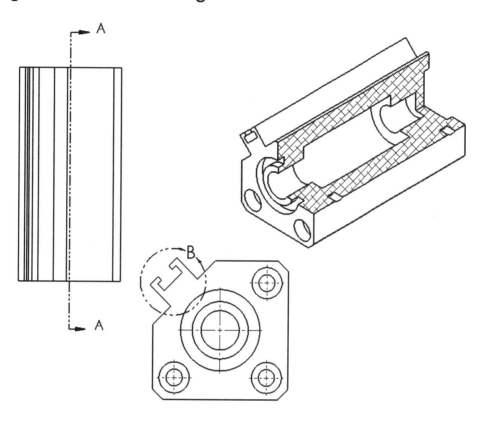

Below are the desired outcomes and usage competencies based on the completion of Chapter 6.

Desired Outcomes:	Usage Competencies:
Three Drawings: • TUBE • ROD • COVERPLATE	• Ability to create the following drawing views: Standard, Isometric, Auxiliary, Section, Broken Section, Detail, Half Section (Cut-away), Crop, Projected Back, and more.
	• Ability to create multi-sheet drawings from various part configurations.

Notes:

Chapter 6 - Drawings and Various Drawing Views

Chapter Objective

Create three drawings: TUBE, ROD and COVERPLATE. Insert the following drawing views: *Front Top, Right, Isometric, Auxiliary, Detail, Section, Crop, Broken Section, Half Section, Revolved Section, Offset Section, Removed, Projected, Aligned Section and more.* Insert, modify, suppress, un-suppress and delete drawing views.

Work between multiple parts, configurations, and sheets to create the required drawing views. Insert annotations and dimensions. Apply a Design Table.

On the completion of this chapter, you will be able to:

- Create a single Sheet drawing.

- Add multiple sheets to a drawing.

- Work between part configurations in a Design Table.

- Insert Predefined views and Named views.

- Insert Auxiliary, Detail, and Section views.

- Insert Broken Section, Half Section, Offset Section and Aligned Section views.

- Add a configuration to a part.

- Insert an Area Hatch.

- Comprehend Orthographic projection: First angle and Third angle.

- Insert dimensions and Annotations.

- Utilize the following SolidWorks tools and commands: *Model View, Projected View, Auxiliary View, Section View, Aligned Section View, Standard 3 View, Broken-out Section View, Horizontal Break View, Vertical Break View, Crop View and Alternate Position View.*

Chapter Overview

A customer approaches the Engineering department to address the current Air Cylinder for a new product application. In the new application, there is an interference concern with the positions of the current Air Cylinder switches.

The engineering team proposes a new design that would re-position the switches in a 45° grooved track.

The design incorporates three individual parts: *TUBE*, *ROD* and *COVERPLATE*. The parts are mated to create the CYLINDER in the Air Cylinder assembly.

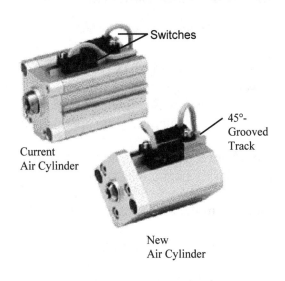

Mates create Geometric relationships between assembly components. As you add mates, you define the allowable directions of linear or rotational motion of the components. You can move a component within its degrees of freedom, visualizing the assembly's behavior.

The Marketing manager for the Air Cylinder product line reviews the new proposed assembly in SolidWorks.

The design team decides to incorporate the new design in its standard product line. The original designer that developed the current Air Cylinder was transferred to a different company division.

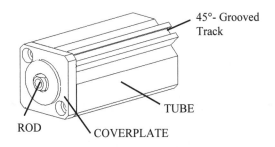

Courtesy of SMC Corporation of America
The feature dimensions for components utilized in this assembly have been modified for educational purposes.

You are part of the CYLINDER project development team. All design drawings must meet the company's drawing standards.

What is the next step? Create drawings for various internal departments, namely: production, purchasing, engineering, inspection and manufacturing.

First, review and discuss the features used to create the three parts. The three parts are:

- ROD

- TUBE

- COVERPLATE

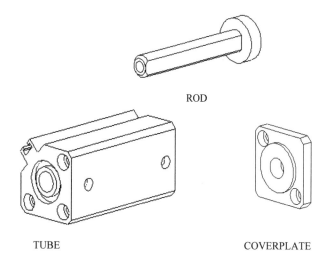

ROD

Second, create three drawings:

- ROD

- TUBE

- COVERPLATE

TUBE   COVERPLATE

A SolidWorks drawing document consists of a single sheet or multiple sheets. The ROD drawing consists of three sheets.

Use three separate drawing sheets to display the required information for the ROD drawing.

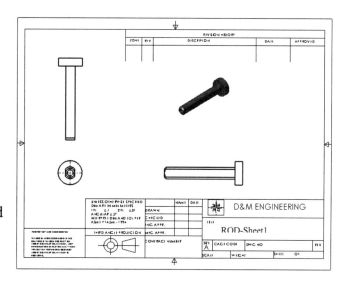

The first drawing sheet utilizes the Short Rod configuration. ROD-Sheet1 contains three Standard views, (Principle views) and an Isometric view.

The three Standard views are:

- Top view

- Front view

- Right view

Utilize the Predefined views in the Drawing template to create the first drawing sheet.

The second drawing sheet, ROD-Sheet2 contains the Long Rod configuration. Use a drawing sheet scale of 2:1 to display the Front detail view. Using a 2:1 scale, the Right view is too long for the drawing sheet.

Use a Vertical Break view to represent the Long Rod configuration with a constant cross section.

Add a Revolved Section view to represent the cross section of the ROD. Position the Revolved Section between the Vertical break.

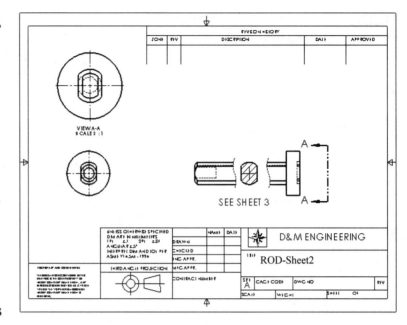

The third drawing sheet, ROD-Sheet3 contains the Long Rod configuration.

Create the Removed view from the Right view in Sheet2. The Removed view is at a 3:1 scale.

Combine two Detail views to construct the Isometric view.

When adding a sheet, if the system can't locate the Sheet format, add the Sheet format in File Location under System Options or Browse to the correct Sheet format location.

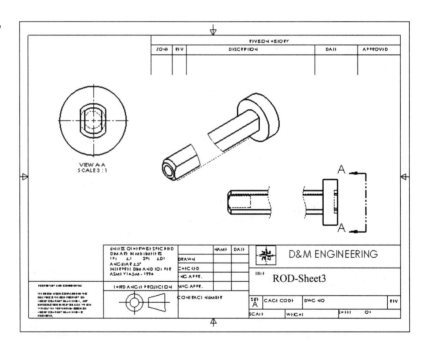

The TUBE drawing consists of one sheet with eight views. The TUBE drawing contains:

Three Standard views and:

1.) Projected Back view

2.) Section view

3.) Detail view

4.) Auxiliary view

5.) Half Section Isometric view

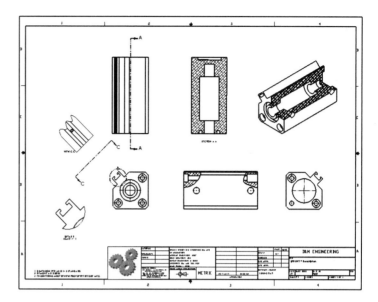

The COVERPLATE drawing consists of two drawing sheets. There are two part configurations:

• Without Nose Holes

• With Nose Holes

The first drawing sheet utilizes the Without Nose Holes configuration.

COVERPLATE-Sheet1 contains the following views: Front view, Right view, and an Offset Section view.

The second drawing sheet utilizes the With Nose Holes configuration.

COVERPLATE-Sheet2 contains the Front view and the Aligned Section view.

Use the DrawCompare tool to highlight the differences between two selected drawings. Click **Tools, Compare, DrawCompare**.

First, let's review the fundamentals of Orthographic projection before you create any drawings.

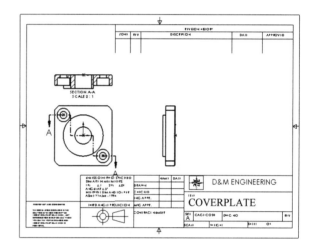

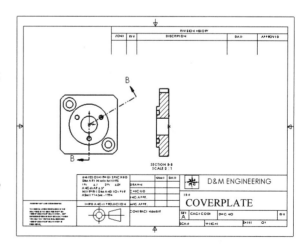

Fundamentals of Orthographic Projection

The three default ⊥ reference planes: Front, Top, and Right represent infinite 2D planes in 3D space. Planes have no thickness or mass.

Orthographic projection is the process of projecting views onto parallel planes with ⊥ projectors.

In Geometric tolerancing, the default reference planes are the Primary, Secondary, and Tertiary ⊥ datum planes. These are the planes used in manufacturing.

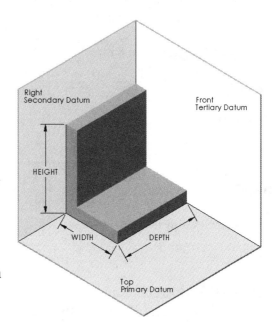

The Primary datum plane contacts the part at a minimum of three points. The Secondary datum plane contacts the part at a minimum of two points. The Tertiary datum plane contacts the part at a minimum of one point.

The part view orientation depends on the Sketch plane of the Base feature. Compare the Front Plane, Top Plane and Right Plane. Each Extruded Base (Boss-Extrude1) feature utilizes an L-shaped 2D profile.

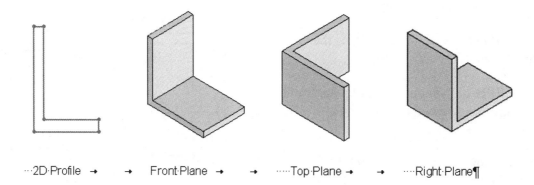

···2D·Profile →   →   Front·Plane →   →   ·····Top·Plane →   →   ····Right·Plane¶

The six principle views of Orthographic projection listed in the ASME Y14.3M standard are: *Top, Front, Right side, Bottom, Rear, & Left side.* SolidWorks Standard view names correspond to these Orthographic projection view names.

ASME Y14.3M Principle View Name:	SolidWorks Standard View:
Front	Front
Top	Top
Right side	Right
Bottom	Bottom
Rear	Back
Left side	Left

In the Third Angle Orthographic projection example below, the standard drawing views are: Front, Top, Right, and Isometric.

There are two Orthographic projection drawing systems.

- First Angle projection

- Third Angle projection

The systems are derived from positioning a 3D object in the first or third quadrant.

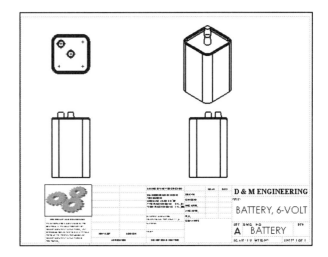

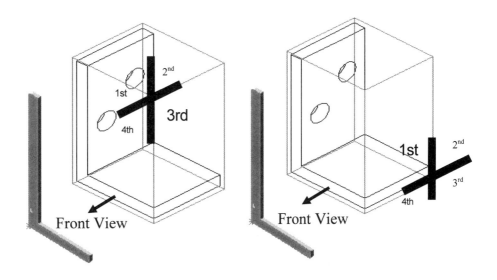

In Third Angle projection, the part is positioned in the third quadrant. The 2D projection planes are located between the viewer and the part.

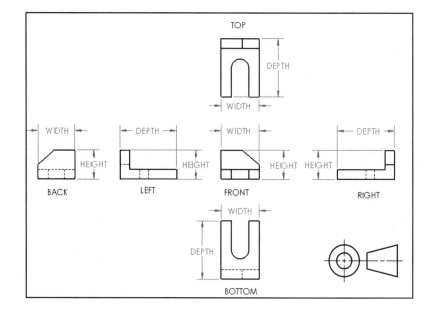

☀ SolidWorks uses BACK view vs. REAR view.

In First Angle projection, the part is positioned in the first quadrant. Views are projected onto the planes located behind the part. The projected views are placed on a drawing.

First Angle projection is primarily used in Europe and Asia. Third angle projection is primarily used in the U.S. and Canada, and is based on the ASME Y14.3M Multi and Sectional View Drawings standard. Designers should have knowledge and understanding of both systems.

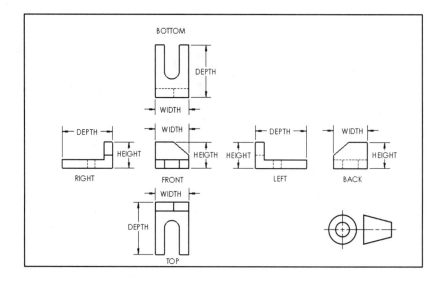

SolidWorks provides the user with numerous view options from the Standard Views, View, and the Heads-up View toolbar. The Heads-up View toolbar provides the following tools: **Zoom to Fit** 🔍, **Zoom to Area** 🔍, **Previous View** 🔗, **Rotate View** ♻, **3D Drawing View** 🔄, Display Style drop-down menu ▢▾, and **Hide/Show Items** 🔗▾.

🔆 **3D Drawing View** 🔄 provides the ability to manipulate the model view in 3D to help select a point, edge or face.

Review the ROD Part and Configurations

Configurations are variations of a part. The ROD part consists of two configurations:

- Short Rod configuration

- Long Rod configuration

The first ROD drawing sheet contains the Short Rod configuration. The second and third ROD drawing sheets contain the Long Rod configuration.

A drawing utilizes views, dimensioning, tolerances, notes, and other related design information from the part. When you modify a feature dimension in a part, the drawing automatically updates. The part and the drawing share the same file structure. Do not delete or move the part document.

🔆 If you did not create the A-ANSI-MM and C-ANSI MM Drawing templates in Chapter 5, utilize the Drawing templates and Sheet formats located in the folder DRAWING-W-SOLIDWORKS-2012\CHAPTER 5-TEMPLATES-SHEETFORMATS on the DVD. Add the folder to the File Locations section under System Options if needed.

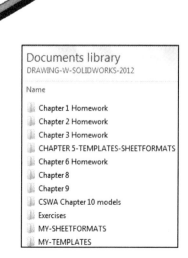

Documents library
DRAWING-W-SOLIDWORKS-2012

Name

- Chapter 1 Homework
- Chapter 2 Homework
- Chapter 3 Homework
- CHAPTER 5-TEMPLATES-SHEETFORMATS
- Chapter 6 Homework
- Chapter 8
- Chapter 9
- CSWA Chapter 10 models
- Exercises
- MY-SHEETFORMATS
- MY-TEMPLATES

☀ *When adding a Sheet to a drawing, if the system can't locate the Sheet format, add the Sheet format in File Location under System Options or Browse to the correct Sheet format location.*

The MY-SHEETFORMATS folder contains the Sheet formats. Note: In some network environments, System Options are valid for the current session of SolidWorks. Add the MY-TEMPLATES tab to the New SolidWorks Document dialog box. If the MY-TEMPLATES tab is not displayed, utilize the System Options, File Locations, Drawing Templates option described in Chapter 5.

Perform the following recommended tasks before starting the ROD drawing:

1. Open the part.

2. View the dimensions in each feature.

3. Move the feature dimensions off the profile.

4. View the configurations of the part.

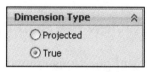

There are two dimension types displayed in a drawing:
- Projected - 2D dimensions.

- True - Accurate model dimensions.

☀ SolidWorks specifies Projected type dimensions for Standard and Custom Orthogonal views and True type dimensions for Isometric, Dimetric, and Trimetric views.

☀ Locate the parts required for this chapter in the DRAWING-W-SOLIDWORKS-2012 file folder on the DVD in the book.

☀ Feature dimensions in the part by default contain the Mark dimension to be imported into a drawing option. The Insert Model Items option places the Marked feature dimensions in the drawing.

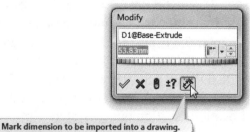

Mark dimension to be imported into a drawing.

🔅 Clarify model items in the part. Position the feature dimensions and annotations off the part before you insert the model items into the drawing.

🔅 Gaps need to be addressed between the model and the extension lines.

🔅 Clutter feature dimensions create clutter drawing views.

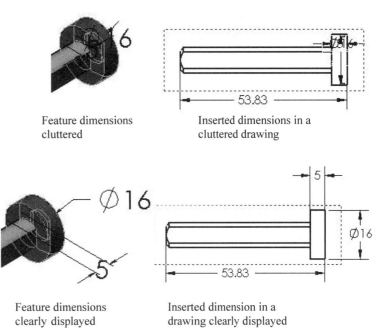

Feature dimensions cluttered

Inserted dimensions in a cluttered drawing

Feature dimensions clearly displayed

Inserted dimension in a drawing clearly displayed

Activity: Review the ROD Part and Configurations

Start a SolidWorks session.
1) Start a **SolidWorks 2012** session.

Open the ROD part.
2) Click **Open** from the Menu bar toolbar.

3) Select the **DRAWING-W-SOLIDWORKS-2012** folder. This folder should be located on your hard drive.

🔅 Copy all files and folders from the DVD in the book to your hard drive. Work directly from your hard drive.
4) Select **Part** for file type.

5) Double-click **ROD**. The Rod is displayed in the Graphics window.

6) Display the **Default** configuration.

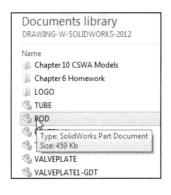

Review the ROD part features.

7) Place the **mouse pointer** over the blue Rollback bar at the bottom of the FeatureManager design tree. The mouse pointer displays a symbol of a hand.

8) Drag the **Rollback** bar upward below the Base-Extrude feature.

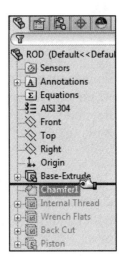

Display the Base-Extrude dimensions.

9) Click **Base-Extrude** from the FeatureManager.

10) Drag the **dimension text** off the model.

11) Click **OK** ✔ from the Dimension PropertyManager or click inside the Graphics window.

Display the Chamfer dimensions.

12) Drag the **Rollback** bar downward below Chamfer1.

13) Click **Chamfer1** from the FeatureManager.

14) Drag the **dimension text** off the model.

15) Click **OK** ✔ from the Dimension PropertyManager or click in the Graphics window.

Display the Internal Thread dimensions.

16) Drag the **Rollback** bar downward below the Internal Thread.

17) Click **Hidden Lines Visible** ⬛ from the Heads-up View toolbar to view the hidden feature.

18) Click **Internal Thread** from the FeatureManager.

19) Drag the **dimension text** off the model.

20) Click **OK** ✔ from the Dimension PropertyManager.

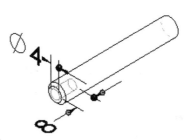

Display the Back Cut dimensions.

21) Drag the **Rollback** bar downward below Back Cut.

22) Click **Back Cut** from the FeatureManager.

23) Click **Wireframe** ⊞ from the Heads-up View toolbar.

24) Drag the **dimension text** off the model.

25) Click **OK** ✔ from the Dimension PropertyManager.

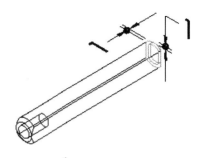

Display the Piston dimensions.
26) Drag the **Rollback** bar downward below Piston.

27) Click **Piston** from the FeatureManager.

28) Drag the **dimension text** off the model.

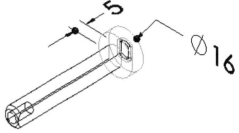

29) Click **OK** ✔ from the Dimension PropertyManager.

Display the ROD part configurations.
30) Click the **ConfigurationManager** tab at the top of the FeatureManager.

31) Double-click the **Long Rod** configuration. View the Long Rod configuration.

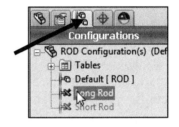

Fit the ROD to the Graphics window.
32) Press the **f** key.

33) Double-click the **Short Rod** configuration. View the Short Rod configuration.

🔆 Press the z key to Zoom out or the middle mouse button. Press the f key to fit the model to the Graphics window.

Return to the ROD FeatureManager.
34) Click the **FeatureManager** tab. The Short Rod is the current configuration.

Fit the ROD to the Graphics window.
35) Press the **f** key.

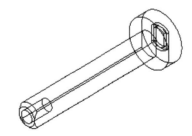

The Internal Thread utilizes an Extruded Cut feature sketched on the Front Plane. Internal Threads require specific notes. Use a Hole Callout in the Drawing to annotate the Internal Thread.

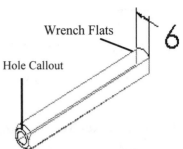

Locate the profile for the Wrench Flats on the Back Plane. The design engineer uses a Symmetric relation with the Right Plane. Add a centerline in the drawing to represent the Wrench Flat symmetry.

☼ Utilize symmetry in the part whenever possible. This conserves rebuild time. Use Symmetric relations in the sketch. Use Mirror All and the Mirror Feature in the part. Symmetric dimension schemes and relations defined in the part require added dimensions in the drawing.

☼ Create fully defined sketches. A minus sign (-) displayed in the FeatureManager indicates an under defined Sketch. Sketch1 through Sketch5 are fully defined. Fully defined sketches provide marked dimensions, address faster rebuild times, and create fewer configuration problems.

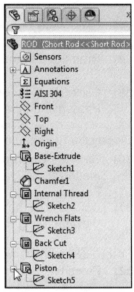

ROD Drawing: Sheet1-Short Rod Configuration

The ROD drawing contains three drawing sheets. Sheet1 contains the Short Rod configuration, three Standard views, (Principle views) and an Isometric view. Insert Standard views and the Isometric view as Predefined views created in the A-ANSI-MM drawing template. The FeatureManager displays the Drawing view names. Predefined views, Named Model views, and Projected views are given a sequential numbered drawing view name.

☼ Rename drawing views for clarity. Click inside the view entry in the FeatureManager. Enter the new name.

Detail views and Section views are labeled with their view name followed by a letter or number. Example: Section view A-A. Reposition the drawing views. Drag the drawing view by its green view boundary or a drawing entity inside the view.

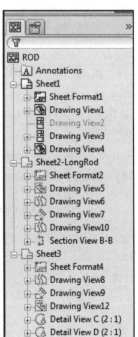

Provide approximately 1in. - 2in., (25mm - 50mm) between each view for dimension placement. The Right and Top views align to the Front view position. The Isometric view is free to move and contains no alignment. The Sheet, View, Edge, and Component contain specific properties. Select the right mouse button on an entity to review the Properties.

To nudge a view, select the view boundary. Press an arrow key to move a view by a set increment. Utilize the System Option, Drawings, Keyboard movement increment, to set the nudge value.

Activity: ROD Drawing-Sheet1

Note: If you did not create the A-ANSI-MM and C-ANSI MM drawing templates in Chapter 5, utilize the Drawing templates and Sheet formats located in the folder DRAWING-W-SOLIDWORKS-2012\CHAPTER 5-TEMPLATES-SHEETFORMATS on the DVD. If needed, add the folder to the File Locations section under System Options. Work directly from your hard drive, not the DVD.

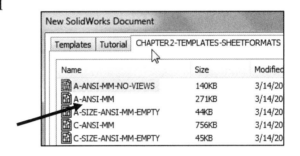

Select the A-ANSI-MM Drawing Template.

36) Click **New** ⬚ from the Menu bar toolbar.

37) Click the **MY-TEMPLATES** tab. Double-click **A-ANSI-MM**.

38) Click **Cancel** from the Model View PropertyManager if needed.

Save the empty drawing.

39) Click **Save As** from the Consolidated Menu bar toolbar.

40) Select **DRAWING-W-SOLIDWORKS-2012** for Save in.

41) Enter **ROD** for File name. Enter **ROD DRAWING** for Description.

42) Click **Save**. The ROD drawing FeatureManager is displayed.

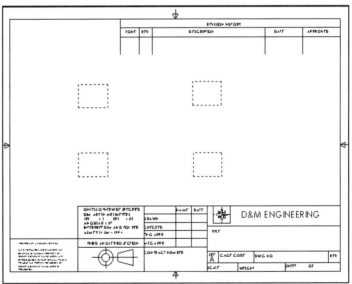

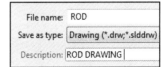

Display the Layer toolbar.
43) Click **View**, **Toolbars**, **Layer** from the Menu bar menu.

44) Select **None** for Layer Properties.

Insert the Predefined Views.
45) Click **Window**, **Tile Horizontal**
 Tile Horizontally from the Menu bar menu. The ROD-Sheet1 drawing and ROD part are displayed.

46) Click and drag the **ROD** ROD (Short Rod) icon from the Part FeatureManager into the drawing Graphics window.

47) **Maximize** the ROD drawing.

If needed; de-activated the Origins.
48) Click **View**, uncheck **Origins** from the Menu bar menu.

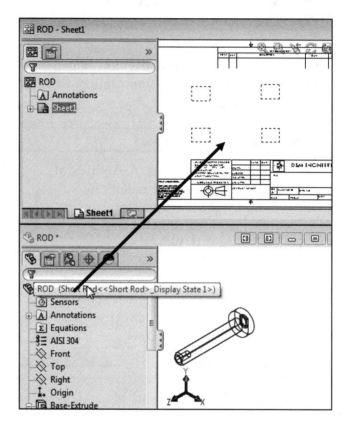

A Parent view is an existing view referenced by other views. The Front view is the Parent view. The Right and Top views are Projected from the Front view. The Right and Top views are called Child views. Child views move relative to Parent views. Retain exact positions between the views, press Shift while dragging the views.

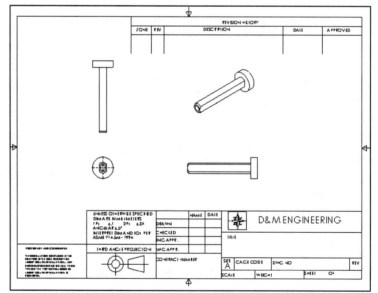

Move the drawing views.

49) Click inside the view boundary of **Drawing View4**, (Isometric view). The mouse pointer displays the Drawing View icon. The view boundary is displayed.

50) Position the **mouse pointer** on the edge of the view until the Drawing Move View icon is displayed.

51) Click and drag the **Isometric** view in an upward direction.

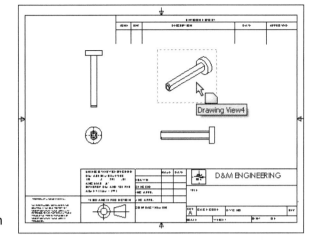

Display the Sheet properties.

52) Position the **mouse pointer** in the middle of the Sheet. The mouse pointer displays the Sheet icon.

53) Right-click in the **sheet area**, (large white space).

54) Click **Properties**. Review the Properties of the Sheet.

55) Click **OK** from the Sheet Properties dialog box.

Display the view properties.

56) Position the **mouse pointer** inside the Top view area. The mouse pointer displays the Drawing View icon.

57) Click inside the **view area**. The view boundary turns blue.

Display the edge and component properties.

58) Locate the mouse pointer on the **vertical line** in the Top view as illustrated. The vertical line turns blue. The mouse pointer displays an Edge icon, the Edge properties and the Component properties.

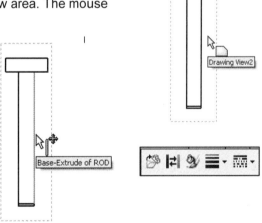

Display the Isometric view shaded.

59) Click inside the **Isometric view** boundary.

60) Click **Shaded With Edges** from the Drawing View4 PropertyManager.

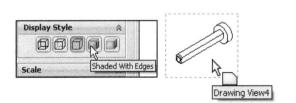

Hide the Top view.

61) Right-click inside the **Top** view boundary.

62) Click the **More arrow** ˅ from the Pop-up menu.

63) Click **Hide**.

64) Click **OK** ✅ from the Drawing View2 PropertyManager.

Save the ROD drawing.

65) Click **Save** 💾.

☀ The FeatureManager icons indicate the visible and hidden views. Modify the view state quickly with the FeatureManager.

The ▦ Drawing View2 icon displays hidden views. The 🞕 Drawing View1 icon displays visible Model views. The 🞕 Drawing View3 icon displays visible Projected views. Utilize Show to display a hidden view. Right-click the view name in the FeatureManager. Select the Show option.

View Boundary Properties and Lock View Options

The view boundary displays different colors to indicate various states as follows:

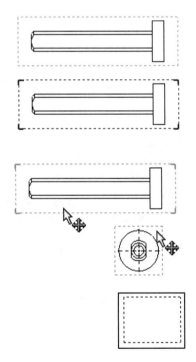

- Dotted blue line indicates the view is selected.

- Dotted pink line with solid corners indicates the view is locked and cannot move until unlocked.

- Dotted blue line with solid corners indicates the view is selected and locked.

- Dotted red line indicates dynamic highlighting.

- Dotted black line indicates an Empty view or Predefined view.

☀ Model geometry and sketch geometry determine the size of the view boundary. Annotations and dimensions do not affect view boundary size. Sketch entities in the drawing are children of the view closest to the initial sketch point.

As a drawing becomes populated with views, utilize the Lock options to control annotation and sketch geometry into the view or the sheet. The Lock View Position, Lock View Focus, and the Lock Sheet Focus options provide the following:

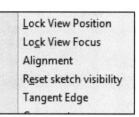

- **Lock View Position**: Secures the view at its current position in the sheet. Right-click in the drawing view to Lock View Position. To unlock a view position, right-click and select Unlock View Position.
- **Lock View Focus**: Adds sketch entities and annotations to the selected locked view. Double-click the view to activate Lock View Focus. To unlock a view, right-click and select Unlock View Focus or double click outside the view boundary.
- **Lock Sheet Focus**: Adds sketch entities and annotations to the selected sheet. Double-click the sheet to activate Lock Sheet Focus. To unlock a sheet, right-click and select Unlock Sheet Focus or double click inside the sheet boundary.

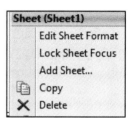

ROD Drawing: Sheet2 - Long Rod Configuration

The second sheet of the ROD drawing, ROD-Sheet2 utilizes the Long Rod configuration.

Add ROD-Sheet2. Copy the Front view from Sheet1 to Sheet2. Select the Long Rod configuration.

Insert a Projected Right view. Use a Sheet scale of 2:1 to display the Front details.

The Right view is too long for the sheet using the scale of 2:1. Insert a Broken (or interrupted) view with a vertical break in the Right view. The Broken view represents the Long Rod with a constant cross section. Dimensions associated with the Broken view reflect the actual model values.

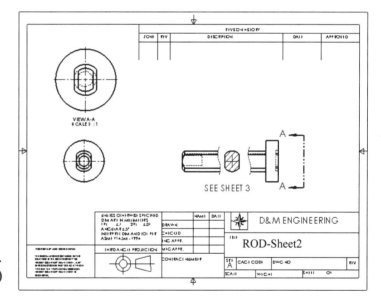

The Add Sheet tab is located at the bottom of the Graphics window.

Activity: ROD Drawing-Sheet2 Projected View and Break View

Add Sheet2 to the ROD drawing.

66) Click the **Add Sheet** tab located at the bottom of the Graphics window. Sheet2 is displayed. Note: At this time, there is a bug with SP1.0. If needed, Browse and apply the correct Sheet format from the MY-SHEETFORMATS folder.

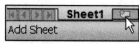

67) Rename **Sheet2** to **Sheet2-LongRod**.

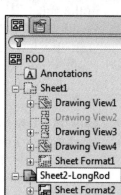

☼ The Custom a-format is the default Sheet format. Sheet2-LongRod is displayed.

Copy the Front view from Sheet1 to Sheet2.

68) Click the **Sheet1** tab. Click inside **Drawing View1**, (Front) view.

Copy the view.

69) Click **Edit**, **Copy** from the Menu bar menu

70) Click the **Sheet2-LongRod** tab.

71) Click a view **position** in the lower left corner.

Paste the view.

72) Click **Edit**, **Paste** from the Menu bar menu. Drawing View5 is displayed.

Modify the view Scale.

73) Click inside the **Drawing View5** view boundary. The Drawing View5 PropertyManager is displayed.

74) Check the **Use custom scale** box.

75) Select **User Defined**.

76) Enter **2:1**. Click **OK** ✓ from the Drawing View5 PropertyManager.

Modify the ROD configuration.

77) Right-click **Properties** in the Drawing View5 view boundary.

78) Select **Long Rod** from the Use Named Configuration drop-down menu. Click **OK**.

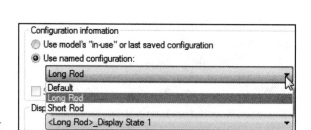

Insert a Projected view.

79) Click **Projected View** ⊞ from the View Layout toolbar.

80) Click a **position** to the right of the Front view. DrawingView6 is displayed.

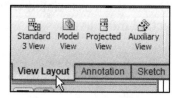

Modify the Scale to fit the drawing.
81) Click inside the **Drawing View6** boundary.

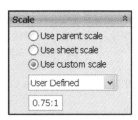

82) Check the **Use custom scale** box.

83) Select **User Defined**.

84) Enter **.75**:**1**.

85) Click **OK** ✓ from Drawing View6 PropertyManager.

86) Drag **Drawing View6** in Sheet2.

Insert a Vertical Zig Zag Break in the Right view.
87) Click inside the **Drawing View6** boundary.

88) Click **Break** 〽 from the View Layout toolbar. The Broken View PropertyManager is displayed. Vertical is the default setting. Gap equals 10mms.

89) Click a **position** as illustrated to create the left vertical break line towards the Internal Thread.

Left vertical break line   Right vertical break line

90) Click a **position** as illustrated to create the right vertical break line towards the Piston.

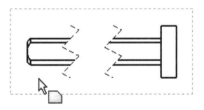

91) Click **OK** ✓ from the Broken View PropertyManager.

92) Right-click inside the **Drawing View6** boundary.

93) Click **Un-Break View**. View the results.

94) Right-click inside the **Drawing View6** boundary.

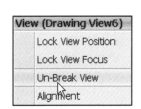

95) Click **Break View**.

96) Click inside the **Drawing View6** boundary.

97) Check the **Use parent scale** box.

Modify the Break line style.

98) Click on the left **Break line**. The Broken View PropertyManager is displayed.

99) Select **Curve Cut** to display the curved break line.

100) Enter **20mm** for Gap.

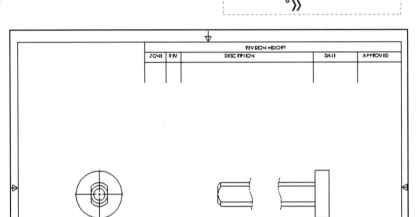

101) Click **OK** ✔ from the Broken View PropertyManager.

Save the ROD drawing.

102) **Rebuild** the drawing.

103) Click **Save** 💾 .

💡 Modify the Break Lines display. Right-click on the Break line. Select: *Straight Cut, Curve Cut, Zig Zag Cut,* or *Small Zig Zag Cut*.

💡 Utilize Options, Document Properties, Line Font to modify the Break Lines Font for the drawing document.

💡 The Line Format toolbar controls: *Layer Properties, Line Color, Line Thickness, Line Style, Hide / Show Edges, Color Display Mode* for selected entities.

💡 When you right-click a component in an assembly drawing, you can open either the part or assembly.

ROD Drawing: Sheet3 - Long Rod Configuration

Add ROD-Sheet3. Sheet3
utilizes a Removed view.
Utilize a Removed view
when additional space is
required to display the view.

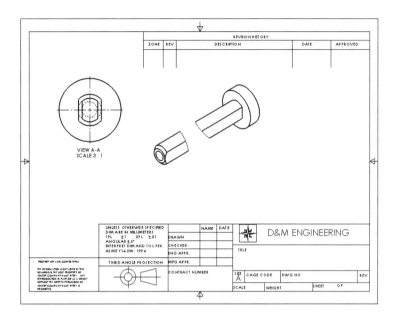

There is no Removed view
tool. Use an Auxiliary view
off the right edge of the
Broken view to create a
Removed view.

Copy the Removed view
from ROD-Sheet2 to ROD-
Sheet3.

Utilize the Auxiliary view
A-A arrows to indicate that
the view is not projected
from the Broken view.

Use upper case letters, Example: View A-A to associate the viewing plane to the
Removed view. Indicate the sheet name below the view name when a Removed view
does not fit on the same sheet.

🔅 Combine Drawings tools and work outside the sheet boundary to produce the
Removed view, Revolved Section view, and Broken Isometric view.

🔅 Click the View Palette 🖳 icon in the Task Pane.
Click the drop-down arrow from the View Palette menu
to view an active saved model or click the Browse button
to locate a model. Click and drag the desired view/views
into the active drawing Sheet.

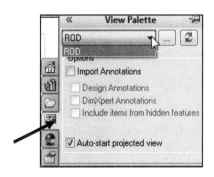

🔅 *When adding a Sheet to a drawing, if the system
can't locate the Sheet format, add the Sheet format in
File Location under System Options or Browse to the
correct Sheet format location.*

Activity: ROD Drawing - Sheet3 Removed View

Insert a Removed view.
104) Click inside the **Right view** boundary.

105) Click **Auxiliary view**  from the View Layout toolbar. The Auxiliary View PropertyManager is displayed.

106) Click the **right vertical edge** of the Right view as illustrated. The Auxiliary view and arrows are displayed.

107) Hold the **Ctrl** key down.

108) Click a **position** above the Front view.

109) Release the **Ctrl** key.

Modify the Scale of the Top view.
110) Click **Use custom scale**.

111) Select **User Defined**.

112) Enter **3:1**. Click **OK** 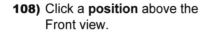 from the Drawing View 7 PropertyManager.

113) Drag the **VIEW A-A, SCALE 3:1** text below the Top view.

114) **Rebuild** the drawing.

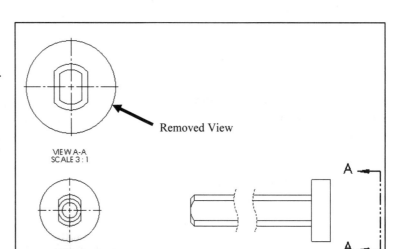

VIEW A-A
SCALE 3 : 1

Removed View

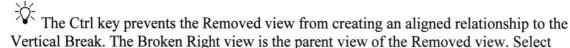

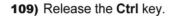 The Ctrl key prevents the Removed view from creating an aligned relationship to the Vertical Break. The Broken Right view is the parent view of the Removed view. Select both views to copy the Removed view to Sheet3.

Add Sheet3 to the ROD drawing.
115) Click the **Add Sheet** tab. The third Sheet is displayed. Note: At this time, there is a bug with SP1.0. If needed, Browse and apply the correct Sheet format from the MY-SHEETFORMATS folder.

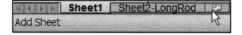

116) **Save** the drawing.

Copy the Removed view from Sheet2 to Sheet3.

117) Click the **Sheet2-LongRod** tab.

118) Hold the **Ctrl** key down.

119) Click the **Broken Right** view.

120) Click the **Removed View A-A**. The Multiple Views PropertyManager is displayed.

121) Release the **Ctrl** key. Press **Ctrl + C**. Click **Yes**.

Paste the views.

122) Click the **Sheet3** tab. Click a **position** on the left top side of Sheet3.

123) Press **Ctrl + V**. The two views are pasted on Sheet3.

124) Move the views in Sheet3 as illustrated. Zoom out. Press the **z** key approximately 2 times.

125) Drag the **Break Right view** off Sheet3 to the right of the Title block as illustrated.

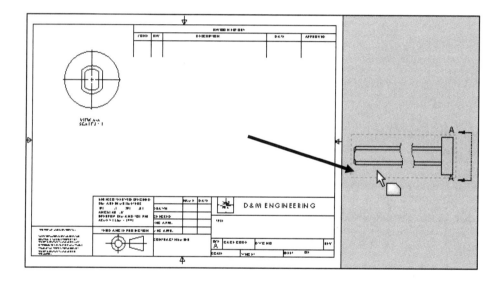

Modify Annotations.

126) Click the **VIEW A-A** text.

127) Right-click **Edit Text in Window**.

128) Enter **SEE SHEET2** on the third line.

129) Click **OK**.

130) Click **inside** Sheet3 to deselect.

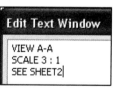

Move the Removed view on Sheet2.

131) Click the **Sheet2-LongRod** tab.

132) Click and drag the **Removed view** boundary to the left of Sheet2 as illustrated.

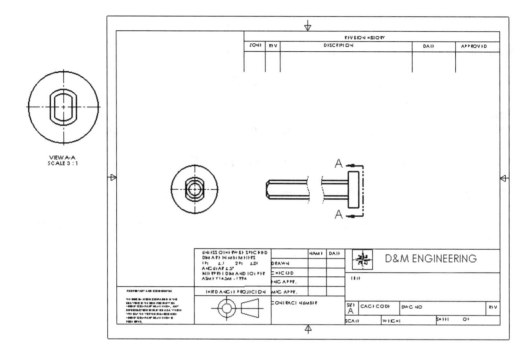

Add a Note.

133) Click the **Annotation** tab from the CommandManager.

134) Click **Note** $\mathbf{A}$ from the Annotation toolbar.

135) Click a **position** below the View A-A arrows.

136) Enter **SEE SHEET 3**.

137) Click **OK** ✅ from the Note PropertyManager.

138) Drag the **View A-A** arrows to the right of the view.

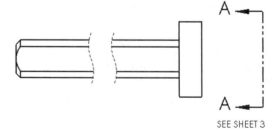

SEE SHEET 3

The Parent view is the original view utilized to create the Child views: *Auxiliary, Section* and *Detail*. Position the Child views on the same drawing sheet as the Parent view. If no space exists on the current sheet, move the Child view to a new Sheet. Label the Child view with the Parent view Sheet number. Utilize the Note tool from the Annotate toolbar, "See Sheet X" where X is the number of the Parent sheet.

Sheets larger than B size contain Zone letters and numbers inside their margins. Place the Zone location below the "SEE SHEET #" text for drawing sizes larger than B. Letters and numbers in the sheet boundary create a grid indicating the exact zone location.

Example: SEE SHEET 2
ZONE A2

ROD Drawing - Revolved Section

A Revolved Section represents the cross section of the Rod. There is no Revolved Section tool. Copy the Broken Right view. Utilize a Section view to create the Revolved Section between the two Break lines. Align the Revolved Section horizontally to the Right view.

Activity: ROD Drawing-Revolved Section

Increase the default break line gap from 10mm to 25mm.

139) Click **Options**, **Document Properties** tab from the Menu bar toolbar.

140) Click the **Detailing** folder under Document Properties.

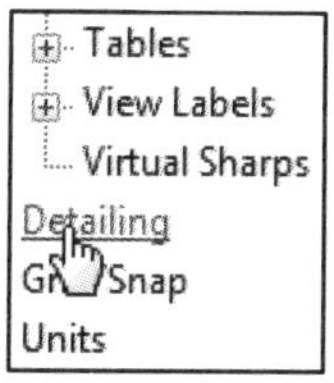

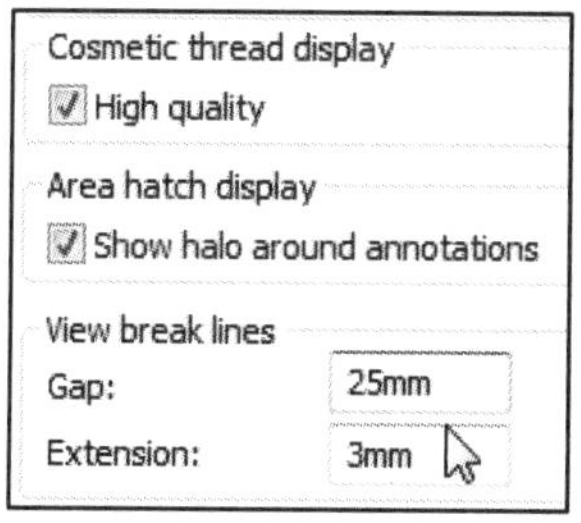

141) Enter **25** in the View break lines Gap box.

142) Click **OK** from the Document Properties - Detailing dialog box.

143) **Rebuild** the drawing.

144) Click **Save**.

Zoom in on the Graphics window.

145) Press the **z** key until Sheet2 is approximately ½ its original size.

Copy and Paste the Vertical Break Right view.

146) Click inside the **Vertical Break** view boundary; Drawing View6.

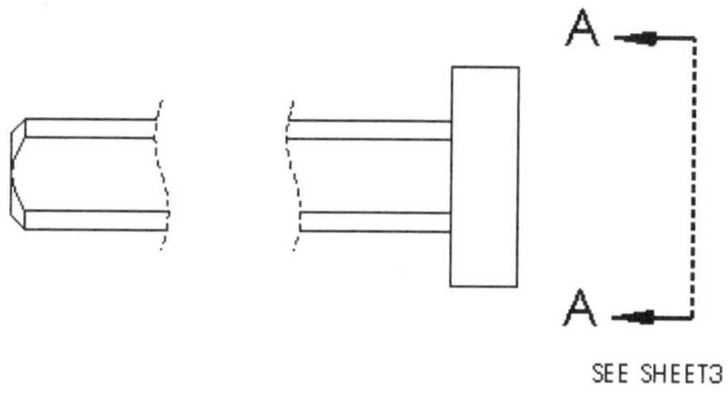

147) Click **Ctrl + C**.

148) Click a **position** above the Right view.

149) Click **Ctrl + V**.

150) Drag the copied **view** off the sheet boundary to the right of the Vertical Break Right view.

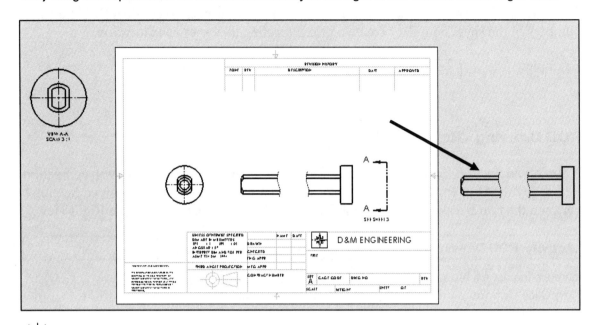

💡 To copy a view outside the sheet boundary, select a view to copy. Click a position inside the sheet boundary. Then drag the new view off the sheet boundary.

Align the views.

151) Right-click inside the **copied Right view**.

152) Click **Alignment**.

153) Click **Align Horizontal by Origin**. The mouse pointer displays the Alignment

icon 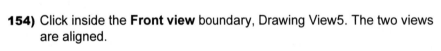.

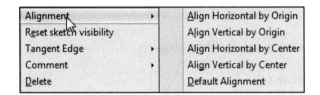

Alignment ▶	Align Horizontal by Origin
Reset sketch visibility	Align Vertical by Origin
Tangent Edge ▶	Align Horizontal by Center
Comment ▶	Align Vertical by Center
Delete	Default Alignment

154) Click inside the **Front view** boundary, Drawing View5. The two views are aligned.

Create a Revolved Section with a Section view.

155) Click inside the copied **Right view** boundary to the right of the sheet boundary.

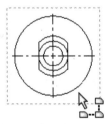

156) Click the **View Layout** tab from the CommandManager.

157) Click **Section View** ⤢ from the View Layout toolbar. The Section View PropertyManager is displayed. The Line Sketch tool is displayed

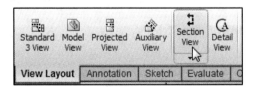

158) Sketch a **vertical line** to the left of the copied Vertical Break and to the right of the Internal Thread feature. **Flip** the arrows to the left if required.

159) Place the **cross section** between the Vertical Break Lines.

Set the Scale.
160) Check the **Use custom scale** box.

161) Select **User Defined** from the drop-down menu.

162) Enter **.75:1**.

163) Click **OK** ✔ from the Section View PropertyManager. Note: If you clicked a position inside of the view boundary of Drawing View6 on the previous page, the text: SEE SHEET3 would be displayed.

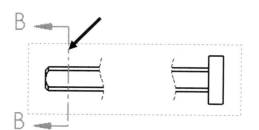

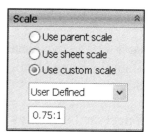

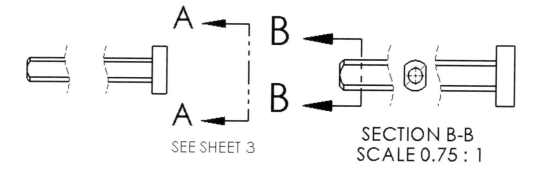

SEE SHEET 3

SECTION B-B
SCALE 0.75 : 1

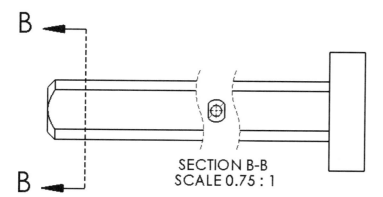

SECTION B-B
SCALE 0.75 : 1

SEE SHEET3

Save the ROD drawing.

164) Click **Save** 🖫 .

ROD Drawing-Broken Isometric View

The Horizontal Break and Vertical Break options work only in 2D views. A Broken Isometric view utilizes two Detail views. Create a front Detail view and then a back Detail view.

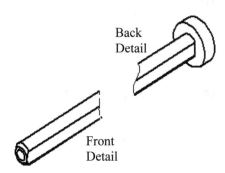

Back Detail

Front Detail

Position the two Detail views. Utilize a Sketch Line to align the Front Detail and the Back Detail. Create the Sketch Line on the Construction Drawing layer.

Select the Detail views and utilize the Default Alignment option to move both views together. Create layers in a drawing document for construction geometry and dimensions.

Sketched geometry in the drawing links to the current view. Select the view and the view boundary turns blue. Sketch the geometry and the geometry moves with the view. Specify line color, thickness and line style. Add New entities to the active layer. Turn layers on/off to simplify drawings. Shut layers off when not in use.

Activity: ROD Drawing-Broken Isometric View

Create a Broken Isometric view.
165) Click the **SHEET3** tab. **Zoom out** on the Sheet boundary.

Insert an Isometric view.
166) Click **Model View** 🖼 from the View Layout toolbar. ROD is an active part document.

167) Click **Next** ➡. *Isometric is selected by default.

168) Click a **position** above the Right view, off the ROD-Sheet3 boundary. The Drawing View12 PropertyManager is displayed.

169) Right-click inside the **Drawing View12** view boundary.

170) Click **Properties**.

171) Select the **Long Rod** configuration.

172) Click **OK**. Click **OK** ✔ from the Drawing View12 PropertyManager.

173) Click and drag the **views** as illustrated.

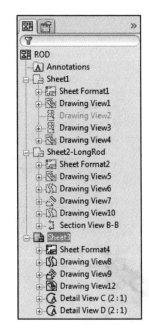

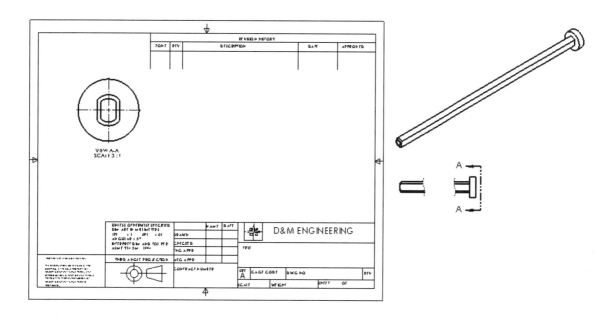

Create a Detail C view.

174) Zoom in on the Internal Thread.

175) Click the **Sketch** tab from the CommandManager.

176) Click **Spline** 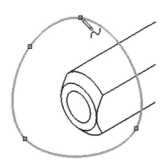 from the Sketch toolbar.

177) Sketch a **closed Spline** around the Internal Thread.

178) Click **OK** from the Spline PropertyManager.

179) Click **Detail View** from the View Layout toolbar. The Detail View PropertyManager is displayed.

180) Enter **2:1** for view scale.

181) Click a **position** to the right of the Removed view in the Sheet boundary as illustrated.

182) Click **OK** from the Detail View C PropertyManager.

Create Detail D.

183) Click the **Sketch** tab from the CommandManager.

184) Click **Spline** from the Sketch toolbar.

185) Sketch a **closed Spline** around the Piston end as illustrated.

DETAIL C
SCALE 2 : 1

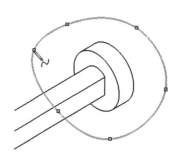

186) Click **OK** ✔ from the Spline PropertyManager.

187) Click **Detail View** Ⓐ from the View Layout toolbar. The Detail View PropertyManager is displayed.

188) Enter **2:1** for view scale.

189) Click a **position** in Sheet3 as illustrated.

190) Click **OK** ✔ from the Detail View PropertyManager. View the results.

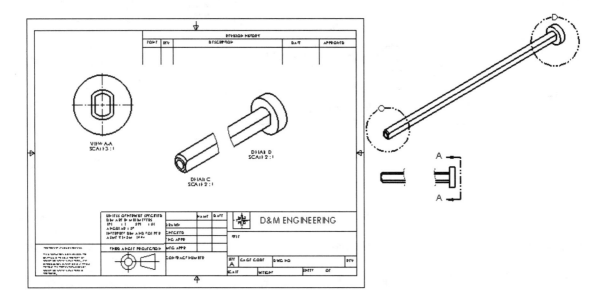

Do not delete the Parent views outside the Sheet boundary. The Detail C and Detail D text are dependent on the Isometric view. Sketching Splines for Broken Isometric views requires practice. Sketch the Spline back portion in Detail C similar to the Spline front portion in Detail D. Right-click on the Detail Circle. Select Edit Sketch to return to the original Spline.

Display the Layer toolbar.
191) Click **View**, **Toolbars**, **Layer** from the Menu bar menu.

Display the Layers dialog box.
192) Click the **Layer Properties** 🗇 icon.

Create a new layer.
193) Click the **New** button.

194) Enter **Construction** for Name.

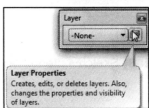

195) Enter **Construction View Lines** for Description. Note: The layer is on when the Light Bulb 💡 is yellow.

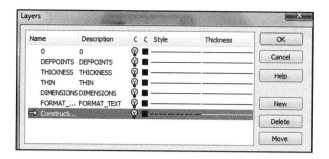

196) Select **Red** for Color.

197) Select **Dashed** for Style.

198) Click **OK** from the Layers dialog box.

Sketch a line.
199) Click inside the **Detail C** view boundary.

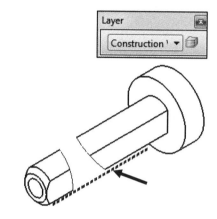

200) Click **Line** ╲ from the Sketch toolbar.

201) Sketch a **line parallel** to the lower profile line on Detail C as illustrated.

Move the Detail D view.
202) Drag **Detail D** until the bottom edge is approximately aligned with the red Line.

Lock View position.
203) Click inside the **Detail C** view boundary.

204) Hold the **Ctrl** key down.

205) Click inside the **Detail D** view boundary.

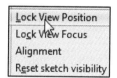

206) Release the **Ctrl** key.

207) Right-click **Lock View Position**.

Hide the red line.
208) Click the **Layer Properties** 🖾 icon.

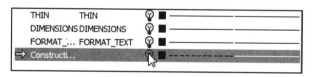

209) Click the **Light Bulb** 💡 to turn off the Construction layer.

210) Click **OK** from the Layers dialog box.

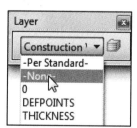

Return to the default layer.
211) Select **None** from the Layer toolbar.

Fit the drawing to the Graphics window.
212) Press the **f** key.

Save the ROD drawing.
213) Rebuild the drawing.

214) Click **Save** 💾 .

Close all parts and drawings.
215) Click **Windows**, **Close All** from the Menu bar menu.

🔍 More Information

Additional details on Drawing Views, Hide, Add Sheet, Horizontal Break, Vertical Break, Line Font, Dimension Type, Align, Spline, Note, and Layers are available in SolidWorks Help Topics.

 **Review**

The ROD drawing consisted of three sheets. Sheet1 contained the Front, Top, Right, and Isometric views for the Short Rod configuration. The Drawing template in Project 2 stored the Predefined views.

Sheet2 contained a copied Front view and a Vertical Break Right view. The views utilized the Long Rod configuration. The Revolved Section utilized the Section view positioned outside the sheet boundary.

Sheet3 contained a Removed view and a Broken Isometric view. The Removed view utilized an Auxiliary view on Sheet2. The Broken Isometric view was created with two Detail views.

Review the TUBE Part

Perform the following recommended tasks before starting the TUBE drawing:

- Verify the TUBE part

- View and move feature dimensions

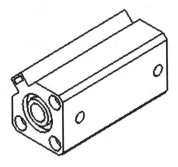

Position feature dimensions off the part before creating the drawing. Dimension schemes defined in the part require changes in the drawing. Design engineers use different dimensioning schemes than those required by manufacturing engineers.

Example 1: The design engineer references the depth dimensions 27.75mm and 32.75mm to the Front Plane for the Tube Extrusion feature. The engineer's analysis calculations also reference the Front Plane.

The manufacturing engineer requires an overall depth of 60.50mm (27.75mm + 32.75mm) referenced from the front face. Create the overall depth dimension of 60.50mm for a drawing.

Example 2: The design engineer references the depth dimensions to the Front Plane for the Stoke Chamber (Depth1 = 17.50mm and Depth2 = 17.50mm).

The manufacturing engineering requires an overall depth of 35.00mm.

Example 3: An Extruded Cut feature creates the Stroke Chamber as an internal feature. Display the Stroke Chamber dimensions in the Section view of the drawing. Reference added dimensions from the front face in the Section view.

Activity: Review the TUBE Part

Review the TUBE part.

216) Click **Open** ⬚ from the Menu bar toolbar.

217) Double-click **TUBE** from the DRAWING-W-SOLIDWORKS-2012 folder. The TUBE FeatureManager is displayed.

Execute various display modes.

218) Click **Hidden Line Visible** ⬚ from the Heads-up View toolbar. Internal features are displayed.

219) Click **Hidden Lines Removed** ⬚ from the Heads-up View toolbar. Internal features are hidden.

Review the TUBE part features.

220) Place the **mouse pointer** over the blue Rollback bar at the bottom of the FeatureManager design tree.

221) Drag the **Rollback** bar upward to below the tube extrusion feature.

222) Click **tube extrusion** from the FeatureManager.

223) Drag the **dimension text** off the model.

224) If needed, flip the **dimension arrows** to view the text.

225) Click **OK** ✔ from the Dimension PropertyManager.

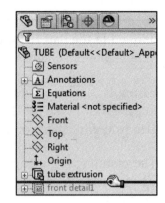

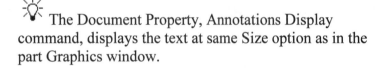

💡 The Document Property, Annotations Display command, displays the text at same Size option as in the part Graphics window.

Display Front Detail feature dimensions.

226) Drag the **Rollback** bar downward below the front detail1 feature.

227) Click on **front detail1**.

228) Drag the **dimension text** off of the model. The front detail1 is an Extruded Cut feature. A 17mm circle is sketched Coincident to the Origin on the front face.

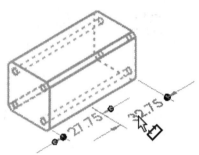

View the feature dimensions.

229) Drag the **Rollback** bar downward below the stroke chamber feature.

230) Click **Hidden Line Visible** ⬚ from the Heads-up View toolbar.

231) Click **stroke chamber** from the FeatureManager.

232) Drag the **dimension text** off the model.

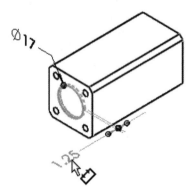

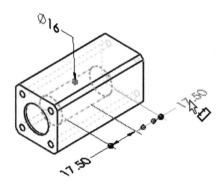

Display the Nose feature dimensions.
233) Drag the **Rollback** bar downward below the nose feature.

234) Click the **nose** feature from the FeatureManager. The Nose feature requires a Detail view.

Display the Bore feature dimensions.
235) Drag the **Rollback** bar downward below the bore feature.

236) Click the **bore** feature from the FeatureManager. The Cut requires a Section view. The circular sketch profile is extruded on both sides of the front plane with two different Depth options.

237) Drag the **dimension text** off the model.

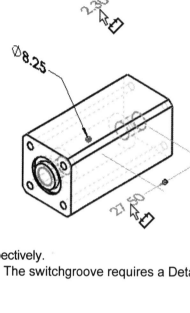

Display the Port feature dimensions.
238) Drag the **Rollback** bar downward below the ports feature.

239) Click the **ports** feature from the FeatureManager.

240) Drag the **dimension text** off the model.

Display the 45 AngleCut, switchgroove, and the M2.0 hole respectively.
241) Drag the **Rollback bar** downward under switchgroove. The switchgroove requires a Detail view. The M2.0 hole requires an Auxiliary view.

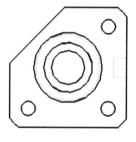

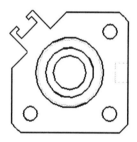
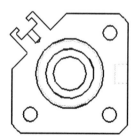

45 AngleCut   SwitchGroove   M2.0 hole

Display the Cbore Front and Cbore Rear
242) Right-click on the **switchgroove** feature.

243) Click **Roll to End**. The Rollback bar is positioned at the end of the FeatureManager.

244) Click the **Cbore Front** feature from the FeatureManager. The feature is displayed in blue in the Graphics window.

245) Rotate the part to view the Rear Detail and Cbore Rear features. The Rear Detail and Cbore Rear requires a Back Projected view in the drawing.

246) Click **Isometric** view from the Heads-up View toolbar.

247) Click **OK** from the Dimension PropertyManager.

TUBE Drawing

The TUBE drawing consists of a single drawing sheet with eight views. The eight views are: three Standard views, a Projected Back view, Section view, Detail view, Auxiliary view, and a Half Section Isometric (Cut away) view.

The Half Section Isometric view requires two part configurations named: *Entire Part* and *Section Cutaway*.

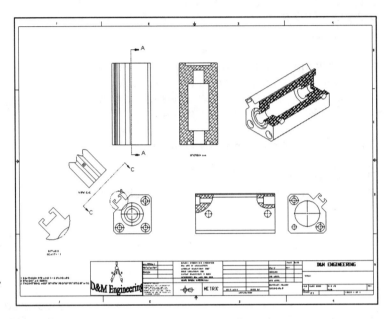

Utilize an A-ANSI-MM Drawing template. Insert the four Predefined views: Front, Top, Right, and Isometric. There is not enough space on an A-size drawing. You have two options: enlarge the sheet size or move additional views to multiple sheets. How do you increase the sheet size? Utilize Sheet Properties.

The Sheet Properties, Size option modifies an A-size drawing to a C-size drawing. Utilize the Sheet format you created in Chapter 5.

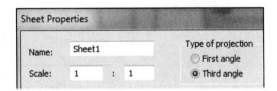

Projected views display the part or assembly by projecting an Orthographic view using the First angle or Third angle projection. Recall that Third angle projection is set in Sheet Properties in the Drawing template. Insert a Project view to create the Back view. Provide approximately 1in. - 2in., (25mm - 50mm) between views.

Activity: TUBE Drawing

Create the TUBE drawing.

248) Click **New** ☐ from the Menu bar toolbar.

249) Click the **MY-TEMPLATES** tab.

250) Double-click **A-ANSI-MM** from the SolidWorks Document dialog box.

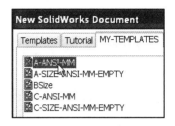

Save the drawing.

251) Click **Save As** from the Consolidated Menu bar toolbar.

252) Select **DRAWING-W-SOLIDWORKS-2012** for Save in folder.

253) Enter **TUBE** for File name.

254) Enter **TUBE DRAWING** for Description.

255) Click **Save**.

Insert the Predefined views.

256) Click **Window**, **Tile Horizontally** from the Menu bar menu. Drag the **TUBE** 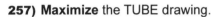 icon from the Part FeatureManager into the drawing Graphics window. The Front, Top, Right, and Isometric views are displayed in the drawing.

257) **Maximize** the TUBE drawing.

If needed, deactivate the Origins.

258) Click **View**, uncheck **Origins** from the Menu bar menu.

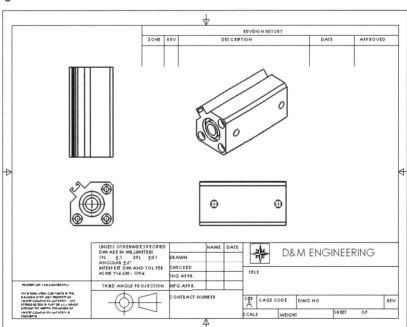

Modify Sheet Properties.

259) Right-click in the **Graphics window**.

260) Click **Properties**. Enter **2:1** for sheet Scale.

261) Select **C (ANSI) Landscape** for Sheet Format/Size.

262) Click the **Browse** button.

263) Double-click **C-FORMAT** from the MY-SHEETFORMATS folder.

264) Click **OK** from the Sheet Properties dialog box.

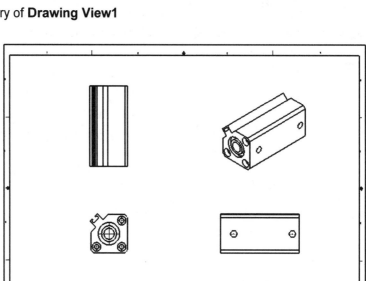

Move the TUBE drawing views.

265) Click inside the view boundary of **Drawing View1** (Front). The view boundary is displayed in blue.

266) Position the **Front** view as illustrated.

267) Position the **Top** view as illustrated.

268) Drag the **Isometric** view as illustrated.

269) Position the **Right** view as illustrated.

Add a Projected Back view to the TUBE drawing.

270) Click inside the view boundary of **Drawing View3**, (Right). The view boundary is displayed in blue.

271) Click **Projected View** ⊞ from the View Layout toolbar. The Projected View PropertyManager is displayed.

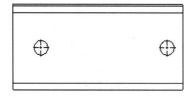

272) Drag the **mouse pointer** to the right of the Right view.

273) Click a **position** for the Projected Back view. Drawing View5 is displayed.

Save the TUBE drawing.

274) Click **Save** 💾 .

TUBE Drawing-Section View and Detail View

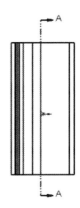

How many views are utilized in a drawing? The number of views in a drawing depends on how many views are required to define the true shape and size of the part.

The TUBE part requires additional drawing views to display interior features and to enlarge features. Display the interior TUBE part features with a Section view.

A Section view defines a cutting plane with a sketched line in a view perpendicular to the view. Create a Full Section view by sketching a section line in the Top view.

A Detail view enlarges an area of an existing view. Specify location, shape and scale. Create a Detail view from a Section view at a 4:1 scale.

Activity: TUBE Drawing-Section View and Detail View

Add a Section view to the TUBE drawing.

275) Display the Origins. Click **View**, check **Origins** from the Menu bar menu.

276) Click inside the view boundary of **Drawing View2**, (Top). The view boundary is displayed in blue.

277) Click **Section View** ⌐ from the View Layout toolbar. The Section View PropertyManager is displayed.

278) Sketch a **vertical section line** Coincident with the Right Plane, through the Origin. The line must extend pass the profile lines.

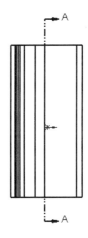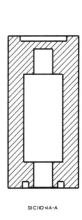

☼ If needed, right-click Edit Sketch on the Section line, to locate the sketched Section line at the part Origin. Select the line. Select the origin. Add a Coincident relation. Save and exit the sketch.

279) Click a **position** to the right Drawing View2 (Top) view. The section arrows point to the right. If required, click **Flip direction**.

280) Click **OK** ✅ from the Section View A-A PropertyManager.

When you create a Section view, you can specific the distance of the cut, so the Section view does not create a cut of the entire drawing view. Do not display origins on the final drawing. This is for illustration purposes only.

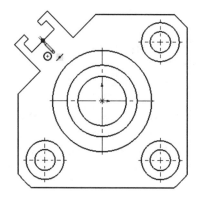

Add a Detail view to the TUBE drawing.
281) **Zoom in** on the upper left corner of Drawing View1.

282) Click **Detail View** ⒶΑ from the View Layout toolbar. The Circle Sketch tool is activated.

283) Click the **middle** of the switchgroove in the Front view as illustrated.

284) Drag the **mouse pointer** downwards as illustrated.

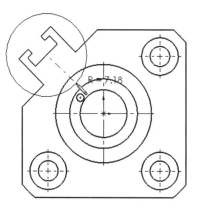

285) Click a **position** just below the large circle to create a sketched circle.

286) Click the **position** to the bottom left of DrawingView1, (Front). The Detail View name is B.

Set the scale.
287) Check the **Use custom scale** box.

288) Enter **4:1** in the Custom Scale text box.

289) Click **OK** ✅ from the Detail View B PropertyManager.

290) Drag the text **B** off the profile lines.

Save the TUBE drawing.
291) Click **Save** 💾 .

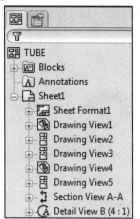

DETAIL B
SCALE 4 : 1

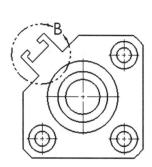

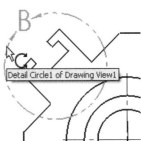

To modify the size of the Detail view, position the mouse pointer on the Detail circle. The mouse pointer displays the

Detail icon. Right-click and select Edit Sketch. Drag the circumference of the sketch circle. Click OK from the Circle PropertyManager. Click Rebuild to update the Detail view.

The Detail view profile is a circle. When a non-circular view is required, sketch the closed profile first. Then select the Detail view.

Verify view names. The A, B, & C view names increment sequentially for Section views, Detail views and Auxiliary views. If you delete the view, the view name still increments by a letter. Modify the view name in the PropertyManager for a specific view.

TUBE Drawing-Broken-out Section View, Auxiliary View and Crop View

A Broken-out Section view removes material to a specified depth to expose the inner details of an existing view. A closed profile defines a Broken-out Section view.

An Auxiliary view displays a plane parallel to an angled plane with true dimensions. A primary Auxiliary view is hinged to one of the six principle views. Create a primary Full Auxiliary view that references the Front view.

Display the M2.0 Hole information. Create a Partial Auxiliary view from the Full Auxiliary view. Sketch a closed profile in an active Auxiliary view. Use the Crop view tool to create a Partial Auxiliary view.

Activity: TUBE Drawing-Broken-out Section View, Auxiliary View, and Crop View

Add the first Broken-out Section view to the TUBE drawing.
292) Click inside the view boundary of **Drawing View3**, (Right).

293) Click **Hidden Line Visible** . The hidden lines do not clearly define the internal front features of the part.

Create a Broken-out Section view.
294) Click the **Sketch** tab from the CommandManager. The Sketch toolbar is displayed.

295) Click **Spline** from the Sketch toolbar.

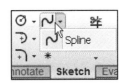

296) Sketch a **closed Spline** in the top left corner. The Spline contains the Cbore Front feature.

297) Click **Broken-out Section** 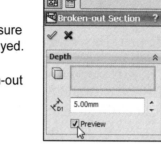 from the Layout View toolbar. The Broken-out Section PropertyManager is displayed.

298) Enter **5**mm for Depth.

299) Check the **Preview** box to insure that the Cbore Front is displayed.

300) Click **OK** ✓ from the Broken-out Section PropertyManager.

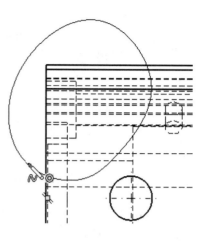

🔆 In an assembly, you can exclude components and fasteners in a Broken-out Section view.

Add a second Broken-out Section view to the TUBE drawing.
301) Click the **Sketch** tab from the CommandManager.

302) Click **Spline** ∿ from the Sketch toolbar.

303) Sketch a **closed Spline** in the top right corner of Drawing View3. The Spline contains the Cbore Rear feature.

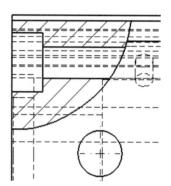

304) Click **Broken-out Section**  from the View Layout toolbar.

305) Enter **5**mm for Depth.

306) Check the **Preview** box.

307) Click **OK** ✓ from the Broken-out Section PropertyManager.

308) Click **inside** Drawing View3.

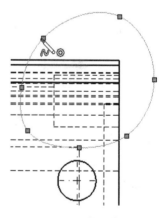

Second Broken-out Section view

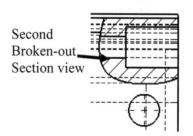

Display no hidden lines.

309) Click **Hidden Lines Removed** .

310) Click **OK** from the Drawing
View3 PropertyManager.

Fit the drawing to the Sheet.
311) Press the **f** key.

Deactivate the Origins.
312) Click **View**, uncheck **Origins** from
the Menu bar menu.

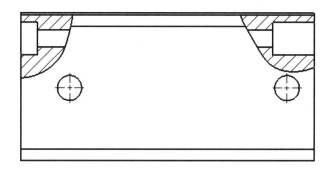

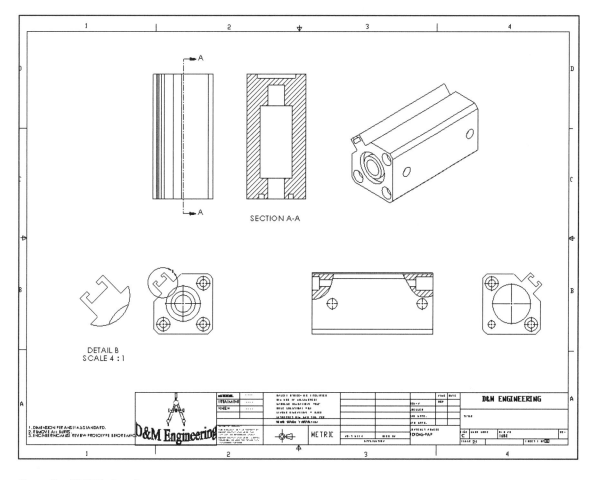

Save the TUBE drawing.
313) Click **Save** .

Add an Auxiliary view to the TUBE drawing.
314) **Zoom in** on the left top side of Drawing View1.

315) Click the **left angled edge** as illustrated.

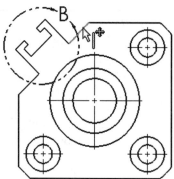

316) Click **Auxiliary View** from the View Layout toolbar.

317) Click a **position** to the upper left of Drawing View1 (Front). The location selected is the center of the Full Auxiliary view.

318) Enter **C** for the View Name.

319) Click **OK** ✔ from the Drawing View PropertyManager.

Fit the Drawing to the Sheet.
320) Press the **f** key.

Position the view arrows.
321) Click **Line C-C**.

322) Drag the **midpoint** and position it between the Auxiliary view and Front view.

323) Click each **endpoint** and drag it towards the midpoint.

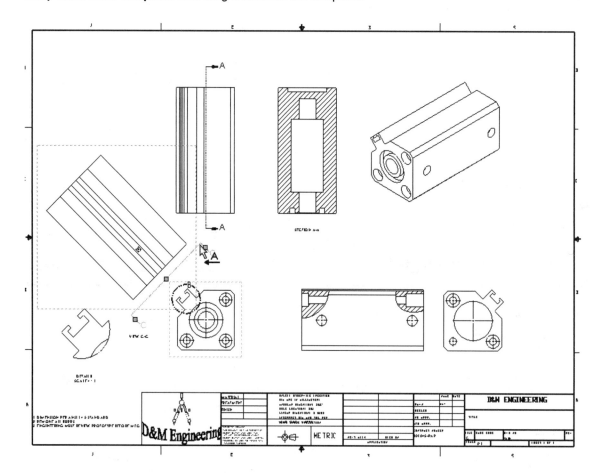

Sketch a closed profile in the active Auxiliary view.

324) Click the **Sketch** tab from the CommandManager.

325) Click **Spline** 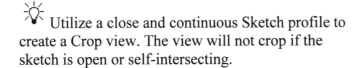 from the Sketch toolbar. The first point is Coincident with the left line of the switchgroove.

326) Sketch **7 Points** to create the closed Spline. The last point is Coincident with the right line of the switchgroove.

Sketch three lines.

327) Click **Line** ＼ from the Sketch toolbar.

328) Sketch the **first line**, the mouse pointer displays Endpoint inference.

329) Sketch the **second line** Collinear with the bottom edge of the Auxiliary view. The first point and second point display Endpoint inference.

330) Sketch the **third line**. The last point must display Endpoint interference with the first point of the Spline.

331) Right-click **Select**.

332) Window-Select the **three lines** and the **Spline**. The Properties PropertyManager is displayed. The selected entities are displayed in the Selected Entities box.

💡 Utilize a close and continuous Sketch profile to create a Crop view. The view will not crop if the sketch is open or self-intersecting.

Crop the view.

333) Click **Crop View** ⬚ from the View Layout toolbar to display the partial Auxiliary view.

334) Click **OK** ✅ from the Properties PropertyManager.

Fit the drawing to the Sheet.
335) Press the **f** key.

Position the view.
336) Drag the **C-C view arrow** between the Auxiliary view and the Front view.

337) Drag the **VIEW C-C** text below the Auxiliary view.

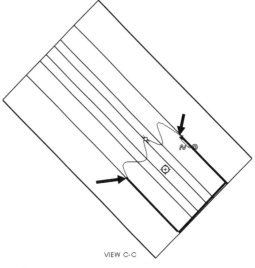

VIEW C-C

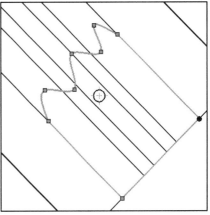

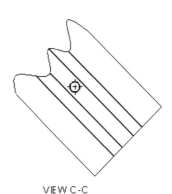

VIEW C-C

338) Click **OK** ✔ from the Note PropertyManager.

Save the TUBE drawing.
339) Click **Save** 🖫 .

💡 Position views in other locations on the sheet when space is limited. The Auxiliary and Section views are aligned to their Parent view. Press the Ctrl key before selecting the Auxiliary and Section view tools in order to position the views anywhere on the sheet.

TUBE Drawing-Half Section Isometric (Cut-Away) View

A Half Section Isometric view in the TUBE drawing requires a Cut feature created in the part. The Extruded Cut feature removes ¼ of the TUBE part. Create an Extruded Cut feature. Create a Design Table to control the Suppressed State of the Extruded Cut feature.

A Design Table is an Excel spreadsheet that represents multiple configurations of a part. The Design Table contains configuration names, parameters to control and assigned values for each parameter.

The TUBE part consists of two configurations:

- Entire Part

- Section Cut

Add the Section Cut Configuration as an Isometric view.

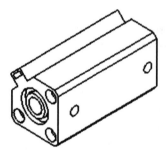
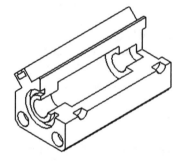

Entire Part

Insert an Area Hatch pattern in the Isometric view. A Hatch Pattern, (section lining or cross sectioning) represents an exposed cut surface based on the material.

The Hatch type, ANSI38(Aluminum) represents the TUBE material.

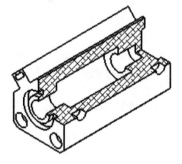

Hatch Cut

Activity: TUBE Drawing-Half Section Isometric-Cut Away View

Open the TUBE part.

340) Right-click inside the **Front view** boundary.

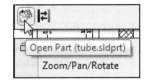

341) Click **Open Part**. The TUBE FeatureManager is displayed

Insert a cut.

342) Click **Front view** from the Heads-up View toolbar.

343) Right-click the **front face** of the TUBE in the Graphics window.

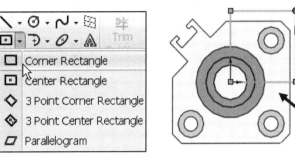

344) Click **Sketch** from the Context toolbar.

345) Click **Corner Rectangle** from the Consolidated Sketch toolbar.

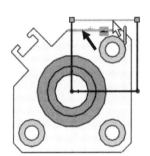

346) Sketch a **rectangle** through the Origin as illustrated.

347) Right-click **Select** to deselect the sketch tool.

Add a Collinear relation between the top horizontal line and the top edge.

348) Click the **top horizontal** line.

349) Hold the **Ctrl** key down.

350) Click the **top edge**.

351) Release the **Ctrl** key.

352) Click **Collinear** from the Add Relations box.

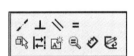

Right-click and use the Pop-up Context toolbar to insert Geometric relations.

353) Add a **Collinear** relation between the right vertical line and the right edge.

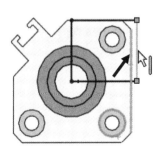

Add an Extruded Cut Feature.

354) Click the **Features** tab from the CommandManager.

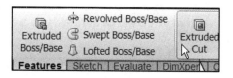

355) Click **Extruded Cut** from the Feature toolbar. The Cut-Extrude PropertyManager is displayed.

356) Select **Through All** for End Condition in Direction 1.

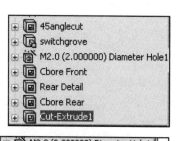

357) Click **OK** from the Cut-Extrude PropertyManager. Cut-Extrude1 is displayed.

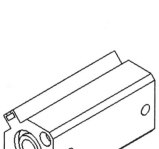

358) Click **Isometric**. View the Cut-Extrude feature.

Suppress the Cut-Extrude1 feature.

359) Right-click **Cut-Extrude1** from the FeatureManager.

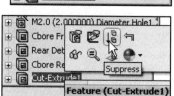

360) Click **Suppress**.

Insert a Design Table.

361) Click **Insert**, **Tables**, **Design Table** from the Menu bar menu.

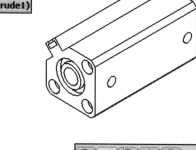

362) Check the **Blank** box for Source.

363) Click **OK** from the Design Table PropertyManager.

364) Click **$STATE@Cut-Extrude1** from the Parameters box.

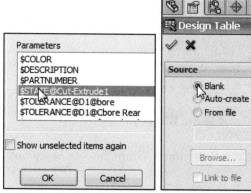

365) Click **OK** from the Add Rows and Columns dialog box. The Design Table for the TUBE is displayed in the upper left corner. $STATE@Cut-Extrude1 is displayed in Cell B2.

Rename the first configuration.

366) Rename the text **First Instance** to **Entire Part**.

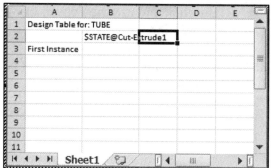

Create the second configuration.
367) Enter **Section Cut** in Cell A4.

368) Enter **S** in Cell B3.

369) Enter **U** in Cell B4.

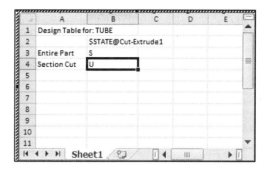

Close the Design Table.
370) Click inside the **Graphics window**.

371) Click **OK**. Both TUBE configurations are created.

☀ Click Edit, Design Table, Edit Table from the Menu bar menu to access an existing Design Table or Right-click the Design Table icon in the ConfigurationManager and select Edit Table.

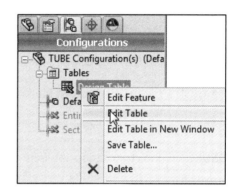

☀ The Design Table abbreviation for Suppressed is S. The abbreviation for Unsuppressed is U.

Display the TUBE part configurations.
372) Double-click **Entire Part** from the ConfigurationManager.

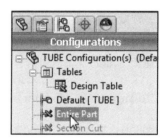

373) Double-click **Section Cut** from the ConfigurationManager. View the results.

Display the TUBE part default configuration.
374) Double-click **Default** from the ConfigurationManager.

Return to the TUBE part FeatureManager.
375) Click the **Part FeatureManager** 🏢 tab.

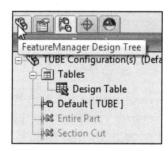

Save the TUBE part.
376) Click **Save** 💾 .

Open the TUBE drawing.
377) Right-click **Tube (Default)** from the FeatureManager.

378) Click **Open Drawing**. The TUBE drawing is displayed.

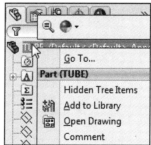

Select the TUBE configuration.

379) Right-click **Properties** in the Isometric view boundary, Drawing View4.

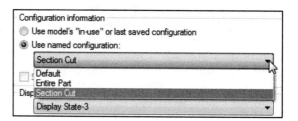

380) Select **Section Cut** from the Named Configuration drop-down menu.

381) Click **OK** from the Drawing View Properties dialog box. The Section Cut configuration is displayed.

Insert Area Hatch.

382) Click the **inside top face** as illustrated.

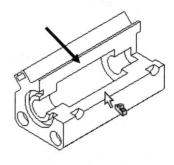

383) Hold the **Ctrl** key down.

384) Click the **inside bottom face** as illustrated.

385) Release the **Ctrl** key.

386) Click the **Annotation** tab from the CommandManager.

387) Click **Area Hatch/Fill** ▨ from the Annotation toolbar.

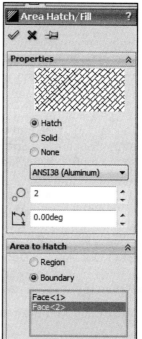

Change the Area Hatch type.

388) Select **ANSI38 (Aluminum)** from the Pattern drop-down menu.

389) Select **2** from the Scale drop-down menu.

390) Click **OK** ✅ from the Area Hatch/Fill PropertyManager.

Fit the drawing to the Sheet.

391) Press the **f** key.

Save the TUBE drawing.

392) Click **Save** 💾 .

The Section view and Broken-out Section view require the Aluminum Property for the Area Hatch.

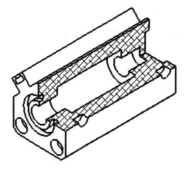

Activity: TUBE Part-Edit Material

Open the TUBE part.

393) Right-click inside the **Isometric view** boundary.

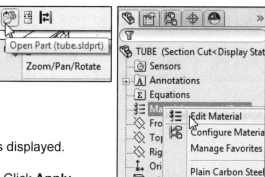

394) Click **Open Part**. The TUBE FeatureManager is displayed.

Set Material type.

395) Right-click **Material** in the FeatureManager.

396) Click **Edit Material**. The Material dialog box is displayed.

397) Expand Aluminum Alloys. Select **6061 Alloy**. Click **Apply**.

398) Click **Close** from the Material dialog box.

Return to the TUBE drawing.

399) Click **Window**, **Tube-Sheet1** from the Menu bar menu. **Rebuild** the drawing to display the Aluminum hatch pattern in the remaining views.

400) Click **Save** .

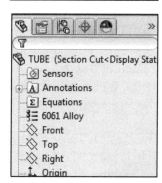

Close all files.

401) Click **Windows**, **Close All** from the Menu bar menu.

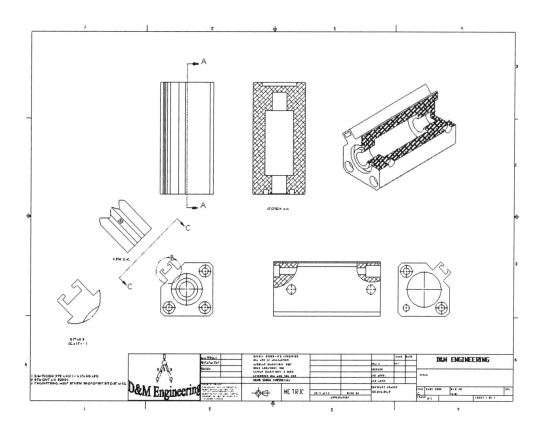

The views required for the TUBE drawing are complete. Insert dimensions and notes for the TUBE drawing in Chapter 7. Note: Utilize Detail View option to create a detail of a preexisting Detail View of a Crop View.

 More Information

Additional details on Drawing Views, Section, Detail, Auxiliary, Area Hatch, Design Tables, Sheet Properties and Broken-out Section are available in Online help. Keywords: Drawing Views (auxiliary, configuration, detail), Model View, Section views, Auxiliary views, Detail views, Design Tables(Suppress), Broken-out Section and Spline.

 Review

The TUBE drawing consisted of a single sheet with eight different views. Sheet Properties were utilized to modify the Sheet size from A to C. The Section view was created by sketching a vertical line in the Top view. The Detail view was created by sketching a circle in the Front view. A Partial Auxiliary view utilized the Crop view tool. The Right view was modified with the Broken-out Section tool.

The Design Table controlled the suppression state of an Extruded Cut feature in the TUBE part. The Isometric view utilized the Section Cut configuration. The Area Hatch utilized the Aluminum material in the Isometric view.

COVERPLATE Drawing

Create the COVERPLATE drawing. The COVERPLATE drawing consists of two part configurations. The first part configuration is With Nose Holes.

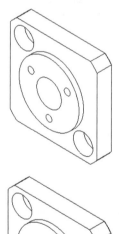

The second part configuration is Without Nose Holes. COVERPLATE-Sheet 1 contains an Offset Section view. COVERPLATE-Sheet2 contains an Aligned Section view.

The Start command when creating a new drawing box is checked by default. To view the Drawing toolbar, click View, Toolbars, Drawing from the Menu bar menu.

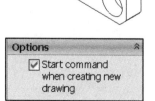

Insert a new Front view with the Model View tool. Delete the Predefined views created with the drawing template. Create a new layer to locate and hide all Center marks on a single layer. Insert an Offset Section view and a Right view.

Copy the Front view from Sheet1 to Sheet2. Modify the configuration. Insert an Aligned Section view.

Activity: COVERPLATE Drawing

Open the COVERPLATE part.
402) Click **Open** from the Menu bar toolbar.

403) Double-click the **COVERPLATE** part.

Display the dimensions.
404) Click on each **feature name**. View the dimensions.

Display the COVERPLATE part configurations.
405) Drag the **Split Bar** downward to split the FeatureManager.

406) Click the **ConfigurationManager** tab.

407) Double-click **With Nose Holes** configuration.

408) Double-click **Without Nose Holes** configuration.

409) Double-click **Default [COVERPLATE]** configuration.

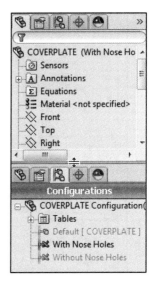

Create the COVERPLATE drawing.
410) Click **New** from the Menu bar toolbar.

411) Double-click the **A-ANSI-MM** drawing template. COVERPLATE is the open document displayed in the Model View PropertyManager.

412) Click **Next** from the Model View PropertyManager.

413) Click ***Front** from the Orientation box.

414) Click a **position** in the lower left corner of the drawing.

Set the View Scale.
415) Click **Use custom scale**.

416) Select **User Defined**.

417) Enter **1.5:1**.

418) Click **OK** from the Projected View PropertyManager. Drawing View5 is displayed in the FeatureManager.

Delete the Predefined empty views.
419) Hold the **Ctrl** key down.

420) Click **Drawing View1**, **Drawing View2**, **Drawing View3** and **Drawing View4**.

421) Release the **Ctrl** key. Press the **Delete** key.

422) Click **Yes to all** to delete the four predefined views. Drawing View5 is displayed.

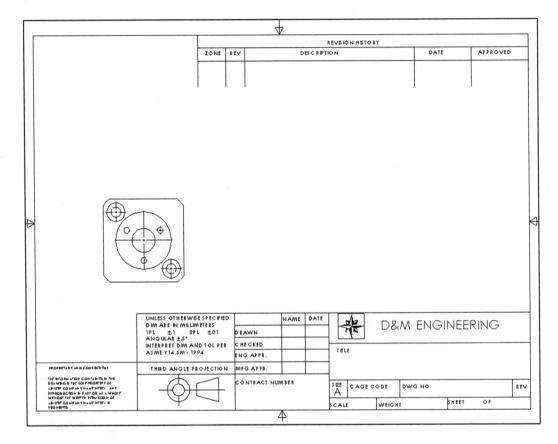

Modify the configuration.
423) Right-click **Properties** inside the Front view boundary, (Drawing View5).

424) Select **Without Nose Holes** for view configuration. Click **OK**.

Display the Layers dialog box.
425) Click **Layer Properties** 🗐 icon.

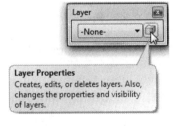

Layer Properties
Creates, edits, or deletes layers. Also, changes the properties and visibility of layers.

Create a new layer.
426) Click the **New** button. Enter **Centermarks** for Name.

427) Click the **Light Bulb** 💡 icon to turn off layer display. Click **OK**.

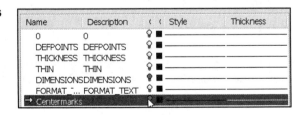

Name	Description	((	Style	Thickness
0	0	💡 ■		
DEFPOINTS	DEFPOINTS	💡 ■		
THICKNESS	THICKNESS	💡 ■		
THIN	THIN	💡 ■		
DIMENSIONS	DIMENSIONS	💡 ■		
FORMAT_...	FORMAT_TEXT	💡 ■		
→ Centermarks		■		

Place the Center marks on the new layer.

428) Hold the **Ctrl** key down.

429) Click the **Center marks** in the Front view.

430) Release the **Ctrl** key.

431) Select **Centermarks** for layer.

432) Click **OK** ✅ from the Center Mark PropertyManager.

433) Click **Save** 🖫.

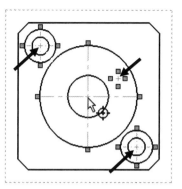

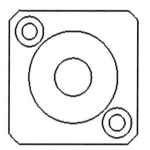

💡 Control Center mark display before you insert dimensions.

Control Center marks with two options:
- **Option 1**: When the Document Property, Auto insert on view creation option is checked, place Center marks on a separate layer. Turn off the layer to add dimensions and construction geometry in the drawing.
- **Option 2**: Uncheck the Auto insert on view creation option to control individual Center marks. Save the setting in the Drawing template. Position dimensions, then apply the Center Mark tool from the Annotation toolbar.

Display the None layer.

434) Click **Layer** drop-down menu.

435) Click **None** for current layer.

Copy the Front view.

436) Click inside the **Front view** boundary. Press **Ctrl + C**.

Add COVERPLATE-Sheet2.

437) Right-click the **Sheet1** tab.

438) Click **Add Sheet**.

Copy the Front view from Sheet1 to Sheet2.

439) Click a **position** on the left side of Sheet2.

440) Press **Ctrl + V**. Right-click **Properties** in the view boundary.

441) Select **With Nose Holes** from the Configuration text box.

442) Click **OK**. A pattern of 3 holes is displayed.

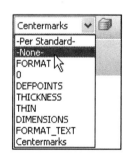

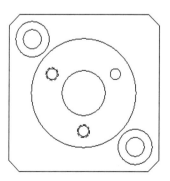

Return to the COVERPLATE-Sheet1.
443) Click the **Sheet1** tab.

Save the COVERPLATE drawing.
444) Click **Save As** from the Menu bar toolbar.

445) Enter **COVERPLATE** for Drawing Name.

446) Enter **COVERPLATE DRAWING** for Description.

447) Click **Save** 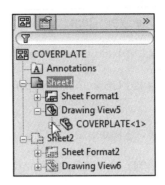 .

COVERPLATE Drawing-Offset Section View and Aligned Section View

Create an Offset Section view by drawing a sketched line. Draw sketch lines in perpendicular segments. Section A-A displays the offsets in a single plane.

In the ASME Y14.3M standard, an Aligned Section occurs when features lend themselves to an angular change in the direction of the cutting plane. The bent cutting plane and features rotate into a plane perpendicular to the line of sight of the sectional view. Create an Aligned Section with a sketched line.

Activity: COVERPLATE Drawing-Offset Section View and Aligned Section View

---

Display the Origin and Temporary Axes on Sheet1.
448) Click **View**, check **Origins** from the Menu bar menu.

449) Click **View**, check **Temporary Axes** from the Menu bar menu.

Select the view.
450) Click inside the **Front view** boundary.

Sketch an open contour with 5 connecting center line segments.
451) Click **Centerline** from the Sketch toolbar.

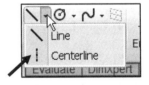

452) Position the **mouse pointer** on the circumference of the upper left Cbore. The center point is displayed.

453) Drag the **mouse pointer** directly to the left. A blue dashed line, aligned with the center point is displayed.

454) Click the **start point** to the left of the vertical profile line.

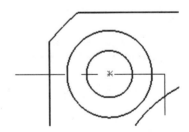

455) Drag the mouse pointer over the **circumference** of the Bore to display the center point.

456) Sketch a **vertical centerline** to the left of the Bore circle.

457) Sketch a **horizontal centerline** through the center of the Bore.

458) Drag the mouse **pointer** over the circumference of the lower right Cbore to display the center point.

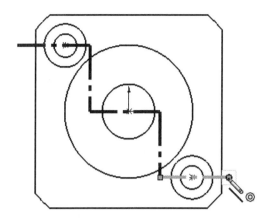

459) Sketch a **vertical centerline**. Sketch a horizontal centerline.

460) Place the **end point** of the last line segment to the right of the vertical profile line.

Add Relations to the Center points.

461) Click **Point** ✳ from the Sketch toolbar. The Point ✳ icon is displayed.

462) Click the center point of the **top left circle** and the **bottom right circle**.

463) Right-click **Select** to deselect the Point Sketch toolbar.

464) Click the **center point** of the left circle.

465) Hold the **Ctrl** key down.

466) Click the **first horizontal line**.

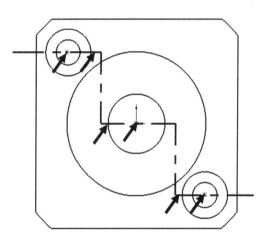

467) Release the **Ctrl** key.

468) Click **Coincident**.

469) Click the **center point** of the right circle.

470) Hold the **Ctrl** key down.

471) Click the **third horizontal** line.

472) Release the **Ctrl** key.

473) Click **Coincident**.

474) Click the **Origin**.

475) Hold the **Ctrl** key down.

476) Click the **second horizontal** line.

477) Release the **Ctrl** key.

478) Click **Coincident**.

479) Click **OK** ✅ from the Properties PropertyManager.

480) Select the five **Center line segments**.

Create the Offset Section view.
481) Click **Insert**, **Drawing View**, **Section** from the Menu bar menu or click Section View from the View Layout toolbar.

482) Click a **position** above the Front view as illustrated.

483) The section arrows point downward. If required, click **Flip direction**.

484) Click **OK** ✅ from the Section View A-A PropertyManager.

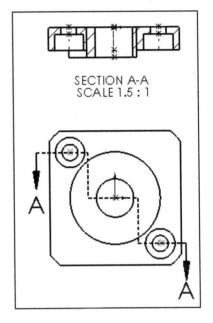

485) Click **Save**.

Deactivate the Origins and Temporary Axes.
486) Click **View**, uncheck **Origins** from the Menu bar menu.

487) Click **View**, uncheck **Temporary Axes** from the Menu bar menu.

Modify the Edit Pull-down menu.
488) Click **Edit**, **Customize menu** from the Menu bar menu.

489) Check **Update View**. View the default settings.

🔆 Update the view if light hatching appears across the view boundary. Utilize Update View to update a single view. Utilize Update All Views or Rebuild to update all drawing views.

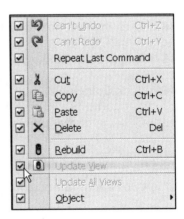

Add a Projected Right view.

490) Click inside the **Front view** boundary.

491) Click **Projected View** 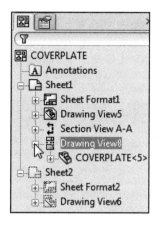 from the View Layout toolbar.

492) Click a **position** to the right of the Front view.

493) Click **Hidden Lines Removed**.

494) Click **OK** ✅ from the Projected View PropertyManager

Save the COVERPLATE drawing.

495) Click **Save** 💾.

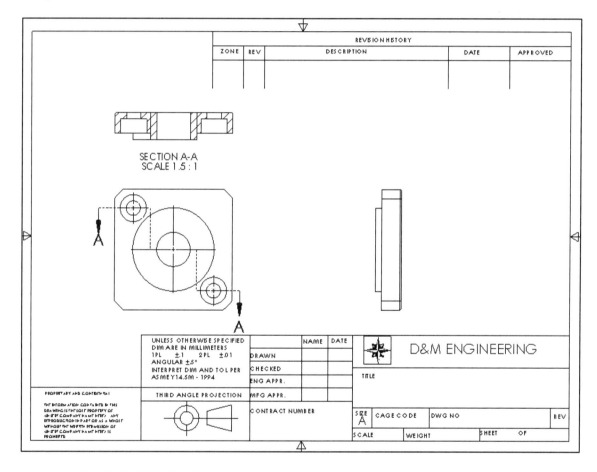

Return to COVERPLATE-Sheet2.

496) Click the **Sheet2** tab. Display the **Origins**.

Create an Aligned Section view.

497) Click inside the **Drawing View6** view boundary. The PropertyManager is displayed.

498) Click the **Sketch** tab from the CommandManager.

499) Click **Centerline** ⁝ from the Sketch toolbar.

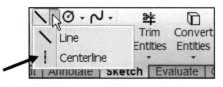

500) Sketch a **vertical centerline** through the bottom hole to the Origin.

501) Sketch an angled **centerline** from the Origin though the right hole as illustrated. The endpoint must extend beyond the right profile. Note: Delete the Center mark if required.

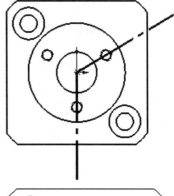

Add Relations to the center points.
502) Click **Point** ＊ from the Sketch toolbar.

503) Click the **center point** of the top right circle.

504) Right-click **Select**.

505) Click the **center point** of the circle.

506) Hold the **Ctrl** key down.

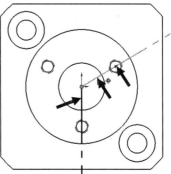

507) Click the **angled line**.

508) Release the **Ctrl** key.

509) Click **Coincident**.

510) Click **OK** ✅ from the PropertyManager.

Project an aligned view from the vertical line.
511) Click the **vertical line**.

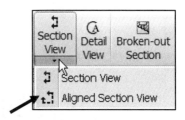

512) Click **Aligned Section View** ᵗↃ from the Consolidated View Layout toolbar.

513) Click a **position** to the right of the Front view.

514) Click **OK** ✅ from the Section View B-B PropertyManager.

515) **Deactivate** the Origins.

Save the COVERPLATE drawing.
516) Click **Save** 💾.

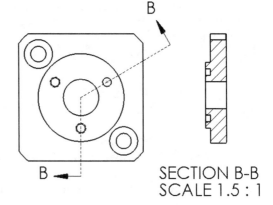

SECTION B-B
SCALE 1.5 : 1

Additional View Options and View Properties

There are additional options for Section views and Aligned Section views. When do you use a Section view versus an Aligned Section view? Answer: Utilize two sketch line segments for the Aligned Section view. Utilize one, three or more sketch line segments and arc segments for the Section view.

Select a vertical or horizontal sketched line before you create the Aligned view. Otherwise, the bent sketched line creates the aligned view at an angle.

Create a Half Section view by sketching two perpendicular line segments for the section line. The available Section view options are: *Partial section, Display only cut faces(s), Auto hatching*, and *Display surface bodies*.

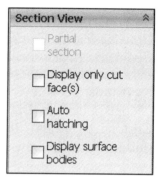

The Partial section option creates a portion of the Section view when the section line is smaller than the view geometry. The Display only cut face(s) option shows only the surfaces cut by the section line in the Section view. The Auto hatching option displays the hatch pattern for the model material. The Display surface bodies' option only displays the surface of the model.

The Right Projected view on Sheet 1 utilized the View tools to set the entire view to Hidden Lines Visible or Hidden Lines Removed.

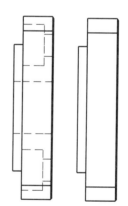

View Properties list the view type, model file and configuration name. The Show Hidden Edges option controls the display of a feature's hidden lines in a specific view.

As models become complex, hidden lines are difficult to distinguish. One technique is to create multiple views and display only specific features with hidden lines.

Bore feature only, Show Hidden Edges

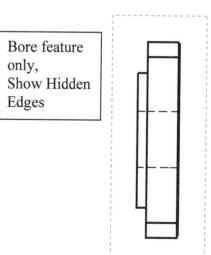

Example: Right-click Properties in the Right view, select Show Hidden Edges. Expand the Drawing FeatureManager. Expand Sheet1. Expand the Right view, Drawing View8. Click the Bore feature.

To display the Bore feature hidden edges, set the display mode option in the drawing view to Hidden Lines Removed.

More Information

Additional details on Offset Section, Aligned Section, Update Drawing Views, Configurations, Customizing menus, Show and Geometric Relations are available in SolidWorks help.

Keywords: Section view (Drawings, Aligned), Section lines (stepped), Update (Drawing views), Drawing (configurations), Customize (menus), Relations (geometric, add) and Show (hidden edges in drawing).

 **Review**

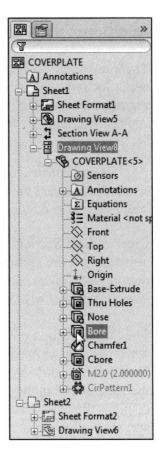

The COVERPLATE drawing consisted of two Sheets. Sheet1 utilized the Without Nose Holes Configuration. A sketched line with five line segments created the Offset Section view. You utilized Geometric relations to define the sketched line relative to the center points of the Cbore.

Sheet2 utilized the With Nose Holes Configuration. A sketched line with two segments created the Aligned Section view. You customized the Edit Pull-down menu by adding the Update Views option.

Use the Lock View Position command to prevent a view from being moved by dragging.

Use the Lock View Focus command when you need a view to remain active as you work within it. This allows you to add sketch entities to a view, even when the mouse pointer is close to another view. You can be sure that the items you are adding belong to the view you want.

Multi-view Drawings - View Layout toolbar

The information in this section is provided in order to create additional Multi-view drawings and to understand the tools which are available in the View Layout toolbar. There are no step-by-step instructions in this section.

Multiple views represent the true shape of the part. The Model View tool selects a Named view from the part Orientation list. The default orientation is the Current Model view. The View Layout toolbar contains numerous tools to create Multiple view drawings.

They are:

Standard 3 View: Provides the ability to create three related default Orthographic views of a part or assembly displayed at the same time.

Model View: Provides the ability to create a new drawing. Note: SolidWorks part and assembly documents support 3D annotations according to the ASME Y14.41-2003 standard. Annotation views are indicated by an A on the view icon.

Projection View: Provides the ability to create a Projected view from a previously defined Orthogonal view.

Auxiliary View: Provides the ability to create an Auxiliary view by selecting an angled edge from a previously defined view. An Auxiliary View is similar to a Projected view, but it is unfolded normal to a reference edge in an existing view.

Section View: Provides the ability to create a Section View cutting the Parent view with a section line. The Section view can be a straight cut section or an offset section defined by a stepped section line. The section line can also include Concentric arcs.

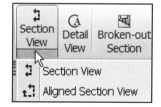

- *Aligned Section View*: Provides the ability to create an Aligned Section view in a drawing through a model, or portion of a model, that is aligned with a selected section line segment. The aligned section view is similar to a Section view, but the section line for an aligned section comprises two or more lines connected at an angle.

Detail View: Provides the ability to create a Detail view in a drawing to display how a portion of a view, usually at an enlarged scale. This detail may be of an Orthographic view, a Non-planar (Isometric) view, a Section view, a Crop view, an Exploded assembly view, or another Detail view.

Broken-out Section View: A Broken-out Section is part of an existing drawing view, not a separate view. A closed profile, usually a Spline, defines the Broken-out section. Material is removed to a specified depth to expose inner details. Specify the depth by setting a number or by selecting geometry in a drawing view.

Break: Provides the ability to apply a broken (or interrupted) view in a drawing. Broken views make it possible to display the drawing view in a larger scale on a smaller size drawing sheet. Note: Reference dimensions and model dimensions associated with the broken area reflect the actual model values.

Crop view: You can crop any drawing view except a Detail View, a view from which a Detail View has been created, or an Exploded view. A Crop view can save steps because you do not create a new view. For example, instead of creating a Section View and then a Detail View, then hiding the unnecessary Section View, you can just crop the Section View directly.

Alternative Position view: Provides the ability to superimpose one drawing view precisely on another. The Alternate Position is displayed by default with phantom lines. Alternate Position Views are often used to show the range of motion of an assembly.

How do you create a single view drawing? Answer: Create the drawing by using a Named view with the Model view tool or apply the View Palette. Use a Parametric note to represent material thickness from the Annotation toolbar.

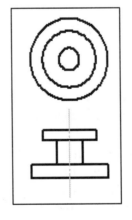

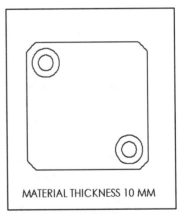

MATERIAL THICKNESS 10 MM

How do you create a two view drawing? Answer: There are three options:

2 View Drawing   1 View Drawing

- **Option 1**: Create the Standard views: Front, Top, and Right. Hide one of the views.

- **Option 2**: Create a Named view with the Model view tool. Insert a Projected view.

- **Option 3**: Apply the View Palette tool from the Task Pane and click and drag the required views.

Develop the part based on the assembly and symmetry. Orient the part based on its position in the assembly. Orient the part to build symmetry between features and sketch geometry. Create a new drawing for the assembly and part before these documents are complete. Utilize the drawing to understand assembly layout, interference and part fabrication.

Use the Model view tool, Rotate view tool, 3D Drawing View tool and the Projection view tool to orient the part in a fabrication drawing. Select the view orientation that minimizes hidden lines and outlines the profile of the feature. The ASME Y14.3M standard defines other view types not required in this chapter. These views are applied to different types of drawings.

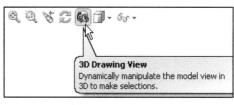

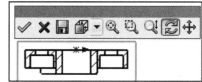

Auxiliary View

A Primary Auxiliary view: VIEW A is aligned and adjacent to the angled edge of the principle Front view.

A Secondary Auxiliary view: VIEW B is aligned and adjacent to a Primary Auxiliary view, VIEW A. Select an edge in the Primary Auxiliary.

In SolidWorks, Secondary Auxiliary views are created from a Primary Auxiliary view. Use the Auxiliary View to create the Secondary Auxiliary view.

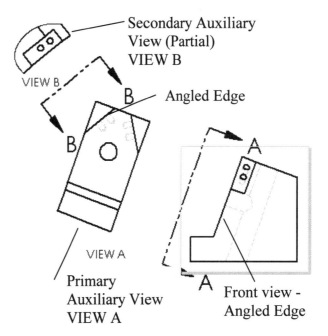

Rotate Drawing View

Views can be rotated to fit within the sheet boundary. The angle and direction of rotation is placed below the view title.

Example: A Front view and Projected Left view are displayed in an A-size drawing.

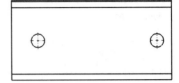

Review the steps to Rotate the Front View using the Rotate View tool

Click inside the Drawing view boundary.

Click Rotate View  from the Heads-up View toolbar.

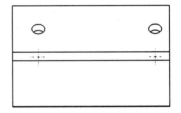

Enter the Drawing view angle from the Rotate Drawing View dialog box. Example: 45°.

The Left view depends on the Front view and rotates by 45°. Note: Select Rotate View 🔄 and drag the view boundary in the Graphics window. The view rotates freely.

Review the steps to Rotate the Front View using the 3D Drawing View tool

Click inside the view boundary. Select the 3D Drawing View 🔄 tool from the Heads-up View toolbar. The Pop-up Context toolbar is displayed.

Click and rotate the selected drawing view to display the required edge, face, or vertex. Select the required sketch entity.

Click OK from the Pop-up Context toolbar to exit 3D Drawing View.

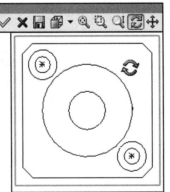
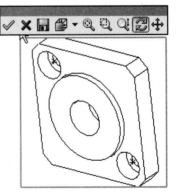

Steps to create a new Rotated View

Select the Section View ⤴ tool. Sketch a straight section line above the Front view. Click the view boundary to rotate.

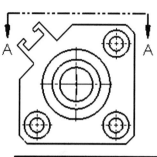

Click Rotate ↻ from the Heads-up View toolbar. Enter the Drawing view angle from the Rotate Drawing View dialog box.

Break alignment of the rotated view to position the view in a new location. Right-click Alignment, click Break Alignment. Realign the view if required.

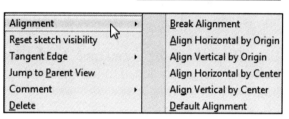

Add a note with view name, rotated angle and direction. Example: VIEW A-A, ROTATED 90 CCW.

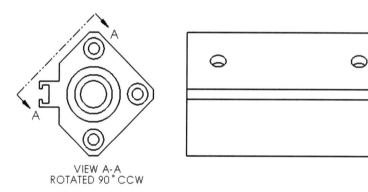

VIEW A-A
ROTATED 90° CCW

Perspective View in a part

A Perspective view is the view normally seen by the human eye. Parallel lines recede into the distance to a vanishing point.

Utilize **View**, **Display**, **Perspective** to create a perspective view of the active model.

Create a Perspective view short cut key. Press the space bar on your keyboard. The Orientation dialog box is displayed.

Click the New View 👋 tool. The Name View dialog box is displayed.

Enter Perspective for View name. Click OK. The Perspective view is added to the Orientation dialog box.

Utilize the Perspective view from the Heads-up View toolbar.

Utilize Model View to add a Perspective view into a drawing.

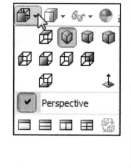

💡 Modify the document units directly from the Graphics window as illustrated.

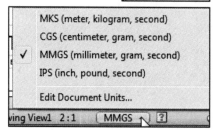

Alternative Position View

The Alternative Position 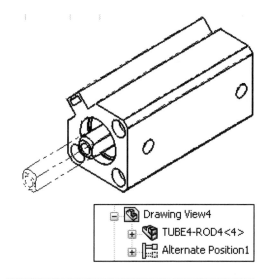 tool displays two configurations of an assembly in a drawing.

Click the Alternative Position tool from the View Layout toolbar. There are two options:

Define the Alternate Position in the drawing.

Create a configuration in the assembly and reference the Alternate Position in the drawing.

Suppress mates in the assembly to create the Alternate Position. The Alternate Position displays the first configuration in dark visible lines and the second configuration in light gray line style. The FeatureManager displays the Alternate Position configuration in the drawing and in the assembly.

Empty View

The Empty view tool creates a blank view not tied to the part or assembly. Utilize Insert, Empty from the Menu bar menu to create the view.

Insert multiple sketched entities, dimensions, relations and annotations into an Empty view. Move, Hide, and Layer Properties apply to an Empty view.

Utilize the Lock View Focus option from the Pop-up menu to link all inserted entities to the Empty view. Geometry inserted outside the view boundary maintains its relationship with the Empty view.

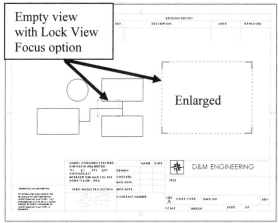

Relative To Model View

The Relative To Model tool defines an Orthographic view based on two orthogonal faces or places in the model. Utilize Tile Horizontal to display the drawing and the model.

Select the drawing for the active window. Select Insert, Drawing View, Relative To Model from the Menu bar menu.

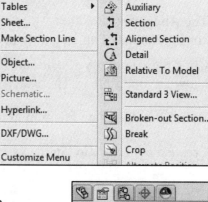

The Graphics window displays the model. Select the First orientation from the model. This is the primary reference in the drawing. Select the Second orientation from the model. This is the secondary reference in the drawing.

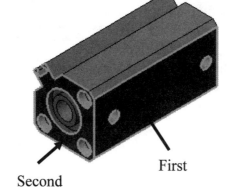

First

Second

Click OK from the Relative View PropertyManager to return to the drawing. Position the view on the drawing.

Name additional drawing views required in the part. Position the model in the graphics window. Press the space bar to invoke the current View Orientation list. Select New View and enter the view name. Views created in the model are accessible in the drawing.

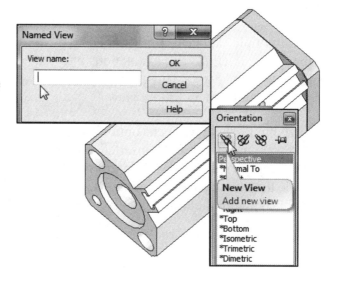

Chapter Summary

In this chapter, you displayed and created Standard, Isometric, Auxiliary, Section, Broken-out Section, Detail, and Half Section (Cut-away) views.

Feature dimensions in the part were positioned off the profile. Part configurations were reviewed. You obtained the ability create a new drawing, use SolidWorks Drawing tools and other related view commands.

You reviewed the Fundamentals of Orthographic projection for first angle and third angle projection systems. You created multi-sheet drawings from various part configurations. The three drawings that you created were:

1. TUBE drawing

2. ROD drawing

3. COVERPLATE drawing

The ROD drawing consisted of three Sheets. The TUBE drawing consisted of a single Sheet. The COVERPLATE drawing consisted of two Sheets. Practice creating drawings, views and more options in the project exercises. Insert dimensions from the part and create new annotations in Chapter 4.

Chapter Terminology

Alternate Position View: A drawing view superimposed in phantom lines on the original view. Utilized to show range of motion of an assembly.

Area hatch: Apply a crosshatch pattern or solid fill to a model face, to a closed sketch profile, or to a region bounded by a combination of model edges and sketch entities. Area hatch can be applied only in drawings.

Auxiliary view: An Auxiliary View is similar to a Projected View, but it is unfolded normal to a reference edge in an existing view.

Balloon: Labels parts in an assembly, typically including item numbers and quantity. In drawings, the item numbers are related to rows in a bill of materials (BOM). Create balloons in a drawing document or in a note.

Bill of Materials: A table inserted into a drawing to keep a record of the parts used in an assembly.

Broken out Section: A drawing view that exposes inner details of a drawing view by removing material from a closed profile, usually a spline.

CommandManager: The CommandManager is a Context-sensitive toolbar that dynamically updates based on the toolbar you want to access. By default, it has toolbars embedded in it based on the document type. When you click a tab below the Command Manager, it updates to display that toolbar. For example, if you click the **Sketches** tab, the Sketch toolbar is displayed.

ConfigurationManager: The ConfigurationManager is located on the left side of the SolidWorks window and provides the means to create, select, and view multiple configurations of parts and assemblies in an active document. You can split the ConfigurationManager and either display two ConfigurationManager instances, or combine the ConfigurationManager with the FeatureManager design tree, PropertyManager, or third party applications that use the panel.

Copy and Paste: Utilize copy/paste to copy views from one sheet to another sheet in a drawing or between different drawings.

Detail view: A portion of a larger view, usually at a larger scale than the original view. Create a detail view in a drawing to display a portion of a view, usually at an enlarged scale. This detail may be of an orthographic view, a non-planar (isometric) view, a section view, a crop view, an exploded assembly view, or another detail view.

Drawing: A 2D representation of a 3D part or assembly. The extension for a SolidWorks drawing file name is .SLDDRW. Drawing refers to the SolidWorks module used to insert, add, and modify views in an engineering drawing.

Edit Sheet: The drawing sheet contains two modes. Utilize the Edit Sheet command to insert views and dimensions.

Edit Sheet Format: The drawing sheet contains two modes. Utilize the Edit Sheet Format command to add or modify notes and Title block information. Edit in the Edit Sheet Format mode.

Empty View: An Empty View creates a blank view not tied to a part or assembly document.

Extruded Cut feature: Projects a sketch perpendicular to a Sketch plane to remove material from a part.

FeatureManager: The FeatureManager design tree located on the left side of the SolidWorks window provides an outline view of the active part, assembly, or drawing. This makes it easy to see how the model or assembly was constructed or to examine the various sheets and views in a drawing. The FeatureManager and the Graphics window are dynamically linked. You can select features, sketches, drawing views, and construction geometry in either pane.

First Angle Projection: Standard 3 Views are in either third angle or first angle projection. In first angle projection, the front view is displayed at the upper left and the other two views are the top and left views.

Handle: An arrow, square, or circle that you drag to adjust the size or position of an entity such as a view or dimension.

Heads-up View toolbar: A transparent toolbar located at the top of the Graphics window.

Layers: Simplifies a drawing by combining dimensions, annotations, geometry and components. Properties such as: display, line style, and thickness are assigned to a named layer.

Lock View Focus: Adds sketch entities and annotations to the selected locked view. Double-click the view to activate Lock View Focus. To unlock a view, right-click and select Unlock View Focus or double click outside the view boundary.

Lock View Position: Secures the view at its current position in the sheet. Right-click in the drawing view to Lock View Position. To unlock a view position, right-click and select Unlock View Position.

Lock Sheet Focus: Adds sketch entities and annotations to the selected sheet. Double-click the sheet to activate Lock Sheet Focus. To unlock a sheet, right-click and select Unlock Sheet Focus or double click inside the sheet boundary.

Menus: Menus provide access to the commands that the SolidWorks software offers. Menus are Context-sensitive and can be customized through a dialog box.

Model: 3D solid geometry in a part or assembly document. If a part or assembly document contains multiple configurations, each configuration is a separate model.

Mouse Buttons: The left, middle, and right mouse buttons have distinct meanings in SolidWorks. Use the middle mouse button to rotate and Zoom in/out on the part or assembly document.

Model View: A specific view of a part or assembly. Standard named views are listed in the view orientation dialog box such as isometric or front. Named views can be user-defined name for a specific view.

Origin: The model origin is displayed in blue and represents the (0,0,0) coordinate of the model. When a sketch is active, a sketch origin is displayed in red and represents the (0,0,0) coordinate of the sketch. Dimensions and relations can be added to the model origin, but not to a sketch origin.

Parent View: A Parent view is an existing view in which other views are dependent on.

Projected View: Projected views are created for Orthogonal views using one of the following tools: Standard 3 View, Model View, or the Projected View tool from the View Layout toolbar.

Relative view: The Relative View defines an Orthographic view based on two orthogonal faces or places in the model.

Section line: A line or centerline sketched in a drawing view to create a section view.

Section view: Create a Section View in a drawing by cutting the Parent view with a section line. The section view can be a straight cut section or an offset section defined by a stepped section line. The section line can also include concentric arcs.

Sheet Format: A document that contains the following: page size and orientation, standard text, borders, logos, and Title block information. Customize the sheet format to save time. The extension for the sheet format filename is .SLDDRT.

Sheet: A page in a drawing document.

Spline: A sketched 2D or 3D curve defined by a set of control points.

Standard views: The three orthographic projection views, Front, Top and Right positioned on the drawing according to First angle or Third angle projection.

Suppress: Removes an entity from the display and from any calculations in which it is involved. You can suppress features, assembly components, and so on. Suppressing an entity does not delete the entity; you can unsuppress the entity to restore it.

System Feedback: Feedback is provided by a symbol attached to the cursor arrow indicating your selection. As the cursor floats across the model, feedback is provided in the form of symbols riding next to the cursor.

Third Angle Projection: Standard 3 Views are in either third angle or first angle projection. In third angle projection, the default front view from the part or assembly is displayed at the lower left, and the other two views are the top and right views.

Toolbars: The toolbar menus provide shortcuts enabling you to access the most frequently used commands. Toolbars are Context-sensitive and can be customized through a dialog box.

View Palette: Use the View Palette, located in the Task Pane, to insert drawing views. It contains images of standard views, annotation views, section views, and flat patterns (sheet metal parts) of the selected model. You can drag views onto the drawing sheet to create a drawing view.

Questions:

1. Name the three default Reference Planes: _____, _____ and
_____ .

2. Identify the six principle drawing views in Orthographic Projection:
_____, _____, _____, _____,
_____, _____ .

3. Name the two Orthographic projection systems: _____,
_____ .

4. A drawing contains multiple _____ of a part.

5. True or False. Delete the part when a drawing is complete.

6. True of False. All drawings contain a single part configuration.

7. A Design Table is inserted into two document types. Identify the two documents.

8. Describe the difference between View properties and Sheet properties.

9. Identify the tool from the View Layout toolbar that is used to browse and create a
view in a drawing.

10. Describe the procedure to copy a view from one sheet to another sheet in the same
drawing.

11. True or False. Drawing Layers exist in a SolidWorks drawing.

12. Identify the command used to change the Scale of a Detailed view.

13. Describe the procedure to display internal features, "view" of a part in a drawing.

14. You created a multi-sheet drawing. On the first sheet, the correct Sheet format is
displayed. On the second sheet, an incorrect Sheet format is displayed. Identify the
procedure to modify the Sheet Properties to display the correct Sheet format.

15. The Alternative Position view tool is located in the View Layout toolbar. Identify the
menu location to find additional information on the Alternative Position view tool.

16. Identify the following View Layout tools:

A········· B········· C········· D········· E········· F········· G········· H········· I

Exercises:

Exercise 6.1: FLATBAR - 3 HOLE Drawing

Note: Dimensions are enlarged for clarity. Utilize inch, millimeter, or dual dimensioning.

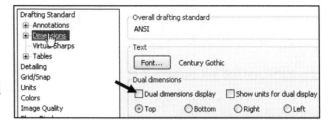

- Create the ANSI-IPS Third Angle
  Projection FLATBAR - 3HOLE drawing. First create the part from the drawing - then create the drawing. Use the default A (ANSI)-Landscape Sheet Format/Size.

- Insert a Shaded Isometric view. No Tangent Edges displayed.

- Insert a Front and Top view. Insert dimensions. Insert 3X - EQ. SP. Insert the Company and Third Angle Projection icon. Add a Parametric Linked Note for MATERIAL THICKNESS. Note: All needed icons are located in the Chapter 6 Homework folder on the DVD. Copy the folder to your hard drive.

- Hide the Thickness dimension in the Top view. Insert needed Centerlines.

- Insert Custom Properties for Material (2014 Alloy), DRAWNBY, DRAWNDATE, COMPANYNAME, etc.

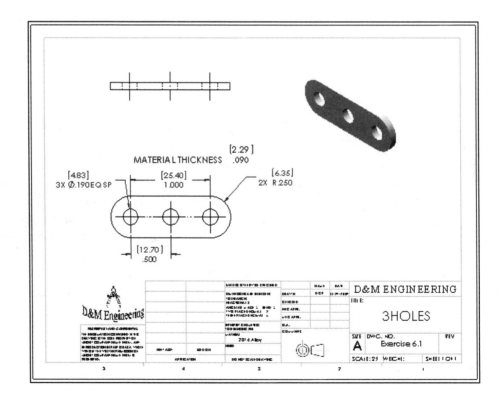

Exercise 6.2: CYLINDER Drawing

Create the ANSI - IPS - Third Angle CYLINDER drawing.

- First create the part from the drawing - then create the drawing. Use the default A (ANSI)-Landscape Sheet Format/Size.

- Insert the Front and Right view as illustrated. Insert dimensions. Think about the proper view for your dimensions!

- Insert Company and Third Angle projection icons. The icons are available in the homework folder. Note: All needed icons are located in the Chapter 6 Homework folder on the DVD. Copy the folder to your hard drive.

- Insert needed Centerlines and Center Marks. Insert Custom Properties: Material, Description, DrawnBy, DrawnDate, CompanyName, etc. Note: Material is AISI 1020.

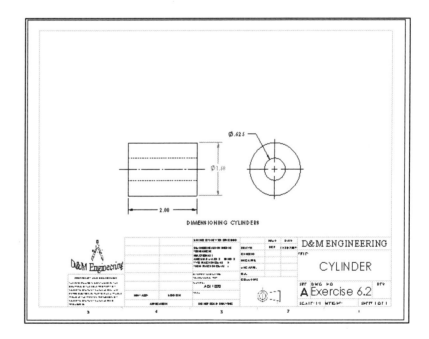

- Utilize the Mass Properties tool from the Evaluate toolbar to calculate the volume and mass of the CYLINDER part. Set decimal places to 4.

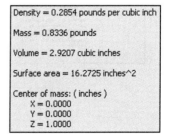

Density = 0.2854 pounds per cubic inch

Mass = 0.8336 pounds

Volume = 2.9207 cubic inches

Surface area = 16.2725 inches^2

Center of mass: (inches)
    X = 0.0000
    Y = 0.0000
    Z = 1.0000

Exercise 6.3: PRESSURE PLATE Drawing

Create the ANSI - IPS - Third Angle PRESSURE PLATE drawing.

- First create the part from the drawing - then create the drawing. Use the default A-Landscape Sheet Format/Size.

- Insert the Front and Right view as illustrated. Insert dimensions. Think about the proper view for your dimensions!

- Insert Company and Third Angle projection icons. The icons are available in the homework folder. Note: All needed icons are located in the Chapter 6 Homework folder on the DVD. Copy the folder to your hard drive.

- Insert needed Centerlines and Center Marks.

- Insert Custom Properties: Material, Description, DrawnBy, DrawnDate, CompanyName, etc. Note: Material is 1060 Alloy.

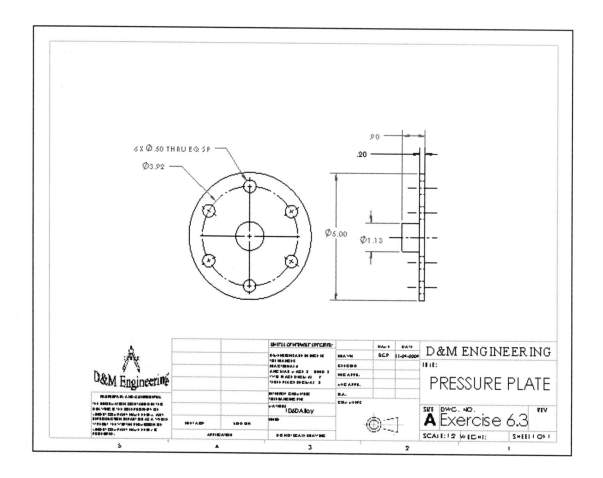

Exercise 6.4: LINKS Assembly Drawing

- Create the LINK assembly. Utilize three different FLATBAR configurations and a SHAFT-COLLAR. You are the designer. Create the four needed parts.

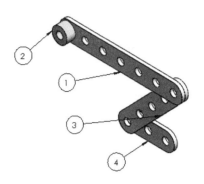

- Create the LINK assembly drawing as illustrated. Use the default A-Landscape Sheet Format/Size.

- Insert Company and Third Angle projection icons. The icons are available in the homework folder. Remove all Tangent Edges. Note: All needed icons are located in the Chapter 6 Homework folder on the DVD. Copy the folder to your hard drive.

- Insert Custom Properties: Description, DrawnBy, DrawnDate, CompanyName, etc.

- Insert a Bill of Materials as illustrated with Balloons.

ITEM NO.	PART NUMBER	DESCRIPTION	QTY.
1	GIDS-SC-10009-7	7 HOLES	1
2	GIDS-SC-10012-3-16	SHAFT-COLLAR	1
3	GIDS-SC-10009-5	5 HOLES	1
4	GIDS-SC-10009-3	3 HOLES	1

D&M ENGINEERING

TITLE:

LINK

A Exercise 6.4

Exercise 6.5: PLATE-1 Drawing

Create the ANSI - MMGS - Third Angle PLATE-1 drawing.

- First create the part from the drawing - then create the drawing. Use the default A-Landscape Sheet Format/Size.

- Insert the Front and Right view as illustrated. Insert dimensions. Think about the proper view for your dimensions!

- Insert Company and Third Angle projection icons. The icons are available in the homework folder.

- Insert needed Centerlines and Center Marks.

- Insert Custom Properties: Material, Description, DrawnBy, DrawnDate, CompanyName, etc. Note: Material is 1060 Alloy.

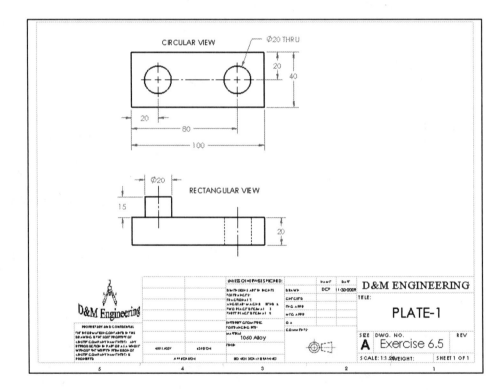

Exercise 6.6: FLATE-PLATE Drawing

Create the ANSI - IPS - Third Angle PLATE-1 drawing.

- First create the part from the drawing - then create the drawing. Use the default A-Landscape Sheet Format/Size. Remove all Tangent Edges.

- Insert the Front, Top, Right and Isometric view as illustrated. Insert dimensions. Think about the proper view for your dimensions!

- Insert Company and Third Angle projection icons. The icons are available in the homework folder. Note: All needed icons are located in the Chapter 6 Homework folder on the DVD. Copy the folder to your hard drive.

- Insert needed Centerlines and Center Marks.

- Insert Custom Properties: Material, Description, DrawnBy, DrawnDate, CompanyName, Hole Annotation, etc. Note: Material is 1060 Alloy

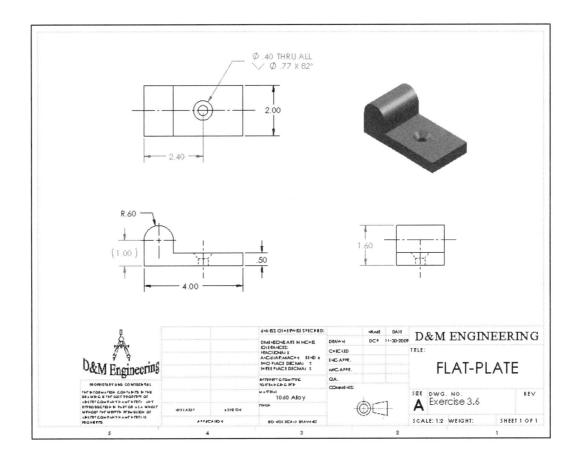

Exercise 6.7: LINKAGE-2 Drawing

- Create a new drawing named, LINKAGE-2.

- Insert an Isometric view, shaded view of the LINKAGE-2 Assembly. The LINKAGE-2 Assembly is located in the Chapter 6 Homework folder on the DVD.

- Define the PART NO. Property and the DESCRIPTION Property for the AXLE, FLATBAR- 9HOLE, FLATBAR - 3HOLE and SHAFT COLLAR.

- Save the LINKAGE-2 assembly to update the properties. Return to the LINKAGE-2 Drawing. Insert a Bill of Materials with Auto Balloons as illustrated.

- Insert the Company and Third Angle Projection icon. Insert Custom Properties for DRAWNBY, DRAWNDATE and COMPANYNAME

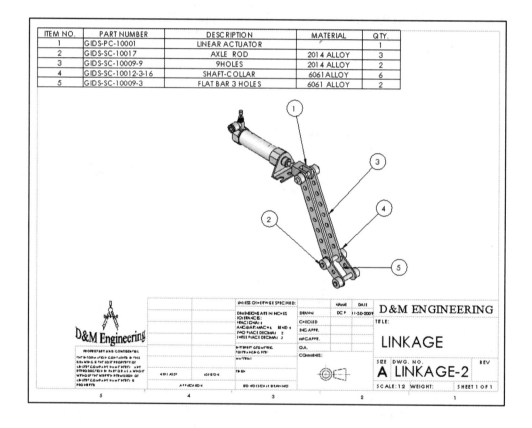

ITEM NO.	PART NUMBER	DESCRIPTION	MATERIAL	QTY.
1	GIDS-PC-10001	LINEAR ACTUATOR		1
2	GIDS-SC-10017	AXLE ROD	2014 ALLOY	3
3	GIDS-SC-10009-9	9HOLES	2014 ALLOY	2
4	GIDS-SC-10012-3-16	SHAFT-COLLAR	6061 ALLOY	6
5	GIDS-SC-10009-3	FLAT BAR 3 HOLES	6061 ALLOY	2

Exercise 6.8: eDrawing

Create an eDrawing of the LINKAGE-2 drawing. A SolidWorks eDrawing is a compressed document that does not require the corresponding part or assembly. SolidWorks eDrawing is animated to display multiple views and dimensions. Review the eDrawing On-line Help for additional functionality.

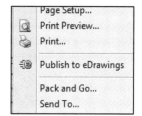

- Click Publish to eDrawing from the Menu bar menu.

- Click the Play button.

- Click the Stop button.

- Save the LINKAGE-2 eDrawing.

- Return to the LINKAGE2 drawing.

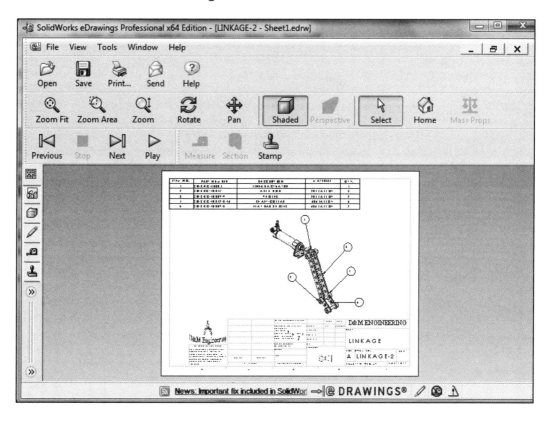

Notes:

Chapter 7

Fundamentals of Detailing

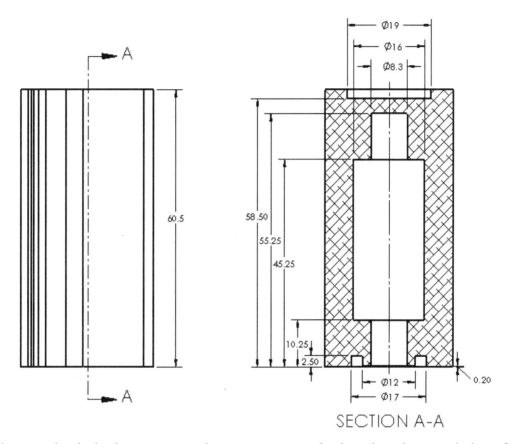

SECTION A-A

Below are the desired outcomes and usage competencies based on the completion of Chapter 7. Note: Drawing refers to the SolidWorks module used to insert, add, and modify views in an engineering drawing. Detailing refers to the SolidWorks module used to insert, add, and modify dimensions and notes in an engineering drawing.

Desired Outcomes:	Usage Competencies:
Two Detail drawings: • TUBE drawing with detailing • COVERPLATE drawing with detailing	• Ability to insert, add and modify dimensions.
	• An understanding of inserting and adding Annotations.
	• Knowledge of dimensioning standards.

Notes:

Chapter 7 - Fundamentals of Detailing

Chapter Objective

Details are the drawing dimensions and notes required to document part features. Create two detailed drawings:

- TUBE

- COVERPLATE

On the completion of this chapter, you will be able to:

- Insert and modify drawing view dimensions.

- Add and address Annotations.

- Insert Hole Callouts, Center Marks, and Centerlines.

- Use various methods to move, hide, show, suppress, and un-suppress drawing views.

- Apply the ASME Y14.5 standard for Types of Decimal Dimensions.

- Add Modifying Symbols and Hole Symbols.

- Utilize the following SolidWorks tools and commands: *Smart Dimension, Model Items, Autodimension, Note, Linear Note, Balloon, AutoBalloon, Magnetic line, Surface Finish, Weld Symbol, Geometric Tolerance, Datum Feature, Datum Target, Hole Callout, Area Hatch/Fill, Block, Center Mark* and *Centerline.*

Chapter Overview

You inserted and added views for the TUBE, ROD and COVERPLATE drawings in Chapter 6. In this Chapter, you will insert, add, and modify dimensions and obtain an understanding of inserting and adding various annotations in a drawing.

Details are the drawing dimensions and annotations required to document part features. There are two types of dimensions: Inserted dimensions and Added dimensions. Inserted dimensions are feature dimensions.

Feature dimensions are created in the part and inserted into the drawing. Inserted dimensions are associative. Modify a dimension in the drawing and the feature dimension is modified in the part.

Added drawing dimensions are called Reference dimensions. Reference dimensions are driven by part features. Driven dimensions are called Reference dimensions. You cannot edit a Driven or Reference dimension.

Add annotations such as: Notes, Hole Callouts, and Center Marks to the drawing document from the View Layout toolbar.

The design intent of this project is to work with dimensions inserted from parts and to incorporate them into the drawings. Explore methods to move, hide, and add dimensions to adhere to a drawing standard.

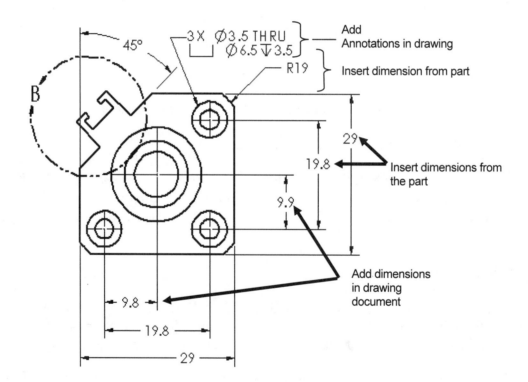

Work between multiple parts, drawings, and sheets. Add annotations to the drawing that reference part dimensions.

A goal of this book is to expose various SolidWorks design tools and features. The most direct way may not always be shown.

There are other solutions to the dimensioning schemes illustrated in this chapter. The TUBE, COVERPLATE, and exercise drawings are sample drawings; they are not complete. A drawing requires tolerances, materials, Revision Tables, Engineering Change Orders, and other notes prior to production and release.

Review a hypothetical "worse case" drawing situation. You just inserted dimensions from a part into a drawing. The dimensions, extensions lines and arrows are not in the correct locations. How can you improve the position of these details? Answer: Apply an engineering drawing standard.

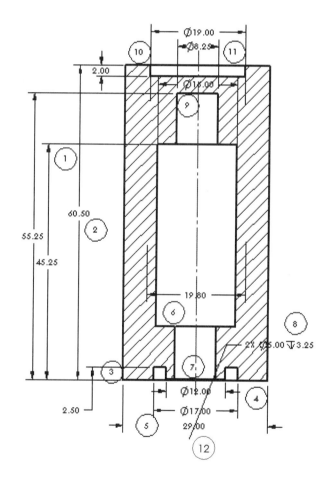

No:	Situation:
1	Extension line crosses dimension line. Dimensions not evenly spaced.
2	Largest dimension placed closest to profile.
3	Leader lines overlapping
4	Extension line crossing arrowhead.
5	Arrow gap too large.
6	Dimension pointing to feature in another view. Missing dimension – inserted into Detail view (not shown).
7	Dimension text over centerline, too close to profile.
8	Dimension from other view – leader line too long.
9	Dimension inside section lines.
10	No visible gap.
11	Arrows overlapping text.
12	Incorrect decimal display with whole number (millimeter), no specified tolerance.

Dimensions are displayed in millimeters in this chapter.

The illustrations in this book are based on SolidWorks SP1.0. The illustrations may vary slightly per your SolidWorks release.

The ASME Y14.5M standard defines an engineering drawing standard. Review the twelve changes made to the drawing to meet the standard.

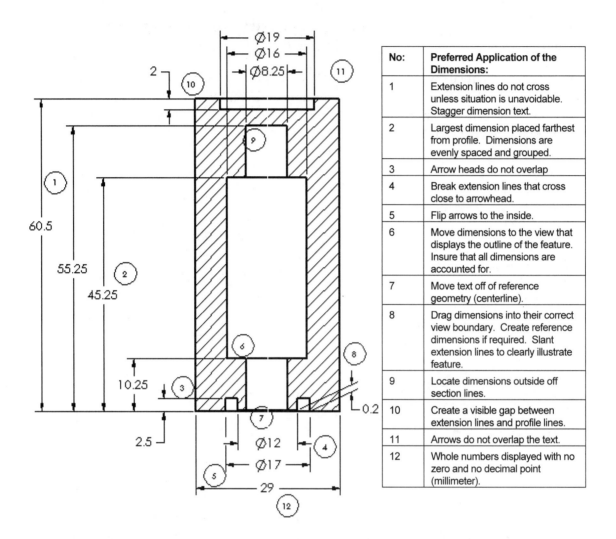

No:	Preferred Application of the Dimensions:
1	Extension lines do not cross unless situation is unavoidable. Stagger dimension text.
2	Largest dimension placed farthest from profile. Dimensions are evenly spaced and grouped.
3	Arrow heads do not overlap
4	Break extension lines that cross close to arrowhead.
5	Flip arrows to the inside.
6	Move dimensions to the view that displays the outline of the feature. Insure that all dimensions are accounted for.
7	Move text off of reference geometry (centerline).
8	Drag dimensions into their correct view boundary. Create reference dimensions if required. Slant extension lines to clearly illustrate feature.
9	Locate dimensions outside off section lines.
10	Create a visible gap between extension lines and profile lines.
11	Arrows do not overlap the text.
12	Whole numbers displayed with no zero and no decimal point (millimeter).

Apply these dimension practices to the TUBE, COVERPLATE, and exercise drawings. Manufactured parts utilize detailed drawings. A mistake on a drawing can cost your company substantial loss in revenue. The mistake could result in a customer liability lawsuit. In other words, as the designer, dimension and annotate your parts clearly to avoid common problems.

Leading zeros, trailing zeros, and number of zeros to the right of the decimal point are important in dimension and tolerance display. Address it either in the Document Properties section or in the Dimension PropertyManager.

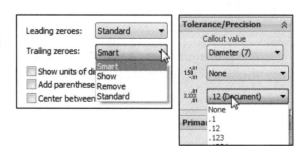

There are different rules for the display of decimal dimensions and tolerances based on millimeter and inch units. Review the below table.

TYPES of DECIMAL DIMENSIONS (ASME Y14.5M)			
Description:	**UNITS: MM**	**Description:**	**UNITS: INCH**
Dimension is less than 1mm. Zero precedes the decimal point.	0.9 0.95	Dimension is less than 1 inch. Zero is not used before the decimal point.	.5 .56
Dimension is a whole number. Display no decimal point. Display no zero after decimal point.	19	Express dimension to the same number of decimal places as its tolerance. Add zeros to the right of the decimal point. If the tolerance is expressed to 3 places, then the dimension contains 3 places to the right of the decimal point.	1.750
Dimension exceeds a whole number by a decimal fraction of a millimeter. Display no zero to the right of the decimal.	11.5 11.51		

TOLERANCE DISPLAY FOR METRIC AND INCH DIMENSIONS (ASME Y14.5M)		
Description:	**UNITS: MM**	**UNITS: INCH**
Dimensions less than 1	0.5	.5
Unilateral Tolerance	$36\,^{0}_{-0.5}$	$1.417\,^{+.005}_{-.000}$
Bilateral Tolerance	$36\,^{+0.25}_{-0.50}$	$1.417\,^{+.010}_{-.020}$
Limit Tolerance	14.50 11.50	.571 .463

Leading zeros, trailing zeros, and number of zeros to the right of the decimal point are important in dimension and tolerance display. Address it either in the Document Properties section or in the Dimension PropertyManager.

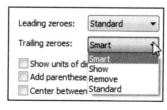

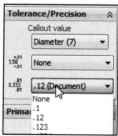

The SolidWorks dimensioning standard is set to ANSI. Trailing zeroes is set to Smart. The primary unit is millimeters in this chapter.

SolidWorks displays a leading zero for millimeter dimensions less than one. SolidWorks displays no decimal point and no zero after the decimal point for whole number dimensions.

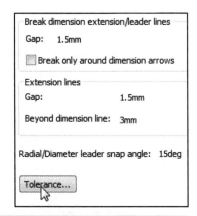

 Click **Options**, **Document Properties** tab, **Dimensions** folder, **Tolerance** button to control tolerance type.

Click **Options**, **Document Properties** tab, **Dimensions** folder to address precision.

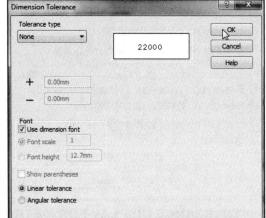

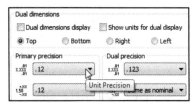

Access the Tolerance/Precision option for an active drawing document either from the Dimension PropertyManager or the dimension Pop-up palette in the Graphics window to save mouse travel to the Dimension PropertyManager.

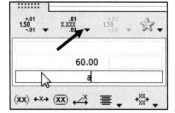

- Example 1: Set Precision Primary Units to .12 places. The drawing dimension displays 0.55. The number of decimal places is two. No change is required.

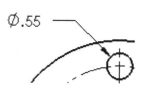

Example 2: The drawing dimension displays 0.50. Control individual dimension precision through the Dimension Properties Tolerance/Precision text box or the dimension Pop-up palette in the Graphics window to save mouse travel to the Dimension PropertyManager.

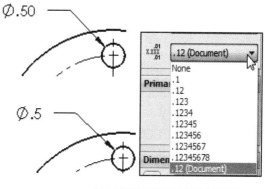

Modify the dimension Primary Units display to .X, (one decimal place). The drawing dimension displays 0.5.

General tolerance values apply to all dimensions on a drawing except reference dimensions and material stock sizes. Tolerance values are displayed with 1, 2 and or 3 decimal places.

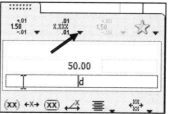

Values differ for machined parts, plastic parts, sheet metal parts, castings and other manufacturing processes.

- Example: 1PL is ±0.2. The dimension 0.9 has a tolerance value of ±0.2. The feature dimension range is 0.7mm - 1.1mm. The tolerance equals 1.1mm - 0.7mm = 0.4mm.

- Example: 2PL is ±0.05. The dimension 0.95 has a tolerance value of ±0.05. The feature dimension range is 0.90mm - 1.00mm. The tolerance equals 1.00mm - 0.90mm = 0.10mm.

UNLESS OTHERWISE SPECIFIED
DIM ARE IN MILLIMETERS
1PL   ±0.2   2PL   ±0.05
ANGULAR ±.5°
INTERPRET DIM AND TOL PER
ASME Y14.5M - 1994

The Document Property, Leading zeroes has three options:

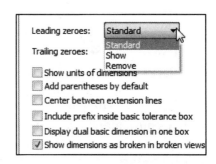

- **Standard**: Zeros are displayed based on the dimensioning standard.

- **Show**: Zeros before decimal points are displayed.

- **Remove**: Zeros are not displayed.

The Document Property, Trailing zeroes has four options:

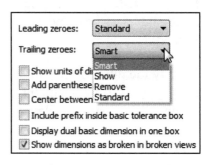

- **Smart**: Trailing zeros are trimmed for whole metric values. (Conforms to ANSI and ISO standards.)

- **Show**: Dimensions have trailing zeros up to the number of decimal places specified in Options, Document Properties tab, Units.

- **Remove**: All trailing zeros are removed.

- **Standard**: Trims trailing zeroes to the ASME Y14.5M-1994 standard.

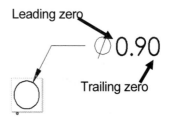

Trailing zeroes, Smart option removes all zeros to the right of the decimal point for whole numbers. The Show option displays the number of zeros equal to the number of places specified in the Units option. The Remove option displays no trailing zeros to the right of the dimension value. The Standard option trims trailing zeroes to the ASME Y14.5M-1994 standard.

Set the Trailing zeroes option to Smart. Control individual dimensions with the Primary Units Precision option. The Trailing zeroes option does not affect tolerance display. The Tolerance/Precision display for a drawing is located in the Dimension PropertyManager. In the drawing, the Tolerance/Precision box determines specific display for individual dimensions.

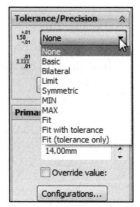

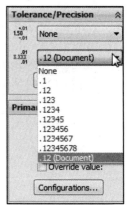

Tolerance Type

A Tolerance type is selected from the available drop down list in the Dimension PropertyManager. The list is dynamic. A few examples of Tolerance type display are listed below:

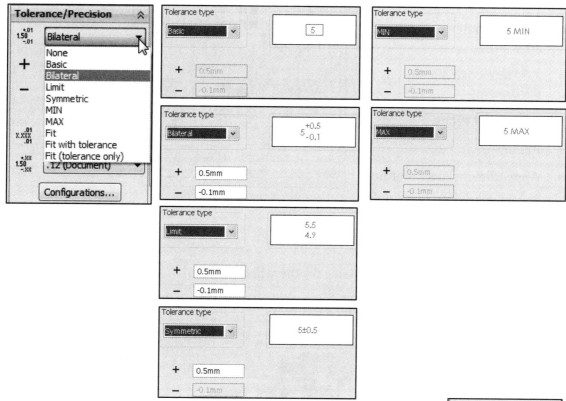

- Example: View the illustrated model. Review the Tolerance, Precision, and Dimension Text in the model.

- 9X Ø.4.83 THRU EQ SP - Nine holes Through All Equally Spaced with a diameter of 4.83. Precision is set to two decimal places.

- 2X R.6.35 - Two corners with a radius of 6.35. Precision is set to two decimal places.

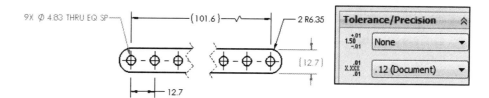

TUBE Drawing-Detailing

Detailing the TUBE drawing
requires numerous steps.
Example:

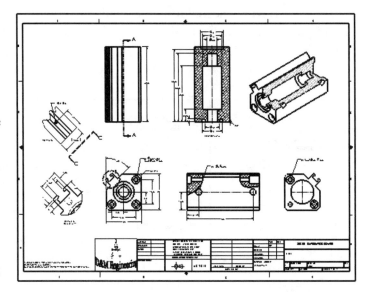

- Insert part dimensions into
  the Tube drawing.

- Reposition dimensions to the
  appropriate view.

- Add reference dimensions to
  the drawing.

- Add Annotations.

- Review each view.

- Apply dimensions according
  to your company's standard.

There are two methods to import
model items from the part into the drawing:

- **Entire model**: Inserts model items for the whole model.

- **Selected feature**: Inserts model items for the feature you select
  in the Graphics window.

There are four methods to
import model items from the
assembly into the drawing.

- **Entire model**: Inserts
  model items for the
  whole model.

- **Selected feature**: Inserts
  model items for the
  feature you select in the
  Graphics window.

- **Selected component**:
  Inserts model items for
  the component you select in the Graphics window.

- **Only assembly**: Inserts model items for assembly features
  only.

How do you reposition numerous dimensions and annotations? Answer: One view at a time. Use the following tips:

- Hide views temporarily when not in use.

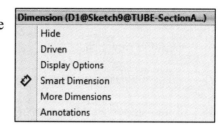

- Hide dimensions that are no longer required. Utilize a layer to turn on/off dimensions. Utilize Hide/Show to control dimension display. Do not delete them. It takes less time to show a hidden dimension than to create one.

- Temporarily move views to see dimensions on top of other views.

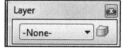

- Deactivate the dimension parenthesis when creating baseline dimensions.

- Review each feature to determine if all feature dimensions and Geometric relations are accounted for in the appropriate view.

- Review each view for center marks, center lines, hole callouts and other annotations.

Work with layers to control the display of dimensions. Create the two new layers named; Details and HideDims. Insert dimensions from the part on the Details layer. Add dimensions and annotations on the Details layer. Move dimensions inserted from the part and not required to detail the drawing to the HideDims layer. The HideDims layer is turned off.

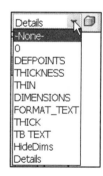

SolidWorks truncates layer names to 26 characters, converts lower case letters to upper case letters and replaces typed spaces in layer names with underscores. Review the view names in the FeatureManager before you Insert Dimensions. Dimensions are displayed in a specific order. First, SolidWorks imports dimensions into all section views and detail views. Next, the dimensions are positioned in the standard views.

Activity: TUBE Drawing-Detailing

Open the TUBE drawing.

1) Click **Open** from the Menu bar toolbar.

2) Select **Drawing** for file type. Double-click **TUBE**.

3) Uncheck the **Dual dimensions display** box in the Document Properties box.

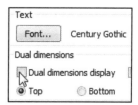

Display the Layer toolbar.

4)   Check **View**, **Toolbars**, **Layer** from the Menu bar menu.

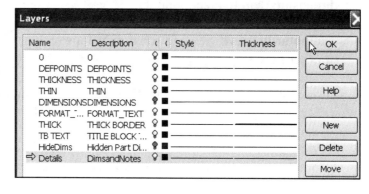

Create a new layer

5)   Click the **Layer Properties** icon.

Layer Properties
Creates, edits, or deletes layers. Also, changes the properties and visibility of layers.

6)   Click the **New** button.

7)   Enter **HideDims** for Name.

8)   Enter **Hidden Part Dims** for Description.

9)   Click the **Light Bulb** to turn the HideDims layer off. Select **Red** for Color. Click **OK**.

10)   Click the **New** button. Enter **Details** for Name.

11)   Enter **DimsandNotes** for Description. The Layer is On when the Light Bulb is yellow.

12)   Enter **Blue** for Color. Accept the default Style and Thickness. Click **OK**. Details layer is the current layer.

Insert dimensions for the entire model.

13)   Click a **position** inside the sheet boundary and outside any view boundary. Note: No Drawing view boundaries are selected.

14)   Click **Model Items** from the Annotation toolbar.

15)   Select **Entire model**. Accept the defaults.

16)   Click **OK** from the Model Items PropertyManager. The dimensions are displayed in blue.

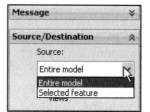

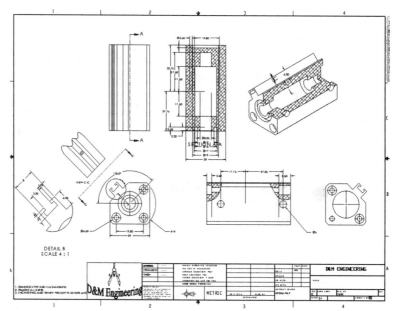

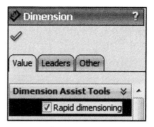

Rapid dimensioning provides the ability to enable or disable the rapid dimension manipulator. Select to enable; clear to disable. This setting persists across sessions. You can use the rapid dimension manipulator to place dimensions so they are evenly spaced and easier to read. When the rapid dimension manipulator creates dimensions on a symmetric centerline, any dimensions that might overlap are staggered for drawings in the ANSI standard. See SolidWorks help for additional information.

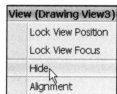

Temporarily hide views when not in use.

17)   Right-click inside the **Right view** boundary; Drawing View3.

18)   Click **Hide**.

Hide dimensions from the Half Section Isometric view.

19)   Click inside the **Half Section Isometric view** boundary.

20)   Drag the **view** to the right, away from the Section view dimensions.

21)   Click and drag the **dimension text** until you view each dimension.

22)   Hold the **Ctrl** key down.

23)   Click the **11**, **3**, **1** and **6.30** dimension text.

24)   Release the **Ctrl** key.

25)   Select the **HideDims** layer from the Dimension PropertyManager.

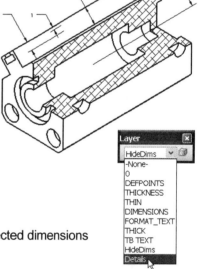

26)   Click **OK** ✔ from the Dimension PropertyManager. The selected dimensions are hidden.

27)   Select the **Details** layer from the Layer toolbar.

Save the TUBE drawing.

28)   Click **Save** 💾 .

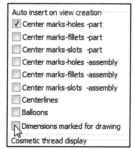

Marked dimensions can be inserted automatically as the views are created using the option **Tools**, **Options**, **Document Properties**, **Detailing**, **Auto insert on view creation**.

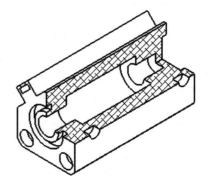

For dimensions placed on a hidden layer, hide and delete commands may not completely remove all of the graphic bits. If the dimensions are not erased completely, click Rebuild.

Hide Dimensions

What command do you select when dimensions are no longer required? Answer: There are two options: HideDims layer or the Hide command.

Number of Dimensions:	Command Sequence:
One or two dimensions	Select the dimensions. Right-click, Hide.
Many dimensions	Place the dimensions on the HideDims layer. Turn off the HideDims layer.

Hide dimensions versus delete dimensions. Use caution when deleting a dimension. You may require the dimension in the future. How do you restore the hidden dimensions? Answer: Utilize View, Hide/Show Annotations from the Menu bar menu. The hidden dimensions are displayed in a small box.

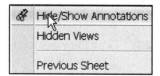

Show Dimensions

Click on the dimension text to display the Dimension PropertyManager. Dimensions placed on the HideDims layer remain turned off. To display the layer, click On ♀ from the Layers dialog box. The dimensions added to a drawing are called Reference dimensions. Model dimensions drive Reference dimensions.

Model dimensions are created in a part or an assembly. A Reference dimension cannot be changed. The dimension for the overall length and Stroke Chamber are defined from the Front reference plane. The part dimension scheme was the engineer's intent. As the detailer, define the dimensions to a base line. Hide the dimensions to avoid superfluous dimensions.

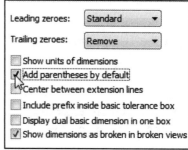

Reference dimensions may be displayed with parentheses. Uncheck the Dimensions Document Property, Add parentheses by default option to conserve design time.

DimXpert applies dimensions in drawings so that manufacturing features, patterns, slots, pockets, etc. are fully-defined. Click the DimXpertManager tab or the DimXpert tab from the CommandManager to access the available DimXpert tools. DimXpert is part of the SWIFT family of features. DimXpert is explored later in the book.

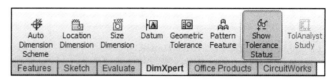

The ASME Y14.5M-1994 standard uses parenthesis to represent an Overall and an Intermediate Reference dimension. Control the dimensions that contain a parenthesis to adhere to your company's drawing standard. Select Properties on the dimension text.

Uncheck the Display with parenthesis option to control the individual Reference dimensions.

Overall Reference Dimension

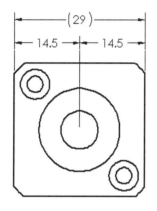

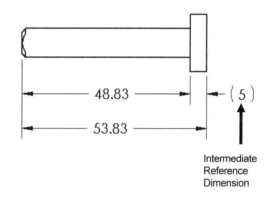

Intermediate
Reference
Dimension

TUBE Detailing-Section View, Top View and Detail View

There are numerous techniques utilized to detail a view. Start with the Section view. The Model Items tool from the Annotate toolbar inserted the majority of the required dimensions into the Section view.

Move the Section view away from the Top view to view the dimensions. The Top view requires an overall vertical dimension. Modify the Precision of the dimension to one decimal place.

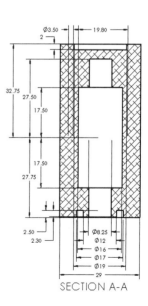

SECTION A-A

Place inserted part dimensions not required on the HideDims layer. Insert a Baseline Dimension for the vertical dimensions, modify extension lines and center dimension text. Move dimensions from the Section view to the Front view.

There is a horizontal dimension required to describe Front-Detail1 in the Section view. The Ø17 dimension was created in the TUBE part.

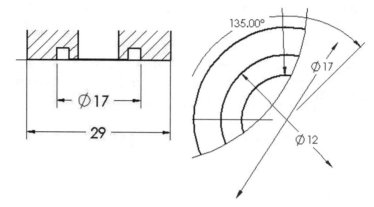

🔆 Where is the dimension? Answer: Look for the dimension in the Detail view if the Ø17 is not displayed in the Section view.

SolidWorks inserts dimensions into the Section view and Detail view. Then SolidWorks inserts dimensions into the remaining views.

The Ø17 text is located in the Detail view if the Detail view contains the Front-Detail1 feature. A small part of the circle is displayed in the Detail view. The leader line is long and extends into the boundary of the Front view.

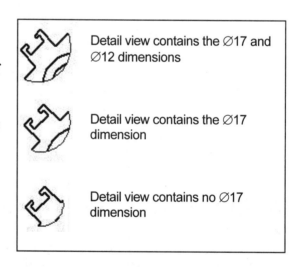

Detail view contains the Ø17 and Ø12 dimensions

Detail view contains the Ø17 dimension

Detail view contains no Ø17 dimension

Move the Ø17 text from the Detail view to the Section view. Create a vertical dimension referencing the bottom horizontal edge. Use the Hole Callout to dimension the Counterbore. Move dimensions and add dimensions to the Front and Detail view.

🔆 Driven or Reference Dimensions can be added directly to the drawing at any time to supplement or replace the model dimensions. Several methods can be used including Standard dimensions, Baseline, Chamfer or Ordinate. They can also be added using the Autodimension tool.

Activity: TUBE Drawing Detailing-Section View, Top View, and Detail View

Temporarily move the Section view.

29) Drag the **Section view** boundary to the right until the dimension text is off the Top view.

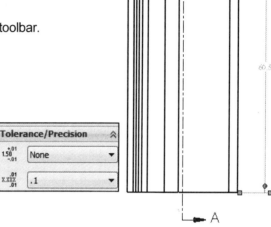

Create the overall depth dimension.

30) Click inside the **Top view** boundary. If needed, **hide** all dimensions in the Top view.

31) Click **Smart Dimension** ✎ from the Sketch toolbar.

32) Click the **right vertical line** in the Top view.

33) Position the **60.50** dimension text to the right of the Top view. A visible gap exists between the extension lines and the right vertical profile lines.

34) Select **.1** from the Primary Unit Precision text box. The 60.5 dimension text is displayed.

35) Click **OK** ✔ from the Dimension PropertyManager. View the results.

Hide the vertical dimensions in the Section view A-A as illustrated.

36) Click the **vertical dimensions**.

37) Select the **HideDims** layer.

38) Click **OK** ✔ from the Dimension PropertyManager.

Insert Baseline dimensions.

39) Select the **Details** layer from the Layer toolbar.

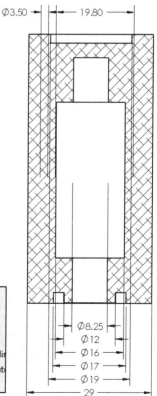

Create the first dimensions for the Stroke Chamber.

40) Click inside the **Section view A-A** view boundary.

41) Click **Smart Dimension** ✎ from the Sketch toolbar.

42) Right-click **More Dimensions**.

43) Click **Baseline**. The Baseline icon is displayed.

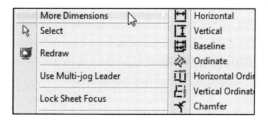

44) Click the **lower left horizontal line** of the Stroke Chamber as illustrated. Click the **left horizontal line** of the Nose as illustrated.

45) Click the **left horizontal line** of the Tube Extrusion as illustrated.

Create the other dimensions.

46) Click the **left horizontal line** of the Stroke Chamber as illustrated.

47) Click the **left horizontal line** of the Bore as illustrated.

48) Click the **left horizontal line** of the Cbore as illustrated. Right-click **Smart Dimension**.

49) Click **OK** ✔ from the Dimension PropertyManager.

50) Drag the **dimension text** to the left as illustrated.

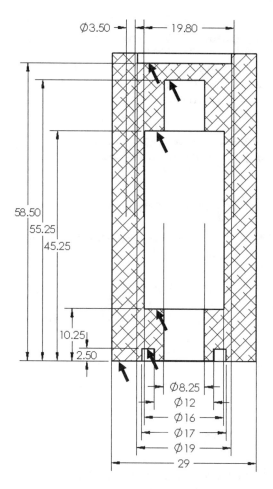

🔆 All drawing views with dimensions require internal gaps between the visible feature line and extension lines. Zoom in on the dimension, click the dimension, and create the gap with the blue control points.

🔆 DimXpert differs from Autodimension in two key ways: DimXpert Recognizes patterns, linear and polar dimensions with instance counts and countersink holes, and DimXpert produces predictable results. Example: When you select an edge in DimXpert, only the feature represented by the edge is dimensioned. With autodimensioning, you may get unwanted dimensions to several features.

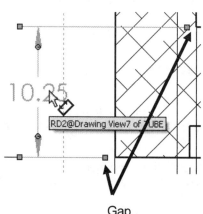

Gap

🔆 Set the depth of section views in parts by specifying how far beyond the section view line you want to see. Previously, this functionality existed in assembly drawings only. This is available under Section Depth in the Section View PropertyManager.

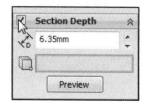

Select a line segment, not a point, to create a linear dimension. Fillet and Chamfer features remove points.

Center the dimension text between the extension lines.

51) Right-click on the **10.25** dimension text.

52) Click **Display Options**.

53) Click **Center Dimension**.

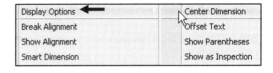

54) Click **OK** ✓ from the Dimension PropertyManager.

Baseline dimensions are aligned. Right-click Properties, Break Alignment to remove aligned dimensions. Click Show Alignment to display dimensions that are aligned. Uncheck the Center Dimension to position text along the extension lines.

55) Review the dimensions and view positions. If required, click and drag the **Section view**, **dimensions** and the **extension lines** of the vertical dimensions to create needed gaps.

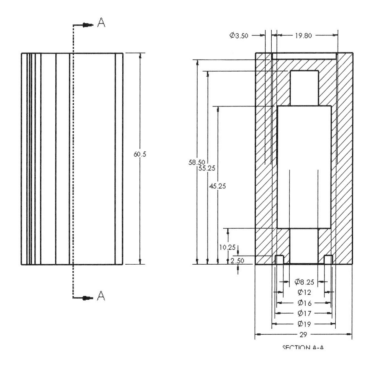

The vertical dimensions are equally spaced and positioned off the profiles. The Top and Section views are adequately spaced. The text and arrows are visible. There is a gap between the profile and vertical extension lines.

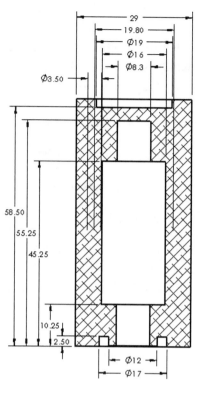

Move the bottom horizontal dimensions to the top in the Section view.

56) Click and drag the ⌀8.25 bottom horizontal dimension text to the top of the Section view A-A approximately 10mm above the top horizontal profile.

57) Set Primary Unit Precision to **.1**.

58) Drag each **extension line** to the top vertex of the Bore to create a gap.

59) Click and drag the ⌀**16** text upward above the ⌀8.3 text.

60) Drag the extension lines to the **top vertex** of the Bore.

61) Repeat for the other **illustrated dimension** text.

Align the top horizontal dimensions.
62) Hold the **Ctrl** key down.

63) Click the ⌀**8.3**, ⌀**16**, and ⌀**19** dimension text.

64) Release the **Ctrl** key.

65) Click **Tools**, **Dimensions**, **Align Parallel/Concentric** from the Menu bar menu.

66) Click **OK** ✓ from the Dimension PropertyManager.

☀ The Dimension Document Property, Offset distances, From last dimension option controls the spacing between parallel dimensions.

Move dimensions from the Section view A-A to the Front view.
67) Press the **z** key until the Front view and the Section view are displayed.

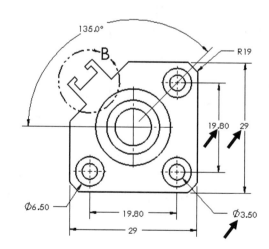

68) Click the **29** dimension text in the Section view. Hold the **Shift** key down.

69) Drag the **29** dimension text to the inside of the Front view.

70) Release the **Mouse button**. Release the **Shift** key.

71) Perform the same procedure for **19.8** and ⌀**3.50** in the Section view. Note Position the text in the Front view in the next section.

72) Hide the **11** dimension with the Hide option.

🔆 The Leaders tab in the Dimension PropertyManager Provides the ability to access the Witness/Leader Display box. The Witness/Leader Display box provides the ability to select arrow style, direction, and type.

🔆 Selecting multiple entities becomes a challenge on a large drawing. To move, copy, or modify multiple entities, select the first entity. Hold the Ctrl key down and select the remaining entities. The first selection clears all previously selected entities.

Move the horizontal dimension text.

73) Click the ⌀**12** dimension text at the bottom of the Section view.

74) Drag the ⌀**12** dimension text upward to a position 10mm below the bottom horizontal profile line.

75) Drag each **extension line** off the profile. Do not use the Nose vertex. The Nose feature is too close to the bottom horizontal line of the Tube to utilize the vertex.

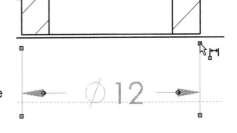

🔆 Use the dimension Pop-up palette in the Graphics window to save mouse travel to the Dimension PropertyManager. The dimension palette appears when you insert or select a dimension so you can easily change the dimension's properties and formatting.

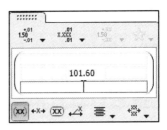

Align the horizontal dimensions.

76) Click the ⌀**12** dimension text.

77) Hold the **Ctrl** key down.

78) Click the ⌀**17** dimension.

79) Release the **Ctrl** key.

80) Click **Tools**, **Dimensions**, **Align Parallel/Concentric** from the Menu bar menu.

81) Click **OK** ✔ from the Dimension PropertyManager.

Position the Section A-A text below the bottom horizontal dimensions.

82) Center the **Section A-A** text.

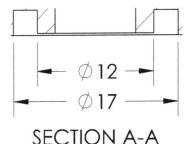

Insert a Centerline.

83)   Click inside the **Section view A-A** boundary.

84)   Click **Centerline** ⊞ from the Annotation toolbar.

85)   Click **OK** ✔ from the Centerline PropertyManager.

💡 Insert Centerlines quickly. Utilize the view boundary, two edges, two sketched entities (expect Splines), face or feature to manually insert a Centerline annotation. Utilize the Offset text option to position the text angled, outside the dimension arrows.

Add a vertical dimension with Offset.

86)   Click **Smart Dimension** ✧ from the Sketch toolbar.

87)   Click the **horizontal line** of the Nose.

88)   Click the **bottom horizontal line** of the Tube Extrusion.

89)   Click a **position** directly to the right.

90)   Drag the **dimension** to the right, off the Section view.

91)   Click **OK** ✔ from the Dimension PropertyManager.

Display offset text.

92)   Click the **0.20** dimension text.

93)   Click the **Value** tab in the Dimension PropertyManager

94)   Click the **Offset Text** button.

💡 To slant the dimension, position the mouse pointer at the end of the extension line. Drag the extension line to create the angled dimension.

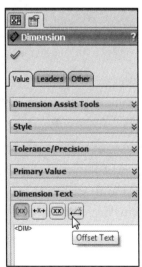

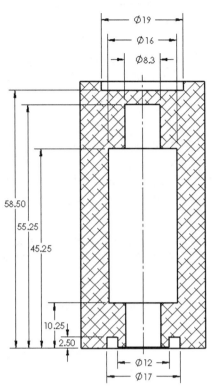

SECTION A-A

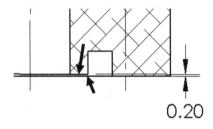

0.20

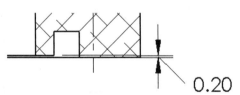

0.20

95) Select **.1** from the
Tolerance/Precision text box. The
0.2 dimension is displayed.

96) Click **OK** ✓ from the Dimension
PropertyManager.

Save the TUBE drawing.
97) Click **Save** 🖫 .

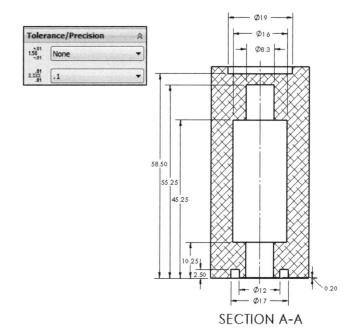

SECTION A-A

TUBE Drawing-Detailing Detail View, and Front View

Review the status of the Front view and Detail view. Dimensions are not clear or
Dimensions are on top of each other. Dimensions are too far or too close to the profile.

Hide the 11 and 135° dimensions in the Detail view or Front view with the Hide option.
Replace the 135° obtuse angle with an acute angle. Create an acute angle dimension from
a construction line Collinear with the left vertical edge in the Front view.

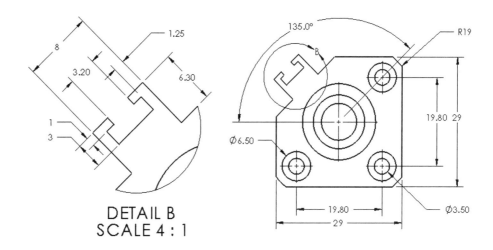

DETAIL B
SCALE 4 : 1

Activity: TUBE Drawing-Detailing Detail View and Front View

Hide the dimensions.

98) Click inside the **Detail view** boundary.

99) Click **Hidden Lines Visible** ⬚ from the Display Style box.

100) If required, click inside the **Front view** boundary. Right-click the **11** dimension text.

101) Click **Hide**.

102) Right-click the **135.0°** angle text.

103) Click **Hide**. Note: The location of the 11 and 135.0° dimension depends on the size of the Detail view.

104) Click inside the **Detail view** boundary. Drag the **1** dimension text approximately 10mm away from the profile. **Flip** the arrows if necessary.

105) Drag the **3** text to the left of the **1** text.

106) Select the **1** dimension text.

107) Hold the **Ctrl** key down.

108) Select the **3** dimension text.

109) Release the **Ctrl** key.

110) Click **Tools**, **Dimensions**, **Align Parallel/ Concentric** from the Menu bar menu.

111) Click **OK** ✔ from the PropertyManager.

112) Drag the **8**, **3.20** and **1.25** dimension text away from the profile.

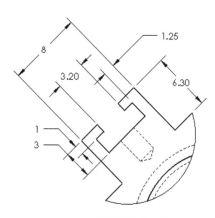

DETAIL B
SCALE 4 : 1

🔅 A break is required when the extension lines cross the dimension lines.

Create a break.

113) Click the **3.20** horizontal dimension.

114) Check the **Break Lines** check box.

115) Check the **Use document gap** box.

116) Click **OK** ✔ from the Dimension PropertyManager.

Set the Precision
117) Click the **3.20** dimension. Hold the **Ctrl** key down.

118) Click the **6.30** dimension. Release the **Ctrl** key.

119) Select **.1** from the Primary Unit Precision text box. The dimensions 3.2 and 6.3 are displayed.

120) Click **OK** ✅ from the Dimension PropertyManager.

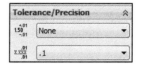

Align the dimensions.
121) Click the **8** dimension. Hold the **Ctrl** key down.

122) Click the **3.2** and **1.25** dimension.

123) Release the **Ctrl** key.

124) Click **Tools**, **Dimensions**, **Align Parallel/Concentric** from the Menu bar menu.

125) Position the **DETAIL B** text below the profile.

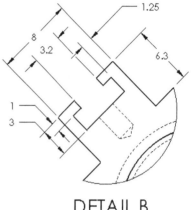

Save the TUBE drawing.
126) Click **Save** 💾 .

DETAIL B
SCALE 4 : 1

🔅 The default Break dimension extension/leader lines Gap value is set in Tools, Options, Document Properties, Dimensions, Break dimension extension/leader lines for an active drawing document.

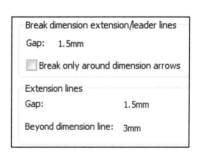

🔅 If the Hide option is utilized to hide an annotation, and you want to display the annotation on the sheet, select View, Hide/Show Annotations from the Menu bar menu. The hidden annotations are displayed in gray. Click the needed annotation to be displayed.

Move and Hide dimensions in the Front view.
127) Click inside the **Drawing View1** view boundary.

128) Drag the vertical **29** dimension text off the profile to the right.

129) Drag the vertical **19.80** dimension to the right.

130) Select **.1** from the Primary Unit Precision text box.

131) Drag the horizontal **29** dimension text below the profile.

132) Drag the horizontal **19.80** dimension below the profile.

133) Select **.1** from the Primary Unit Precision text box.

134) Drag the **R19** dimension upward. The arrow of the leader line is aligned to the centerpoint of the arc.

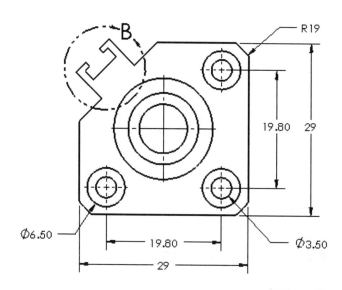

Edit the Radius text. Note: The TUBE Default part configuration document needs to be activtive.

135) Click the **R19** text.

136) Enter **3X** in the Dimension text box.

137) Press the **space bar**. Click **OK** ✓ from the Dimension PropertyManager.

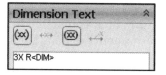

Hide dimensions.

138) Click the ∅**3.50** dimension text. Hold the **Ctrl** key down.

139) Click the ∅**6.50** dimension text. Release the **Ctrl** key.

140) Select **HideDims** layer.

141) Click **OK** ✓ from the Dimension PropertyManager.

142) Select the **Details** layer from the Layer toolbar.

Dimension the angle cut.

143) Click **Smart Dimension** ✏ from the Sketch toolbar.

144) Click the **left vertical profile line** and the **top angled edge**.

145) Position the **dimension** inside the acute angle.

146) Select **None** from the Primary Units Precision box.

147) Click **OK** ✓ from the Dimension PropertyManager.

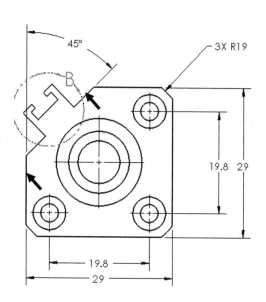

Save the TUBE drawing.

148) Click **Save** 🖫 .

🔅 Edge selection is important. Select the top angled edge, not the bottom angle edge. The bottom angle edge extension line overlaps the profile line and does not produce a gap.

TUBE Drawing-Detailing Right View, Back View, and Holes

The Right view contains a series of holes that require annotations. Display the Right view. Reposition dimensions and add annotations. The Back view requires additional annotations to detail a Counterbore.

Simple Holes and other circular geometry utilize various display options: *Display As Radius, Display As Linear, Define by Hole Wizard, Show Parentheses and Show as Inspection.*

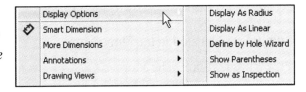

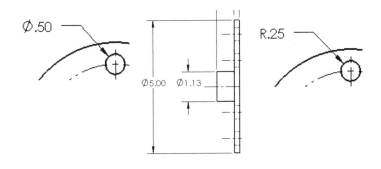

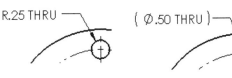

🔅 You can also utilize the Dimension PropertyManager - Leaders tab to affect the display option: *Outside, Inside, Smart, Arrow type, Radius, Diameter, Linear, Perpendicular to Axis, and Use document bend length.*

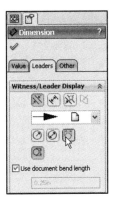

Flip arrows by selecting the
blue control point on the
arrowhead. Arrows
alternate between the
outside position and the
inside position.

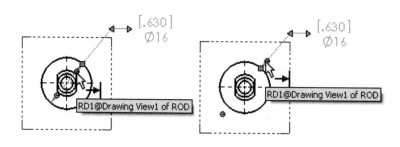

Counterbore holes in the
Right view require a note.
Use the Hole Callout to
dimension the holes. The
Hole Callout function

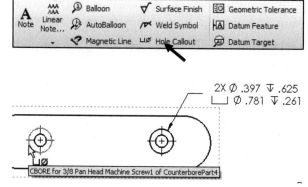

creates additional notes required to
dimension the holes. The dimension
standard symbols are displayed
automatically when you insert holes
created with the Hole Wizard feature.

Symbols are located in the Dimension

Properties text box. The More More...
button displays additional Symbol libraries.
Symbols are also accessed from the

Variables Variables button.

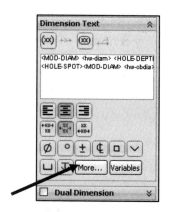

A few command commands are:

- <MOD-DIAM>: Diameter symbol ⌀.

- <MOD-DEG>: Degree symbol °.

- <MOD-PM>: Plus / Minus symbol ±.

- <MOD-CL>: CenterLine symbol ℄.

- <MOD-BOX>: Square symbol ▫.

- <HOLE-SINK>: CounterSink symbol ∨.

- <HOLE-SPOT>: Counterbore symbol ⌴.

- <HOLE-DEPTH>: Depth/Deep symbol ↧.

- <DIM>: Dimension value.

The text in brackets <>, indicates the <library name – symbol name>. Place the number of holes (3) and the multiplication sign (X) before the diameter dimension. Example: 3X<MOD-DIAM><DIM> THRU EQ SP is displayed on the drawing as: 6X Ø.50 THRU EQ SP.

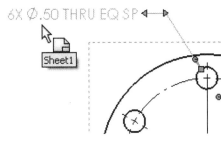

Two Extruded Cut features created the Counterbore in the Front view. The third Extruded Cut feature created the Counterbore in the Back. The Extruded Cut features did not produce the correct Counterbore Hole Callout according to a dimensioning standard. Utilize the Hole Callout tool to create the correct annotation. The mouse pointer displays the Hole Callout ⌴ø icon, when the Hole Callout tool is active.

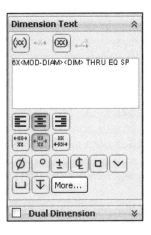

Create two Parametric notes to represent the Counterbore in the Front and Back view. A Parametric note contains dimensions from a part or drawing. Modify the dimension and the Parametric note to reflect the new value. Utilize the Centerline tool and Center Mark tool from the Annotation toolbar. Centerlines are composed of alternating long and short dash lines. The lines identify the center of a circle, axes, or cylindrical geometry.

Center Marks represent two perpendicular intersecting centerlines. Adjust adjacent extension lines after applying Center Marks.

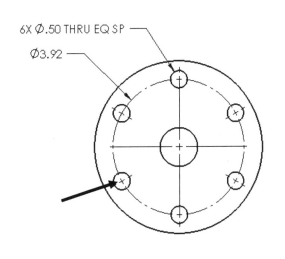

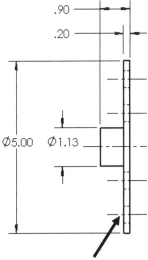

Activity: TUBE Drawing-Detailing Right View, Back View and Holes

Display the Right view.

149) Right-click **Drawing View3** in the FeatureManager.

150) Click **Show**.

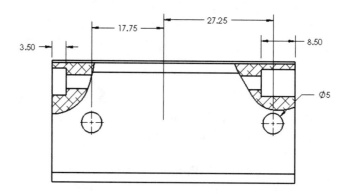

Hide dimensions.

151) Click the ⌀**5** dimension text.

152) Press the **Ctrl** key.

153) Click the **3.50, 8.50, 17.75,** and **27.25** dimension text.

154) Release the **Ctrl** key.

155) Select the **HideDims** layer.

156) Click **OK** ✓ from the Dimension PropertyManager.

157) Select the **Details** layer from the Layer toolbar.

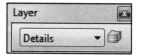

Dimension the Ports.

158) Click **Hole CallOut** ⊔⌀ from the Annotation toolbar.

159) Select the **circumference** of the left Port.

160) Click a **position** above the profile.

161) Enter **2X** before the <MOD-DIAM> text.

162) Click **Yes** to the Break Link with Model dialog box.

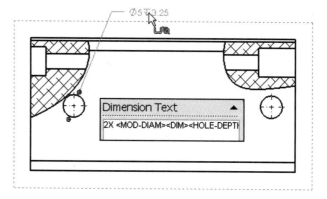

163) Press the **space** key.

164) Click **OK** ✅ from the Dimension PropertyManager.

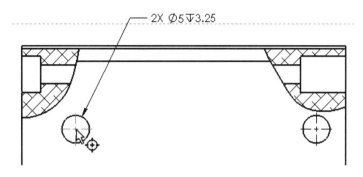

🔅 Inserting text into a Hole Callout annotation in the drawing produces the Break Link with the Model dialog box. Modify the part dimension from ∅5 to ∅6 and the drawing annotation updates. Manually edit the dimension text from ∅5 to ∅6 in the Hole Callout and the part dimension remains unchanged.

Add the vertical and horizontal dimensions.

165) **Hide** the Center Marks on the Port holes.

166) Click **Smart Dimension** ◇ from the Annotation toolbar.

167) Click the **bottom horizontal edge**.

168) Click the left side of the **circumference** of the first circle. Click a **position** to the left of the vertical profile line. The 14.50 dimension text is displayed.

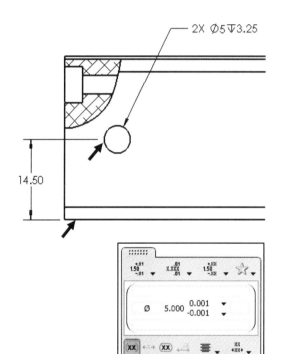

🔅 Use the dimension palette in the Graphics window to save mouse travel to the Dimension PropertyManager. The dimension palette appears when you insert or select a dimension so you can easily change the dimension's properties and formatting. You can change the tolerance, precision, style, text, and other formatting options in the palette without going to the PropertyManager.

🔅 A goal of this book is to expose various SolidWorks design tools and features. The most direct way may not always be shown.

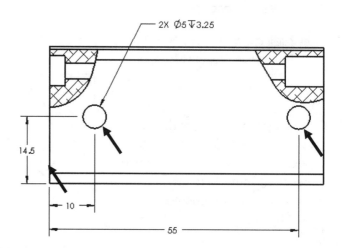

169) Select **.1** from the Primary Unit
Precision text box. The 14.5
dimension text is displayed.

170) Repeat for above procedure for the
horizontal dimensions; **10** and **55**.
Note: Click the lower left vertical
edge to the gap.

Save the TUBE drawing.

171) Click **Save** 💾 .

🔅 Select edges, not vertices when
creating linear dimensions. Select the
circumference of the circle not the
Center Mark annotation when
referencing the center point of circular
geometry.

Show the HideDims layer.

172) Click the **Layer Properties** 🗇 icon.

173) Click the **light bulb** to display the HideDims layer.

174) Click **OK** from the Layers dialog box. The dimensions are
displayed in red.

FORMAT_...	FORMAT_TEXT	♀ ■ —
THICK	THICKNESS	♀ ■ —
TB TEXT	TITLE BLOCK...	♀ ■ —
HideDims	Hidden Part Di...	♀ ■ —
⇒ Details	DimsandNotes	⚡ ■ —

175) Click the ⌀**3.50** dimension text in the
Front view.

176) Hold the **Ctrl** key down.

177) Click the ⌀**6.50** dimension text.

178) Release the **Ctrl** key.

179) Select the **Details** layer from the
Dimension PropertyManager.

180) Click **OK** ✅ from the PropertyManager.
The dimensions are on the Details
layer, and are displayed in blue.

Modify the Precision.

181) Select **.1** Primary Unit Precision for the
⌀3.5 and ⌀6.5 dimension text.

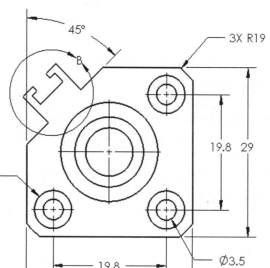

Insert a Note.

182) Click **Note** **A** from the Annotation toolbar.

183) Click the **circumference** of the top right Counterbore in the Front view

184) Click a **position** to the top right of the view. Note: The Details layer is the active layer in the drawing.

185) Enter **3X**.

186) Click the ⌀**3.5** dimension text in the Front view.

187) Enter **THRU**.

188) Press the **Enter** key.

189) Click the **Add Symbol** button.

190) Select **Hole Symbols** for Symbol library.

191) Click **Counterbore (Spotface)**.

192) Click **OK**.

193) Click the ⌀**6.5** dimension text.

194) Enter**<HOLE-DEPTH>**.

195) Press the **space** bar.

196) Enter **3.5**.

197) Click **OK** from the Note PropertyManager.

Hide the diameter dimensions.

198) Click the ⌀**3.5** dimension in the Front view.

199) Hold the **Ctrl** key down.

200) Click the ⌀**6.5** dimension.

201) Release the **Ctrl** key.

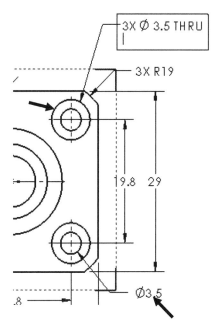

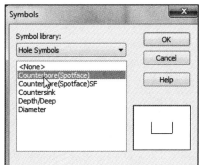

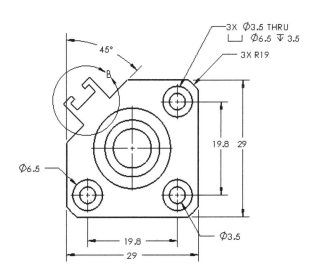

202) Select the **HideDims** layer from the Dimension PropertyManager.

203) Click **OK** ✔ from the PropertyManager. The dimension text is displayed in red.

204) Click the **Details** layer from the Layers toolbar.

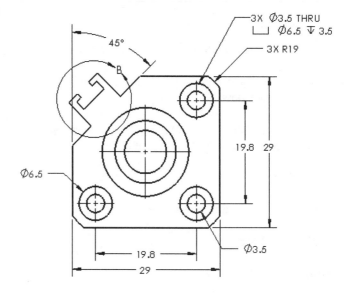

Modify the layer.
205) Click the ⌀**8.50** dimension text in the Right view.

206) Select the **Details** layer from the PropertyManager.

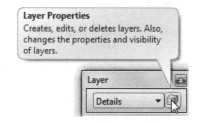

Add a Note to the Counterbore Rear.
207) Click **.1** for Primary Unit Precision. The 8.5 dimension is displayed.

208) Click **OK** ✔ from the Dimension PropertyManager.

209) Double-click on the **Cbore note** in the Front view.

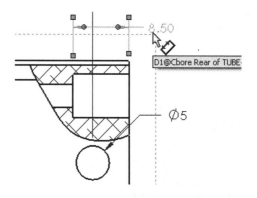

Copy the text.
210) Select the **second line** of text.

211) Right-click **copy**.

212) Click **OK** ✔ from the Note PropertyManager.

213) Click **Note A** from the Annotation toolbar.

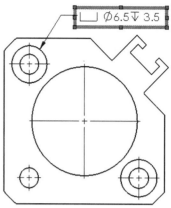

214) Click the **circumference** of the top left Counterbore in the Back view.

215) Click a **position** for the Note.

Paste the Note.
216) Click-right **Paste**.

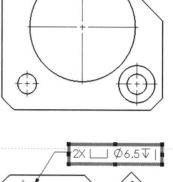

Edit the Note.
217) Enter **2X** at the start of the line.

218) Press the **space** bar.

219) Delete the **3.5** Note text.

220) Click the **8.5** dimension text in the Right view. Click **OK** ✓ from the Note PropertyManager.

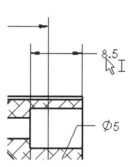

Hide the 8.5 dimension.
221) Click the **8.5** dimension text in the Right view.

222) Select the **HideDims** layer from the Dimension PropertyManager.

223) Click **OK** ✓ from the Dimension PropertyManager.

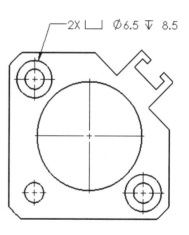

224) Turn the **HideDims layer off**.

225) Click the **Details** layer from the Layers toolbar.

💡 Delete automatically inserted Center Marks in the Right view before you investigate the next step.

Add Center Marks and a Centerline to the Right view.
226) Click **Center Mark** ⊕ from the Annotation toolbar. Note you options for Slot center marks.

227) Click the **Linear Center Mark** button.

228) Check the **Connection lines** box.

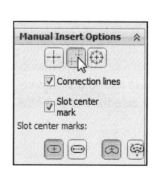

229) Click the circumference of the **left Port** in the Right view.

230) Click the circumference of the **right Port** in the Right view.

231) Click **OK** ✅ from the Center Mark PropertyManager. The two Center Marks and Centerline are displayed.

232) Drag the **centerlines** and **extension** lines off the Center Marks. Do not overlap the Center Marks.

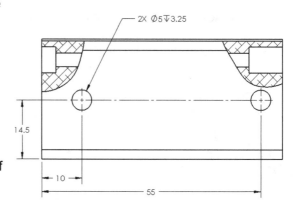

🔅 The desired Centerline did not work if you select the top/bottom edges. The top edge is the Switch feature, not the extruded Tube feature. To display the Centerline for this feature, select Hidden Lines Visible. Select the silhouette top and bottom edges of the Bore feature to create the Centerline.

🔅 To specify tolerance in the Hole Callout, insert the Hole Callout. Click inside the Dimension Text box and select the Tolerance type.

$$2X \ \varnothing 5^{+0.5}_{\quad 0} \ \overline{\mathbb{V}} \ 3.3$$

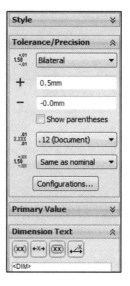

TUBE Drawing-Adding Dimensions

Add dimensions with the Smart Dimension tool in the drawing. The TUBE holes utilized symmetry in the initial Base sketch.

The profile contains horizontal and vertical construction lines sketched from the Origin to a midpoint. A Symmetric relationship with vertical and horizontal construction lines create a fully defined sketch. No additional dimension is required from the Origin to the center point of the hole.

Create new dimensions to locate the holes in relationship to the center of the Bore. Adjust all vertical and horizontal dimensions. Stagger and space dimension text for clarity. Create a gap between the extension lines and the Center Mark. The Auxiliary view is the last view to move and to add dimensions. Use a Hole Callout to specify size and depth. Add a dimension to locate the center of the hole. Move extension lines off the profile.

Activity: TUBE Drawing-Adding Dimensions

Create a vertical dimension in Drawing View1.

233) Click **Smart Dimension** ✧ from the Sketch toolbar.

234) Click the **circumference** of the small right bottom hole.

235) Click the **circumference** of the center circle.

236) Drag the **9.90** dimension to the right of the vertical profile line. Note: If required, delete the small **Center Mark** at the center of the Front view.

237) Click **.1** for Primary Unit Precision. The 9.9 dimension is displayed.

238) Drag the other vertical **dimensions** to the right. **Flip** the dimension arrows if required.

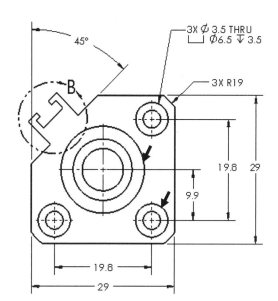

🔅 The Arc Condition option in the Dimension PropertyManager provides the ability to set the dimension between arcs or circles. The First arc condition specifies where or the arc or circle the distance is measured. The Second arc condition specifies where on the second selected item the

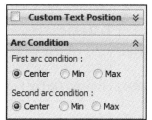

distance is measured, when both items are arcs or circles.

Align dimensions.
239) Click the **9.9** dimension text.

240) Hold the **Ctrl** key down.

241) Click the **19.8** and **29** dimension text.

242) Release the **Ctrl** key.

243) Click **Tools**, **Dimensions**, **Align Parallel/Concentric** from the Menu bar menu.

244) Click **OK** ✅ from the Dimension PropertyManager.

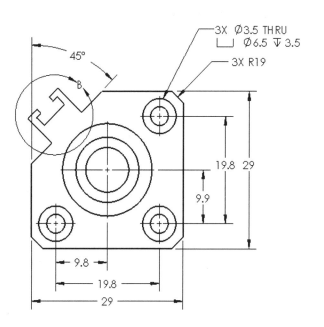

Create a horizontal dimension.

245) Click **Smart Dimension** 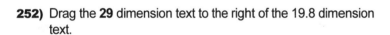 from the Sketch toolbar.

246) Click the **circumference** of the small left bottom hole.

247) Click the **circumference** of the center bottom hole.

248) Drag the **dimension** below the horizontal profile line.

249) Click a **position**. Note: Clicking the position will provide the 9.80 dimension text.

250) Click **.1** for Primary Unit Precision. The 9.8 dimension is displayed.

251) Drag the other horizontal **dimensions** downward. **Flip** the dimension arrows if required.

252) Drag the **29** dimension text to the right of the 19.8 dimension text.

253) Click the **9.8** dimension text.

254) Hold the **Ctrl** key down.

255) Click the **19.8** and **29** dimension text.

256) Release the **Ctrl** key.

257) Click **Tools**, **Dimensions**, **Align Parallel/Concentric** from the Menu bar menu.

258) Click **OK**  from the PropertyManager.

Add a Hole Callout to the Auxiliary view.
259) **Hide** the Center Mark in the Auxiliary view.

260) Click **Hole Callout** ⌴⌀ from the Annotation toolbar.

261) Click the **circumference** of the Hole.

262) Click a **position** to the top left corner of the view. The depth of the Hole is calculated by the Hole Wizard.

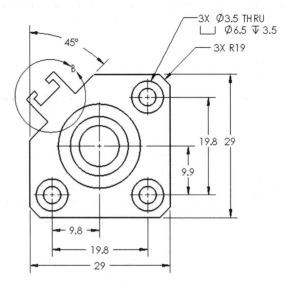

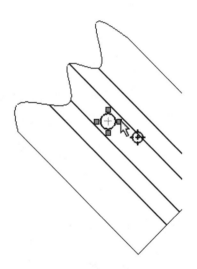

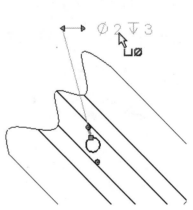

Add dimensions.

263) Click **Smart Dimension** 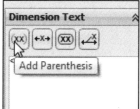 from the Annotation toolbar.

264) Click the **circumference** of the small hole.

265) Click the **bottom edge**.

266) Click a **position** to the right off the profile.

267) Click the **left edge**.

268) Click the **right edge**.

269) Click a **position** below the profile.

Modify the reference dimension.

270) Click the **18.88** dimension text.

271) Click **Add Parentheses** in the Dimension Text box.

Insert a Center Mark.

272) Click **Center Mark** 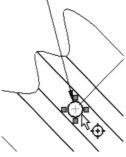 from the Annotation toolbar. The Center Mark PropertyManager is displayed. Single Center Mark is the default option.

273) Click the **center circle** as illustrated.

274) Click the **Single Center Mark** box.

275) Enter **0** for Angle to rotate the Center Mark.

276) Click **OK** from the Center Mark PropertyManager.

Fit the Model to the Sheet.

277) Press the **f** key.

Save the TUBE drawing.

278) Click **Save** .

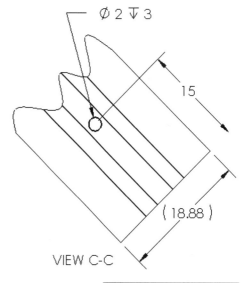

VIEW C-C

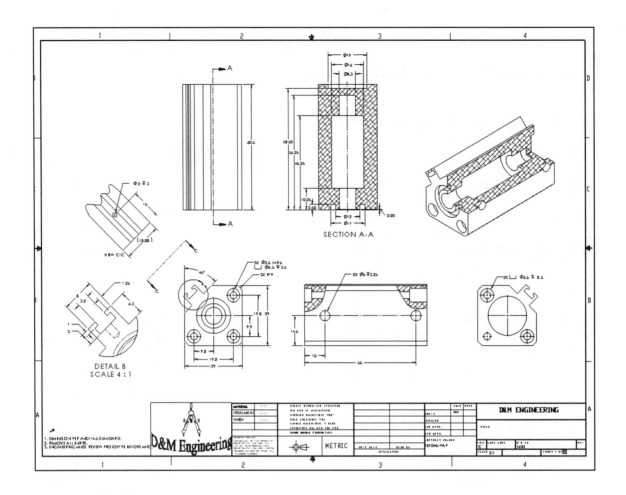

More Information

Additional details on Dimension, Layer, Insert Model Items, Hide/Show, Document Properties, Display Options, Align, Precision, Break Dimension Lines, Symbols, Hole Callout, Center Mark, Centerline and Parametric Note are available in SolidWorks help.

Keywords: Dimensions (align, copy, display, driven, move and reference), Layers (drawing), Insert (dimensions into drawings), Hide (dimensions, drawing views), Options (drawings) Display (drawing views), Align (dimensions), Precision(display), Break Lines, Symbols (in note text), Hole Callouts, and Parametric note.

Use the dimension palette in the Graphics window to save mouse travel to the Dimension PropertyManager. The dimension palette appears when you insert or select a dimension so you can easily change the dimension's properties and formatting. You can change the tolerance, precision, style, text, and other formatting options in the palette without going to the PropertyManager.

Review

The TUBE drawing consisted of a single sheet with eight different views. Each view contained dimensions and annotations. You utilized layers to hide and display dimensions and annotations.

Feature dimensions were inserted from the part into the drawing. Dimensions were relocated in the view and moved to different views. Added dimensions were created in the drawing. Display options and alignment were used to modify the dimensions. Hole Callout annotations utilized symbols and dimension values to create
Parametric notes.

Detailing Tips

The Hole Wizard feature created the M2 hole in the part. The M2 hole sketch utilized a Midpoint and Horizontal Geometric relation. No dimensions were required to position the hole.

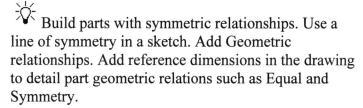

Where do you create dimensions? Do you return to the part and change your dimension scheme to accommodate the drawing? Answer: No. Build the dimensioning scheme and design intent into the part.

Build parts with symmetric relationships. Use a line of symmetry in a sketch. Add Geometric relationships. Add reference dimensions in the drawing to detail part geometric relations such as Equal and Symmetry.

Modify part sketches and features to accommodate a drawing. Fully defined sketches are displayed in black. Drag sketch dimensions off the profiles. Insert part dimensions into the drawing.

Position dimensions in the best view to document the feature.

Move dimensions with the Shift key. Copy dimensions with the Ctrl key. Select a position inside the new view boundary to place the dimensions.

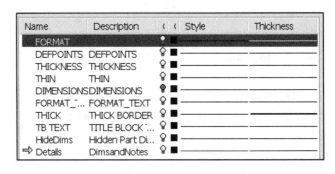

Utilize drawing layers to hide unwanted part dimensions, annotations, and construction geometry created in the drawing.

Add additional layers to control notes and various line fonts. Control the Layer display with the On/Off option.

The TUBE drawing contained dimensions from over 10 features. The Insert Model Items, Entire model option, displayed numerous dimensions. How do you display hundreds of feature dimensions for a part? Answer: Utilize the following tips:

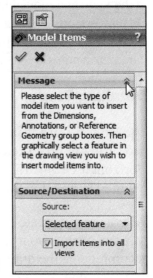

Organize dimension and annotation display with the FeatureManager. Select the feature from the FeatureManager. Select Insert Model Items, Selected Feature option. Repeat for multiple features from the top to the bottom of the FeatureManager.

Utilize a two-view approach. Create a copy of the view and position the new view outside the sheet boundary. The copy of the view is called the "sloppy copy". Select the sloppy copy view boundary. Select Insert Model Items for the selected view. Utilize Ctrl-Select to choose multiple dimensions. Move the required dimensions from the sloppy copy to the original view inside the sheet boundary.

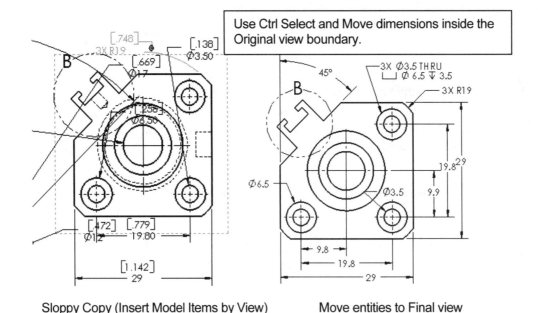

Sloppy Copy (Insert Model Items by View)   Move entities to Final view

Create multiple part configurations with a Design Table. Configurations conserve design time and provide a record of the changes in a single part file.

Example: A Design Table controls the Suppressed/UnSuppressed State of the all around Fillet features. Utilize the Suppress configuration in the drawing. Replace the Fillet features with a note. To modify the note attachment point to the bent leader line, first position the note on the drawing. Select the note and then select the Attachment Leader Style

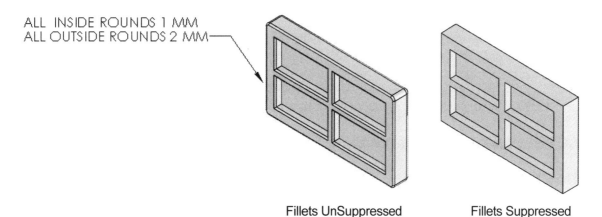

ALL INSIDE ROUNDS 1 MM
ALL OUTSIDE ROUNDS 2 MM

Fillets UnSuppressed   Fillets Suppressed

Drawings contain multiple sheets and views. The Lock Sheet Focus and the Lock View Focus options assist in complex drawings.

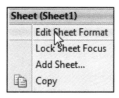 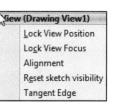

System Options, Drawings, Automatically scale new drawing views option scales new drawing views to fit the drawing sheet, regardless of the paper size selected.

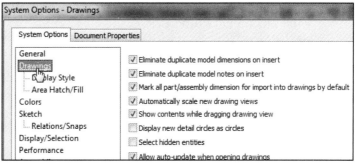

Selecting the preferred view with the mouse is difficult when view boundaries overlap. Sketch entities belong to the view closest to the mouse pointer when you begin sketching.

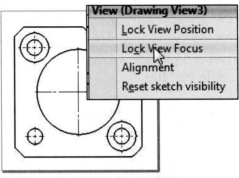

NOTE STAYS WITH VIEW

Lock Sheet Focus and Lock View Focus temporarily halt Dynamic drawing view activation. The Lock Sheet Focus allows you to add entities to the sheet. Entities reference the sheet not a view.

Lock View Focus allows you to add entities to a view, even when the mouse pointer is close to another view. Entities reference only the Locked View.

To reactivate the Dynamic drawing view activation option, right-click in the sheet boundary and select Unlock Sheet Focus, or right-click in the locked view boundary and select Unlock View Focus.

☼ Double-click any view boundary to activate the Dynamic drawing view activation option.

☼ Utilize the arrow keys to move views or notes by small increments.

COVERPLATE Drawing-Detailing

The COVERPLATE utilizes Geometric relationships such as Symmetric to define the position of the features. The ∅8.25 dimension requires a Precision value of 2 decimal places.

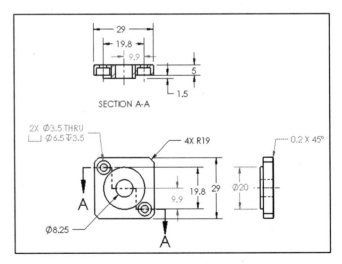

All of the remaining dimensions require a Precision value of 1 or None.

Modify the Document Properties Precision value to 1 decimal place. Review the geometric relations. What additional dimensions and annotations are required in the drawing? Answer: Locate the Counterbore with respect to the Center Hole with a linear dimension in the drawing. Add a Chamfer annotation in the drawing.

The COVERPLATE-Sheet1 Front view utilizes the Without Nose Holes configuration. Activate the part configuration to modify the dimension in the Front view. You cannot edit a dimension in the sheet unless the configuration is active

A Cosmetic Thread displays the major and minor diameter of a thread. Control a Cosmetic Thread as an annotation in the part or in the drawing. The Hole Wizard tapped hole contains a Cosmetic Thread option. Insert a Cosmetic Thread into COVERPLATE-Sheet2. Activate the With Nose Holes part configuration to modify the annotation.

Activity: COVERPLATE Drawing-Detailing

Set Document Precision to 1 decimal place.
279) Open the COVERPLATE drawing.

280) Click the **Sheet1** tab.

281) Click **Options** ⬚, **Document Properties** tab, **Dimensions** from the Menu bar toolbar.

282) Select **1** for Primary precision dimension value.

283) Select **.12** for Tolerance Precision.

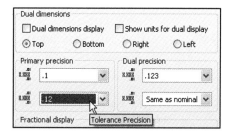

284) Click the **Units** folder.

285) Select **None** for Angular dimension value.

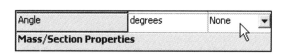

286) Click **OK** from the Document Properties – Units dialog box.

Create a Hole Callout.
287) Click **Hole Callout** ⊔ø from the Annotation toolbar. The Hole Callout PropertyManager is displayed.

288) Click the **Counterbore circumference** in Drawing View5.

289) Click a **position** above the profile.

290) Enter **2X** in the Dimension Text box.

291) Click **Yes** in the Break Link with Model dialog box.

292) Click the **space** bar.

293) Click **OK** ✔ from the Dimension PropertyManager.

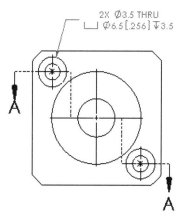

Insert the Model Item for individual features.

294) Click the **circumference** of the small center Bore feature in the Front view.

295) Hold the **Ctrl** key down.

296) Click the **circumference** of the large center Nose feature.

297) Release the **Ctrl** key.

298) Click **Model items** from the Annotation toolbar. The Model Items PropertyManager is displayed. Click **Selected Feature** from the Source/Destination box.

299) Click **OK** from the Model Items PropertyManager. Two dimensions are displayed.

300) Click the ⌀**8.25** dimension text. Click the **Leaders** tab.

301) Click **Diameter** from the Witness/Leader Display dialog box.

302) Click the **Value** tab. **Uncheck** the Dual Dimension box.

303) Click **OK** from the Dimension PropertyManager.

304) Click the ⌀**8.25** dimension text.

305) Click the ⌀**20 dimension** text. Note: Later move the ⌀**20 dimension** text to the right view.

306) **Uncheck** the Dual Dimension box.

307) Click **OK** from the Dimension PropertyManager.

308) **Eliminate** all dual dimensions in the drawing view as illustrated.

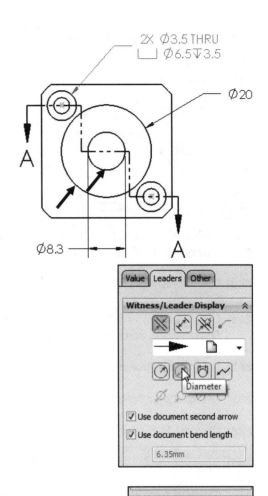

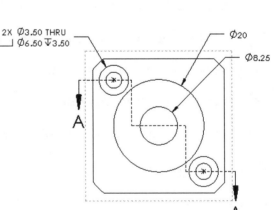

One of the goals in this book is to inform the SolidWorks user on different ways to perform the same function.

Insert the Model Item for the Section view.

309) Click inside the **Section view** boundary.

310) Click **Model Items**  from the Annotation toolbar. The Model Items PropertyManager is displayed.

311) Select **Entire model** from the Source/Destination box.

312) Click **OK** ✔ from the Model Items PropertyManager. The dimensions are displayed.

313) **Eliminate** all dual dimensions in the Drawing. Un-check the Dual dimensions display box from Document Properties.

314) **Eliminate** all trailing zeros on the dimensions.

315) Hide the ∅**6.5**, ∅**3.5** and the **3.5** dimension text.

316) Drag the horizontal dimensions **29** and **19.8** 10mm away from the Profile line. A gap exists between the extension lines and profile.

Open the part.

317) Right-click in the **Section view A-A** boundary.

318) Click **Open Part**. The COVERPLATE is displayed in the Graphics window.

🔆 The view utilizes the Without Holes Configuration.

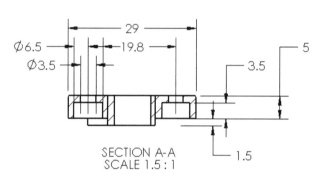

SECTION A-A
SCALE 1.5 : 1

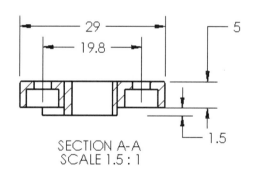

SECTION A-A
SCALE 1.5 : 1

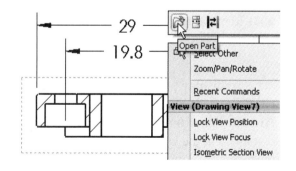

Select the No Holes Configuration.

319) Click the **ConfigurationManager** ⊞ tab.

320) Double-click **Without Nose Holes**.

Return to the FeatureManager.

321) Click the **FeatureManager** tab.

Return to the COVERPLATE drawing

322) Right-click on the **COVERPLATE** name in the FeatureManager.

323) Click **Open Drawing**. The COVERPLATE drawing is displayed.

Insert Centerlines.

324) Click inside the **Section View A-A** boundary.

325) Click **Centerline** ⊞ from the Annotation toolbar. A centerline is displayed.

Add a dimension.

326) Click **Smart Dimension** ⟡ from the Annotation toolbar.

327) Click the **Centerline** of the Hole as illustrated.

328) Click the **Centerline** of the right Counterbore as illustrated.

329) Drag and click the **dimension** off the profile.

330) Click **OK** ✓ from the Dimension PropertyManager.

331) **Eliminate** trailing zeros on the dimension.

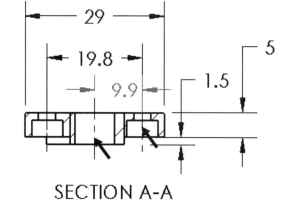

SECTION A-A

To display a hidden dimension in the Graphics window which is not on a layer, click **View**, **Hide/Show Annotations** from the Menu bar menu. The Hidden dimensions are displayed in the Graphics windows. Click the **dimension** to show in the Graphics window. Click **View**, **Hide/Show Annotation** from the Menu bar menu to return to the Graphics window.

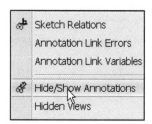

Insert the remaining dimensions.
332) Click a **position** in the sheet boundary.

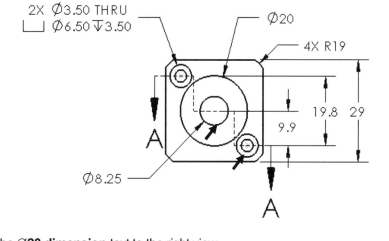

333) Click **Model Items** ✎ from the Annotation toolbar.

334) Select **Entire Model**.

335) Click **OK** ✔ from the Model Items PropertyManager. Note: If needed, modify the drawing view scale to 1:1 to fit the inserted dimensions. Move the ⌀**20 dimension** text to the right view.

336) **Eliminate** all trailing zeros.

Create a vertical dimension in the Front view.
337) Click inside the **Front view** boundary. Click **Smart Dimension** ✎ .

338) Click the **circumference** of the right Counterbore. Click the **circumference** of the small center circle. Click a **position** to the right of the profile. Click **OK** ✔ from the PropertyManager.

☀ Apply the 3D Drawing View 🖥 tool from the Heads-up View toolbar to select difficult edges or faces in a drawing view.

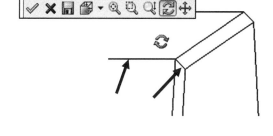

☀ If the extension line references the arc tangent, drag the endpoint of the extension line to the center point to create a center-to-center dimension.

Create a Chamfer dimension in the Right view.
339) Click inside the **Right view** boundary.

340) **Zoom in** on the top right corner.

341) Click the **Smart Dimension** ✎ tool.

342) Right-click **More Dimensions** from the Pop-up menu. Click **Chamfer**.

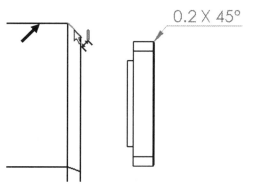

343) Click the small **angled edge**. Click the top **horizontal edge**.

344) Click a **position** to place the dimension.

345) Click **OK** ✔ from the Dimension PropertyManager.

View the hidden lines in the Right view.
346) Click inside the **Right view** boundary.

347) Click **Hidden Lines Visible**.

Modify Drawing View Properties to display the Bore feature.
348) Right-click **Properties** in the Right view.

349) Click the **Show Hidden Edges** tab.

350) **Expand** the FeatureManager for the Drawing View8 (Right).

351) Click the **Bore** feature.

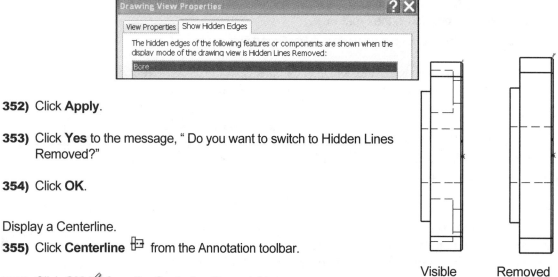

352) Click **Apply**.

353) Click **Yes** to the message, " Do you want to switch to Hidden Lines Removed?"

354) Click **OK**.

Display a Centerline.
355) Click **Centerline** 🎔 from the Annotation toolbar.

356) Click **OK** ✔ from the Centerline PropertyManager.

Visible   Removed

🔅 Control individual line display with the Show/Hide option. Control individual Line font. Right-click a component in the drawing. Select Component Line Font. Select the Type of edge, Line style, Line weight and Layer. Click OK.

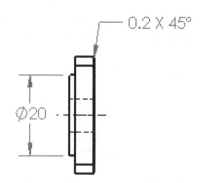

Save the COVERPLATE drawing.

357) Click **Save** 💾 .

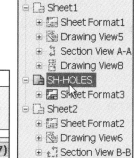

Add a new Sheet.

358) Right-click on the **Sheet1** tab.

359) Click **Add Sheet**. Sheet3 is the default Sheet Name.

360) Enter **SH-HOLES** for sheet name.

Modify the sheet order.

361) Drag **SH-HOLES** upward in the FeatureManager.

362) Position **SH-HOLES** below Sheet1.

Open the COVERPLATE part.

363) Open **COVERPLATE**. Select the **With Nose Holes** configuration.

364) Expand the **M2.0 Diameter Hole1** feature in the FeatureManager.

365) Right-click **Sketch7**. Click **Show**.

Insert a Relative view into the SH-HOLES Sheet.

366) Click **Windows**, **Tile Horizontal** from the Menu bar menu.

367) Click inside **COVERPLATE-SH-HOLES** Sheet.

368) Click **Insert**, **Drawing View**, **Relative to Model** from the Menu bar menu. The Relative View PropertyManager is displayed.

369) Click the **front face** of the COVERPLATE part for First orientation as illustrated.

370) Click the **right face** of the part for the Second orientation as illustrated. Click **OK** ✅ from the Relative View PropertyManager.

Place the view.

371) Click a **position** on the left side of the SH-HOLES sheet.

372) Create a Custom Scale of **2:1** for the Relative view.

373) Click **OK** ✅ from Drawing View10 PropertyManager.

Insert Dimensions for the M2.0 hole.

374) Click **Model Items** ⊗ from the Annotation toolbar.

375) Click the **Hole Wizard Locations** ⊕ box.

376) Click the **Hole Callout** box.

377) Click **Selected feature**.

378) Click the **top right hole** (Seed feature).

379) Click **OK** ✓ from the Model Items PropertyManager.

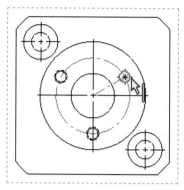

380) Drag the **30°** dimension text off the profile.

381) Right-click the ∅**14** dimension text.

382) Click **Display Options**.

383) Click **Display As Diameter**.

384) Drag the **dimensions** off the Profile.

385) Click **OK** ✓ from the PropertyManager.

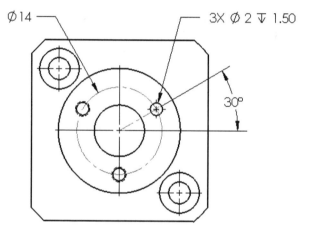

Create an Angular dimension.

386) If needed, hide the **Center Marks** in the top right M2 circle and the center circle.

387) Click **View**, check **Origins** from the Menu bar menu.Sketch a **centerline** from the Origin to the center of the top right M2 circle.

388) Sketch a **centerline** from the Origin to the center of the top left M2 circle.

389) Click the **Smart Dimension** ⊗ tool.

390) Click the **first centerline**. Click the **second centerline**.

391) Click a **position** above the profile.

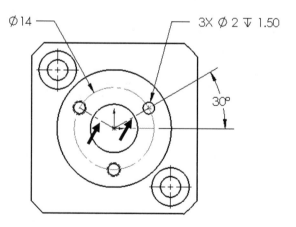

392) Click **OK** from the Make Dimension Driven dialog box.

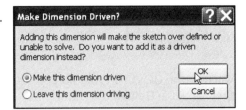

393) Click the **120°** text in the Graphics window.

394) Enter **3X** before the dimension text as illustrated.

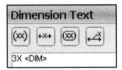

Add a Cosmetic Thread.
395) Click the **right M2 hole** (Edge<1>).

396) Click **Insert**, **Annotations**, **Cosmetic Thread** ⋓ from the Menu bar menu. The Cosmetic Thread PropertyManager is displayed.

397) Select **None**.

398) Select **Blind**.

399) Enter **1.5** for Depth. Accept the defaults.

400) Click **OK** ✓ from the Cosmetic Thread PropertyManager.

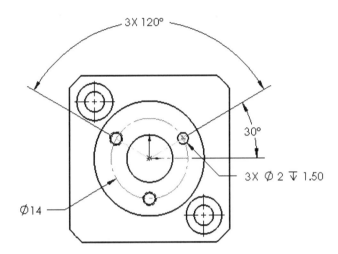

Display the Cosmetic Thread in the FeatureManager.
401) Expand the COVERPLATE FeatureManager.

402) Expand the Hole Wizard feature. The Cosmetic Thread is added to the M2.0 hole feature.

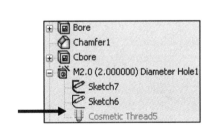

Save the COVERPLATE drawing.

403) Click **Save** 💾 .

Return to the COVERPLATE part.

404) Click the **Default** configuration.

405) Click **Save** 💾 .

406) Click **Windows**, **Close All** from the Menu bar menu.

The Cosmetic Thread represents the outside thread diameter of the hole or the inside thread diameter of a boss. Insert the Cosmetic Thread Annotation in the part, assembly or drawing.

The Hole Wizard, Tapped Hole also utilizes the Cosmetic Thread option. Add Cosmetic thread with thread callout option in the part creates the corresponding Hole Callout in the drawing. The Cosmetic Thread is a sub-entry in the CirPattern1 feature.

Insert and add dimensions and annotations as an exercise to complete the COVERPLATE drawings.

You added annotations in the COVERPLATE drawing. In Chapter 5 create annotations in a new part and insert annotations into a drawing. Utilize Model Items to insert the following: Datums, Datum Targets, Geometric tolerances, Notes, Surface finish, and Weld annotations.

More Information

Additional details on Dimension Precision, Hole Callout, Aligned Section View, Section View, Chamfer, Relative View, View Properties, Grid and Cosmetic Thread are available in SolidWorks help.

Review

The COVERPLATE drawing consisted of three Sheets. Sheet1 utilized an Aligned Section view. Sheet2 utilized an Offset Section view. Sheet3 was renamed SH-HOLES and utilized a Relative view.

An Aligned Section required two sketched line segments. The Offset Section required 5 sketched line segments. Additional options for the Section views were discussed.

The Dimension, Chamfer option inserted an annotation for the Chamfer feature. The Chamfer option required the chamfered edge, reference line and a placement position for the annotation. You utilized the Drawing View Properties to control the display of the hidden lines of the Bore feature. Sheet SH-HOLES was positioned in the FeatureManager as the second sheet in the drawing. The Relative view utilized the part to locate the front and right faces.

The M2 Hole Wizard dimensions were inserted into the drawing.

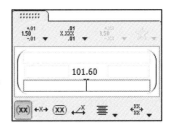 The Dimension palette saves mouse travel to the Dimension PropertyManager to modify dimension, tolerance, leader and more. The dimension palette appears when you insert or select a dimension so you can easily change the dimension's properties and formatting. You can change the tolerance, precision, style, text, and other formatting options in the palette without going to the PropertyManager.

Modifying Features

The design process is dynamic. We do not live in a static world. Explore the following changes to the COVERPLATE, With Nose Holes configuration in Exercise 4.1.

Decrease the Boss diameter to ⌀17. The drawing dimension decreases. The Dimension text position is unchanged. Feature changes in the part that modify size require simple or no changes in the drawing.

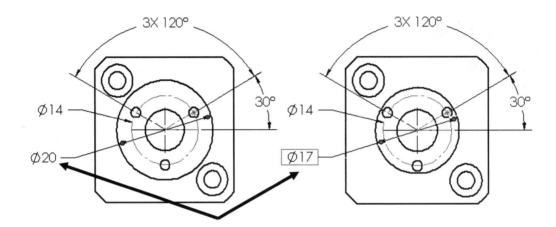

When a part has multiple configurations, dimension changes modify one or more configurations. Modify the 30° to 45° dimensions in the drawing. Check the This Configuration option from the Modify box.

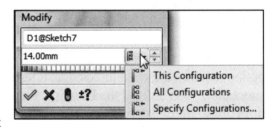

The part configuration COVERPLATE-With Nose Holes controls the 30° dimension. The COVERPLATE-With Nose Holes is the current configuration of the part.

☼ If you receive a warning message, "the part was saved in a different configuration", open the part and set the configuration to With Nose Holes before you change a dimension.

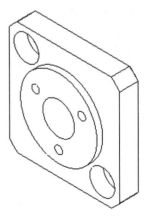

☼ Change the number of holes from 3 to 4 in the Circular Pattern. The change from 3 to 4 instances requires a drawing modification.

The number of instances, changes from 3 to 4. Modify the angle from 30° to 45°. Add new centerline and Center Marks.

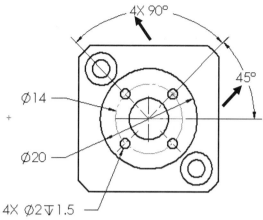

Insert the part Reference geometry into the drawing. Utilize Insert Model Items to display Axes, Curves, Planes, Surfaces, Points, Routing points and Origins.

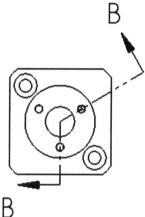

Control the display of Reference geometry through the View menu: Planes, Axes, Temporary Axes, Origins, Coordinate Systems, Sketches, etc. The options in the View menu control the display for the entire sheet.

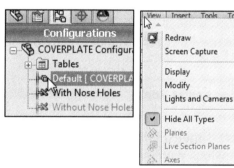

How do you control the display of a plane in a single drawing view? Answer: Create configurations to control the state of a plane in the part. The State Property controls the Suppress/Unsuppress reference geometry such as: *Plane, Axis, Coordinate System, and Point.*

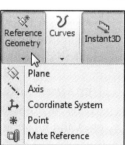

Additional Information-Dimension PropertyManager and Dimensioning Features

The following section explores the Dimension PropertyManager, Document Properties, and dimension display options. The information provides definitions and examples. There are no step-by-step instructions in this section.

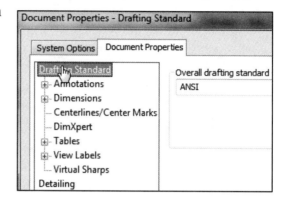

Document Properties contain the Detailing default settings for the entire drawing document. Individual Properties control the selected dimension display through the Dimension PropertyManager and the Dimension Properties dialog box.

The Dimension PropertyManager is displayed on the left side of the Graphics window when you select a drawing dimension. Three are three tabs: *Value*, *Leaders*, and *Other*. The Value tab is the default tab.

Dimension PropertyManager

Provides the ability to insert specify document-level drafting settings for all dimensions. If you select multiple dimensions, only the properties that apply to all the selected dimensions are available.

The Dimension PropertyManager provides the following options:

Dimension Assist Tools

- **Smart dimensioning**. Provides the ability to create dimensions with the Smart Dimension tool.

- **Rapid dimensioning**. Provides the ability to enable or disable the rapid dimension manipulator. Select to enable; clear to disable. This setting persists across sessions.

- **DimXpert**. Provides the ability to apply dimensions to fully define manufacturing features (patterns, slots, pockets, fillets, etc.) and locating dimensions, using DimXpert for drawings.

Style

The Style box provides the ability to define styles, similar to paragraph styles in word processing documents, for dimensions and various annotations (Notes, Geometric Tolerance Symbols, Surface Finish Symbols, and Weld Symbols). When you use styles with annotations, you can repeat commonly used symbols. With styles, you can

- Save a dimension or annotation property as part of a style.

- Name styles so that they can be referenced.

- Apply styles to multiple dimensions or annotations.

- Add, update, and delete styles.

- Save and load styles. You can also load styles saved from other documents and located in other folders.

Style Type:	File extension:
Dimensions	.sldfvt
Notes	sldnotfvt
Geometric Tolerance Symbols	.sldgtolfbt
Surface Finish Symbols	.sldsffvt
Weld Symbols	.sldweldfvt

Styles live in the original model. Modify an inserted dimension in the drawing and the Favorites in the drawings change the Favorites in the part.

Tolerance/Precision

The Tolerance/Precision box defines a Callout value. Select a dimension in an active drawing. The Tolerance/Precision box provides the following options:

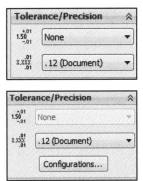

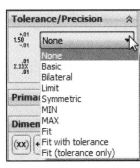

- **Tolerance Type**: Select from the drop-down menu: (None, Basic, Bilateral, Limit, Symmetric, etc). The list is dynamic. Example: Types for chamfer dimensions are limited to None, Bilateral, and Symmetric.

- **Maximum Variation**: Input a value.

- **Minimum Variation**: Input a value.

- **Show parentheses**: Parentheses are available for Bilateral, Symmetric, and Fit with tolerance types. When selected, parentheses bracket the tolerance values. Parenthesis are available for Fit with tolerance if you specify Hole Fit or Shaft Fit, but not both.

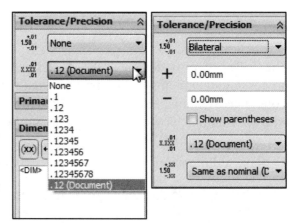

- **Primary Unit Precision**: Select the number of digits after the decimal point from the drop-down menu for the dimension precision.

- **Tolerance Precision**: Select the number of digits after the decimal point for tolerance values.

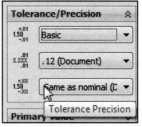

- **Classification**: Available only for Fit, Fit with tolerance, or Fit (tolerance only) types. Classification can be User Defined, Clearance, Transitional, or Press. Select a classification from the list. When you select either Hole Fit or Shaft Fit, the list for the other category (Hole Fit or Shaft Fit) is filtered based on the classification.

- **Hole Fit**: Available only for Fit, or Fit with tolerance, or Fit (tolerance only) types. Select from the lists, or type any text.

- **Shaft Fit**: Available only for Fit, or Fit with tolerance, or Fit (tolerance only) types. Select from the lists, or type any text.

- **Fit tolerance display**: Available only for Fit, Fit with tolerance, or Fit (tolerance only) types. Choose from:

  o **Stacked with line display**, **Stacked without line display**, and **Linear display**

- **Configurations**: For parts and assemblies only. Provides the ability to apply the dimension tolerance to specific configurations for driven dimensions only.

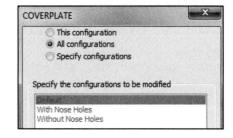

⚡ See SolidWorks help for additional information and details.

Primary Value

The Text Dimension box provides the ability to add tolerances to a dimension that you have overridden add, or modify the selected dimension in the drawing.

- **Name box**: Displays the name of the select entity.

- **Dimension Value**. Displays the selected dimension in the drawing view.

- **Override value**: Select to override the primary value. If you clear **Override value**, the dimension returns to its original value but retains the tolerance.

- **Configurations**: For parts and assemblies only. Provides the ability to apply the dimension tolerance to specific configurations for driven dimensions only.

Text Dimension

The Text Dimension box provides the ability to add, or modify the selected dimension in the drawing. Select the drawing dimension. The dimension is displayed automatically in the center text box, represented by <DIM>. Place the pointer anywhere in the text box to insert text. If you delete <DIM>, you can reinsert the value by clicking Add Value. The Text Dimension box provides the following options:

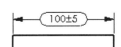

- **Add Parenthesis:** Inserts Parenthesis around the dimension.

- **Center Dimension:** Centers the dimension.

- **Inspection Dimension**: Inserts an Inspection dimension.

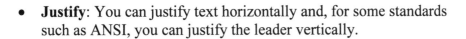

- **Offset Text:** Offset text relative to the dimension.

- **Justify**: You can justify text horizontally and, for some standards such as ANSI, you can justify the leader vertically.

  o **Horizontal - Left Justify, Center Justify, Right Justify**

  o **Vertical - Top Justify, Middle Justify, Bottom Justify**

- **Symbols**: Click to place the pointer where you want a symbol. Click a symbol icon (for Diameter, Degree, etc) or click the More option to access the Symbol Library. The symbol is represented by its name in the text box, and the actual symbol is displayed in the Graphics window.

Dual Dimension

The Dual Dimension box provides the ability to specify that the dimension is displayed in both the document's unit system and the dual dimension units. Both units are specified in **Tools**, **Options**, **Document Properties**, **Units**.

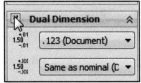

- **Primary Unit Precision:** Select the number of digits after the decimal point from the list for the dimension value.

- **Tolerance Precision:** Select the number of digits after the decimal point for tolerance values.

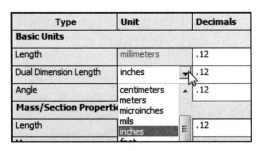

New in SolidWorks 2012 is the ability to modify the document units directly from the Graphics window as illustrated.

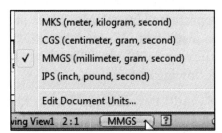

Dimension Leaders PropertyManager

The Dimension Leaders PropertyManager is document and dimension dependent.

If you select multiple dimensions, only the properties that apply to all the selected dimensions are available. The Leaders tab in the Dimension PropertyManager provides the following options:

Witness/Leader Display

The Witness/Leader Display box provides the ability to position the following:

- **Leader display location**: **Outside, Inside, Smart, and Directed Leader**.

- **Arrow style**: Provides the ability to select **13 Arrow Styles**.

- **Leader display**: **Radius, Diameter, Linear, Multi-jog Leader, Two Arrows / Solid Leader, Two Arrows / Open Leader, One Arrow / Solid Leader, One Arrow / Open Leader.**

- **Use document bend length**. Checked by default.

- **Use document second arrow**. Checked by default.

 Smart specifies that arrows automatically appear outside of extension lines if the space is too small to accommodate the dimension text and the arrowheads.

Arrow style and Leader display are document dependent.

Leader Style

You can define Leader styles, similar to paragraph styles in word processing documents, for dimensions and various annotations (Notes, Geometric Tolerance Symbols, Surface Finish Symbols, and Weld Symbols).

Break Line

The Break Lines box provides the ability to select the dimension and extension lines to break when crossing other dimension or extension lines in drawings:

- **Use document gap**: Select to use the document default set in Tools, Options, Document Properties, Dimensions.

- **Gap**: Enter a value if you do not use the document's default.

Custom Text Position

The Custom Text Position box provides the following options: **Solid leader, aligned text, Broken leader, horizontal text, and Broken leader, aligned text**.

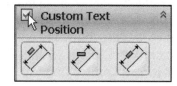

 See SolidWorks help for additional information and details.

Arc Condition

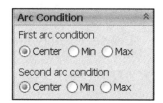

The Arc Condition box provides the ability to set how to dimension between an arc or a circle:

- **First arc condition**: Provides the ability to specify where on the arc or circle the distance is measured.

- **Second arc condition**. Provides the ability to specify where on the second item the distance is measured, when <u>both</u> items are arcs or circles.

Example: The **First arc condition** is **Center**, and the **Second arc condition** is set as illustrated.

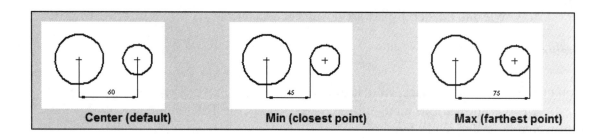

Dimension Other PropertyManager

The Dimension Other PropertyManager provides the ability to specify the display of dimensions. If you select multiple dimensions, only the properties that apply to all the selected dimensions are available.

Override Units

The Override Units box provides the ability to override the document's units defined in the Units options section. Specify the unit type for the selected dimension. The available options depend on the type of dimensions that you selected. For example, an **Angular Unit** can be **Degrees**, **Deg/Min**, **Deg/Min/Sec**, or **Radians**.

Text Fonts

The Text Fonts box provides the following options:

- **Dimension font:** Provides the ability to specify the font used for the dimension. Either select **Use document's font**, as defined in the Annotations Font section, or clear the check box and click the Font option to select a new font type, style, and size for the selected items.

- **Tolerance font.** Provides the ability to specify the font used for the tolerance dimension. Select **Use dimension font** to use the same font as for dimensions. Clear **Use dimension font** to specify **Font scale** or **Font height**.

- **Fit tolerance font** (For **Fit** tolerance types only). Select **Use dimension font** to use the same font as for dimensions. Clear **Use dimension font** to specify **Font scale** or **Font height**.

Options

The Options box provides the following two options: **Read only** and **Driven**.

The Driven option specifies that the dimension is driven by other dimensions and conditions, and cannot be changed.

Layer

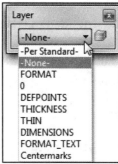

The Layer box provides the ability to select a layer in the drawing.

Dimension Properties Dialog Box

The Dimension Properties dialog box contains additional options to control the selected dimension.

In tight spaces control the arrow, extension line, and dimension line display.

Both arrowheads do not fit in the tight space. Modify the bottom arrowhead to a straight line.

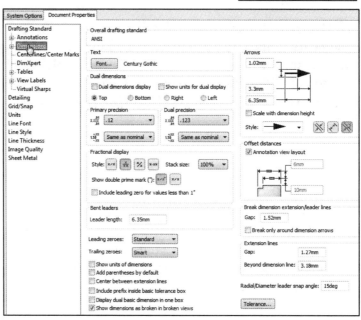

For the document, the Document Properties, Dimensions: *Angle, Arc Length, Chamfer, Diameter, Hole Callout, Linear, and Radius* folders address Leaders to control leader lines and text.

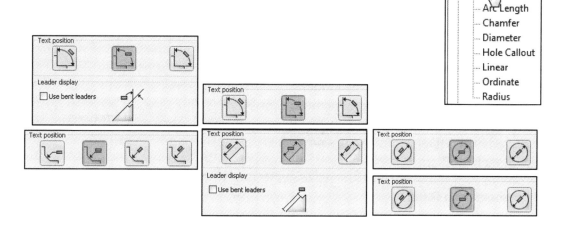

Hide Dimension Line, Hide Extension Line, and Driven

Additional Dimension options are available with the Right-click Pop-up menu. Hide the Extension Line. Right-click on the Extension Line. Select the Hide Extension Line command.

Right-click on the Dimension Line. Select Hide Dimension Line. Select the left and right lines between the dimension to hide both lines.

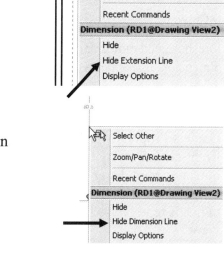

Modify an inserted model dimension to a Driven dimension in the drawing. Other dimensions and conditions drive a Driven dimension. Check the Driven option in the Pop-up menu or in the Dimension PropertyManager Options box.

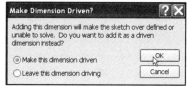

Dimension Schemes

There are various dimension schemes for arcs. The dimensioning scheme of the part utilized symmetry and equal relations between the two arcs.

How do you determine the design intent of a sketch, if you did not create the model? Answer: Review the geometric relations.

Locate Display\Delete Relations 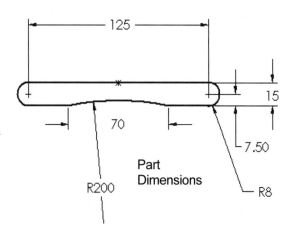 in the Sketch toolbar.

Foreshortened Radii

The Dimension tool draws large radii outside the sheet boundary or overlaps a second view. A Foreshortened radius inserts three line segments on the leader line.

When you dimension to a foreshortened radius or diameter, the dimension also appears as a zigzag.

Check the Foreshortened radius check box in the Dimension Leaders PropertyManager or Right-click Display Options, Foreshortened. Drag the blue endpoints of the foreshortened radius if required to fit within the view.

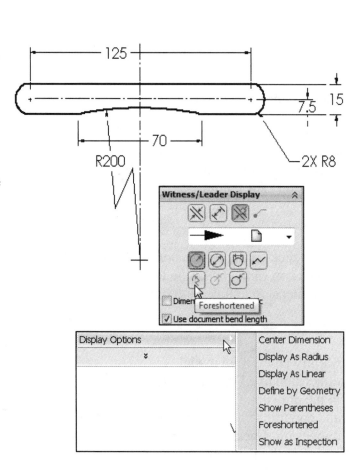

Partially Rounded Ends, Center/Min/Max Arc Condition

The distance between the two center points of the arc determines the current overall dimension, 125. Return to the part sketch to redefine the dimension scheme.

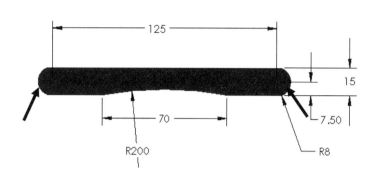

Delete the overall dimension. Click Smart Dimension. Select each arc to redefine the overall length. Do not select the center point.

Select the dimension, 125. Click Max for the First arc condition from the Dimension Leaders PropertyManager. Click Max for the Second arc condition. Click OK from the PropertyManager. The overall arc dimension is 141.

Save and Exit the sketch. Return to the drawing.

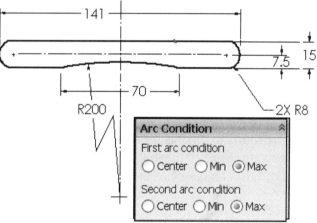

Modify the dimension in the drawing. Enter 2X for the radius text. Add center marks to indicate the center of the radii. Create a gap. Add centerlines to complete the drawing. The Max and Min arc condition options appear when dimensions reference arc edges. The Max and Min arc conditions options do not appear when dimensions reference arc center points.

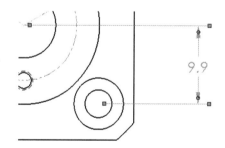

In the drawing, drag the extension line to modify the Max, Min, Center arc condition.

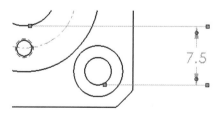

Display Option, Offset Text

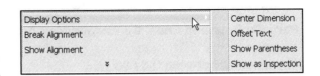

The Pop-up Display Options controls the dimension display. In tight spaces, utilize the Offset Text to position the dimension text off the dimension line.

Slotted Holes

Slotted Holes utilized symmetry in the part. Redefine the dimensions for the Slot Cut according to the ASME 14.5M standard. The ASME 14.5M standard requires that the dimension references the arc edge.

The Radius value is not dimensioned. Select each arc to create a center/min/max arc condition in the part.

Insert the part into the drawing. The end radii are indicated.

No dimension is labeled. There are three methods to dimension a slot in the drawing. Modify the dimension properties to create one of the following:

Method 1: Select Center for the First Arc condition. Select Center for the Second Arc condition.

Create a linear dimension between the two vertical lines of the slot. Create a radial dimension. Delete the radius value.

Enter the text 2X R. Add two Center Marks and a Centerline between the two arcs.

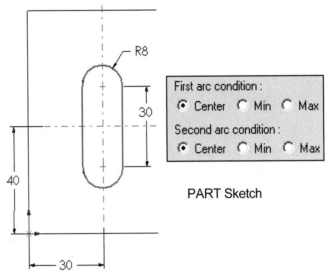

PART Sketch

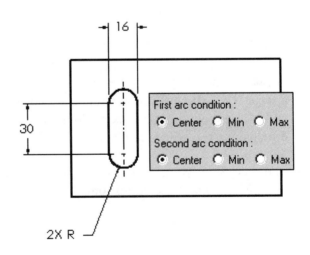

Method 2: Use a Note with a Leader Line. Enter the text of the overall width and height of the Slot. Use a radial dimension.

Enter the 2X R text. Add two intersecting centerlines.

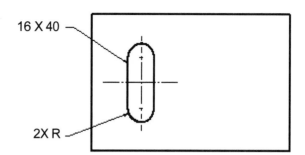

Method 3: Select Max for the First Arc condition. Select Max for the Second Arc condition.

Create a linear dimension between the two vertical lines of the slot.

Create a radial dimension. Delete the radius value. Enter 2X R text.

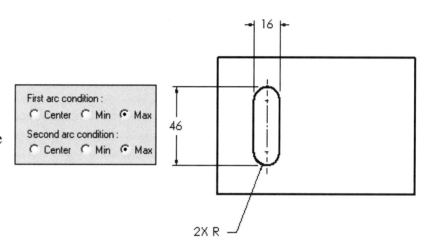

Grid/Snap

The Document Properties, Dimensions, Snap text to grid option positions the dimension text at the grid snap points in a drawing or sketch. The snap points are located at the intersection of two perpendicular grid lines. Control Grid and Snap options through the Document Properties, Grid/Snap option.

Location of Features

The information is provided to you in order to explore other dimensioning methods.

Rectangular coordinate dimensioning locates features with respect to one another, from a datum or an origin.

There are two methods:

- **Base Line Dimensioning**

- **Ordinate Dimensioning**

Base Line Dimensioning

Create Base Line Dimensions. Select a Base Line. Select a feature (hole). Select a location for the dimension text.

Select the remaining features in order from smallest to largest.

Base Line dimensions are aligned dimensions. To insert a new dimension between existing dimensions, break the alignment with the text closest to the new value.

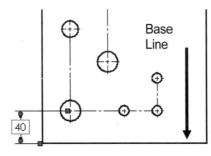
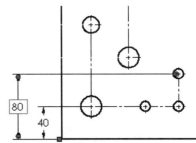
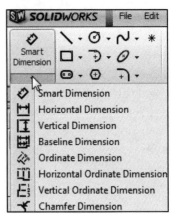

Ordinate Dimension

Create Horizontal Ordinate Dimensions.
Select Tools, Dimension, Horizontal Ordinate
from the Menu bar menu or use
Autodimension PropertyManager.

Select the Origin or vertex for a zero location.
All other dimensions are measured from this
location.

Select a location for the
dimension text below the
profile. Select a feature
(hole). Select the remaining
features in order from left
to right.

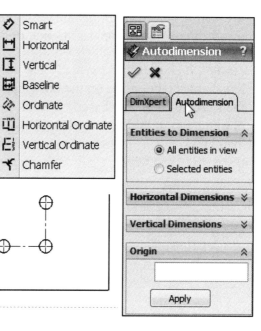

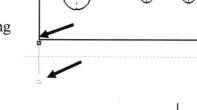

Create Vertical Ordinate
Dimensions. Select
Vertical Ordinate. Select the Origin of vertex for
zero location.

Select a location for the dimension text off the
profile. Select a feature (hole).

Select the remaining features in order from
bottom to top. Extension lines will jog to fit
dimension text.

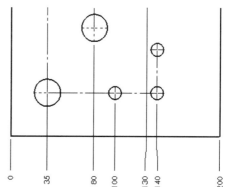

Select Help, Ordinate
Dimensions to view the .avi file
from SolidWorks.

Baseline Dimensioning and
Ordinate Dimensioning
produce reference dimensions.
They are driven dimensions
from the part.

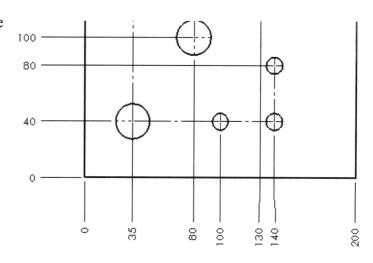

Part features drive Baseline and Ordinate dimensions. To insert a new Ordinate dimension, right-click on an existing dimension. Click Add to Ordinate.

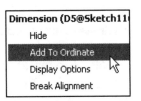

Hole Tables label holes on the drawing. The labels locate each hole based on an X-Y coordinate system. Explore Hole Tables in Chapter 8.

Hole Table for TABLE-PLATE-LABELS			
TAG	X LOC	Y LOC	SIZE
A1	35	40	Ø25 THRU
A2	80	100	Ø25 THRU
A3	80	180	Ø25 THRU
A4	130	260	Ø25 THRU
B1	35	140	Ø20 THRU
B2	130	210	Ø20 THRU
C1	100	40	Ø12 THRU
C2	140	40	Ø12 THRU
C3	140	80	Ø12 THRU

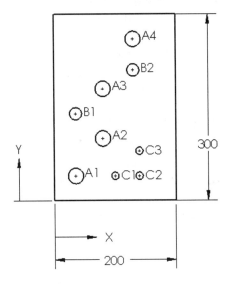

View Layout Toolbar and Annotation Toolbar

The CommandManager displays the Annotation toolbar and the View Layout toolbar. In Chapter 6 and Chapter 7 you utilized the default tools in the View Layout and the Annotation toolbars.

Locate additional tools in the Menu bar menu:

- **Insert, Drawing View**

- **Insert, Annotations**

- **Tools, Dimensions**

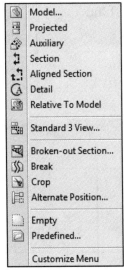

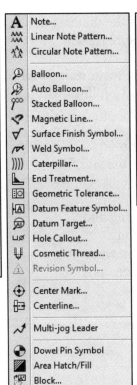

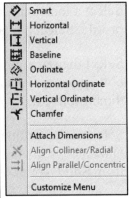

Utilize the Tools, Customize from the Menu bar menu to modify a toolbar. Select the Commands tab to insert additional tools.

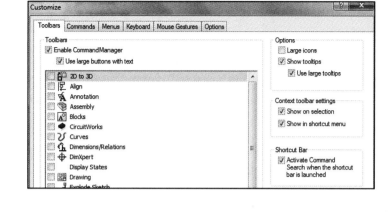

Chapter Summary

You created two detailed drawings in this chapter:

- Detailed TUBE drawing

- Detailed COVERPLATE drawing

You addressed and applied the following tools: *Smart Dimension, Model Items, Autodimension, Note, Linear Note, Balloon, AutoBalloon, Magnetic line, Surface Finish, Weld Symbol, Geometric Tolerance, Datum Feature, Datum Target, Hole Callout, Area Hatch/Fill, Block, Center Mark* and *Centerline*.

You inserted, added, and modified dimensions along with obtaining an understanding of inserting and adding notes in the detailed drawings.

You were exposed to various methods to move, hide, and add dimensions that adhere to a drawing standard.

Review the additional dimensioning options in the Dimension PropertyManager, Dimension Property dialog box and Pop-up menu. Apply your skills to detail the ROD drawing and other drawings in the chapter exercises.

Chapter Terminology

Annotation: An annotation is a text note or a symbol that adds specific information and design intent to a part, assembly, or drawing. Annotations in a drawing include: specific note, hole callout, surface finish symbol, datum feature symbol, datum target, geometric tolerance symbol, weld symbol, balloon, and stacked balloon, center mark, centerline marks, area hatch, and block.

AutoDimension: The Autodimension tool provides the ability to insert reference dimensions into drawing views such as baseline, chain, and ordinate dimensions.

Baseline dimensions: Dimensions referenced from the same edge or vertex in a drawing view.

Balloon: Labels parts in an assembly, typically including item numbers and quantity. In drawings, the item numbers are related to rows in a bill of materials (BOM). Create balloons in a drawing document or in a note.

Bill of Materials: A table inserted into a drawing to keep a record of the parts used in an assembly.

Broken out Section: A drawing view that exposes inner details of a drawing view by removing material from a closed profile, usually a spline.

Center Mark: A cross that marks the center of a circle or arc.

Centerline: An axis of symmetry in a sketch or drawing displayed in a phantom font.

ConfigurationManager: The ConfigurationManager is located on the left side of the SolidWorks window and provides the means to create, select, and view multiple configurations of parts and assemblies in an active document. You can split the ConfigurationManager and either display two ConfigurationManager instances, or combine the ConfigurationManager with the FeatureManager design tree, PropertyManager, or third party applications that use the panel.

CommandManager: The CommandManager is a Context-sensitive toolbar that dynamically updates based on the toolbar you want to access. By default, it has toolbars embedded in it based on the document type. When you click a tab below the Command Manager, it updates to display that toolbar. For example, if you click the **Sketches** tab, the Sketch toolbar is displayed.

Copy and Paste: Utilize copy/paste to copy views from one sheet to another sheet in a drawing or between different drawings.

Cosmetic thread: An annotation that represents threads.

Crosshatch: A pattern (or fill) applied to drawing views such as section views and broken-out sections

Detailing: Detailing refers to the SolidWorks module used to insert, add, and modify dimensions and notes in an engineering drawing.

Design Table: An Excel spreadsheet that is used to create multiple configurations in a part or assembly document.

Dimension: A value indicating the size of feature geometry.

Dimension Line: A line that references dimension text to extension lines indicating the feature being measured.

DimXpert for Parts: A set of tools that applies dimensions and tolerances to parts according to the requirements of the ASME Y.14.41-2003 standard.

Document: A file containing a part, assembly, or drawing.

Drawing: A 2D representation of a 3D part or assembly. The extension for a SolidWorks drawing file name is .SLDDRW. Drawing refers to the SolidWorks module used to insert, add, and modify views in an engineering drawing.

Edit Sheet: The drawing sheet contains two modes. Utilize the Edit Sheet command to insert views and dimensions.

Edit Sheet Format: The drawing sheet contains two modes. Utilize the Edit Sheet Format command to add or modify notes and Title block information. Edit in the Edit Sheet Format mode.

Equation: Creates a mathematical relation between sketch dimensions, using dimension names as variables, or between feature parameters, such as the depth of an extruded feature or the instance count in a pattern.

Extension line: The line extending from the profile line indicating the point from which a dimension is measured.

Face: A selectable area (planar or otherwise) of a model or surface with boundaries that help define the shape of the model or surface. For example, a rectangular solid has six faces.

FeatureManager: The FeatureManager design tree located on the left side of the SolidWorks window provides an outline view of the active part, assembly, or drawing. This makes it easy to see how the model or assembly was constructed or to examine the various sheets and views in a drawing. The FeatureManager and the Graphics window are dynamically linked. You can select features, sketches, drawing views, and construction geometry in either pane.

First Angle Projection: Standard 3 Views are in either third angle or first angle projection. In first angle projection, the front view is displayed at the upper left and the other two views are the top and left views.

Foreshortened radius: Helpful when the centerpoint of a radius is outside of the drawing or interferes with another drawing view: Broken Leader.

Fully defined: A sketch where all lines and curves in the sketch, and their positions, are described by dimensions or relations, or both, and cannot be moved. Fully defined sketch entities are displayed in black.

Geometric Tolerance: A set of standard symbols that specify the geometric characteristics and dimensional requirements of a feature.

Graphics window: The area in the SolidWorks window where the part, assembly, or drawing is displayed.

Heads-up View toolbar: A transparent toolbar located at the top of the Graphic window.

Hole Callouts: Hole callouts are available in drawings. If you modify a hole dimension in the model, the callout updates automatically in the drawing if you did not use DimXpert.

Leader: A solid line created from an annotation to the referenced feature.

Model Item: Provides the ability to insert dimensions, annotations, and reference geometry from a model document (part or assembly) into a drawing.

Ordinate dimensions: Chain of dimensions referenced from a zero ordinate in a drawing or sketch.

Origin: The model origin is displayed in blue and represents the (0,0,0) coordinate of the model. When a sketch is active, a sketch origin is displayed in red and represents the (0,0,0) coordinate of the sketch. Dimensions and relations can be added to the model origin, but not to a sketch origin.

Rebuild: A tool that updates (or regenerates) the document with any changes made since the last time the model was rebuilt. Rebuild is typically used after changing a model dimension.

Reference dimension: Dimensions added to a drawing document are called Reference dimensions, and are driven; you cannot edit the value of reference dimensions to modify the model. However, the values of reference dimensions change when the model dimensions change.

Relative view: A relative (or relative to model) drawing view is created relative to planar surfaces in a part or assembly.

Rollback: Suppresses all items below the rollback bar.

Parametric note: A Note that references a SolidWorks dimension or property.

Precision: Controls the number of decimal places displayed in a dimension.

Silhouette edge: A curve representing the extent of a cylindrical or curved face when viewed from the side.

Suppress: Removes an entity from the display and from any calculations in which it is involved. You can suppress features, assembly components, and so on. Suppressing an entity does not delete the entity; you can unsuppress the entity to restore it.

Tangent Edge: The transition edge between rounded or filleted faces in hidden lines visible or hidden lines removed modes in drawings.

Weld Finish: A weld symbol representing the parameters you specify.

Questions:

1. Dimensions in a drawing are _____ from a part or _____ in the drawing.

2. Drawing Notes, Hole Callout, and Center Mark tools are located in the SolidWorks _____ toolbar.

3. Identify the order in which dimensions are inserted into a drawing with the various views: Standard views, Section views and Detail views.

4. True or False. Feature dimensions are inserted into an Empty drawing.

5. Identify the command to select when dimensions are no longer required.

6. Describe a Reference dimension in SolidWorks.

7. Describe the procedure to move a part dimension from one view to a different view.

8. List and describe three methods to dimension simple holes and circular geometry.

9. True or False. Cosmetic Threads added in the drawing are automatically inserted into the referenced part.

10. A drawing references multiple part configurations. A dimension is changed on a drawing. Identify the three Modify options that appear in the Modify dialog box.

11. Name three different types of Reference geometry created in a part that is inserted into a drawing.

12. Describe the procedure to create a Foreshortened radius.

13. Identify the arc conditions that are required when dimensioning the overall length of a slot.

14. Provide a definition for Baseline Dimensioning.

15. Provide a definition for Ordinate Dimensioning.

16. Identity the following symbols:

Exercises

Exercise 7.1:

Open the COVERPLATE part. Decrease the Boss diameter to Ø17.

Open the COVERPLATE drawing. Modify the M2 hole location from 30° to 45°.
Change the number of M2 holes from 3 to 4 in the Circular Pattern.

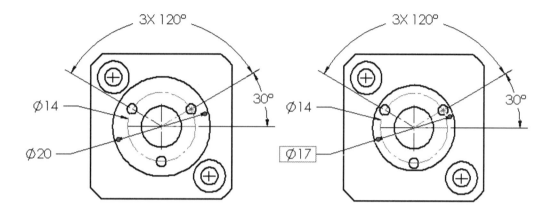

Add a new centerline and redefine the dimension. Reposition the dimensions and edit the
note quantity of M2 holes from 3 to 4. Insert Center Marks to complete the drawing.

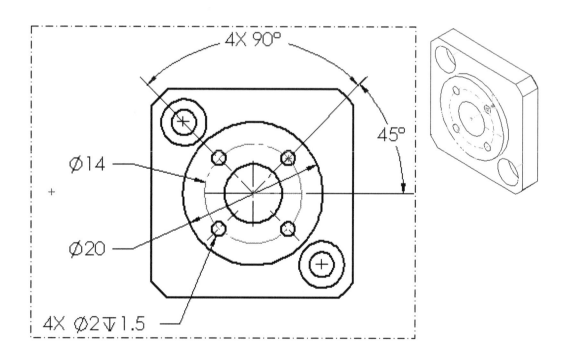

Exercise 7.2:

Create a new drawing for the RADIUS-ROUNDED END part. Locate the part in the DRAWING-W-SOLIDWORKS-2012\Exercises folder. Add a Foreshorten Radius for the R200.

Create an overall dimension for the partially rounded ends. Modify the Radius text according to the ASME standard. Add Centerlines and Center Marks.

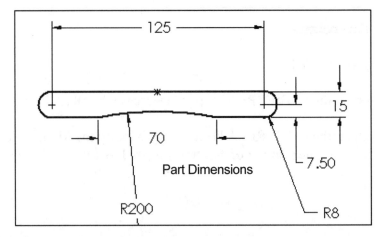

Part Dimensions

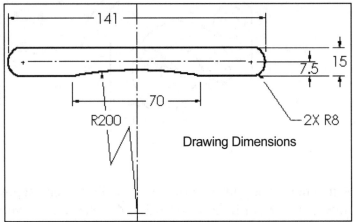

Drawing Dimensions

Exercise 7.3:

Dimension chamfers in the drawing. Create a new part called C-BLOCK. Sketch an L-shaped Extruded Base feature. Add two different size CHAMFER features. The dimensions are not provided.

Create the C-BLOCK drawing. Insert chamfer dimensions into a drawing. Click Smart Dimension from the Sketch toolbar. Right-click in the Graphics window. Select Chamfer. The mouse pointer changes to   .

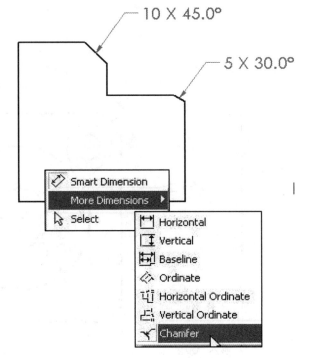

Select the chamfered edge. Select one of the lead-in edges. Click in the Graphics window to place the dimension and to display the CHAMFER.

Exercise 7.4:

Create a new drawing for the SLOT-PLATE part located in the DRAWING-W-SOLIDWORKS-2012\Exercises folder. Redefine the dimensions for the Slot Cut according to the ASME 14.5M Standard. The ASME 14.5M Standard requires an outside dimension for a slot. The Radius value is not dimensioned. Select each arc to create a center/min/max arc condition in the part. Insert the part into the drawing. The end radii are indicated by 2X R.

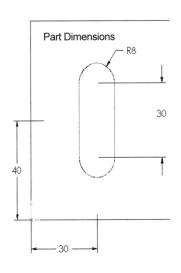

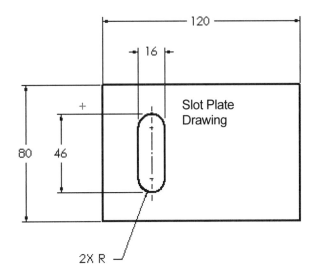

Exercise 4.7:

Create a new drawing for the TABLE-PLATE part located in the DRAWING-W-SOLIDWORKS-2012\Exercises folder.

Rectangular coordinate dimensioning locates features with respect to one another, from a datum or an origin. Dimension the TABLE-PLATE with Base Line Dimensioning.

Insert Center Marks and Centerlines to complete the drawing.

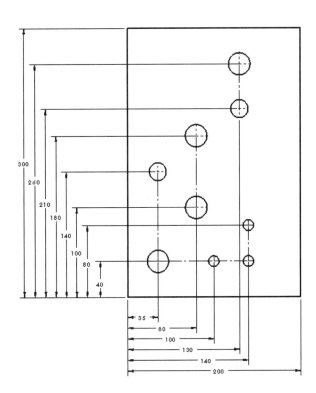

Exercise 7.6:

Create a new drawing for the TABLE-PLATE part located in the DRAWING-W-SOLIDWORKS-2012\Exercise folder. Dimension the TABLE-PLATE with Ordinate Dimensioning.

Insert Center Marks and Centerlines to complete the drawing.

To insert an Ordinate dimension for a new feature, right-click on an existing dimension and select the Add to Ordinate option.

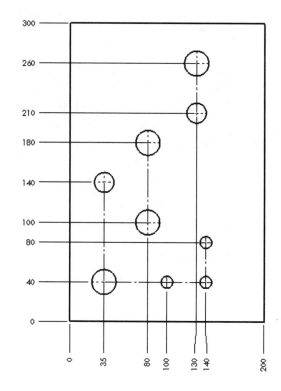

Exercise 7.7:

Detail the ROD Drawing.

The ROD requires dimensions for both the Long and Short part configuration. Dimension the Short configuration on Sheet1. Dimension the Long configuration on Sheet2 and Sheet3 in this section.

Utilize Hole Callout, Center Mark and Centerline from the Annotations toolbar.

Utilize the Display As Radius option for the Front view diameter dimension.

Modify the 2X R4. Utilize the Displays As Linear option.

Modify the 8 dimension. Utilize the Display As Diameter option.

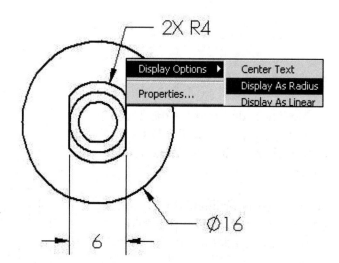

Exercise 7.8:

Create a new drawing for the MOUNTINGPLATE-CYLINDER part located in the Exercise folder. The MOUNTING-CLYLINDER contains a square pattern of 4 holes. The location of the holes corresponds to the initial sketch of the TUBE Base Extrude feature. Four holes are used in order for the TUBE to be mounted in either direction.

Utilize Document Property, Remove Trailing zeroes option. Review the 2 PATTERN and 3 PATTERN part configurations. Insert the part dimensions into the drawing. Add dimensions in the drawing. Hide superfulous dimensions.

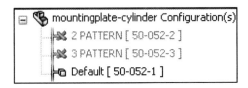

ASME Y14.5M defines a dimension for a repeating feature in the following order: number of features, an X, a space and the size of the feature. Example: 12X $\varnothing$3.5.

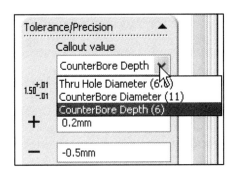

Create a drawing called MOUNTINGPLATE-CYLINDER with two sheets. Modify the CounterBore Depth Callout value to include Tolerance +0.2/-0.5.

Sheet1 contains the 3 PATTERN configuration.
Sheet2 contains the 2 PATTERN configuration.

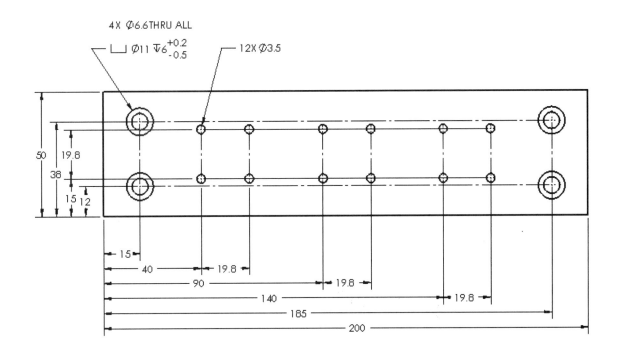

Notes:

Chapter 8

Assembly Drawings

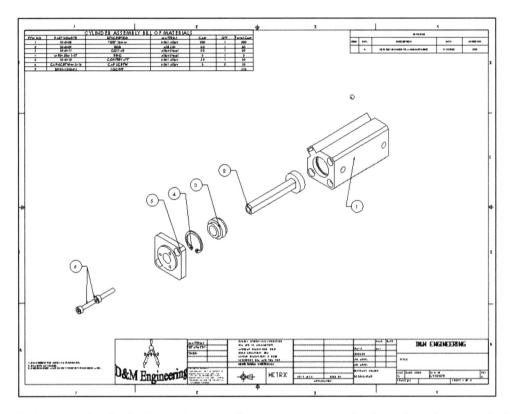

Below are the desired outcomes and usage competencies based on the completion of Chapter 8.

Desired Outcomes:	Usage Competencies:
Two Drawings and a Assembly: • CYLINDER assembly with Custom Properties and a Design Table	• Ability to create an assembly with multiple configurations.
	• An understanding of Custom Properties and SolidWorks Properties.
• CYLINDER drawing • COVERPLATE4 drawing	• Ability to create an assembly drawing using multiple part and assembly configurations.
• Bill of Materials and Revision Table.	• Knowledge to develop and incorporate a Bill of Materials and Revision Tables.

Notes:

Chapter 8 - Assembly Drawings

Chapter Objective

You will create the
following in this chapter:

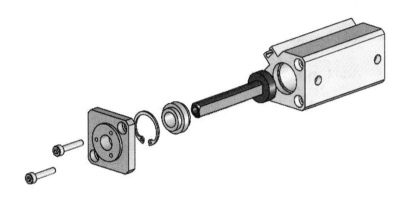

- CYLINDER assembly
  with Custom Properties
  and a Design Table.

- CYLINDER drawing
  with multiple sheets
  and a Bill of Materials.

- COVERPLATE4
  drawing with a
  Revision Table.

Insert an Isometric
Exploded view in the CYLINDER assembly. Add Custom
Properties to each part to describe: Material, Mass, Description,
and Cost parameters. Insert a Design Table in the CYLINDER
assembly to create six different configurations of the assembly.

Insert a Revision Table into the COVERPLATE4 drawing and the
CYLINDER drawing. An Engineering Change Order (ECO)
requires a Revision letter in the Revision Table and the Title blocks
of the part and assembly drawings. Create three sheets for the
CYLINDER drawing:

- Sheet1: Isometric Exploded view, Balloon labels, and a Bill of
  Materials.

- Sheet2: Multiple configurations of the CYLINDER assembly
  with corresponding Bill of Materials.

- Sheet3: Show/Hide options and configurations in drawing
  views.

Create a single sheet for the COVERPLATE4 drawing:

- Sheet1: Insert a Revision Table and Revisions.

On the completion of this chapter, you will be able to:

- Insert an assembly with multiple configurations into a drawing.

- Display the Exploded view in the drawing.

- Insert Balloons and Bill of Materials.

- Edit and format the Bill of Materials.

- Add Custom Properties to the components of the CYLINDER assembly.

- Link Custom Properties in the drawing.

- Modify View Properties in the drawing.

- Insert Revisions and modify the REV linked property in the Title block.

- Utilize the following SolidWorks tools and commands: *Custom Properties*, *Note*, *Balloon, Auto Balloon, Stacked Balloon, Bill of Materials, Exploded View, Revision Table, Design Library* and *View Palette*.

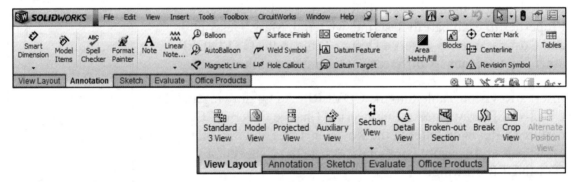

Chapter Overview

The Manufacturing and Marketing department requires a CYLINDER drawing. Marketing needs part and assembly views for their on-line catalog. Manufacturing requires a Bill of Materials for the assembly configuration.

Creating a Bill of Materials is an automatic function that uses a table similar to the Hole Table and the Revision Table. Changes at the assembly level (deletions, reordering, additions and so on) are reflected in the BOM.

The CYLINDER drawing consists of multiple configurations of the CYLINDER assembly and the Bill of Materials.

Sheet1 contains an Exploded Isometric View with a Bill of Materials.

The Revision Table, REV letter is linked to the REV letter in the Title block of the drawing.

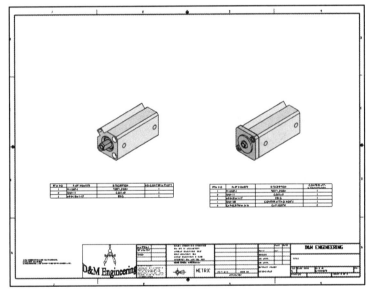

Sheet2 contains two CYLINDER configurations. The COVERPLATE and CAP-SCREWS are suppressed in the top left Isometric view.

The two parts: COVERPLATE and CAP-SCREWS are unsuppressed in the top right Isometric view.

The Bill of Materials reflects the two different configurations.

Insert Custom properties in a part - they propagate to the Design Table. Insert Custom properties in a Design Table - they propagate to the part if the link is active.

A goal of this book is to expose various SolidWorks design tools and features. The most direct way may not always be shown.

Sheet3 contains the CUTAWAY, Default CYLINDER configuration, and the CYLINDER Design Table.

Sheet3 also contains two Front views of the COVERPLATE part. The left Front view displays the WithNoseHoles configuration. The right Front view displays the WithoutNoseHoles configuration.

Link the Notes positioned below the Front views to the COVERPLATE part configuration.

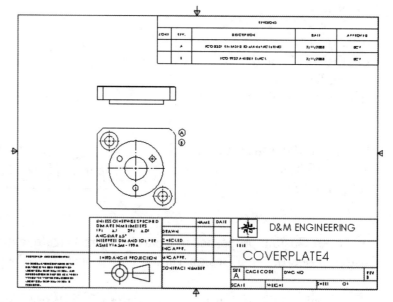

COVERPLATE4-Sheet1 contains the Revision Table. The Revision Table, REV letter is linked to the REV letter in the Title block of the drawing.

☼ *When adding a Sheet to a drawing, if the system can't locate the Sheet format, add the Sheet format in File Location under System Options or Browse to the correct Sheet format location.*

⌖ Utilize the CYLINDER assembly and other components: CAP-SCREW-M3x16, COLLAR, COVERPLATE4, RING, ROD4, TUBE4, and TUBE4-ROD4 located in DRAWING-W-SOLIDWORKS-2012\Chapter 8 folder on the DVD in the book. Copy all needed files and folders to your hard drive.

The components contain the parts, Design Tables, and Custom Properties required for the three sheets in the CYLINDER drawing. Work between five different document types in this project: drawing, assembly, part, Design Table and Bill of Materials. The illustrations specify the document type.

⌖ Utilize Ctrl Tab to toggle between the open drawing, assembly and part.

⌖ SMC Corporation of America manufactures the CYLINDER assembly. The model files were obtained from 3D ContentCentral. The components were modified for educational purposes.

The RING and CAP-SCREW-M3x16 parts were obtained from the SolidWorks\toolbox and modified for the chapter.

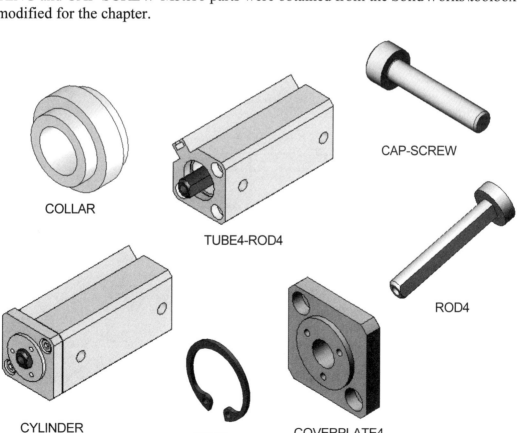

COLLAR

CAP-SCREW

TUBE4-ROD4

ROD4

CYLINDER

RING

COVERPLATE4

CYLINDER Assembly-Exploded View

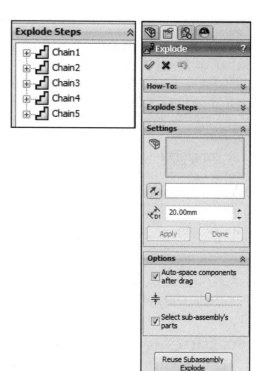

The Exploded view  tool utilizes the Explode PropertyManager.

An Exploded view illustrates how to assemble the components in an assembly.

Create an Exploded view in this section with seven steps. Click and drag components in the Graphics window.

The Manipulator icon ⋏ indicates the direction to explode. Select an alternate component edge for the Explode direction. Drag the component in the Graphics window or enter an exact value in the Explode distance box. Manipulate the top-level components in the assembly.

Access the Explode View 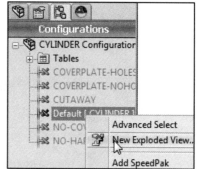 tool from the following locations:

- Click the **ConfigurationManager** tab. Right-click **Default**. Click **New Exploded View**. The Explode PropertyManager is displayed.

- Click the **Exploded View** tool in the Assembly toolbar. The Explode PropertyManager is displayed.

- Click **Insert, Exploded View** from the Menu bar menu. The Explode PropertyManager is displayed.

🔅 The illustrations in this book are based on SolidWorks SP1.0. The illustrations may vary slightly per your SolidWorks release.

Activity: CYLINDER Assembly-Exploded View

Open the CYLINDER assembly.

1) **Open** the CYLINDER assembly in the DRAWING-W-SOLIDWORKS-2012\Chapter 8 folder which you copied from the DVD in the book to your hard drive.

Insert an Exploded view.

2) Click **Exploded View** from the Assembly toolbar. The Explode PropertyManager is displayed.

Create Explode Step1.

3) **Expand** the fly-out FeatureManager in the Graphics window.

4) Click **CAP-SCREW-M3x16<1>** and **CAP-SCREW-M3x16<2>**.

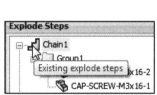

5) Enter **180**mm in the Explode distance box or use the on-screen ruler with the control points.

6) Check the **Auto-space components after drag** box.

7) Check the **Select-sub-assembly's parts** box.

8) Click **Reverse direction**, if required.

9) Click **Apply**.

10) Click **Done**. Chain1/Group1 is created. View the illustration.

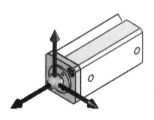

Click and drag with the Manipulator icon to move the component in the assembly using the control points with the on-screen ruler.

Fit the Model to the Graphics window.
11) Press the **f** key.

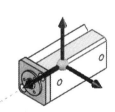

For a more realistic assembly animation, create the Explode Steps in the order to disassemble the physical components.

Create Explode Step2.
12) Click **COVERPLATE4<1>** from the FeatureManager.

13) Drag the **blue/orange manipulator handle** to the left approximately 100mms.

14) Click **Done**. Chain2 is created.

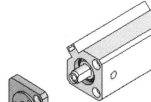

Create Explode Step3.

15) Click **RING<1>** from the FeatureManager.

16) Drag the **blue/orange manipulator handle** to the left approximately 50mms.

17) Click **Done**. Chain3 is created.

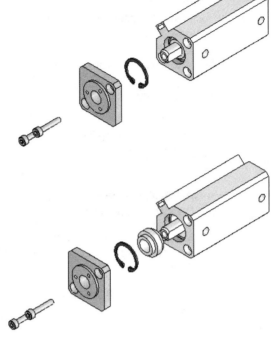

Create Explode Step4.

18) Click **COLLAR<1>** from the FeatureManager.

19) Drag the **blue/orange manipulator handle** to the left approximately 30mms.

20) Click **Done**.

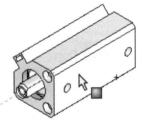

Create Explode Step5.

21) Click **Tube4<1>** from the Graphics Window as illustrated.

22) Drag the **blue/orange manipulator handle** to the right approximately 70mms.

23) Click **Done**. View the results.

24) Click **OK** ✓ from the Explode PropertyManager.

Display the Exploded view steps in the ConfigurationManager.

25) Click the **ConfigurationManager** 🔧 tab.

26) **Expand** Default.

27) **Expand** ExplView1 to display Explode the ConfigurationManager.

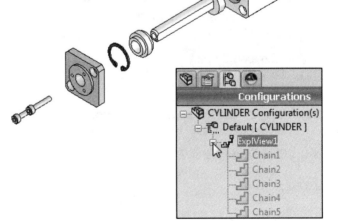

28) Right-click on **ExplView1**.

29) Click **Animate collapse**. View the animation.

30) Click **Close** ⊠ from the Animation Controller.

Return to the CYLINDER assembly.

31) Click the CYLINDER **FeatureManager** 🗐 tab.

Save the CYLINDER assembly.

32) Click **Save** 🖫 .

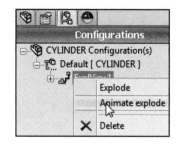

☼ When the Animation Controller is open, commands in SolidWorks are not accessible. Close the Animation Controller toolbar to return to SolidWorks.

☼ Click the **Animation1** tab/**Motion Study1** tab at the bottom of the Graphics window to perform a Motion Study on the assembly. Click the **Model** tab to return to a SolidWorks Graphics window.

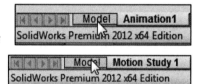

CYLINDER Assembly Drawing-Insert Balloons

The CYLINDER assembly drawing contains an Isometric Exploded view. Utilize View Properties to display the Exploded view. Use Balloon annotations to label components in an assembly. The Balloon contains the Item Number listed in the Bill of Materials. A Balloon displays different end conditions based on the arrowhead geometry reference.

Drag the endpoint of the arrowhead to modify the attachment and the end condition.

- Edge/vertex: - Arrowhead.

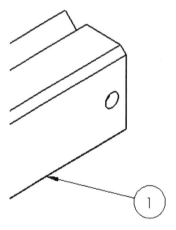

- Face/surface: - Dot.

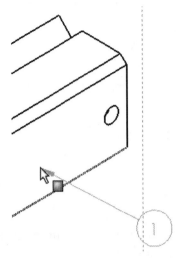

- Unattached: - Question mark.

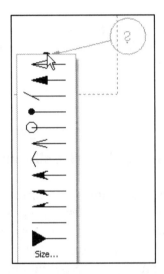

⚡ Click the dimension, right-click the control point to select the correct arrow style.

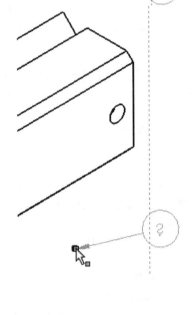

⚡ View mouse pointer feedback to distinguish between a vertex in the model and the attachment point in a Balloon.

The attachment point displays the Note ⌖ icon for a Balloon and the Point ⌐ icon for point geometry.

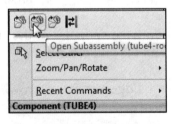

⚡ When you right-click an Assembly in an Assembly drawing, you can either open the part, subassembly or the assembly.

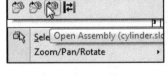

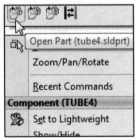

The Document Template, Drafting Standards, Balloons option defines the default arrow style and Balloons options.

The Balloons option controls: *Single balloon*, *Stacked balloons*, *Balloon text*, *Bent leaders*, and *Auto Balloon Layout* options.

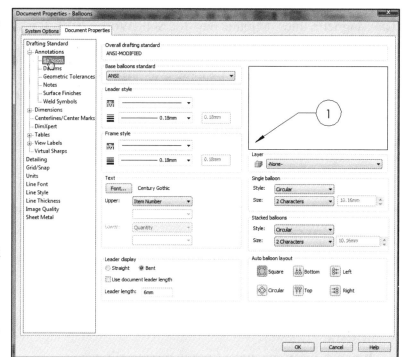

The Auto Balloon Layout option determines the display of the Balloons and the ability to use the insert magnetic lines tool. Square Layout is the default. The Top Layout displays the Balloons horizontally aligned above the model. The Left Layout displays the Balloon vertically aligned to the left of the model.

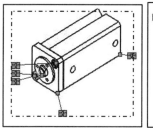

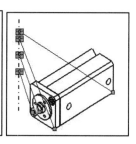

Square (Default)   Top Layout   Left Layout

Modify the selected Balloon with Balloon Properties. The Circular Split Line Style displays the Item Number in the Upper portion of the circle and the Quantity in the Lower portion of the Circle. The Insert magnetic lines (s) tool is selected by default.

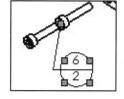

The Magnetic lines option is new for SolidWorks 2012. It is a convenient way to align balloons along a line at any angle.

You attach balloons to magnetic lines, choose to space the balloons equally or not, and move the lines freely, at any angle, in the drawing.

- You can have multiple magnetic lines in a drawing view.

- Magnetic lines do not print.

- Balloons maintain their alignment when the magnetic lines are not visible.

- When you drag a balloon onto another balloon on a magnetic line, the balloons swap positions.

- You can insert balloons before or after inserting magnetic lines.

- You can insert magnetic lines automatically when you use the Auto Balloon command.

To manually insert a Magnetic line, click **Magnetic Line** (Annotations toolbar) or click **Insert, Annotations, Magnetic Line** from the Menu bar menu.

Select the Balloon option from the Annotation toolbar or Right-click Annotations in the Graphics window, or click Insert, Annotations from the Menu bar menu.

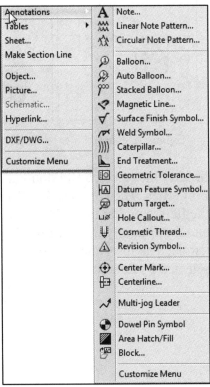

The Balloon option inserts a single item with a leader. The Auto Balloon option inserts Balloons based on the view boundary and the BOM type. The Stacked Balloon option contains multiple item numbers with a single leader from the Pop-up menu.

Activity: CYLINDER Assembly Drawing-Insert Balloons

Create a drawing from the assembly.

33) Click **Make Drawing from Part/Assembly** from the Menu bar toolbar.

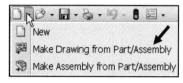

34) Double-click the **C-ANSI-MM** drawing template from the MY-TEMPLATES tab.

35) Drag the **Isometric view** boundary to the upper right corner of Sheet1.

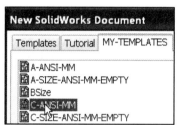

36) Click inside the **Top** predefined view.

37) Hold the **Ctrl** key down.

38) Click inside the **Front** and **Right** predefined views.

39) Release the **Ctrl** key.

40) Press the **Delete** key.

41) Click **Yes to All**. If required, **deselect** the Origins.

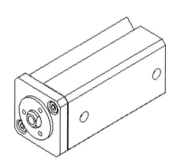

Save the CYLINDER drawing.

42) Click **Save As** from the Menu bar toolbar.

43) Enter **CYLINDER** for File name.

44) Click **Save**.

Display the Exploded view state.

45) Right-click inside the **Isometric view** boundary.

46) Click **Properties**.

47) Check the **Show in exploded state** box.

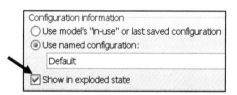

48) Click **OK** from the Drawing View Properties dialog box. The Isometric view displays the Exploded state.

Fit the Model to the Graphics window.
49) Press the **f** key.

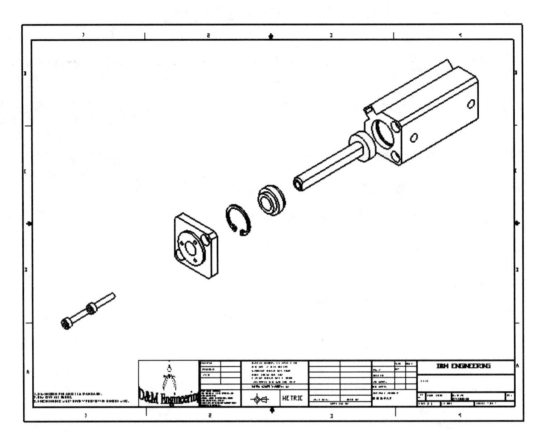

Insert Balloons to label each component.
50) Click inside the **Isometric view** boundary.

51) Click **AutoBalloon** 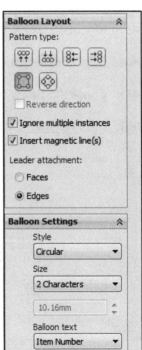 from the Annotation toolbar. The Auto Balloon PropertyManager is displayed. Six balloons are displayed in the Isometric view. Note the magnetic lines between the balloons. Use the magnetic lines to align the balloons.

52) Click **OK** ✓ from the Auto Balloon PropertyManager.

Modify the Balloons.
53) **Window-select** the six balloons in the Graphics window. The Balloon PropertyManager is displayed.

54) Click the **More Properties** button.

55) Click **Bent Leader**  for Leader display.

Modify the Font.

56) Uncheck the **Use document font** box.

57) Click the **Font** button. The Choose Font dialog box is displayed.

58) Enter **5**mm for font Height.

59) Click **OK**.

60) Click **OK** ✔ from the Note PropertyManager.

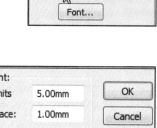

Move the Balloons.

61) Click the **arrowhead** on **Balloon 1**.

62) Click and drag the **arrow head** to the middle of the TUBE face as illustrated. The arrow head changes shape per the Engineering Standard. The arrow head shape is different for an edge vs. a face.

63) Drag each **Balloon** into position. Leave space between the Balloon numbers.

Create two leader lines.

64) Zoom in on the two CAP-SCREWS.

65) Click the **Arrow head** on the CAP-SCREW.

66) Hold the **Ctrl** key down.

67) Drag and drop the **arrowhead** from the edge of the first CAP-SCREW to the edge of the second CAP-SCREW. Note: The Arrow head type for an edge vs. a surface.

68) Release the **Ctrl** key.

69) Click **OK** ✔ from the PropertyManager.

Save the CYLINDER drawing.

70) Click **Save** 🖫 .

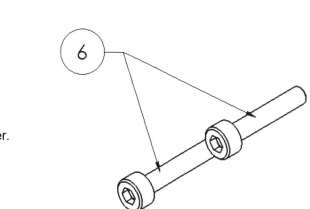

.

CYLINDER Assembly Drawing-Bill of Materials

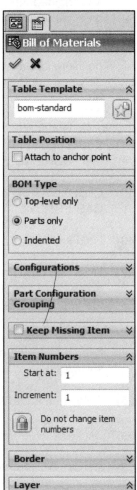

The Bill of Materials (BOM) is a table that lists essential information on the components in an assembly. Insert a Bill of Materials (BOM) into the CYLINDER drawing. The BOM is linked to the Properties of the CYLINDER components. There are two options to create a BOM in the drawing:

- Table option

- Excel spreadsheet option

Investigate the Table option in this activity. The first BOM Table inserted into the CYLINDER drawing requires additional work. The information is incomplete. Utilize the Component Properties tool to define the majority of information located in the BOM.

ITEM NO.	PART NUMBER	DESCRIPTION	MATERIAL	QTY.
1	TUBE4			1
2	ROD4			1
3	10-0411			1
4	MP043BM1-17	RING	Material <not specified>	1
5	10-0410	COVERPLATE	6061 Alloy	1
6	MP04-M3-05-16	CAP SCREW	Material <not specified>	2

The foundation for the BOM is the BOM template. The template contains the major column headings. The default BOM template, bom-standard.sldbomtbt contains the following column headings: ITEM NO., PART NUMBER, DESCRIPTION, QTY. (QUANTITY).

The SolidWorks\lang\<language> folder contains additional BOM templates:

- MATERIAL

- STOCK-SIZE

- VENDOR

- WEIGHT

The bom-all.sldbomtbt contains the default column headings. A BOM template also contains User Defined Custom headings. The User Defined Custom headings are linked to Custom Properties in the part or assembly. Define Custom Properties with the ConfigurationManager or a Design Table.

Create a Custom-BOM template. Start with a pre-defined BOM template. Insert additional headings. Right-click Save BOM template and select the MY-TEMPLATES folder. Open the Custom-BOM template through the Table Template option.

The BOM Table Anchor point locates the BOM at a corner of the drawing. The BOM Table moves when the Attach to anchor option is unchecked. The BOM Type contains three options:

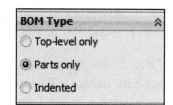

- **Top level only**: Lists parts and sub-assemblies, but not sub-assembly components.

- **Parts only**: Does not list sub-assemblies. Lists sub-assembly components as individual items.

- **Indented assemblies**: Lists sub-assemblies. Indents sub-assembly components below their sub-assemblies. Select Show numbering to display item numbers for sub-assembly components.

Summary Table:

Utilize the **Top level only** option (for assemblies that contain sub-assemblies) to display the highest level components in the FeatureManager.

ITEM NO.	PART NUMBER
1	TUBE4-ROD4
2	10-0411
3	MP04-3BM1-17
4	10-0410
5	MP04-M3-05-16

Utilize the **Parts only** option to display the parts in an assembly in the BOM.

ITEM NO.	PART NUMBER
1	TUBE4
2	ROD4
3	10-0411
4	MP04-3BM1-17
5	10-0410
6	MP04-M3-05-16

Utilize the **Indented** option to display sub-assembly components below their sub-assemblies in the BOM.

ITEM NO.	PART NUMBER
1	TUBE4-ROD4
	TUBE4
	ROD4
2	10-0411
3	MP04-3BM1-17
4	10-0410
5	MP04-M3-05-16

By default, component order in the assembly determines their ITEM NO. in the BOM. The occurrence of the same component in an assembly defines the value in the QTY column.

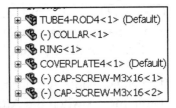

The PART NUMBER is the SolidWorks File name, Example: TUBE4.

DESCRIPTION is the text entered in the Description box. The Description box is blank.

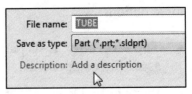

Define Description as a Custom Property in the next section. Create a Parts level only Bill of Materials with the SolidWorks BOM Template, bom-material.sldbomtbt for Sheet1. Create a Top level only Bill of Materials with the bom-standard.sldbomtbt for Sheet2.

Activity: CYLINDER Assembly Drawing-Bill of Materials

Insert the default Bill of Materials.
71) Click inside the **Isometric view** boundary.

72) Click **Bill of Materials** from the Consolidated Tables toolbar.

73) Double-click **bom-material.sldbomtbt** from the SolidWorks\lang\english folder.

74) Click the **Parts only** box.

75) Click **OK** from the Bill of Materials PropertyManager. The Bill of Materials is attached to the mouse pointer.

76) Click a **position** in the upper left corner of the sheet. View the results.

Existing BOM tables can be modified after creation to include additional columns, formatting or changed settings.

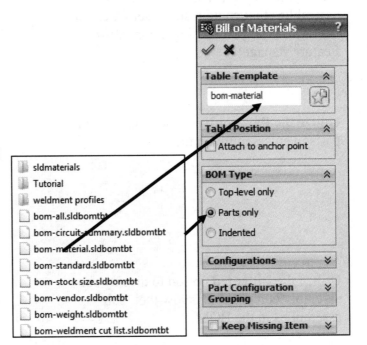

77) **Zoom in** to enlarge the BOM. The RING and CAPSCREW components were taken from the SolidWorks Toolbox. Note the information in the Material column. The order in your BOM may differ than illustrated. ·

ITEM NO.	PART NUMBER	DESCRIPTION	MATERIAL	QTY.
1	TUBE4			1
2	ROD4			1
3	10-0411			1
4	MP043BM1-17	RING	Material<not specified>	1
5	10-0410	COVERPLATE	6061 Alloy	1
6	MP04-M3-05-16	CAPSCREW	Material<not specified>	2

Information in the current BOM is incomplete. The Custom Properties in the parts/components are linked to the PART NUMBER, DESCRIPTION, MATERIAL, and QTY. columns in the BOM. Create additional Custom Properties in the parts and in the BOM to complete the BOM in the drawing.

Materials Editor and Mass Properties

The BOM contains a Material column heading. The Materials Editor provides a list of predefined and user defined materials and their physical properties. Access the Materials Editor through the FeatureManager.

Utilize the density and volume of the material to determine the mass of the part. Select Tools, Mass Properties to calculate mass and other physical properties of the part. The physical properties of the part depend on different configurations. Review the Mass Properties for each part configuration.

Activity: Materials Editor and Mass Properties

Edit and Insert material for TUBE4.
78) **Expand** TUBE4-ROD4<1> in the Drawing FeatureManager.

79) Right-click the **TUBE4<1>** part in the Drawing FeatureManager.

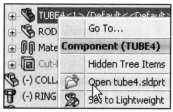

80) Click **Open tube4.sldprt**. The TUBE4 FeatureManager is displayed

81) Right-click **6061 Alloy** from the TUBE4 (Default) FeatureManager. Part material information in the BOM is not transferred to the drawing until you address it in the Custom Properties section. You will do this in the next section.

82) Click **Edit Material**. The Materials dialog box displayed. View the available information on the material.

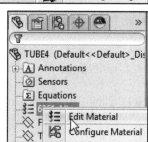

83) Click **Apply**.

84) Click **Close** from the Materials dialog box.

Display the Mass Properties.

85) Click **Mass Properties** from the Evaluate tab in the CommandManager. The Mass Properties dialog box is displayed.

86) Click the **Options** button.

87) Enter **4** for Decimal Places.

88) Click **OK**. The Mass 92.3617g is display. The Density 0.0027g/mm^3 is determined from the assigned material.

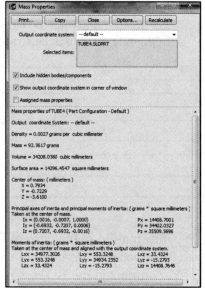

89) Click **Close** from the Mass Properties dialog box.

Insert material for ROD4.

90) **Open** the ROD4 part.

91) Right-click **Material** from the FeatureManager.

92) Click **Edit Material**.

93) **Expand** Steel.

94) Select **AISI 304**.

95) Click **Apply**. Click **Close** from the Material dialog box.

Calculate the Mass Properties for the ROD4 Default.

96) Click **Mass Properties** from the Evaluate tab in the CommandManager. The Mass Properties dialog box is displayed.

97) Click the **Options** button.

98) Click **Use custom settings**.

99) Enter **4** for Decimal Places.

100) Click **OK**. View the mass properties.

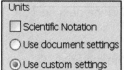

101) Click **Close** from the Mass Properties dialog box.

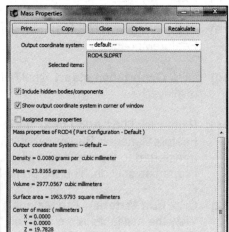

View the ShortRod and LongRod Mass Properties.
102) Double-click the **ShortRod** Configuration.

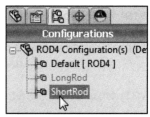

103) Click **Mass Properties** from the Evaluate tab in the CommandManager. View the mass properties.

104) Click **Close** from the Mass Properties dialog box.

105) Double-click the **LongRod** Configuration.

106) Click **Mass Properties** from the Evaluate tab in the CommandManager. View the properties.

107) Click **Close** from the Mass Properties dialog box.

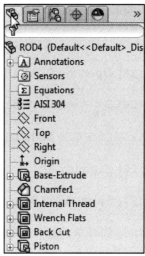

Return to the Default configuration.
108) Double-click **Default** from the ConfigurationManager.

109) **Return** to the FeatureManager.

Close the Mass Property dialog box before you switch to a different configuration. You cannot switch configurations when the Mass Properties dialog box is open. Select the new

configuration and calculate the Mass Properties.

Review the material and mass for COVERPLATE4.
110) **Open** the COVERPLATE4 part from the Chapter 8 folder. The FeatureManager displays 6061 Alloy.

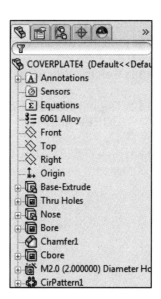

Calculate the Mass Properties for the COVERPLATE4 Default.
111) Click **Mass Properties** from the Evaluate tab in the CommandManager.

112) Click **Options**.

113) Enter **4** for Decimal Places.

114) Click **OK**. The Mass equals 10.8125 grams.

115) Click **Close** from the Mass Properties dialog box.

View the two configurations.
116) Double-click the **WithNoseHoles** Configuration.

117) Click **Mass Properties** from the Evaluate tab in the CommandManager. The Mass equals 10.8125 grams.

118) Click **Close** from the Mass Properties dialog box.

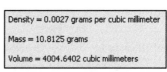

Density = 0.0027 grams per cubic millimeter

Mass = 10.8125 grams

Volume = 4004.6402 cubic millimeters

Density = 0.0027 grams per cubic millimeter

Mass = 10.8507 grams

Volume = 4018.7774 cubic millimeters

119) Double-click the **WithoutNoseHoles** Configuration.

120) Click **Mass Properties** from the Evaluate tab in the CommandManager. The Mass equals 10.8507 grams.

121) Click **Close** from the Mass Properties dialog box.

Return to the Default configuration.
122) Double-click **Default**.

Apply material to the COLLAR part.
123) Open the COLLAR part.

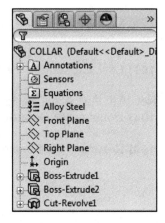

124) Right-click **Material**.

125) Click **Edit Material**.

126) Expand Steel.

127) Select **Alloy Steel**.

128) Click **Apply**.

129) Click **Close** from the Material dialog box. The FeatureManager displays the Material.

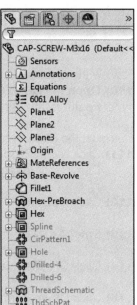

130) Repeat the above process for the **RING**.

131) Select **Alloy Steel** for Material.

132) Repeat the above process for the **CAP-SCREW-M3x16**.

133) Select **6061 Alloy** for Material.

The TUBE4, ROD4, CAP-SCREW-M3x16, COLLAR, and COVERPLATE4 parts, CYLINDER assembly and CYLINDER drawing - Sheet1 remain open in the next activities. Properties modified in the part require a rebuild to update the drawing BOM.

Configuration Properties

In a previous chapter, you linked Custom Properties and SolidWorks Properties to Notes in the Sheet format. In this chapter, cell entries in the BOM are linked to Properties created in the part and assembly. Create Properties in the part with two techniques: **Configuration Properties** and **Design Table**.

Access the Configuration Properties through the ConfigurationManager. The BOM requires a part number. There are three options utilized to display the Part number in the BOM:

- **Document Name (file name)**. Note: Default setting.

- **Configuration Name**

- **User Specified Name**

Utilize two options in this section. The Document name is TUBE4. The current BOM Part Number column displays the Document Name. Utilize the User Specified Name to assign a numeric value.

The Custom button contains the Summary Information, Custom Properties and Configuration Specific options. Utilize the Configuration Specific tab to control the Description, Material. Mass and Cost Properties.

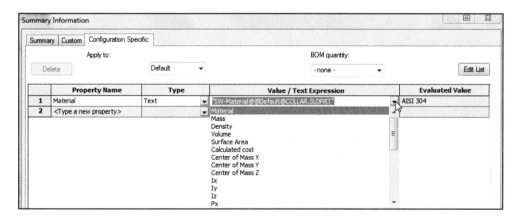

The Description Property links the BOM Description column heading. The TUBE 16MM Value corresponds to the Cell entry in the BOM.

Link the Material Property to the value; "SW-Material@@Default@TUBE4.SLDPRT". This value corresponds to the Material assigned with the Materials Editor. The parameter is in the form:

Property Name@@Configuration Name@Part Name

Link the Mass Property to the value;"SW-Mass@@Default@TUBE4.SLDPRT". The value corresponds to the mass calculated through the Mass Properties tool. Enter values for the Custom Property Cost. Insert the Cost column into the BOM.

The Design Table is an Excel spreadsheet utilized to create multiple configurations of a part or assembly.

Utilize Custom Properties in the Design Table to save time in creating multiple configurations and their properties.

Activity: Configuration Properties

Add Custom Properties to TUBE4.

134) Display the TUBE4 part.

135) Click the **ConfigurationManager**  tab.

136) Right-click **Properties** on the Default [TUBE4] configuration.

Add a User Specified Part number.

137) Select the **User Specified Name** from the drop-down menu.

138) Enter **10-0408** for Part number displayed when used in bill of materials option.

Insert Custom Properties.

139) Click the **Custom Properties** button from the Configuration Properties dialog box.

Add the Material Property.

140) Click the **Configuration Specific** tab.

141) Select **Material** from the Property Name drop-down menu.

142) Select **Material** from the Value / Text Expression box. The "SW-Material@@Default@TUBE4.SLDPRT" value is added to the Value text box.

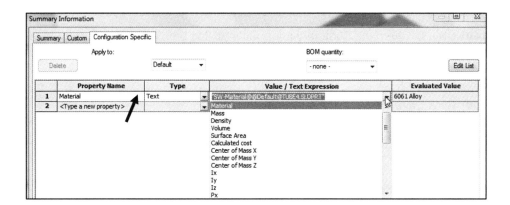

Add the Mass Property.

143) Enter **Mass** in the Property Name box.

144) Select **Mass** from the Value / Text Expression drop-down menu. The "SW-Mass@@Default@ TUBE4.SLDPRT" value is added to the Value text box.

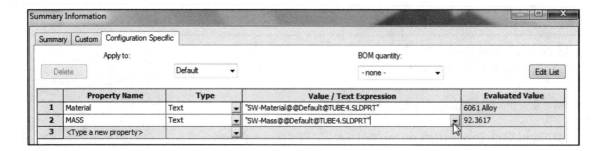

Add a Description Property.
145) Select **Description** from the Property Name drop-down menu.

146) Enter **TUBE 16MM** in the Value / Text Expression box.

Add a Cost Property.
147) Select **Cost** from the Property Name drop-down menu.

148) Enter **200** in the Value / Text Expression box.

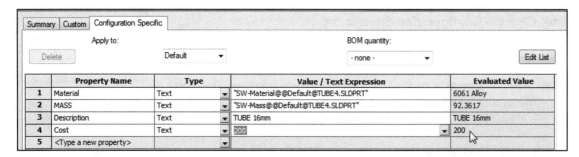

149) Click **OK** from the Summary Information dialog box. Click **OK** ✅ from the Configuration Properties PropertyManager. **Return** to the FeatureManager.

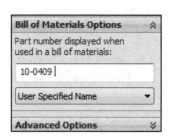

Save the TUBE4 part.
150) Click **Save** 🖫 .

Add Custom Properties to the ROD4 part.
151) **Open** the ROD4 (Default) part.

152) Click the **ConfigurationManager** 🔠 tab.

153) Right-click **Properties** on the Default configuration.

Add a User Specified Part number.
154) Select the **User Specified Name** from the drop-down menu.

155) Enter **10-0409** for Part number displayed when used in bill of materials option.

156) Click the **Custom Properties** button.

Add a Material Property.
157) Click the **Configuration Specific** tab.

158) Select **Material** from the Property Name drop-down menu.

159) Select **Material** from the Value / Text Expression box. The "SW-Material@@Default@ROD4.SLDPRT" value is added to the box.

Add a Mass Property.
160) Enter **Mass** in the Property Name box.

161) Select **Mass** from the Value / Text Expression box. The "SW-Mass@@Default@ROD4.SLDPRT" value is added to the Value text box.

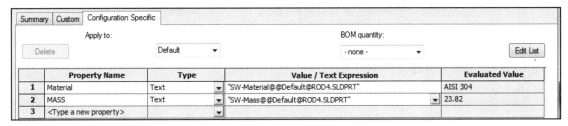

Add a Description Property.
162) Select **Description** from the Property Name drop-down menu.

163) Enter **ROD** in the Value / Text Expression box.

Add a Cost Property.
164) Select **Cost** from the Property Name drop-down menu.

165) Enter **50** in the Value / Text Expression box.

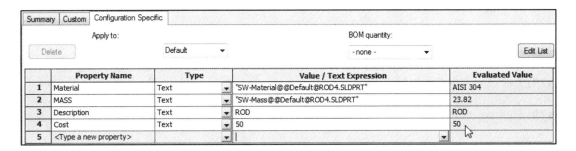

166) Click **OK** from the Summary Information dialog box.

167) Click **OK** ✅ from the Configuration Properties PropertyManager.

168) Click the **Part** FeatureManager icon.

Save the ROD4 part.
169) Click **Save** 💾 .

Review Custom Properties for COVERPLATE4.
170) Open COVERPLATE4 (Default).

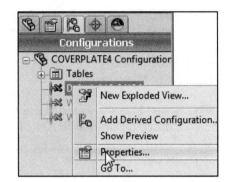

171) Click the **ConfigurationManager** 🔖 tab.

172) Right-click **Properties** on the Default configuration.

173) Click the **Custom Properties** button. View the Names and Values for the Properties: Material, Mass, Description and Cost.

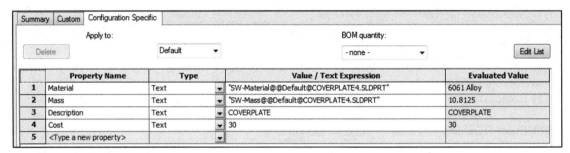

	Property Name	Type	Value / Text Expression	Evaluated Value
1	Material	Text	"SW-Material@@Default@COVERPLATE4.SLDPRT"	6061 Alloy
2	Mass	Text	"SW-Mass@@Default@COVERPLATE4.SLDPRT"	10.8125
3	Description	Text	COVERPLATE	COVERPLATE
4	Cost	Text	30	30
5	<Type a new property>			

174) Click **OK** from the Summary Information dialog box.

175) Click **OK** ✔ from the Configuration Properties PropertyManager.

176) Return to the FeatureManager.

Edit the COLLAR part.
177) Open the COLLAR part.

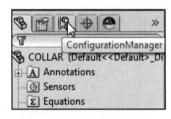

178) Click the **ConfigurationManager** 🔖 tab.

179) Right-click **Properties** on the Default configuration.

180) Select the **User Specified Name** from the drop-down menu.

181) Enter **10-0411**.

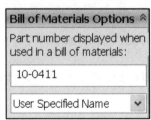

182) Click the **Custom Properties** button.

183) Select **Description** from the Property Name drop-down menu.

184) Enter **COLLAR** for Value / Text Expression.

Add a Material Property.
185) Select **Material** from the Property Name drop-down menu.

186) Select **Material** from the Value / Text Expression box.

Add a Cost Property.
187) Enter **Cost** in the Property Name drop-down menu. Enter **20** in the Value / Text Expression box.

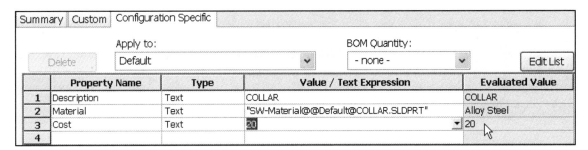

188) Click **OK**. Click **OK** ✔ from the Configuration Properties PropertyManager.

Edit the Ring Part.
189) **Open** the RING part. Click the **ConfigurationManager** tab. Right-click **Properties** on the Default configuration.

190) Click the **Custom Properties** button.

Add a Material Property.
191) Click the **Configuration Specific** tab.

192) Select **Material** from the Property Name drop-down menu.

193) Select **Material** from the Value / Text Expression box.

Add a Cost Property.
194) Select **Cost** from the Property Name drop-down menu. Enter **5** in the Value / Text Expression box.

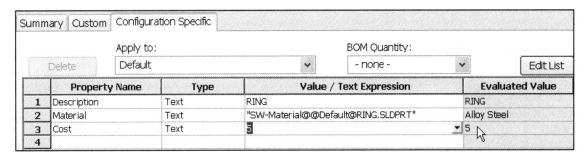

195) Click **OK**. Click **OK** ✔ from the Configuration Properties PropertyManager.

If needed, modify the CAP-SCREW-M3x16.

196) Open **CAP-SCREW-M3x16**. Click the

ConfigurationManager 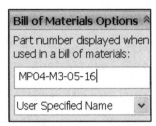 tab. Right-click **Properties** on the Default configuration. Select the **User Specified Name** from the drop-down menu. Enter **MP04-M3-05-16**. Click the **Custom Properties** button. View the information.

Bill of Materials Options
Part number displayed when used in a bill of materials:
MP04-M3-05-16
User Specified Name

Summary	Custom	Configuration Specific			

Apply to: **Default**   BOM Quantity: **- none -**   Delete   Edit List

	Property Name	Type	Value / Text Expression	Evaluated Value
1	Description	Text	CAP SCREW	CAP SCREW
2	Material	Text	"SW-Material@@Default@CAP-SCREW-M3x16.SL	6061 Alloy
3	Cost	Text	5	5
4				

197) Click **OK**. Click **OK** ✓ from the Configuration Properties PropertyManager.

Design Table

A Design Table is an Excel spreadsheet utilized to create configurations and control parameters in a part or assembly.

Cell A1   **Design Table Parameters**

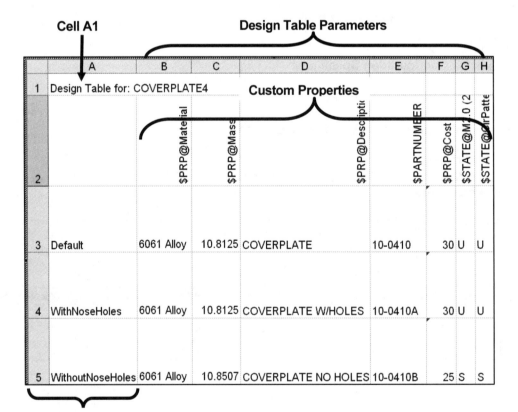

Custom Properties

Configuration Names

The model name associated with the Design Table is located in Cell A1. Define the configuration names in the first column of an Excel spreadsheet. Define the parameters in the second row.

Enter values in the Cells that correspond to the configuration name and the parameter name. Leave Cell A2 blank.

Entering parameters into a Design Table is a cumbersome task. Utilize the Auto-create option to load all configured parameters and their associated values from a part or assembly. Utilize the Design Table to create multiple configurations for the ROD part and the CYLINDER assembly.

The current ROD Default Configuration contains Custom Properties: Mass, Material, Description and Cost. The Design Table with the Auto create option inserts the Custom Property parameters in Row 2.

Custom Properties begin with the prefix, $PRP@. Enter user defined values for the BOM Part Number in the Design Table. The Property, $PARTNUMBER displays three options in a Design Table:

- **$D Document Name (filename)**

- **$C Configuration Name**

- **User defined**

Additional part and assembly control parameters control Configuration, State, Color, Comment and Dimension. All parameters begin with a $, except Dimension.

Enter parameters carefully. The "$", "@" and "<>" symbol format needs to match exactly for the result to be correct in the BOM.

The Summary of Design Table Parameters is as follows:

Summary of Design Table Parameters:		
Parameter Syntax (header Cell)	**Legal Values** (body Cell)	**Default if Value** is Left Blank
Parts only:		
$configuration@part_name	configuration name	not evaluated
$configuration@<feature_name>	configuration name	not evaluated
Parts and Assemblies:		
$comment	any text string	empty
$part number	any text string	configuration name
$state@feature_name	Suppressed, S Unsuppressed, U	Unsuppressed
dimension @feature	any legal decimal value for the dimension	not evaluated
$parent	parent configuration name	property is undefined
$prp@ property	any text string	property is undefined
$state@equation_number@equations	Suppressed, S Unsuppressed, U	Unsuppressed
$state@lighting_name	Suppressed, S Unsuppressed, U	Unsuppressed
$state@sketch relation@sketch name	Suppressed, S Unsuppressed, U	Unsuppressed
$sw-mass	Any legal decimal value for mass of a component.	The calculated value of mass in the Mass Properties option
$sw-coq	Any legal decimal value for the center of gravity in x, y, z.	The calculated cog in the Mass Properties option.
$user_notes	any text string	not evaluated
$color	32-bit integer specifying RGB (red, green, blue) color. See Online Help, Color for more info	zero (black)
Assemblies only:		
$show@component<instance>	Yes, Y No, N	No
$state@component<instance>	Resolved, R, Suppressed, S	Resolved
$configuration@component<instance>	configuration name	Component's "in-use" or last saved configuration NOTE: If the component uses a derived configuration, and the value is left blank, the configuration used is linked to its parent.
$never_expand_in_BOM	Yes (never expand) No (allow to expand)	No

Perform two activities with Design Tables. In the first activity, review the Design Table for COVERPLATE4. Insert a Design Table into the ROD4.

Review the updates in the Bill of Materials. In the second activity, insert a Design Table into the CYLINDER assembly. Control multiple configurations in the CYLINDER drawing views.

Activity: Design Table

Review the COVERPLATE4 Design Table.

198) Open COVERPLATE4. Click the **ConfigurationManager** tab.

199) Right-click the **Design Table** folder as illustrated.

200) Click **Edit Table**. Review the Parameters for the Design Table.

Enlarge the Design Table.
201) Drag the **lower right corner** downward.

202) Click a **position** in the Graphics window to close the Design Table and to return to SolidWorks.

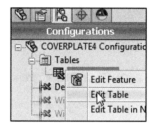

	A	B	C	D	E	F	G	H
1	Design Table for: COVERPLATE4							
2		$PRP@Material	$PRP@Mass		$PRP@Description	$PARTNUMBER	$PRP@Cost	$STATE@M2.0 (2	$STATE@CirPatte
3	Default	6061 Alloy	10.8125	COVERPLATE		10-0410	30	U	U
4	WithNoseHoles	6061 Alloy	10.8125	COVERPLATE W/HOLES		10-0410A	30	U	U
5	WithoutNoseHoles	6061 Alloy	10.8507	COVERPLATE NO HOLES		10-0410B	25	S	S

Insert a Design Table.
203) Open the ROD4 (Default) part.

204) Click **Insert, Tables, Design Table** from the Menu bar menu. The Design Table PropertyManager is displayed.

Select the parameters.
205) Check the **Auto-create** box.

206) Check the **New parameters** box.

207) Check the **New configurations** box.

208) Check **Warn when updating design table** in the Options box.

209) Click **OK** 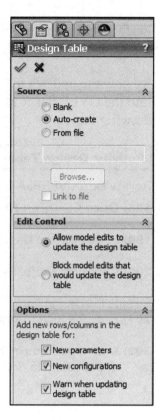 from the Design Table PropertyManager.

	A	B	C	D	E	F	G	H	I	J
1	Design Table for: ROD4									
2		$DESCRIPTION	$PARTNUMBER	$COLOR	$PRP@Material	$PRP@Mass	$PRP@Description	$PRP@Cost	D1@Base-Extrude	
3	Default	Default	10-0409	9871013	AISI 304	23.82	ROD	50	53.83	
4	ShortRod	ShortRod	$C	9871013	AISI 304				53.83	
5	LongRod	LongRod	$C	9871013	AISI 304				200	
6										

Copy the Material cell.
210) Copy **AISI 304** to Cell E4, and Cell E5.

 Click a position outside the Design Table to exit EXCEL and return to a SolidWorks session. To return to the Design Table, right-click Design Table in the ConfigurationManager. Select Edit Table.

Note: Your column numbers may vary per the illustration.

Edit the Part number column.
211) Click Cell **C4**. Enter **10-0409S**.

212) Click Cell **C5**. Enter **10-0409L**.

D	E	F
$COLOR	$PRP@Material	$PRP@Mass
9871013	AISI 304	23.82
9871013	AISI 304	
9871013	AISI 304	

Edit the Mass column.
213) Click Cell **F4**.

214) Enter **"SW-Mass@@ShortRod@ROD4.SLDPRT"**.

215) Click Cell **F5**.

216) Enter **"SW-Mass@@LongRod@ROD4.SLDPRT"**.

Edit the Description column.
217) Click Cell **G4**.

218) Enter **ROD 16MM SHORT**.

219) Click Cell **G5**.

220) Enter **ROD 16MM LONG**.

Edit the Cost column.
221) Click Cell **H4**.

222) Enter **50**.

223) Click Cell **H5**.

224) Enter **100**.

225) Click inside the **Graphics window**.

226) Rebuild the model.

227) Return to the Design Table to view the updates.

The parameter, SW-Mass is case sensitive. Your color cell numbers may vary slightly for the illustration.

	A	B	C	D	E	F	G	H
1	Design Table for: ROD4							
2		$PARTNUMBER	$COLOR	$PRP@Material		$PRP@Mass	$PRP@Description	$PRP@Cost	D1@Base-Extrude
3	Default	10-0409	9871013	AISI 304		23.82 ROD		50	53.83
4	ShortRod	10-0409S	11314333	AISI 304		23.82 ROD 16MM SHORT		50	53.83
5	LongRod	10-0409L	11314333	AISI 304		74.11 ROD 16MM LONG		100	200
6									

Bill of Materials - Part 2

The Custom Properties in the TUBE4, ROD4, and COVERPLATE4 parts produce changes to the BOM. Return to the CYLINDER Sheet1. Rebuild the drawing to update the BOM.

Editing Cells

The BOM requires additional changes. Double-clicking a cell brings up the Context toolbar with items specific to the selected cell. The Context toolbar provides the ability to change the header, border, text and layer settings for the entire table.

Editing Columns

Hovering over a cell displays the Editing Table icon. Click a cell to display the Context toolbar. The toolbar's buttons reflect the available options for the type of table and

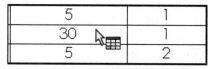

selections, (rows, column, and cells).

To access a table's PropertyManager, click the move table icon in the upper left corner or Right-click the table, and click Properties from the Pop-up menu.

Click the vertical arrows as illustrated to insert a row. Click the Horizontal arrows as illustrated to insert a column.

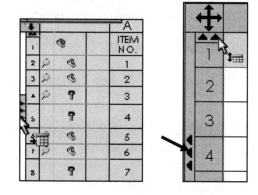

🔅 The illustrations in this book are based on SolidWorks SP1.0. The illustrations may vary slightly per your SolidWorks release.

🔅 SolidWorks informs you when you edit a cell; either to keep or to break the link to the external model.

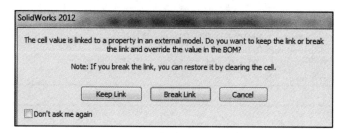

The Table Properties option returns you to the BOM PropertyManager.

The Insert tool provides the ability to insert a column to the Right or Left side of the selected column or a Row above or below the selected row.

The Select tool provides the ability to select a Table, Column, or Row.

The Formatting tool provides the ability to format the width of a column, the height of a row, or the entire table.

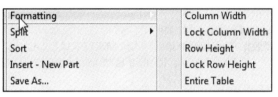

The Formatting Entire Table tool displayed the Entire Table dialog box.

The Sort tool provides the ability to sort selected items in the Bill of Materials. The Sort tool displays the Sort dialog box. Select the sort by item from the drop-down menu and check either ascending or descending order.

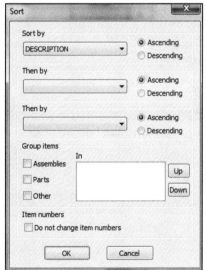

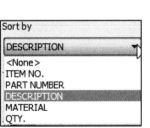

Activity: Bill of Materials-Part 2

Update to the CYLINDER-Sheet1 drawing.
228) Open the CYLINDER drawing-Sheet1. View the updated BOM.

Bill of Material - Insert Column

ITEM NO.	PART NUMBER	DESCRIPTION	MATERIAL	QTY.
1	10-0411	COLLAR	Alloy Steel	1
2	MP043BM1-17	RING	Alloy Steel	1
3	10-0410	COVERPLATE	6061 Alloy	1
4	MP04-M3-05-16	CAP SCREW	6061 Alloy	2
5	10-0408	TUBE 16MM	6061 Alloy	1
6	10-0409	ROD	AISI 304	1

Insert a column called COST.
229) Right-click inside the **MATERIAL** cell. The Pop-up toolbar is displayed.

230) Click **Insert**. Click **Column Right**.

231) Select **Column Properties**.

232) Select **Cost** from the Custom Property drop-down menu. Cost is inserted into the Bill of Materials.

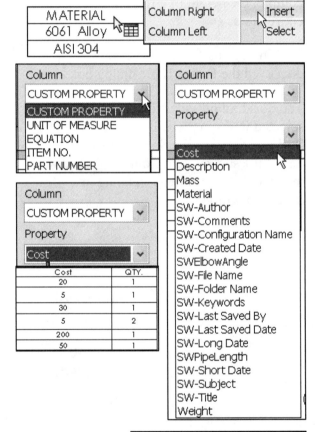

233) Position the **mouse point** on the column line between COST and QTY. Hovering over a column divider changes the mouse pointer.

234) Drag the **column divider line** to the left, to shrink the column by half as illustrated.

Bill of Materials - Header

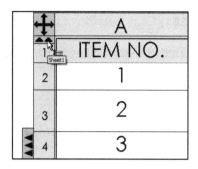

Insert the BOM Title.

235) Click **inside** the ITEMS NO. cell

236) Click the **vertical up-arrows**. The Bill of Materials header is displayed. Note: BOM Table is displayed by default.

237) Enter **CYLINDER ASSEMBLY BILL OF MATERIALS** for Title in the Header box.

238) Click **outside** of the Bill of Materials.

Insert a bulk item in the BOM.

239) Right-click inside **Cell Item No 6**.

240) Click **Insert**, **Row Below**. Row No. 7 is displayed.

241) Double-click the **Cell** to the right of Item No 7.

242) Click **Yes** to the question; Continue editing the Cell?

243) Enter **DP01-1010-23** for the PART NUMBER.

244) Double-click inside the **Cell** to the right of DP01-1010-23.

245) Click **Yes**.

246) Enter **LOCTITE** for DESCRIPTION.

247) Click **outside** of the Bill of Materials.

Modify the Item Column Order.

248) Click inside the **ITEM NO. 1** Cell.

249) **Position** the mouse pointer on number 3 as illustrated.

250) Click and drag the **first column Cell** downward as illustrated.

251) Click **outside** of the Bill of Materials.

252) Press the **f** key to the drawing in Sheet1. The balloons displayed the updated Bill of Materials.

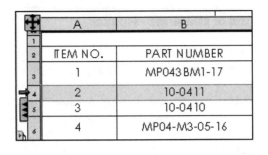

A	B
ITEM NO.	PART NUMBER
1	MP043 BM1-17
2	10-0411
3	10-0410
4	MP04-M3-05-16

Return to the original Item No. order.
253) Click inside the **Items NO. 2** Cell. Position the mouse pointer on number 4.

254) Click and drag the **column Cell** upwards. The Bill of Materials returns to the original order.

255) Click **outside** of the Bill of Materials.

256) Press the **f** key to the drawing in Sheet1. The balloons displayed the updated Bill of Materials

A	B
ITEM NO.	PART NUMBER
1	10-0411
2	MP043 BM1-17
3	10-0410
4	MP04-M3-05-16

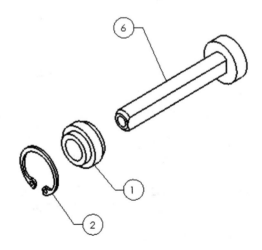

Bill of Materials - Equation

Apply an Equation to the Bill of Materials in a new Column. The Equation tool from the Edit Tables Context toolbar displays the Equation editor.

Insert the Total Cost Column.
257) Click the **Qty** cell.

258) Right-click **Insert**, **Column Right**.

259) Enter **Total Cost** for Title.

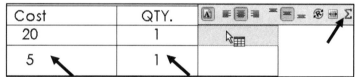

Apply the Equation tool.
260) Click the **cell** under the Total Cost header as illustrated.

261) Click the **Equation** Σ tool from the Context toolbar. The Equation editor is displayed.

262) Click the **20** Cost cell.

263) Enter the multiplication * symbol

264) Click the **1** QTY Cost cell.

265) Click **OK** ✅. View the results. 20 is displayed with the Equation icon.

266) **Perform** the above procedure for the rest of the Cost and QTY columns.

Cost	QTY.	Total Cost
20	1	20
5	1	
30	1	
5	2	
200	1	
50	1	

Enter Total Cost.

267) Click inside the illustrated **cell** to create the Total Cost sum.

268) Click the **Equation** Σ tool from the Context toolbar. The Equation editor is displayed.

269) Select the **SUM** Function from the drop-down menu.

270) Click **inside** cell G3. SUM(G3) is displayed.

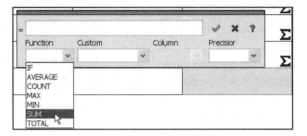

271) Enter: as illustrated.

272) Click **inside** cell G8. SUM(G3:G8) is displayed.

273) Click **OK** ✓. The value for Total Cost, 315 is calculated by the Equation.

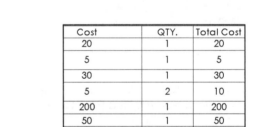

Modify the BOM Table Font size.

274) Click **CYLINDER ASSEMBLY BILL OF MATERIALS** in the Header box.

275) Modify the Font to **5mm**.

276) Select **Bold**.

Cost	QTY.	Total Cost
20	1	20
5	1	5
30	1	30
5	2	10
200	1	200
50	1	50
		315

277) Click **Inside** the Sheet. View the results.

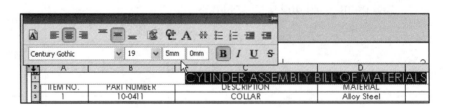

Fit the drawing to the Graphics window.

278) Press the **f** key.

Save the CYLINDER drawing.

279) Click **Save** 🖫 . Your order in the BOM may differ per the illustration.

💡 You can double click in the PART, DESCRIPTION or Cost column to link directly back to modify the part.

ITEM NO.	PART NUMBER	DESCRIPTION	MATERIAL	Cost	QTY.	Total Cost
\multicolumn{7}{c}{CYLINDER ASSEMBLY BILL OF MATERIALS}						
1	10-0411	COLLAR	Alloy Steel	20	1	20
2	MP043BM1-17	RING	Alloy Steel	5	1	5
3	10-0410	COVERPLATE	6061 Alloy	30	1	30
4	MP04-M3-05-16	CAP SCREW	6061 Alloy	5	2	10
5	10-0408	TUBE 16MM	6061 Alloy	200	1	200
6	10-0409	ROD	AISI 304	50	1	50
7	DP01-1010-23	LOCTITE				315

An Engineering Change Order is issued to modify the COLLAR from Alloy Steel to 6061 Alloy. Do you modify the BOM in the drawing? Answer: No. Return to the COLLAR part and update the Material in the Materials Editor. Investigate additional BOM options in the project exercises.

The CYLINDER assembly contains the default configuration for the TUBE, ROD and COVERPLATE parts. How do you modify the assembly to support multiple configurations of the ROD and COVERPLATE in a drawing? Answer: With a Design Table.

CYLINDER Assembly-Design Table

Design Tables control parameters in an assembly. Create a Design Table in the CYLINDER assembly with three different configurations of the COVERPLATE:

- NO-COVERPLATE (Suppressed COVERPLATE Component).

- COVERPLATE-HOLES uses the WithNoseHoles Configuration.

- COVERPLATE-NOHOLES uses the WithoutNoseHoles Configuration.

Insert three CYLINDER assembly configurations into a drawing. The TUBE, ROD, and COVERPLATE parts are set to their Default configurations. Utilize the configurations in the CYLINDER drawing views.

3	Default	Default
4	NO-COVERPLATE	Default
5	COVERPLATE-HOLES	WithNoseHoles
6	COVERPLATE-NOHOLES	WithoutNoseHoles

The TUBE4-ROD4 assembly contains two configurations:

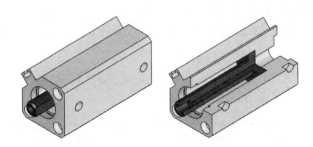

- Default

- CutAway

Utilize the CutAway configuration in the CYLINDER Design Table for Sheet2.

Activity: CYLINDER Assembly-Design Table

Create a Design Table in the CYLINDER assembly.
280) Open the CYLINDER assembly.

281) Click **Insert**, **Tables**, **Design Table** from the Menu bar menu. Accept the defaults. Note your options in the Design Table PropertyManager.

282) Click **OK** ✅ from the Design Table PropertyManager.

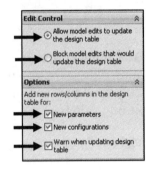

	A	B	C	D
1	Design Table for: CYLINDER			
2				
3	Default			

283) Enter **NO-COVERPLATE** in Cell A4.

284) Enter **COVERPLATE-HOLES** in Cell A5.

285) Enter **COVERPLATE-NOHOLES** in Cell A6.

286) Enter **NO-HARDWARE** in Cell A7.

287) Drag the **column bar** between Column A and Column B to the right until the full Configuration Names are displayed.

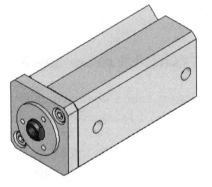

To avoid creating a Hyperlink in EXCEL, insert a single apostrophe 'before a parameter that contains the @ symbol. The COVERPLATE4<1> parameter is the same as the FeatureManager component name. The Component Name is case sensitive. Do not interchange upper and lower case letters. Use dashes and underscores, not spaces.

	A
1	Design Table for: CYLINDER
2	
3	Default
4	NO-COVERPLATE
5	COVERPLATE-HOLES
6	COVERPLATE-NOHOLES
7	NO-HARDWARE

Insert the COVERPLATE parameters

288) Enter **$CONFIGURATION@COVERPLATE4<1>** in Cell B2.

289) Enter **Default** in Cell B3.

290) Enter **Default** in Cell B4.

291) Enter **WithNoseHoles** in Cell B5.

292) Enter **WithoutNoseHoles** in Cell B6.

293) Enter **Default** in Cell B7.

294) Enter **$STATE@COVERPLATE4<1>** in Cell C2.

295) Enter **R** for Resolved in Cell C3, Cell C5, Cell C6 and C7.

296) Enter **S** for Suppress in Cell C4.

297) Enter **$STATE@CAP-SCREW-M3x16<*>** in Cell D2.

298) Enter **S** for Suppress in Cell D4 and Cell D7.

299) Enter **R** for Resolved in Cell D3, Cell D5 and Cell D6.

The <*> symbol indicates all instances for the CAP-SCREW-M3x16.

	A	B	C	D
1	Design Table for: CYLINDER			
2		$CONFIGURATION@COVERPLATE4<1>	$STATE@COVERPLATE4<1>	$STATE@CAP-SCREW-M3x16<*>
3	Default	Default	R	R
4	NO-COVERPLATE	Default	S	S
5	COVERPLATE-HOLES	WithNoseHoles	R	R
6	COVERPLATE-NOHOLES	WithoutNoseHoles	R	R
7	NO-HARDWARE	Default	R	S

Display the configurations.

300) Click a **position** outside the Design Table. Four assembly CYLINDER configurations are created.

301) Click **OK**.

Verify the configurations.

302) Double-click on **NO-COVERPLATE**.

303) Double-click on **COVERPLATE-HOLES**.

304) Double-click on **COVERPLATE-NOHOLES**.

305) Double-click on **NO-HARDWARE**.

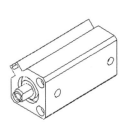 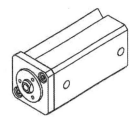 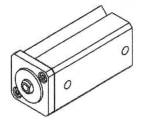 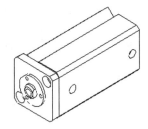

Return to the default configuration.

306) Double click the **Default** configuration.

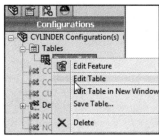

Edit the Design Table.

307) Right-click **Design Table** in the ConfigurationManager.

308) Click **Edit Table**.

309) Click **Cancel** to the Add Rows and Columns dialog box.

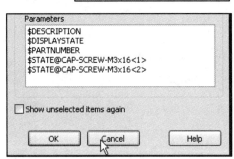

Enter the CUTAWAY configuration.

310) Enter **CUTAWAY** in Cell A8.

311) Enter **Default** in Cell B8. Enter **S** in Cell C8 and Cell D8.

312) Enter **$CONFIGURATION@TUBE4-ROD4<1>** in Cell E2.

313) Enter **Default** in Cell E3 - Cell E7.

314) Enter **CutAway** in Cell E8.

Add User_Notes.
315) Enter **$USER_NOTES** in Cell F2. SolidWorks does not calculate $USER_NOTES.

Enter the following notes displayed in Cells F3 through F8.
316) Enter **BASIC** in Cell F3 and Cell F4.

317) Enter **ANODIZED COVER** in Cell F5, Cell F6 and Cell F7.

318) Enter **SEE INTERNAL FEATURES** in Cell F8.

	A	B	C	D	E	F
1	Design Table for: CYLINDER					
2			$CONFIGURATION@COVERPLATE4<1>	$STATE@COVERPLATE4<1>	$STATE@CAP-SCREW-M3x16<*>	$CONFIGURATION@TUBE4-ROD4<1>	$USER_NOTES
3	Default	Default	R	R	Default	BASIC
4	NO-COVERPLATE	Default	S	S	Default	BASIC
5	COVERPLATE-HOLES	WithNoseHoles	R	R	Default	ANODIZED COVER
6	COVERPLATE-NOHOLES	WithoutNoseHoles	R	R	Default	ANODIZED COVER
7	NO-HARDWARE	Default	R	S	Default	ANODIZED COVER
8	CUTAWAY	Default	S	S	CutAway	SEE INTERNAL FEATURES

Update the configurations.
319) Click a **position** outside the Design Table.

320) Click **OK**.

Verify all CYLINDER configurations before creating additional views in the CYLINDER drawing.
321) Double-click each CYLINDER **configuration**. View the results in the Graphics window.

322) Double-click the **Default** configuration.

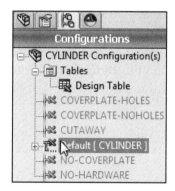

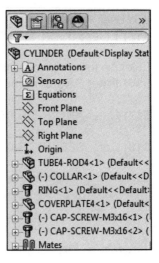

☀ To delete a configuration, select the Configuration name in the ConfigurationManager. The Row entries are removed from the Design Table.

Save the CYLINDER assembly.
323) Click the **FeatureManager** tab.

324) Click **Save** 🖫 .

The design table can include a column for configuration-specific colors. The value is a 32-bit integer that specifies RGB (red, green, blue). If no value is specified, zero (black) is applied.

If you know the 32-bit integer value of a color, you can type the number directly into the design table in a column with the **$COLOR parameter** as the header. If you do not know the 32-bit integer value, you can calculate it in the design table with the RGB component values.

☀ Color is an important property for visualization and machining purposes. One company provided the following colors as an example:

- Red - As Cast

- Blue - Machined Surface

- Orange - High Finish

The following table lists some typical colors, their components and the equivalent integer values.

Color	Red	Green	Blue	Integer
Black	0	0	0	0
Red	255	0	0	255
Orange	255	128	0	33023
Green	0	255	0	65280
Blue	0	0	255	16711680
Purple	255	128	255	16744703
Turquoise	0	255	255	16776960
White	255	255	255	16777215

CYLINDER Drawing-Multiple Configurations

Multiple configurations created in the CYLINDER Design Table allow you to insert various configurations into the drawing. Specify the configuration in the Properties of the current view. Modify the display options in the View Properties. Work between the three Sheets in the CYLINDER drawing.

Activity: CYLINDER Drawing-Multiple Configurations

Add Sheet2.
325) Open the CYLINDER drawing.

326) Click the **Add Sheet** icon at the bottom of the Graphics window. Sheet2 is displayed.

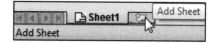

Add Sheet3.
327) Click the **Add Sheet** icon at the bottom of the Graphics window. Sheet3 is displayed.

Copy the Sheet1 Drawing View to Sheet2.
328) Click the **Sheet1** tab.

329) Click inside the **Isometric Drawing view** boundary of Sheet1.

330) Click **Ctrl + C**.

331) Click the **Sheet2** tab.

332) Click a **position** in Sheet2.

333) Click **Ctrl + V**.

Hide the Balloons.
334) Window-select the **Balloons**. The Balloon PropertyManager is displayed.

335) Right-click **Hide**.

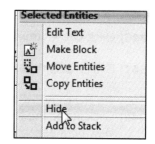

Drawing View #'s and Sheet Format #'s depend on the number of views you inserted and deleted. Your entries in the FeatureManager can vary to the illustrations in the next section.

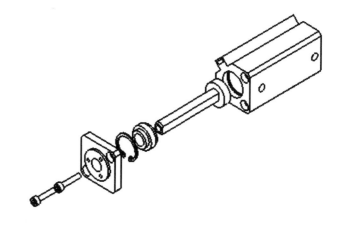

Modify View Properties.
336) Right-click **Properties** in the Isometric view boundary.

337) Uncheck **Show in exploded state**.

338) Select **NO-COVERPLATE** for the Use named configuration.

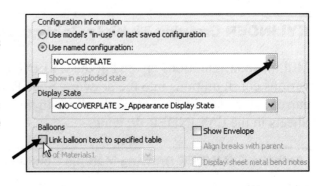

339) Un-check the **Link balloon text to specified table** box.

340) Click **OK** from the dialog box.

341) Hide all balloons if needed.

Insert a Bill of Material.
342) Click inside the **Isometric view** boundary. Click **Bill of Materials** 🗊 from the Consolidated Tables toolbar.

343) Select **bom-standard** for the Table Template.

344) Select **Top level only** for BOM Type.

345) Check **NO-COVERPLATE** for Configurations. Uncheck all other configurations.

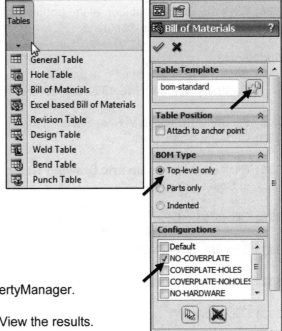

346) Click **OK** 🗸 from the Bill of Materials PropertyManager.

347) Click a **position** below the Isometric view. View the results.

Copy the NO-COVERPLATE view.
348) Click inside the **NO-COVERPLATE** view boundary.

349) Click **Ctrl + C**.

350) Click a **position** to the right of the view.

351) Click **Ctrl + V**.

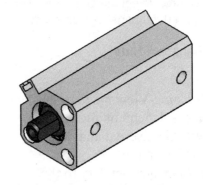

ITEM NO.	PART NUMBER	DESCRIPTION	NO-COVERPLATE/ QTY.
1	99-1007-1	TUBE4_ROD4	1
2	10-0411	COLLAR	1
3	MP043BM1-17	RING	1

Modify the View Properties.

352) Right-click **Properties** in the view boundary of the new Isometric view.

353) Click **COVERPLATE-NOHOLES** for the Use named configuration.

354) Click **OK**.

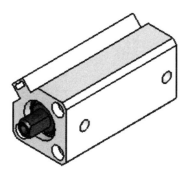 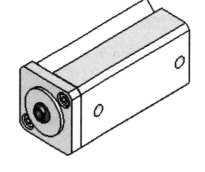

FTM NO	PART NUMBER	DESCRIPTION	NO COVERPLATE/QTY
1	99 1007 1	TUBE4_ROD4	1
2	10-0411	COLLAR	1
3	MP043BM1 17	RING	1

Insert a Bill of Materials.

355) Click inside the **Isometric view** boundary.

356) Click **Bill of Materials** from the Consolidated Tables toolbar. The Bill of Materials PropertyManager is displayed.

357) Select **bom-standard** for the Table Template.

358) Select **Top level only** for BOM Type.

359) Select **COVERPLATE-NOHOLES**.

360) Click **OK** from the Bill of Materials PropertyManager.

361) Click a **position** below the second Isometric view.

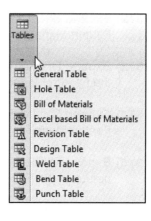

Tables

- General Table
- Hole Table
- Bill of Materials
- Excel based Bill of Materials
- Revision Table
- Design Table
- Weld Table
- Bend Table
- Punch Table

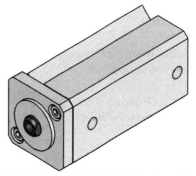

ITEM NO.	PART NUMBER	DESCRIPTION	COVERPLATE-NOHOLES/QTY.
1	99-1007-1	TUBE4_ROD4	1
2	10-0411	COLLAR	1
3	MP043BM1-17	RING	1
4	10-0410B	COVERPLATE NO HOLES	1
5	MP04-M3-05-16	CAP SCREW	2

Insert views into Sheet3.

362) Click the **Sheet3** tab.

363) Click **Model View**  from the View Layout toolbar.

364) Click **Browse**.

365) Double-click the Default **CYLINDER** assembly configuration from the Open dialog box.

366) Select *****Right** from the View Orientation list.

367) Click a **position** on the upper left side of Sheet3.

368) Click **OK** ✅ from the Projected View PropertyManager.

369) Right-click **Properties** in the view boundary.

370) Click the **Show Hidden Edges** tab.

371) **Expand** CYLINDER in the drawing FeatureManager.

372) **Expand** Sheet 3 in the drawing FeatureManager.

373) **Expand** DrawingView7 (Right) in the FeatureManager.

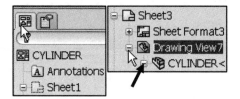

374) **Expand** CYLINDER in the FeatureManager.

375) **Expand** TUBE4-ROD4<1> default in the FeatureManager.

376) Click **ROD4<1> Default** in the FeatureManager.

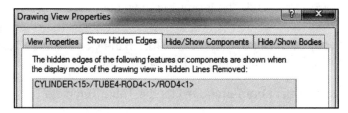

377) Click **Apply**.

378) Click **OK** from the Drawing View Properties dialog box.

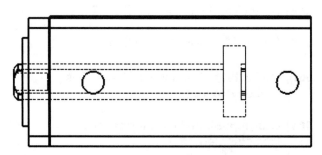

379) Rename **Drawing View7** to **Drawing View7-Right**.

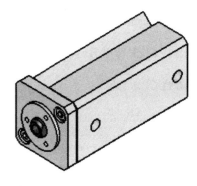

Copy the Right view.
380) Click inside the **Right** view boundary.

381) Click **Ctrl + C**.

382) Click a **position** to the right of the view.

383) Click **Ctrl + V**.

384) Click inside the **view** boundary.

385) Click ***Isometric** from the
Model View
PropertyManager.

386) Click **Shaded with Edges**.

387) Click **OK** ✅ from the
PropertyManager.

388) Rename **Drawing View8** to
Drawing View8-Isometric.

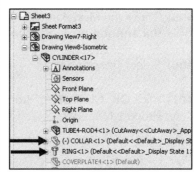

Modify the Properties.
389) Right-click **Properties** in the
Isometric view boundary.

390) Select **CUTAWAY** for Use named configuration.

391) Click the **Hide/Show
Components** tab.

392) Click **COLLAR<1>** from the
Sheet 3, Drawing View8
(Isometric) FeatureManager.

393) Click **RING<1>**. Click **Apply**.

394) Click **OK** to hide the COLLAR and RING parts.

Insert COVERPLATE4 configurations.
395) Click **Model View** 🖼 from the View Layout toolbar.

396) Click **Browse**. Double-click **COVERPLATE4**.

397) Select ***Front** for View Orientation. Click a **position** on the
left side of Sheet3.

398) Click **OK** ✅ from the Projected View PropertyManager.

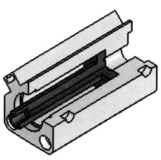

Modify the View Properties.
399) Right-click **Properties** in the Front view.

400) Click **WithNoseHoles** for Use named configuration.

401) Click **OK**.

Insert a Linked Note.
402) Click **Note** $\mathbf{A}$ from the Annotation toolbar.

403) Click a **position** below the profile, inside the view boundary.

404) Click **Link to Property**.

405) Check the **Model in view to which the annotation is attached** box.

406) Select **Description**.

407) Click **OK**. Click **OK** ✓ from the Note PropertyManager.

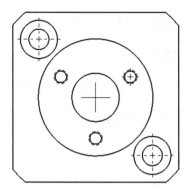

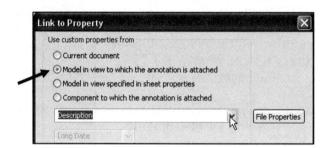

Utilize Lock View Focus to attach an Annotation to the selected view. For custom properties, the Model in view to which annotation is attached option displays when an Annotation references the view. When you move a view, the attached annotations move with the view.

Copy the Front view.
408) Click inside the **Front view** boundary.

409) Click **Ctrl + C**.

410) Click a **position** to the right of the view.

411) Click **Ctrl + V**. The Linked Note copies with the view.

Modify the View Properties.
412) Right-click **Properties** in the copied view.

413) Click **WithoutNoseHoles** for Use named configuration.

414) Click **OK**.

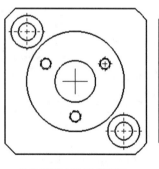
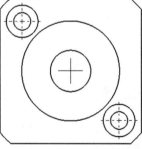

COVERPLATE W/HOLES   COVERPLATE NO HOLES

Align the Front view.
415) Right-click **Alignment** on the COVERPLATE W/HOLES view.

416) Select **Align Horizontal by Origin**.

417) Click **inside** the COVERPLATE NO HOLES view.

Align the Notes.
418) Click the **COVERPLATE W/HOLES** note.

419) Hold the **Ctrl** key down.

420) Click the **COVERPLATE NO HOLES** note.

421) Release the **Ctrl** key. Right-click **Align**. Click **Align Bottom**.

422) Click **OK** ✅ from the Note PropertyManager.

⯐	Align Left
⯑	Align Right
⯒	Align Top
⯓	Align Bottom
⯔	Align Horizontal
⯕	Align Vertical

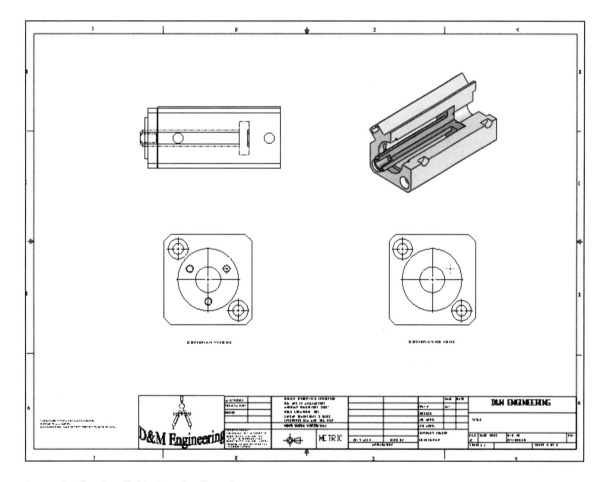

Insert the Design Table into the Drawing.
423) Click inside the **CutAway Isometric** view bounday.

424) Click **Insert**, **Tables**, **Design Table** from the Menu bar menu.

425) Click a **postion** in the left corner of Sheet3.

426) **Modify** the scale and position of the drawing views to fit the Sheet.

Design Table for: CYLINDER		$CONFIGURATION@COVERPLATE4<1>	$STATE@COVERPLATE4<1>	$STATE@CAP-SCREW-M3x16<*>	$CONFIGURATION@TUBE4-ROD4<1>	$USER_NOTES
Default	Default	R	R	Default	BASIC
NO-COVERPLATE	Default	S	S	Default	BASIC
COVERPLATE-HOLES	WithNoseHoles	R	R	Default	ANODIZED COVER
COVERPLATE-NOHOLES	WithoutNoseHoles	R	R	Default	ANODIZED COVER
NO-HARDWARE	Default	R	S	Default	ANODIZED COVER
CUTWAY	Default	S	S	CutAway	SEE INTERNAL FEATURES

Save the Sheet1 BOM as a custom BOM Template.
427) Click the **Sheet1** tab.

428) Right-click the **BOM table** in Sheet1.

429) Click **Save as**.

430) Select the **MY-TEMPLATES** folder.

431) Enter **BOM-MATERIAL-COST** for file name.

432) Click **Save**.

Save the CYLINDER drawing and close all doucments.
433) Click **Save** 💾 .

434) Click **Windows**, **Close All** from the Menu bar menu.

Review the following additional tips on Bill of Materials and Design Tables.

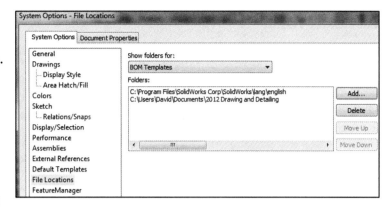

⌖ Locate a custom BOM template quickly. Add the MY-TEMPLATE folder to the System Options, File Locations, BOM Templates for a default BOM Template folder location.

There are two options to create a Bill of Materials in an assembly drawing:

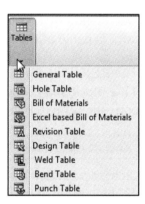

- SolidWorks table generated Bill of Materials.

- Excel generated Bill of Materials.

⌖ A drawing contains only one BOM creation option.

⌖ An Excel generated BOM utilizes Microsoft Excel 2000 or later.

⌖ Work quickly between the Design Table in the drawing and the Design Table in the part or assembly. If you double-click the Design Table in the drawing, you return to the Design Table in the part or assembly.

⌖ Modify the Design Table to display only the specific rows and columns of information. Utilize the Excel Hide option.

⌖ A goal of this book is to expose various SolidWorks design tools and features. The most direct way may not always be shown.

Revision Table

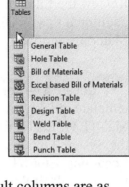

The Revision Table lists the Engineering Change Order (ECO) in the top right section of the drawing. An ECO documents changes that occur to a component. The Engineering department maintains each ECO with a unique document number. In this chapter, the ECO 8531 releases the drawing to manufacturing.

The current Revision block on the drawing was imported from AutoCAD. Delete the current Revision block lines and text. Utilize the Consolidated Tables toolbar to create a Revision Table. The default columns are as follows: Zone, Rev, Description, Date and Approved.

The Zone column utilizes the row letter and column number contained in the drawing border. Position the REV letter in the Zone area. Enter the Zone letter/number. Enter a Description that corresponds to the ECO number. Modify the date if required. Enter the initials/name of the engineering manager who approved the revision.

The REV. column in the Revision Table is a Sheet Property. Create a Linked Note in the Title block and utilize the Revision Sheet Property. The current Revision of the drawing corresponds to the letter in the last row of the Revision Table.

Activity: Revision Table

Create a new drawing.
435) Open the **COVERPLATE4** part.

436) Click **Make Drawing from Part/Assembly** from the Menu bar toolbar.

437) Double-click **A-ANSI-MM** from the MY-TEMPLATES folder.

438) **Delete** the Right view and the Isometric view.

Edit the Sheet Format.
439) Right-click in the **Graphics window**.

440) Click **Edit Sheet Format**.

Delete the current Revision Table.
441) **Zoom in** on the upper right corner of the Sheet Format.

442) Window-select the **Revision Table**. The Revision Table is displayed in blue.

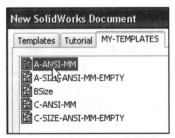

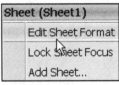

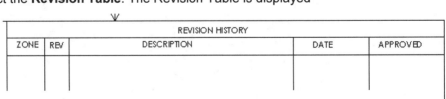

REVISION HISTORY				
ZONE	REV	DESCRIPTION	DATE	APPROVED

443) Right-click **Delete**.

Return to the drawing sheet.
444) Right-click in the **Graphics window**.

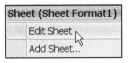

445) Click **Edit Sheet**.

446) Rebuild the drawing.

Fit the drawing to the Graphics window.
447) Press the **f** key.

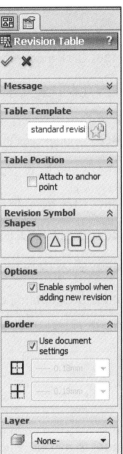

Insert a Revision Table.
448) Click **Revision Table** from the Consolidated Tables toolbar. The Revision Table PropertyManager is displayed.

449) Select the **standard revision** Table Template

450) Click the **Circle Revision** Symbol Shape.

451) Check the **Enable symbol when adding new revision** option. Accept the default settings.

452) Click **OK** ✔ from the Revision Table PropertyManager. The Revision Table is displayed in the upper right corner.

453) Drag the **Revision Table** header downward to the inside upper right sheet boundary.

The Enable symbol when adding new revision option displays the

Revision Symbol on the mouse pointer when you execute the Add Revision command. Position the revision symbol on the drawing that corresponds to the change.

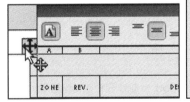

REVISIONS					
ZONE	REV.	DESCRIPTION		DATE	APPROVED

Insert the first row.
454) Right-click the **Revision Table**.

455) Click **Revisions, Add Revision**.
The Revision letter, A and the
current date are displayed in the
Revision Table. The Revision
Symbol is displayed on the mouse pointer.

Revisions		Add Revision
Insert	▶	

Position the Revision Symbol.
456) Click a **position** in the Front view.

457) Click **OK** ✔ from the Revision Symbol PropertyManager.

Edit the Revision Table.
458) Double-click the **text box** under the Description column.

459) Enter **ECO 8531 RELEASED TO MANUFACTURING**.

460) Click **outside** of the table.

461) Double-click the **text box** under the APPROVED column.

462) Enter Documentation Control Manager's Initials, Example: **DCP**.

463) Click **outside** of the table.

		REVISIONS		
ZONE	REV.	DESCRIPTION	DATE	APPROVED
	A	ECO 8531 RELEASED TO MANUFACTURING	2/24/2012	DCP

Edit the Sheet Format.
464) Right-click a **position** in the Sheet boundary.

465) Click **Edit Sheet Format**.

Insert a Linked Note for Revision.
466) Click **Note A** from the Annotation
toolbar.

467) Click a **position** below the REV text in
the Title block.

468) Click **Link to Property** ⬚.

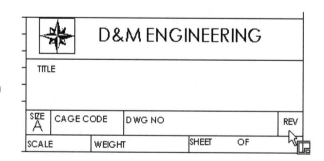

469) Select **Revision** from the drop-
down list.

470) Click **OK**.

471) Click **OK** ✓ from the Note
PropertyManager.

Return to the drawing sheet.
472) Right-click a **position** in the sheet
boundary.

473) Right-click **Edit Sheet**.

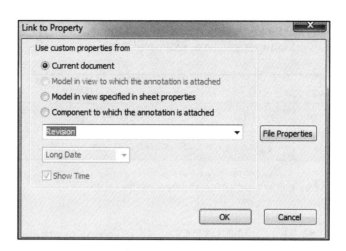

Save the COVERPLATE4 drawing.
474) Click **Save**.

475) Enter **COVERPLATE4** for File name.

Insert a Revision Table into the CYLINDER drawing.
476) Open the CYLINDER drawing.

477) Click the **Sheet1** tab.

Insert a Revision Table.
478) Click **Revision Table** from the Consolidated Tables toolbar. Accept the
defaults.

479) Click **OK** ✓ from the Revision Table
PropertyManager.

480) Drag the **Revision Table** header
downward to the inside upper right
sheet boundary.

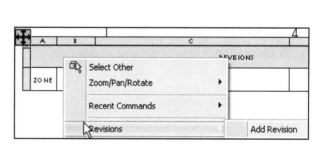

Insert the first row.
481) Right-click the **Revision Table**.

482) Click **Revisions**, **Add Revision**.

Position the Revision Symbol.
483) Click a **position** in the Isometric view to place the A Rev. letter.

484) Click **OK** ✓ from the PropertyManager.

Edit the Revision Table.
485) Double-click the **text box** under the Description column.

486) Enter **ECO 8531 RELEASED TO MANUFACTURING**.

487) Click a **position** outside of the table.

488) Double-click the **text box** under the APPROVED column. Enter Documentation Control Manager's Initials, Example: **DCP**.

REVISIONS				
ZONE	REV.	DESCRIPTION	DATE	APPROVED
	A	ECO 8531 RELEASED TO MANUFACTURING	2/24/2012	DCP

489) Click a **position** outside of the table.

The C-ANSI-MM Drawing Template utilizes the $PRPSHEET:"Revision" property defined in the Sheet Properties. Utilize the $PRP:"Revision" property to link the REV letter in the Title block to the current REV letter in the Revision Table.

Edit the Sheet Format.
490) Right-click a **position** in the Sheet boundary.

491) Click **Edit Sheet Format**.

Modify the Linked Note for Revision.
492) Double-click the Note below the REV text in the Title block.

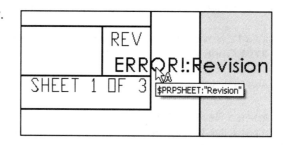

493) Click **Delete**.

494) Click **Link to Property** .

495) Select **Revision** from the drop down list.

496) Click **OK**.

497) Click **OK** ✔ from the Note: PropertyManager.

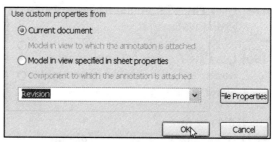

Return to the drawing sheet.
498) Right-click a **position** in the sheet boundary.

499) Click **Edit Sheet**.

Save the CYLINDER drawing.
500) Click **Save** .

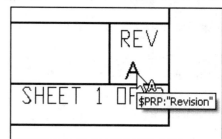

Return to the COVERPLATE4 drawing.
Insert the second row.
501) Open the **COVERPLATE4** drawing.

502) Right-click the **Revision Table**.

503) Click **Revisions**, **Add Revision**.

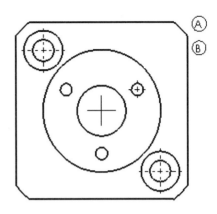

Position the Revision Symbol.
504) Click a **position** in the Front view to place the B Rev. letter.

505) Click **OK** ✔ from the Revision PropertyManager.

Note: The REV letter in the Title block displays the latest revision of the drawing.

Edit the Revision Table.
506) Double-click the **text box** under the Description column.

507) Enter **ECO 9932 ANODIZE BLACK** for DESCRIPTION.

508) Enter **DCP** for APPROVED.

		REVISIONS		
ZONE	REV.	DESCRIPTION	DATE	APPROVED
	A	ECO 8531 RELEASED TO MANUFACTURING	2/24/2012	DCP
	B	ECO 9932 ANODIZE BLACK	2/24/2012	DCP

509) Click a **position** outside of the table.

Save the COVERPLATE4 drawing.
510) Click **Save** 💾 .

511) Click **Windows**, **Close All** from the Menu bar menu.

The File Properties button in the Link to Property box lists the Custom Properties of the sheet and their current values. When the Revision Table is inserted into the drawing, the Revision Custom Property is added to the list.

The Revision Table example shows how to control a REV. value through the $PRP:"Revision" property. The original C-ANSI-MM Template utilized $PRPSHEET:"Revision" property. Companies also control the REV. value by combining a Revision Custom Property in the part and a Linked Note in the drawing. Product Data Management systems, (PDM) control document revisions based on the Revision rules in your company's engineering documentation practices.

Only Sheet1 displays the current REV. You will have to update the Title block in every sheet. Is there a more efficient method to control notes in the Title block? Answer: Yes. Develop a Sheet Format with Drawing Specific SolidWorks Properties and Custom Properties. Insert the Revision Table into the Drawing Template.

For Revision A, the CYLINDER drawing and the COVERPLATE4 drawing utilized the same ECO 8531 number to release the documents to manufacturing. For Revision B, only the COVERPLATE4 drawing was modified. Does the COVERPLATE4 drawing require Revision B? Answer: This "up-rev" action depends on company policy for updating revisions on assemblies. In this case, since the form, fit and function of the CYLINDER assembly did not change, the drawing remained at Rev A.

The default A-size SolidWorks Sheet Format contains Custom Properties defined in the Title block. Set Drawing Specific System Properties: SW-Sheet Name, SW-Sheet Scale, SW-Sheet Format Size, and SW-Template Size in the Sheet Properties dialog box.

Additional Information

The following section explores additional tools and functions as they relate to assembly drawings. Explore these techniques in the chapter exercises. There are no step-by-step instructions.

Section View and Broken-out Section

The Section View and Broken-out Section View contain additional options for assemblies.

A Section View in the assembly starts similar to a Section View in the part. Sketch a line in the Parent view. Click Section View from the View Layout toolbar. The Section View dialog box displays the Section Scope option. Expand the FeatureManager that corresponds to the Sheet and Drawing View #. Select the components to exclude from the section cut. Example: COLLAR and RING.

The Auto hatching option creates alternate pattern hatching between components. The excluded components are not hatched.

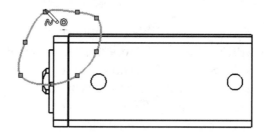

The Materials Editor determines the hatch pattern. A Broken-out Section in the assembly starts similar to a Broken-out Section View in the part. Sketch a Spline (Closed Profile) in the area of the Parent view to break away.

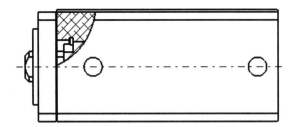

The Depth reference requires a value or an edge reference. The Preview check box displays a yellow cross arrow symbol indicating the Depth.

Hide Behind Plane

The Hide Behind Plane option hides components of an assembly drawing behind a plane. This option provides a quicker selection method than to select individual components.

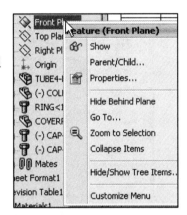

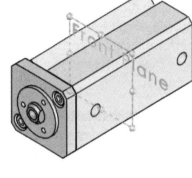

Only the components that are completely behind the plane become hidden. Example: COVERPLATE, CAP-SCREW, COLLAR and RING.

Display an Isometric view in the drawing. Select the CYLINDER Front Plane from the FeatureManager. Right-click Hide Behind Plane. Enter 25mm for Distance.

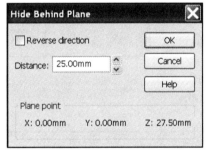

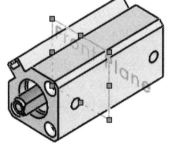

The X, Y and Z coordinates of the plane distance are shown in the Hide Behind Plane dialog box. The default offset distance is 0.

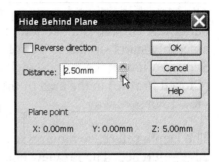

Show the hidden components. Right-click Properties in the current view. Select Hide/Show Components. Delete the component from the hidden list.

Large Assembly Drawing Performance

System Options, Drawings contains the settings for drawings that improve performance. Large assembly drawings are system memory intensive.

Check Automatically hide component on view creation. Review the available options, and uncheck any un-needed option to save system memory and time for large assembly drawings.

Set the default display style to Hidden lines removed and default display quality to Draft Quality. View SolidWorks Help for additional information on opening and saving a Large Assembly and a Large Assembly drawing.

Splitting A BOM

The BOM can be split (Split options) into smaller tables by dividing horizontally or vertically. The split portion retains the column titles and can be dragged anywhere on the drawing. The Merge Table option brings a Split BOM back together.

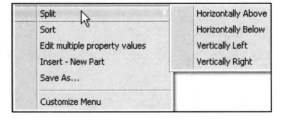

	A	B	C	D	E
1	ITEM NO.	PART NUMBER	DESCRIPTION	MATERIAL	QTY.
2	1	TUBE4			1
3	2	ROD4			1
4	3	10-0411			1

	A	B	C	D	E
	ITEM NO.	PART NUMBER	DESCRIPTION	MATERIAL	QTY.
5	4	MP043BM1-17		Material <not specified>	1
6	5	10-0410		6061 Alloy	1
7	6	MP04-M3-05-16		Material <not specified>	2

Menu: Zoom/Pan/Rotate, Recent Commands, Insert, Select, Delete, Hide, Formatting, Sort, Merge Tables, Edit multiple property values

Create assembly drawings early in the assembly process. As additional components are added to the assembly, the views and BOMs update in the drawing.

Dragging A BOM

Drag the split portion of the table away from the original using the upper left handle as illustrated and "snap" it onto the upper edge of the sheet format if needed.

Creating a BOM Template

Customized BOM templates can be created by saving the current BOM to a file. Columns and formatting are saved in the template.

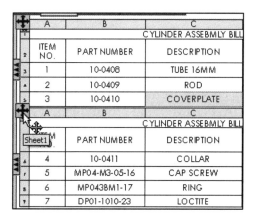

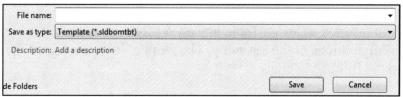

Tabulated Bill of Materials

A Tabulated Bill of Materials can be used when the assembly contains multiple configurations. The tabulation affects only the QTY.column. See SolidWorks Help for additional information.

eDrawings

An eDrawing is a compressed document of a SolidWorks part, assembly, or drawing. An eDrawing provides animation, view, measure, section and markup.

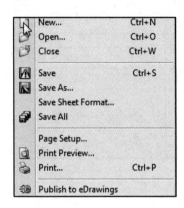

In a multi sheet drawing, select the sheets to create the eDrawing. An eDrawing can be sent via email to a vendor without the corresponding part, assembly or drawing documents.

Export

Export is the process to save a SolidWorks document in another format. Exported files are used in: other CAD/CAM, rapid prototyping, web, or graphics software applications.

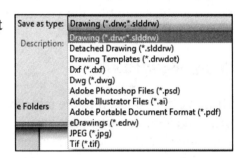

Chapter Summary

You developed the following in this chapter: CYLINDER assembly with Custom Properties and a Design Table, CYLINDER drawing with multiple sheets and a Bill of Materials.

You inserted an Isometric Exploded view in the CYLINDER assembly and assigned Custom Properties to each part to describe: Material, Mass, Description and Cost parameters. The CYLINDER assembly consisted of the TUBE4, ROD4, COLLAR, RING, COVERPLATE4, and CAP-SCREW-M3x16 parts from the Chapter 8 folder on the DVD.

You inserted a Design Table in the CYLINDER assembly to create six different configurations of the assembly. The Design Table contained the Custom Properties linked to the Bill of Materials.

Three sheets of the CYLINDER drawing were developed:

- Sheet1: Isometric Exploded view, Balloon labels, and a Bill of Materials.

- Sheet2: Various configurations of the CYLINDER assembly with corresponding Bill of Materials.

- Sheet3: Multiple documents and component display.

Try the exercises at the end of this project before going on to Project 6.

Chapter Terminology

Anchor point: The origin of the Bill of Material in a sheet format.

Assembly: An assembly is a document that consists of components and features. A component consists of a single part or an assembly. Components are mated together. The extension for a SolidWorks assembly file name is .SLDASM.

Attachment Point: An attachment point is the end of a leader that attaches to an edge, vertex, or face in a drawing sheet.

Balloon: A balloon labels the parts in the assembly and relates them to item numbers on the bill of materials (BOM) added in the drawing. The balloon item number corresponds to the order in the Feature Tree. The order controls the initial BOM Item Number.

Bill of Materials: A table inserted into a drawing to keep a record of the parts used in an assembly.

BOM: Abbreviation for Bill of Materials.

Broken-out Section: A broken-out section exposes inner details of a drawing view by removing material from a closed profile. In an assembly, the Broken-out Section displays multiple components.

Cell: Area to enter a value in an EXCEL spreadsheet, identified by a Row and Column.

CommandManager: The CommandManager is a Context-sensitive toolbar that dynamically updates based on the toolbar you want to access. By default, it has toolbars embedded in it based on the document type. When you click a tab below the Command Manager, it updates to display that toolbar. For example, if you click the **Sketches** tab, the Sketch toolbar is displayed.

Component: A part or sub-assembly within an assembly.

ConfigurationManager: The ConfigurationManager is located on the left side of the SolidWorks window and provides the means to create, select, and view multiple configurations of parts and assemblies in an active document. You can split the ConfigurationManager and either display two ConfigurationManager instances, or combine the ConfigurationManager with the FeatureManager design tree, PropertyManager, or third party applications that use the panel.

Configurations: Variations of a part or assembly that control dimensions, display and state of a model.

Copy and Paste: Utilize copy/paste to copy views from one sheet to another sheet in a drawing or between different drawings.

Datum Feature: An annotation that represents the primary, secondary and other reference planes of a model utilized in manufacturing.

Design Table: An Excel spreadsheet that is used to create multiple configurations in a part or assembly document.

Document: A file containing a part, assembly, or drawing.

Dimension: A value indicating the size of feature geometry.

Dimension Line: A line that references dimension text to extension lines indicating the feature being measured.

DimXpert for Parts: A set of tools that applies dimensions and tolerances to parts according to the requirements of the ASME Y.14.41-2009 standard.

Drawing: A 2D representation of a 3D part or assembly. The extension for a SolidWorks drawing file name is .SLDDRW.

Edit Sheet: The drawing sheet contains two modes. Utilize the Edit Sheet command to insert views and dimensions.

Edit Sheet Format: The drawing sheet contains two modes. Utilize the Edit Sheet Format command to add or modify notes and Title block information. Edit in the Edit Sheet Format mode.

Exploded view: A configuration in an assembly that displays its components separated from one another

Export: The process to save a SolidWorks document in another format for use in other CAD/CAM, rapid prototyping, web, or graphics software applications.

FeatureManager: The FeatureManager design tree located on the left side of the SolidWorks window provides an outline view of the active part, assembly, or drawing. This makes it easy to see how the model or assembly was constructed or to examine the various sheets and views in a drawing. The FeatureManager and the Graphics window are dynamically linked. You can select features, sketches, drawing views, and construction geometry in either pane.

First Angle Projection: Standard 3 Views are in either third angle or first angle projection. In first angle projection, the front view is displayed at the upper left and the other two views are the top and left views.

Fully defined: A sketch where all lines and curves in the sketch, and their positions, are described by dimensions or relations, or both, and cannot be moved. Fully defined sketch entities are displayed in black.

Geometric Tolerance: A set of standard symbols that specify the geometric characteristics and dimensional requirements of a feature.

Graphics window: The area in the SolidWorks window where the part, assembly, or drawing is displayed.

Heads-up View toolbar: A transparent toolbar located at the top of the Graphic window.

Hole Callouts: Hole callouts are available in drawings. If you modify a hole dimension in the model, the callout updates automatically in the drawing if you did not use DimXpert.

Leader: A solid line created from an annotation to the referenced feature.

Mass Properties: The physical properties of a model based upon geometry and material.

Model Item: Provides the ability to insert dimensions, annotations, and reference geometry from a model document (part or assembly) into a drawing.

Origin: The model origin is displayed in blue and represents the (0,0,0) coordinate of the model. When a sketch is active, a sketch origin is displayed in red and represents the (0,0,0) coordinate of the sketch. Dimensions and relations can be added to the model origin, but not to a sketch origin.

Parametric note: A Note that references a SolidWorks dimension or property.

Precision: Controls the number of decimal places displayed in a dimension.

Revision Table: The Revision Table lists the Engineering Change Orders (ECO), in a table form, issued over the life of the model and the drawing. The current Revision letter or number is placed in the Title block of the Drawing.

Section Scope: Specifies the components to be left uncut when you create an assembly drawing section view.

Sheet: A page in a drawing document.

Stacked Balloon: A group of balloons with only one leader. The balloons can be stacked vertically (up or down) or horizontally (left or right).

Task Pane: The Task Pane is displayed when you open the SolidWorks software. It contains the following tabs: SolidWorks Resources, Design Library, File Explorer, Search, View Palette, Document Recovery, and RealView/PhotoWorks.

Toolbars: The toolbars provide shortcuts enabling you to access the most frequently used commands. When you enable the Add-in application in SolidWorks, you can also display their associated toolbars.

Questions:

1. An assembly is comprised of _____.

2. True or False. Parts contained in an assembly cannot be opened from within that assembly.

3. Describe the procedure in a drawing to display an Exploded view and a Collapsed view.

4. True or False. A Design Table is used to create multiple configurations in an assembly.

5. True or False. A Design Table is used to create multiple configurations in a part.

6. True or False. A Design Table is used to create multiple configurations in a drawing.

7. Describe the types of Drawing views you can create from an assembly.

8. Describe the procedure to copy a drawing view from Sheet1 to Sheet2 utilizing the FeatureManager.

9. Identify the column that contains the configuration names in a Design Table.

10. True or False. The Materials Editor contains a library of materials and their properties.

11. Identify the location to create an Exploded view.

12. Describe the function of a Balloon annotation.

13. The Part Number column in the Bill of Materials displays the _____ name by default.

14. Describe the procedure to add the Material to the part and to the Bill of Materials.

15. Describe the procedure to add the Mass Property to the part and to the Bill of Materials.

16. Describe the procedure to add the Cost Property to the part and the Bill of Materials.

17. Describe the function of the $STATE variable in the part Design Table.

18. A drawing can contain multiple configurations of a _____ and an _____.

Exercises

Exercise 8.1:

Create an assembly drawing for the TUBE4-ROD4 assembly. The TUBE4-ROD4 assembly contains two configurations. Create a new configuration for the assembly that utilizes the LongRod configuration. The ShortRod Configuration Cost is $200 and the Long Rod is $250.

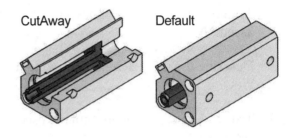

The drawing contains two sheets. Insert three Isometric views on Sheet1. Each view uses a different configuration. Add a Bill of Materials to each view. Add the Cost Column to the BOM.

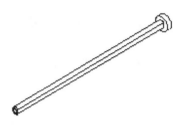

Insert a Front view and Right view for the ROD part. Display the ShortRod and LongRod configuration on Sheet2.

Exercise 8.2:

An Engineering Changer Order is issued to modify the COLLAR part from Alloy Steel to 7079 Alloy. Open the COLLAR part in the Chapter 8 folder on the DVD in the book and update the Material in the Materials Editor. Open the CYLINDER drawing to update the BOM.

Exercise 8.3:

Insert a Sheet4 into the CYLINDER drawing. Insert a Right view and a Section view.

Hide the COLLAR and RING parts in the Section View Section Scope.

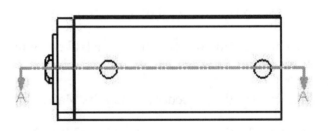

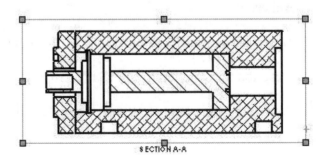

SECTION A-A

Exercise 8.4:

On Sheet4 in the CYLINDER
drawing, create a Right view.
Project a Front view. Insert a
Broken-out Section. Locate the
Distance at the center of the Bore
hole.

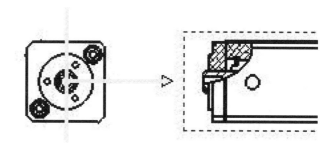

Exercise 8.5:

An Engineering Change Order is issued to create a new configuration of the CYLINDER
assembly. Create a new configuration of the CAP-SCREW-M3x16 that is 20mm in
length.

Utilize the CYLINDER assembly Design Table to control the CAP-SCREW-M3x20 part.
Update the Bill of Materials on Sheet1 to utilize the CAP-SCREW-M3x20.

Exercise 8.6:

Note: The RACK assembly project in Exercise 8.6 through 8.10 must be completed in
order. Knowledge of assembly modeling Concentric and Coincident Mates is required.
The chapter utilizes SW\Toolbox. If you do not have the Toolbox application, dimensions
for the hardware utilize the dimensions in Exercise 8.7.

RACK Assembly Project.

Create a new assembly named RACK.
Insert the MOUNTINGPLATE-
CYLINDER as the base component in
the assembly, fixed to the Origin. The
default configuration contains three sets
of holes. Insert the CYLINDER
component.

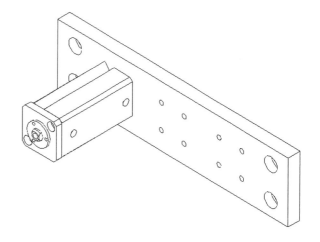

Open the CYLINDER assembly. Delete
the two CAP-SCREW-M3x16 parts.
You will insert new fasteners with
Toolbox at the top level of the RACK
assembly.

Mate the Cbore holes of the TUBE with the two diagonal holes of the MOUNTINGPLATE-CYLINDER. Mate the back face of the TUBE and the front face of the MOUNTINGPLATE-CYLINDER.

Create a Component Pattern in the RACK assembly. Click Insert, Component Pattern, Use an Existing Feature Pattern (Derived). Select CYLINDER as the Seed Component from the assembly FeatureManager. Select LPattern1 as the Pattern feature in the MOUNTINGPLATE-CYLINDER.

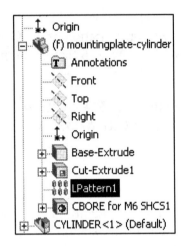 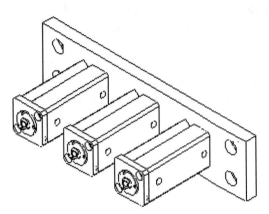

Exercise 8.7:

Add hardware to the RACK assembly. Utilize the SolidWorks Toolbox to obtain hardware part files. The SolidWorks Toolbox is a set of industry standard bolts, screws, nuts, pins, washers, structural shapes, bearings, PEM inserts and retaining rings.

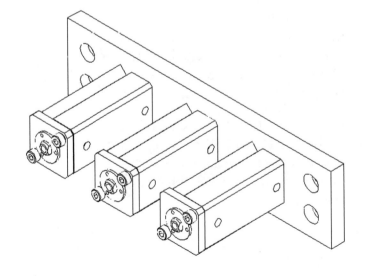

The SolidWorks parts are inserted into an assembly. An M4x0.7x16 and M4x0.7x20 socket head cap screws and M4 washers complete the RACK assembly.

Note: Below are the part dimensions for the actual hex socket head cap screw and washer.

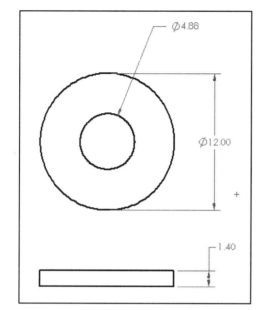
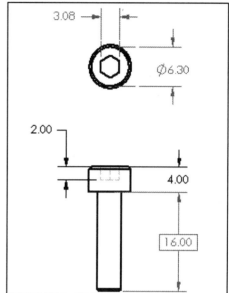

To utilize Toolbox, select Toolbox from the Add-Ins option. Insert an M4X0.7X16 Socket Head Cap Screw. Click the bottom left Cbore circle on the first CYLINDER. Select the Hardware option. Click the Bolts and Screws Tab. Select ANSI Metric, Socket Head Cap Screw, M4X0.7. Select 16 for Fastener Length. Click Create. The M4X0.7 Socket Head Cap Screw component is created and automatically mated to the CYLINDER assembly. Repeat for the second Cbore circle on the first CYLINDER.

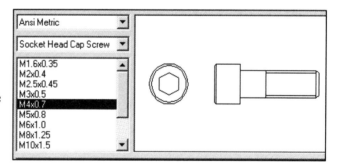

Edit the derived Component pattern. Select the two M4x0.7 Socket Head Cap Screws for the Seed Component from the FeatureManager. The Socket Head Caps Screws are displayed on the other components.

Insert a M4 Washer and an
M4X0.7X20 Socket Head Cap Screw
to the back face of the
MOUNTINGPLATE-CLYLINDER.

Before submitting the
MOUNTINGPLATE-CYLINDER
drawing to the machine shop, check
material and hardware availability with
the parts department. No metric size
socket head cap screws are in the stock
room. There are only ¼″ and ½″ flat
plate stock available in the machine
shop. What do you do? Modify your
design to reflect inch components.

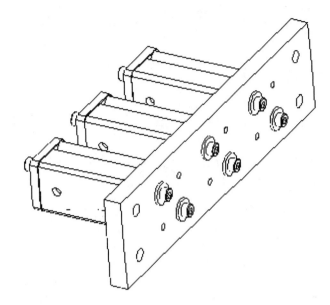

Exercise 8.8:

Create an Exploded view for the RACK assembly.

Create a new drawing, RACK. Add Balloons to the MOUNTINGPLATE-CYLINDER,
CYLINDER and M4X0.7X16 Socket Head Cap Screw. Add a Stacked Balloon to the
M4X0.7X20 Socket Head Cap Screw. Select the M4Washer.

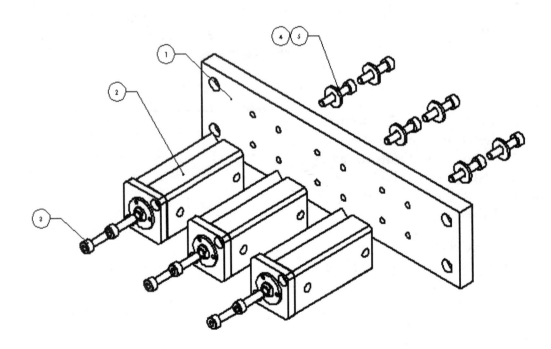

Insert a top level Bill of Materials to the Exploded view in the RACK drawing.

Add the Custom Property Description in the Configuration Manager for the MOUNTINGPLATE-CYLINDER and hardware. Add the PART NUMBERs necessary to complete the Bill of Materials.

RACK ASSEMBLY BILL OF MATERIALS			
ITEM NO.	PART NUMBER:	DESCRIPTION	QTY.
1	50-052-1	MOUNTING PLATE	1
2	99-0531	CYLINDER ASSEMBLY	1
3	5126-16	CAP SCREW 16MM	6
4	5126-20	CAP SCREW 20MM	6
5	5226-1	WASHER 4MM	6

Exercise 8.9:

The MOUNTINGPLATE-CYLINDER part has two configurations named: 2-PATTERN and 3-PATTERN. Review the configurations for the MOUNTING PLATE-CYLINDER part.

Design Table for: MOUNTINGPLATE-CYLINDER	
	D1@LPattern1
2-PATTERN	2
3-PATTERN	3

Control the configurations in the RACK assembly.

Create a Design Table for the RACK assembly. Add two RACK assembly configurations: 2-CYLINDER and 3-CYLINDER.

Enter $CONFIGURATION@MOUNTINGPLATE-CYLINDER<1>. Enter configuration names: 2-PATTERN and 3-PATTERN.

Design Table for: RACK	
	$CONFIGURATION@MOUNTINGPLATE-CYLINDER<1>
2-CYLINDER	2-PATTERN
3-CYLINDER	3-PATTERN

Sheet2 contains the MOUNTINGPLATE-CYLINDER, 2-PATTERN configuration.

Only one Exploded view can exist per assembly. Delete the Stacked Balloons. The hardware quantities are displayed in the Bill of Materials.

RACK ASSEMBLY BILL OF MATERIALS			
ITEM NO.	PART NUMBER	DESCRIPTION	QTY
1	50-052-2	2PATTERN	1
2	99-0531	CYLINDER ASSEMBLY	1
3	5126-16	CAP SCREW 16MM	4
4	5126-20	CAP SCREW 20MM	4
5	5226-1	WASHER 4MM	4

Add new Explode Steps to display the hardware in both a vertical and horizontal direction. Exploded view lines are 3D curves that are added to the Exploded view in the assembly.

Hint. Click Insert, Explode Line Sketch in the CYLINDER assembly. The Route Line PropertyManager is displayed. Click the circular edges of the corresponding cap screw and holes in order from left to right. Click OK. Repeat for the remaining hardware.

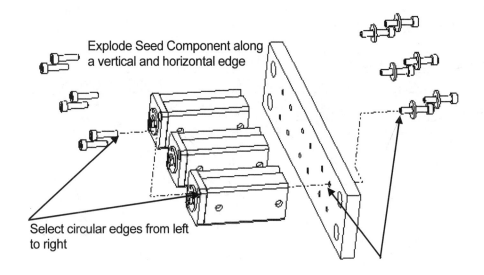

Explode Seed Component along a vertical and horizontal edge

Select circular edges from left to right

Add the Custom Property Description in the Configuration Manager for the MOUNTINGPLATE-CYLINDER and hardware. Add the PART NUMBER to the components necessary to complete the Bill of Materials for the 2PATTERN configuration.

Add the Property $Color. The 2PATTERN MOUNTINGPLATE-CYLINDER is Red. The 3PATTERN is Blue.

Exercise 8.10:

Create an eDrawing of the RACK assembly.

Set the Large Assembly Mode options. Assembly Drawings contain hundreds of components. Utilize Large Assembly Mode, drawing settings to optimize performance.

Work in the Shaded display mode for large assemblies to conserve drawing time.

Create a RapidDraft™ drawing of MOUTINGPLATE-CYLINDER part. RapidDraft™ drawings are designed to open and work in drawing files without the model files being loaded into memory. Select File, Open.

Check the Refer to Help for more information on RapidDraft™ and Large Assembly Mode.

☑ Move components by dragging
☐ Prompt before changing mate alignments on edit
☐ Save new components to external files

Large assemblies
☑ Use Large Assembly Mode to improve performance whenever working with an assembly containing more than this number of components: 500

When Large Assembly Mode is active:
☑ Do not save auto recover info
☑ Hide all planes, axes, sketches, curves, annotations, etc.
☑ Do not display edges in shaded mode
☐ Suspend automatic rebuild

Notes:

Chapter 9

Datums, Feature Control Frames, Geometric Tolerancing and other Drawing Symbols

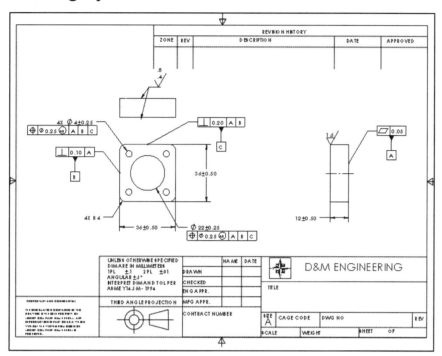

Below are the desired outcomes and usage competencies based on the completion of Chapter 9.

Desired Outcomes:	Usage Competencies:
• VALVEPLATE1 drawing • VALVEPLATE1-GDT drawing	• Ability to insert and edit: Dimensions, Feature Control Frames, Datums, Geometric Tolerancing, Surface Finishes and Weld Symbols using DimXpert.
• VALVEPLATE1-GDT eDrawing • ASME14-41 drawing	• Ability to insert and edit: Dimensions, Features Control Frames, Datums, and Geometric Tolerancing manually in a drawing.
• PLATE-TUBE drawing • PLATE-CATALOG drawing	• Skill to develop and edit a Design Table in EXCEL. • Knowledge to create, apply, and save Blocks and Parametric Notes in a drawing.

Notes:

Notes:

Chapter 9 - Geometric Tolerancing and other Symbols

Chapter Objective

Create five drawings: *VALVEPLATE1, VALVEPLATE1-GDT, VALVEPLATE1-GDT eDrawing, PLATE-TUBE, PLATE-CATALOG*. Modify the *ASME14-41* drawing.

On the completion of this chapter, you will be able to:

- Apply DimXpert and the DimXpertManager:
  - Plus and Minus option
  - Geometric option
- Knowledge of the DimXert toolbar.
- Knowledge of the View Palette.
- Modify dimensions to contain None, Bilateral, and Limit Tolerance.
- Insert Parametric notes.
- Insert Datums, Feature Control Frames, Geometric Tolerances, Surface Finishes, and Weld Symbols.
- Develop a Minimum Content Drawing.
- Insert a Weld Bead assembly feature.
- Format a Design Table in EXCEL.
- Create, Insert, and Save Blocks.
- Understand Fit types.

In this chapter, utilize the following SolidWorks tools and commands: *Smart Dimension, Model Items, Autodimension, Note, Balloon, AutoBalloon, Surface Finish, Weld Symbol, Geometric Tolerance, Datum Feature, Hole Callout, Area Hatch/Fill, Insert Block*, and *DimXpert*.

🔅 DimXpert provides the ability to import dimensions and tolerances you created using The DimXpert tool for parts into drawings. DimXpert is not associative. DimXpert does not import annotations into an Isometric drawing view.

🔅 TolAnalyst™ is a tolerance analysis tool used to study the effects tolerances and assembly methods have on dimensional stack-up between two features of an assembly. The result of each study is a minimum and maximum tolerance stack, a minimum and maximum root sum squared (RSS) tolerance stack, and a list of contributing features and tolerances.

☼ TolAnalyst™ performs a tolerance analysis called a study, which you create using a four-step procedure. TolAnalyst is only available in SolidWorks Premium.

Chapter Overview

As a designer, you work on multiple projects. Each project involves a different type of drawing.

- **VALVEPLATE1 drawing**: Open the VALVEPLATE1 part. Apply DimXpert: Plus and Minus option. Insert dimensions and Geometric tolerances. Create the VALVEPLATE1 drawing with the View Palette tool. Insert three drawing views. Hide the Top view. Insert a Centerline and Hide Tangent Edges in the Right view. Display None and Bilateral tolerance.

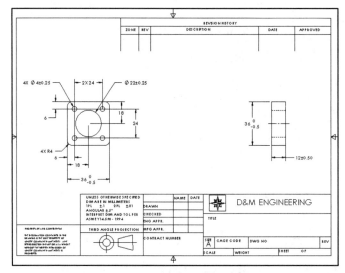

- **VALVEPLATE1-GDT drawing**: Open the VALVEPLATE1-GDT part. Apply DimXpert: Geometric option. Insert Datums, Feature Control Frames, and Geometric Tolerances. Edit Feature Control Frames. Create the VALVEPLATE1-GDT drawing using the View Palette tool. Insert three drawing views. Insert the Surface Finish symbol on the Top and Right view. Create multiple Leaders to the Surface Finish symbol. Insert Hide Tangent Edges in the Top and Right view.

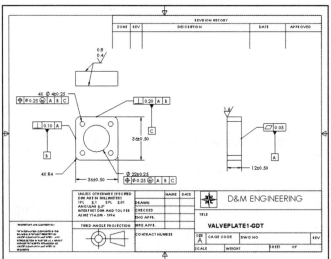

- **VALVEPLATE1-GDT eDrawing**: Send a SolidWorks eDrawing outside to a machine shop for quotation. The VALVEPLATE1-GDT eDrawing is a compressed stand alone document.

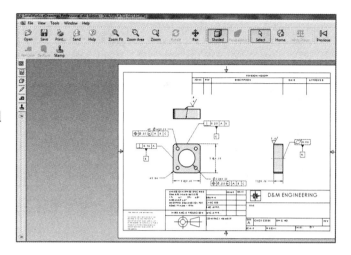

- **ASME14-41 drawing**: Open the ASME14-41-Rev-A part. Apply DimXpert: Geometric option. View the Inserted Datums, Feature Control Frames, and Geometric Tolerances. Modify the ASME14-41 drawing. Manually insert Datums, Feature Control Frames, Dimensions, and Geometric tolerances into an Isometric view on multiply drawing sheets. Note: DimXpert does not import annotations into an Isometric drawing view.

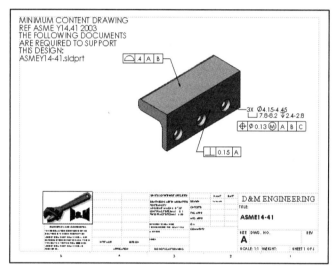

A goal of this book is to expose various SolidWorks design tools and features. The most direct way may not be shown.

The illustrations in this book are based on SolidWorks SP1.0. The illustrations may vary slightly per your SolidWorks release.

- **PLATE-TUBE drawing**:
Open the PLATE-TUBE
assembly. Create the
PLATE-TUBE drawing. The
PLATE-TUBE drawing is a
conceptual customer
drawing. The customer is
concerned about the
cosmetic appearance of a
weld.

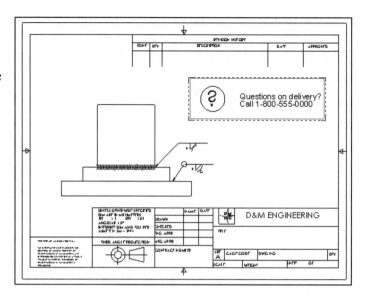

Insert the Weld Bead assembly
feature between the TUBE and
PLATE parts in the PLATE-
TUBE assembly.

Add a second PLATE
component to the PLATE-TUBE
assembly. Create a Weld Symbol
as a separate annotation in the
PLATE-TUBE drawing.

- **PLATE-CATALOG
drawing**: The PLATE-
CATALOG drawing is used
for the on-line catalog. The
PLATE-CATALOG drawing
utilizes a Design Table.
Format the Design Table in
EXCEL.

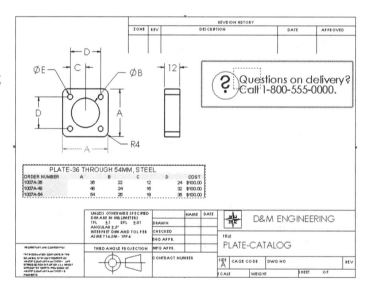

Each of the created drawings in
this chapter display examples of
applying various types of
symbols in SolidWorks.

This chapter requires you to
work between multiple
documents: Drawings, Parts,
Assemblies and Design Tables.

Drawing Template

The PLATE-TUBE drawing and PLATE-CATALOG drawing utilize different model
views. The current A-ANSI-MM Drawing template contains four views. Modify the font
height for the Surface Finish Symbols and Weld Symbols. Create a new Drawing
template from the A-ANSI-MM with no Predefined views.

Activity: Drawing Template

Open an existing Drawing template.

1)   Click **New** from the Menu bar toolbar.

2)   Double-click the **A-ANSI-MM** template from the MY-TEMPLATES tab.

3)   Hold the **Ctrl** key down. Select **Drawing View 1** through **Drawing View 4** from the FeatureManager.

4)   Release the **Ctrl** key. Right-click **Delete**.

5)   Click **Yes to All**.

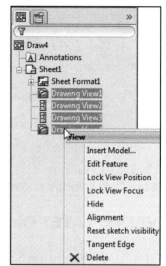

Set the Document Properties.

6)   Click **Options** , **Document Properties** tab from the Menu bar toolbar.

7)   Click the **Detailing** folder.

Clear the Auto insert on view creation box.

8)   Uncheck the **Center marks-holes** and **all other** options.

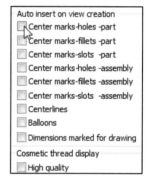

Set the Annotations Font Height.

9)   Expand the **Annotations** folder.

10)   Click the **Surface Finishes** folder.

11)   Click the **Font** button.

12)   Enter **3** mm for Height.

13)   Click **OK** from the Choose Font dialog box.

14)   Click the **Weld Symbols** folder.

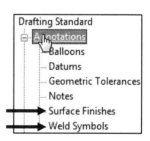

15)   Click the **Font** button. The Choose Font dialog box is displayed.

16)   Enter **3mm** for Height.

17)   Click **OK** from the Choose Font dialog box.

18)   Click **OK** from the Document Properties - Weld Symbols dialog box.

Save the Drawing template.

19) Click **Save As** from the Menu bar toolbar.

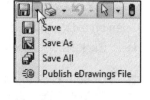

20) Select **Drawing Template** for Files of type.

21) **Browse** to the DRAWING-W-SOLIDWORKS-2012\MY-TEMPLATES folder. Note: You created this folder in an earlier chapter.

22) Enter **A-ANSI-MM-NO-VIEWS** for file name.

23) Click **Save**.

Close all documents.

24) Click **Windows**, **Close All** from the Menu bar toolbar.

VALVEPLATE1 Part – DimXpert

The Auto Dimension Scheme tool automatically applies dimensions and tolerances to the manufacturing features of a part. Supported manufacturing features are: Boss, Chamfer, Cone, Cylinder, Discrete feature types, Fillet, Counterbore hole, Countersink hole, Simple hole, Intersect circle, Intersect line, Intersect plane, Notch, Plane, Pocket, Slot Surface, Width and Sphere.

The dimensions and tolerances conform to the ASME Y14.41-2003 standard. The DimXpert application stores the features, dimensions and tolerances that comprise it in the DimXpertManager, a tree structure similar to the FeatureManager Design tree.

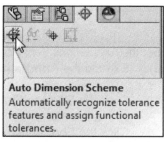

DimXpert speeds the process of adding reference dimensions by applying dimensions in drawings so that manufacturing features, such as patterns, slots, and pockets, are fully-defined.

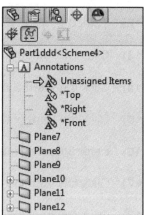

The DimXpert tool is accessible in the Dimension PropertyManager. You select a feature's edge to dimension, then DimXpert applies all associated dimensions in that drawing view for the feature.

Colors are used to help visualize the status of the features, presented as fully, under or over defined like sketches.

Feature Recondition

When you applyDimXpert dimensions to manufacturing features, DimXpert uses the following methods in this order to recognize features:

- Model feature recognition

- Topology recognition

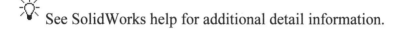 See SolidWorks help for additional detail information.

Settings for DimXpert

Settings exist for DimXpert at the part level, they are: Part type: Prismatic and Turned, Tolerance type: Plus and Minus and Geometric, and Pattern Dimensioning: linear, and polar. See SolidWorks Help for additional information.

Reference Features

Defines the **Primary**, **Secondary**, and **Tertiary** reference features (for **Plus and Minus** schemes) or datums (for **Geometric** schemes).

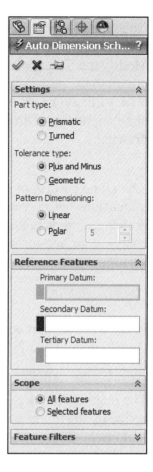

Click **Tools**, **Options**, **Document Properties**, **DimXpert** to view the available settings.

Block Tolerance vs. General Tolerance

Under Tools, Options, Document Properties, DimXpert there are settings for Methods: Block Tolerance and General Tolerance. General Tolerance is selected by default. If Block Tolerance is selected, all of the feature types are set to these values. In General Tolerance, individual settings for each feature type is available.

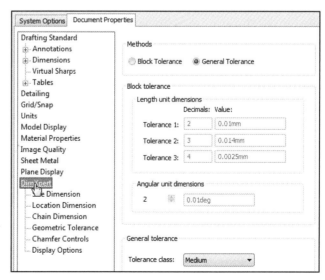

Open the VALVEPLATE1 part from the DVD. View the three Extrude features, Linear Pattern feature, and the Fillet feature. Modify the Sketch plane. Apply the DimXpert: Plus and Minus option to the part. Apply View Palette to create the VALVEPLATE1 drawing. Insert three drawing views with annotations from DimXpert. Work between the part and drawing.

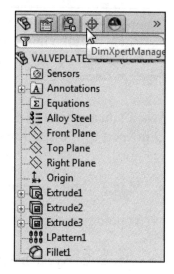

☼ DimXpert is not fully associative. Modify all DimXpert dimensions before you insert the part and annotations into the drawing. Care is required to apply DimXpert correctly on complex surfaces or with some existing models.

☼ Do not dimension the Mounting Holes from the part edges. Dimension the Mounting Hole from the Center Hole axis.

The majority of the part features reside on the top face. Redefine the part orientation so that the top face is parallel with the Front Plane.

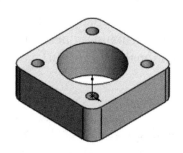
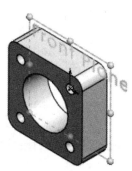

Activity: VALVEPLATE1 Part - DimXpert Plus and Minus Option

Open the part and modify the plane orientation.

25) Click **Open** 📂 from the Menu bar toolbar.

26) **Browse** to the DRAWING-W-SOLIDWORKS-2012 folder.

27) Double-click the **VALVEPLATE1** part. The VALVEPLATE1 FeatureManager is displayed.

Redefine the part orientation.

28) **Expand** Extrude1 from the FeatureManager.

29) Right-click **Sketch1**.

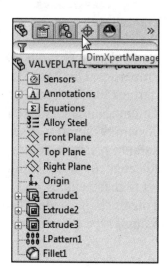

30) Click **Edit Sketch Plane** 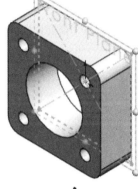 from the Context toolbar. The Sketch Plane PropertyManager is displayed. Top Plane is displayed.

Modify the Sketch Plane from Top Plane to Front Plane.
31) **Expand** VALVEPLATE1 from the Graphics window.

32) Click **Front Plane** from the Flyout FeatureManager. Front Plane is displayed in the Sketch Plane / Face box.

33) Click **OK** 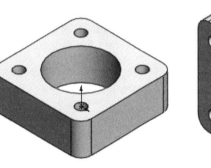 from the Sketch Plane PropertyManager. View the model in the Graphics window. The model is displayed on the Front Plane.

Access DimXpert from the DimXpertManager ⊕ tab or from the DimXpert tab in the CommandManager.

The DimXpertManager provides the ability to list the tolerance features defined by the DimXpert in chronological order and to display the available tools.

Apply DimXpert to the VALVEPLATE1 part.
34) Click the **DimXpertManager** ⊕ tab.

35) Click the **Auto Dimension Scheme** 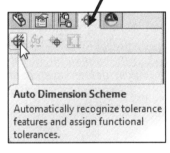 tool from the DimXpertManager. The Auto Dimension PropertyManager is displayed. Prismatic, Plus and Minus, and Linear are selected by default.

The Auto Dimension Scheme option is used to automate the process of recognizing features and adding functional tolerances. Starting with datum selection, features and planes can be added to define the scope of the scheme.

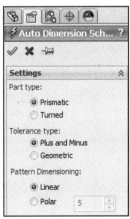

A key difference between the *Plus and Minus* option versus the *Geometric* option is how DimXpert controls the four-hole pattern, and how it applies tolerances to interrelate the datum features when in *Geometric* mode. You will apply both options in this chapter.

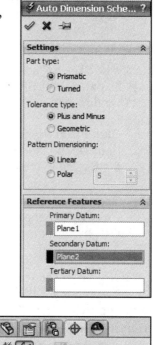

Select type of Scheme.
36) Check the **Prismatic** box.

Select the Primary Datum.
37) Click the **back face** of the model. Plane1 is displayed in the Primary Datum box. Note: Plus and Minus and Linear should be selected by default.

Select the Secondary Datum.
38) Click **inside** the Secondary Datum box.

39) Click the **left face** of the model. Plane2 is displayed in the Secondary Datum box. Two planes are selected.

40) Click **OK** ✓ from the Auto Dimension PropertyManager.

Display an Isometric view.
41) Click **Isometric view**. View the dimensions. View the features displayed in green and yellow. Green is fully constrained. Yellow is under constrained. *Note: Additional dimensions are required for manufacturing. This is NOT a fully defined system at this time. Three mutually Perpendicular planes are required.*

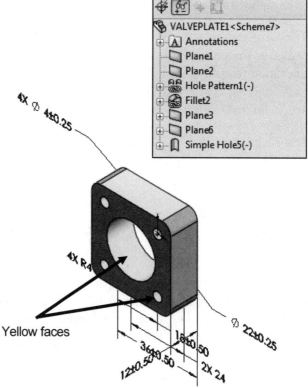

Yellow faces

The DimXpertManager displays either *no mark*, *(+)*, or a *(-)* sign next to the Plane or Feature.

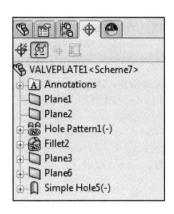

- Features with *no mark* after the name are fully constrained, as illustrated in the VALVEPLATE1 DimXpertManager and are displayed in green.

- Features with the *(+)* sign following the name are over constrained and are displayed in red in the Graphics window.

- Features with the *(-)* sign following the name are under constrained and are displayed in yellow in the Graphics window.

☼ DimXpert dimensions and tolerances are magenta-colored by default.

☼ For DimXpert - features means manufacturing features. For example, in the CAD world, you create a "shell" feature, which is a type of "pocket" feature in the manufacturing world.

☼ When you apply DimXpert dimensions to manufacturing features, DimXpert uses the following two methods in this order to recognize features: *Model feature recognition*, and *Topology recognition*.

☼ The Feature Selector is a floating, Context sensitive toolbar that you can use to distinguish between different DimXpert feature types. The available Feature Selector choices depend on the selected face and the active command.

The order of features in the Feature Selector is based on their complexity:

- Basic features like planes, cylinders, and cones are located on the left.

- Composite features like counterbore holes, notches, slots, and patterns are located in the middle.

- Compound features like compound holes and intersect points are located on the right. Compound features require additional selections.

☼ Within DimXpert, a single face can typically define multiple manufacturing feature types that require different dimensions and tolerances.

42) Click each **Plane** and **feature** in the Show Tolerance Status FeatureManager. The selected item is displayed in blue.

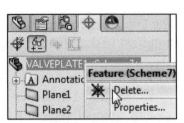

Delete the DimXpert Scheme.

43) Right-click **VALVEPLATE1** from the DimXpertManager.

44) Click **Delete**.

45) Click **Yes**.

Create a New Scheme which is fully constrained.

46) Click the **Auto Dimension Scheme** tool from the DimXpertManager. The Auto Dimension PropertyManager is displayed. Prismatic, Plus and Minus, and Linear should be selected by default.

Select the Primary Datum.

47) Click the **back face** of the model. The selected plane is displayed in the Primary Datum box.

Select the Secondary Datum.

48) Click **inside** the Secondary Datum box.

49) Click the **left face** of the model. The selected plane is displayed in the Secondary Datum box.

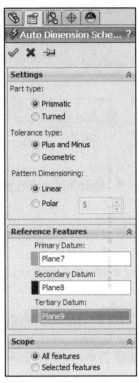

Select the Tertiary Datum.

50) Click **inside** the Tertiary Datum box.

51) Click the **top face** of the model. The selected plane is displayed in the Tertiary Datum box.

52) Click **OK** from the Auto Dimension PropertyManager.

53) Click **Isometric view**. View the dimensions. All features are displayed in green.

54) **Drag** all dimensions off the model.

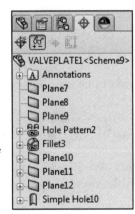

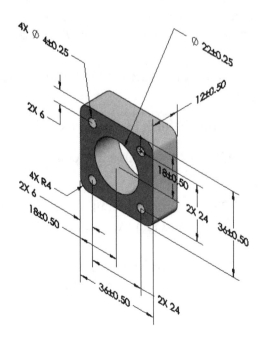

Modify Tolerance and dimensions in the part.

55) Click the **36 horizontal** dimension text. The DimXpert PropertyManager is displayed.

Create a Bilateral Tolerance.

56) Select **Bilateral** from the Tolerance Type drop-down menu.

57) Enter **0** for Maximum Variation.

58) Repeat the above procedure for the **36 vertical** dimension text.

59) Click **OK** ✅ from the DimXpert PropertyManager. View the results.

Remove Instance Count from the part.

60) Click the **2X 6 vertical** dimension text.

61) Hold the **Ctrl** key down.

62) Click the **2X 6 horizontal** dimension text.

63) Click the **2X 24 vertical** dimension text.

64) Click the **2X 24 horizontal** dimension text.

65) Release the **Ctrl** key.

66) **Uncheck** the Instance Count box from the Dimension Text dialog box. View the results.

Remove a tolerance from the part.

67) Click the **18 vertical** dimension text.

68) Hold the **Ctrl** key down.

69) Click the **18 horizontal** dimension text.

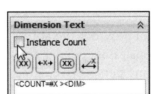

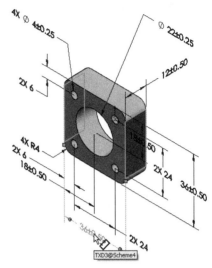

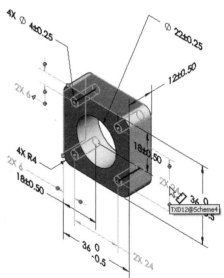

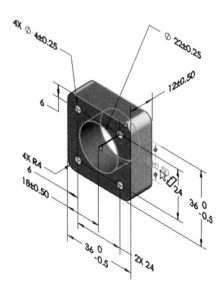

70) Release the **Ctrl** key.

71) Select **None** for Tolerance Type. View the results.

72) Click **OK** ✅ from the DimXpert PropertyManager.

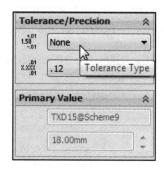

DimXpert toolbar

The DimXpert toolbar provides tools for placing dimensions and tolerances on a part. Below are the following DimXpert tools:

- The *Auto Dimension Scheme* ✤ tool provides the ability to automatically apply dimensions and tolerances to the manufacturing features of a part.

- The *Location Dimension* ▦ tool provides the ability to apply linear and angular dimensions between two DimXpert features, (excluding surface, fillet, chamfer, and pocket features).

- The *Size Dimension* ▣ tool provides the ability to place tolerance size dimensions on DimXpert features.

- The *Pattern Feature* ᴀᴀ tool provides the ability to create or edit pattern features and collection features.

- The *Datum* ꞁ▲ tool provides the ability to define datum features. The tool supports these feature types: *Boss, Cylinder, Notch, Plane, Simple Hole, Slot,* and *Width.*

- The *Geometric Tolerance* ▤ tool provides the ability to apply geometric tolerances to DimXpert features. Note: When you apply geometric tolerances to features defined as datums or to features with pre-existing size tolerances, DimXpert automatically places the feature control frame and pre-existing annotation in an annotation group.

- The *Show Tolerance Status* ⅋ tool provides the ability to identify the manufacturing features and faces that are fully constrained, under constrained, and over constrained from a dimensioning and tolerancing perspective. Note: The DimXpert identification process is unlike that used in sketches, which utilizes dimensional and geometrical relationships to determine the constraint status of the sketch entities. DimXpert is based solely on dimension and tolerance constraints. Geometrical relationships, such as Concentric relationships, are not considered.

- The *Copy Tolerance Scheme* ✤ tool provides the ability to copy a DimXpert tolerance scheme from one configuration of a part to another configuration. Note: Copied schemes are not synchronized with the Source configuration. Making changes to one scheme has no affect on the other.

- The *Delete All Tolerances* ✳ tool provides the ability to delete the entire DimXpert database. Note: To reinstate the DimXpert database, click **Undo** from the Menu bar toolbar.

☼ Various drawing standards display Tolerance zeros differently. The ASME Y14.5M standard states for millimeter dimensions, that there is no decimal point associated with a unilateral tolerance on a 0 value. There is no +/- sign associated with the unilateral tolerance on a 0 value.

A unilateral tolerance is similar to a SolidWorks bilateral tolerance; with one tolerance value set to 0. The other tolerance value contains a +/- sign. Select Bilateral Tolerance in SolidWorks when a unilateral tolerance is required.

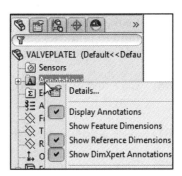

$$\phi\ 22^{+0.4}_{\ \ 0}$$

Decimal inch tolerance rules differ from millimeter rules. Explore decimal unilateral tolerance at the end of this chapter.

DimXpert Annotations and Drawings

The dimensions and annotations generated when dimensions schemes are created are considered DimXpert Annotations. These annotations, combined with the planes that hold them, are very useful which creating drawing views. In the next section, insert DimXpert annotations into a drawing.

Activity: VALVEPLATE1 Drawing - View Palette

73) Click the **FeatureManager** tab.

74) Right-click the **Annotations** folder from the FeatureManager.

75) **Uncheck** the Show DimXpert Annotations box. View the results in the Graphics window.

Display the DimXpert Annotations.
76) Right-click the **Annotations** folder from the FeatureManager.

77) **Check** the Show DimXpert Annotations box.

78) Click **Save**.

🔆 To modify the default DimXpert color, click **Options**, **Colors**. Under Color scheme settings, select **Annotations**, **DimXpert** and pick the new color.

Create a new VALVEPLATE1 drawing. Apply the DimXpert Annotations.

79) Click the **Make Drawing from Part/Assembly** from the Menu bar toolbar.

80) Click the **MY-TEMPLATES** tab.

81) Double-click the **A-ANSI-MM-NO-VIEWS** drawing template.

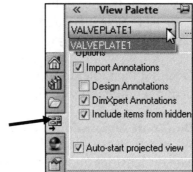

🔆 In the A-ANSI-MM-NO-VIEWS Template, there are no Pre-defined views and Auto insert on view creation Center Marks option is unchecked.

Insert three drawing views using the View Palette.

82) Click the **View Palette** tab in the Task Pane. VALVEPLATE1 is displayed in the drop-down menu.

83) Check the **Import Annotations** box.

84) Check the **DimXpert Annotations** box.

85) To include all annotations that may be in annotation views other than the default Front, Top and Right, click **the Include items from hidden features** box. Note: The (A) next to the drawing view informs the user that DimXpert Annotations are present.

86) Click and drag the **(A) Front** view into Sheet1 in the lower left corner.

87) Click a **position** directly above the Front view.

88) Click a **position** directly to the right of the Front view. Three views are displayed.

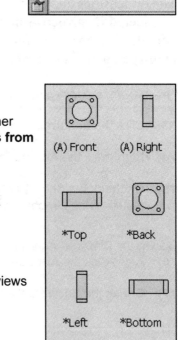

89) Click **OK** ✅ from the Project View PropertyManager.

Modify the Sheet Scale.
90) Right-click in the **sheet boundary**.

91) Click **Properties**. Enter **1:1** for Scale.

92) Click **OK** from the Sheet Properties dialog box.

93) If required, click **Options**, **Document Properties** tab from the Menu bar toolbar.

94) **Uncheck** the Dual dimensions display box from the Document Properties - Dimensions dialog box.

95) Click **OK**. Click and drag the **dimensions** off the model as illustrated. Move any dimensions if needed as illustrated.

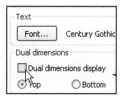

At this time, you can NOT insert extension line gaps when using DimXpert.

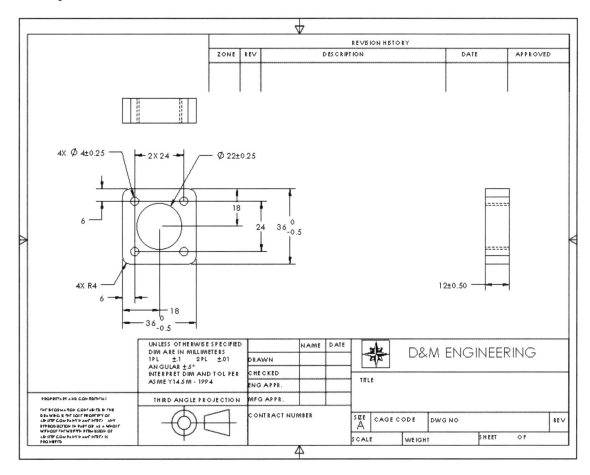

Hide the Top view.
96) Right-click **inside** the Top view boundary.

97) Click **Hide**.

98) Click **OK** ✅ from the Drawing View2 PropertyManager

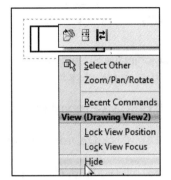

🔆 To displayed a hidden dimension, click View, Hide/Show Annotations. The Hidden Annotations are displayed in the drawing.

Insert a Centerline in the Right view.
99) Click **Centerline** 🔲 from the Annotation toolbar. Check the Select View box.

100) Click **inside** the Right view boundary.

101) Click **OK** ✅ from the Centerline PropertyManager. Note: The Right view is displayed with Hidden Lines Visible.

Hide Tangent edges in the Right view.
102) Click inside the **Right view** boundary.

103) Right-click **Tangent Edge**.

104) Check **Tangent Edges Removed**.

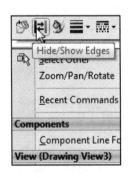

Hide small hole edges.
105) If needed, click **Hidden Lines Visible** 🔲 from the Display Style dialog box.

106) Hold the **Ctrl** key down.

107) Click the **four silhouette edges** as illustrated. Note the silhouette icon.

108) Right-click **Hide/Show Edges**.

109) Release the **Ctrl** key.

110) Hide the Centerlines.

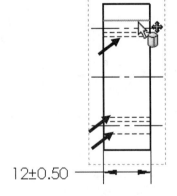

111) Click **Save**  .

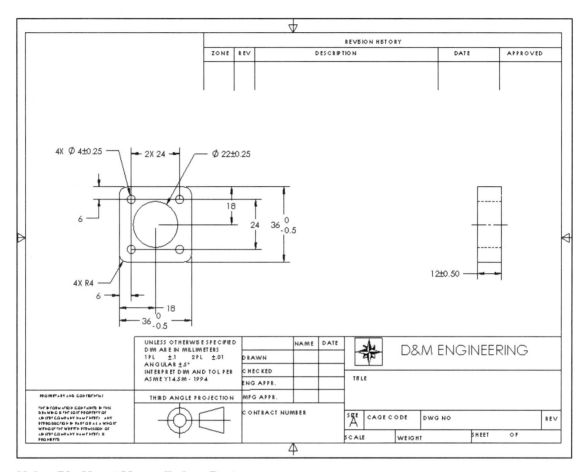

Using DimXpert Manually in a Part

SolidWorks provides the ability to apply DimXpert manually. In the next section, add datums, dimensions and geometric tolerance using the manual method.

> **Activity: Vise Assembly - DimXpert Manual Method in a Part**

Open the assembly and apply the DimXpert Manual Method.

112) Click **Open** from the Menu bar toolbar.

113) **Browse** to the DRAWING-W-SOLIDWORKS-2012 folder.

114) Double-click the **Vise** assembly. The Vise FeatureManager is displayed.

Add a Datum to the base component.

115) Right-click **base** from the FeatureManager.

116) Click **Open Part**.

117) Click **Tools**, **DimXpert**, **Datum** or click the
DimXpert tab from the CommandManager and click
the **Datum** tool. The Datum Feature
PropertyManager is displayed. The default Datum
label is A. The label is attached to the mouse
pointer.

118) Click the **top face** of the part to located the Datum.

119) Click a **position above** the datum.

120) Click **OK** from the Datum Feature
PropertyManager. View the results.

Insert a dimension using DimXpert.

121) Click **Tools**, **DimXpert**, **Size Dimension** or
click the **DimXpert** tab from the
CommandManager and click the Size
Dimension tool.

122) Click the **right face** as illustrated.

123) Click **Create Width
Feature**.

124) Click the
**opposite
face** as
illustrated.

125) Click **OK**
from the Pop-
up menu.

126) Place the
dimension
off the model.
The
DimXpert
PropertyMan
ager is
displayed.

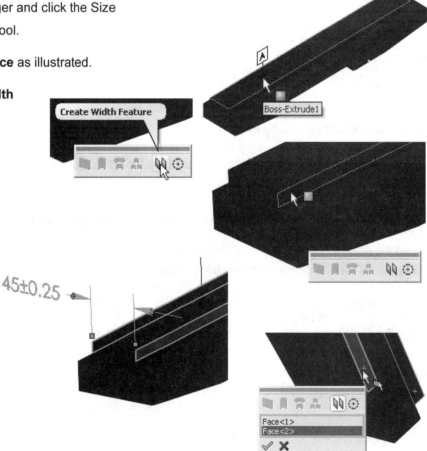

45±0.25

Set the Tolerance of the dimension.
127) Set Tolerance/Precision to **limit**.

128) Enter Maximum Variation: **-0.12**mm.

129) Enter Minimum Variation: **-0.20**mm.

130) Set **Tolerance Precision** as illustrated.

131) Click **OK** from the DimXpert
PropertyManager.

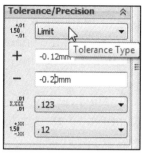

132) **Save** and **close** the part. The Vise assembly
is displayed.

133) Open the **jaw1 part** from the vise assembly.
The jaw1 FeatureManager is displayed.

134) Insert **datums A, B and C** as shown using
DimXpert. Follow the above procedure.

Insert a dimension using DimXpert.
135) Click **Tools**, **DimXpert**, **Size Dimension** or
click the **DimXpert** tab from the
CommandManager and click the Size
Dimension tool.

136) Add a **size dimension between the inner
faces** as illustrated.

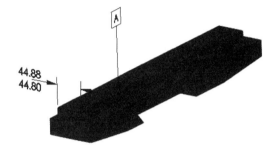

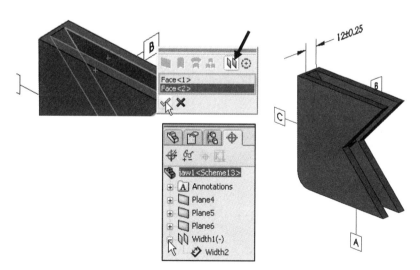

The Geometric Tolerance symbol can be added to a face or dimension of the model. It is created in the same way as the annotation geometric tolerance symbol in a drawing.

The Primary, Secondary and Tertiary datum names must exist before adding them to the geometric tolerance symbol.

Insert Geometric Tolerance to the part.
137) Click the **size dimension.**

138) Click **Tools**, **DimXpert**, **Geometric Tolerance** or click the **DimXpert** tab from the CommandManager and click the **Geometric Tolerance** tool. The Properties dialog box is displayed.

139) Click the **Symbol drop-down** arrow.

140) Click the **Position** ⊕ symbol.

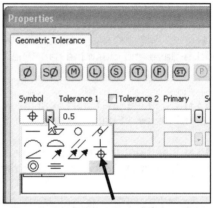

141) Enter **0.0** for Tolerance 1.

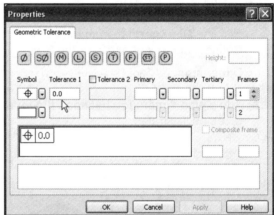

142) Click the **Max Material Condition** Ⓜ **symbol**.

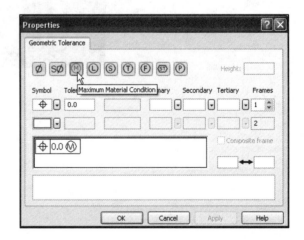

143) Click the **Primary datum** drop-down menu.

144) Enter **A**.

145) Click **OK** ✅.

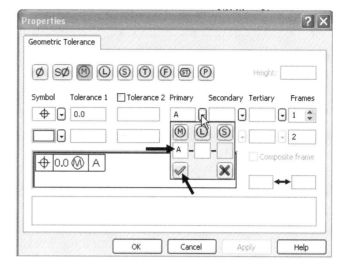

146) Click the **Secondary datum** drop-down menu.

147) Enter **B**.

148) Click **OK** ✅.

149) Click **OK** from the Properties dialog box. View the results.

150) Save and **Close** all models.

🔆 Double-click the Feature Control frame as illustrated to displayed the Properties dialog box.

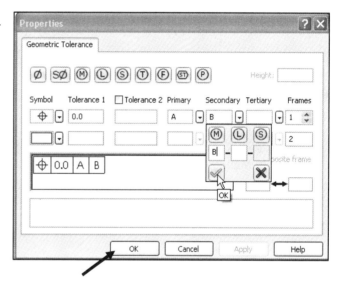

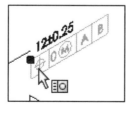

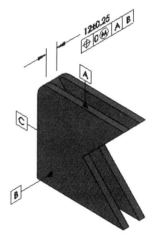

🔅 The Annotation PropertyManager is displayed each time you add new DimXpert dimensions. If you do not update the annotations at that time, you must click View, Hide/Show Annotations from the Menu bar menu to display the updated annotations.

VALVEPLATE1-GDT Part - Datums, Feature Control Frames, Geometric Tolerances, and Surface Finish

Open the VALVEPLATE1-GDT part from the DVD. View the three Extrude features, Linear Pattern feature, and Fillet feature. Apply the DimXpert: Geometric option to the part. View the inserted Datums, Feature Control Frames, and Geometric tolances.

Edit the Feature Control Frames. Create the VALVEPLATE1-GDT drawing using the View Palette. Insert three drawing views. Insert Surface Finish on the Top and Right view. Create multiple Leaders to the Surface Finish symbol in the Top view. Insert Hide Tangent Edges in the Top and Right view.

Activity: VALVEPLATE1-GDT Part - DimXpert: Geometric option

Open the VALVEPLATE1-GDT part.

151) Click **Open** 📂 from the Menu bar toolbar.

152) Double-click **VALVEPLATE1-GDT** part. The Part FeatureManager is displayed.

Apply DimXpert to the part.

153) Click the **DimXpertManager** ⊕ tab.

154) Click the **Auto Dimension Scheme** ⊕ tool from the DimXpertManager. The Auto Dimension PropertyManager is displayed. Prismatic and Plus and Minus is selected by default. In this section, select the Geometric option.

🔅 DimXpert: Geometric option provides the ability to locate axial features with position and circular run out tolerances. Pockets and surfaces are located with surface profiles.

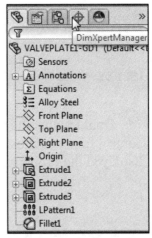

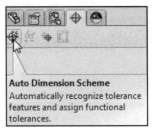

155) Check the **Geometric** box as illustrated. Prismatic is selected by default.

Select the three Datums.

156) Click the **back face** of the model. Plane1 is displayed in the Primary Datum box.

157) Click **inside** the Secondary Datum box.

158) Click the **left face** of the model. Plane2 is displayed in the Secondary Datum box.

159) Click **inside** the Tertiary Datum box.

160) Click the **top face** of the model. Plane3 is displayed in the Tertiary Datum box.

161) Click **OK** ✅ from the Auto Dimension PropertyManager.

162) Click **Isometric view**. View the Datum's, Feature Control Frames, and Geometric tolerances. All features are displayed in green.

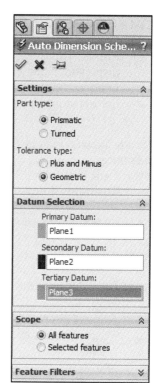

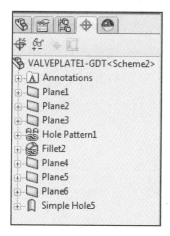

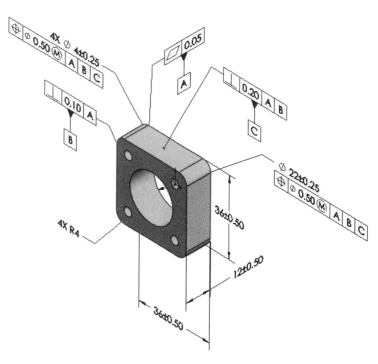

Edit a Feature Control Frame in the part.

163) Double-click the illustrated Feature Control Frame. The Properties dialog box is displayed. Note: You need to click in the correct location.

Modify the 0.50 feature tolerance.

164) Click **inside** the Tolerance 1 box.

165) Delete the existing text.

166) Enter **0.25**.

167) Click **OK** from the Properties dialog box.

168) Repeat the above procedure for the second Position Feature Control Frame. View the results.

169) Click **Save**.

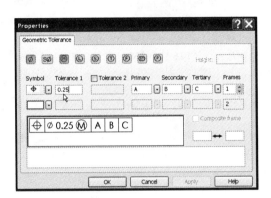

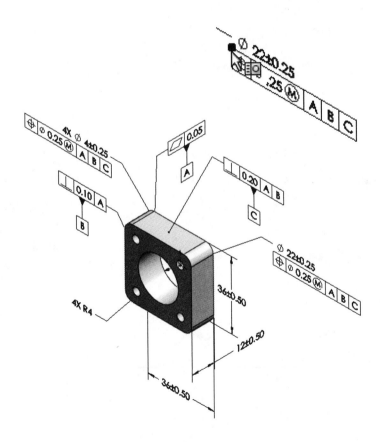

Activity: VALVEPLATE1-GDT Drawing - View Palette

Create the VALVEPLATE1-GDT drawing.

170) Click the **Make Drawing from Part/Assembly** in the Menu bar toolbar.

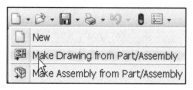

171) Click the **MY-TEMPLATES** tab.

172) Double-click the **A-ANSI-MM-NO-VIEWS** drawing template.

In the A-ANSI-MM-NO-VIEWS Template, there are no Pre-defined views and Auto insert on view creation Center Marks option is unchecked.

Insert three views from the View Palette.

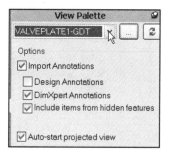

173) Click the **View Palette** tab in the Task Pane. VALVEPLATE1-GDT is displayed in the drop-down menu.

174) Check the **Import Annotations** box.

175) Check the **DimXpertAnnotations** box.

176) Check the **Include items from hidden features** box. Note: The (A) next to the drawing view informs the user that DimXpert Annotations are present.

177) Click and drag the **(A) Front** view into Sheet1 in the lower left corner.

178) Click a **position** directly above the Front view.

179) Click a **position** directly to the right of the Front view. Three views are displayed.

180) Click **OK** from the Projected View PropertyManager.

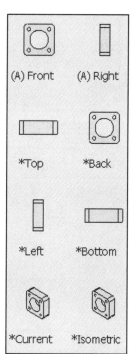

Modify the Sheet Scale.

181) Right-click in the **sheet boundary**.

182) Click **Properties**.

183) Enter **1:1** for Scale.

184) Click **OK** from the Sheet Properties dialog box.

185) Uncheck the Dual dimensions display box.

186) Click and drag the **dimensions** off the model as illustrated.

Save the VALVEPLATE1-GDT drawing.

187) Click **Save** 🖫 . Accept the default name.

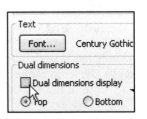

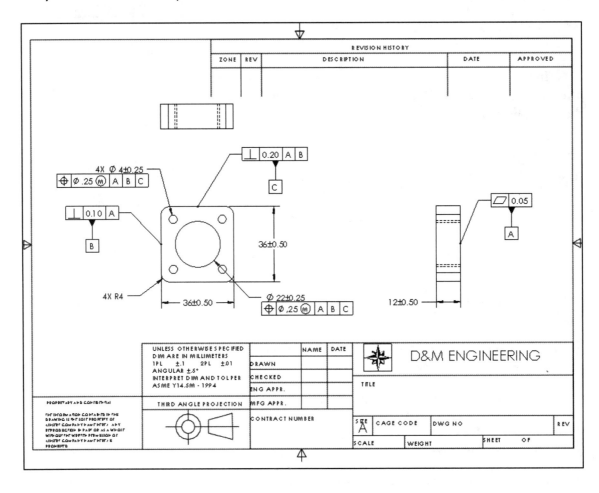

Activity: VALVEPLATE1-GDT Drawing- Surface Finish

Insert the Surface Finish symbol with a Bent Leader into the Top View.
188) Zoom in on the Top view.

189) Click **Surface Finish** ⱱ from the Annotation toolbar.

190) Click **Basic** for Symbol.

191) Enter **0.8** micrometers for Maximum Roughness.

192) Enter **0.4** micrometers for Minimum Roughness.

193) Click **Leader**.

194) Click **Bent Leader**.

195) Click the **top horizontal edge** of the Top view for the arrowhead attachment.

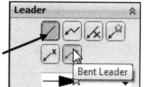

196) Click a **position** for the Surface Finish symbol

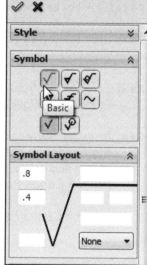

197) Click **OK** ✅ from the Surface Finish PropertyManager.

Create multiple Leaders to the Surface Finish symbol.
198) Hold the **Ctrl** key down.

199) Click the tip of the **arrowhead**.

200) Drag the **arrowhead** to the bottom edge of the Top view.

201) Release the **Ctrl** key. **Release** the mouse button.

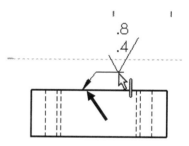

Remove the Tangent Edge in the Top view.
202) Click inside the **Top view**.

203) Right-click **Tangent Edge**.

204) Check **Tangent Edges Removed**.

205) Display **Hidden Edges Removed** in the Top View.

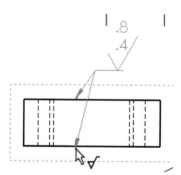

Insert Surface Finish symbol in the Right View.
206) Display **Hidden Edges Removed** in the Right view.

207) Click the **top horizontal edge** in the Right view.

208) Click **Surface Finish** ∇ from the Annotation toolbar.

209) Select the **Machining Required** option for Symbol.

210) Enter **1.6** micrometer for Maximum Roughness.

211) Click **No Leader** .

212) Click the **top horizontal edge** of the Right view.

213) Click **OK** from the Surface Finish PropertyManager.

214) Drag the **Surface Finish Symbol** to the left of the profile line as illustrated. Display **Hidden Edges Removed**.

215) Insert a Centerline in the Right view.

Save the VALVEPLATE drawing.

216) Click **Save** .

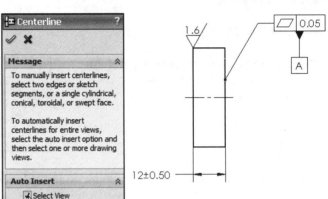

The Surface Finish PropertyManager contains additional options that refer to the machining process required to complete the part.

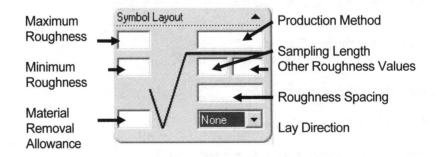

To utilize a specific Finish in the Title Block, add the Custom Property, Finish in the Part. Link the Finish box in the Title Block to the Finish Property. The Greek Letter, m, is obtained from the SWGrekc Font.

Name	Value	Type
Finish	1.8	Text

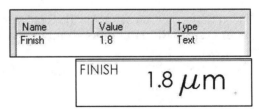

eDrawing

An outside machine shop will manufacture the VALVEPLATE1-GDT. Send a SolidWorks eDrawing of the VALVEPLATE1-GDT to the machine shop for a price quotation. Create a SolidWorks eDrawing.

Activity: eDrawing

Create an eDrawing.
217) Click **File**, **Publish to eDrawings** from the Menu bar menu.

The Mark-up options are available in eDrawings Professional software application.

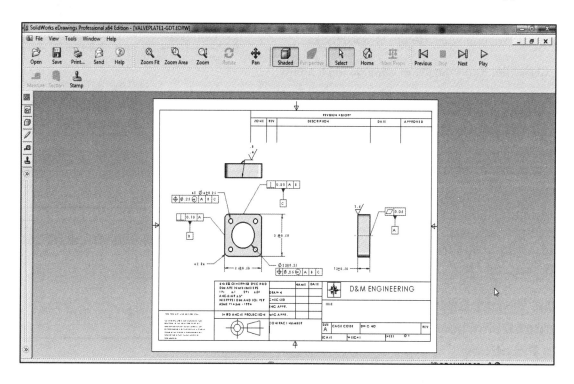

Display the views.
218) Click the **Play** button. View the three views.

219) Click **Stop**.

View the Full Sheet.
220) Click **Home**.

Save the eDrawing.
221) Click **Save**.

222) Accept the default file name.

223) Click **Save**.

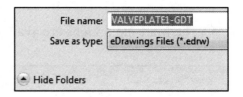

Exit the eDrawing module. Return to SolidWorks.

224) Click **File**, **Exit** from the eDrawings Main menu.

Close all parts and drawings.
225) Click **Windows**, **Close** All from the Menu bar toolbar.

Additional eDrawing
Save As type options
include: *.zip, *htm, *exe,
*bmp, *tif, and *jpg.

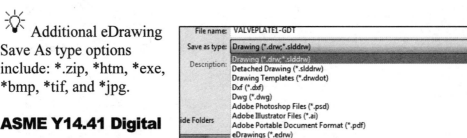

ASME Y14.41 Digital Product Definition Data Practices

ASME Y14.41 describes the rules for applying dimensions and tolerances to a 3D model and a 3D model and 2D drawing. There are two digital formats:

- Model only digital format.

- Model and drawing digital format.

Why does this standard become important in SolidWorks? Answer: The SolidWorks designer requires a standard to control parts, assemblies, and drawings in electronic form.

Example for Model only digital format: An engineer supplies a 3D model file electronically to a manufacturing prototype vendor in Mexico. The part requires a key tolerance within a specified range. The engineer inserts Geometric tolerances into the 3D model file and emails the file to the vendor.

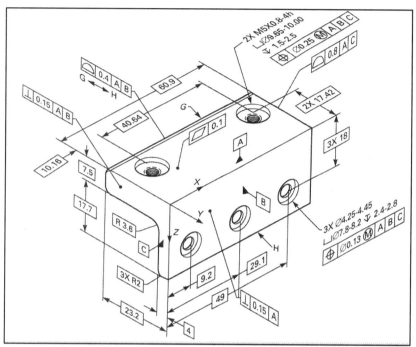

Y14.41 Digital Product and Data Definition Practices
Reprinted from ASME Y14.41-2003, by permission of
The American Society of Mechanical Engineers. All rights reserved.

Example for Model and drawing digital format: A design engineer supplies a 2D eDrawing to the local machine shop to create a tooling drawing. Mating parts contain critical dimensions.

The designer creates all geometric tolerances in the part and inserts model items into the drawing. Part configurations control the Section views. View orientation controls named views. The drawing references the model filename.

A drawing (electronic, eDrawing, or paper) combined with a corresponding electronic model file becomes a Minimum Content Drawing (MCD). The MCD contains key dimensions, tolerances and annotations required to manufacture the part. The MCD usually is not fully detailed.

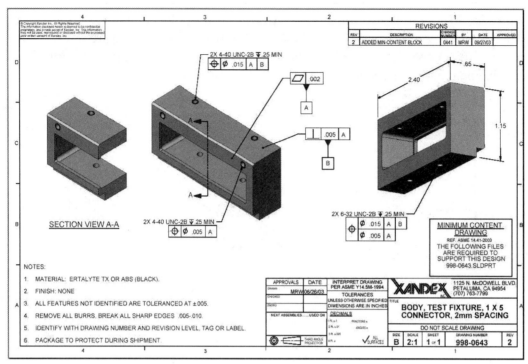

Tooling Drawing (Minimum Content Drawing)
Courtesy of XANDEX, Inc. Petaluma, CA, USA

Modify a ASME14-41 Drawing

Utilize the Y14.41 standard to modify the ASME14-41 drawing. Open the ASME14-41-Rev-A part. Apply DimXpert: Geometric option. View the Inserted Datums, Feature Control Frames, and Geometric Tolerances. Open the ASME14-41 drawing. Insert Datums, Feature Control Frames, Dimensions and Geometric Tolerances into an Isometric drawing view on multiple drawing sheets. Note: A this time, DimXpert does not import annotations into an Isometric drawing view.

Activity: Open the ASME14-41 Part - Modify the ASME14-41 Drawing

Open the ASME14-41 part.
226) Open the ASME14-41-Rev-A part in the DRAWING-W-SOLIDWORKS-2012 folder. The model is displayed in the Graphics window.

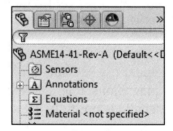

Set Dimensioning standard to **ANSI** under **Tools, Options, Document Properties, Detailing** to display annotations according to the ASME standard. Standards other than ANSI are not yet supported in DimXpert.

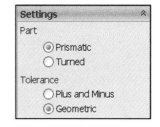

Apply DimXpert to the part.

227) Click the **DimXpertManager** ⊕ tab.

228) Click the **Auto Dimension Scheme** 🌼 icon from the DimXpertManager. The Auto Dimension PropertyManager is displayed.

229) Check the **Prismatic** box.

230) Check the **Geometric** box.

Three mutually Perpendicular planes are required.

231) Click the **Top face** of the model. Plane1 is displayed in the Primary Datum box.

232) Click **inside** the Secondary Datum box.

233) Click the **Right face** of the model. Plane2 is displayed in the Secondary Datum box.

234) Click **inside** the Tertiary Datum box.

235) Click the **Front face** of the model. Plane 3 is displayed in the Tertiary Datum box.

236) Click **OK** ✔ from the Auto Dimension PropertyManager. View the results. The model is displayed in green and is fully constrained.

237) Click and drag the **annotation** off the model.

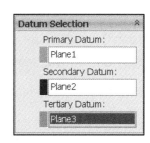

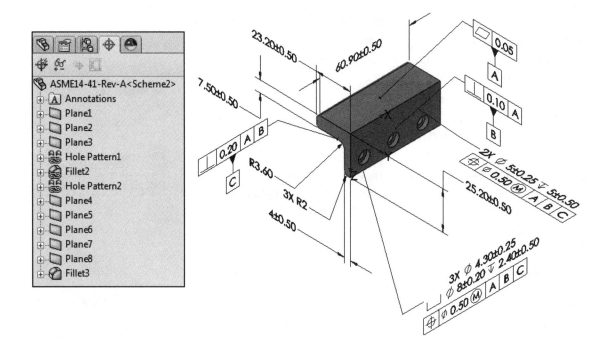

ASME Y14.41 requires a Coordinate System X, Y, Z symbol. Utilize Insert, Reference Geometry, Coordinate System.

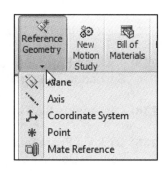

ASME Y14.41 requires a Section Plane in the drawing. The Section Plane configuration contains a rectangular sketch with a line indicating the cut direction.

Modify the ASME14-41 drawing.

238) Open the ASME14-41drawing from the DRAWING-W-SOLIDWORKS-2012 folder.

Insert Geometric Tolerances and Notes.

239) Click **Model Items** ⊗ from the Annotation toolbar.

240) Select **Entire model** from the Source/Destination box.

241) Click the **Notes** box from the Annotations dialog box.

242) Click the **Geometric tolerances** box from the Annotations dialog box.

243) Click **OK** ✓ from the Model Items PropertyManager.

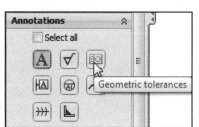

244) Position the **annotations** in the view as illustrated.

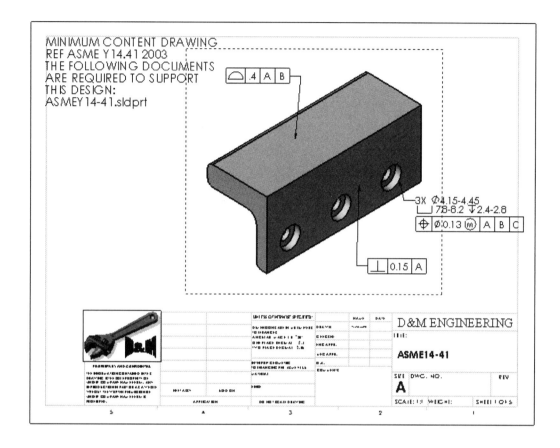

Modify the arrowhead to a dot for the annotations that references a top face.

245) Click the **arrowhead tip** as illustrated on the top face. The Geometric Tolerance PropertyManager is displayed.

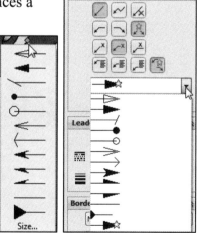

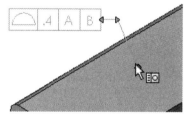

246) Right-click and select the **dot arrowhead**.

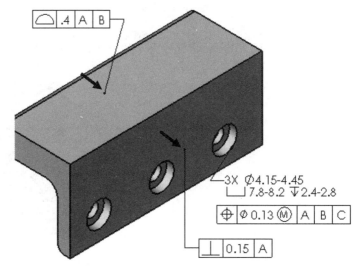

Insert overall dimensions on Sheet2.
247) Click the **Sheet2** tab.

248) Click inside the **Isometric view** boundary.

249) Click **Smart Dimension** ◇ from the Annotation toolbar.

250) Check the **Smart dimensioning** box.

251) Insert three overall **dimensions** for width, height, and depth as illustrated.

To dimension in an Isometric view, select edges not vertices. Avoid selecting fillets and chamfers.

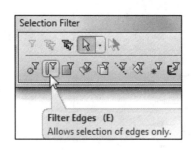

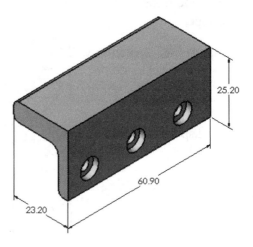

Insert Geometric Tolerances and Datum Features.
252) Click the **Sheet3** tab.

253) Click **Datum Feature** ⊢Ⓐ from the Annotation toolbar.

254) Click the **top face** in the Isometric view for Datum A.

255) Click a **position** above the top face.

256) Click the **Perpendicular** Feature Control Frame for Datum B. Click a **position** below the Feature Control Frame as illustrated.

257) Click **OK** ✅ from the Datum Feature PropertyManager.

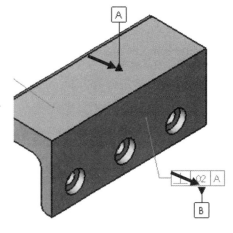

Review Sheet4.
258) Click the **Sheet4** tab. Click inside the **Isometric view** boundary.

259) Right-click **Properties**.

260) Select **large-100mm** for Use name configuration.

261) Click **OK** from the Drawing Views Properties box.

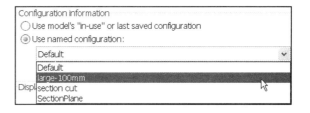

Review Sheet 5.
262) Click the **Sheet 5** tab.

263) Click inside the **Isometric** view boundary.

264) Click **Model Items** ✑ from the Annotation toolbar.

265) Select **Entire model** from the Source/Destination box.

266) Click the **Notes** box from the Annotations dialog box.

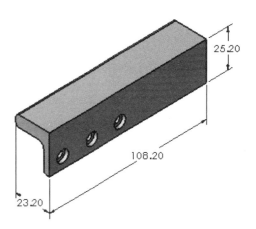

267) Click the **Geometric tolerances** box from the Annotations dialog box.

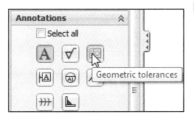

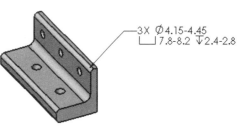

268) Click **OK** ✓ from the
PropertyManager.

Copy the Annotation.
269) Click the **Note**.

270) Click **Ctrl + C**.

271) Click a **position** to the top left
of the profile.

272) Click **Ctrl + V**.

273) Drag the **arrowhead** to the
back hole edge.

274) **Hide** the first Note.

275) **Hide** the other annotations
as illustrated.

Save the ASME14-41 drawing.
276) Click **Save** 💾.

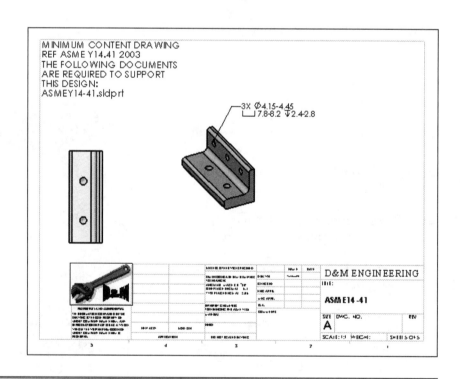

Review the notes created in the 3D part and inserted into the Isometric view in the drawing. Modify the note attachment point to reference the appropriate geometry.

PLATE-TUBE Assembly Drawing and Weld Symbols

Open the PLATE-TUBE assembly from the DRAWING-W-SOLIDWORKS-2012 folder. The customer requires a concept drawing of the PLATE-TUBE assembly. The TUBE part is welded to the PLATE part. Explore the procedures to create Weld symbols:

- Weld Bead Assembly Feature

- Weld Symbol Annotation

Insert the Weld Bead Assembly feature between the TUBE and PLATE parts in the PLATE-TUBE assembly. A Weld symbol automatically attaches to the Weld Bead. Utilize the Model Items tool to insert the Weld symbol into the Left drawing view.

Add a second PLATE component to the PLATE-TUBE assembly. Create a Weld symbol as a separate annotation in the PLATE-TUBE drawing.

The PLATE-TUBE assembly is created with three components:

- PLATE1-W<1> (Default)

- TUBE1-W<1>

- PLATE1-W<2> (Large Plate)

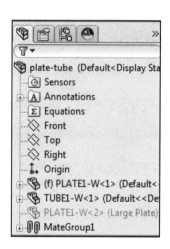

PLATE1-W<2> (Large Plate) is suppressed for the first portion of this activity.

Weld beads use a simplified display. They are displayed as graphical representations in models. No geometry is created. The weld beads are lightweight and do not affect performance.

Activity: PLATE-TUBE Assembly Drawing and Weld Symbols

Create a Weld Bead in the PLATE-TUBE assembly.

277) Open the PLATE-TUBE assembly from the DRAWING-W-SOLIDWORKS-2012 folder.

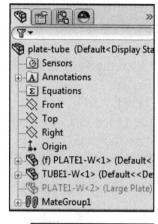

Create a Weld bead between the PLATE1-W<1> and TUBE1-W<1> components.

278) Click **Insert, Assembly Feature, Weld Bead** from the Menu bar menu. The Weld Bead PropertyManager is displayed.

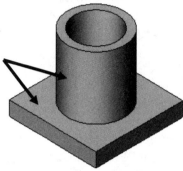

- Weld paths are supported between two bodies. You cannot define a weld path among three or more bodies or between the faces of one body.

- Gaps between faces are supported.

- Gaps between edges are not supported. Edges must lie on the surface of a body.

The Smart Weld Section tool provides the ability to let you drag the pointer over the faces where you want to apply a weld bead.

Select the weld faces.

279) Click the **outside cylindrical face** of the TUBE1-W component.

280) Click the **top face** of the PLATE1-W<1> component.

281) Enter **6.00** for Bead size.

282) Check the **Selection** button.

283) Click **Define Weld Symbol**. The ANSI Weld dialog box is displayed.

284) Click the **Weld Symbol** button as illustrated.

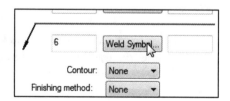

285) Select **Fillet** from the ANSI Weld Symbols drop down menu.

286) Click **OK**.

287) Select **Concave** for Surface Shape as illustrated.

288) Click **OK** from the ANSI Weld dialog box.

289) Click **OK** ✅ from the Weld Bead PropertyManager. View the results. A Weld Folder is displayed in the FeatureManager.

290) Right-click the **Weld Folder** folder in the FeatureManager.

291) Click **Show Cosmetic Welds**. View the results in the Graphics window.

Save the PLATE-TUBE assembly.

292) Click **Save** 💾.

🔆 You can edit the weld bead feature as you would any feature by right-clicking in the FeatureManager design tree and clicking Edit Feature.

🔆 View the additional options in the Weld Bead PropertyManager to create various gaps and pitch with the bead.

🔆 Due to the weight of the Bead feature, it is not displayed in the Drawing.

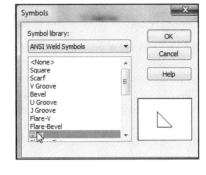

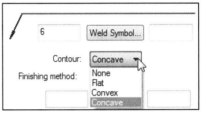

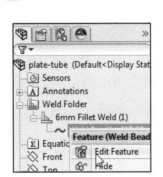

Create a new PLATE-TUBE drawing.

293) Click **New** ⬚ from the Menu bar toolbar.

294) Double-click **A-MM-ANSI-NO-VIEWS** from the MY-TEMPLATES folder. The Model View PropertyManager is displayed. Plate-Tube is the active document.

295) Click **Next** ➡ from the Model View PropertyManager.

296) Click ***Right** for View Orientation. Note: Third Angle Projection!

297) Enter **.75:1** for Scale.

298) Click a **position** to the left of the Sheet.

299) Click **OK** ✓ from the Projected View PropertyManager.

Save the PLATE-TUBE drawing.

300) Click **Save** 💾. Accept the default name. Due to the weight of the Bead feature, it is not displayed in the Drawing.

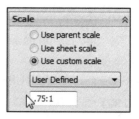

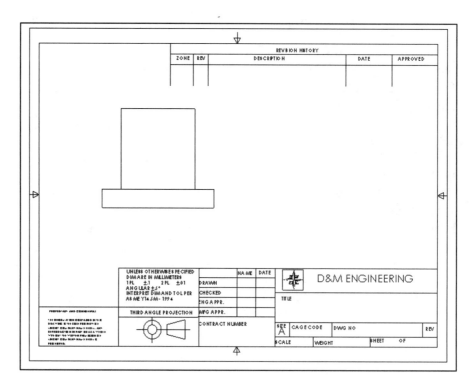

Insert the Model Items Weld Symbols.
301) Click **inside** the drawing view.

302) Click **Model Items** 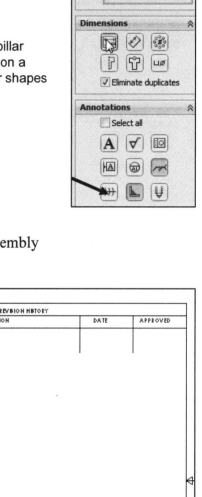 from the Annotation toolbar.

303) Select **Entire model** from the Source/Destination box.

304) Uncheck the Dimensions, Marked for Drawing option. Note: No Dimensions are inserted.

305) Click **End Treatment** from the Annotations box.

306) Click **Weld Symbols** from the Annotations box.

307) Click the **Caterpillar** from the Annotations box. The caterpillar symbol represents the position and length of a weld bead on a drawing. The symbol comprises repeated circular or linear shapes along an edge.

308) Uncheck any other options.

309) Click **OK** ✓ from the Model Items PropertyManager.

310) Drag the **Weld Symbol** off the profile.

The Weld attachment point inserted from a Weld Assembly feature cannot be modified.

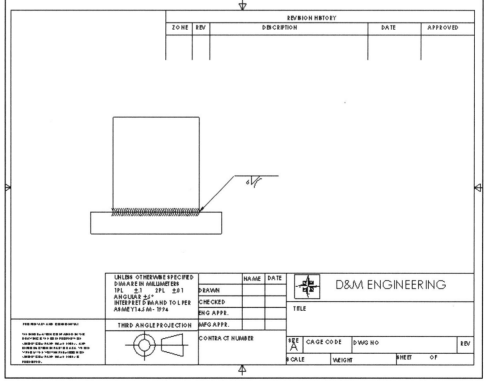

🔆 The Weld Symbol dialog box corresponds to the standard location of elements, a welding symbol as defined by AWS A2.4:1997.

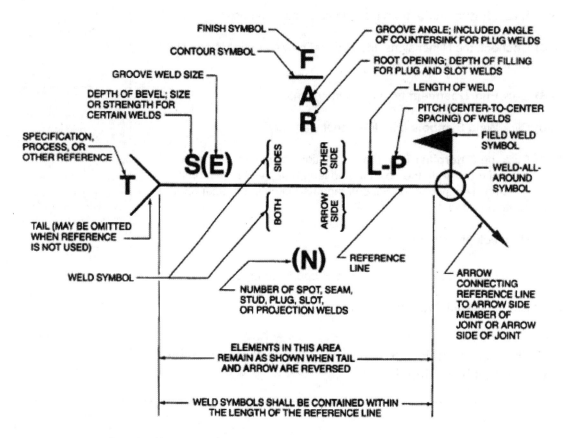

Standard Location of Elements of a Welding Symbol (AWS A2.4:1997)

Return to the PLATE-TUBE assembly.
311) Click **Window**, **PLATE-TUBE** from the Menu bar menu.

312) Right-click **PLATE1-W<2> (Large Plate)** in the assembly FeatureManager.

313) Click **Unsuppress**.

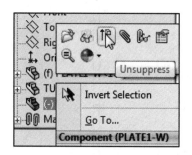

Return to the PLATE-TUBE drawing.
314) Press **Ctrl + Tab**.

315) Click the **right intersection** as illustrated.

316) Click **Weld Symbol** 📐 from the Annotation toolbar.

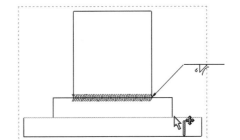

317) Click the **Around** check box to indicate that the weld extends completely around the joint.

318) Click the second Weld **Symbol** button.

319) Select **Fillet**. Click **OK**.

320) Enter **6** for Bead size.

321) Select **Convex** for Contour.

322) Select **G-Grinding** for Finish Method.

323) Click **OK** from the Properties dialog box.

324) Drag the **Weld Symbol** off the profile line as illustrated.

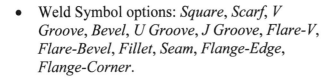

Save the PLATE-TUBE drawing.

325) Click **Save** 💾.

The ANSI Weld Properties dialog box contains Weld Symbols, Contour options, and Finishing method options:

- Weld Symbol options: *Square, Scarf, V Groove, Bevel, U Groove, J Groove, Flare-V, Flare-Bevel, Fillet, Seam, Flange-Edge, Flange-Corner.*

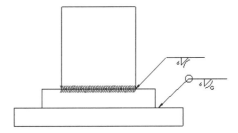

- Contour options: *None, Flat, Convex,* or *Concave.*

- Finishing method: *None, Chipping, Grinding, Hammering, Machining, Rolling,* or *Unspecified.*

Additional Weld options are available for ISO and GOST standards.

Save Rebuild time. Save Weld Symbols created in the drawing onto a Weld layer. Turn off the Weld layer when not required. Suppress Weld Beads created in the assembly.

When a weld is required on both sides, select the Arrow Side option and the Other Side option. Enter all weld options for the Arrow Side. Enter all options for the Other Side.

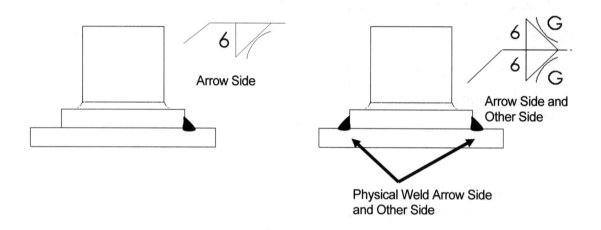

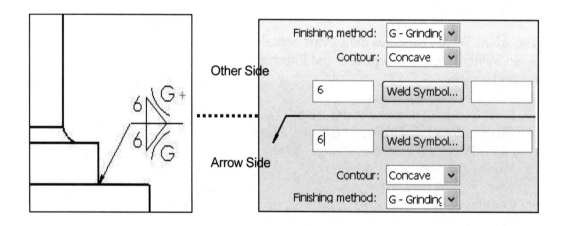

Example: Weld Arrow Side and Other Side

PLATE-CATALOG Drawing, Design Table, and EXCEL Formatting

Create the PLATE-CATALOG drawing for the company's online catalog. The PLATE-CATALOG drawing utilizes a Design Table. Review the PLATE-CATALOG configurations. The PLATE-CATALOG part contains three configurations:

- 1007A-36

- 1007A-48

- 1007A-54

The configurations names represent the family part number (1007A -). The last two digits represent the square plate size: 36mm squared, 48mm squared and 54mm squared.

Create the PLATE-CATALOG drawing. Insert dimensions from the PLATE-CATALOG Default part. Modify the PLATE-CATALOG drawing to contain symbolic representations of the dimensions. Utilize EXCEL tools to format the Design Tables. Example: The letter A replaces the dimension 36. Insert the Design Table into the drawing. Modify the Design Table to represent the various configurations as a family of parts.

Activity: PLATE-CATALOG Drawing, Design Table and EXCEL Formatting

Open the PLATE-CATALOG part.
326) Open the PLATE-CATALOG part from the DRAWING-W-SOLIDWORKS-2012 folder.

Review the PLATE-CATALOG configurations.
327) Click the **ConfigurationManager** tab.

328) Double click **1007A-54**.

329) Double click **1007A-48**.

330) Double-click **1007A-36**.

Edit the Design Table.
331) Right-click **Design Table**.

332) Click **Edit Table**. The Design Table PropertyManager is displayed.

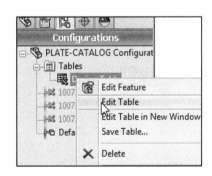

View the table.

	A	B	C	D	E	F	G
1	Design Table for: PLATE-CATALOG						
2		D1@Sketch1	D1@Sketch2	D2@Sketch3	D3@LPattern1	D4@LPattern1	
3	1007A-36	36	22	12	24	24	
4	1007A-48	48	24	16	32	32	
5	1007A-54	54	26	18	36	36	

◄ ◄ ► ►◄ \ Sheet 1 /

333) Click a **position** in the sheet boundary to exit the Design Table.

Create a PLATE-CATALOG drawing.

334) Click **New** ⬜ from the Menu bar toolbar.

335) Double-click **A-MM-ANSI-NO-VIEWS** from the MY-TEMPLATES folder.

336) Click **Cancel** ✖ from the Model View PropertyManager.

337) Click **Model View** 📷 from the View Layout toolbar.

338) Select **PLATE-CATALOG**.

339) Click **Next** ➡.

340) Click ***Top**.

341) Click a **position** on the left of the sheet as illustrated.

342) Click a **position** to the right of the first view as illustrated.

343) Enter **1:1** for Custom Scale.

344) Click **OK** ✔ from the Drawing View PropertyManager.

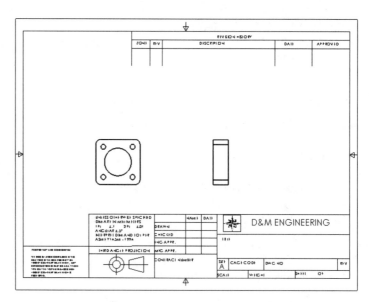

Save the PLATE-CATALOG drawing.
345) Click **Save As** from the Menu bar toolbar. Accept the default name.

346) Click **Save**.

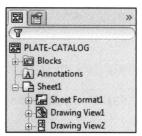

Modify the configuration.
347) Right-click **Properties** in Drawing View1. Note: The Top view is the Front view in the drawing.

348) Select **1007A-36** for the current Used named configuration. Click **OK**.

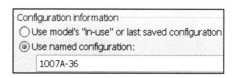

Increase the dimension height.
349) Click **Options** 📋, **Document Properties** tab from the Menu bar toolbar.

350) Click the **Dimensions** folder. Click the **Font** button.

351) Enter **5**mm for Height in the Units text box.

352) Click **OK** from the dialog box.

353) Click **OK**.

Insert Model dimensions.
354) Click a **position** inside Sheet1.

355) Click **Model Items** ✣ from the Annotation toolbar.

356) Select **Entire model** from the Source/Destination box.

357) Click **OK** ✔ from the Model Items PropertyManager.

358) Drag the **dimensions** approximately 10mm away from the profile as illustrated.

359) If required, uncheck the **Dual dimensions display** box.

Hide all superficial dimensions.
360) **Hide** the 36 dimension text in the right view.

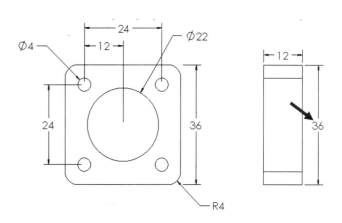

Add an overall horizontal dimension in Drawing View1.

361) Click **Smart Dimension** .

362) Click the **left** and **right vertical lines**.

363) Click a **position** below the profile for the 36 horizontal dimension text.

364) Drag the **extension lines** off the profile.

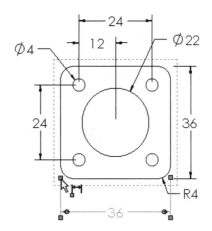

Modify dimensions to text symbols.

365) Click the **36 horizontal** dimension text.

366) Select the **<DIM>** text.

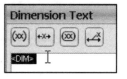

367) Press **Delete**.

368) Click **Yes** to the question, Do you want to continue?

369) Enter **A**.

370) Click **OK** from the Dimension PropertyManager.

371) Click the **36 vertical** dimension text.

372) Select the **<DIM>** text.

373) Press **Delete**.

374) Click **Yes** to the question, Do you want to continue?

375) Enter **A**.

376) Click **OK** from the Dimension PropertyManager.

377) Click the **⌀22** dimension text.

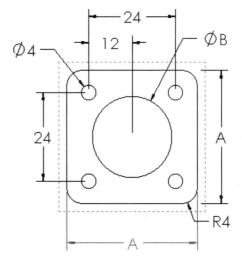

378) Select the **<DIM>** text.

379) Press **Delete**.

380) Click **Yes** to the question, Do you want to continue?

381) Enter **B**.

382) Click **OK** from the Dimension PropertyManager.

383) Click the **12** dimension text in the Front view.

384) Select the **<DIM>** text.

385) Press **Delete**.

386) Click **Yes** to the question, Do you want to continue?

387) Enter **C**.

388) Click **OK** ✓ from the Dimension PropertyManager.

389) Click the **24 horizontal** dimension text.

390) Select the **<DIM>** text.

391) Press **Delete**. Click **Yes** to the question, Do you want to continue?

392) Enter **D**. Click **OK** ✓ from the Dimension PropertyManager.

393) Click the **24 vertical** dimension text.

394) Select the **<DIM>** text. Press **Delete**.

395) Click **Yes** to the question, Do you want to continue?

396) Enter **D**.

397) Click **OK** ✓ from the Dimension PropertyManager.

398) Click the **⌀4** dimension text.

399) Select the **<DIM>** text.

400) Press **Delete**.

401) Click **Yes** to the question, Do you want to continue?

402) Enter **E**.

403) Click **OK** ✓ from the Dimension PropertyManager.

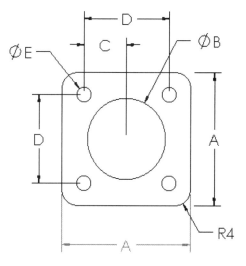

☼ When letters replace the <DIM> placeholder, the part dimensions update to reflect both the letter and the dimension value. Example: 36 is replaced with A36.

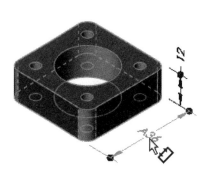

Return to the part. Note: You need Microsoft Excel to perform the following steps.

404) Press **Ctrl + Tab** to display the PLATE-CATALOG part.

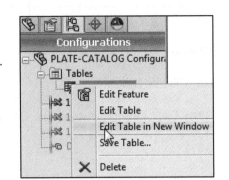

Edit the Design Table in an EXCEL window.

405) Right-click **Design Table** in the ConfigurationManager.

406) Click **Edit Table in New Window**. The Microsoft Excel dialog box is displayed.

Format the Design Table in Excel. Utilize Microsoft Excel functions, Excel Main menu, Toolbars, and Pop-up menus. Note the procedure will be different depending on your version of Excel.

Expand the Design Table.

407) Click and drag the **lower right corner** of the Design Table to display all entries.

Hide Row 1 and Row 2.

408) Click **Row 1**.

409) Drag the mouse pointer to **Row 2** in the Row frame. Both Row 1 and Row 2 are selected.

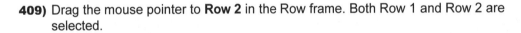

	A	B	C	D	E	F
	A1		fx	Design Table for: PLATE-CATALOG		
1	Design Table for: PLATE-CATALOG					
2		D1@Sketch1	D1@Sketch2	D2@Sketch3	D3@LPattern1	D4@LPattern1
3	1007A-36	36	22	12	24	24
4	1007A-48	48	24	16	32	32
5	1007A-54	54	26	18	36	36
6						

410) Right-click **Hide**. Row 3 is now displayed as the first row.

	A	B	C	D	E	F
	A1		fx	Design Table for: PLATE-CATALOG		
3	1007A-36	36	22	12	24	24
4	1007A-48	48	24	16	32	32
5	1007A-54	54	26	18	36	36
6						

Insert 2 Rows.
411) Click **Row 3** in the Row frame.

412) Right-click **Insert**. Row 3 is the new row.

413) Repeat the same steps for a second row.

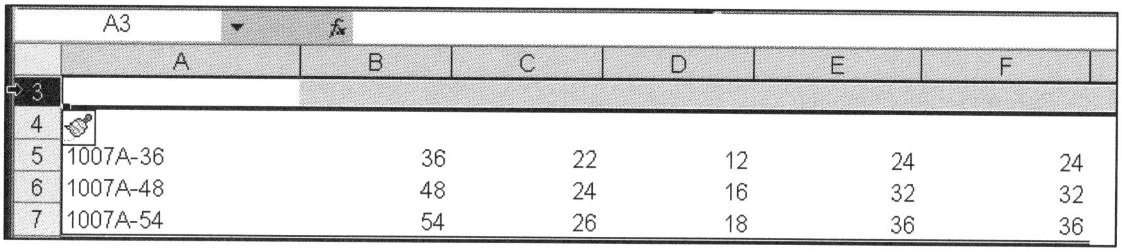

	A	B	C	D	E	F
3						
4						
5	1007A-36	36	22	12	24	24
6	1007A-48	48	24	16	32	32
7	1007A-54	54	26	18	36	36

Hide Column F.
414) Click **Column F**.

415) Right-click **Hide**. Column G is displayed to the right of Column E.

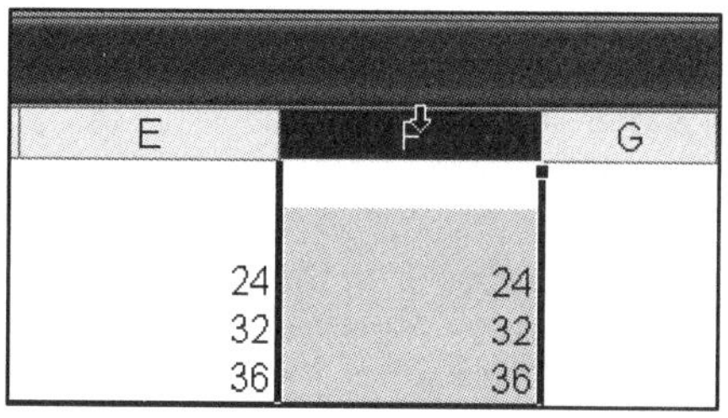

Modify the Hyperlink option.
416) Remove all Hyperlinks in your table directly from Microsoft Excel. The procedure will be different depending on your version of Excel.

E		G
24		24
32		32
36		36

The "@" symbol creates a hyperlink in the Design Table if the AutoFormat option remains checked.

Add Title and Headers. The procedure will be different depending on your version of Excel.
417) Click **Cell A3.**

418) Hold the left mouse button down.

419) Drag the mouse pointer to **Cell G3**

420) Release the left mouse button.

421) Right-click **Format Cells** Format Cells...

422) Click the **Alignment** tab.

423) Click the **Merge cells** check box.

424) Select **Center** for Horizontal.

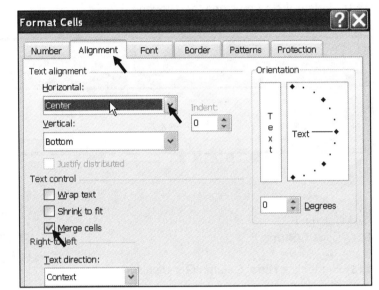

425) Click **OK** from the Format Cells dialog box.

426) Enter **PLATE – 36 THROUGH 54 MM, STEEL** for the title.

427) Click **Cell A4.**

428) Enter **ORDER NUMBER**.

429) Click **Cell B4**. Enter **A**. Click **Cell C4**. Enter **B**.

430) Click **Cell D4**. Enter **C**. Click **Cell E4**. Enter **D**. Note: D3@LPattern1 appears.

431) Delete and enter **D**.

Increase the Column A width.
432) Click the **vertical line** between Column A and Column B in the Column frame.

433) Drag the **vertical line** to the right until ORDER NUMBER is completely displayed.

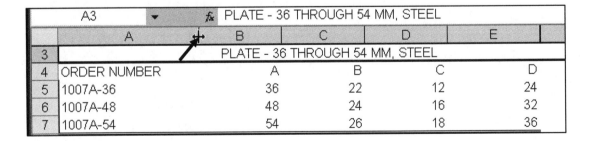

Format the A, B, C, and D Column text. The procedure will be different depending on your version of Excel.

434) Click **Cell B4.**

435) Hold the left mouse button down.

436) Drag the mouse pointer to **Cell E7**.

437) Release the left mouse button.

438) Right-click **Format Cells**.

439) Click the **Alignment** tab.

440) Click **Center** from the Horizontal drop down list.

441) Click **OK**.

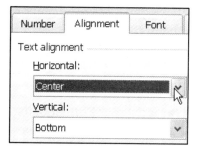

Format Column G for COST.

442) Click **Cell G4**. Enter **COST**.

443) Drag the mouse pointer to **Cell G7**.

444) Right-click **Format Cells**.

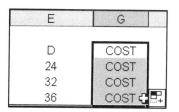

445) Click the **Number** tab.

446) Click **Currency** from the Category list. The default Decimal place is 2.

447) Click **OK**.

448) Click **Cell G5**.

449) Enter **100**. The currency value $100.00 is displayed.

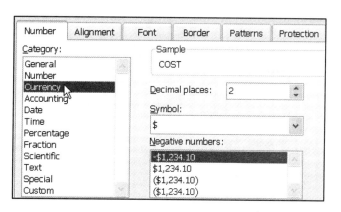

450) Click **Cell G5**. The Fill handle is located in the bottom right corner of the cell.

451) Position the **mouse pointer** over the small black square. The mouse pointer displays a black cross.

452) Click the **left mouse button**.

453) Drag the **mouse pointer** downward to **Cell G7**. The value $100.00 is displayed in Cell G6 and Cell G7.

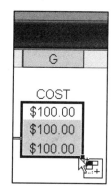

Remove Gridlines.
454) Click **Tools**, **Options** from the Microsoft Excel Main menu.

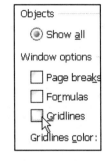

455) Click the **View** tab.

456) Uncheck the **Gridlines** check box.

457) Click **OK**.

Increase the title size.
458) Click **Cell A3**.

459) Right-click **Format Cells**.

460) Click the **Font** tab.

461) Select **14** for Size.

462) Click **OK**.

Add Borders.
463) Click **Cell A3**.

464) **Hold** the left mouse button down.

465) Drag the mouse pointer to **Cell G7**

466) **Release** the left mouse button.

467) Right-click **Format Cells**.

468) Click the **Border** tab.

469) Click the **Outline** button.

470) Select the **double line border** Style.

471) Click **OK**.

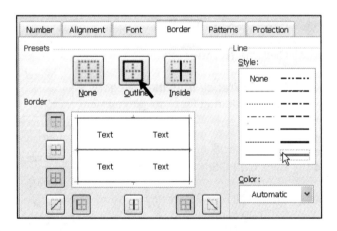

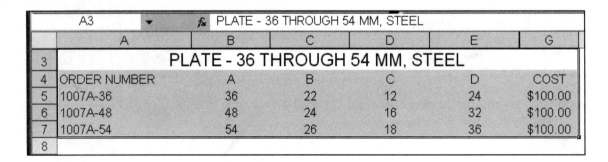

A3		f_x	PLATE - 36 THROUGH 54 MM, STEEL		
	A	B	C	D	E	G
3	PLATE - 36 THROUGH 54 MM, STEEL					
4	ORDER NUMBER	A	B	C	D	COST
5	1007A-36	36	22	12	24	$100.00
6	1007A-48	48	24	16	32	$100.00
7	1007A-54	54	26	18	36	$100.00
8						

Add pattern color.

472) Click **Cell A4**. **Hold** the left mouse button down.

473) Drag the mouse pointer to **Cell G4**

474) Release the left mouse button.

475) Right-click **Format Cells**.

476) Click the **Patterns** tab.

477) Select a **light blue color** for shading.

478) Click **OK**.

479) Click **Cell A4**. **Hold** the left mouse button down.

480) Drag the mouse pointer to **Cell A7**

481) Release the left mouse button.

482) Right-click **Format Cells**.

483) Click **Patterns**.

484) Select a **light blue color** for shading.

485) Click **OK**.

A4		f_x	ORDER NUMBER			
	A	B	C	D	E	G
3	PLATE - 36 THROUGH 54 MM, STEEL					
4	ORDER NUMBER	A	B	C	D	COST
5	1007A-36	36	22	12	24	$100.00
6	1007A-48	48	24	16	32	$100.00
7	1007A-54	54	26	18	36	$100.00
8						

The Family Cell indicates the start of the SolidWorks parameters.

Create comment rows above and columns to the right of the Family Cell. The Family Cell displays the word, Family in the Name box. The text Family does not display in the Cell or Formula area.

Family		f_x	
	A		B
3	PLATE - 36		
4	ORDER NUMBER		A
5	1007A-36		36
6	1007A-48		48
7	1007A-54		54
8			

You inserted comments into Row 3 and Row 4. Move Family Cell Row 2 below Row 4 for the Design Table to work properly. The procedure will be different depending on your version of Excel.

Unhide Row 1 and Row 2.
486) Right-click on the **Row 3 top line** in the Row frame.

487) Click **Unhide**.

488) Perform the same procedure for Row 2.

Cut/Insert Row 2.
489) Select **Row 2** in the Row frame.

490) Right-click **Cut**.

491) Select **Row 5** in the Row frame.

492) Right-click **Insert Cut Cells**. The dimension parameters row is below the ORDER NUMBER row.

Insert the Cost Custom Property.
493) Click **Cell G4**. Enter **$prp@cost**.

	A	B	C	D	E	G
1	Design Table for: PLATE-CATALOG					
2	PLATE - 36 THROUGH 54 MM, STEEL					
3	ORDER NUMBER	A	B	C	D	COST
4		D1@Sketch1	D1@Sketch2	D2@Sketch3	D3@LPattern1	$prp@cost
5	1007A-36	36	22	12	24	$100.00
6	1007A-48	48	24	16	32	$100.00
7	1007A-54	54	26	18	36	$100.00
8						

Column Custom Properties in the Design Table are accessible as Linked Notes in the Drawing.

Insert a new Column.
494) Select **Column A** in the Column frame.

495) Right-click **Insert**.

496) Enter **Catalog Title** in Cell A2 for comment.

497) Enter **Catalog Values** in Cell A3.

498) Double-click the **Column A – Column B** frame to resize the column width.

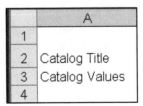

Verify the B4 Family Cell.
499) Click **Cell B4**. The word, Family appears in the Name box.

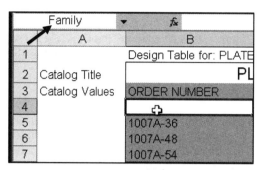

☀ Enter the text, Family in the Name Box for the Cell name if required.

Hide Rows and Columns.
500) Select **Row1**.

501) Right-click **Hide**.

502) Select **Row4**.

503) Right-click **Hide**.

504) Select **Column A** in the Column frame.

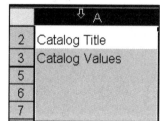

505) Right-click **Hide**.

	B	C	D	E	F	H	I
2	PLATE - 36 THROUGH 54 MM, STEEL						
3	ORDER NUMBER	A	B	C	D	COST	
5	1007A-36	36	22	12	24	$100.00	
6	1007A-48	48	24	16	32	$100.00	
7	1007A-54	54	26	18	36	$100.00	
8							

Save and Update EXCEL.
506) Click **File**, **Save Copy As** from the EXCEL Main menu.

507) **Browse** and **select** the DRAWING-W-SOLIDWORKS 2012 folder.

508) Enter **TABLE-PLATE-CATALOG** to save a copy in EXCEL format.

509) Click **Save**.

Update the linked Design Table in SolidWorks.
510) Click **File**, **Update** from the EXCEL Main menu.

511) Click **File**, **Exit** from the EXCEL Main menu.

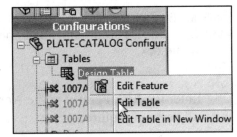

Return to SolidWorks and the PLATE-CATALOG part.
512) Right-click **Design Table** from the FeatureManager.

513) Click **Edit Table**.

514) Resize the EXCEL window to display Cell B2
      through H7. The Design Table window in the part
      determines the Design Table display in the drawing.

	B	C	D	E	F	H
2	PLATE - 36 THROUGH 54 MM, STEEL					
3	ORDER NUMBER	A	B	C	D	COST
5	1007A-36	36	22	12	24	$100.00
6	1007A-48	48	24	16	32	$100.00
7	1007A-54	54	26	18	36	$100.00
8						
9						

Insert a Design Table into the drawing.
515) Press **Ctrl-Tab** to display the PLATE-CATALOG
      drawing.

516) Click inside the **Drawing View1** boundary.

517) Click **Design Table** from the Annotation toolbar.

518) Drag the **Design Table** below the Front view.

Enlarge the Design Table.
519) Right-click the **Design Table**.

520) Click **Reset Size**.

521) Drag the **corner handle** to the right.

522) Click **inside** the sheet.

As an exercise, add Center Marks and
Centerlines to complete the PLATE-CATALOG drawing.

Save the PLATE-CATALOG drawing.

523) Click **Save** 💾 .

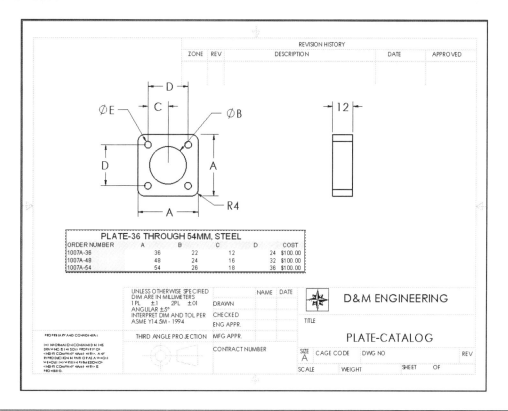

PLATE-36 THROUGH 54MM, STEEL					
ORDER NUMBER	A	B	C	D	COST
1007A-36	36	22	12	24	$100.00
1007A-48	48	24	16	32	$100.00
1007A-54	54	26	18	36	$100.00

🔆 Save Time, Reuse Design Tables and their parameters. You saved the Design Table, TABLE-PLATE-CATALOG.XLS as an Excel Spread Sheet. Insert Excel Spread Sheets into other part and assembly documents. Utilize Insert, Design Table, From File option.

Utilize consistent names in Design Tables. Example: $PRP:Material is the variable name for Material in all Design Tables. Utilize the comment entry "ORDER NUMBER" in the same Cell location for all Catalog drawings. Insert Comments above and to the left of the Family Name Cell.

Plan your Catalog drawings. Identify the comments and the parameters to display in the drawing. Insert additional comments, formulas and values not required in a Design Table by leaving a blank column or row. The Design Table does not evaluate Cell entries placed after the column space.

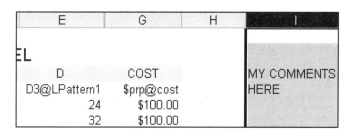

Blocks

Blocks can be used to create standard notes, labels and any other custom symbols that SolidWorks does not provide. Blocks consist of the following elements: *text*, *sketched entities*, *Area Hatch* and *Single Balloon*. Blocks are symbols that exist on one or more drawings. Save Blocks in the current file folder or create a symbol library.

Set the Block file folder location in Tools, Options, System Options, File Locations when creating symbol libraries.

In the next example, make a new Block. Combine text and a rectangle. Save the Block to the current file folder. Insert the new Block. Modify the Properties of the Block.

The Block PropertyManager controls the Source Name of the Block to insert. Specify Location by selecting a position with the mouse pointer or entering the exact X, Y coordinates.

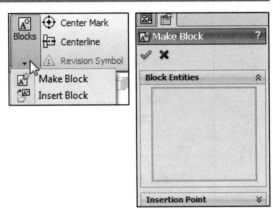

Scale and Rotate a Block in Block Display. Select Leader arrow style and Layer for the Block.

Insert an Empty View. Insert sketch geometry and annotations. The new geometry references the Empty View.

🔆 An Empty View is not required to create a Block. Block geometry can reference the sheet.

The Design Library, Add File Location option, creates a reference to a folder that contains Blocks. Position the mouse pointer on the Block icon to display a preview.

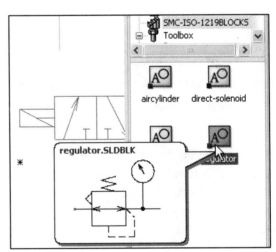

🔆 Blocks can be created from sketch geometry and notes and be used locally (within a drawing) or be saved to a file for use in any drawing.

Activity: Blocks

Insert an Empty View.

524) Click **Insert**, **Drawing View**, **Empty** from the Menu bar menu.

525) Click a **position** to the right of the PLATE-CATALOG Right view.

526) Right-click the **Empty view boundary**.

527) Click **Lock View Focus**. The blue view boundary, with filled corners indicates a locked view. Added geometry will reference the Empty view.

Add Notes.

528) Click **Note** $\mathbf{A}$ from the Annotation toolbar.

529) Click a **position** inside the Empty view; Drawing View3.

530) Click the **No Leader** box.

531) Enter **Questions on delivery?**

532) Press the **enter** key.

533) Enter **Call 1-800-555-0000** on the second line.

534) Select the **text**.

535) Modify the Font height to **5mm**.

536) Click **OK** from the Note Property Manager.

Questions on Delivery?
Call 1-800-555-0000

537) Click **Note** $\mathbf{A}$ from the Annotation toolbar.

538) Click a **position** to the left of the Note.

539) Click **No Leader** .

540) Enter **?**.

Question on delivery?
Call 1-800-555-0000

541) Click **OK** from the Note Property Manager.

542) Click the **?** mark. The Note PropertyManager is displayed.

543) Expand the Border dialog box.

544) Select **Circular** from the drop-down menu. Tight Fit is selected by default.

545) Uncheck the Use document font box.

546) Click the **Font** button.

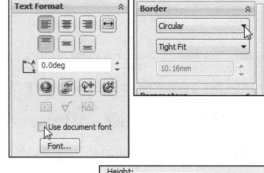

547) Select **14**mm for Font height.

548) Click **OK** from the Choose Font dialog box.

549) Click **OK** ✅ from the Note PropertyManager.

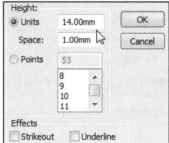

Sketch a rectangle around the two Notes.

550) Click **Corner Rectangle** ▣ from the Sketch toolbar.

551) Sketch a **rectangle** around the two notes as illustrated.

552) Click **OK** ✅ from the Rectangle PropertyManager.

Display the Line Format toolbar. Modify the Line color and thickness.

553) Click **View**, **Toolbars**, **Line Format** from the Menu bar menu. The Line Format toolbar is displayed.

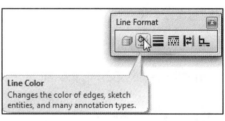

554) Click the **Line Color** 🖊 tool from the Line Format toolbar.

555) Select a **Blue Color Swatch**.

556) Click **OK**.

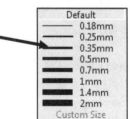

557) Click the **Line Thickness** ≡ tool from the Line Format toolbar.

558) Select **Medium** Thickness.

Create a new Block.

559) Click inside the **Sheet** boundary.

560) Hold the **Ctrl** key down.

561) Select the two **Notes** and the **Rectangle**.

562) Release the **Ctrl** key.

563) Click **Make Block** from the consolidated Blocks toolbar. The selected block entities are displayed in the Block Entities dialog box.

564) Click **OK** ✓ from the Make Block PropertyManager. Blocks is displayed in the drawing FeatureManager.

Save the Block.

565) Click **Tools**, **Block**, **Save** from the Menu bar menu.

566) Enter **QUESTION-BLOCK** for File name.

567) Click **Save**. Note: Blocks contain the file extension .sldblk.

Position the Block.

568) Drag the **Empty view** to the right side of the sheet boundary. The QUESTION-BLOCK moves with the Empty view.

Save the PLATE-CATALOG drawing.

569) Click **Save** 🖫 .

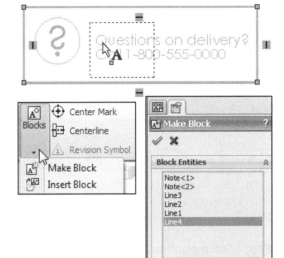

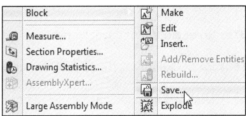

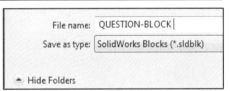

The Block contains one insertion point. Insert the Block into the PLATE-TUBE drawing. Modify the scale and layer for the QUESTION-BLOCK.

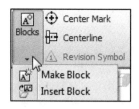

Insert a Block.
570) Open the PLATE-TUBE drawing.

571) Click a **position** to the right of the Front view.

572) Click **Insert Block** from the Annotation toolbar.

573) Click the **Browse** button.

574) Double-click **QUESTION-BLOCK**.

575) Click a **position** to the right of the Front view. The Block is displayed.

576) Click **OK** 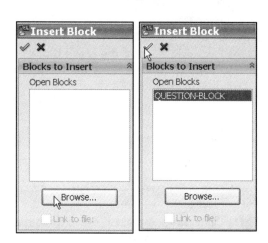 from the Insert Block PropertyManager.

Create a new layer.
577) Click **Layer Properties** from the Layer toolbar.

578) Click the **New** button.

579) Enter **Notes** for Layer Name.

580) Enter **Customer Notes** for Description.

581) Click **OK** from the Layers dialog box.

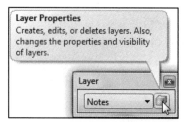

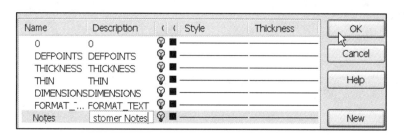

Modify the Properties of the block.

582) Click **QUESTION-BLOCK** in the Sheet. The QUESTION-BLOCK PropertyManager is displayed.

583) Enter **0.9** for Block Scaling.

584) Select **Notes** from the Layer drop-down menu.

585) Click **OK** ✔ from the QUESTION-BLOCK PropertyManager.

Save the PLATE-TUBE drawing.

586) Click **Save** 🖫.

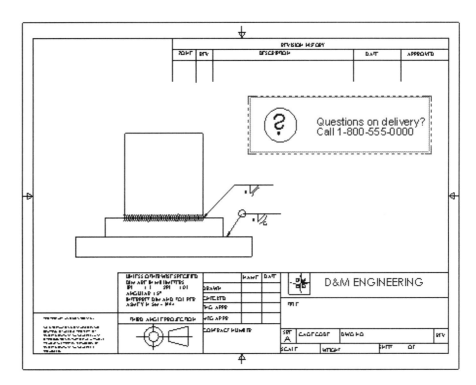

Additional Information

Blocks

Utilize Blocks in a drawing to represent components for pneumatic, mechanical and HVAC systems.

Example: Import the .dxf file ISO-1219 pneumatic symbols. Select the drawing option on Import. Create individual Blocks in SolidWorks.

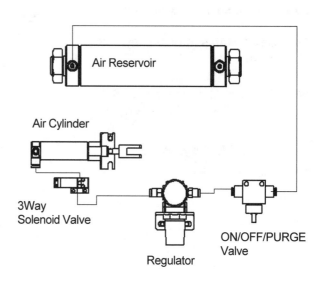

Pneumatic Components Diagram
Courtesy of SMC Corporation of America and
Gears Educational Systems.

Utilize Blocks in the exercises at the end of this project. Each pneumatic symbol is a separate Block. Sketch lines connect the symbols to display the airflow.

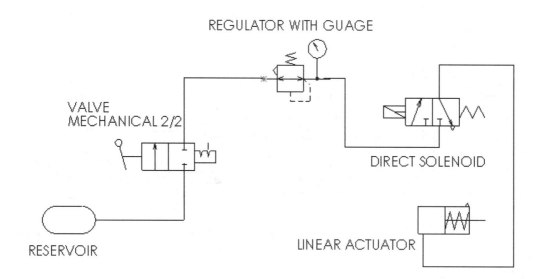

ISO-1219 Symbols – Blocks
Courtesy of SMC Corporation of America

Geometric Tolerance Symbols

A relationship exists between the Geometric Tolerance Symbols and the lower case letters in the SW-GDT Font. In EXCEL, select the SW-GDT Font type for Column H.

The letters, a through z, display various Geometric Tolerancing, and Hole Symbols.

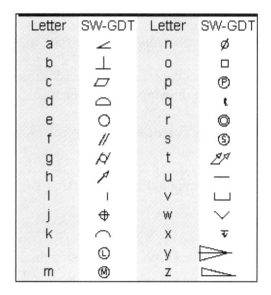

Types of Fits

Utilize Fit tolerances for dimensions for shafts and holes. The Tolerance options are Fit, Fit with tolerance, Fit (tolerance only). The Classification options User Defined, Clearance, Transitional and Press. There are Hole Fit and Shaft

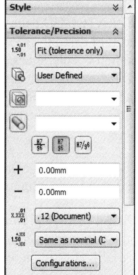

Fit designations depending on the geometry. An example utilizing Fit with Design Tables is explored in the chapter exercises. See SolidWorks Help for additional information.

☀ The SolidWorks 2012 Reference Guide is available online in .pdf format. The .pdf document contains additional tools and options.

The project exercises explore additional techniques with symbols, Hole Tables, Types of Fits in the drawing. The Appendix explores 2D-3D conversion and layout sketches.

Chapter Summary

You created five drawings: VALVEPLATE1, VALVEPLATE1-GDT, VALVEPLATE1-GDT eDrawing, PLATE-TUBE, PLATE-CATALOG. You modified the ASME14-41 drawing.

You created the VALVEPLATE1 drawing. You opened the VALVEPLATE1 part. Applied the DimXpert tool using the Plus and Minus option. Inserted dimensions and Geometric tolerances. Created the VALVEPLATE1 drawing using the View Palette tool. Inserted three drawing views. Inserted a Centerline and Hide Tangent Edges in the Right view. Displayed None and Bilateral tolerance.

You created the VALVEPLATE1-GDT drawing. You opened the VALVEPLATE1-GDT part. Apply the DimXpert tool using the Geometric option. Inserted Datums, Feature Control Frames, and Geometric Tolerances. Edited the Feature Control Frames. Created the VALVEPLATE1-GDT drawing with the View Palette tool. Inserted three drawing views. Inserted the Surface Finish symbol on the Top and Right view. Created multiple Leaders to the Surface Finish symbol. Inserted Hide Tangent Edges in the Top and Right view.

You created the VALVEPLATE1-GDT eDrawing. The VALVEPLATE1-GDT eDrawing is a compressed stand alone document.

You modified the ASME14-41 drawing. Manually inserted Datums, Feature Control Frames, Dimensions, and Geometric tolerances into an Isometric view on multiply drawing sheets. The ASME14-41 drawing consisted of five sheets.

You created the PLATE-TUBE drawing. Inserted the Weld Bead assembly feature between the TUBE and PLATE parts in the PLATE-TUBE assembly.

Added a second PLATE component to the PLATE-TUBE assembly. Created a Weld Symbol as a separate annotation in the PLATE-TUBE drawing.

You created the PLATE-CATALOG drawing. The PLATE-CATALOG drawing utilized a Design Table.

Chapter Terminology

ASME: American Society of Mechanical Engineering, publisher of ASME Y14 Engineering Drawing and Documentation Practices that controls drawing, dimensioning and tolerancing.

AWS: American Welding Society, publisher of AWS A2.4, Standard Location of Elements of a Welding Symbol.

Block: A symbol in the drawing that combines geometry into a single entity.

Cell: Area to enter a value in an EXCEL spreadsheet, identified by a Row and Column.

Component: A part or sub-assembly within an assembly.

Configurations: Variations of a part or assembly that control dimensions, display and state of a model.

CommandManager: The CommandManager is a Context-sensitive toolbar that dynamically updates based on the toolbar you want to access. By default, it has toolbars embedded in it based on the document type. When you click a tab below the Command Manager, it updates to display that toolbar. For example, if you click the **Sketches** tab, the Sketch toolbar is displayed.

ConfigurationManager: The ConfigurationManager is located on the left side of the SolidWorks window and provides the means to create, select, and view multiple configurations of parts and assemblies in an active document. You can split the ConfigurationManager and either display two ConfigurationManager instances, or combine the ConfigurationManager with the FeatureManager design tree, PropertyManager, or third party applications that use the panel.

Copy and Paste: Utilize copy/paste to copy views from one sheet to another sheet in a drawing or between different drawings.

Datum Feature: An annotation that represents the primary, secondary and other reference planes of a model utilized in manufacturing.

Design Table: An Excel spreadsheet that is used to create multiple configurations in a part or assembly document.

Dimension: A value indicating the size of feature geometry.

Dimension Line: A line that references dimension text to extension lines indicating the feature being measured.

Dimension Tolerance: Controls the dimension tolerance values and the display of non-integer dimensions. The tolerance types are *None, Basic, Bilateral, Limit, Symmetric, MIN, MAX, Fit, Fit with tolerance,* or *Fit (tolerance only).*

DimXpert for Parts: A set of tools that applies dimensions and tolerances to parts according to the requirements of the ASME Y.14.41-2003 standard.

Document: A file containing a part, assembly, or drawing.

Drawing: A 2D representation of a 3D part or assembly.

Edit Sheet Format: The drawing sheet contains two modes. Utilize the Edit Sheet Format command to add or modify notes and Title block information. Edit in the Edit Sheet Format mode.

eDrawing: A compressed document that does not require the referenced part or assembly. eDrawings are animated to display multiple views in a drawing.

Exploded view: A configuration in an assembly that displays its components separated from one another

Export: The process to save a SolidWorks document in another format for use in other CAD/CAM, rapid prototyping, web, or graphics software applications.

Family Cell: A named empty cell in a Design Table that determines indicates the start of the evaluated parameters and configuration names. Locate Comments in a Design Table to the left or above the Family Cell.

FeatureManager: The FeatureManager design tree located on the left side of the SolidWorks window provides an outline view of the active part, assembly, or drawing. This makes it easy to see how the model or assembly was constructed or to examine the various sheets and views in a drawing. The FeatureManager and the Graphics window are dynamically linked. You can select features, sketches, drawing views, and construction geometry in either pane.

First Angle Projection: Standard 3 Views are in either third angle or first angle projection. In first angle projection, the front view is displayed at the upper left and the other two views are the top and left views.

Fully defined: A sketch where all lines and curves in the sketch, and their positions, are described by dimensions or relations, or both, and cannot be moved. Fully defined sketch entities are displayed in black.

Geometric Tolerance Symbol: Set of standard symbols that specify the geometric characteristics and dimensional requirements of a feature.

Hole Table: A table in a drawing document that displays the positions of selected holes from a specified origin datum. The tool labels each hole with a tag. The tag corresponds to a row in the table.

Line Format: A series of tools that controls Line Thickness, Line Style, Color, Layer and other properties.

Parametric Note: A Note annotation that links text to a feature dimension or property value.

Precision: The number of decimal places displayed for a dimension value.

Revision Table: The Revision Table lists the Engineering Change Orders (ECO), in a table form, issued over the life of the model and the drawing. The current Revision letter or number is placed in the Title block of the Drawing.

Sheet: A page in a drawing document.

Surface Finish: An annotation that represents the texture of a part.

Weld Bead: An assembly feature that represents a weld between multiple parts.

Weld Symbol: An annotation in the part or drawing that represents the parameters of the weld.

Questions:

1. Datum Feature, Geometric Tolerance, Surface Finish and Weld Symbols are located in the _____ Toolbar.

2. True or False. A SolidWorks part file is a required attachment to email a SolidWorks eDrawing.

3. Describe the procedure to create a Basic dimension.

4. Dimensions on the drawing are displayed with three decimal places. You require two decimal places on all dimensions except for one diameter dimension. Identify the correct Document Property options.

5. Describe the procedure to create a Unilateral Tolerance.

6. Datum Symbols A, B and C in the VALVEPLATE1 drawing represent the _____, _____, and _____ reference planes.

7. Describe the procedure to attach a Feature Control Frame to a dimension.

8. Surface Finish symbols are applied in the _____ and in the _____.

9. Describe the procedure to create multiple leader lines that attach to the same symbol.

10. A Weld Bead is created in the _____. A Weld Symbol is created in the _____.

11. _____ combine text and sketched entities, Area Hatch and single Balloons to create symbols in a drawing document.

12. Format Design Tables using _____.

13. True or False. In a Minimum Content Drawing, the designer adds every dimension in the drawing in order to manufacture the part.

14. Describe the purpose of a Family Cell in a Design Table.

15. Identify the annotations created in the part and inserted into the drawing.

16. In your opinion, why would a Rapid Prototype manufacturer accept a Minimum Content Drawing or an eDrawing from a designer?

Exercises:

Exercise 9.1:

Create a new drawing for the part, ANGLEPLATE2 located in the DRAWING-W-SOLIDWORKS 2012\Exercise file folder.

Insert a Front view, Bottom view,gand Auxiliary view. Use Geometric relations when constructing centerlines. The centerline drawn between the Front view and the Auxiliary view is perpendicular to the angled edge.

Insert the Feature Control Frame before applying Datum Reference Symbols, (Example Datum E).

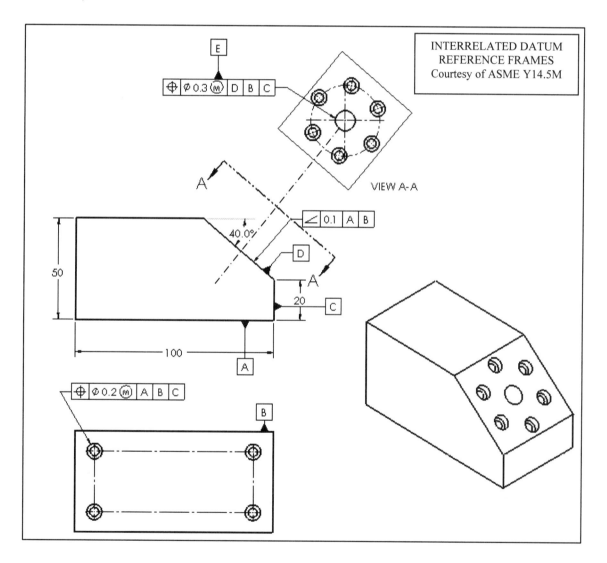

Exercise 9.2:

Create a new drawing for the part, FIG5-28 located in the DRAWING-W-SOLIDWORKS-2012\Exercises file folder. View A is created with an Auxiliary view from the angled edge in the Right view. Crop the Auxiliary view.

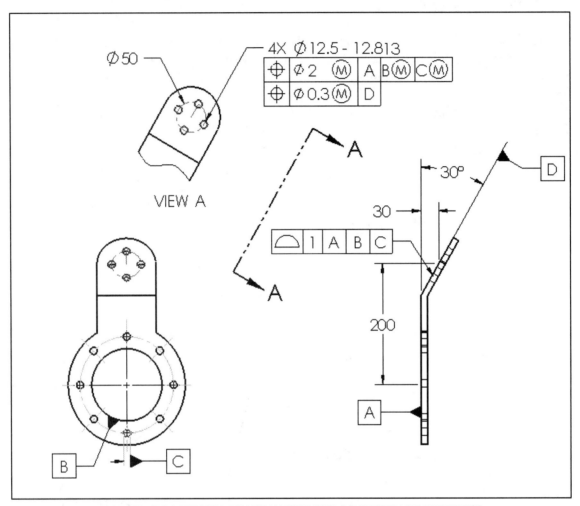

MULTIPLE POSITIONAL TOLERANCING FOR A PATTERN OF FEATURES
COURTESY ASME Y14.5M

Use spaces to align Feature Control Frames 1 and 2.

Insert Datum Feature Symbols to circular pattern features. Utilize a Linear Diameter Dimension.

Modify the Display options to display only the Second Dimension line.

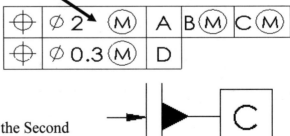

Exercise 9.3:

Investigate three different fits for a 16mm shaft and a 16mm hole using the HOLE part, SHAFT part and HOLE-SHAFT assembly configurations, Table 9.1.

TabLE 9.1 TYPE of FIT (MILLIMETERS ASME B4.2)				
Type of Fit	MAX/MIN	HOLE	SHAFT	FIT
Close Running Fit	MAX	16.043	16.000	0.061
	MIN	16.016	15.982	0.016
Loose Running Fit	MAX	16.205	16.000	0.315
	MIN	16.095	15.890	0.095
Free Sliding Fit	MAX	16.024	16.000	0.035
	MIN	16.006	15.989	0.006

Create the HOLE part. Use the nominal dimension ∅16mm for the Hole feature and ∅16mm for the diameter of the Shaft. Set units to millimeters, 3 decimal places. Insert a Design Table for the HOLE that contains 6 different configurations.

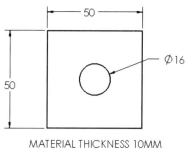

Create the SHAFT part. Insert a Design Table for the SHAFT that contains 6 different configurations. The Min value is before the Max value. Format the columns in Excel to three decimal places.

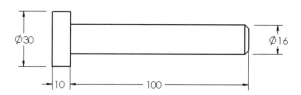

Create the HOLE-SHAFT assembly. Insert a new Design Table into the assembly that contains 6 configurations

	A	B	C	D	E
1	Design Table for: HOLE-SHAFT				
2		$CONFIGURATION@HOLE<1>	$STATE@HOLE<1>	$CONFIGURATION@SHAFT<1>	$STATE@SHAFT<1>
3	CLOSE-MAX	H-CLOSE-MAX	R	S-CLOSE-MIN	R
4	CLOSE-MIN	H-CLOSE-MIN	R	S-CLOSE-MAX	R
5	LOOSE-MAX	H-LOOSE-MAX	R	S-LOOSE-MIN	R
6	LOOSE-MIN	H-LOOSE-MIN	R	S-LOOSE-MAX	R
7	FREE-MAX	H-FREE-MAX	R	S-FREE-MIN	R
8	FREE-MIN	H-FREE-MIN	R	S-FREE-MAX	R

Create a new Excel document, HOLE-SHAFT-COMBINED.XLS. Copy cells A3 through A8 in the Design Table HOLE-SHAFT to column A. Copy cells B3 through B8 in the Design Table HOLE to column B. Copy cells B3 through B8 in the Design Table SHAFT to column C. Insert the formula =B2-C2 in column D to calculate the Fit.

HOLD-SHAFT-COMBINED

	A	B	C	D
1		HOLE	SHAFT	FIT
2	CLOSE-MAX	16.043	15.982	0.061
3	CLOSE-MIN	16.016	16.000	0.016
4	LOOSE-MAX	16.205	15.890	0.315
5	LOOSE-MIN	16.095	16.000	0.095
6	FREE-MAX	16.024	15.989	0.035
7	FREE-MIN	16.006	16.000	0.006

Create a new drawing that contains the HOLE-SHAFT assembly, the SHAFT part and the HOLE part. Insert Balloons for the two components in the assembly. Modify the Ballon Property from Item Number to Custom. Enter H for the HOLE and S for the SHAFT.

Insert the Excel Worksheet, HOLE-SHAFT-COMBINED. Click Insert, Object, Microsoft Excel. Add dimensions.

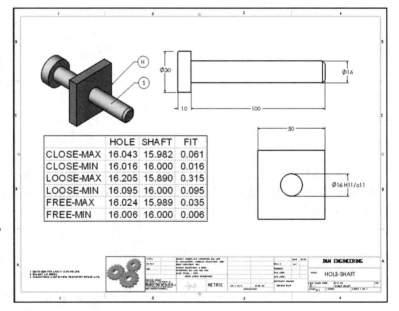

Open the Hole part. Select the LOOSE-MAX configuration. Select Clearance for Type of Fit for ∅16. Select H11 for Hole Fit. Select c11 for Shaft Fit.

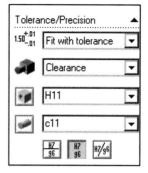

HOLE/SHAFT Metric Fit (ASME B4.2)		
Clearance Fit	Hole	Shaft
Loose running	H11/c11	C11/h11
Free running	H9/d9	D9/h9
Close running	H8/f7	F8/h7

Create a HOLE drawing. Select the HOLE, default configuration for the Front view. Copy the view two times. Select the LOOSE-MAX configuration. The ISO symbol Hole/Shaft Classification is displayed on the Hole diameter dimension. Modify the dimensions in the other two views to create a Free Running and Close Running Clearance Fit.

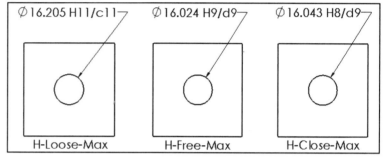

Exercise 9.4:

Create a new drawing for the part, TABLE-PLATE-LABELS located in the DRAWING-W-SOLIDWORKS 2012\Exercises file folder. Insert a Hole Table. A Hole Table displays the positions of selected holes from a specified Origin. The Hole Table tool labels each hole with a tag, which corresponds to a row in the Hole Table in the drawing.

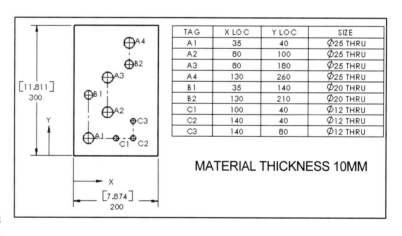

TAG	X LOC	Y LOC	SIZE
A1	35	40	∅25 THRU
A2	80	100	∅25 THRU
A3	80	180	∅25 THRU
A4	130	260	∅25 THRU
B1	35	140	∅20 THRU
B2	130	210	∅20 THRU
C1	100	40	∅12 THRU
C2	140	40	∅12 THRU
C3	140	80	∅12 THRU

MATERIAL THICKNESS 10MM

Utilize Insert, Tables, Hole Table. Select the lower left vertex for Hole Origin. Select the front face of the Front view for Holes. Insert Center Marks, overall dimensions and a Parametric note for Material Thickness. The Parametric note links to the depth dimension.

Exercise 9.5:

A U.S. company designs components and specifies basic welding joints in inch units. Two ½ inch plates are welded together with an intermittent fillet weld to form a T shape. The BASE PLATE is 19.00in x 6.00in.

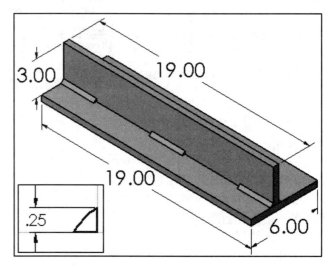

The SECOND PLATE is 19.00in x 3.00in. The .25in Radius weld is placed on both sides of the SECOND PLATE. The weld bead is placed at 8.00in intervals. Parts, assembly and drawings are in inch units, 2 decimal places.

Create the BASE PLATE and SECOND PLATE parts. Create the T-PLATE assembly. A SolidWorks Weld Bead Assembly Feature creates a continuous bead.

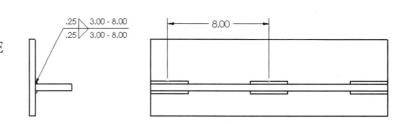

Create the Weld Bead part with a .25in Radius. Insert a Component Pattern, Linear Pattern in the assembly.

Create a T-PLATE drawing. Insert a Weld Symbol on the Arrow side option and the Other side option. Add dimensions to complete the drawing.

Exercise 9.6:

Import the DRAWING-WITH-SOLIDWORKS 2012\EXERCISES\AUTOCAD-DWG\LOGIC-GATES.dwg file as a SolidWorks drawing.

Explode the blocks and increase the line thickness.

Create a new block for each logic gate. Save the blocks. Utilize their logic name for file name.

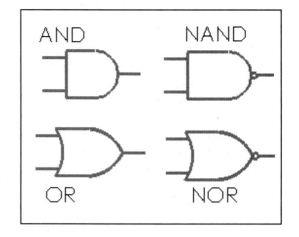

Exercise 9.7:

Create the new drawing, SCHEMATIC
DIAGRAM for the pneumatic
components.

The pneumatic components utilized in
the PNEUMATIC TEST MODULE
Assembly are:

- Air Reservoir

- Regulator

- ON/OFF/PURGE Valve –
  Mechanical 2/2

- 3Way Solenoid Valve

- Air Cylinder – Linear Actuator

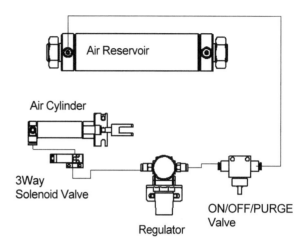

Pneumatic Components Diagram
Courtesy of SMC Corporation of America and
Gears Educational Systems.

ISO-1219 Pneumatic Symbols are created as SolidWorks Blocks. The Blocks are stored
in the Exercise Pneumatic ISO Symbols folder. Utilize the Design Library and create a
new folder location for the ISO-Symbols.

Utilize Insert, Block. Insert the Blocks into a B-size drawing. Enter 0.1 for Scale. Label
each symbol. Utilize the Line tool to connect the pneumatic symbols.

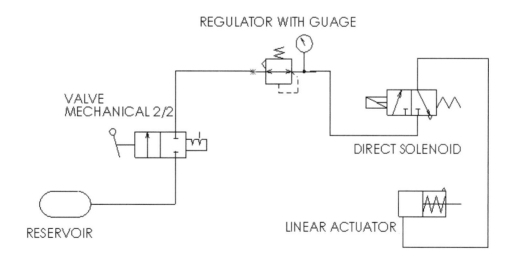

ISO-1219 Symbols
Courtesy of SMC Corporation of America

Notes:

Chapter 10

Introduction to the Certified SolidWorks Associate Exam

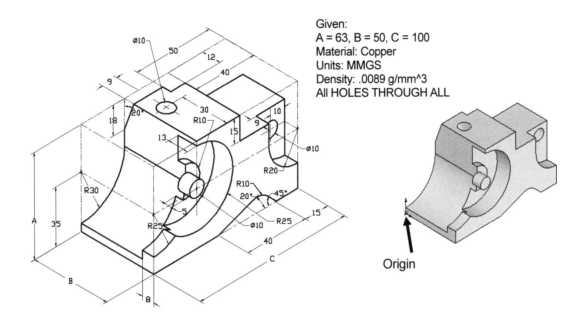

Given:
A = 63, B = 50, C = 100
Material: Copper
Units: MMGS
Density: .0089 g/mm^3
All HOLES THROUGH ALL

Origin

Below are the desired outcomes and usage competencies based on the completion of Chapter 10.

Desired Outcomes:	**Usage Competencies:**
• Procedure and process knowledge	• Familiarity of the CSWA exam.
• Exam categories:	• Comprehension of the skill sets to past the CSWA exam.
○ Drafting Competencies, Basic Part Creation and Modification, Intermediate Part Creation and Modification, Advanced Part Creation and Modification, and Assembly Creation and Modification	• Awareness of the question types.
	• Capability to locate additional CSWA exam information.

Notes:

Chapter 10 - Certified SolidWorks Associate CSWA Exam

Chapter Objective

Provide a basic introduction into the curriculum and categories of the Certified SolidWorks Associate CSWA exam. Awareness to the exam procedure, process, and required model knowledge needed to take and past the CSWA exam. The five exam categories are:

- Drafting Competencies

- Basic Part Creation and Modification

- Intermediate Part Creation and Modification

- Advanced Part Creation and Modification

- Assembly Creation and Modification

Introduction

DS SolidWorks Corp. offers various stages of certification. Each stage representing increasing levels of expertise in 3D CAD design: Certified SolidWorks Associate CSWA, Certified SolidWorks Professional CSWP and Certified SolidWorks Expert CSWE along with specialty fields in Simulation, Sheet Metal, and Surfacing.

The CSWA Certification indicates a foundation in and apprentice knowledge of 3D CAD design and engineering practices and principles. The main requirement for obtaining the CSWA certification is to take and pass the on-line proctored 180 minute exam (minimum of 165 out of 240 points). The new CSWA exam consists of fourteen questions in five categories.

Intended Audience

The intended audience for the CSWA exam is anyone with a minimum of 6 - 9 months of SolidWorks experience and basic knowledge of engineering fundamentals and practices. SolidWorks recommends that you review their SolidWorks Tutorials on Parts, Assemblies, and Drawings as a prerequisite and have at least 45 hours of classroom time learning SolidWorks or using SolidWorks with basic engineering design principles and practices.

To prepare for the CSWA exam, it is recommended that you first perform the following:

- Take a CSWA exam preparation class or review a text book written for the CSWA exam.

- Complete the SolidWorks Tutorials

- Practice creating models from the isometric working drawings sections of any Technical Drawing or Engineering Drawing Documentation text books.

- Complete the sample CSWA exam in a timed environment, available at www.solidworks.com.

Additional references to help you prepare are as follows:

- **SolidWorks Users Guide**, SolidWorks Corporation, 2012.

- ***Official Certified SolidWorks® Associate Examination Guide, Version 3; 2011, 2010, 2009** Planchard & Planchard, SDC Pub., Mission, KS.

- **Engineering Drawing and Design**, Jensen & Helsel, Glencoe, 1990.

- **Drawing and Detailing with SolidWorks**, Planchard & Planchard, SDC Pub., Mission, KS 2010.

*For detail exam information see the Official Certified SolidWorks Associate Examination Guide book. The primary goal of this book is not only to help you pass the CSWA exam, but also to ensure that you understand and comprehend the concepts and implementation details of the CSWA process.

CSWA Exam Content

The CSWA exam is divided into five key categories. Questions on the timed exam are provided in a random manor. The following information provides general guidelines for the content likely to be included on the exam. However, other related topics may also appear on any specific delivery of the exam. In order to better reflect the contents of the exam and for clarity purposes, the guidelines below may change at any time without notice.

- *Drafting Competencies*: (Three questions - multiple choice - 5 points each).

  - Questions on general drawing views: Projected, Section, Break, Crop, Detail, Alternate Position, etc.

- *Basic Part Creation and Modification*: (Two questions - one multiple choice / one single answer - 15 points each).

  - Sketch Planes:

    - Front, Top, Right

  - 2D Sketching:

    - Geometric Relations and Dimensioning

  - Extruded Boss/Base Feature

  - Extruded Cut feature

  - Modification of Basic part

🔅 In the *Basic Part Creation and Modification* category there is a dimension modification.

- *Intermediate Part Creation and Modification*: (Two questions - one multiple choice / one single answer - 15 points each).

  - Sketch Planes:

    - Front, Top, Right

  - 2D Sketching:

    - Geometric Relations and Dimensioning

> A00006: Drafting Competencies - To create drawing view 'B' it is necessary to select drawing view 'A' and insert which SolidWorks view type?

> B22001: Basic Part (Hydraulic Cylinder Half) - Step 1
> Build this part in SolidWorks.
> (Save part after each question in a different file in case it must be reviewed)
>
> Unit system: MMGS (millimeter, gram, second)
> Decimal places: 2
> Part origin: Arbitrary
> All holes through all unless shown otherwise.
> Material: Aluminium 1060 Alloy

Screen shots from the exam.

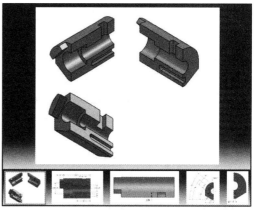

> D12801: Intermediate Part (Wheel) - Step 1
> Build this part in SolidWorks.
> (Save part after each question in a different file in case it must be reviewed)
>
> Unit system: MMGS (millimeter, gram, second)
> Decimal places: 2
> Part origin: Arbitrary
> All holes through all unless shown otherwise.
> Material: Aluminium 1060 Alloy
>
> A = 134.00
> B = 890.00
>
> Note: All geometry is symmetrical about the plane represented by the line labeled F"" in the M-M Section View.
>
> What is the overall mass of the part (grams)?

Screen shots from the exam.

- Extruded Boss/Base Feature

- Extruded Cut Feature

- Revolved Boss/Base Feature

- Mirror and Fillet Feature

- Circular and Linear Pattern Feature

- Plane Feature

- Modification of Intermediate Part:

  - Sketch, Feature, Pattern, etc.

- Modification of Intermediate part

- *Advanced Part Creation and Modification:*
  (Three questions - one multiple choice / two
  single answers - 15 points each).

  - Sketch Planes:

    - Front, Top, Right, Face, Created Plane,
      etc.

    - 2D Sketching or 3D Sketching

  - Sketch Tools:

    - Offset Entities, Convert Entitles, etc.

  - Extruded Boss/Base Feature

  - Extruded Cut Feature

  - Revolved Boss/Base Feature

  - Mirror and Fillet Feature

  - Circular and Linear Pattern Feature

  - Shell Feature

  - Plane Feature

  - More Difficult Geometry Modifications

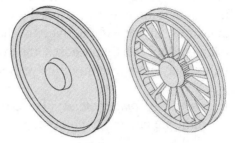

Screen shots from the exam.

C12801: Advanced Part (Bracket) - Step 1
Build this part in SolidWorks.
(Save part after each question in a different file in
case it must be reviewed)

Unit system: MMGS (millimeter, gram, second)
Decimal places: 2
Part origin: Arbitrary
All holes through all unless shown otherwise.
Material: AISI 1020 Steel
Density = 0.0079 g/mm^3

A = 64.00
B = 20.00
C = 26.50

What is the overall mass of the part (grams)?

Screen shots from the exam.

- *Assembly Creation and Modification*: (Two different assemblies - four questions - two multiple choice / two single answers - 30 points each).

  - Insert the first (fixed) component

  - Insert all needed components

  - Standard Mates

  - Modification of key parameters in the assembly

Download the needed components in a zip folder during the exam to create the assembly.

Note: To apply for CSWA Provider status for your institution, go to www.solidWorks.com/cswa and fill out the CSWA Provider application. It is as easy as that.

A total score of 165 out of 240 or better is required to obtain your CSWA Certification.

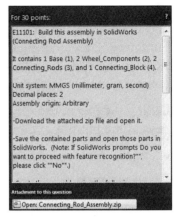

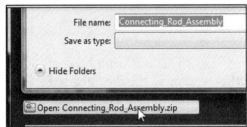

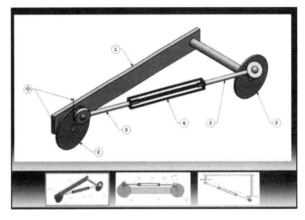

Screen shots from the exam.

⚙ You are allowed to answer the questions in any order. Use the Summary Screen during the CSWA exam to view the list of all questions you have or have not answered.

During the exam, use the control keys at the bottom of the screen to:

- *Show the Previous the Question*

- *Reset the Question*

- *Show the Summary Screen*

- *Move to the Next Question*

⚙ Do NOT use feature recognition when you open the downloaded components for the assembly in the CSWA exam. This is a timed exam. Manage your time. You do not need this information.

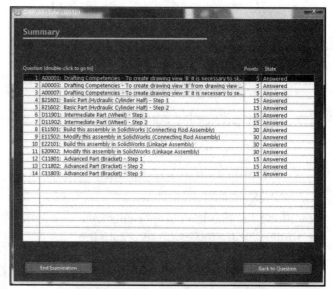

Screen shots from the exam.

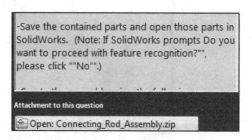

-Save the contained parts and open those parts in SolidWorks. (Note: If SolidWorks prompts Do you want to proceed with feature recognition?"", please click ""No"".)

Attachment to this question

Open: Connecting_Rod_Assembly.zip

During the exam, SolidWorks provides the ability to click on a detail view below (as illustrated) to obtain additional details and dimensions during the exam.

⚙ No Simulation (CosmosXpress) questions are on the CSWA exam.

⚙ No Sheetmetal questions are on the CSWA exam.

⚙ FeatureManager names were changed through various revisions of SolidWorks. Example: Extrude1 vs. Boss-Extrude1. These changes do not affect the models or answers in this book.

⚙ No Surface questions are on the CSWA exam.

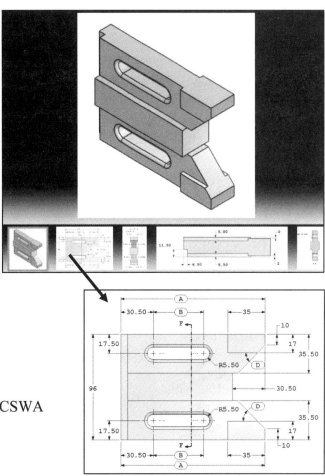

Screen shots from the exam.

About the CSWA exam

Most CAD professionals today recognize the need to become certified to prove their skills, prepare for new job searches, and to learn new skill, while at their existing jobs.

Specifying a CSWA or CSWP certification on your resume is a great way to increase your chances of landing a new job, getting a promotion, or looking more qualified when representing your company on a consulting job.

Exam Day

You will need:

- A computer with SolidWorks installed on it in a secure environment.

- An internet connection.

- A valid email address.

- A voucher ID code (Provided by the CSWA Provider).

- ID: Student, ID, drivers license, etc.

Log into the Tangix_TesterPRO site (http://www.virtualtester. com/solidworks) and click the Download TesterPRO Client link to start the exam process.

Click the Run button and follow the directions.

After you click the Start Examination button. You have 180 minutes (3 hours) to complete the exam. Good luck!

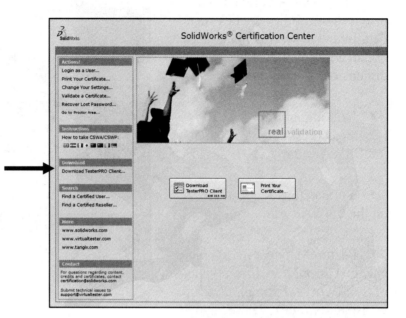

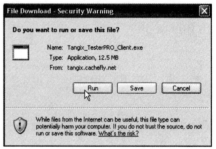

Screen shots from the exam.

The exam generates unique questions for each student.

Click on different images to display additional views as illustrated.

Read the questions slowly, view the additional views, model your part or assembly and then select the correct answer.

The exam uses a multi-question single answer format or a fill in the blank format.

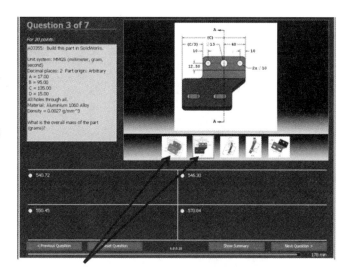

Screen shots from the exam.

In the Basic Part Creation and Modification, Intermediate Part Creation and Modification, Advanced Part Creation and Modification, and Assembly Creation and Modification categories, you will be required to read and interpret all types of drawing views.

Click the Next Question button to procedure to the next question in the exam.

You can also click in the image itself to zoom in on that area.

Below are examples for a part and an assembly screen shot in the CSWA exam.

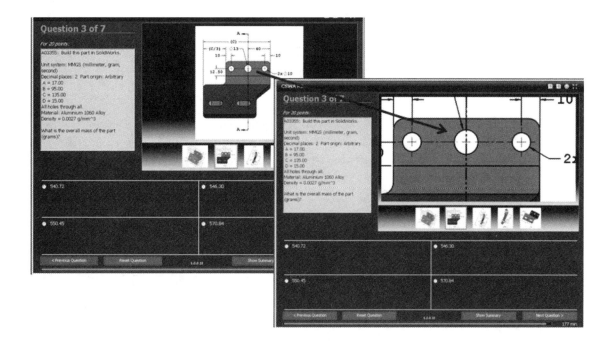

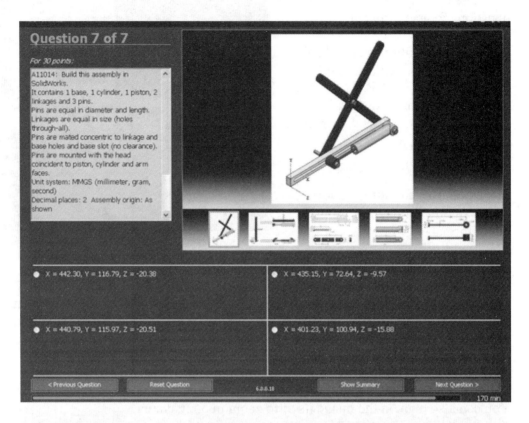

For 30 points:

A11014: Build this assembly in SolidWorks.
It contains 1 base, 1 cylinder, 1 piston, 2 linkages and 3 pins.
Pins are equal in diameter and length.
Linkages are equal in size (holes through-all).
Pins are mated concentric to linkage and base holes and base slot (no clearance).
Pins are mounted with the head coincident to piston, cylinder and arm faces.
Unit system: MMGS (millimeter, gram, second)
Decimal places: 2 Assembly origin: As shown

● X = 442.30, Y = 116.79, Z = -20.38   ● X = 435.15, Y = 72.64, Z = -9.57

● X = 440.79, Y = 115.97, Z = -20.51   ● X = 401.23, Y = 100.94, Z = -15.88

| < Previous Question | Reset Question | 6.0.0.18 | Show Summary | Next Question > |

170 min

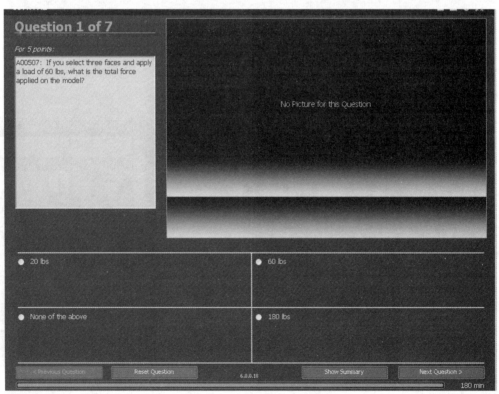

For 5 points:

A00507: If you select three faces and apply a load of 60 lbs, what is the total force applied on the model?

No Picture for this Question

● 20 lbs   ● 60 lbs

● None of the above   ● 180 lbs

| < Previous Question | Reset Question | 6.0.0.18 | Show Summary | Next Question > |

180 min

Click the Show Summary button to display the current status of your exam.

This is a timed exam. Skip a question and move on it you are stuck. You can also go back to the question you skipped anytime in the exam.

At the completion of the exam, Click the End Examination button. Click Yes to confirm.

Candidates receive a score report along with a score breakout by exam section.

For detail exam information see the Official Certified SolidWorks Associate Examination Guide book. The primary goal of this book is not only to help you pass the CSWA exam, but also to ensure that you understand and comprehend the concepts and implementation details of the CSWA process.

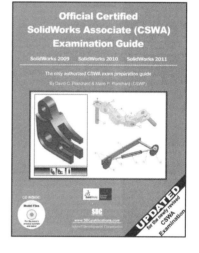

Drafting Competencies

Drafting Competencies is one of the five categories on the CSWA exam. There are three questions - multiple choice format - 5 points each and requires general knowledge and understanding drawing view methods, and basic 3D modeling techniques. Spend no more than 10 minutes on each question in this category for the exam. Manage your time.

A00006: Drafting Competencies - To create drawing view 'B' it is necessary to select drawing view 'A' and insert which SolidWorks view type?

Screen shots from the exam.

Sample Questions in the category

In the *Drafting Competencies* category, an exam question could read:

Question 1: Identify the view procedure. To create the following view, you need to insert a:

- A: Open Spline

- B: Closed Spline

- C: 3 Point Arc

- D: None of the above

The correct answer is B.

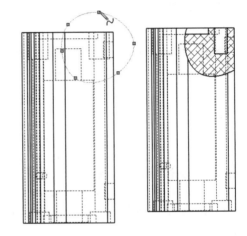

Question 2: Identify the illustrated view type.

- A: Crop view

- B: Section view

- C: Projected view

- D: None of the above

The correct answer is A.

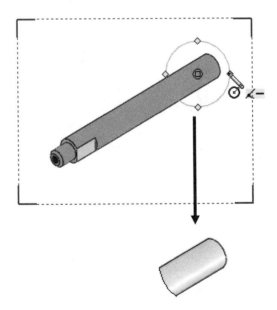

Question 3: Identify the illustrated Drawing view.

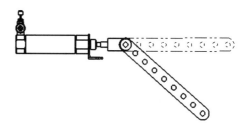

- A: Projected View

- B: Alternative Position View

- C: Extended View

- D: Aligned Section View

The correct answer is B.

Question 4: Identify the illustrated Drawing view.

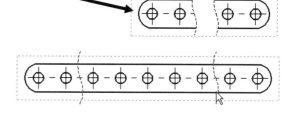

- A: Crop View

- B: Break View

- C: Broken-out Section View

- D: Aligned Section View

The correct answer is B.

Question 5: Identify the illustrated Drawing view.

- A: Section View

- B: Crop View

- C: Broken-out Section View

- D: Aligned Section View

The correct answer is D.

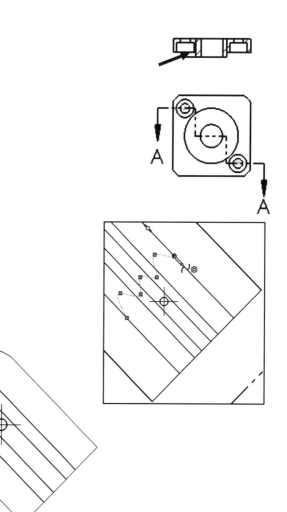

Question 6: Identify the view procedure. To create the following view, you need to insert a:

- A: Rectangle Sketch tool

- B: Closed Profile: Spline

- C: Open Profile: Circle

- D: None of the above

The correct answer is a B.

Basic Part Creation and Modification and Intermediate Part Creation and Modification

Basic Part Creation and Modification and Intermediate Part Creation and Modification is two of the five categories on the CSWA exam.

There are two questions on the CSWA exam in the *Basic Part Creation and Modification* category. One question is in a multiple choice single answer format and the other question (Modification of the model) is in the fill in the blank format. Each question is worth fifteen (15) points for a total of thirty (30) points.

You are required to build a model, with six or more features and to answer a question either on the overall mass, volume, or the location the Center of mass for the created model relative to the default part Origin location. You are then requested to modify the part and answer a fill in the blank format question.

There are two questions on the CSWA exam in the *Intermediate Part Creation and Modification* category. One question is in a multiple choice single answer format and the other question (Modification of the model) is in the fill in the blank format. Each question is worth fifteen (15) points for a total of thirty (30) points.

You are required to build a model, with six or more features and to answer a question either on the overall mass, volume, or the location the Center of mass for the created model relative to the default part Origin location. You are then requested to modify the model and answer a fill in the blank format question.

The main difference between the *Basic Part Creation and Modification* category and the *Intermediate Part Creation and Modification* or the *Advance Part Creation and Modification* category is the complexity of the sketches and the number of dimensions and geometric relations along with an increase in the number of features.

🔆 Spend no more than 40 minutes on the question in these categories. This is a timed exam. Manage your time.

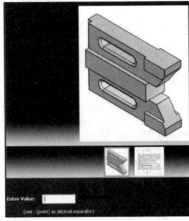

B22001: Basic Part (Hydraulic Cylinder Half) - Step 1
Build this part in SolidWorks.
(Save part after each question in a different file in case it must be reviewed)

Unit system: MMGS (millimeter, gram, second)
Decimal places: 2
Part origin: Arbitrary
All holes through all unless shown otherwise.
Material: Aluminium 1060 Alloy

D12801: Intermediate Part (Wheel) - Step 1
Build this part in SolidWorks.
(Save part after each question in a different file in case it must be reviewed)

Unit system: MMGS (millimeter, gram, second)
Decimal places: 2
Part origin: Arbitrary
All holes through all unless shown otherwise.
Material: Aluminium 1060 Alloy

A = 134.00
B = 890.00

Note: All geometry is symmetrical about the plane represented by the line labeled F'" in the M-M Section View.

What is the overall mass of the part (grams)?

Screen shots from the exam.

Sample Questions in these categories

Question 1: Build the illustrated model from the provided information. Locate the Center of mass relative to the default coordinate system, Origin.

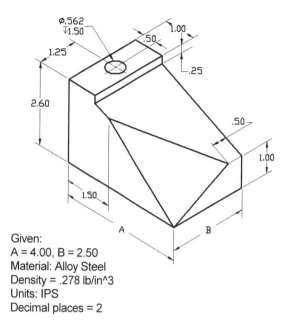

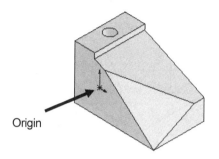

Origin

Given:
A = 4.00, B = 2.50
Material: Alloy Steel
Density = .278 lb/in^3
Units: IPS
Decimal places = 2

- A: X = -1.63 inches, Y = 1.48 inches, Z = -1.09 inches

- B: X = 1.63 inches, Y = 1.01 inches, Z = -0.04 inches

- C: X = 43.49 inches, Y = -0.86 inches, Z = -0.02 inches

- D: X = 1.63 inches, Y = 1.01 inches, Z = -0.04 inches

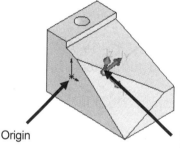

Origin

Center of mass relative to the part Origin

The correct answer is B.

In the *Basic Part Creation and Modification and Intermediate Part Creation and Modification* category of the exam; you are required to read and understand an engineering document, set document properties, identify the correct Sketch planes, apply the correct Sketch and Feature tools, and apply material to build a part.

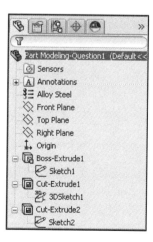

💡 Note the Depth/Deep ⊽ symbol with a 1.50 dimension associated with the hole. The hole Ø.562 has a three decimal place precision. Hint: Insert three features to build this model: Extruded Base, and two Extruded Cuts. Insert a 3D sketch for the first Extruded Cut feature. You are required to have knowledge in 3D sketching for the exam.

💡 All models for this chapter are located on the DVD in the book.

Question 2: Build the illustrated model from the provided information. Locate the Center of mass of the part?

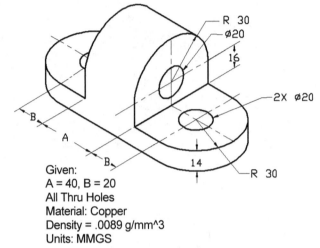

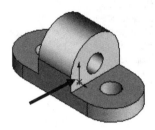

Given:
A = 40, B = 20
All Thru Holes
Material: Copper
Density = .0089 g/mm^3
Units: MMGS

- A: X = 0.00 millimeters, Y = 19.79 millimeters, Z = 0.00 millimeters

- B: X = 0.00 inches, Y = 19.79 inches, Z = 0.04 inches

- C: X = 19.79 millimeters, Y = 0.00 millimeters, Z = 0.00 millimeters

- D: X = 0.00 millimeters, Y = 19.49 millimeters, Z = 0.00 millimeters

- The correct answer is A.

Question 3: Build the illustrated model
from the provided information. Locate the
Center of mass of the part.

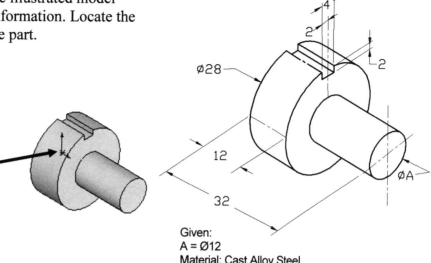

Given:
A = Ø12
Material: Cast Alloy Steel
Density = .0073 g/mm^3
Units: MMGS

- A: X = 10.00 millimeters, Y = -79.79 millimeters,
  Z: = 0.00 millimeters

- B: X = 9.79 millimeters, Y = -0.13 millimeters,
  Z = 0.00 millimeters

- C: X = 9.77 millimeters, Y = -0.10 millimeters,
  Z = -0.02 millimeters

- D: X = 10.00 millimeters, Y = 19.49 millimeters,
  Z = 0.00 millimeters

- The correct answer is B.

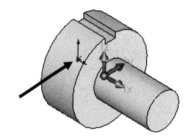

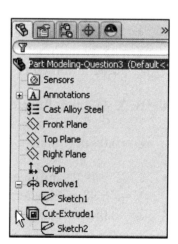

Question 4: Build the illustrated model from the provided information. Locate the Center of mass of the part.

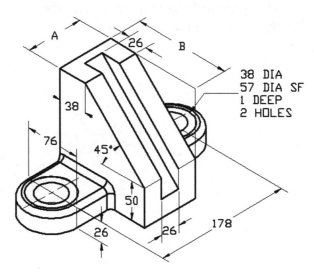

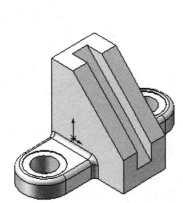

There are numerous ways to build this model. Think about the various features that create the model. Hint: Insert seven features to build this model: Extruded Base, Extruded Cut, Extruded Boss, Fillet, Extruded Cut, Mirror, and a second Fillet. Apply symmetry.

In the exam, create the left half of the model first, and then apply the Mirror feature. This is a timed exam.

- A: X = 49.00 millimeters,
  Y = 45.79 millimeters,
  Z = 0.00 millimeters

- B: X = 0.00 millimeters,
  Y = 19.79 millimeters,
  Z = 0.04 millimeters

- C: X = 49.21 millimeters,
  Y = 46.88 millimeters,
  Z = 0.00 millimeters

- D: X = 48.00 millimeters,
  Y = 46.49 millimeters,
  Z = 0.00 millimeters

The correct answer is C.

Given:
A = 76, B = 127
Material: 2014 Alloy
Density: .0028 g/mm^3
Units: MMGS
ALL ROUNDS EQUAL 6MM

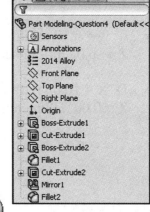

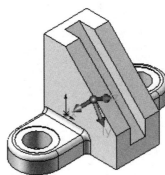

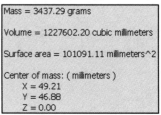

Mass = 3437.29 grams

Volume = 1227602.20 cubic millimeters

Surface area = 101091.11 millimeters^2

Center of mass: (millimeters)
  X = 49.21
  Y = 46.88
  Z = 0.00

Question 5: Build the illustrated model from the provided information. Locate the Center of mass of the part.

🔆 Think about the various features that create this model. Hint: Insert five features to build this part: Extruded Base, two Extruded Bosses, Extruded Cut, and Rib. Insert a Reference plane to create the Extruded Boss feature.

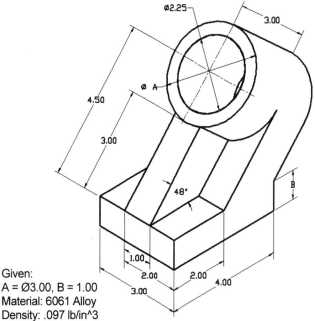

Given:
A = Ø3.00, B = 1.00
Material: 6061 Alloy
Density: .097 lb/in^3
Units: IPS
Decimal places = 2

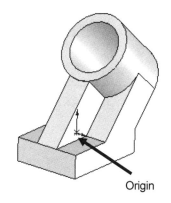

Origin

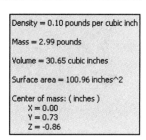

- A: X = 49.00 inches, Y = 45.79 inches, Z = 0.00 inches

- B: X = 0.00 inches, Y = 19.79 inches, Z = 0.04 inches

- C: X = 49.21 inches, Y = 46.88 inches, Z = 0.00 inches

- D: X = 0.00 inches, Y = 0.73 inches, Z = -0.86 inches

The correct answer is D.

🔆 All models for this chapter are located on the DVD in the book.

Advanced Part Creation and Modification

Advanced Part Creation and Modification is one of the five categories on the CSWA exam. The main difference between the *Advanced Part Creation and Modification* and the *Basic Part Creation and Modification* category and the *Intermediate Part Creation and Modification* is the complexity of the sketches and the number of dimensions and geometric relations along with an increase number of features.

There are three questions - one multiple choice / two single answers - 15 points each. The question is either on the location of the Center of mass relative to the default part Origin or to a new created coordinate system and all of the mass properties located in the Mass Properties dialog box: total overall mass, volume, etc.

Sample Questions in the category

In the *Advanced Part Creation and Modification* category, an exam question could read:

Question 1: Build the illustrated model from the provided information. Locate the Center of mass of the part.

C12801: Advanced Part (Bracket) - Step 1
Build this part in SolidWorks.
(Save part after each question in a different file in case it must be reviewed)

Unit system: MMGS (millimeter, gram, second)
Decimal places: 2
Part origin: Arbitrary
All holes through all unless shown otherwise.
Material: AISI 1020 Steel
Density = 0.0079 g/mm^3

A = 64.00
B = 20.00
C = 26.50

What is the overall mass of the part (grams)?

Screen shots from the exam.

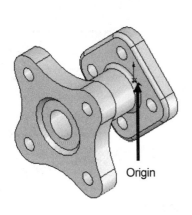

Origin

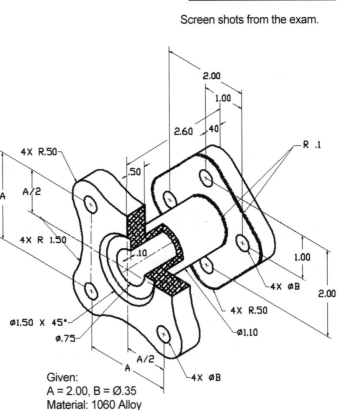

4X R.50
A
A/2
4X R 1.50
.10
Ø1.50 X 45°
Ø.75
A/2
A
4X ØB
2.00
1.00
2.60 .40
.50
R .1
1.00
4X ØB
2.00
4X R.50
Ø1.10

Given:
A = 2.00, B = Ø.35
Material: 1060 Alloy
Density: 0.097 lb/in^3
Units: IPS
Decimal places = 2

Think about the steps that you would take to build the illustrated part. Identify the location of the part Origin.

Start with the back base flange. Review the provided dimensions and annotations in the part illustration.

The key difference between the *Advanced Part Creation and Modification* and the *Basic Part Creation and Modification* category and the *Intermediate Part Creation and Modification* is the complexity of the sketches and the number of features, dimensions, and geometric relations. You may also need to locate the Center of mass relative to a created coordinate system location.

Mass = 0.59 pounds

Volume = 6.01 cubic inches

Surface area = 46.61 inches^2

Center of mass: (inches)
 X = 0.00
 Y = 0.00
 Z = 1.51

- A: X = 1.00 inches, Y = 0.79 inches, Z = 0.00 inches

- B: X = 0.00 inches, Y = 0.00 inches, Z = 1.04 inches

- C: X = 0.00 inches, Y = 1.18 inches, Z = 0.00 inches

- D: X = 0.00 inches, Y = 0.00 inches, Z = 1.51 inches

The correct answer is D.

All models for this chapter are located on the DVD in the book.

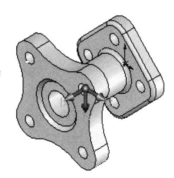

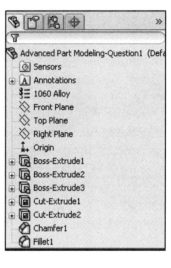

Question 2: Build the illustrated model from the provided information. Locate the Center of mass of the part.

Hint: Create the part with eleven features and a Reference plane: Extruded Base, Plane1, two Extruded Bosses, two Extruded Cuts, Extruded Boss, Extruded Cut,

Extruded-Thin, Mirror, Extruded Cut, and Extruded Boss.

Given:
A = 3.500, B = 4.200, C = 2.000,
D = 1.750, E = 1.000
Material: 6061 Alloy
Density: 0.097 lb/in^3
Units: IPS
Decimal places = 3

Think about the steps that you would take to build the illustrated part. Create the rectangular Base feature. Create Sketch2 for Plane1. Insert Plane1 to create the Extruded Boss feature: Extrude2. Plane1 is the Sketch plane for Sketch3. Sketch3 is the sketch profile for Extrude2.

- A: X = 1.59 inches, Y = 1.19 inches, Z = 0.00 inches

- B: X = -1.59 inches, Y = 1.19 inches, Z = 0.04 inches

- C: X = 1.00 inches, Y = 1.18 inches, Z = 0.10 inches

- D: X = 0.00 inches, Y = 0.00 inches, Z = 1.61 inches

The correct answer is A.

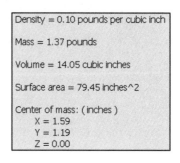

Density = 0.10 pounds per cubic inch

Mass = 1.37 pounds

Volume = 14.05 cubic inches

Surface area = 79.45 inches^2

Center of mass: (inches)
  X = 1.59
  Y = 1.19
  Z = 0.00

Question 3: Build the illustrated model from the provided information. Locate the Center of mass of the part. Note the coordinate system location of the model as illustrated.

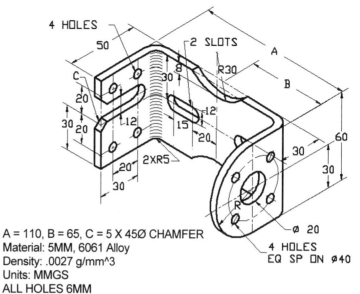

A = 110, B = 65, C = 5 X 45Ø CHAMFER
Material: 5MM, 6061 Alloy
Density: .0027 g/mm^3
Units: MMGS
ALL HOLES 6MM

Where do you start? Build the model. Insert thirteen features: Extruded-Thin1, Fillet, two Extruded Cuts, Circular Pattern, two Extruded Cuts, Mirror, Chamfer, Extruded Cut, Mirror, Extruded Cut, and Mirror.

Think about the steps that you would take to build the illustrated part. Review the provided information. The depth of the left side is 50mm. The depth of the right side is 60mm

Create Coordinate System1 to locate the Center of mass.

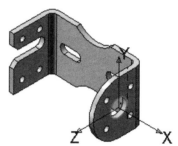

Coordinate system: +X, +Y. +Z

☼ The SolidWorks software displays positive values for (X, Y, Z) coordinates for a reference coordinate system. The CSWA exam displays either a positive or negative sign in front of the (X, Y, Z) coordinates to indicate direction as illustrated, (-X, +Y, -Z).

- A: X = -53.30 millimeters, Y = -0.27 millimeters, Z = -15.54 millimeters

- B: X = 53.30 millimeters, Y = 0.27 millimeters, Z = 15.54 millimeters

- C: X = 49.21 millimeters, Y = 46.88 millimeters, Z = 0.00 millimeters

- D: X = 45.00 millimeters, Y = -46.49 millimeters, Z = 10.00 millimeters

The correct answer is A.

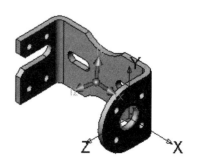

Question 4: Build the illustrated model from the provided information. Locate the Center of mass of the part.

Hint: Insert twelve features and a Reference plane: Extruded-Thin1, two Extruded Bosses, Extruded Cut, Extruded Boss, Extruded Cut, Plane1, Mirror, five Extruded Cuts.

Think about the steps that you would take to build the illustrated part. Create an Extrude-Thin1 feature as the Base feature.

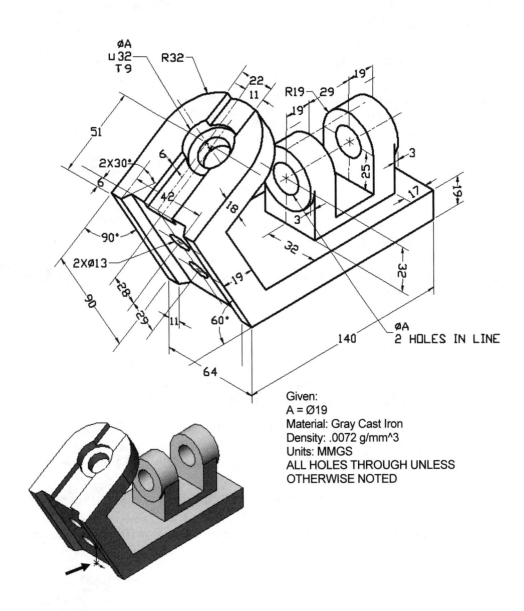

Given:
A = Ø19
Material: Gray Cast Iron
Density: .0072 g/mm^3
Units: MMGS
ALL HOLES THROUGH UNLESS
OTHERWISE NOTED

- A: X = -53.30 millimeters, Y = -0.27 millimeters, Z = -15.54 millimeters

- B: X = 53.30 millimeters, Y = 1.27 millimeters, Z = -15.54 millimeters

- C: X = 0.00 millimeters, Y = 34.97 millimeters, Z = 46.67 millimeters

- D: X = 0.00 millimeters, Y = 34.97 millimeters, Z = -46.67 millimeters

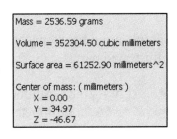

The correct answer is D.

☼ Due to software rounding, you may view a negative -0.00 coordinate location in the Mass Properties dialog box.

Question 5: Build the illustrated model from the provided information. Locate the Center of mass of the part.

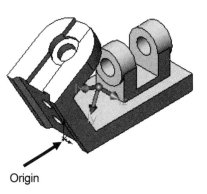

Origin

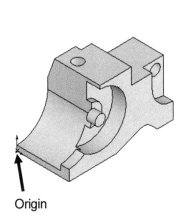

Origin

Given:¶
A·=·63,·B·=·50,·C·=·100¶
Material:·Copper¶
Units:·MMGS¶
Density:·.0089·g/mm^3¶
All·HOLES·THROUGH·ALL¶

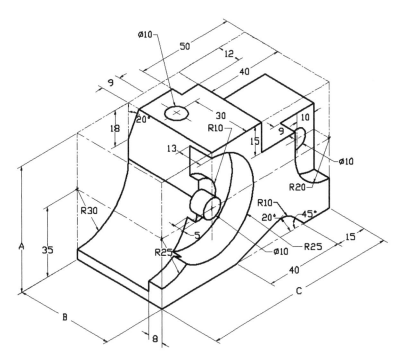

The center point of the top hole is located 30mm from the top right edge.

Think about the steps that you would take to build the illustrated part.

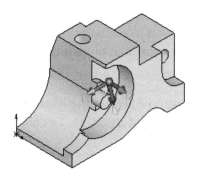

Mass = 1280.33 grams

Volume = 143857.58 cubic millimeters

Surface area = 26112.48 millimeters^2

Center of mass: (millimeters)
    X = 26.81
    Y = 25.80
    Z = -56.06

- A: X = 26.81 millimeters, Y = 25.80 millimeters, Z = -56.06 millimeters

- B: X = 43.30 millimeters, Y = 25.27 millimeters, Z = -15.54 millimeters

- C: X = 26.81 millimeters, Y = -25.75 millimeters, Z = 0.00 millimeters

- D: X = 46.00 millimeters, Y = -46.49 millimeters, Z = 10.00 millimeters

The correct answer is A.

This example was taken from the SolidWorks website, **www.solidworks.com/cswa** as an example of an Advanced Part on the CSWA exam. This model has thirteen features and twelve sketches.

☼ There are numerous ways to create the models in this chapter.

Assembly Creation and Modification

Assembly Creation and Modification is one of the five categories on the CSWA exam. In the last two section of this chapter, a *Basic Part Creation and Modification, Intermediate Part Creation and Modification,* or an *Advanced Part Creation and Modification* was the focus.

The *Assembly Creation and Modification* category addresses an assembly with numerous sub-components.

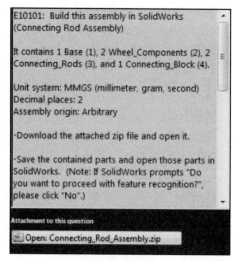

E10101: Build this assembly in SolidWorks (Connecting Rod Assembly)

It contains 1 Base (1), 2 Wheel_Components (2), 2 Connecting_Rods (3), and 1 Connecting_Block (4).

Unit system: MMGS (millimeter, gram, second)
Decimal places: 2
Assembly origin: Arbitrary

-Download the attached zip file and open it.

-Save the contained parts and open those parts in SolidWorks. (Note: If SolidWorks prompts "Do you want to proceed with feature recognition?", please click "No".)

Attachment to this question

Open: Connecting_Rod_Assembly.zip

Screen shots from the exam.

Knowledge to insert Standard mates is required in this category.

There are four questions on the CSWA exam in the Assembly Creation and Modification category: (Two different assemblies - four questions - two multiple choice / two single answers - 30 points each).

You are required to download the needed components from a provided zip file and insert them correctly to create the assembly as illustrated. You are then requested to modify the assembly and answer fill in the blank format questions.

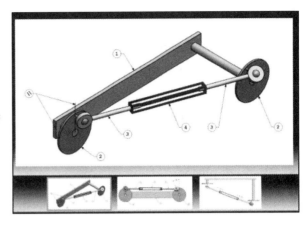

Screen shots from the exam.

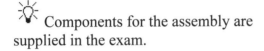 Components for the assembly are supplied in the exam.

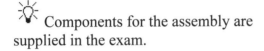 Do NOT use feature recognition when you open the downloaded components for the assembly in the CSWA exam. This is a timed exam. Manage your time. You do not need this information.

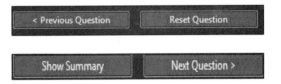

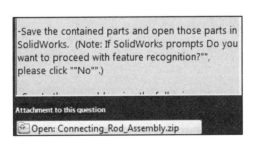

Sample Questions in the category

In the *Assembly Creation and Modification* Assembly Modeling category, an exam question could read:

Build this assembly in SolidWorks (Chain Link Assembly). It contains 2 long_pins (1), 3 short_pins (2), and 4 chain_links (3).

- Unit system: MMGS (millimeter, gram, second)
- Decimal places: 2
- Assembly origin: Arbitrary

IMPORTANT: Create the Assembly with respect to the Origin as shown in the Isometric view. (This is important for calculating the proper Center of Mass). Create the assembly using the following conditions:

1. Pins are mated concentric to chain link holes (no clearance).

2. Pin end faces are coincident to chain link side faces.

A = 25 degrees, B = 125 degrees, C = 130 degrees

What is the center of mass of the assembly (millimeters)?

Hint: If you don't find an option within 1% of your answer please re-check your assembly.

A) X = 348.66, Y = -88.48, Z = -91.40

B) X = 308.53, Y = -109.89, Z = -61.40

C) X = 298.66, Y = -17.48, Z = -89.22

D) X = 448.66, Y = -208.48, Z = -34.64

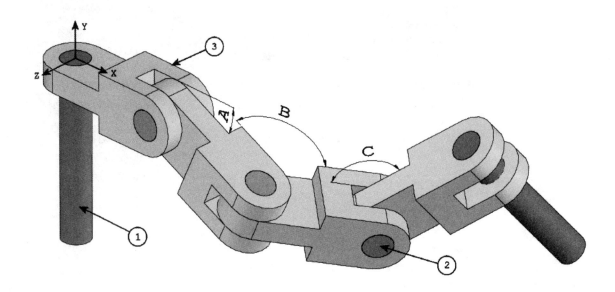

There are no step by step procedures in this section.

Download the *needed components* from the Chapter 10 CSWA Models folder on the DVD in the book to create the assembly.

Below are various Assembly FeatureManagers that created the above assembly and obtained the correct answer.

The correct answer is:

A) X = 348.66, Y = -88.48, Z = -91.40

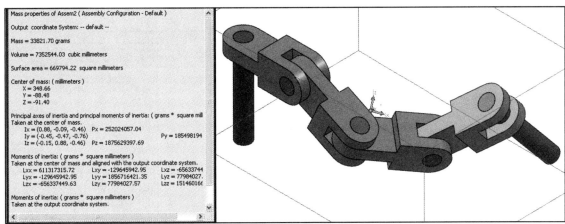

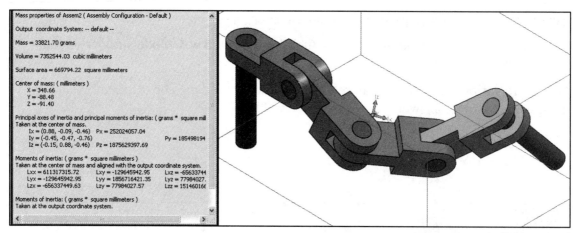

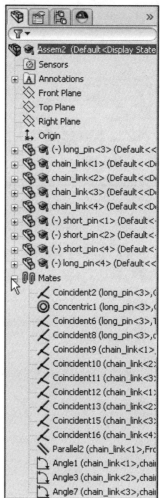

Appendix

Engineering Changer Order (ECO)

D&M Engineering Change Order		ECO # _____ Page 1 of __

Product Line	☐ Hardware ☐ Software ☐ Quality ☐ Tech Pubs	Author Date Authorized Mgr. Date

Change Tested By

Reason for ECO(Describe the existing problem, symptom and impact on field)

D&M Part No.	Rev From/To	Part Description	Description	Owner

ECO Implementation/Class		Departments	Approvals	Date	
All in Field	☐	Engineering			
All in Test	☐	Manufacturing			
All in Assembly	☐	Technical Support			
All in Stock	☐	Marketing			
All on Order	☐	DOC Control			
All Future	☐				
Material Disposition		ECO Cost			
Rework	☐	DO NOT WRITE BELOW THIS LINE (ECO BOARD ONLY)			
Scrap	☐	Effective Date			
Use as is	☐	Incorporated Date			
None	☐	Board Approval			
See Attached	☐	Board Date			

This text follows the ASME Y14 Engineering Drawing and Related Documentation Practices for drawings. Display of dimensions and tolerances are as follows:

TYPES of DECIMAL DIMENSIONS (ASME Y14.5M)			
Description:	**UNITS: MM**	**Description:**	**UNITS: INCH**
Dimension is less than 1mm. Zero precedes the decimal point.	0.9 0.95	Dimension is less than 1 inch. Zero is not used before the decimal point.	.5 .56
Dimension is a whole number. Display no decimal point. Display no zero after decimal point.	19	Express dimension to the same number of decimal places as its tolerance. Add zeros to the right of the decimal point. If the tolerance is expressed to 3 places, then the dimension contains 3 places to the right of the decimal point.	1.750
Dimension exceeds a whole number by a decimal fraction of a millimeter. Display no zero to the right of the decimal.	11.5 11.51		

TABLE 1 TOLERANCE DISPLAY FOR INCH AND METRIC DIMENSIONS (ASME Y14.5M)		
DISPLAY:	**UNITS: INCH:**	**UNITS: METRIC:**
Dimensions less than 1	.5	0.5
Unilateral Tolerance	$1.417^{+.005}_{-.000}$	$36^{\ 0}_{-0.5}$
Bilateral Tolerance	$1.417^{+.010}_{-.020}$	$36^{+0.25}_{-0.50}$
Limit Tolerance	.571 .463	14.50 11.50

SolidWorks Keyboard Shortcuts

Listed below are some of the pre-defined keyboard shortcuts in SolidWorks:

Action:	Key Combination:
Model Views	
Rotate the model horizontally or vertically:	**Arrow** keys
Rotate the model horizontally or vertically 90 degrees.	**Shift** + **Arrow** keys
Rotate the model clockwise or counterclockwise	**Alt** + left of right **Arrow** keys
Pan the model	**Ctrl** + **Arrow** keys
Magnifying glass	**g**
Zoom in	**Shift + z**
Zoom out	**z**
Zoom to fit	**f**
Previous view	**Ctrl + Shift + z**
View Orientation	
View Orientation menu	**Spacebar**
Front view	**Ctrl + 1**
Back view	**Ctrl + 2**
Left view	**Ctrl + 3**
Right view	**Ctrl + 4**
Top view	**Ctrl + 5**
Bottom view	**Ctrl + 6**
Isometric view	**Ctrl + 7**
Normal To view	**Ctrl + 8**
Selection Filters	
Filter edges	**e**
Filter vertices	**v**
Filter faces	**x**
Toggle Selection Filter toolbar	**F5**
Toggle selection filters on/off	**F6**
File menu items	
New SolidWorks document	**Ctrl + n**
Open document	**Ctrl + o**
Open From Web Folder	**Ctrl + w**
Make Drawing from Part	**Ctrl + d**
Make Assembly from Part	**Ctrl + a**
Save	**Ctrl +s**
Print	**Ctrl + p**
Additional shortcuts	
Access online help inside of PropertyManager or dialog box	**F1**
Rename an item in the FeatureManager design tree	**F2**
Rebuild the model	**Ctrl + b**
Force rebuild – Rebuild the model and all its features	**Ctrl + q**
Redraw the screen	**Ctrl + r**

Cycle between open SolidWorks document	**Ctrl + Tab**
Line to arc/arc to line in the Sketch	**a**
Undo	**Ctrl + z**
Redo	**Ctrl + y**
Cut	**Ctrl + x**
Copy	**Ctrl + c**
Additional shortcuts	
Paste	**Ctrl + v**
Delete	**Delete**
Next window	**Ctrl + F6**
Close window	**Ctrl + F4**
View previous tools	**s**
Selects all text inside an Annotations text box	**Ctrl + a**

 In a sketch, the **Esc** key un-selects geometry items currently selected in the Properties box and Add Relations box. In the model, the **Esc** key closes the PropertyManager and cancels the selections.

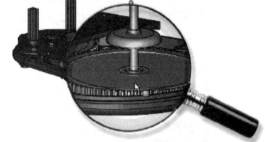

 Use the **g** key to activate the Magnifying glass tool. Use the Magnifying glass tool to inspect a model and make selections without changing the overall view.

 Use the **s** key to view/access previous command tools in the Graphics window.

Windows Shortcuts

Listed below are some of the pre-defined keyboard shortcuts in Microsoft Windows:

Action:	Keyboard Combination:
Open the Start menu	Windows Logo key
Open Windows Explorer	Windows Logo key + E
Minimize all open windows	Windows Logo key + M
Open a Search window	Windows Logo key + F
Open Windows Help	Windows Logo key + F1
Select multiple geometry items in a SolidWorks document	Ctrl key (Hold the Ctrl key down. Select items.) Release the Ctrl key.

Helpful On-Line Information

The SolidWorks URL: http://www.solidworks.com contains information on Local Resellers, Solution Partners, Certifications, SolidWorks users groups, and more.

Access 3D ContentCentral using the Task Pane to obtain engineering electronic catalog model and part information.

Use the SolidWorks Resources tab in the Task Pane to obtain access to Customer Portals, Discussion Forums, User Groups, Manufacturers, Solution Partners, Labs, and more.

Helpful on-line SolidWorks information is available from the following URLs:

- http://www.dmeducation.net

    Helpful tips, tricks and what's new in SolidWorks.

- http://www.mechengineer.com/snug/

    News group access and local user group information.

- http://www.nhcad.com

    Configuration information and other tips and tricks.

- http://www.dmeducation.net

    Helpful tips, tricks and what's new in SolidWorks.

- http://www.topica.com/lists/SW

    Independent News Group for SolidWorks discussions, questions and answers.

*On-line tutorials are for educational purposes only. Tutorials are copyrighted by their respective owners.

.

Notes:

INDEX